Indian Heritage, Art and Culture

For Civil Services Examinations

(Preliminary & Main)

Third Edition

Indian Heritage, Art and Culture

For Civil Services Examinations

(Preliminary & Main)

Third Edition

Madhukar Kumar Bhagat

G. K. PUBLICATIONS (P) LTD.

Title : Indian Heritage, Art and Culture (Preliminary & Main) 3ed

Language : English

Author's Name : Madhukar Kumar Bhagat

Typeset & Published by :

Career Launcher Infrastructure (P) Ltd.

A-45, Mohan Cooperative Industrial Area, Near Mohan Estate Metro Station, New Delhi - 110044

Marketed by :

G.K. Publications (P) Ltd.

Plot No. 9A, Sector-27A, Mathura Road, Faridabad, Haryana-121003

ISBN : **978-93-94168-96-1**

Printer's Details : Printed in India, New Delhi.

For product information :

Visit *www.gkpublications.com* or email to *gkp@gkpublications.com*

Dedicated to

Maa, Papa,
Bhaiya,
Garima,
Pranshu and Prabhav,

for family is
the fountainhead
of values and culture.

सिद्धिर्भवति कर्मजा

Success is born of action

–The Bhagvad Gita

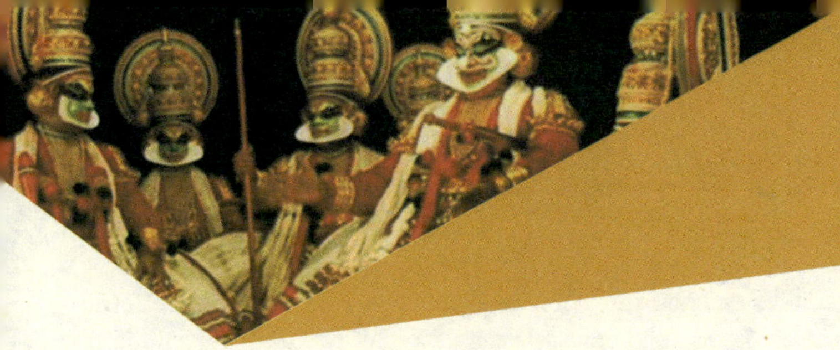

Preface to the First Edition

The term 'Culture' is usually understood to be the collective values of the society manifested through its numerous institutions as well as in the dispositions, attitudes and manners of its individual members. These in turn find expression in the various art forms—tangible and intangible, abstract ideas, beliefs and even in the material objects.

The Indian social landscape with its continuous and unbroken evolution of at least 5000 years has offered sufficient space for Indian culture to evolve into enchanting diverse forms. One cannot help but marvel at the distinct cultural waves which have swept our country through the ages and their confluences which have bloomed into new forms of culture. Truly, it has been the strength of Indian culture to assimilate the influences rather than to annihilate it.

Thus, our culture and art forms as we see them today, are a heritage of centuries of cultural tradition and evolution. Even to capture a glimpse of it is a colossal task, albeit a satisfying one. This is what this book has endeavoured to do.

The various aspects of Indian culture, right from the Indus Valley and the Vedic culture to the post-independence and modern culture, have been captured in this book. Although the subject of culture is wide, encompassing its numerous manifestations, the focus here has been on the need of the aspirant from the perspective of the civil-services examination. Considering that the scope of study of Indian culture is extremely diverse and a vast one, while the time of an average aspirant is limited, every effort has been made to capture the essence of all topics relevant. Thus, conciseness and preciseness are the twin hallmarks of this book.

The book begins with a detailed analysis of the topics and their relevance from the perspective of the civil-services examination. It also brings out the relative importance of the topic of 'Culture' in the scheme of the Preliminary and the Main examination as well the significance of the various sub-topics. Understandably, all the topics/subtopics are not equally important (from the examination perspective) and the book therefore helps the aspirants to prioritise.

Another unique aspect of the book is that it incorporates sufficient number of model questions for the Preliminary and the Main examination. These are analogous to what one may expect in the examination itself. The Preliminary questions section (Appendix-1) contains 100 model objective type multiple choice questions while the section on questions for the Main Examination (in Appendix 3) contains 20-20 questions each, which are fully solved or contain/indicate the important points to be covered. Relevant illustrations and photographs have also been provided at appropriate places to help the reader to grasp the nuances of the subject better.

Writing the book has been a long, enriching and satisfying journey for me and I thank the publishers for trusting me with this project and themselves putting in a lot of hard work.

I sincerely hope the book will kindle an avid interest in topic of Indian culture and also help the aspirants of civil-services in grasping the nuances of this topic and emerging with flying colours.

Wishing all the very best

Madhukar Kumar Bhagat

Preface to the First Edition

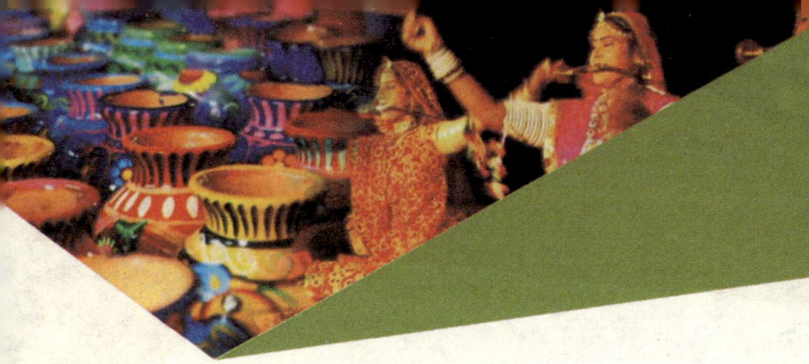

Preface To The Second Edition

It is just two years since the first edition of this book was published and here we are with the second edition. At the outset I am extremely thankful to all the dear readers for their warm sincere and positive responses and kind words of appreciation which has encouraged us to venture further in this enduring journey.

So what's new in this edition of the book? Well! To begin with, this edition has been launched in colour with nearly 275 images/pictures. This truly marks a paradigm shift in publication approach pertaining to the topic of Indian culture or rather any other topic of the Civil Services examination (CSE) preparation. Colour images not only enhance the quality of the pictures enabling the readers' better appreciation of the works of art, monuments, emblems, seals, sculptures, temples, paintings and numerous other artefacts displayed in this book but also create a succinct and lingering mental imagery , so essential for grasping the substance of the topic and its timely recollection.

But that is not all. Nearly 65 objective types multiple choice questions have been added to the 100 questions of the first edition, thus creating a sizeable set of questions for practice for the Preliminary examination. Besides, 10 fully solved quality essay type questions have also been added taking their tally to 50 .This will indeed be a value addition for the aspirants of the Main examination. Further, the book has been also been comprehensively re-edited and typographical errors, if any, have duly been corrected.

The Civil Services aspirant is always burdened with a humongous range of syllabus and acute paucity of time. Accordingly, the objective of this book has been to assist the readers escape this twin paradox by keeping the coverage precise as well as concise. Short chapters in chronological sequence, summary tables, inset boxes, chapter end identification of important topics to focus upon, topic wise analysis of past year questions, application type practice questions akin to the Preliminary and Main examination; all of these features endeavour to resolve the aspirants perpetual struggle of coping with burgeoning syllabus in constrained preparation time.

Thus, we can confidently say that we fully understand the readers' need and hence this book. Finally, wishing our dear readers success through right knowledge in all endeavours.

Madhukar Kumar Bhagat

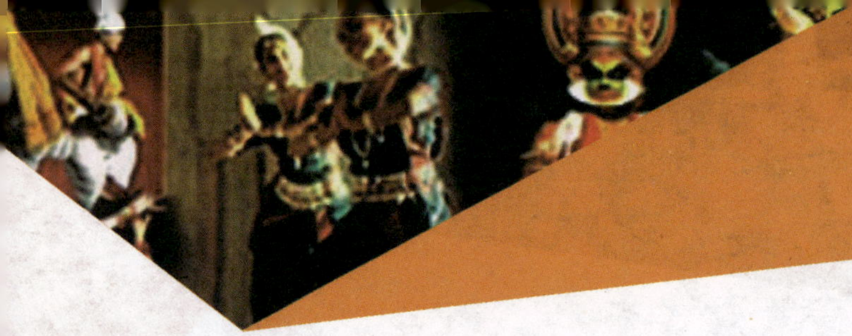

Preface to the Third Edition

The Third Edition of this widely appreciated book has been updated with two key features:

1. Solved Questions related to Indian culture from 2020 and 2021 GS Main Paper I
2. A 22-page write up titled '*The Essence of Indian Culture and the Phases of Cultural Evolution in India*'.

This write up encapsulates the highlights of Indian culture during the period of Ancient India while simultaneously exploring the important phases of cultural evolution in Ancient India.

Ancient India is a very important topic in the UPSC and any aspirant must have a good grasp of the important landmarks of this period.

Some of the key periods described in this write up are

(a) The Indus Valley Civilisation

(b) The Vedic Culture

(c) The Dravidian Culture

(d) Jainism, Buddhism and Sramana traditions

(e) The Puranic Age

We are hopeful that this write-up will be a valuable addition to the book and will also enhance the reader's appreciation of the period.

Madhukar Kumar Bhagat

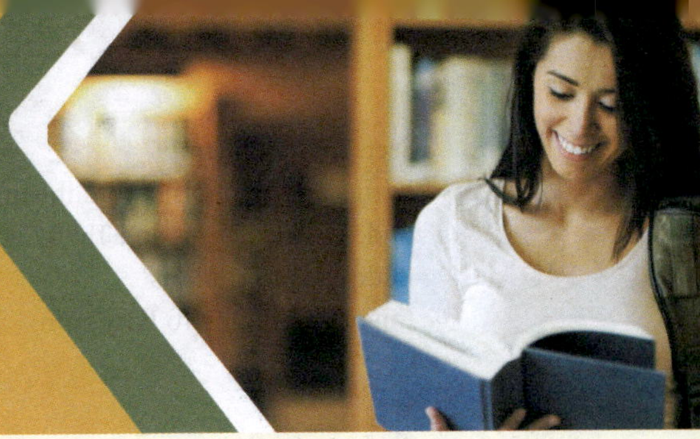

Contents

CHAPTER 1

INDIAN HERITAGE, ART AND CULTURE: How to Approach the Topic

SIGNIFICANCE OF THE TOPIC FOR THE CIVIL SERVICES EXAMINATION

Indian culture is an interesting as well as a significant topic from the perspective of both the Preliminary and the Main examination. It encompasses a variety of questions ranging from religious philosophies in ancient India to music and dance in modern times, from architecture of temples and forts in the medieval period to religious reforms and Sufism. Thus, it not only offers a great variety to read, but also includes those topics with which the aspirants are invariably able to connect with personally owing to their knowledge of cultural heritage of India and their abiding personal interest.

But the topic also poses a challenge to the aspirants. It embraces a period of study of more than 2500 years, including diverse topics like religious philosophies to modern day art, for which no singular source of reference would suffice. **It is here that a book like this is handy which offers an easy access to all what an aspirant needs to know, compiled in a systematic and concise manner which is easy to understand.**

What to Study?

This is a question which every aspirant asks. But before one embarks on the journey of preparation for this topic, it is prudent to understand what is expected of an aspirant, as far as the examination is concerned. One ought to determine the realm of study accordingly. This topic contributes questions in Preliminary as well as the Main examination. However, the nature of questions is quite different in both the examinations. As such the orientation of study should also be different.

THE PRELIMINARY EXAMINATION AND THE TOPIC OF CULTURE: A QUICK LOOK

The Preliminary examination has seen an increasing number of questions being asked from 'culture', particularly after 2011, when the new pattern of the Preliminary examination was introduced. Over the years, at an average 8–10 questions arise from this topic, although yearly variations do take place. The year wise distribution of questions (out of total of 100) is being given here.

Considering that 'culture' is one among eight subjects from which questions are being asked in the 'Prelims', **a weightage of 10% in the examination is good enough to warrant a thorough study of this topic**.

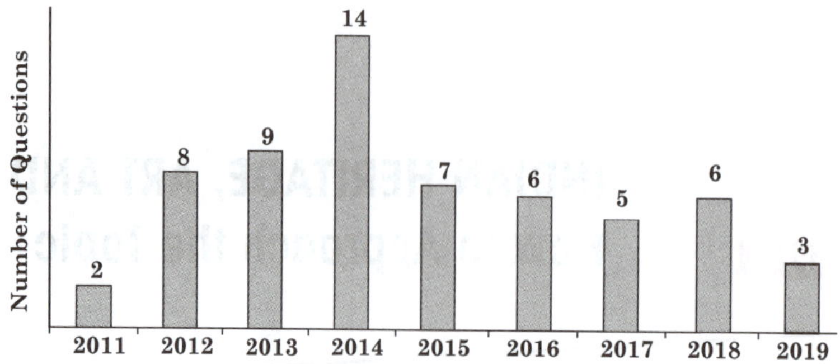

What to Study in the Preliminary Examination

The notification of the Preliminary examination does not prescribe any syllabus for the topic of culture. Rather, it does not specify 'culture' to be a separate topic in itself. Apparently, it is considered by the UPSC to be a part of the topic of history. However, the nature of questions arising in the Preliminary examination are such that mere reading of the standard History books would not enable coverage of all or even some of the questions. This is so as many topics such as dance, music, theatre, or other performing arts are not covered in the history text books. Further, the perspective of coverage of topics like religious philosophies (of Hinduism, Buddhism, Jainism), art, and architecture in ancient and medieval India may be quite meagre or quite different from what is actually required in the test.

THE PRELIMINARY EXAMINATION AND THE TOPIC OF CULTURE: A DETAILED LOOK

It is important to know not only as to how many questions are being asked from this topic but as to which are the areas of 'Indian culture', from which questions are arising. An analysis of the questions which have arisen in the past five years and the areas from which they are figuring are being given below (along with the question number in the Question Paper Series A).

Topic Wise Distribution of Questions in the Preliminary Examination

	2015	2014	2013	2012	2011
1. Religions **(a) Hinduism/ Vedic culture** **(b) Buddhism & Buddha** **(c) Jainism** **(d) Other religions**	Q. No. 39; Places associated with the life of Buddha	Q. No. 47; Six systems of the Indian philosophy Q. No. 54; Satyamev Jayate; referred in which Upanishad? Q. No. 25; Places associated with life of Buddha.	Q. No. 58; Sankhya Philosophy. Q. No. 36; Chaitya & Viharas Q. No. 37; Nirvana in Buddhism Q. No. 47; Jain doctrine	Q. No. 22; Features common to Buddhism & Jainism. Q. No. 72; Buddha; Bhumi sparsh mudra, its significance Q. No. 73; Vedic Aryan religion	Q. No. 77; Jain philosophy

2. Art & Sculpture in Ancient India & Indus valley			Q. No. 4; Rock-cut architecture Q. No. 57; Ajanta caves, Sanchi stupa		Q. No. 92; Indus Valley civilisation
3. Literature, music, dance, & other art forms in ancient India		Q. No. 87; Kalaripayattu martial art	Q. No. 6; Hieun Tsang account Q. No. 79; Tribhanga dance posture		
4. Bhakti movement & Sufism		Q. No. 90; Saint Dadu Dayal & Madhavacharya	Q. No. 52 Guru Nanak, Dadu Dayal, Tyagraja	Q. No. 69; Sufism, its practice & features	
5. Temple and their Art & architecture (ancient & medieval India)	Q. No. 54; Different temples & locations	Q. No. 85; Temples and images		Q. No. 24; Nagara, Dravida, and Vesara style of temple architecture	
6. Palaces, forts, architecture and other art forms, medieval India	Q. No. 41; Introduction of arches & domes in India	Q. No. 93; Ibadat Khana, Fathehpur Sikri			
7. Dance forms in modern times		Q. No. 83; Sattriya dance Q. No. 88; Dances & States		Q. No. 68; Kuchipudi & Bharatnatyam	
8. Other art forms in modern times, viz. music, paintings craft, folk art, language	Q. No. 75; The language recently given classical language status Q. No. 96; Kalamkari	Q. No. 8; Language recently given classical language status Q. No. 76; Towns associated with sarees/fabric Q. No. 91; Maganiyars, folk musicians		Q. No. 67; Dhrupad	

9. Social reforms, current cultural trends, other/miscellaneous	Q. No. 15; Places of pilgrimage & location Q. No. 99; Geographical location status given to certain products	Q. No. 84; National Calendar, Saka Era Q. No. 89; Buddhist monasteries		Q. No. 74; Brahmo Samaj	

As can be seen, the distribution of questions is not uniform amongst all the subtopics of culture. There are **nine broad areas** (as highlighted above) from which the questions are emanating. Further, the topic of the religious philosophies and religions (particularly, Hinduism, Buddhism, and Jainism) account for the maximum number of questions. As such, the focus of candidates should also be on such topics. Although a candidate should endeavour to make a wide coverage of all the topics (if time permits), where time is a matter of constraint, an aspirant must make effort to cover thoroughly at least the subtopics given in the next section.

IMPORTANT TOPICS FOR THE PRELIMINARY EXAMINATION

- **Vedic Culture** Vedanta, Hindu scriptures, (viz. what are Shrutis, Smritis, Nyaya; Vedas, Samhita, Aranyakas, Upanishads, etc.) and other texts, deities, and various forms of Hinduism (viz. Nirguna, Shaguna, Shaivism, Vaishnavism, etc.), important personalities and their contribution, etc.
- **Buddhism and Jainism** Teachings and philosophy of Buddhism and Jainism, similarities and differences, scriptures of Buddhists (Tripittakas), various forms of Buddhism (Hinayana, Mahayana, Tibetan Buddhism and other forms, and sects), Boddhisattvas scriptures of Jainism, Tirthankars, etc.
- **Temples and rock-cut art and architecture** viz. Ajanta and Ellora, other caves and architecture, stupas (Sanchi), and other important monuments of ancient India.
- **Temple architecture in medieval India** Nagara, Dravida, and Vesara architectural styles, temple frescoes, murals, prominent temples, special features (viz. their claim to fame), important palaces, and forts in medieval India.
- **Sufism and Bhakti movement** Prominent personalities associated with it and their philosophy and contribution.
- **Various dance forms of different regions of India** Persons/personalities associated with it, particularly in modern times.

THE MAIN EXAMINATION AND THE TOPIC OF CULTURE: AN ANALYSIS

Approach of Study

From the perspective of the Main examination, the topic of culture is an altogether different ball-game. The approach has to be quite different from that of the Preliminary examination. While wide coverage and knowledge of subject is more important for the Preliminary examination, it is the application of knowledge and analysis of the acquired information which are called for in the Main examination. This is particularly true for the examinations held since Mains 2013 wherein the new pattern (in the Main examination) was introduced.

The Syllabus of the Main Examination

The topic of culture figures in the General Studies Paper-I of the Main examination and the UPSC does specify a syllabus for it. However this only gives a brief outline mentioning the following.

"Indian culture will cover salient aspects of art forms, literature, and architecture from ancient to modern times."

Thus, the syllabus in itself does not throw much light on what needs to be covered. Further, the ambit of the words 'art form', 'literature', and 'architecture' is quite expansive. As such, to understand what and how much to study, one has to analyse the questions which are figuring in the Main examination in the past years. Those of the time period from 2011–2016 are given below:

Questions of Past Years' in Mains (2011-2018)

Main Examination 2018

Q.1 *Safeguarding the Indian art heritage is the need of the moment. Discuss* **(10 marks)**

Q.2 *Assess the importance of the accounts of the Chiness and Arab travellers in the reconstruction of the history of India.* **(10 marks)**

Q.3 *The Bhakti movement received a remarkable re-orientation with the advent of Sri Chaitanya Mahaprabhu. Discuss.* **(15 marks)**

Main Examination 2017

Q.1 *How do you justify the view that the level of excellence of Gupta numismatic art is not at all noticeable in later times?* **(10 marks)**

Main Examination 2016

Q.1 *Early Buddhist Stupa-art, while depicting folk motifs and narratives successfully expounds Buddhist ideals. Elucidate.* **(12.5 marks)**

Q.2 *Krishnadeva Raya, the King of Vijayanagar, was not only an accomplished scholar himself but was also a great patron of learning and literature. Discuss.* **(12.5 marks)**

Q.3 *To what extent globalisation has influenced the core of cultural diversity in India? Explain.* **(12.5 marks)**

Main Examination 2015

Q.1 *The ancient civilisation in Indian subcontinent differed from those of Egypt, Mesopotamia, and Greece in that its culture and traditions have been preserved without breakdown to the present day. Comment.* **(12.5 marks)**

Q.2 *Mesolithic rock-cut architecture of India not only reflects the cultural life of the times but also a fine aesthetic sense comparable to modern painting. Critically evaluate this comment.* **(12.5 marks)**

Q.8 *Describe any four cultural elements of diversity in India and rate their relative significance in building a national identity.* **(12.5 marks)**

Main Examination 2014

Q.1 *To what extent has the urban planning and culture of the Indus Valley Civilisation provided inputs to the present day urbanisation? Discuss.* **(12.5 marks)**

Q.2 *Gandhara sculpture owed as much to the Romans as to the Greeks. Explain.* **(12.5 marks)**

Q.3 *Taxila university was one of the oldest universities of the world with which were associated a number of renoned learned personalities of different disciplines. Its stratetgic location caused its fame to flourish, but unlike Nalanda, it is not considered as a university in the modern sense. Discuss.* **(12.5 marks)**

Q.4 *Sufis and medival mystic mytic saints failed to modify either the religious ideas and practices or the outward structure of Hindu/Muslim societies to any appreciable extent. Comment.* **(12.5 marks)**

Main Examination 2013

Q.1 *Though not very useful from the point of view of a connected political history of South India, the Sangam literature portrays the social and economic conditions of its time with remarkable vividness. Comment.* **(10 marks)**

Q.2 (a) *Discuss the 'Tandava' dance as recorded in early Indian inscriptions.* **(5 marks)**

(b) *Chola architecture represents a high watermark in the evolution of temple architecture. Discuss.* **(5 marks)**

Main Examination 2012

Q.1 (d) *The 'flute-playing Krishna' theme is very popular in Indian art. Discuss.* **(15 marks)**

(i) *Comment on the significance of fire in Zoroastrianism.* **(15 marks)**

Q.4 (b) *Comment on the Bagurumba folk dance* **(5 marks)**

Main Examination 2011

Q.8 *Attempt the following in not more than 50 words each:* **(5 × 4 = 20 marks)**

(a) *Distinguish either between the 'Moatsu' and 'Yemshe' festivals of Nagaland or the 'Losar' and 'Khan' festivals of Arunachal Pradesh.*

(b) *Write a sentence each on any five of the following traditional theatre forms:*

(i) *Bhand Pather*

(ii) *Swang*

(iii) *Maach*

(iv) *Bhaona*

(v) *Mudiyettu*

(vi) *Dashavatar*

(c) *What are the major different styles of unglazed pottery making in India?*

(d) *List the classical dance forms of India as per the Sangeet Natak Akademi.*

Number of Questions and Weightage of Culture

As can be seen from the above set of questions, **every year three to four questions worth 30–40 marks are being asked from the topic on culture**. This would be 12%–15% of the total marks of G.S. Paper-I, which includes other topics such as 'Indian and Modern World History', 'Indian and World Geography', social, developmental, and women related issues. Considering the vast coverage of other topics, the weightage assigned (12%–15%) to culture is a fair and an important one.

Nature of Questions

The nature of questions particularly since 2013, is based on analysis and application of knowledge. They are not straightforward ones where recall and presentation of the appropriate information would suffice. Rather, the questions are of the type 'critically evaluate', 'comment', 'discuss', 'describe', etc. This implies that although knowledge of the subject would be a prerequisite to attempt such questions, surely that would not suffice. Application and analysis of that information is what is being asked for. Considering the pressures of time in the examination, it may not always be possible for the aspirants to analyse the issues then and there and to formulate an appropriate answer. As such, from the perspective of the Main examination, whenever one is studying a topic of culture, it is very important to keep on thinking as to what application based/analytical questions can arise and what will be the broad points to dwell upon. Many such questions are also given in this book to guide the aspirants.

IMPORTANT TOPICS FOR THE MAIN EXAMINATION

Although wide and thorough coverage of all topics is desirable, it may not always possible or practicable to do so. *Considering the trend of past years' questions, the emphasis of candidates should be on the following topics.*

- **Ancient India art, architecture, cultural heritage** with special emphasis on:
    (a) **Indus valley civilisation**, culture town planning, seals, important cities, and salient findings.
    (b) **Buddhism, Jainism, and Vedic culture**.
    (c) **Various schools of art and architecture in ancient India** (viz. Kushana, Gandhara, etc.), rock-cut architecture, influence of Greek and Roman styles, etc.
    (d) **Sangam literature** and other important literary achievements in ancient India.
- **Sufism and Bhakti Movement** in medieval India, other socio religious ideas, impact on society, and various personalities associated with these movements.
- **Temple architecture in medieval India** and other art forms associated with them, viz. sculpture, paintings, etc.

PART 1

Art and Culture in Ancient India

CHAPTER

2 The Indus Valley Civilisation And Harappan Culture

If I were asked under what sky the human mind has most fully developed some of its choicest gifts, has most deeply pondered on the greatest problems of life and has found solutions, I should point to India.

Max Mueller

WHAT IS THE INDUS VALLEY CIVILISATION?

The Indus Valley Civilisation dates back to nearly 4500 BP (before present) and is the earliest known urban culture in the Indian subcontinent. Among the many sites of this civilisation discovered so far, the Harappan site was the first to be discovered in 1921 and hence the civilisation is also referred to as the Harappan Civilisation or Harappan Culture.

In 1922, another great city of this lost civilisation, called Mohenjo-daro (meaning; mound of the dead) was discovered. A number of other sites such as **Chanhudaro, Lothal, Kalibangan, Dholavira, etc.** have subsequently been discovered. These indicate that the civilisation had spread to vast areas now located in present day Pakistan, Gujarat, Rajasthan, Punjab, and Jammu region in India and even in many parts of Afghanistan.

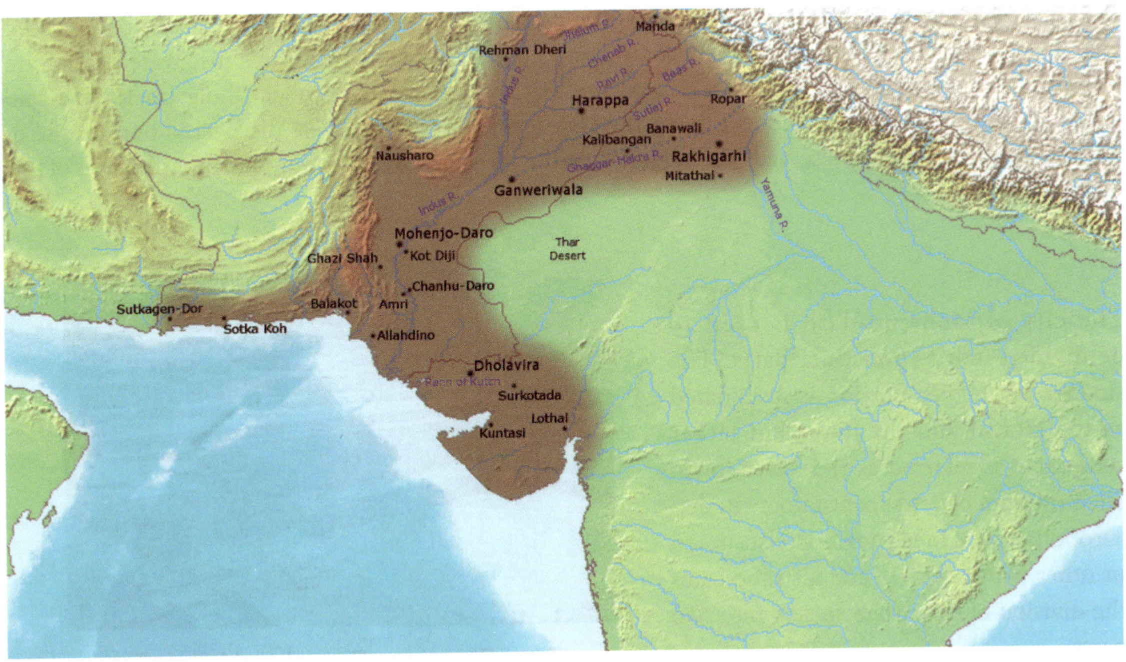

Indus Valley Civilisation (shaded region)

Over 1000 such settlements have been discovered up till now in the valley of river Indus and the adjoining rivers and their tributaries (hence the name Indus Valley Civilisation). Out of these, nearly 100 sites have been excavated. The sites of Harappa, Mohenjo-daro, Dholavira, Ganeriwala, and Rakhigarhi were found to be among the major urban centres.

PERIOD AND PHASES OF GROWTH

This civilisation is said to have flourished for nearly 2000 years between 3300 BCE to 1300 BCE. Thus, it was a contemporary of the Egyptian and Mesopotamian civilisation, the two other great civilisations of the ancient world. The phase of growth of this culture can be divided into three parts. The period 2600 BCE to 1900 BCE represents the mature Harappan Civilisation. This phase was preceded and succeeded by the early Harappan and the late Harappan phases.

SALIENT FEATURES OF THE HARAPPAN CULTURE

The Harappan culture is known for some of its very distinct features. These include the **development of urban centres, planning of towns, streets, sewage system, the great baths, and granaries**. The discovery of numerous artefacts, seals and statues, standard weights and measures which are unique to this culture, also throw light on the art, culture, science and technology, government, agriculture, religion, script, and other aspects of social life.

Urban Growth

One of the most important features and achievements of this culture was the growth of urban centres and cities which flourished in this civilisation. After its extinction, such cities and urban centres emerged only a 1000 years later in the Indian subcontinent. The important urban centres discovered so far are Harappa, Mohenjo-daro, and Ganeriwala in the present day Pakistan and Lothal, Dholavira, Kalibangan, Rakhi, and Rupar in India. Amongst these, the Harappan site is the earliest discovered but the site of Mohenjo-daro was better preserved. The latter reveals the excellent town planning and other features of this civilisation.

Town Planning

The city of Mohenjo-daro is seen to be divided into two distinct parts. The smaller but higher portion is designated as the citadel and the lower but larger settlement is referred as the lower town. Such division of settlement into a citadel/ acropolis and a lower town is also noted in other urban centres and also indicates the division of this urban society into two parts.

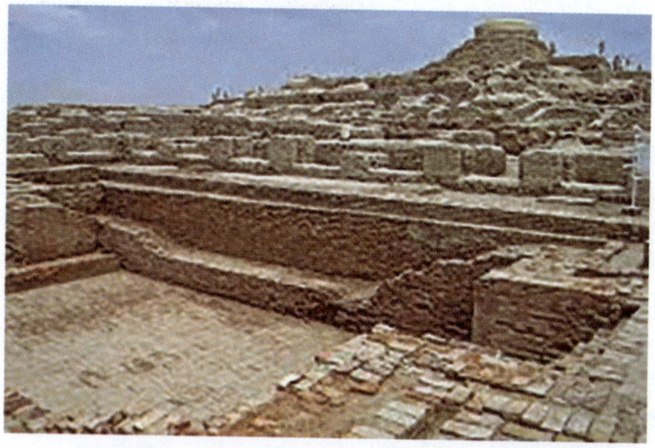

Town Planning : Citadel and Lower Town

The citadel which was built on a higher ground had walls fortifying it from all sides. The structures and houses were built on mud and burnt brick platform. These structures include many important ones like the great bath, the warehouse, the pillared hall, etc. which appear to have been used for public purposes.

The lower town was of much larger area than the citadel but built on a lower ground. Like the citadel, it was walled, apparently to keep the flood waters away. The houses and structures too have been found to be built on raised platforms made of mud and burnt bricks. The bricks were of standard size and ratio (of length, breadth, and height) and similar/standard bricks were employed in all settlements in this culture.

Streets and Town Planning

The streets of the urban centres were running at right angles in east–west and north–south directions, resembling a grid pattern. These were wide (as much as 30–35 ft), with corners rounded making them suitable for wheeled and heavy vehicles like carts. They also had arrangement for street lighting. The streets along with the efficient drainage system seems to have been constructed first and the houses built around them later, indicating existence of advanced town planning and municipal system.

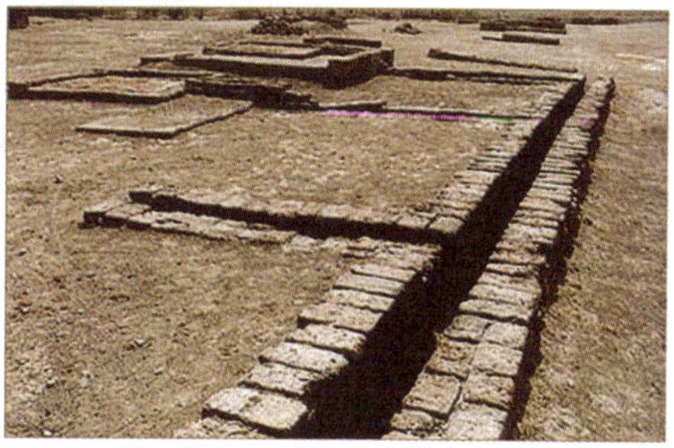

Drainage Mohenjo-daro

The Drainage System

This civilisation had developed an advanced and efficient drainage system not found amidst other contemporary civilisations. Each house had its private drinking well and a bathroom. The water from them ran through clay pipes into underground drains which ran into main drains. These main drains were made up of bricks set in mortar and had large cross-sections to accommodate even a large waterflow. The house drains were first emptied into a cesspit or a sump in which the solid matter would first settle allowing the water to drain in the main drain. The latter had sumps at regular intervals to enable its cleaning. The above is indicative of not only the advancement in municipal system and importance attached to social and personal hygiene, but also of proper planning and good knowledge of brick-mortar construction.

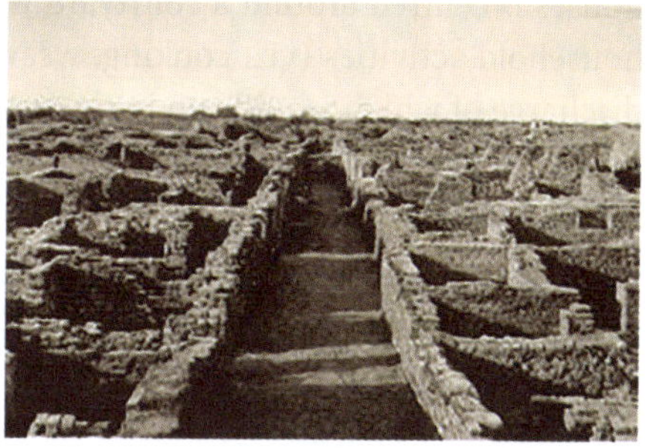

Street image Mohenjo-daro

The Great Bath

The Great Bath of Mohenjo-daro is one of the most important finds of this civilisation. Located on the citadel it was apparently used for ceremonial bathing purposes. The structure is rectangular in shape (approximate dimensions 12m by 7m and depth 2.43m). It was accessible from two wide staircases each on the northern and the southern side. The tank was watertight, as it was made of tightly fitting bricks with coating of mud and gypsum plaster. The pool had an array of rooms located on one side of it with a well located in one of the rooms, which was used for drawing water for the pool.

The Great Bath is a reflection of the achievement of this civilisation in the field of engineering and construction technology. Besides, it also indicates the social significance attached to religious/ceremonial matters in public life.

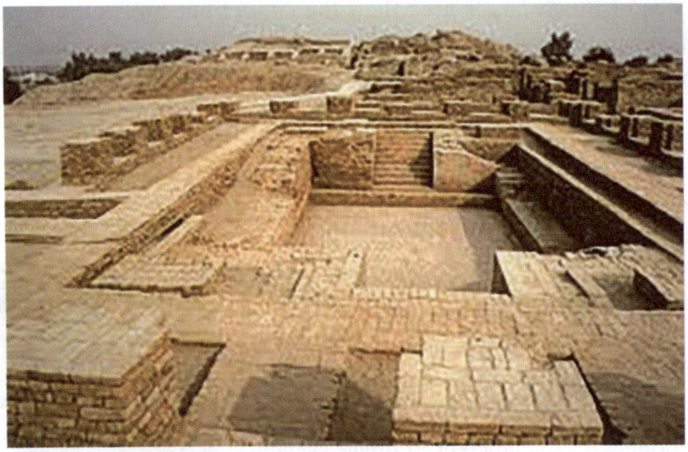

The Great Bath of Mohenjo-daro

Domestic House Planning and Architecture

The domestic house planning and architecture is evident in the lower town of Mohenjo-daro. The houses were constructed along the roads and drains (which were planned and constructed first). Each of the houses is centred around a courtyard with rooms built around it. The courtyard could be the centre of household activities (viz. cooking, weaving, etc). Each house had a separate bathroom with a well, the discharge of which would run in the system of drains.

Great Granary

Evidence has also been found of a large warehouse type structure at Harappa which is also referred to as the Great Granary.

Dockyard at Lothal

The existence of a channel based docking system at Lothal (literally meaning *Loth-Sthal*; or mound of the dead) in the state of Gujarat, is an important find of the Harappan culture. The dockyard was connected to a river channel through which boats could reach the sea following the tidal system. The dock and the channel could be locked during a low tide and unlocked during high tide thus allowing navigation. The town also boasted of a citadel or acropolis and a lower town. Bead making, jewellery making, and making of other metallurgical products flourished in this centre. It was also an important trading town.

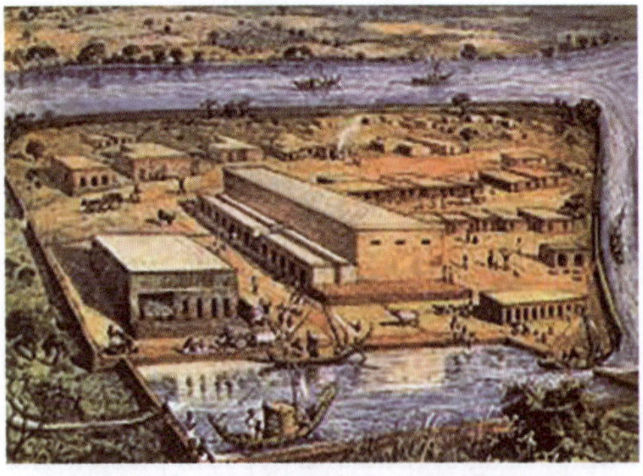

Pictographic picture of Lothal

Indus Script

The Indus script has not been deciphered as yet and may have been a **pictographic** one. A large number of characters of this script (nearly 400) have been discovered so far, primarily on the numerous seals and ceramic pots excavated. Most of the inscriptions are short with the longest being of 26 signs (found in what is called a signboard over a structure in Dholavira). What is known, is that the characters were written from right to left as in some seals/inscriptions, many characters are seen to be squeezed for want of space towards the left end.

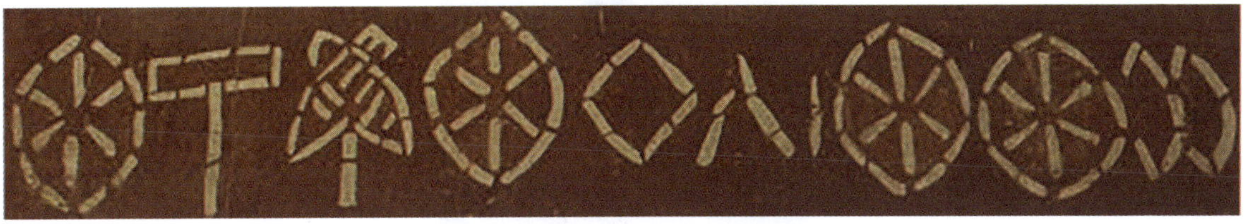

Signboard Dholavira

Weights and Measures

The culture had also developed an accurate system of weights and measures. The weights were made of cubical pieces of stone called **Cherts**. While the lower weights were binary in nature (ratio of 1:2:4:8, etc.) the higher weights were of decimal base. At Lothal, an ivory scale (to measure length) was found showing smallest division of 1.704 mm.

The use of accurate weights and measures indicates advancement in science and mathematics and growth of trade and commerce in the civilisation.

Seals, Pottery and Other Artifacts

A number of seals, pottery, jewellery, and other artifacts have been discovered which throw light on the art and craft of this culture. Chanhudaro (in Pakistan) was an important centre of such crafts which included bead making, metal works, making of seals and artifacts, pottery, and sheet cutting. A variety of stones, viz. steatite, quartz, and jasper crystal were used. Besides, terracotta, faience, and metals like copper, bronze, and even gold were used. The above are indicative of high standards of craftsmanship, knowledge of metallurgy and foundry, besides flourishing trade and commerce.

Important Seals and Artifacts

(a) **Shiva Pashupati seal:** The seal depicting a figure seated cross legged in a yogic posture with a horned head dress. The figure is surrounded by a number of animals (elephant, buffalo, tiger, rhinoceros, and antelope) and is considered to be a **proto-Shiva** or early form of Shiva/Pashupati/Rudra venerated in later and contemporary Hinduism.

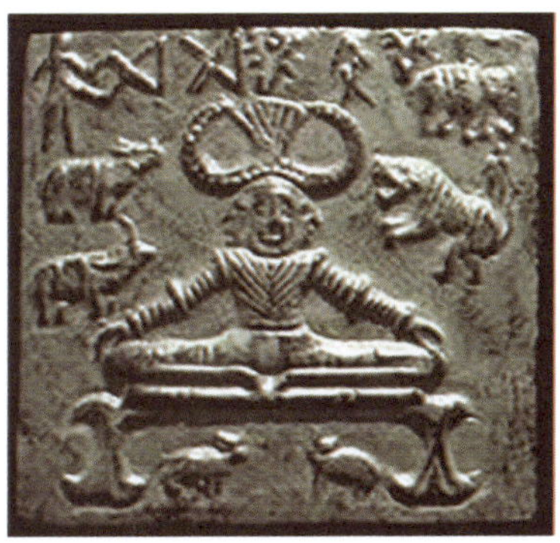

Pashupati Seal

(b) **Mother Goddess figurine:** This is a terracotta figurine of a woman adorned with jewellery and imposing fan shaped headgear. Many such figurines have been found. They are considered to be a depiction of the Mother Goddess. The images of proto-Shiva and of the Mother Goddess indicate religious belief of people of this civilisation. Further, it also indicates a link with the subsequent Hindu tradition and belief in similar/identical gods and goddesses.

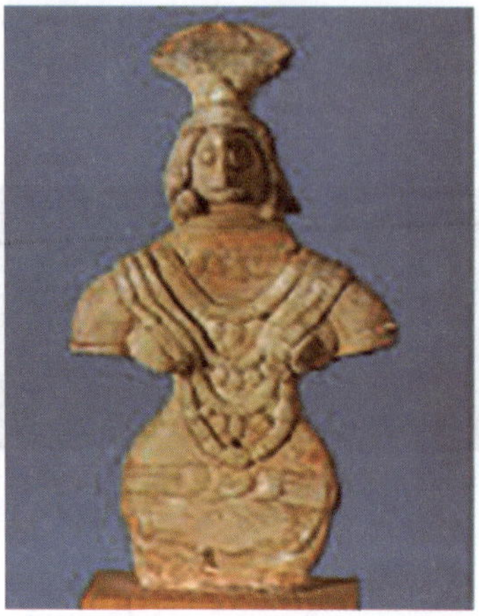

Mother Goddess Figurine

(c) **Priest King statue:** It is a famous stone (steatite) statue of a bearded man believed to be a priest king. The bust (statue) has a fillet or a ribbon headband with a circular inlay ornament. Similar ribbon with fillet is found on the forearm. The figure is draped in a shawl with trefoil pattern.

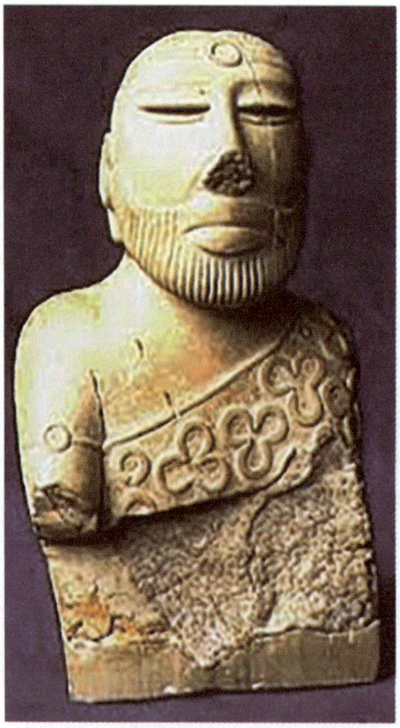

Priest King statue

(d) **The Dancing Girl statue:** This small bronze statue of a dancing girl found in Mohenjo-daro, is an excellent example of art and metallurgy of this period. The statue is dated to around 2500 BC. It depicts a naked girl striking a dancing posture with one hand on her hips. A number of bangles are seen in the other arm. She is also wearing a necklace. The arms are shown to be unusually long.

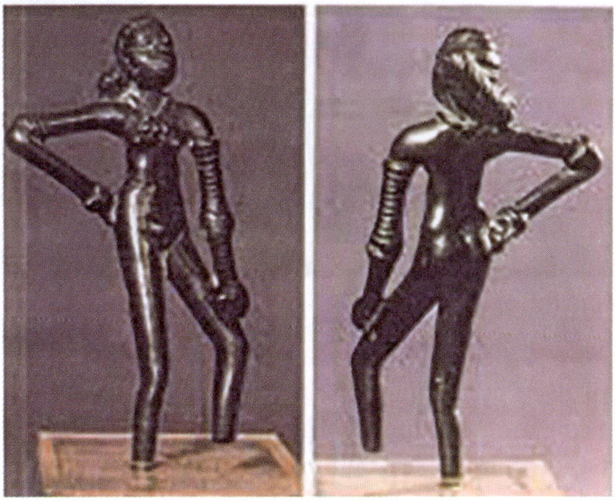

Dancing Girl statue

(e) **The Bull seal:** This seal shows a humped bull and has good depiction of the features of the animal. A number of seals with animal depictions have been found. All this are indicative of knowledge of wild animals and hunting.

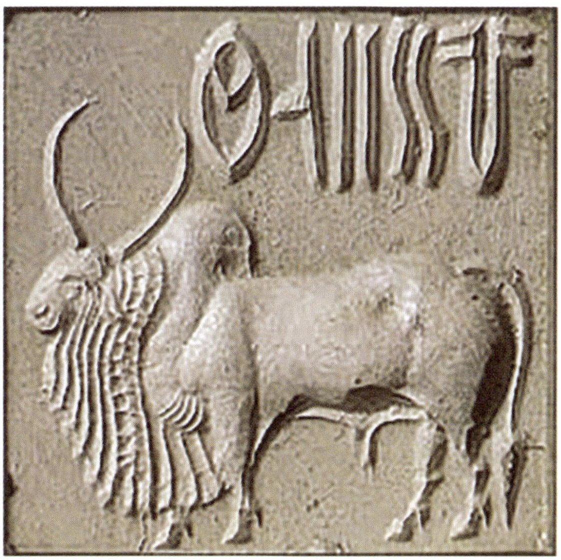

Bull Seal

(f) **The Unicorn seal:** It is another important seal depicting a unicorn which is a mythical animal (a horse with a single horn).

(g) **The Male Torso:** This is another red sand statue depicting the male torso. The figure has socket holes in the arms and neck for attachment of arms and neck. The proportions of the male body (torso) are well shown.

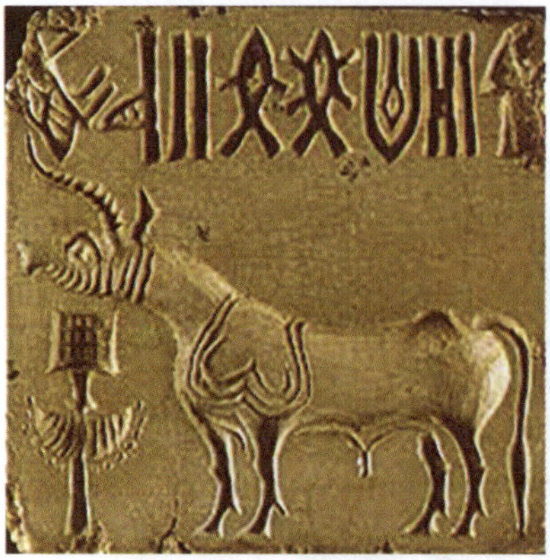

Unicorn Seal

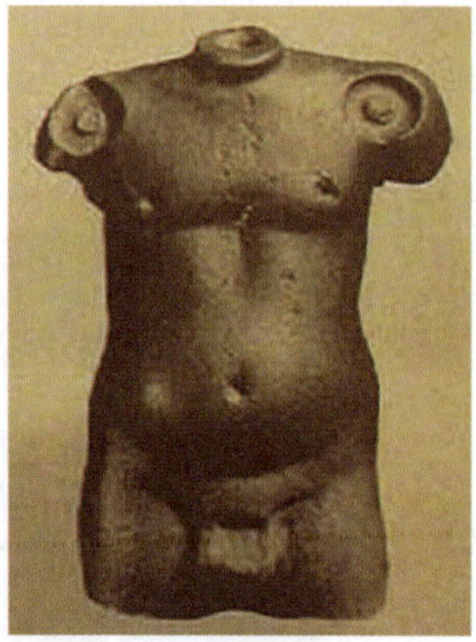

Male Torso

Utility and Significance of Seals

Over 4000 seals and similar artifacts pertaining to the Harappan period have been discovered so far. The seals are believed to be used for sealing the consignment of goods and securing them (by placing a mark of the seal on the opening). The presence of an intact seal on the consignment at the destination was a sign the goods being secure. Besides, the seals were also an indication of the identity of the sender. The discovery of a large number of seals at various sites is an indication of the flourishing trade and commerce and also of the fact that this urban civilisation was not just an agriculture dependent economy. The symbols on the seal indicate the existence of a script. The numerous figures throw light on the socio religious and other aspects of the culture.

Society and Government

From the archeological findings it is noted that the Harappan bricks, seal weights, etched uniformly irrespective of not being produced in same centre and being found in different places. The uniformity in bricks is especially noteworthy as they had common ratio of length, breadth, and height. Further, the existence of town planning, establishment of settlements near the source of raw material, etc. all point towards existence of some kind of central authority. However, lack of discovery of large and distinct structures such as palaces (as found in Mesopotamian and Egyptian sites) suggests that the authority may not have been a monarch or a king. Thus, the society could have been egalitarian with distribution of power in hands of many. Some historians even suggest that each of the various sites could have had separate rulers. However, the latter is less likely considering the uniformity in weights and measures, bricks, and artifacts.

Burials and Belief in Afterlife

At some of the Harappan sites, burial chambers have been discovered which are generally in the form of pits. In some burial pits, brick linings were also found indicating existence of social differences. Some of the dead were buried along with items of jewellery and pottery indicating belief in afterlife.

Trade and Commerce

Trade and commerce was an important sector of this culture's economy as evident from the numerous seals and artifacts. The raw material used in production were sourced from different places, viz. copper from Oman (as chemical analysis shows Omani copper and Harappan artifacts to have traces of nickel, thus indicating common origin). Similarly, Harappan artifacts have been found at different sites too, viz. Harappan jars (pottery with a layer of black clay) found at Omani sites. The trade and commerce could have been carried through land or through sea. Seals depicting ships have been discovered besides dockyard of Lothal which is further indicative of sea trade.

Agriculture

Discovery of grains at some of the Harappan sites and terracotta models of plough found at Cholistan and Banawali (Haryana) point towards prevalence of agriculture. Terracota figurines, statue, and seals of bulls also suggest that oxen might have been used for ploughing. Evidence of ploughed fields has been found at Kalibangan (Rajasthan). Irrigation is thought to have been carried by use of wells or reservoirs which were found at Dholavira (Gujarat). Some traces of canals have also been identified at Shortughai, a Harappan site in Afghanistan. Barley and wheat were the major cultivated cereal crops.

IMPORTANT HARAPPAN SITES AND THEIR SIGNIFICANCE

Sites & Present Location	Significance and Archaeological Discoveries
Mohenjo-daro (in Pakistan)	• Discovered in 1922, amongst the better preserved sites. • Existence of **citadel** and **lower town** • Discovery of **Great Bath**, pillared hall, granary planned roads, sewage system
Harappa (in Pakistan)	• Earliest discovered (in 1921), **one of the largest sites**, but less preserved as ruin—bricks were used for ballast for laying tracks in early British Rule and also lost due to theft. • The **Great Granary**
Lothal (in Gujarat)	• Existence of earliest dockyard and acropolis • Discovery of **weights and measures** • Flourishing centre of beads and gem making
Dholavira (in Gujarat)	• Discovery of large water reservoirs (built of stone) drawing water from channels and rivulets • One of the five large settlements of Harappan culture • Large signboard containing a number of characters
Rakhigarhi (in Haryana)	• Important and large site (nearly 33 square km) • Discovery of artifacts 5000 years old (early Harappan phase) • Paved roads, rain water collection, drainage system, granary, bronze artifacts, bangles, etc. • Discovery of female skeletons with shell bangles and gold armlet. 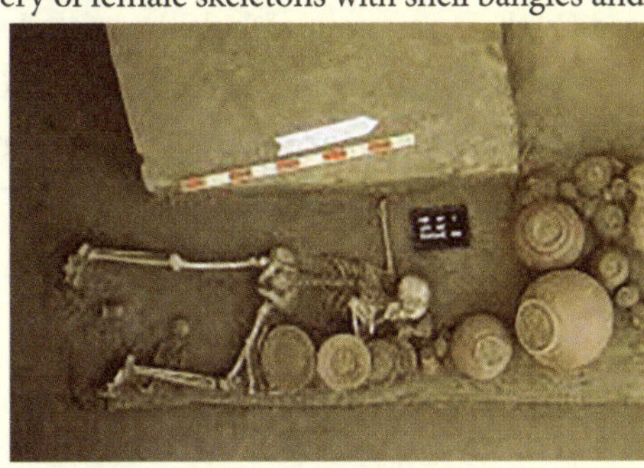 **Burial and Skeleton**

Kalibangan (in Rajasthan)	• Literally means black bangles owing to discovery of a number of terracotta black bangles at this site • Represents early Harappan phase • Fortified settlement citadel and fire altars discovered
Kot Diji (in Pakistan)	• Settlement of early Harappan phase • Existence of citadel and lower town • Discovery of defensive wall with a mud brick revetment with bastions
Ganeriwala (in Pakistan)	• Among the largest cities of Harappan civilisation (80 hectares)

OTHER IMPORTANT FEATURES OF THE HARAPPAN CULTURE

- **Fabric and cloth:** Cotton was commonly used as fabric for clothing, although wool could also have been used. Findings of spindles indicate that weaving and spinning was known. Needles and buttons have been discovered indicating that perhaps stitching was also known. Dress or fabric has not survived but statues and figurines suggest that two pieces of cloth were used by men and women. One piece resembled a dhoti covering the lower body. Other portion was worn over the left shoulder under the right arm.

- **Games, sports, and entertainment:** Objects similar to dice games and clay carts have been found. Hunting is believed to be common as seen from a number of seals carrying images of animals. Dancing and singing were popular as seen from the bronze statue of the dancing girl.

- **Religion:** Discovery of seal of Shiva Pashupati (proto-Shiva) and figurines believed to be of Mother Goddess, indicate presence of religious beliefs comparable to very early Hinduism. However, historians believe that religion does not seem to have a predominant influence on the society.

IMPORTANT TOPICS TO FOCUS ON

- Harappan civilisation's town planning, street system, and drainage system.
- Important structures excavated and their significance, viz. the Great Bath (Mohenjo-daro), granary, dockyard (Lothal), reservoir (Dholavira), citadels, and lower towns.
- Important seals, figurines, and artifacts, and information gathered/inferences drawn therefrom.
- Governance, religious practices, trade and commerce, and script.

CHAPTER 3

Hinduism

> Hinduism alone is by itself a vast and complex thing, not so much a religion as a great diversified and yet subtly unified mass of spiritual thought, realisation and aspiration
>
> **Sri Aurobindo**

AN INTRODUCTION

Hinduism is the oldest organised and living religion of the world. At present it has more than 10 million followers which is roughly 14% of the world population. It is the third largest religion (after Christianity and Islam) in the world with wide geographical distribution of its followers. Believers of this faith are in majority in the demography of India, Nepal, and Mauritius and are present in more than 100 countries and with more than 100,000 population in nearly 35 countries. However, over 98% of Hindu population is concentrated in South Asia (India; 1 billion, Nepal; 23 million, Bangladesh; 13.5 million, Pakistan; 3.6 million).

Hinduism as a religion does not have an origin at a single point of time, a singular religious preacher to whom it could own its genesis, a singular scripture to which its philosophy can be attributed, or even a single faith which can define it. It is a conglomeration of beliefs, faiths, and philosophies. It is a religion which has grown over nearly 4000 years. Numerous scriptures (the *Vedas*, the *Puranas*, the *Ramayana*, the *Mahabharata*, the *Gita*, and others) contain its philosophy. Numerous sages and reformers have contributed to its growth as it has evolved assimilating numerous beliefs and philosophies in it.

The very word 'Hinduism' is of later origin, referring to the people in the valley of river Sindhu (Indus) and beyond it. The coinage of the term 'Hindu' is Persian in nature and over a period it acquired a religious connotation. In the early period of this growth, the faith has been referred to *Sanatan Dharma* (the eternal or universal religion), or *Varnashram Dharma*, a faith based on fulfillment of duties based on *Varna* (class) and *Ashram* (stage of life), or a *Vaidik Dharma* (a faith based on principles of the Vedas).

A BRIEF HISTORY

The Vedic religion and texts are said to be nearly 3500 years old. The growth of the Vedic faith has been divided into several periods of development.

The Vedic Phase

The period from 1500 BCE to 500 BCE is usually referred as the Vedic period. The four Vedas, the Rigveda, the Samveda, the Atharvaveda, and the Yajurveda are said to have been composed in this period, the Rigveda being of the earliest origin amongst the four.

Early Vedic Phase and Later Vedic Phase

The Vedic phase is further divided into the **early Vedic phase** (1500–1000 BCE) **and later Vedic phase** (1000–500 BC). The advent of Buddhism and Jainism marked the next phase in the growth of the Vedic religion (500 BCE to 200 BCE). This was a period of upheavals as there was opposition to the Brahmanical superiority, animal sacrifices and challenge to the authority of the ritualistic/tradition of the Vedas by the two upcoming faiths.

The Golden Period of Hinduism

The next 700 to 800 years, i.e., 200 BCE to 500 CE can be described as a **golden period for growth of Hinduism.** This phase also coincides in history with the Gupta period. The six branches of Hindu philosophy—*Nyaya, Vaisheshika, Samkhya, Yoga, Purva Mimansa,* and *Vedanta* came into vogue in this period. The growth of the Puranas or the advent of the Puranic Hindu culture succeeds this period.

The Age of Adi Shankara and Advaita Vedanta

Towards the end of this phase came the doctrine of *Advaita Vedanta* propounded and consolidated by **Sri Adi Shankaracharya** (8th century CE). He unified the various sects and streams of Hinduism in vogue then and founded the **four Mathas** (monasteries) which gave a formal structure to Hinduism and helped in its revival. This was followed by the emergence of *Vishista Advaita* (propounded by **Ramanuja** in 12th century CE) and *Dwaitvad* (propounded by **Madhavacharya** in the 13th century).

The Bhakti Movement

The **Bhakti movement** in medieval period (15th century CE to 17th century CE) was another important epoch in the growth of Hinduism. It began in the southern part of the country and spread to the northern and eastern parts. Ramananda, Vallabhacharya, Tukaram, Namdeva, Mirabai, Nanak, Kabirdas, Soordas, Tulsidas, Chaitanya, etc. are associated with it. The movement influenced reform within Hinduism, rather than giving it a new philosophy. It emphasised on devotion as a path for salvation regardless of caste, gender, or other differences. It was further characterised as *Nirguna* Bhakti (devotion to formless god) or *Saguna* Bhakti (specific gods and goddesses with attributes).

The Modern Era and Phase of Reforms

The eighteenth and the nineteenth centuries saw another phase of reforms and revival in Hinduism—Brahmo Samaj, Arya Samaj, Prathana Samaj, Ramakrishna Mission, etc. Reformists like Raja Ram Mohun Roy, Dayananda Saraswati, Ishwar Chandra Vidyasagar, Vivekananda, and others, endeavoured to purge it of many social events like sati, child marriages, untouchability, and caste systems and base it on Vedantic philosophy or principles as laid in various scriptures or schools of philosophical thought.

SCRIPTURES AND PHILOSOPHIES OF HINDUISM

Scriptures and philosophies of Hinduism form a crucial area of study of the topic of culture. Many questions, particularly in the Preliminarily Examination, arise from this topic which requires an understanding of the areas such as the six ancient philosophies, the Vedic religion, and the scriptures like Samhitas, Upanishads, Puranas, etc.

A brief account of the important scriptures and the salient Hindu philosophy is given herein.

Classification of Scriptures

The Hindu scriptures can broadly be classified into two broad categories—the *Smritis* and the *Shrutis*. This classification is based on the purported origin of the scriptures.

(a) The Shrutis: The word *Shruti* literally means 'what is heard'. The *Shruti* refer to the class of scriptures and texts which were 'heard' by the sages and seers in ancient times. They are believed to be of divine origin. Thus, these scriptures were purportedly revealed to them due to their divine knowledge and understanding and the sages communicated this knowledge to the world. The *Shrutis* comprise the most authoritative texts of Hindu philosophy and religion. These include the four Vedas.

(b) The Smritis: These refer to the Hindu scriptures which are considered to be of human origin and can be attributed to a specific author unlike the *'Shrutis'* which were considered to be of primordial or non-human origin. *Smriti* means what is remembered. Thus, the composer of these texts recalled the occurrences of event and facts and captured them in the form of texts. The eighteen Puranas, authored by sage *Veda Vyasa* and the two epics *Ramayana* (by sage Valmiki) and *Mahabharata* (by sage Veda Vyasa) fall in this category. The epics are also referred to as **'*Itihasa*'**. The other Hindu scriptures would also fall in the category of *Smritis.*

IMPORTANT HINDU SCRIPTURES

The Vedas

The *Vedas* can be said to be the most important scriptures of Hinduism as they contain the central cannons of the Hindu philosophy. The word *Veda* is derived from the root word **'vid'** or **knowledge** or **wisdom**. Thus, Vedas were considered as scriptures containing the sum total of the knowledge of the people. Further, the word 'Vid' also refers to the knowledge which could illuminate the path in the darkness (of ignorance), eventually leading to salvation. Historically, they are said to have been composed between 1500 BCE to 600 BCE. However, recent researches particularly those based on astronomical dating of events described therein, attribute them to be of earlier origin although a formal compilation/categorisation could have occurred later. The six system of Hindu philosophy— **Nyaya, Vaiseshika, Sankhya, Yoga, Purva Mimamsa, and Vedanta** (discussed later) —also accept the authority of the Vedas. These were composed in Sanskrit and their study was largely limited to the Brahmins. The Vedas are four in number: **the Rigveda, the Yajurveda, the Samaveda**, and **the Atharvaveda**. Each of these consists of and includes the Samhitas, the Brahmanas, the Aranyakas, and the Upanishads, as separate parts or layers of the Vedas.

(i) Rigveda: The Rigveda is oldest of all the Vedas. Thus, it is the most ancient of the Hindu scriptures. It is a collection of hymns or *suktas* (1028 in number) for propitiation of various deities. The earliest deities were the various elements of nature (viz. *Agni, Indra, Varun, Soma,* etc.). The latter hymns deal with philosophical and metaphysical questions such as nature of god, origin of universe, *Brahma, Atma,* etc. It is also referred to as the book of *Mantras.*

(ii) Yajurveda: The Yajurveda is a compilation of verses or mantras invoked or chanted in various rituals/ offering by the priests. Thus, it prescribed the modalities for conduct of different *yajnas* and rituals. The earlier portion of Yajurveda (the *Samhita*) contains nearly 1875 *shlokas*. It also includes some important Upanishads, viz. the **Brihad-Upanishad, Aranyaka-Upanishad, Katha-Upanishad, Isha-Upanishad, Tattireya-Upanishad,** etc.

(iii) Samaveda: The Samaveda is a book of chants and hymns notated as melodies. It is the third Veda and shortest in terms of mantras, containing 1874 mantras in total. Many of its verses are derived from the Rigveda which are set in form of musical notations. It has two major parts. These include melody collections in the first part (*Gana*) and the second part contains the verses (*Archika book*). The melody in the first part corresponds to the verse in the second part. Thus, the roots of Indian music and dance are contained in **Samaveda**. It also contains the two important Upanishads — the **Chandoga Upanishad** and **Kena Upanishad**.

(iv) Atharvaveda: The Atharvaveda is the last of the Vedas. The name of this Veda is derived from the word **'Atharvanas'** implying procedures for everyday life. Thus, this Veda contained knowledge having application in daily life ranging from medicine to other physical sciences. However, it was earlier misinterpreted to be a book of magical spells or formulae.

This Veda has nearly 730 hymns and includes **Mundaka, Mandukya**, and **Prashana Upanishads** as a part of it.

Scriptures Comprising the Vedas

(i) Samhitas: The Samhitas are the first of the four parts of the Vedas (also referred as the first layer). They are also referred as the '*Mantra*' as they are a compilation of Mantras or sacred chants and incantations. These chants were invoked for propitiation of elements of nature and deities and the latter were symbolic of the former. The Samhitas are also known by the *Veda* to which it belonged, viz. *Rigveda Samhita* or the '*Rig- Samhita*'.

As the Samhitas, along with the next part of the Vedas, viz. the Brahmanas, contain ritual instructions. They are together referred to as the '*Karma Kanda*' or literally the 'action portion' of the Vedas. In the Hindu school of philosophy, the Samhitas and Brahmanas put together contain the *Purva Mimansa* philosophy (literally meaning 'former inquiry').

(ii) Brahmanas: The second part (or second layer) of the Vedas is referred to as the Brahmanas. They are concerned with the various rituals and rites for propitiation of elements of nature and deities. They also offer explanation to the Mantras as contained in the Samhitas. It is believed that with passage of time it became imperative to explain the meaning of the Mantras which were becoming difficult to understand for the successive generations. Hence came the *Brahmanas* into existence which elaborated upon their meaning and significance. Thus, they were concerned with the proper performance of rituals.

Important Brahmanas

(i) **Aitareya Brahamana** – dealing with Soma sacrifice

(ii) **Kaushitaki Brahmana** – dealing with food sacrifice in Rigveda

(iii) **Satapatha Brahmana** – the largest Brahmana in Yajurveda deals with Vedic rituals.

(iii) Aranyakas: The Aranyakas, the third part of the Vedas, mark a transition from a ritualistic to philosophical and metaphysical thoughts. They offer explanation to the various rituals from a philosophical and different perspective. They are the third part of the Vedas but are also considered by some as extension of or appendices to the Brahmanas.

The *Aranyakas* originates from Sanskrit word '*Aranya*' meaning the forest. This book therefore was also called the 'forest book'. The Aranyakas are believed to have been composed by forest dwelling sages and seers, who eschewed the rituals and emphasised more on their spiritual and philosophical interpretation.

Important Aranyakas

- Aitreya Aranyaka and Kaushitaki Aranyaka of Rigveda
- Taitreya Aranyaka, Katha Aranyaka of Yajurveda
- Chandoga Aranyaka, Kena Aranyaka of Samaveda
- Mundaka and Mandukya Aranyaka pertaining to Atharvaveda

(iv) Upanishads: The Upanishads are the final layer or the concluding part of the Vedas. In a way **they mark the highest point in the Vedic spiritual knowledge** (referred as *Ved-shirsha*). They deal with numerous metaphysical and philosophical questions such as *Brahma* (god), *Atma* (soul), their nature, and relationship which are the focus of the Upanishads.

As they are the concluding portion of the Vedas, they are also referred as the **Vedant** (or the end of the Vedas) and together with the **Aranyakas** they represent the **'Jnan Kand'** or the knowledge portion of the Vedas. The Upanishads along with *Brahma Sutra* and the *Bhagavad Gita* encapsulates the **Vedanta philosophy**. Further, the branch of philosophy **'Uttar Mimansa'** (post analysis) is also based on the teachings contained in Upanishads.

The very word Upanishad is derived from the word '*Sad*' (or *satya*/truth). Thus, Upanishads were considered to be revelatory of truth or true knowledge. It is also thought to mean to sit close to a *guru* and to acquire knowledge. The Upanishads often present this knowledge in the form of a dialogue between a '*guru*' and '*shishya*' (master and disciple). The '*shishya*' raises queries about the philosophical and metaphysical issues (viz. nature of cosmos, *Brahma*, *Atman*, etc.) which the '*guru*' explains.

There are said to be 108 Upanishads of which ten Upanishads **Chandoga, Brihdaranyaka, Aitareya, Tatkriya, Kena, Isha, Mundaka, Mandukya, Katha**, and **Prasna** are considered to be more important.

Itihasa

The word *Itihasa* is derived from the three words, *Iti-Ha-Asa* implying as it happened. Thus, the **Itihasa texts are an account of historical events/history as it happened.** Itihasas come under the classification of the *Smriti* scriptures. The two great Indian epics, the *Ramayana* and the *Mahabharata* are texts/scriptures falling under this category.

(i) The Ramayana: The *Ramayana* is considered to be one of the holy Hindu scriptures. It gives an account of the crown prince Rama, (believed to be an incarnation of Lord Vishnu), and how he vanquishes Ravana and rescues Sita. The Ramayana was written by sage Valmiki in Sanskrit verses. It is divided into seven *kands* (chapters) and contains 24000 verses and is indeed a great piece of ancient literature. Not only does it give a historical account of the life of Rama, but also a social, cultural, and philosophical perspective where Rama represents ideal values, setting an example worth emulation.

There is no unanimity regarding the exact date/period in which Ramayana was written. The generally agreed time frame given by historians is (1500 BC to 600 BC). However, some recent researches based on astronomic dating of events and *nakshatra* position described in Ramayana suggest it to be of older origin.

(ii) The Mahabharata: The great epic was composed by sage Veda Vyasa and is the **longest epic (or poem) ever written**. Its original version is said to contain over a 1,00,000 *shlokas* (longer version) while the shorter version comprises 24000 *shlokas*.

The story recounts the fratricidal war between the Kauravas and the Pandavas which involves all of the remaining dynasties and kingdoms of the time. It gives an account of the political social and cultural life. Further, it is **also a treatise on philosophy and metaphysics** as seen from several chapters/portions of the book, particularly the **Bhagavad Gita**.

(iii) The Bhagavad Gita: The Bhagavad Gita is considered to be the holiest of the Hindu scriptures. Although it is a part of the Mahabharata, owing to its philosophical and spiritual importance, it is considered as a separate and a standalone scripture.

The Gita is a discourse by Lord Krishna to Arjuna given on the battlefield of Kurukshetra, when Arjuna becomes despondent at the prospect of engaging in a war with his cousins, gurus, and dear ones. The scripture is a treatise on topics such as **Dharma** (duty), **Karma Yoga, Bhakti Yoga**, and **Jnan Yoga.** It heavily draws upon the Sankhya and Yoga philosophy as contained in the Upanishads. It further enunciates the philosophy of '*Nishkama Karma*' (detached performance of one's duties).

(iv) Puranas: The word *Purana* literally means, old, or ancient or historical. They are a part of the *Smriti* texts and cover a vast range of religious literature pertaining to legends and stories of various gods and goddesses and their incarnations.

Sage Veda Vyasa is credited with the compilation of the Puranas which are 18 in number. The **Bhagavada Purana** is the most studied and popular of the Puranas. It describes the avatars of lord Vishnu. It also forms the basis of *Gaudiya Vaishnavism* founded by medieval saint in Bengal, Chaitanya Mahaprabhu. Other important Puranas are **Brahma-Purana, Vishnu-Purana, Shiva-Purana,** and **Markendaya-Purana.**

The *Puranas* and the *Itihasas* were the religious literature which was more popular in the masses/ common people as the study of the Vedas was more restricted to the Brahmanical section of the society.

OTHER HINDU SCRIPTURES

Vedangs and Upvedas

Although strictly not a part of the Vedas, the Vedang (literally meaning 'part of the Vedas') and Upvedas (literally meaning 'subsidiary or sub-Veda') are considered to be auxiliary disciplines associated with the study of the Vedas.

(i) Vedang: These are six separate disciplines which aid in the study of the Vedas or are independent subjects in themselves. These are:

(a) ***Nirukta*** – Dealing with etymology; study of obscure phrases and words

(b) ***Vyakaran*** – Study of grammar

(c) ***Kalpa*** – Dealing with religious ceremonies

(d) ***Shiksha*** – Study of phonetics and pronunciation
(e) ***Chandas*** – Study of verses and prosody
(f) ***Jyotisha*** – Study of movement of celestial bodies and astronomy

The first two (*Nirukta* and *Vyakaran*) were essential and common to study of all Vedas while the others aided as well as developed into an independent study.

(ii) Upvedas: There are five recognised Upvedas each dealing with a separate discipline. These are:

(a) ***Arthaveda*** – Dealing with science of sociology, economics, and political systems related to Rigveda.
(b) ***Dhanurveda*** – Science of defence, arms, and armament. It is related to Yajurveda.
(c) ***Gandharvaveda*** – Science of music (includes singing and instruments). It is related to Samaveda.
(d) ***Ayurveda*** – Science of medicines, which is related to Atharvaveda.
(e) ***Sthapathyaveda*** – Science of architecture which is related to Yajurveda.

Dharma Shastras

These were texts which prescribed laws and religious duties pertaining to righteous conduct in the society. They are reflective of the religious and social conditions of the ancient society. Dharma shastras dwell on issues like the '*Aachara*' (rules of daily rituals), '*Vyavahara*' (rules of substantive law and removal of doubts), '*Prayaschitta*' (rules of penance), etc. The important Dharma shastras are **Manu-Smriti, Yajnavalkya-Smriti, Narada-Smriti,** and **Vishnu-Smriti**.

HINDU PHILOSOPHY

The Hindu philosophy is a collection of numerous philosophical doctrines ranging from the '*Shad-Darshan*' (six philosophical schools) propounded in ancient India to the *Advaita Vedanta* (8th century CE) from *Nirguna Brahma* to *Saguna Brahma* and from *Varnashrama-Dharma* to *Bhakti Yoga*. Each has enriched and added to the cumulative philosophical tradition. However, singularly none can be said to represent the Hindu philosophy wholly. *Some of the important philosophical traditions are discussed below:*

The Shad-Darshanas

These refer to the six philosophical systems which emerged in ancient India between 6th century BCE to 4th century CE. They form the core of the Hindu philosophical system. These are **Nyaya, Vaishesika, Samkhya, Yoga, Purva Mimansa**, and **Vedanta.**

(i) Nyaya

They Nyaya school of philosophy is said to be founded in the 2nd century CE by sage Gautama. It deals with **formal reasoning, logic, epistemology, theology, and metaphysics.** *Nyay-sutra* which is the foundational text of this school sheds light on sixteen topics pertaining to logic and reasoning. These are: (a) **Pramana** (epistemology/ proof) (b) **Pramey** (which is to be proven) or ontology (c) **Samasya** (doubt) (d) **Prayojana** (purpose) (e) **Drishtanta** (illustrations or case study) (f) **Siddhanta** (established doctrine) (g) **Avayavya** (premise of a syllgolism) (h) **Tarka** (logical deduction) (i) **Nirnaya** (conclusion) (j) **Vada** (discussion) (k) **Jalpa** (debates with view to defeat an opponent) (l) **Vitanda** (debate without interest in establishing a view) (m) Hetvabhasha (fallacious arguments) (n) Chala (unfair attempt to contradict a statement) (o) Jai (unfair reply to argument), and (p) Nigrasthana (ground for defeat in a debate).

(ii) Vaiseshika

This system of philosophy was founded by sage Kanada (in 1st century CE). It deals with philosophical as well as metaphysical issues. It postulates matter and objects in the physical world to be eventually made up of *Parmanu* (atoms). Earth, water, air, and fire are the four basic substances composing the physical world. These in turn are themselves of two types— 'atomic' (*Parmanu*) and 'composite'. A 'composite' in turn is divided into atoms and atoms are indivisible, indestructible, and invisible.

However, beyond the metaphysical concepts this school also postulates what is *Dharma* and that it is *Dharma* which leads to salvation. Its postulates are contained in the 'Vaisesika-sutra' of Kanada.

(iii) Samkhya

The Samkhya school of philosophy is the oldest of the organised schools of Indian philosophy. The propounder of this school is said to be sage Kapila. This school developed independent of the Vedas and even finds a mention in the *Katha Upanishad* and the *Bhagavad Gita*. Some Jain texts too refer to this system. 'Samkhya Karika' of Isvar Krishna (4th century CE) is the authoritative text of this philosophy.

As per the Samkhya system, the universe comprises of two fundamental entities—the '*Purusa*' (consciousness-person) and *Prakriti* (matter nature). The living being or *Jiva* exists as a result of the bond between the *Purusa* and *Prakriti*.

Prakriti or nature comprises the three Gunas—Sattva (based on knowledge, illuminance, goodness, compassion, positivity, etc.), Rajas (based on activity, passion, impulsiveness, and even chaos), and Tamas (based on ignorance, inaction, negativity, lethargy, destruction etc.). All the three *Gunas* are present in different proportions in different life forms. The Gunas define character of a living thing and lead to pleasure or pain. With true satvic knowledge does a being realise the distinction of *Purusa* from *Prakriti* which eventually leads to the end of the cycle of transmigration of soul or a state of complete freedom or Kaivalya.

This system does not base itself on the teaching in Vedas nor does it believe in a universal being or God. It is considered a rationalist school of Indian philosophy.

(iv) Yoga

The Yoga philosophy emanates from Patanjali's '***Yoga Sutra***' (4th century CE). The essence of this philosophy is also contained in Bhagavad Gita. The Yoga philosophy quite like the Samkhya, does not derive its authority from Vedas and like Samkhya, it believes the cosmos to be a result of interaction between *Purusha* and *Prakriti* and that there is existence of the three Gunas. However, while in the Samkhya system, liberation is achieved by *Prakriti* (nature) enlightening the *Purusha* (which has a lesser proactive role), in the Yoga system, *Purusha* is not a mere spectator and by personal effort and practical action, *Purusha* can attain its own liberation. The Ashtanga Yoga as propounded by Patanjali is the means to such liberation. *It consists of eight limbs which are:*

Yama – comprising *Ahimsa*, eschewing *Asatya* (falsehood), *Aparigraha* (greed/envy), *Asteya* (acquisition), and practicing *Brahmacharya* (sexual restraint)

Niyama – Discipline and observance of rules of simplicity, austerity, and purity

Asana – Physical postures and exercises

Pranayama – Control of breath and mind

Pratyahara – Withdrawal of consciousness/mind from sensory objects

Dharana – Concentration

Dhyana – Meditation

Samadhi – State of union of self with universe or *Kaivalya*

Yoga is recognised by the Hindu philosophy to be categorised as *Raja Yoga* (described in Patanjali's *Ashtanga Yoga* system), *Jnana Yoga, Karma Yoga, and Bhakti Yoga.*

(v) Purva Mimansa The philosophy of Purva Mimansa or Mimansa is contained in the Purva Mimansa Sutra of Jamini. The words *Purva* (former) and *Mimansa* (enquiry) refer to the former part of the Vedas, i.e., to the Samhitas and the Brahmanas or the *Karmkand*. Thus, this school of philosophy is based on the teachings of Vedas as contained in Samhitas and Brahmanas. It considers the Vedas to be eternal and infalliable and emphasises on *Mantras* and rituals as prescribed in Vedas, as of being of primary importance, while the Upanishads were considered to be of secondary importance. Its philosophy concerns more with *Dharma*, and duties of a person or '*Karya*' rather than metaphysical knowledge. This school also helped in development of philosophy of language, linguistics, and philology which influenced other schools.

(vi) Vedanta The word 'Vedant' literally means the 'end of the Vedas'. The philosophy of this school is based on the teachings as contained in the concluding portion of the Vedas, viz. the Upanishads. It is also referred as Uttar Mimansa (or latter enquiry) as opposed to Purva Mimansa.

The Vedantic philosophy is expressed in its classical form in the Vedant Sutras or the Brahmsutras of *Badrayana* (1st century CE) which is akin to a synopsis of the teachings of Upanishads. It also finds expression in the teachings of the 'Bhagavad Gita'. This philosophy emphasised on *Jnana* (or knowledge) and explored metaphysical subjects like *Brahma*, *Atman* (soul), etc. It laid greater stress on acquisition of true knowledge and spiritual development rather on rituals and sacrifices.

The Vedanta school branched out into separate sub-schools based on their philosophies of dualism to monism. Some of these schools are: 'Advaita', 'Vishishta Advaita', 'Dvaita', 'Bheda-abheda', and 'Neo-Vedanta', etc.

Branches of Vedanta

Advaita Vedanta

Advaita literally means 'no two' or sole or unity. Thus, this school of philosophy is based on principle of monoism or unitism that all creation is a reflection of the supreme. Thus, soul was not a separate entity from the Brahman but only its manifestation. Sri Adi Shankarachrya (8th century CE) consolidated the principles of Advaita Vedanta and structured the philosophy in a formal shape.

Vishist Advaita

This philosophy was propunded by Ramanuja (15th century CE). Although it does consider *Jivatama* (soul-living being) to be a reflection of the *Brahma*, however, unlike Advaita school, it does not consider the *Brahma* to be without attributes. Thus, *Brahma* is *Saguna* (with attributes). *Atma* and *Brahma* were distinct entities but mutually inseparable. This philosophy and teachings of Ramanuja also laid the foundation of Vaishnavism.

Dvaita

Madhavacharya (13th century CE) was the propounder of this school of philosophy. It considered *Brahma* (the Universal) and *Atma* (soul) to be two distinct entities. *Brahma* is also identified with a personalised god with attributes which was considered to be lord Vishnu with various incarnations. It also emphasises on '*Bhakti*' as means for salvation of the soul.

Bheda-abheda

This school of philosophy is known to have existed as early as 8th century CE. The word Bheda-abheda literally means 'difference and no difference'. It propounds that *Brahman* (universal/supreme) and *Jivatma* (soul-living being) are distinct and different and yet not different from each other. Bhaskara (8th–9th century CE) and Nimbakara (13th century CE) were important teachers of this school.

Neo-Vedanta

This modern interpretation of Vedanta emerged in the 19th and 20th century. This is the result of thinkers and philosophers like Sri Ramakrishna, Sri Vivekananda, Sri Aurobindo, and other philosophers and teachers. It **is founded on the philosophy of Advaita Vedanta of Shankaracharya** but does not accept the concept of universal illusionism of this school. Rather, it **propounds concept of universal realism**.

VARNASHRAMA DHARMA

The Dharma Shastras

The philosophy of Varnashrama Dharma finds reference in the various Dharma Shastras. The word *Varnashrama Dharma* is composed of three distinct words. *Varna* (here referred to as the class), *Ashrama* (or stage/station in life), and *Dharma* (duty or obligation). Thus, based on *Varna* (class) and *Ashrama* (station), a person was obliged to discharge his duties.

The Shastras identified four Varnas and four Ashrams. The four Varnas are **Brahmans** (priests, preachers, teachers), **Kshatriyas** (kings, soldiers, warriors), **Vaishyas** (merchants, agriculturists, artisans, etc) and **Shudras** (labourers/service providers).

The four ashramas were **Brahmacharya, Grihastha, Vanaprastha,** and **Sanyasa. Brahmacharya** was the first stage of the life where the objective was to acquire knowledge and lead a life of discipline and celibacy. **Grihastha** or the stage of householder, was the next, where one was to choose his occupation as per Varna, marry, and raise a family. **Vanaprastha** was the third stage literally meaning proceeding to the forest. After fulfilling the duties of a householder, with the onset of age, a person could retire from worldly matters and spend more time in spiritual pursuits. **Sanyasa** was the final stage where a person was to detach himself from the society and fully pursue attainment of salvation or *Moksha*. But not all entered the last *Ashrama*.

Depending on the Varna and Ashram, a person was required to discharge his Dharma (duty) as enunciated in the Dharmashastras. The **Varna** system in later phases of Hinduism metamorphosed into the stringent caste system.

Purusharthas

The Purshartha has an important place in the domain of the Hindu philosophy as a beacon to human pursuits. The word *Purushartha* is derived from the two words *Purush* (human being) and *Arth* (purpose). Thus, it literally means, 'the objective or purpose of a human being or his life'. This philosophy advocates four **'Purusharthas'**, the pursuit of which should be the objective of every human being. These are **Dharma, Arth, Kama**, and **Moksha.**

Dharma refers to the social, moral, and ethical duties of a person. These duties would vary from person to person. Fulfillment/discharge of these duties is of prime importance for every person. It signifies the right conduct and appropriate way of living.

Arth refers to the material possessions, wealth, and other resources necessary for the physical existence. Thus, Arth signifies the means of physical sustenance of life.

Kama refers to desire and fulfilment of the sensory needs; be it emotional, aesthetics, or physical.

Moksha refers to the objective of liberation or emancipation of human soul from the Karmic cycle.

Thus, pursuit of the four *Purusharthas* and ultimately *Moksha* was the objective of human life. This philosophy also emphasised on the need for balance between the respective pursuits. In case of any contradiction or clash or disharmony, the pursuit of *Dharma* was considered to be the most important, followed by *Artha* and then *Kama.*

Charvaka Philosophy or Lokayata School

This school of philosophy also referred to as the *Brahasptya*, is a philosophical school of materialism. Brahaspati is said to have laid the foundation of this school but Charvaka was the main propounder. *The essential elements of its philosophy are:*

- The physical world as perceived by the senses is the only world and nothing beyond it exists.
- The school denied the existence of *Brahma* (God) or *Atma* (Soul) and denied that the objective of human life was salvation or unison of *Atma* with Soul. Thus, it was an atheistic school.
- It emphasised on material pursuits and sensory enjoyment as an objective of human life.

SECTS OF HINDUISM

Although a watertight demarcation does not exist between different sects in Hinduism, however, depending on the primary deity being worshipped, there can be said to be three devotional sects in Hinduism. These are *Vaishnavism*, *Shaivism*, and *Shaktism.*

The **Vaishnava** sect worships lord Vishnu and his incarnations (Sri Ram and Sri Krishna) as the primary deity. Lord Vishnu is considered as the creator, sustainer, and destroyer of all the three worlds. Sometimes he is considered as the preserver of the trinity of *Brahma* (creator), *Vishnu* (preserver), and *Mahesh* (destroyer). He is perceived as formless (*Nirguna*) or with form (*Saguna*). There are many *sampradayas* (sub-sects) which fall under Vaishanavism, such as **Sri Vaishanavism** (associated with goddess *Laxmi*), **Ramanandi Sampradaya** (followers of Ramanand), **Swaminarayan Sampraday** (followers of Swaminarayan), **Brahma Sampradaya** (followers of Madhava), **Rudra Sampradava** (followers of Vallabhacharya), **Gaudiya Vaishanavism** (followers of Chaitanya), **Bhagvat sect** (followers of Sri Krishna), etc.

Lord Shiva is the prime deity of the **Shaivism sect.** Shaivism too sometimes takes the form of monism and sometimes dualism (the lord and the devotee are two different entities in dualism). It too has different

Sampradayas such as **Pashupata Shaivism, Saiva Siddhanta, Siddha Siddhanta, Lingayata, Kashmir Shaivism, Shiva Advaita,** etc.

Shaktism refers to the worship of *Shakti* or the divine mother in various forms such as *Durga Kali, Saraswati, Laxmi, Parvati,* etc. Reference to the worship of Mother Goddess is also noted in figurines of Harappan civilisation and along with Shaivism, it is the oldest form of Hinduism. *Shiva* and *Shakti* were often considered to be the two forms of the supreme and complementary cosmic forces.

Smartism is another recognised form of Hinduism where the believers choose to worship any of the Hindu deities.

IMPORTANT TOPICS TO FOCUS ON

- Classification of scriptures and important Hindu scriptures.
- Various Vedas (viz. Rigveda, Yajurveda, Samaveda, and Atharvaveda), the objectives of hymns contained therein, various scriptures comprising Vedas or sections, and their objectives and salient features.
- Other important scriptures and salient points.
- Important Hindu philosophies and their features.

4

CHAPTER

Buddhism

> If there is any religion that could respond to the needs of modern science, it would be Buddhism
>
> **Albert Einstein**

AN INTRODUCTION

Buddhism is the fourth largest religion in the world having nearly 500–550 million followers (7%–8% of the world population). It is concentrated largely in Asia with the maximum Buddhist presence in China and other countries in Southeast Asia (viz. Cambodia, Myanmar, and Thailand), South Asia (Sri Lanka), and East Asia (Japan).

Buddhism as a religion was founded by Gautama Buddha in the 6th century BCE in India. It has a history of more than 2500 years, making it one of the oldest living religions in the world along with Hinduism, Judaism, and Jainism. It is divided into numerous sects, viz. Mahayana, Hinayana, Vajrayana, and Theravada. It has a rich philosophy, captured in the Tripitakas and other Buddhist scriptures. These texts also throw light on the history of the religion and the regions indicating the profound impact on art, culture, and other social aspects of the countries where Buddhism had flourished.

A BRIEF HISTORY

Origin of Buddhism

The history of Buddhism falls under the category of recorded history (unlike early Hinduism). Events and occurrences have been found to be recorded in the various Buddhist texts and accounts of travellers and writers like Faxian and Xuanzang. Further, inscriptions and edicts of emperor Ashoka and other kings which survive to this day on stupas, chaityas, and other rock inscriptions, serve as an important source of information about Buddhism.

As per the accepted historical account, Buddhism originated in the teachings of Buddha (also referred as Gautama, Siddhartha, Shakyamuni, and Tathagata). He was born in 563 BCE to King Suddhodhana (a Sakya ruler of Kapilvastu) and Maya Devi, in Lumbini (in present day Nepal). It is said that owing to predictions of seers, that he would either become a great king or a great sage, his father restricted his life to the comforts of the palace. He was married to Yashodhara and had a son Rahul. Once, in a venture outside the palace, the sight of a sick man, an old man, a corpse, and a monk (referred to as the 'four sights') deeply influenced him. He renounced his worldly life, family, and kingdom in pursuit of the truth.

After many years of asceticism and meditation, Buddha attained enlightenment in Bodh Gaya under a Pipal tree (called the **Bodhi tree**) and hence became **Buddha—one who is enlightened**. He delivered his **first sermon** to his five disciples at Sarnath (Varanasi), an event called the **Dharmachakra Pravartana** or **the turning of the wheel of law**. This marks a formal beginning of the Buddhist religion. This was also the beginning of the **Sangha** (or the order of monks). Buddha spent the rest of his life in preaching in different parts of the country—largely in **Magadh and Kosala** Mahajanpads. He attained **Mahaparinirvana** at Kusinagra (in present day Uttar Pradesh).

Spread of Buddhism

Buddhism soon spread in India and different parts of South Asia and Southeast Asia. The factors existing in the Indian society, viz. —excessive **emphasis on ritualism, brahmanical superiority,** and **caste system**—on one hand and **simple teachings of Buddhism** with emphasis on **ahimsa, equality, compassion,** etc. on the other hand which endeared it to the masses, helped in its growth. Further, patronage and propagation by several emperors and kings also enabled it to spread far and wide. Emperor Ashoka and his missions to Sri Lanka, Southeast Asia, China, patronage of Buddhism, by Menander-I (a Bactrian King in the 2nd Century BCE), by the Kushanas, particularly emperor Kanishka (1st Century CE), by Pala Kings, and by emperor Harsha (6th century CE), were important factors for its spread far and wide. However, with the decline of royal patronage beyond the reign of Harsha and with rejuvenation and consolidation of Hinduism as a result of efforts of Shankaracharya (8th century CE) and other Hindu religious leaders, Buddhism suffered a decline in India, although it continued to spread in other countries outside it.

The Buddhist Councils

Although the Buddhist Sangha came into existence during the lifetime of Buddha, the four Buddhist councils which were held much later helped in better organising the Sangha and the Buddhist texts, structuring them, and spreading the teachings of Buddha.

The **first Buddhist council** took place in 483 BCE in Rajgriha after Buddha's death. It was presided by **Mahakashyapa,** a discipline of Buddha and took place under the **patronage of king Ajatshatru**. The **Vinaya Pitaka** (book of monastic rules and discipline) and **Sutta Pitaka** (sermons/teachings of Buddha) were compiled in this council.

The **second Buddhist council** took place in **Vaishali in 383 BCE** around 100 years after the death of Buddha, where schism between **Sthavirvadins** and **Mahasamghikas** took place.

The third council took place under the patronage of emperor Ashoka in 247 BCE in Patliputra and was presided by **Moggaliputta Tissa**. This council helped in the revision of the Buddhist scriptures and consolidation of their teachings.

The **fourth and last of the councils** took place during the reign of emperor Kanishka in Kashmir and was presided by **Asvaghosh** and **Vasumitra**. Here, the division of Buddhism into **Mahayana** (larger vehicle) and **Hinayana** (smaller vehicle) took place.

TEACHINGS AND PHILOSOPHY

The Buddhist teachings are found in the scriptures called the ***Sutta Pitaka****. The salient points of the teachings are as below.*

- Buddhism emphasises on following the **middle path** for attaining salvation, i.e., a path neither of self-indulgence nor of extreme asceticism or self-penance.
- It bases its philosophy on the **Four Noble Truths** ('*Chattvari Arya Satyani*') and propounds the eightfold path to attain salvation.
- The **Four Noble Truths** are:

(i) The world is transient and impermanent **(Anicca),** human existence is not eternal **(Anatta),** and is filled with sorrow (**Dukkha**).

(ii) **Desire** (craving) is the root cause of sorrow.

(iii) To end sorrow **one must control desire.**

(iv) To control desire one must **follow the eightfold path**.

- **Eightfold path** ('*Arya Ashtanga Marga*')

  (a) *Right view* (b) *Right intention* (c) *Right speech* (d) *Right action* (e) *Right livelihood* (f) *Right concentration* (g) *Right effort* (h) *Right mindfulness.*

- Buddhism **preached against ritualism, idolatry, animal sacrifices, Brahmanism, and caste system.**
- It believed in **existence of soul and its transmigration** or rebirth in different human forms.
- It emphasised on **righteous action** for attaining **salvation or 'Nibbana'** (**Nirvana)** which literally means extinguishing of the ego and desire.
- Buddhist teachings also emphasised on **Ahimsa or non-violence** (although Buddhism was more moderate as compared to Jainism in the extent and strictness to which Ahimsa and its edicts were to be implemented or asceticism was to be adopted).
- Buddha did not believe in god as a creator of the universe or an eternal or unchanging soul. However, Buddhist texts do not contain explicit denial of existence of god. As such, Buddhism is not considered an atheistic religion in a strict sense. Latter Buddhism, particularly Mahayana sect believed Buddha himself to be an eternal god and other five Buddhas to be ruling the heavens and other parts of world (viz. *Amitabha, Vairochana, Akshobhaya, Ratnasambhava,* and *Amogsiddha).*

BUDDHIST SCRIPTURES

The Buddhist philosophy is contained in several important Buddhist scriptures, the most important of which are the **Tripitakas.** It literally means the three baskets (of knowledge and teachings). *These were written in Pali and include:*

(a) The **Vinaya Pitaka**: It contains the details of life of lord Buddha and rules and regulations for functioning of the Sangha.

(b) The **Sutta Pitaka**: This contains the sermons of lord Buddha.

(c) The **Abhidhama Pitaka** – The metaphysical concepts and philosophy of Buddhism are contained in this Pitaka.

Besides the Tripitakas, the **Dhammacakkappavattana Sutta** (discourse on turning of wheel of law), the **Dhammapada** (treasury of truth), **Mahasatipattha Sutta** (four foundation of mindfulness), etc. are some other important Buddhist scriptures.

SECTS IN BUDDHISM

Over a period of time Buddhism divided into several sects, depending on their belief and practice. The important sects in Buddhism are Hinayana, Mahayana, Theravada, and Vajrayana.

(a) **Hinayana:** Literally meaning the **smaller vehicle**, Hinayana emerged as a separate form of Buddhism after the fourth Buddhist council (during the reign of emperor Kanishka). This was the orthodox sect that emphasised on individual salvation by following the original teachings of Buddha (ethical conduct, discipline, and right knowledge). In this sect, unlike in the Mahayana sect, Buddha was not considered as eternal or a god, nor making of his statutes or worship was encouraged. In Hinayana sect, Buddha and events of his life were represented symbolically.

(b) **Mahayana:** Literally meaning the **larger vehicle**, this sect believed in **universal salvation** rather than merely the salvation of individuals. They also followed the concept of **Bodhisattvas** such as *Avlokiteshwara, Vajrapani, Kshitigarbha,* and *Visvapani*. These were venerated souls who had attained personal salvation but took birth on this earth to enable the salvation of other souls. Mahayana sect also accepted making of statues of Buddha in human form and **believed Buddha to be an eternal god**. This sect was propagated by emperor Kanishka and later spread far and wide.

(c) **Theravada:** This literally means the **doctrine of elders**. Like Hinayana, it emphasised on attaining of individual 'nirvana' through mental discipline, appropriate knowledge, and right conduct.

(d) **Vajrayana:** A new form of Buddhism emerged in Bengal and Bihar during the Pala rule under the influence of tantric sects of Hinduism. This sect worships Buddha, Bodhisattvas, and female divinities like Tara.

Buddhism also has regional variations such as **Lamaism of Tibet, Sri Lankan Buddhism, Thai Buddhism, and Japanese Buddhism.**

EVENTS AND SYMBOLS IN BUDDHISM

The Buddhist art, sculptures, and architecture is replete with symbols which are representative of important events in the life of Buddha. These events are the birth of Buddha, his renunciation in search of truth, his attaining of enlightenment, his delivering of the first lecture (or *Dharmachakra Pravartana*), and his death (*Mahaparinirvana*). Some of these symbols are discussed below.

(a) **Lotus:** This represents the birth of Buddha.

(b) **Pipal/Bodhi Tree:** It represents attainment of enlightenment by Buddha.

(c) **Wheel:** This represents the delivering of the first sermon by Buddha at Sarnath or Dharmachakra Pravartana. The eight spokes of the wheel represent the eightfold path of Buddhism.

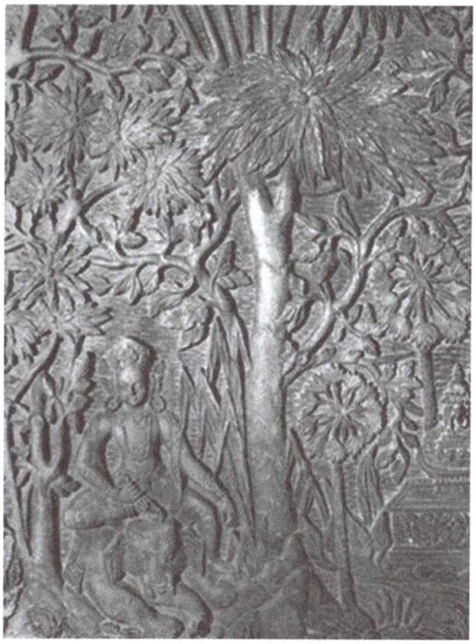

Enlightenment of Buddha under the Bodhi Tree

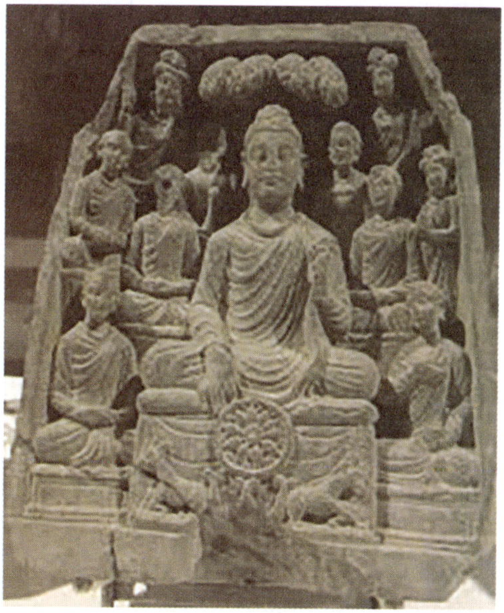

First Sermon of Buddha in Sarnath

(d) **Stupa:** This represents the Mahaparinirvana of Buddha. Sometimes, it also refers to an enlightened Buddha.

(e) **Empty Throne:** This represents the Buddha himself and it is also a reference to his royal ancestry. At times it also signifies the Buddha in meditation.

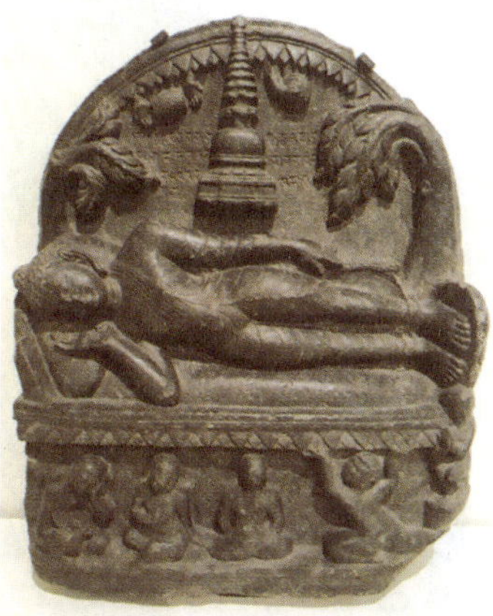

Mahaparinirvana

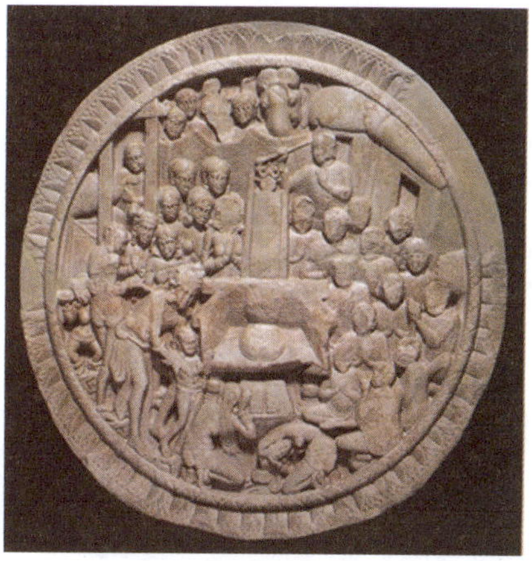

Empty Throne

(f) **Lion:** This symbol traditionally represents strength, power, and royalty and it is also representative of Buddha.

(g) **Footprints:** It is representative of the footprints of the Buddha and his presence.

(h) **Three Jewels (Triratna):** The triple gems represent the Buddha, the *Dhamma* (*Dharma* or his teachings), and the Sangha.

(i) **Deer** – It is a reference to Buddha's first teaching at Deer Park at Sarnath or the *Dharmachakra Pravartana*.

(j) **Elephant** – It represents valour, strength, and wisdom.

Mudras in Buddhism

In early Buddhism, statues of Buddha were not made and Buddha was represented through symbols. The practice of making Buddha's statues came in vogue in the later Buddhist tradition, particularly in the Mahayana form of Buddhism where Buddha was shown in seated or standing pose with various hand gestures called the **'mudras'**. Some of the important ones are described below.

(a) **Dhyana Mudra** – This is among the most common of mudras in which Buddha is depicted. He is shown to be seated in lotus posture while both his hands are placed on the lap. The palm is open and facing upward, with fingers stretched. The right palm is over left and the eyes are closed in **meditation.**

(b) **Abhaya Mudra** – This is a posture of **fearlessness and also blessing**. The right arm of Buddha is shown to be elevated and bent slightly. The palm is facing outward and fingers are extended upwards. This mudra is also a common one showing a peaceful Buddha in benediction.

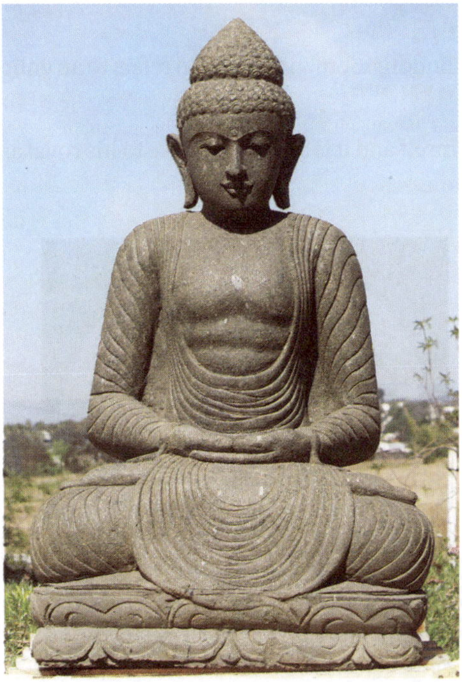

Dhyana Mudra

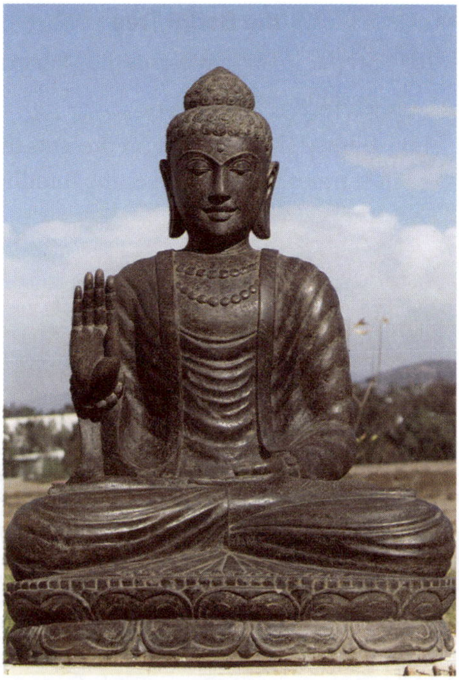

Abhaya Mudra

(c) **Bhumisparsha Mudra** – Buddha is shown to be seated in lotus posture (*Padmasana*) with his right palm hanging on the right knee and the fingers touching the earth. The left hand rests on the lap with palm upwards. It symbolises Buddha calling the earth to be his witness to his **victory over Mara** (Mara is a demon representing passion trying to entice Buddha into worldly pleasures).

(d) **Varada Mudra** – In this mudra, Buddha is shown to be **conferring his grace or blessings**. The arm is shown extended all the way down with the palm facing outward. Buddha is usually depicted in a standing position in this mudra.

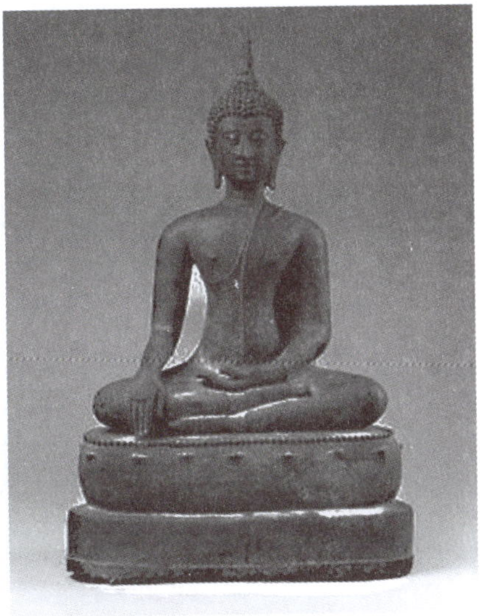

Bhumisparsha Mudra

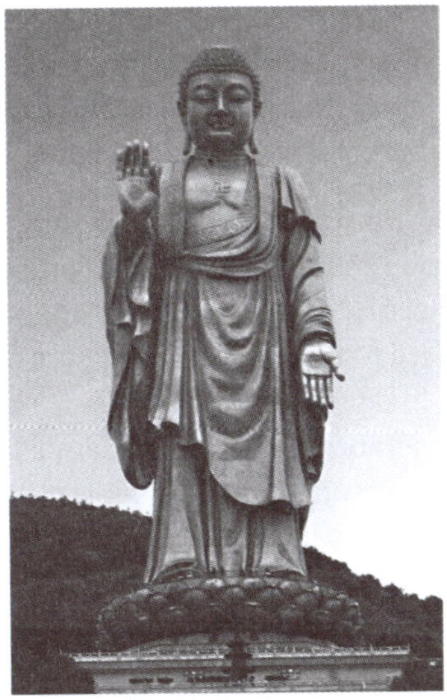

Varada Mudra

(e) **Shraman Mudra** – The hand points downward and away from body and is symbolic of Buddha's **renunciation of worldly pleasures**.

(f) **Chin Mudra** – This mudra is symbolic of **spiritual understanding**. The thumb and index finger are touching and forming a circle, appearing as if grasping a fine object (as a grain of truth). The three remaining fingers are gently stretched outwards.

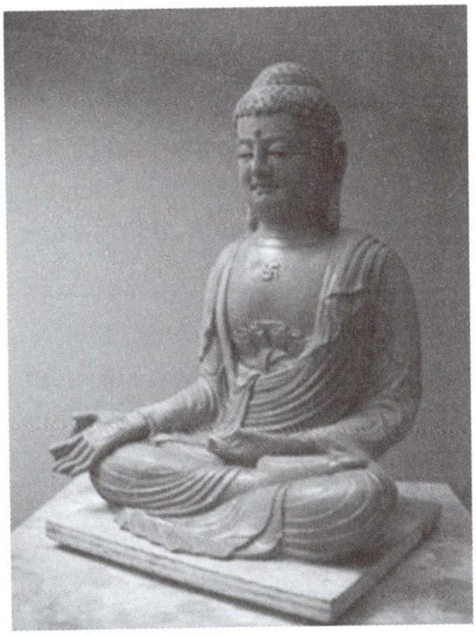

Shraman Mudra

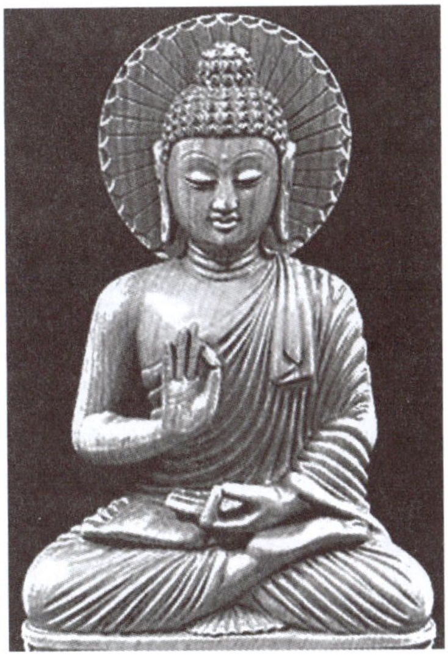

Chin Mudra

BUDDHIST STRUCTURES AND THEIR SIGNIFICANCE

The Buddhists constructed a number of viharas, stupas, and chaityas. Their purposes and significance is briefly explained.

- **Viharas** – These were monasteries or the places of residence of the Buddhist monks where wandering monks took shelter, particularly during the rainy season. Owing to a large number of viharas in the erstwhile Magadh region, it was also called Bihar (a land of viharas)
- **Chaityas** – These were Buddhist shrines which were prayer halls with a stupa at one end of the hall. It had pillars on the side of the pathway which led to the stupa. The purpose of these chaityas was to offer a community place of worship for a large number of Buddhists. Many chaityas were rock-cut structures. Some of the famous ones surviving to this day are **chaityas of Ajanta caves, Bhaja caves, and Kanaheri caves**.

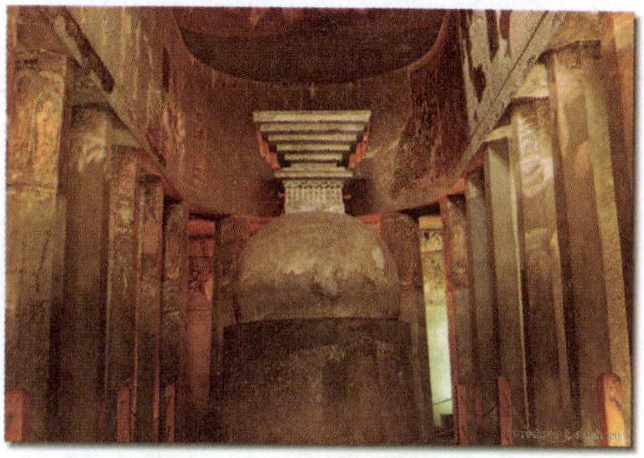

Chaitya

- **Stupa** – A stupa is a hemispherical (mound shape) construction which contains holy relics or cremated remains of Buddha or other monks. Apart from the hemispherical structure, most of the stupas also have a fence around it which serves to separate the sacred space of the stupa. Later, stupas had a balcony atop and a mast also. (See Chapter 5 for structure of a stupa).

> **Origin of Stupa**
>
> As per the *Mahaparinibbana* portion of *Sutta Pitaka*, at the time of death of Buddha (Mahaparinirvana), Ananda and his disciples asked him as to what should be done to his remains. However, Buddha did not want any honour for his remains. But being pressed by Ananda further, Buddha asked for a stupa to be constructed over them which would accord peace to those paying obeisance to it.
>
> It is believed that Buddha's cremated remains were divided into eight portions and a stupa was built in the eight kingdoms associated with the life of Buddha. It is said that later, emperor Ashoka dug up the stupas and distributed the relics in 84000 portions, building stupas over them in different parts of world.

- **Gompas** – Gompas refer to a Buddhist temple (place of worship) or a monastery which is in vogue particularly in the Mahayana form of Buddhism. The structure has a central prayer hall with a statue of Buddha. It usually also houses places of residence of the monks. A large number of gompas exist in Tibet. In India, such structures abound in the Ladakh region.

BUDDHIST INSCRIPTIONS

A large number of Buddhist inscriptions which are on pillars and rocks have survived to this day and throw light on Buddhism, the existing regime, and the society at that point of time. Many of these inscriptions are edicts of king Ashoka (pillar edicts and rock edicts). These are found in areas as far as present day Afghanistan, Pakistan, Bangladesh, Sri Lanka, and Nepal. Some of the important pillar edicts are those at Vaishali (Bihar), Sarnath (Uttar Pradesh), Sanchi (Madhya Pradesh), Amravati (Andhra Pradesh), Kaushambi (Allahabad district of Uttar Pradesh), Lauriya Nandangarh (Bihar), and Kandhar (Afghanistan). The Lion Capital of Ashoka with four lions at Sarnath is also adopted as a national symbol of India.

Rock edicts have been found at Girnar (Gujarat) and Junagadh (Gujarat) besides Nepal, Pakistan, and Afghanistan. These edicts give the moral precepts (Dhamma) of emperor Ashoka and are based on the teachings and philosophy of Buddhism. It exhorted people to follow the word of Buddha and emphasised upon right behaviour, benevolence among people, kindness to prisoners, respect for animal life, etc.

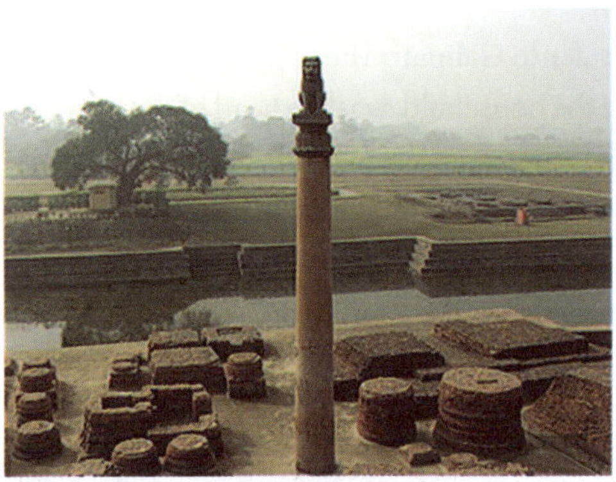

Vaishali Pillar edict

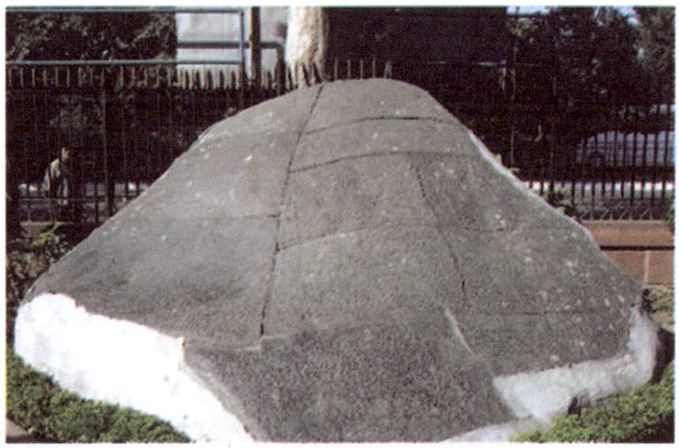

Ashokan Rock Edicts, Girnar

- **Jatakas:** These are a set of stories from the previous births of Buddha (who is believed to be remembering incidents of his previous births). This literature is in Pali and in the stories Buddha (in previous births) is in human or animal form depicting various qualities and virtues.
- **Avadana:** This is Buddhist literature which contains stories and explanation by Buddha of the events of one's life based on the virtues of the previous life. Such stories are also included in the *Vinaya Pitaka* and are also collected separately. *Sarvastivada*, *Divyavdana*, and *Mahavastu* are among the most important *Avadanas*.
- **Sangha and entry of women:** The Sangha or the religious order of Buddhist monks did not initially permit the entry of women in its fold. However, on request and mediation of Ananda, one of the chief disciples of Buddha, women were allowed in the Sangha. The women were referred to as the ***Bhikkhunis***. Buddha's foster mother **Mahapajapati Gotami** was the first woman to be initiated in the order. Many of the women in the order later became ***Theris*** who were women who had attained liberation and were thus respected.

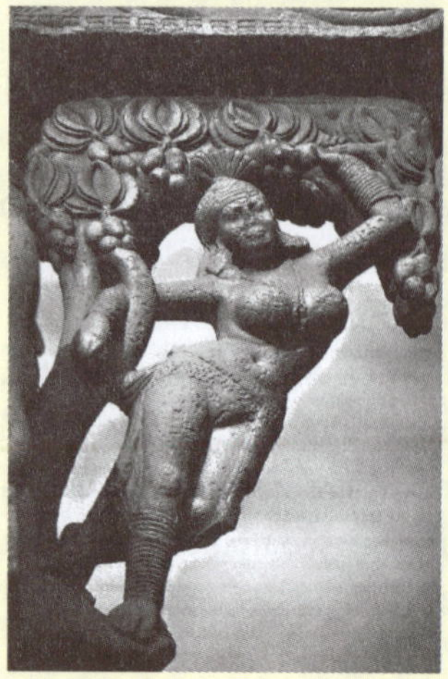

- **Shalabhanjika Motif:** This is the figure of a woman found in Sanchi Stupa, shown to be holding on to a tree and swaying from the edge of a gateway. The beautiful motif is apparently in contradiction of the early Buddhist teachings of renunciation and simplicity. It is believed that the image represented *Shalabhanjika*, a woman whose touch caused trees to bear fruits and was thus considered auspicious. The motif also depicts the influence of extant social norms and culture on Buddhist beliefs and the change it brought in Buddhism. Earlier, Buddhist art and architecture were limited to only depiction of Buddha and that too, only symbolically. Further, this motif also indicates dexterity of the evolving art forms in Buddhism.
- **Gahpati:** Buddhist texts and Ashokan edicts often refer to Gahpati. The gahpati (literal meaning owner of a household) or householder/master/head of the household, was the head of the residence, land, and other resources including the women, children, and workers, who all shared the common residence. The kings and gahpatis are advised by these edicts to be humane and ethical in their conduct. Gahpati were in contrast to the wandering monks who would just have meagre worldly possessions and no permanent/long period of residence.

IMPORTANT TOPICS TO FOCUS ON

- Buddhism teachings and philosophy
- Difference in Buddhist sects
- Mudras, symbols, and their significance
- Buddhist structures and their significance
- Important points of differences between the Buddhist philosophy and the Vedic philosophy

CHAPTER 5

Jainism

> Have benevolence towards all living beings, joy at the site of virtuous, compassion and sympathy for the afflicted, and tolerance towards the indolent and ill behaved
>
> **Tattvartha Sutra**

AN INTRODUCTION

Jainism along with Hinduism and Buddhism is among the oldest of all existing religions. This faith is said to have been propounded by Mahavira in the 6th century BCE. At present there are 4.5 to 5 million Jains in the world and the followers are mostly concentrated in India. However, within India, the followers are spread in almost all the states and union territories. As a community, despite the small numbers (less than 0.5% of the Indian population), it enjoys good prosperity and literacy. Today, it is considered to be a separate religion distinct from Hinduism and has been accorded a minority community status in India.

A BRIEF HISTORY

The philosophy of Jainism is based on the teachings of 24 Tirthankaras. Rishabhnath was the first Tirthankara and Mahavira was the 24th and the last Tirthankara. As a philosophy, Jainism is as old as Vedic Hinduism with Rishabhnath, Arishtanemi, and Ajinatha (Tirthankaras) being referred to in the Vedas. Rishabhnath (also known as Adinath) is also considered as an incarnation of Lord Vishnu in the Puranas.

Jainism flourished as a separate religious philosophy only after the advent of Mahavira, the last Tirthankara. The excessive ritualism, animal sacrifices, etc. which were opposed by the Jain teachings along with its emphasis on Ahimsa, compassion, morality, ethics, and other precepts, enabled it to spread in the country. However, with the regeneration of Hinduism in the 8th century CE, Jainism was pushed to the social fringes and also literally so to the states of Gujarat, Rajasthan, and southern India, where the community still has a greater presence even today.

The Life and Times of Mahavira

Vardhaman (Mahavira) was the son of King Siddhartha (the chief of Jnatrika clan), and queen Trishala. He was born in 599 BC in Kundagrama (Vaishali in present day Bihar). At an age of 30, he renounced his family and kingdom including all worldly possessions, even his clothes, and set out in search of the truth. After 13 years of wandering as an ascetic and performing penance and meditation, on the 10th of Vaishakha, he eventually found true knowledge and thus became **Jina (or the conquer), or Mahavira**

(the great one). He was also referred as Nigrantha (or Nigantha), one who is free from attachments and vices. After attainment of **Kaivalya** (enlightenment—true knowledge) he preached for several years. At the age of 72, he is said to have attained **Nirvana** at **Pavapuri** (Bihar).

TEACHINGS AND PHILOSOPHIES OF JAINISM

The Jain philosophies are based on the teachings of the Tirthankaras compiled in their scriptures called **Agamas**.

The salient points of the Jain philosophy and teachings are discussed below.

Ahimsa

Non-violence or Ahimsa is one of the key Jain philosophies. Emphasis on the practice of Ahimsa is one of the important aspects of Jainism which distinguishes it from other religions. As per Jain philosophy, **the whole world is animated** (has life). This would include even the apparently non-living things such as water, stones, etc. As such, one must practice Ahimsa or non-violence/non-injury particularly to human beings, animals, and even to insects and plants. Intentional harm and absence of compassion makes the act more violent.

The life and conduct of Jains is often shaped by non-violence making vegetarianism essential to their conduct. The strict followers of Jainism travel only on foot and do not travel by vehicles as it could trample insects. Further, they cover their mouth with a white cloth and use a broom (of fine thread called **Ogho** or **Rajoharan**) to sweep where they sit, lest they kill any insect.

Karma and Transmigration of Soul

Jainism believes in **transmigration of soul,** viz. the rebirth in different living forms. A person reaps the fruits of one's Karma and the cycle of birth and rebirth is shaped through one's Karma. Thus, to attain freedom from this cycle or attain **Nirvana** or **Kaivalya**, one must practice the right Karma. Nirvana could be attained by following the **Triratnas—** right conduct, right faith, and right knowledge.

Triratnas

The three jewels, **Samyak Charita** (right conduct), **Samyak Darshana** (right faith), and **Samyak Jnana** (right knowledge) are the core values to be adopted for attaining salvation.

(a) **Samyak Charita** – This refers to right conduct which in turn includes five vows **(Panch-Mahavrata).** These are **Ahimsa** (non injury/non-violence), **Satya** (not lying/telling truth), **Asteya** (non stealing), **Aparigraha** (non possession/non attachment), and **Brahmacharya** (celibacy).

(b) **Samyak Darshana** – Right faith or Samyak Darshan implies; to **understand the true nature of substance**. To do this one must have faith in the teachings of the Tirthankaras which enables a person to distinguish between the right and wrong *Karma*. As per this philosophy, a person ought to believe in **seven Tattvas** which are:

Jiva – or the soul which exists and is immortal

Ajiva – or non soul (matter or material without soul)

Asvana – or influx of auspicious and evil *karmic* matter in the soul

Bandha – or bondage caused by intermingling of the *Karma* and the soul

Samvara – obstruction of the inflow of *karmic* matter into the soul

Nirjara – or separation/dissociation of *karmic* matter from the soul

Moksha – liberation due to separation of *karmic* matter from the soul

(c) **Samyak Jnana** – As per this philosophy the right knowledge is of five kinds. These are:

(1) **Mati** (mental knowledge): obtained through normal faculties

(2) **Sruti** (acquired knowledge): which is verbal or non-verbal acquired words and symbols/signs

(3) **Avadhi** (distant knowledge): of remote things or clairvoyance acquired through higher faculties

(4) **Manahparyay** (para-normal knowledge): or knowledge acquired psychically or telepathically

(5) **Keval** (absolute knowledge): or perfect knowledge which is not subject to perspectives or relative standpoints

There are other kinds of knowledge called **Mithya Jnana** (or invalid knowledge).

Anekantavada

Also known as the philosophy of non-absolutism or of relative pluralism, Anekantavada is among the core and distinguishing philosophies of Jainism. As per this philosophy, "although the truth is one, but owing to different perspectives, different people perceive the same truth differently". Thus, truth can be approached in different ways. This is so as every substance has infinite attributes. Thus, truth as we perceive may not be taken as absolute, rather it is even relative. The concepts of **Syadvada** or 'conditional view points' and **Nayavada** or 'partial viewpoints' further arose from Anekantavada.

The doctrine of Anekantavada is applied by Jains in religion, philosophy, and all fields of life. Thus, it encourages free thinking and helps in reconciliation of different perspectives. At the same time it also forewarns us not to be too dogmatic or a stickler to one's own viewpoint as **truth is not absolute**. Thus, it promotes tolerance of views and reconciles with the philosophy of non-violence.

Other Salient Aspects of Jain Philosophy

- Jainism was opposed to ritualism, animal sacrifices, infallibility of the Vedas, and Brahmanical superiority.
- It laid special emphasis on **renunciation, austerity, and asceticism.**
- It did not consider the existence of God as a creator of universe necessary. While some believe Jainism to be an atheistic religion, it is more appropriately described as a **transtheistic religion** as it does not consider the necessity of a supreme being for enlightenment.

Jain Scriptures

The teachings of Mahavira and other Tirthankars are contained in the Jain scriptures called **'Agamas'**. These Agamas were written in **Prakrit**. They are also called **Jain Shrut**. These scriptures were not originally in written form or documented, as possessions and attachments were not permitted in the Jain philosophy. As such, these scriptures were passed on by oral traditions for many centuries before being documented. It is believed that after the great famine in 350 BCE, many of the Agamas were lost. Subsequently, they were recompiled and documented. But it is also believed by Digambaras that these recompiled Agamas were not the authentic teachings of Lord Mahavira. However, Shwetambaras believe the Agamas to be the teachings of Mahavira himself.

The Agamas were divided into two major groups. These are the **Angagama Sutra** which consist of 12 texts containing direct teachings of Lord Mahavira and **Angabayha Agama Sutras** which provide further explanation to the Angagama Sutras.

Sects in Jainism

The Jains are divided into two sects, the **Digambaras** (meaning sky-clad or naked) and the **Shwetambaras** (meaning white-clad).

The schism of Jainism into the two sects seems to have taken place in around 350 BCE. It is believed during the reign of Chandragupta Maurya when there was a 12 year of famine, Bhadrabahu, leading Jain Muni/scholar went to Karnataka, but on return to Magadha found differences with other Jains on the issue of acceptance of the Agamas and wearing of cloth. This led to the emergence of the two different sects.

Difference in the two sects

- While the Digambara sect prescribes **living naked** and not even having cloth as their possession, the **Shwetambaras** are clad in white clothes.
- Digambaras do not consider the Agamas to contain the teachings of Mahavira and believe that they were lost in the famine but the Shwetambaras believe that the Agamas survived and they represent the teachings of Mahavira.
- The Digambara sect also believes that women cannot be Tirthankaras or attain salvation on account of not being able to practice complete renunciation, as they have to cover their body. This view is not held by the Shwetambaras. They accord the same status to women who have renounced the world and who are referred as sadhvis. They also believe that **Mallinath,** the 19th Tirthankara was a woman who attained salvation and thus women are not precluded from salvation. However, Digambaras do not accept the view of womanhood of Mallinath.

However, the two sects do agree on basic tenets of Jainism, viz. **Triratna**, **Panch-Mahavrata** (five vows), **Ahimsa, Anekantavada,** etc.

JAINISM AND SYMBOLS

In Jain philosophy, symbols occupy an important place. However, unlike Buddhism they are not representative of life or events of any of the Tirthankaras in particular but signify abstract and metaphysical aspects, such as purity of soul, peace, well-being, wisdom, victory over carnal desire, etc.

(a) Ashtamangala: *These are eight auspicious symbols of Jainism and include:*

(1) **Swastika:** This is an auspicious symbol signifying **peace and well-being**. It is customarily drawn in places of worship and religious ceremonies. The four arms of the Swastika are also said to symbolise the **four categories of the world** (or the destiny of worldly beings based on *Karma*). These four categories include the heavenly being (**Deva**), human beings (**Manushya**), animals, birds, and plants (**Triyanch**), and hellish beings (**Narakvasi**).

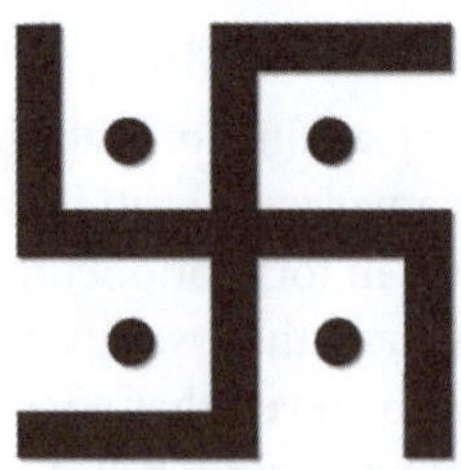

Swastika

(2) **Shrivatsa:** It is said to be a mark on the chest of Mahavira and other Tirthankaras which signifies purity of soul, compassion, and love for all beings.

(3) **Nandavarta:** It is a complex form of Swastika with nine angles or corners, each representing divinity. It is indicative of higher meditative attainment.

(4) **Vardhamanaka:** It is an earthern bowl used as a lamp, symbolic of light (knowledge) banishing darkness (ignorance).

(5) **Bhadrasana:** It is a holy seat representing the seat of Mahavira and other venerated and liberated souls.

(6) **Kalasha:** It is a pot filled with holy water. It signifies purity and wisdom to fill our minds.

(7) **Meen Yugala:** It is a figure of a fish couple considered auspicious and signifying flow of divine life in the cosmic ocean. It is also said to signify victory over carnal desires.

(8) **Darpana:** Mirror (Darpana) signifies reflection of one's true self that is the soul.

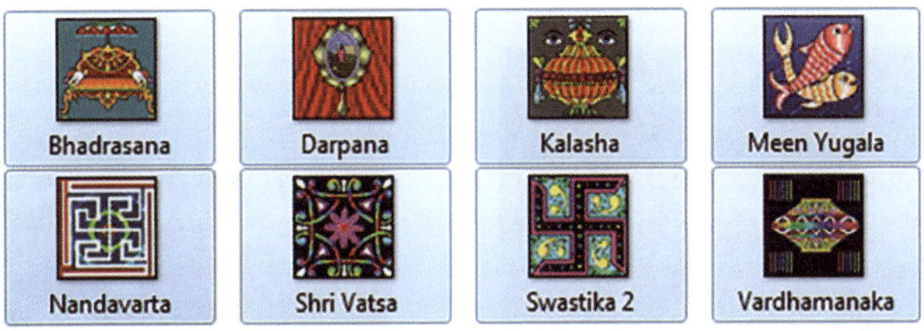

(b) **The Jain emblem:** *This is a congregation of several of the Jain symbols which has been accepted and adopted by all sects. It includes:*

(a) The emblem's outline (signifying the universe and the three worlds).

(b) The Swastika

(c) The Jain palm symbol with Ahimsa (non-violence) inscribed in it, and

(d) The words *Parasparo Graho Jeevanam*, inscribed at the bottom of the emblem, which means all life is bound together by mutual support and interdependence.

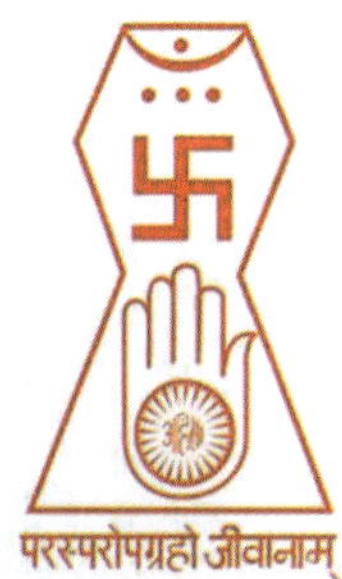

Jain Emblem

Thus, respect for life and others or the concepts of *Ahimsa* and *Anekantavada* are at the core of this philosophy.

JAIN COUNCILS

Historical reference of two councils is obtained in the Jain treatises. The first one took place in the 3rd century BCE under the leadership of monk Sthulibhadra which led to the **compilation of the Agamas**. In the second council held around 800–900 years later in the 5th century CE (held in Valabhi), twelve Angas and Upangas were compiled.

JAIN ART AND ARCHITECTURE

The temples, statues, and rock-cut architecture associated with Jainism survive to this day and throw light on Jain art and architecture. Although Jain art is restricted to religious art and architecture, yet it attained great heights and cast an important influence on the Indian art.

Jain art usually comprises the statues and carvings of Tirthankaras who are shown either seated or standing in a meditative posture and depicted naked. Images of Yaksha and Yakshini are seen guarding the images of Tirthankars. Besides, the art forms usually have symbols and floral motifs. The lack of variety of subjects is more than made up in dexterity of carving which is particularly evident in the **Dilwara Temple** at Mount Abu (in Rajasthan), **Ranakpur temple** (in Rajasthan), and **Palitana temple** at Bhavnagar in Gujarat. The monolithic statue (18 metre high) of Bahubali at Sravanbelogola is another excellent example of Jain architecture.

The rock-cut Jain temples at Udayagiri, Khandagiri caves (in Orissa near Puri), and Ellora caves are also important landmarks of Jain architecture. Quite like many Buddhist caves, these also served as places of residences for the monks but were much simple in nature owing to emphasis on asceticism. They also lacked larger halls for congregation and community prayer.

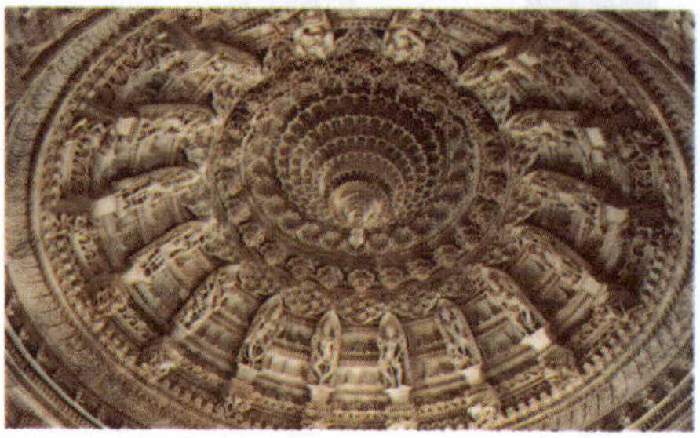

Dilwara Ceiling Architecture

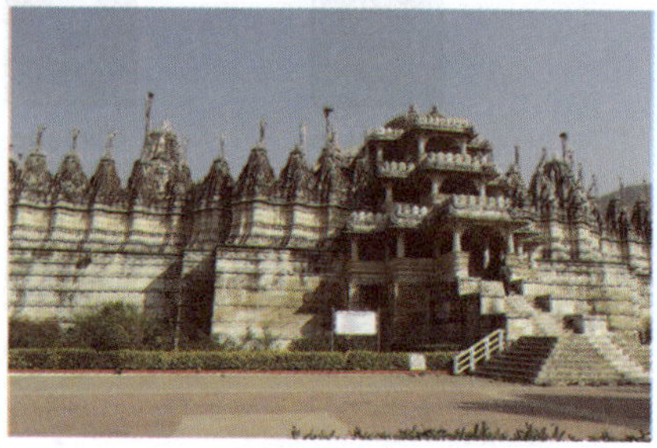

Ranakpur Temple

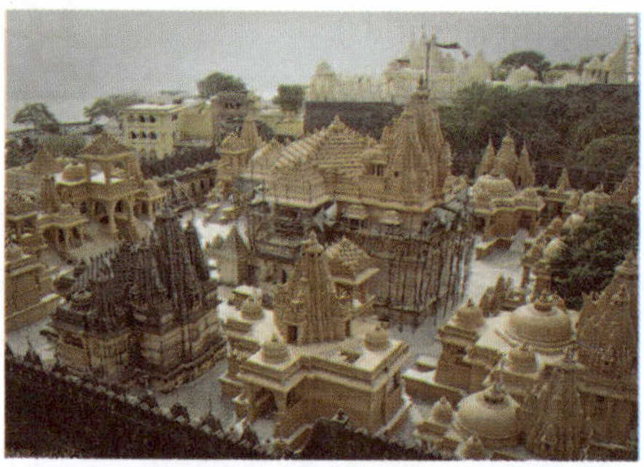

Palitana Temple

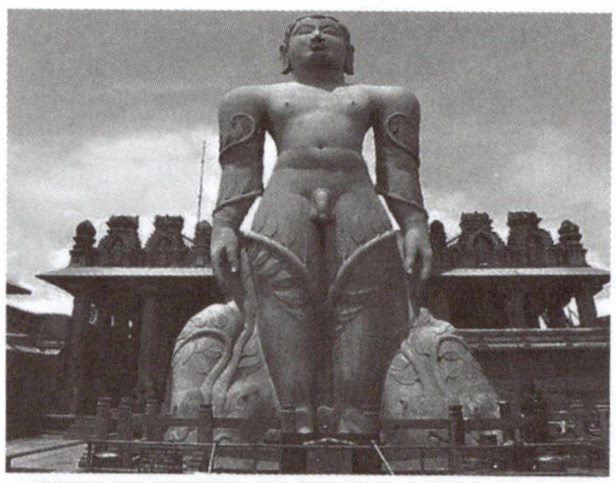

Bahubali Statue

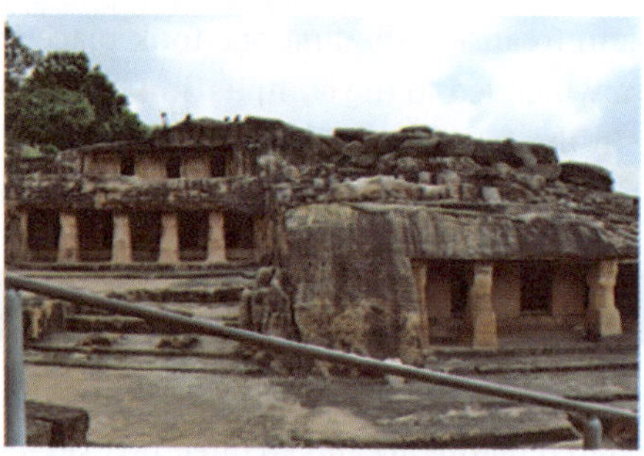

Udayagiri Cave

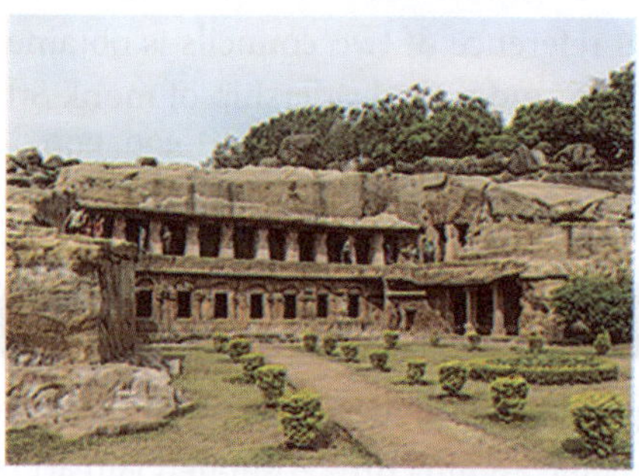

Khandagiri Cave

- **Tirthankaras –** literally the word 'Tirthankara' means one who could show a fordable passage across the sea. Thus, Tirthankaras were those great souls who could guide others across the sea of this continuous life and birth.
- **Arihant –** Arihant refer to those beings who have acquired the true and omniscient knowledge and thus have attained Nirvana or salvation. They are also called **Kevalins** or those possessing **Keval Jnana**. However, these beings continue to remain in human form unlike the **Siddhas** which are liberated souls which have already attained Nirvana and are free from the bondage of life, death, and birth. The **Namokar Mantra** (most important religious mantra of Jains) pays first obeisance to Arihants (as they are accessible to human beings), then to Siddhas, and then to other holy entities.
- **Sammed Shikhar-** or Shikharji is one of the most revered Jain holy place. Located on hill top of Parasnath hills (Giridih District in Jharkhand), it is believed that 20 out of the 24 Tirthankaras and many other saints attained Nirvana here.

IMPORTANT TOPICS TO FOCUS ON

- Teachings of Mahavira and Tirthankaras and Jain philosophy particulars (*Triratna, Panch-Mahavrata* (five vows), *Samyak Jnan,* and *Anekantavada*)
- Two sects of Jainism and differences between them
- Poignant difference in philosophy of Jainism from Hinduism and Buddhism
- Jain art, architecture, and its contribution
- Impact of Jainism on Indian society

CHAPTER 6

Art, Architecture, Sculpture, Literature, And Performing Arts In Ancient India

> What is art? It is the response of man's creative soul to the call of the real
>
> **Rabindranath Tagore**

AN INTRODUCTION

Art, architecture, sculpture, and performing arts in ancient India not only covers a vast period of history but numerous and multifarious subjects as well. The entire period of Indian history up to the beginning of the medieval period (1000–1100 CE) falls in its purview. Many areas of culture such as the Buddhist sculpture and art, rock-cut architecture, various schools of art, pillars and capitals, coins, literature, and other areas of culture too fall in its ambit. In this chapter the period beginning from 300 BCE (beginning of the Mauryan period) to 1000–1100 CE (beginning of the medieval period) is being covered. This period can be broadly subdivided into (a) the **Mauryan** period (b) the **Post Mauryan** period (c) the **Gupta** period, and (d) the **Post Gupta** period.

ART AND ARCHITECTURE IN THE MAURYAN PERIOD

Since the 5th century CE, the social landscape of India (particularly in the Gangetic plane) underwent a change and so did the art and architecture of the period. Buddhism and Jainism, which rejected the supremacy of the Vedas and Brahmanical system and emphasised on Ahimsa and equality, appealed to a vast section of the society and grew rapidly. The patronisation of Buddhism by Mauryan kings, particularly by Ashoka, greatly influenced the religious and political atmosphere as well as the art and culture. As such, the Mauryan art and culture bears a distinct Buddhist stamp on it, as visible in the stupas, chaityas, viharas, pillars and capitals, rock-cut architecture, cave architecture, and sculptures. *These elements of Mauryan culture are discussed below.*

Elements of Mauryan Culture

(a) Viharas: The viharas were **places of residence or monasteries** of Buddhist monks particularly for taking shelter during the rainy season. The erstwhile kingdom of Magadh had a large number of viharas lending it the name Bihar. Initial viharas were simple wooden structures which do not survive to this day. However, some of the viharas do exist in the rock-cut structures in the **Ajanta, Ellora, Karle, Nasik, Bagh, Badami,** and **Kanaheri caves** among others. Many of such viharas are seen to be having a standard or a common plan. It would have a quadrangular court with walls flanking it. Small cells would be present around this central court. These cells would have stone beds, a raised portion of which would serve as a pillow. A small hollow in the wall of the cell would be a space for keeping an earthen lamp.

(b) Chaityas: These were the Buddhist shrines or prayer halls with a stupa at one end of the hall and pillars on the side of the pathway leading to the stupa. They were also community places of worship for the Buddhists. The rock-cut chaityas which exist even today are seen in **Ajanta, Ellora, Karle, Bagh, Nasik, and Kanaheri** caves. Many of these were constructed in the post Mauryan period. However, the chaitya at **Barabar and Nagarjuni caves** are examples of Mauryan art.

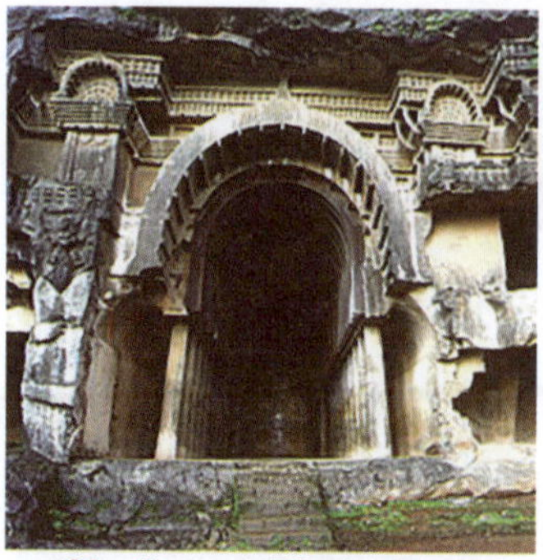

Chaitya at Bhaja Cave

The chaitya at **Bhaja** cave is a typical example of chaitya construction. These consisted of a hall with semicircular roof/apsidal hall. Both the sides of this hall have a number of columns which are sloping inwards. These were imitations of wooden columns. The roof which is semicircular and barrel shaped is having semicircular ribs. These were also features of wooden structures. The columns and walls were finely polished, which was a typical feature of Mauryan art. Thus, the hall and its structures though cut in stone depicted a wooden facade. The pillars were carved exquisitely and had an intricate abacus atop.

(c) Pillars and Capitals: Pillars (stambha) and capitals are important elements depicting the Mauryan art. The object of construction of pillars was to carry inscriptions containing the edicts of kings who commissioned it. Many of the Ashokan pillars carry edicts which were teachings of Buddhist Dhamma.

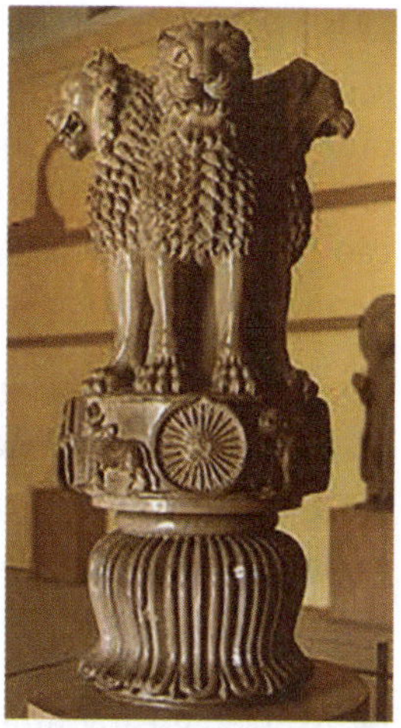

Sarnath pillar lion

The pillars of Mauryan times were **rock-cut stone pillars**. They were a single piece of stone or **monolithic pillars** unlike the contemporaneous Achaemenid pillars which were constructed in pieces. The cutting of round pillars in hard stones reflects the skills of craftsmen of that age. The pillars were highly polished with inscriptions engraved on them. Atop the pillars, **capital figures were carved, such as the lion, the bull, the elephant,** etc. At the base of the capital there would be an **abacus** which would be like **an inverted lotus or a bell**. The pillars, lion capital of Sarnath (Uttar Pradesh), Lauriya Nandangarh (Bihar), Vaishali (Bihar), Rampurva (Champaran in Bihar), and elephant capital at Sansika (Farrukhabad in UP) are well known and belong to the Mauryan period.

(i) *The Sarnath Pillar* – The pillar of **Sarnath carrying atop the lion capital** (the national symbol of India) is the most famous example of Mauryan sculpture. This lion capital (2.31 m high) consists of four parts:

(a) **a bell shaped vase covered with inverted lotus**

(b) **an abacus** with figures of, a horse, a bull, a lion, and elephant on it

(c) **four chakras** (wheels) each having twenty four spokes

(d) **four lions** placed back-to-back looking in the four directions.

All of these elements are symbolic, viz. the lion symbolises Buddha (a fearless roar in all directions of truth and knowledge), the chakra symbolises the turning of the wheel of law. Thus, this capital symbolised the Buddha's historical delivery (at Sarnath) of the first sermon or Dharmachakra Pravartana. The carvings in the figures are especially exquisite. The muscularity of the lion is clearly visible. The polishing is very fine and mirror-like. The original capital also had a 'Dharmachakra' (a large wheel) atop the four lions, but this was broken (and is not a part of the national symbol).

(ii) The pillar at **Lauriya Nandangarh** (3rd century BCE) is another exquisite example of Mauryan art. The pillar (9.8 m high) has a bell shaped inverted lotus. The abacus is decorated with flying geese and a single lion atop.

(iii) Another famous example is the **Vaishali** pillar with a lion capital.

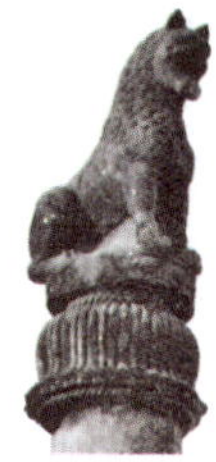

Lauriya Nandangarh Pillar

(d) Stupa: A stupa is a hemispherical (mound shape) construction which **contains holy relics or cremated remains of Buddha** or other monks. Apart from the hemispherical structure, most of the stupas also have a fence around it.

Structure of a Stupa – The semicircular mound of earth is called **anda** which is the structure of the simplest of the stupa. This usually is made up of mud and bricks. The stupas of later period have a balcony above the anda called **harmika** which is representative of the **abode of the gods**. Usually, a mast also arises from the harmika. This is called a **yashti**, atop of which is an umbrella or **chatri**. Some stupas also have a railing surrounding it which serves to separate the sacred space of the stupa. Later, stupas also had an outer circumambulatory path with railings called **vedika** and decorative gateways called **torana**.

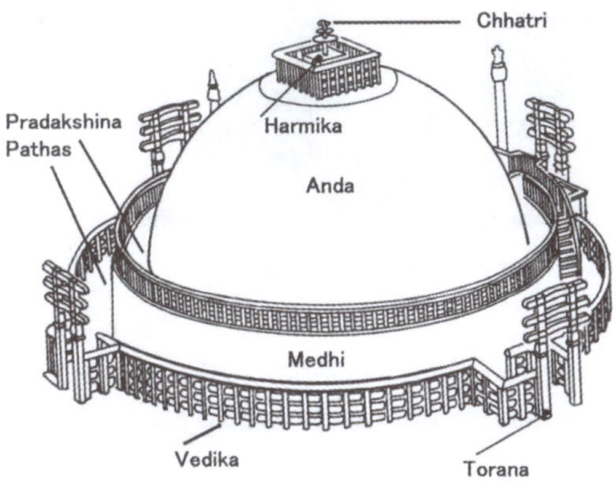

Stupa labelled parts

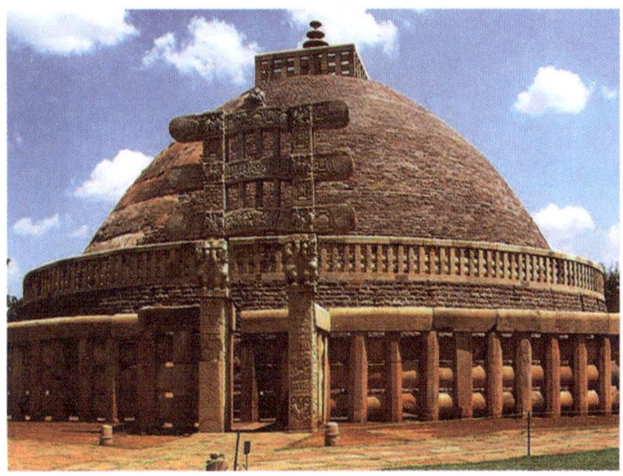

Sanchi Stupa

The stupa at Sanchi (built by emperor Ashoka) with its decorative gateways containing numerous inscriptions, is the most famous one. Other famous stupas of the ancient time are **Dhamekh stupa at Sarnath** (Uttar Pradesh), **Ramabhar stupa at Kushinagar (UP), Vaishali stupa** (Bihar), **Kesariya stupa** (Bihar), and **Amravati stupa** (Andhra Pradesh). However, these stupas are not in the same good state of preservation as the stupa at Sanchi.

(e) Sculptures: The dexterity of the Mauryan sculptures is visible in the various pillars and capitals, the stupas, and the figures on its railing and gateways, the chaityas, and viharas, etc. These represented the class of sculptures commissioned by the king. However, several stone statues have also been found that were not commissioned by the king but by the governors and other rich patrons. The statues of **Yaksha** and **Yakshinis** were quite common in this category and depict the richness of Mauryan art. Some of the important sculptures are described herewith.

- ***Didarganj Yakshini:*** This is a life size free standing statue of a Yakshi (discovered in Didarganj near Patna hence the name). It is a masterpiece of a sculpture. The sandstone figure shows a Yakshi holding a chauri (fly-whisk). It is tall and well-proportioned. The roundness of face, muscular body, and sharp features of nose, lips, and eyes are clearly visible. The upper body is bare with a very well crafted necklace of beads hanging from the neck. The folds of the garment of the lower body are shown by protruding lines creating a transparent effect.

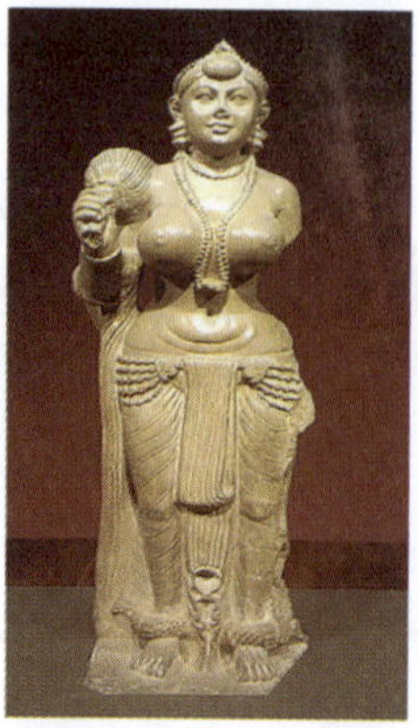

Didarganj Yakshini

- ***Parkham Yaksha:*** This is another great masterpiece of this period. It is a **life size statue of Yaksha made of red sandstone found near Mathura** (presently located in Mathura museum). The muscular body and the folds of garments of the lower body are striking. However, the statue is not as well preserved as that of the Didarganj Yakshini.

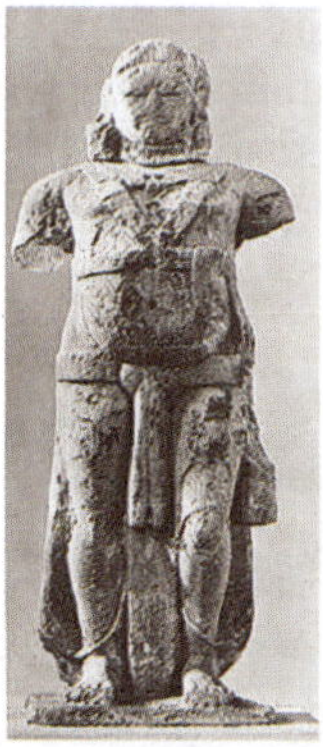

Parkham Yaksha, Mathura

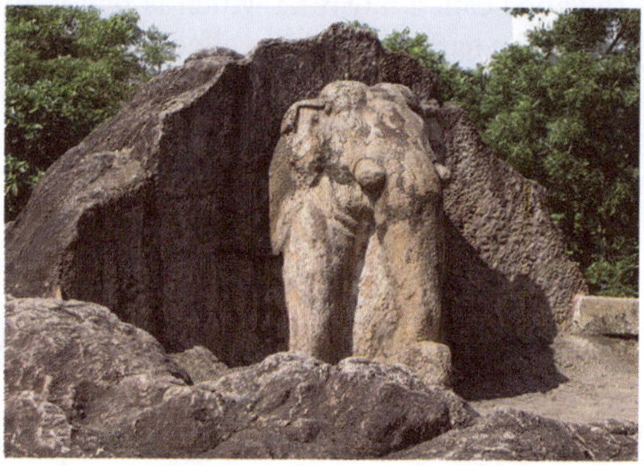

Rock-cut Elephant at Dhauligiri

- ***Rock-cut elephant at Dhauli:*** This monumental rock-cut elephant found at Dhauli (Odisha) is another important specimen of sculpture of this period. Built by emperor Ashoka, the elephant is above a rock edict (inscribed on which is Ashoka's concern for the whole world). This place (Dhauli) is believed to be the site of the Kalinga war.

- ***Rock-cut caves:*** Rock-cut caves are important specimens of art and sculpture of ancient India. Chaityas and viharas too were built at times in rock-cut caves. They reflect the society and culture of the period. Many such rock-cut caves have been found throughout India. The example of Mauryan rock-cut cave is however limited to **Barabar and Nagarjuni** caves near Gaya (Bihar) which are the oldest surviving caves of this category. The outer facade of the Barabar cave has a chaitya arch which is semicircular. The rectangular interior hall has a circular chamber at the back. These chambers are carved out of granite rock and bear highly polished internal surface. Built by emperor Ashoka, the Barabar caves are also called the **Lomas Rishi cave** and was a centre of the followers of the **Ajivika** sect.

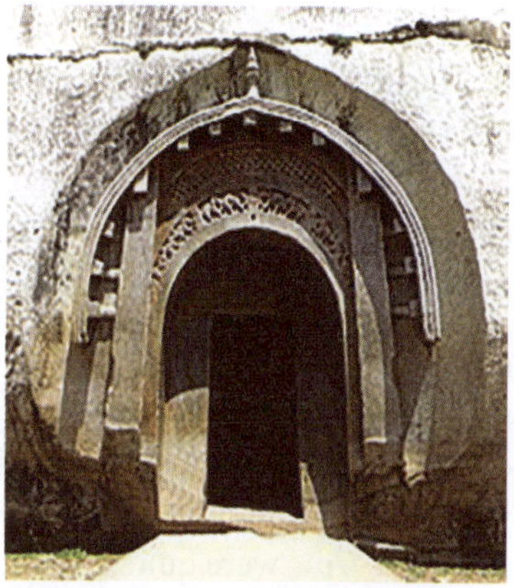

Barabar Cave

(f) Palaces: The Mauryan palaces were another example of the splendour of Mauryan art and architecture. The Ashokan palace, the remains of which can still be seen at **Kumhrar (Patna)**(after 2300 years) had a grand **80 pillared assembly hall**. All the pillars were rock-cut and the remains of a massive pillar of this assembly hall can still be seen at the site of the palace at Kumhrar. Wooden structures with decorative carvings were aplenty and covered the remaining portion of the palace.

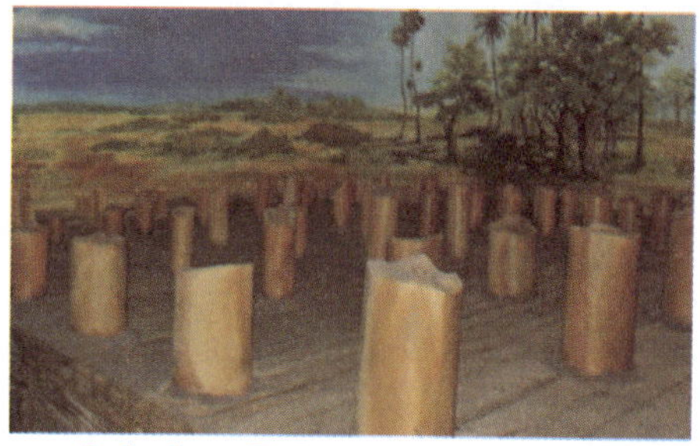

Ashokan Palace site, Kumhrar

(g) Pottery: A variety of Mauryan pottery has been found. Amongst these, the one which was of the highest quality and finish is the **Northern Black Polished Ware** (NBP). It was made of fine alluvial clay and had jet black, deep grey, or metallic steel blue hue. It had a typical lustre and was found in abundance in the Gangetic valley.

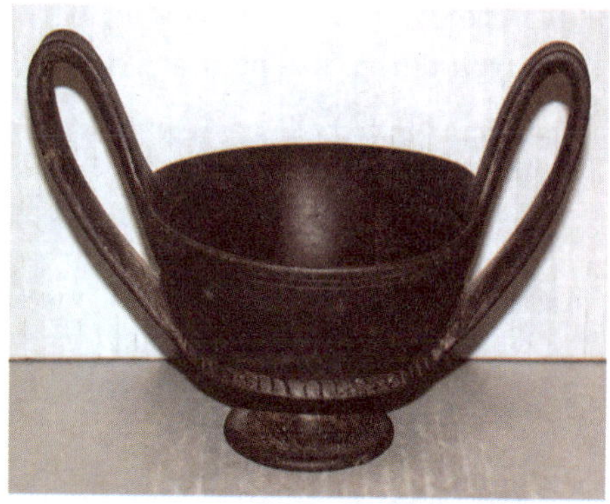

Northern Black Polished Ware

(h) Coins: The coins in the Mauryan period were usually of silver, besides a few of copper. These were of various shapes, sizes, and weights and carried different figures as that of animals, trees, etc. The metal was first cut and the figures were then punched. These punched symbols represented either the royal insignia or the symbols of local guilds issuing it.

ART AND CULTURE IN THE POST MAURYAN PERIOD, GUPTA PERIOD, AND POST GUPTA PERIOD

Art and culture in ancient India has been deeply influenced by the political regime and its patronisation of the religious thought. While in the Mauryan period, Buddhist thought and culture was predominant, in the post Mauryan period, the Gupta period, and the post Gupta period, different social religious influences dominated art and culture.

The various regimes in the period 200 BCE to 1100 CE and their important contribution to art and culture is briefly discussed below.

Post Mauryan Period and Their Influence on Art and Culture

(a) The Sungas: The Sunga dynasty (187 BCE to 75 BCE) founded by **Pushyamitra Sunga**, succeeded the Mauryan dynasty. The Sungas were a **Brahmanical dynasty** and this period also saw rise in **Vaishnavism** and **Shaivism** which reached its peak during the **Gupta period**. During the rule of **Pushyamitra Sunga** (and his successors Agnimitra, Vasumitra, and Devbhuti), the royal patronage shifted from Buddhism to Brahmanism. The salient contribution/developments in field of art and culture in this period are as below:

- **Mathura school of art**, (a counterpart of the Gandhara school of art) flourished in this period.
- Hindu philosophy flourished. Important works such as **Patanjali's Yoga Sutra** and **Mahabhashya** (a treatise on Sanskrit grammar) is said to be composed during this period.
- **Buddhist shrines** such as the s**tupas at Sanchi** and **Baharut** started during the Mauryan period underwent architectural expansions.

(b) Kanva dynasty: The Kanva dynasty (75 BCE to 30 BCE) which overthrew the Sungas was short-lived. Founded by **Vasudeva Kanva**, it was a **Brahmanical dynasty** and continued the support to **Shaivism and Vaishnavism**. This further pushed the Buddhist influence to Central India (from Magadha region and Northern India). This dynasty was brought to an end by the Satavahanas.

(c) The Satavahana Dynasty: This dynasty came to power in the southern part of India (Deccan region) and reached its zenith under the reign of **Gautamiputra Satkarni**. Although they were Hindu kings (descendents of the solar dynasty—Suryavanshi) they were supporters of Buddhism as well as Brahmanism. *Their salient contribution to the cultural landscape is as below:*

- The **grand stupa of Amaravati** (Andhra Pradesh) and other stupas in the Krishna river valley were built during this period.

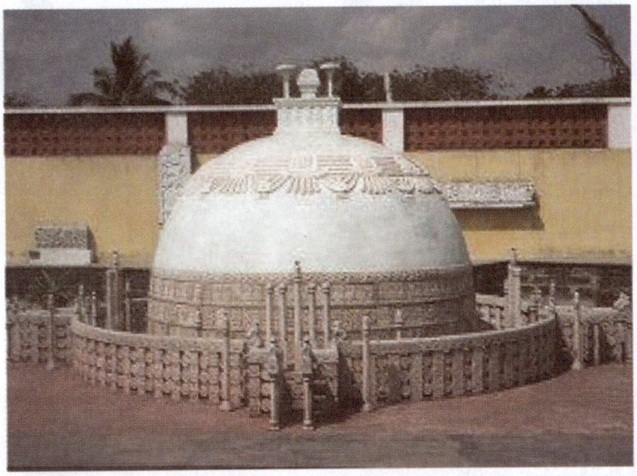

Amaravati Stupa

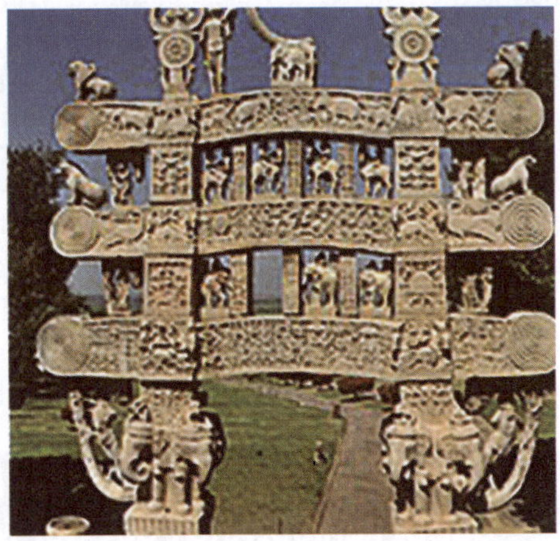

Gateway at Sanchi Stupa

- The **gateways** at the Sanchi stupa is believed to have been started/built by them.
- This regime helped in the **spread of Hindu culture** to Southeast Asia.
- It issued its own **coins** with portrait of rulers.
- **Prakrit** was used in official communications, coins, etc. and as a language of administration.

(d) Kushana Dynasty: The Kushana dynasty came into prominence in the northern and north western part of India in the first century CE. It also covered the present day Pakistan and large parts of Afghanistan. It was established by king Kujula Kadphises (in 78 CE). Emperor **Kanishka** was the most prominent ruler of this dynasty. The early Kushana rulers are believed to have been influenced by Hinduism and called themselves Devaputra (son of gods). Kanishka however, was a supporter of Buddhism and held the **fourth Buddhist council in Kashmir**. The reign had an important influence on Indian art and culture.

- A new form of Buddhism, **Mahayana sect** emerged as a consequence of the **4th Buddhist council**. Mahayana was patronised by Kanishka which helped in its spread not only in India but from Gandhara to China.

- **Saka Calendar** was started from 78 CE which is the national calendar of India.
- The **Gandhara** as well as the **Mathura school of art** flourished at this time. The Gandhara school had more of Greco-Buddhist influence with statues of Buddha having curly hair, sharp features of eyes, lips, etc. The Mathura school was more indigenous. A number of large statues of Kushana rulers was found at Mathura, the most famous being the **headless statue of Kanishka**.
- Gold coins were issued for the first time by Kushana rulers carrying images of the kings.

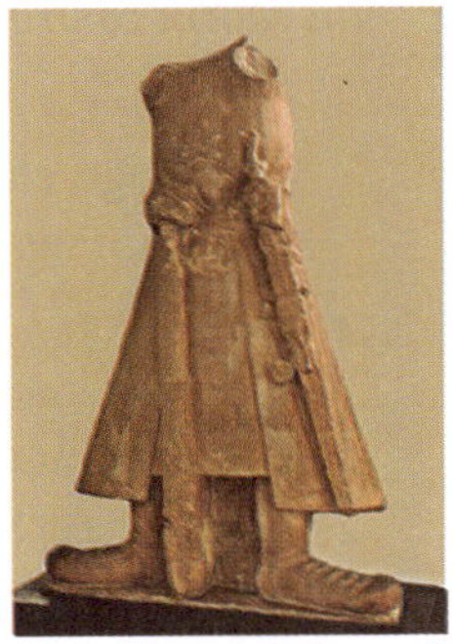

Headless statue of Kanishka

Gupta Period and Their Influence on Art and Culture

Introduction

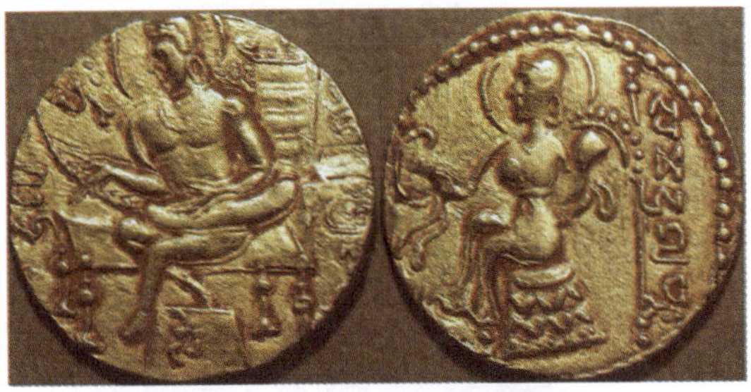

Coin Showing Samudragupta

The Gupta dynasty from 240 CE to 550 CE ushered in a new phase of growth and development in all walks of life. Historians have aptly termed it as a **Golden Age** of Indian history. Not only did areas of human knowledge like art, sculpture, science, technology, mathematics, astronomy, and philosophy flourish in this period but growth of agriculture, commerce, and trade coupled with sound administration and military conquests made it one of the most prominent regimes of its time in the world. Eminent scholars and litterateurs like **Kalidasa** and **Vishnu Sharma**, astronomers, and scientists like **Aryabhatta** and **Varahamihira,** and other personalities like **Vatsayana** who made notable contributions in their respective fields, prospered in this age.

A Brief History of the Gupta Rulers

This empire was founded by Maharaj Srigupta. Chandragupta I, **Samudragupta, and Chandragupta Vikramaditya** (Chandragupta II) were the most notable rulers of this period. Samudragupta who is known for his great military conquests is also referred by historians as the Indian Napoleon. He was himself a poet and musician (coins depict him playing a **veena**). The empire reached its zenith during Chandragupta II (375 CE to 415 CE) when a large part of the Indian subcontinent was directly under this empire or owed suzerainty to it. A detailed account of the Gupta period is obtained in the writings of the Chinese traveller **Faxian** (also referred as *Fahien*) who stayed in India from 405 to 411 CE. The accounts which are the most important source of information of this age, describe a prospering civilisation, able but mild administration, and a glorious account of the rule and the king.

The Guptas were Hindu kings and Hindu art and culture underwent resurgence in this phase. However, they were tolerant of Buddhism and Jainism and contributed to the development of a monastery at Bodhgaya.

Art and Culture in the Gupta Period

Art and culture indeed reached its zenith during this period which included Hindu, Buddhist, and Jain art.

The salient contribution/elements of art and culture of this period is described below.

- **Paintings at Ajanta** – The mural paintings of Ajanta (a world heritage monument) are a contribution of this age, although, earlier the **Satavahanas** and later the **Vakatakas** have also contributed to it. The paintings include images of Bodhisattvas and Jatakas.
- **Sculptures in Gupta period** – The **Dashavatara temple at Deogarh (UP)** which contains the reclining image of Vishnu is a grand example of this age's sculpture. During this phase, both the Gandhara and Mathura school of art flourished. The image of Vishnu at Mathura and seated image of Buddha at Sarnath are the finest examples of sculpture. The sculpture of Varaha at Udayagiri caves near Vidisha (Madhya Pradesh) is another example of great craftsmanship. Further, the standing image of Buddha at Mathura and Buddha's bronze statue are other great examples of sculpture showing the influence of puranic Hinduism as well as Buddhism.

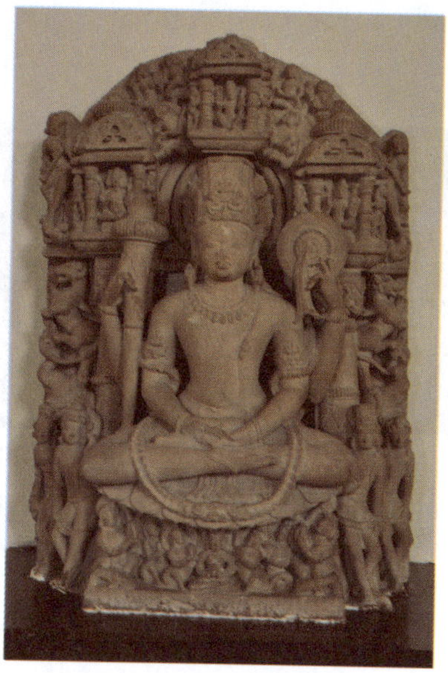

Vishnu at Mathura

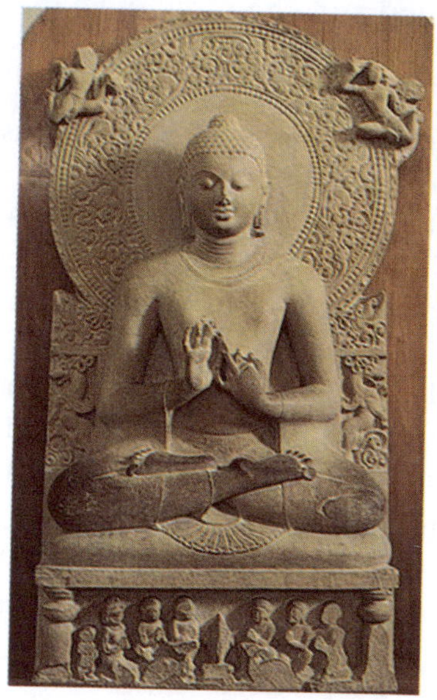

Seated image of Buddha at Sarnath

- Temple architecture evolved during this period as seen from **Dashavatara stone temple (Deogarh)** and the **Chaturmukhlinga Shiva temple at Nachana** (Madhya Pradesh).
- Cave and rock-cut sculpture flourished during this period. This is evident in the **Udayagiri caves** and the **Elephanta caves** (5th to 8th century CE). The latter has the famous **Trimurti** sculpture.
- **Coins** – A number of gold and silver coins of this age have been discovered. These show images of Samudragupta, holding royal sceptre, sacrificing at the altar, holding bow, performing *Ashwamedha Yagna*, playing *Veena*, etc. Coins with images of other rulers are also found.

Post Gupta Period and Their Influence on Art and Culture

(i) The Vakataka dynasty: This dynasty (3rd to 5th century CE) was contemporary of the Guptas and flourished in the Deccan region between the Malwa plateau and the Tungabhadra river. The daughter of

Chandragupta II (Prabhavati Gupta) was married to Rudrasena, a Vakataka king. The Vakatakas were Brahmin kings. They were great patrons of art and literature. Many of the viharas/chaityas were also built during this period. **The paintings** (in cave no. XVI) of **Ajanta** are said be commissioned by Vakataka king Harisena.

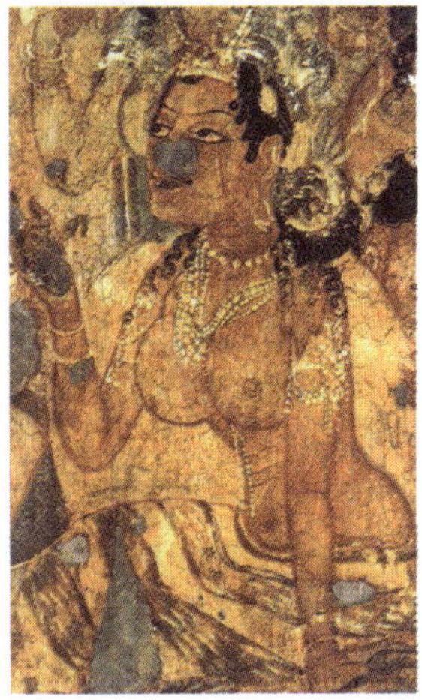

Ajanta Cave Painting

(ii) The Chalukya dynasty: The Chalukya period (6th to 13th century CE), succeeded the Vakatakas and is often referred as **the golden period** in the history of South India. The regime covered large parts of Central and Southern parts of India. **Pulakeshin II** was one of the most important rulers of this dynasty who halted the southward march of King Harsha. Administration, commerce. overseas trade, and art and architecture received a great boost in this phase. The **temples at Aihole** in Karnataka **(a UNESCO world heritage site)**, **rock-cut architecture of Badami** famous for sculptures of Hindu deities (such as Shiva's *Tandava* and Vishnu as *Trivikrama*), temples of **Pattadakal (a world heritage site)**, and many temples of Western Chalukyas are representative of this regime.

(iii) Pala Dyanasty: The Pala dynasty 8th century CE to 12th century CE came in prominence in the Bengal and Bihar region. At the height of this dynasties' influence (during the rule of king Dharmapala), it brought parts of northern and north-western India under its control, though this influence was short-lived. This regime had profound influence on art, sculpture, philosophy, etc. so much so that the Pala period sculpture was referred as a separate school of art. It was famous for its stone (black basalt) palm leaf miniature paintings and bronze statues. The Palas were Buddhist and subjects of art was taken from Mahayana, Vajrayana, and Tantra form of Buddhism. The Mahaviharas of Somapura (Bangladesh), Jagaddala (West Bengal), Odantpura (Bihar), Vikramshila (Bihar) was built during their regime. They were the patrons of Vikramshila and Nalanda universities and the latter reached its pinnacle during the rule of the Palas.

(iv) Pallava dynasty: This dynasty flourished in South India between 6th to 9th century CE and is known for art and architecture, particularly rock-cut temples and monolithic shrines. The Pallavas were Hindu kings and built the famous temple at **Mahabalipuram** (Mammalapuram) and **Kailashnath temple at Kanchipuram**. The structures at Mahabalipuram (**a world heritage site**) are attributed to kings, Mahendraverman-1 (600 to 630 CE) and Narsimhavarman (630 CE to 668 CE). These include rock-cut structures such as the **Panch Rathas** (carved out of a single rock). The **'Arjuna's Penance sculpture'** located here is quite famous. They also include the world famous **shore temples** (which is a complex of three temples by the seashore).

(v) Chandela Dynasty: The Chandela dynasty came in prominence in the early 10th century CE in Central India (Bundelkhand region). The Chandelas were Rajputs (*Chandravanshi*—Lunar dynasty). They are known for the construction of the Hindu and Jain temple complex in **Khajuraho** (Madhya Pradesh) which were built between 950 to 1000 CE. The group of temples are known for the dexterity in carving of erotic sculptures and figures on the temple walls. A UNESCO world heritage site, the most famous amongst these temples are the *Kandariya Mahadev, Laxmana, and Chaustha Yogini temples.*

SCHOOLS OF ART IN ANCIENT INDIA

From the 1st century CE onwards a number of important centres of production of art and sculpture emerged in different parts of India. Each had its unique style and covered a variety of subjects. These are referred to as the schools of art. The most prominent ones were the **Mathura, Gandhara, Amaravati,** and **Sarnath** schools of art. *The salient features and important schools, their subjects and creations are briefly given here.*

The Mathura School of Art

- This school of art developed around **Mathura** region, it being the main production centre while **Kausambi** and **Sarnath** were also important centres of art.
- It developed after 1st century CE but gained in prominence during the **Gupta period** after the 3rd century CE.
- This was an **indigenous school of art** and unlike Gandhara school, it did not have Greek-Hellenistic influence.
- Subjects from **Buddhism, Vaishnavism, Shaivism**, and **Jainism** were incorporated in the sculptures. The earlier Buddhist subjects were the symbols of Buddha (viz. lotus, empty throne, etc.). But later, images of Buddha were incorporated which were modelled around the images of the earlier Yakshas.
- The images of Buddha are either seated or standing with a large **highly decorated halo around them**. The Vaishnavite and Shaiviti images of gods are also found which are represented by their **ayudhas** (weapons).

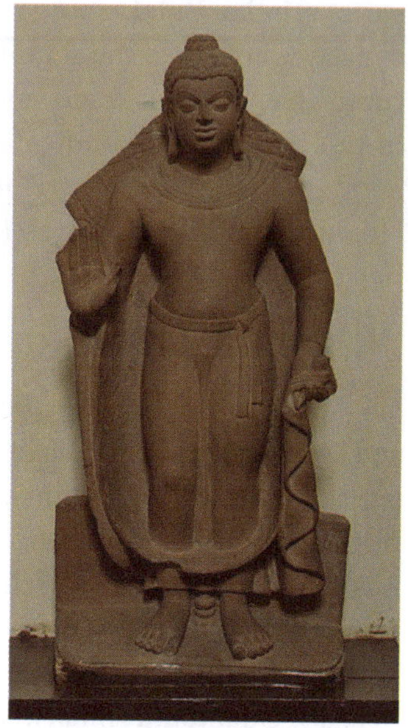

Standing Buddha at Mathura

- The images of this school have a typical boldness and are large and highly decorated. The faces are round and smiling. The features are often fleshier. However, in the images of the 4th and 5th century the fleshiness and massiveness becomes less and the features of body are seen to be tightened. Further, transparent quality in the robes of images of Buddha is also evident.
- The sculptures of this school were made in **spotted sandstone**. Important sculptures include, statue of Lord Vishnu, headless statue of Kanishka, and sandstone image of standing Buddha in *Abhayamudra.*

Gandhara School of Art

- This school of art developed in north-western part of India around Gandhara.
- It flourished in the **Kushana** rule in the 1st century CE specially during the rule of Kanishka when it reached its zenith. The style of the Gandhara school was deeply **influenced by the Greek and Hellenistic art**. Thus, it was a confluence of Indo-Greek art tradition and is also referred as Graeco-Buddhist school of art.

- The themes were mainly Buddhist and subjects included images of Buddha and events from his life. Images of Buddha are shown seated or standing depicting different mudras. The expression is serene. Curly hair, sharp features of eyes, ears, lips, and absence of fleshy heaviness are typical features of the sculptures. The drapery and folds of cloth create an image of transparency. High degree of craftsmanship is depicted and grey and bluish grey standstone is the material largely used in this school. However, mud, lime, and stucco has also been used.
- Important sculptures include the 'Meditating Buddha' (in Dhyan mudra) and Bodhisattva.

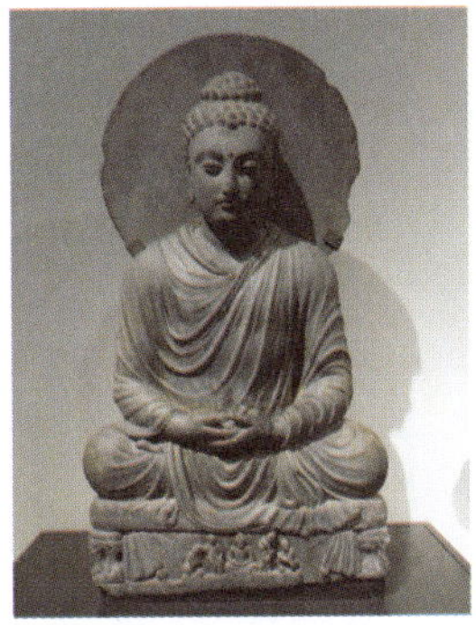

Meditating Buddha

Amaravati School of Art

- This school of art flourished in South India in **Amaravati** and other centres in Krishna and Godavari region valley including Nagarjunakonda, Goli, and Guntapalle.
- Amaravati school dates back to 3rd century BCE and reached its peak during the **Satavahana period**. The school was an **indigenous** one and the images had largely Buddhist subjects though some images of Hindu gods and goddesses were also made.
- Sculptures contain images from the life of Buddha and Jataka tales in form of narratives, viz. scenes of events in the life of Buddha (or Jataka) rather than individual images. Some images of Hindu gods are also found, viz. **Ganesha, Lakshmi,** and ornate bull Nandisvara.
- The sculptures of this school are often depicted with deep emotions, a lot of body movement, and in body postures such as **tribhanga** (three bents of the body). The images and sculptures were made usually in white and at times in green marble.
- The stupa drum slab, image of birth of Buddha (dream of Maya Devi with an elephant above her), Nandisvara, and image of Ganesha and Lakshmi are important sculptures of this school.

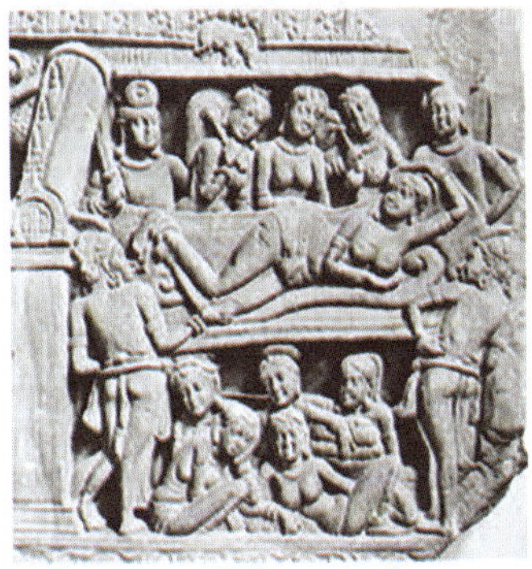

Dream of Maya before Buddha's birth

Stupa Drum Slab

Sarnath School of Art

- **Sarnath** (near Varanasi in Uttar Pradesh) where Buddha delivered the first sermon developed as an important centre of Buddhist art (although Mathura was the main centre of production). This school flourished during the **Gupta period**.

- **Images of Buddha** was the common theme in this school. These images differ from the Mathura images as here the Buddha sculptures have **plain and transparent drapery**. Further, the halo around the head has **little ornamentation** unlike the Mathura images of Buddha which have heavy ornamentation of the halo. The Sarnath images of Buddha are **simple** yet **sublime**.

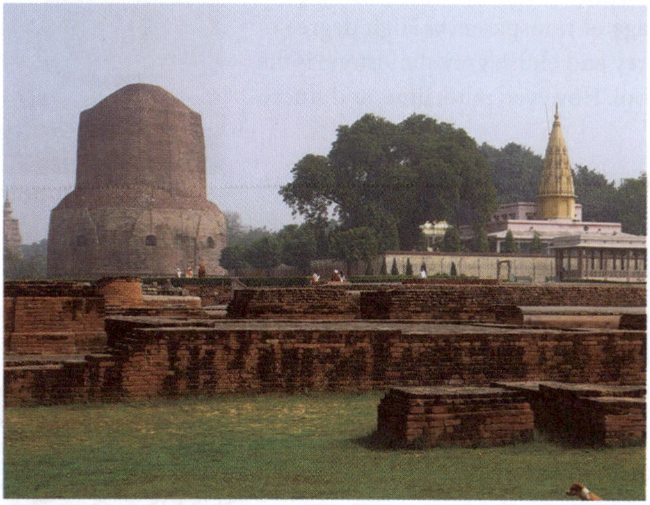

Sarnath

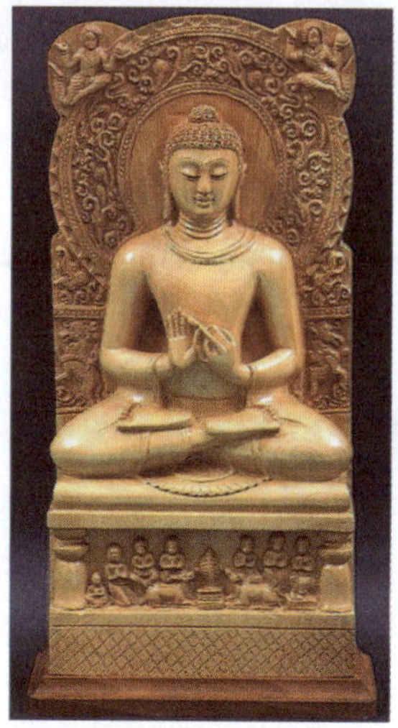

Sarnath Buddha

- Standing figure of **ornamented Tara** (a Buddhist deity) is the best example of this school.

ROCK-CUT ARCHITECTURE

Rock-cut architecture refers to creation of structures (objects of art) by cutting and removal of stones from solid natural rock, till what is left is the structure intended to be created. This style of architecture has been an important form of religious artistic expression in India for centuries. Over 1500 known rock-cut structures survive even today, **the oldest being the Barabar caves** of 3rd century BCE (of Mauryan period). In the post Mauryan period hundreds of such caves were excavated. They were invariably religious in nature and a large number of them were of Buddhist origin. The **Ajanta, Ellora, Bhaja, Kanaheri, Karla, Elephanta, Nashik, Pitalkhora, Junnar, Badami, Udayagiri**, and **Khandagiri** are amongst the most famous of rock-cut caves. Amongst these **Junnar** has the maximum number of caves (more than two hundred). The subjects of the rock-cut structures varied, from simple **chaitya, viharas,** and **temples** to beautiful **sculptures and paintings**. Existence of mural paintings however is unique to Ajanta caves.

The salient features of important caves are being discussed below.

Ajanta Caves

The Ajanta, a UNESCO world heritage site near Aurangabad (Maharashtra) is among the most famous and the most exquisite example of art of ancient India, especially of painting. The caves were discovered in 1819 (by a British hunting expedition). They are excavated in a horseshoe bend of rock surface overlooking a stream. There are 30 caves which were excavated including one which is unfinished. Out of these, five are chaityas while the rest are viharas.

- These caves were built from **2nd century BCE to 6th century CE** in two phases, the first phase beginning from 2nd century BCE while the second phase was from 400 to 650 CE.
- The subject of excavation in all the caves are **Buddhist**. The earlier caves belong to the Hinayana phase while the latter to Mahayana. Images of Buddha, Bodhisattvas, and scenes from *Jatakas* and *Avadanas* are included in the sculptures and paintings. The chaitya caves 19 and 26 contain elaborate carvings with the biggest image being that of **Buddha's Mahaparinibbana** (cave no. 26).

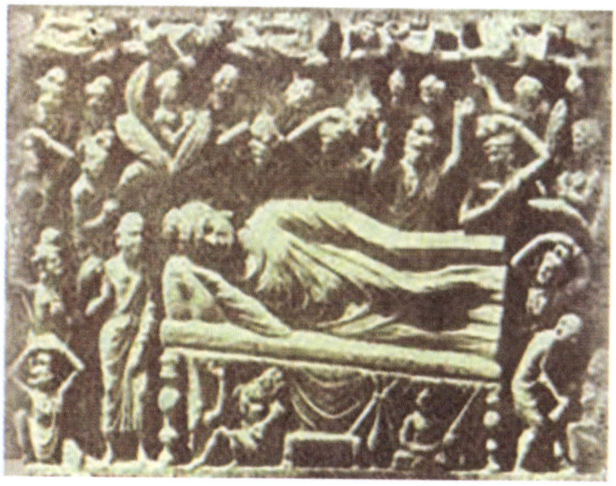

Buddha Mahaparinibbana

- The famous **mural paintings** are found in caves 1, 2, 16, and 17. The lines of the painting are clearly defined with body colours merging with outline creating a volume effect. Limited colours with natural tones have been used (brown, yellowish brown, yellow ochre, and greenish). The different skin colours represent multi-coloured population. The most famous painting is the one of Buddha with Rahul and Yashoda, and another is that of an Apsara.

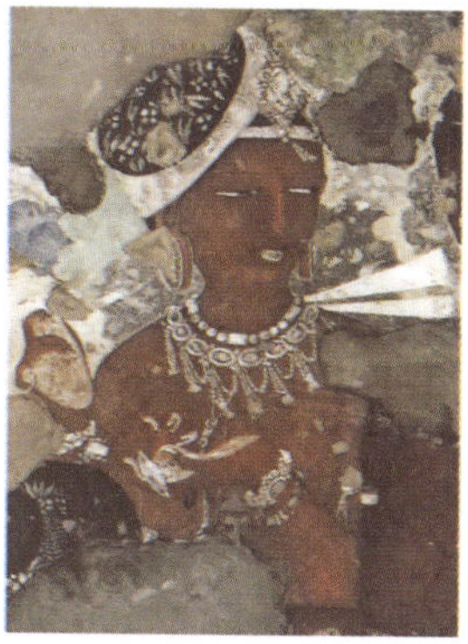

Image of Apsara

- The paintings were done after elaborate surface preparation. Rock surface cut with chisel (with chisel marks left to help greater adhesion) was covered with a ground layer of earth mixed with rock grit, sand, vegetable fibres, paddy husk, and grass. A second layer of mud and ferruginous earth mixed with sand, rock powder, and fine fibrous vegetable material was applied, over which a thin coat of lime wash was applied. Over this surface bold outlines were drawn and colours were painted. These paintings are considered as murals and not frescoes as in these a binding agent was used, whereas in frescoes the painting are executed when the lime wash is still wet which in turn acts as a binding agent.
- Several dynasties and patrons are known to have contributed to the Ajanta caves. These include the **Vakatakas** who were contemporary of Guptas. Varahdeva, minister of Vakataka king Harisena, was patron of cave no. 16.

Ellora Caves

This group of caves near Aurangabad is another UNESCO world heritage site and is said to be an epitome of rock-cut architecture.

- These 32 caves were built between 5th century CE to 11th century CE under the patronage of different dynasties, primarily the **Rashtrakutas** (**Kailasa temple** cave no. 16) and **Yadavas** (Jain group of caves).

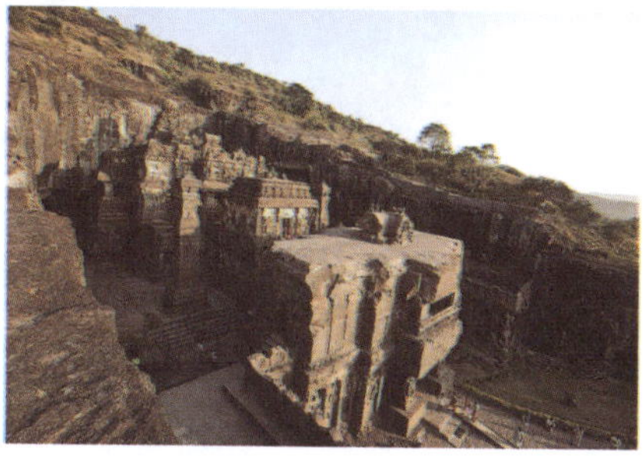

Ellora Cave

- These cave sculptures are a **confluence of Buddhist, Brahmanical, and Jain subjects**. Besides, they represent different styles of architecture and craftsmanship as guilds from Tamilnadu, Karnataka, Vidarbha, etc. carved different caves at different points of time. Many caves are two storeys and some even three storeys which adds to the uniqueness of Ellora. The Buddhist caves (no. 14, 15, 16, 21, and 29) contain the images of Buddha which is guarded by **Vajrapani** and **Padmapani**. Many images of **Tara** and **Bodhisattvas like Amitabha Avlokiteshwara, Vairochana, etc.** are found.

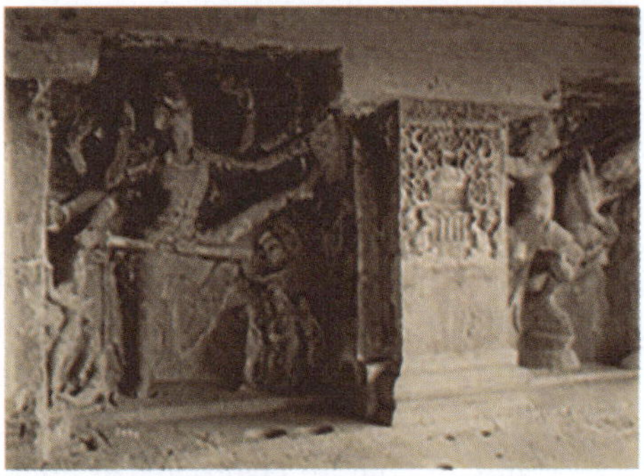

Dashavatara Cave

- The Brahmanical caves are of Shaivism faith (image of **Gajasura Shiva** in cave no. 15) besides images of different **avataras of Vishnu** are also found in **Dashavatara** (cave no. 15).
- The Jain caves (no. 32 to 34) are known for their decorative and ornate images. These are of later period (9th century CE).
- The most famous creation at Ellora is the great **Kailasa temple** (cave no. 16) which is **carved out of a single piece of rock**. Thus, it is the **largest monolithic temple** which even included a courtyard. The temple is dedicated to Lord Shiva. The temple's central shrine has a *lingam* with a roofed '*mandapa*' supported by 16 pillars and a *shikhara* of Dravidian style. An image of Nandi (bull) is seen in the porch in front of the temple.

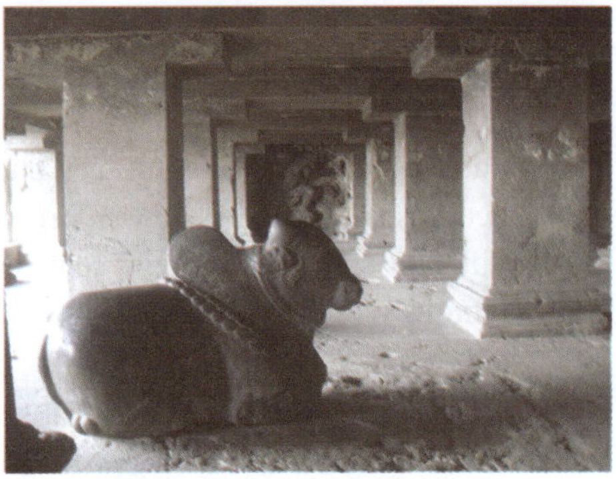

Nandi Bull at Ellora

Elephanta Caves

These caves located on an island near Mumbai are another great exquisite example of rock-cut architecture and is also a UNESCO world heritage site. It derives its name from a **large stone elephant sculpture** found at the entrance.

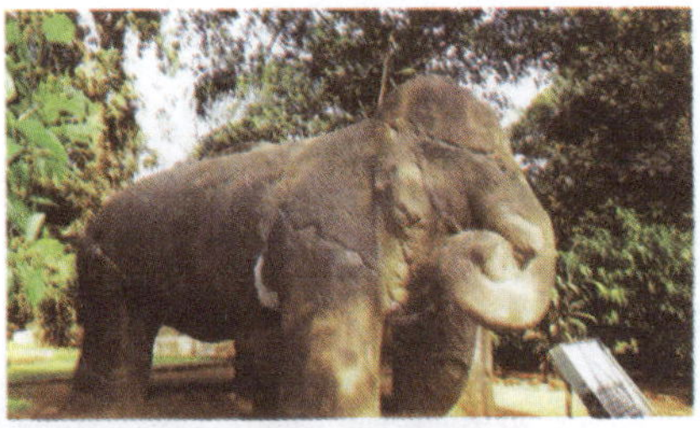

Stone Elephant at Elephanta

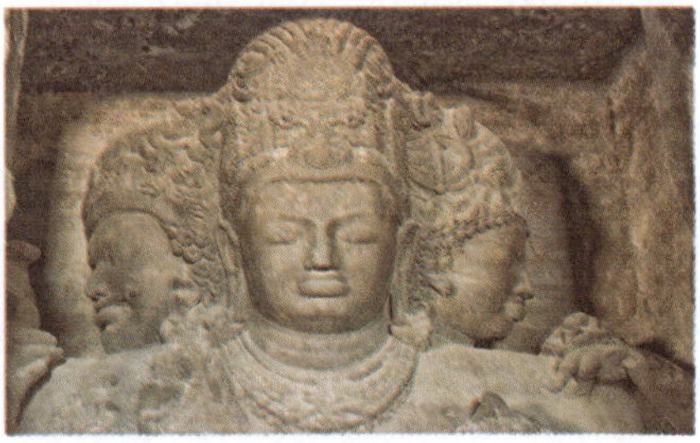

Shiva Trimurti at Elephanta Caves

- The caves are believed to be originally a Buddhist site but later images are of Shaivite faith. The **most famous sculpture is the Trimurti image**.
- The sculptures show **slenderness with a unique light and dark effect**. The caves are believed to be contemporary of Ellora.

Kanaheri Caves

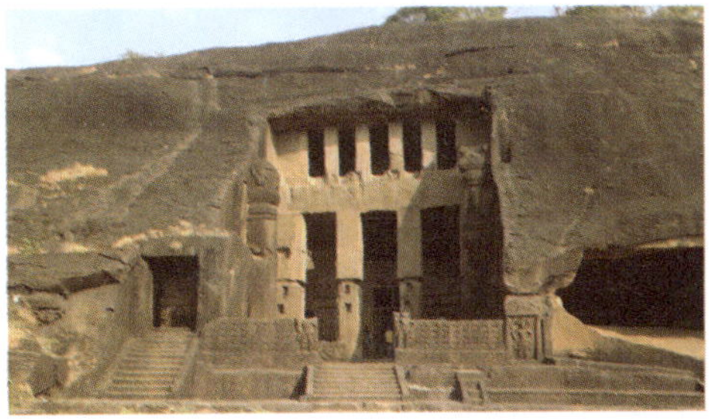

Kanheri Cave

These are 108 rock-cut Buddhist caves located in Mumbai, which date from 100 BCE to 1000 CE. The caves are mostly **viharas** which are spartan in terms of interior carvings and sculptures and contain a stone plinth for a bed. A chaitya hall with a stupa is also present.

- The images in these caves are mostly of **Buddha and Bodhisattvas**. The image of **Avlokiteshwara** is quite prominent.
- Rock inscription in Brahmi and Devnagri script are found indicating donations from different dynasties including that from **Gautamiputra Satkarni** (Satavahana dynasty) and **Amogvarsha** (Rashtrakuta dynasty).
- A unique feature of these caves was construction of canals and cisterns which channelised rainwater into large tanks.

Udayagiri and Khandagiri Caves

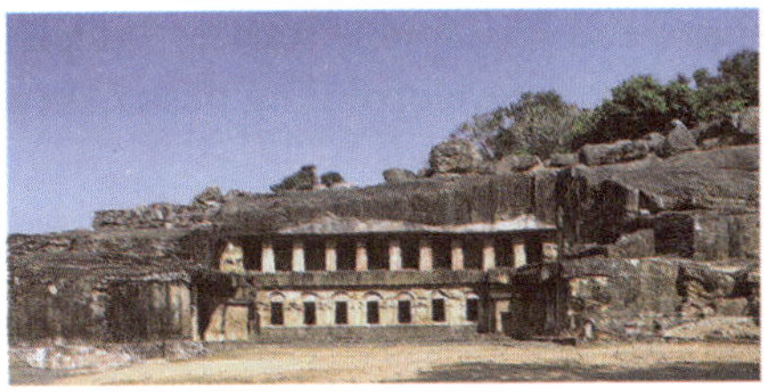

Ranigumpha

The twin hills of Udayagiri and Khandagiri near Bhubaneswar have nearly 33 rock-cut caves (some of them natural caves also). These were built during the reign of king **Kharavela**. These caves are a **Jain complex** used as residence of Jain monks and as such, simple and spartan in architecture. The caves are notable for **Ranigumpha** which is double storeyed and also for the work relief of the 24 Tirthankaras in the **Anantgumpha**.

Guntapalle Caves

These caves are located in Guntapalle in Eluru district of Andhra Pradesh and date to the **second century BCE**. These are Buddhist caves and quite unique as structured stupas and viharas are excavated at one place. It has a chaitya cave which is circular. It has a stupa in the circular hall and a chaitya arch at the entrance.

Junagadh Caves

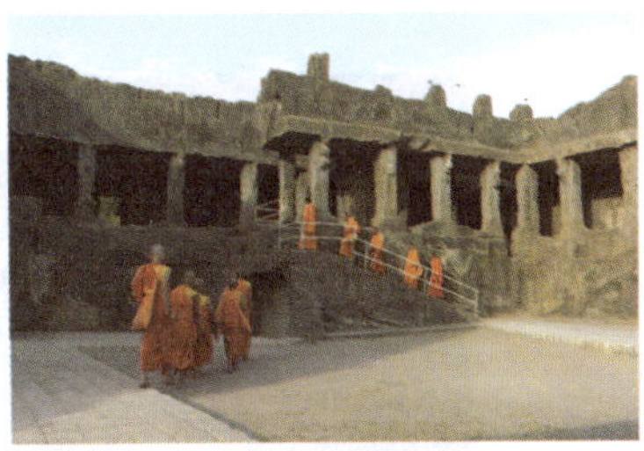

Buddhist Caves of Uperkot

Located in Junagadh (Gujarat) and built during the 1st century to the 4th century CE, these are Buddhist caves built during different regimes. Some date to Ashoka's period while most are of **Satavahana** regime. The most famous are the **Uperkot caves** which were in form of a high citadel in three tiers.

Nasik Caves

These are nearly 24 caves located near Nasik (also called Panduleni). The caves were built from the 3rd century BCE to 2nd century CE and contain subjects of **Hinayana Buddhism**.

Bhaja Caves

These caves are located in Pune near Lonavala. They date to 2nd century BCE and the sculptural subjects belong to **Hinayana Buddhism**. The most prominent cave is the **Chaityagriha** (cave XII) which exhibits a wooden architecture in a rock-cut horseshoe shaped stone ceiling. The pillared verandah has a unique relief. A carving also shows a woman playing *Tabla* and another woman performing dance. These caves are similar to **Karla caves**.

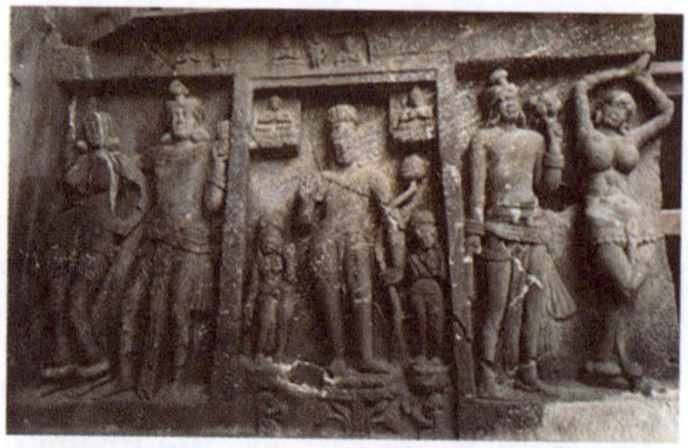

Woman Playing tabla (Bhaja Caves)

EARLY TEMPLES AND ARCHITECTURE

With the rise in Brahmanism in this period and patronage of rulers like the Guptas, early temples began being constructed in ancient India. These temples would have a main deity or a central image of a god. The image narratives on the temples would contain myths from Puranas.

The temples of this period were relatively simple in architecture specially when compared to the much ornate and complex medieval temples. They would be structures with a flat roof which was square in shape and was double storied. Temples with circumambulatory path around **garbhagriha** (sanctum) were first to develop during this phase and with passage of time the architecture evolved (See chapter on temple architecture).

Broadly the temples could be cateogorised as:

(a) **Sandhara** type; those without *pradakshina path* (circumambulatory pathway)

(b) **Nirandhara** type; those with *pradakshina path*

(c) **Sarvatobhadra** type; those which could be accessed from all the sides

Important Temples of this Age

(a) Dashavatara Temple: Located in Deogarh, this temple built in 500 CE (in the Gupta period) is dedicated to Lord Vishnu and depicts his 10 incarnations. The temple is built in stone and bricks and was the first among temples with a shikhara. It is of sarvatobhadra type of construction. The temple is famous for the **reclining statue of Vishnu** on *sheshnag* and has ornate decorations.

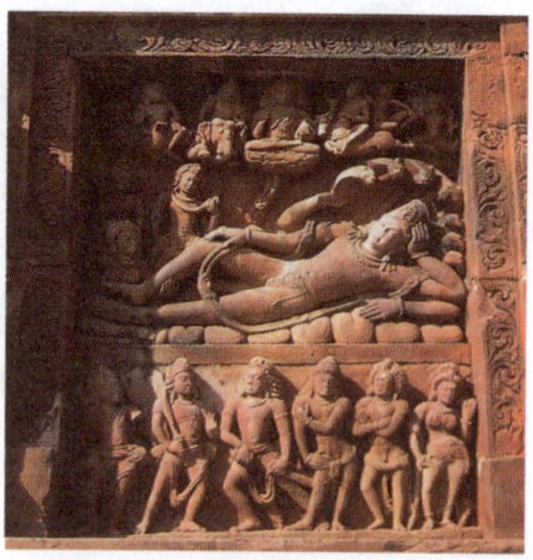

Reclining Vishnu at Deogarh

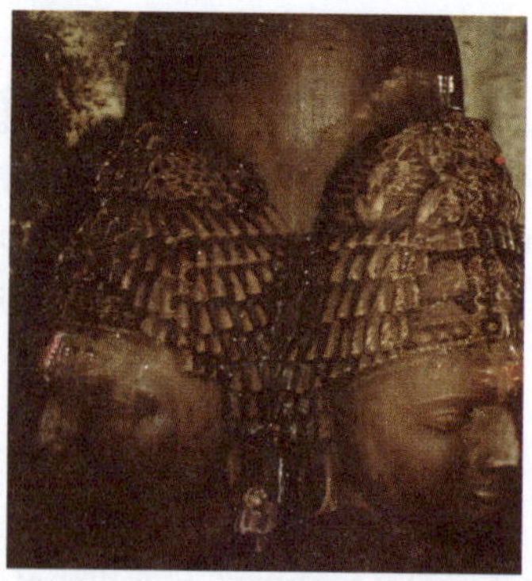

Chaumuknath at Nachna

(b) Nachna Kuthara Temple: This temple, located in Nachna village (Panna in Madhya Pradesh) was built in the Gupta period in the second half of 5th century CE. It has two temples nearby, the Parvati temple (built on a raised platform) and the Chaturmukhi Linga Shiva temple which has a large linga with four faces).

(c) Udayagiri Temples (Vidisha): These rock-cut temples (located in Vidisha, Madhya Pradesh) were built under the patronage of Chandragupta II. It is famous for the **relief sculpture of Lord Vishnu in Varaha avatar** (form of a boar) rescuing Bhumi Devi.

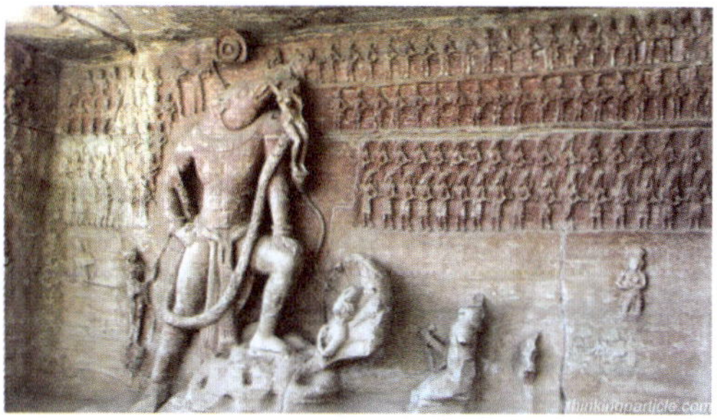

Varaha at Udayagiri Caves

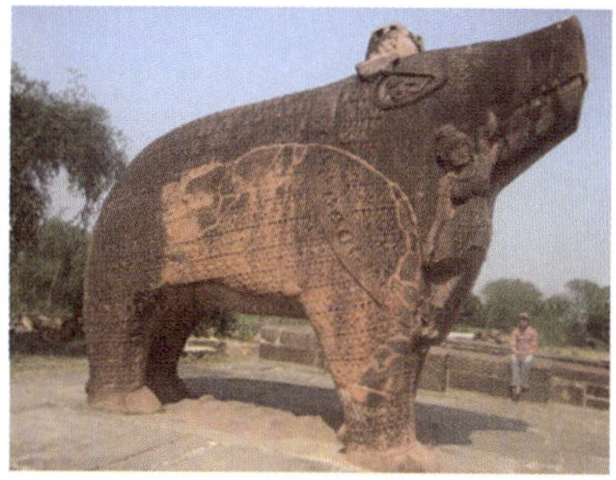

Eran Varaha

(d) Eran Temple: Located in Sagar district (Madhya Pradesh), these temples were dedicated to Lord Vishnu. Though largely in ruins, a mandap of Lord Vishnu's temple and a large statue of Varaha (11.5 feet high) survives today. The site is also known for a *sati* temple and a number of *sati* pillars.

ANCIENT UNIVERSITIES

The existence of several flourishing centres of study and universities in ancient India reflects the importance attached to knowledge and learning. Universities like **Takshshila, Nalanda,** and **Vikramshila,** which were important centres of learning and culture, attracted thousands of scholars, not only from India but from China, Japan, and Southeast Asia, and as far as from Persia and Turkey. Some of these universities, their unique features, and significant contributions to learning and culture is described below.

Takshshila University

Located in Taxila (present day Pakistan) it was the most important centre of learning in ancient India. It was founded in 6th century BCE. It finds reference in Greek texts as a flourishing centre of learning at the time of Alexander's conquest (4th century BCE). Further, it finds glorifying reference even in Faxian's accounts. The university at its peak taught the **Vedas along with 17 shilpas** (disciplines) **including Ayurveda, grammar, philosophy, and archery** (other forms of warfare). Many eminent scholars and personalities associated with this university like **Chanakya** (author of *Arthashastra* and minister of Chandragupta Maurya), **Jivak** (physician of king Bimbisara of Magadh, who also treated Buddha), **Panini, Charaka,** and **Vishnu Sharma** are also said to be associated with it.

Nalanda University

Nalanda was another great university of ancient India which flourished between **5th century CE and 12th century CE in Nalanda (Bihar)**. Glorious description of this university is contained in the accounts of

Faxian, Xuanzang (Chinese traveller who also studied at this university for two years), and I Tsing. The university was founded during the Gupta period and later patronised and supported by **emperor Harsha** and then the Pala kings. The university was the largest residential centre of learning with more than **10,000 scholars** from different parts of India and Asia and **2000 teachers**. Disciplines like **Buddhism, Vedic studies, astronomy, city planning, medicine, grammar, logic, Samkhya,** etc. were taught. Many eminent scholars like Nagarjuna, Aryadeva, Shilbhadra, and Padmasambhava were associated with it. The university is believed to have been burnt by Bakhtiyar Khilji in 12th century CE. It was accorded a UNESCO world heritage site status in 2016.

Vikramshila University

This university was established by the Pala king Dharmapala in the 8th century CE in Vikramshila (near Bhagalpur in Bihar). The university was a centre of Buddhist learning, particularly Mahayana and also Tantrism which had gained prominence by then. Besides, subjects like philosophy, grammar, metaphysics, logic, etc. were also taught to scholars from different parts of India and Asia. More than 1000 scholars and 100 teachers resided at the university.

As per Tibetan accounts, **Vikramshila (Bihar)**, along with **Nalanda (Bihar)**, **Jagdalla** (Bengal), **Odantapuri** (Bihar), and **Somapura** (Bangladesh) formed the five **Mahaviharas**. The latter three were also important universities/seats of learning in ancient India.

Besides the above, **Valabhi University** (Gujarat 6th to 12th century CE) and **Pushpagiri University** (Kalinga in Odisha from 3rd to 11th century CE), were other important universities.

LITERATURE IN ANCIENT INDIA

The ambit of literature is quite vast and expansive and in its broadest sense includes religious literature a well as scientific works, poetry, as well as prose. Like other art forms, literature too flourished during the ancient period, and reached its peak during the end of first millennia BCE and the Gupta period. The transmission of literature was largely oral and manuscripts (if any) do not survive (in original) to this day. The classification of ancient Indian literature can be done on the basis of languages of their composition, viz. **Sanskrit literature, Pali and Prakrit** literature, and **Dravidian literature** (in Tamil, Telugu, Kannada, and Malayalam). Literary works can also be categorised into religious literature which included the Vedic, Buddhist, and Jain literature and the non-religious, classical, and scientific literature.

The Religious Literature

The religious literature pertaining to the Vedic, Buddhist, and Jain literature is one of the earliest and richest texts in the world. The Vedic literature is said to have been composed as early as 1500 BCE to 1200 BCE, while the Buddhist and Jain literature date to a period later than 500 BCE.

Vedic Literature

These comprise the four Vedic texts which were written in Sanskrit, viz. the **Rigveda, Samaveda, Yajurveda**, and **Atharvaveda;** the Rigveda being the most ancient of all. Each of these had four layers, the Samhita, the Brahmana, the Aranyaka, and the Upanishad (See Chapter 3).

Besides the above, the two Sanskrit epics, **Ramayana** and **Mahabharata** are considered to be amongst the earliest and amongst the greatest literary works. While some historians date their age to 1500 BCE to 1000 BCE, some recent researchers put their date to an even earlier period and thus, push the Vedic period to greater antiquity.

The **Puranas** which are 18 in number too fall in the category of religious literature and are said to have been composed around fifth and fourth century BCE (See Chapter 3).

Buddhist Literature

These were composed in Pali and Prakrit and comprised the **Tripitakas**, viz. **Vinaya Pitaka**, **Sutta Pitaka**, and the **Abhidhamma Pitaka**. The Jatakas containing stories of previous lives of Buddha and Avadanas were important non-canonical Buddhist literature (See Chapter 4). *Buddhacharita* by *Ashvagosha* written in Sanskrit (in 1st century CE) is another important Buddhist literature (non-canonical) which is a biographical account of Lord Buddha in the form of an epic poem.

Jain Literature

Written in Prakrit, the Jain canonical texts are an important source of ancient literature. These include **Agamas**. The discourses are divided into the **Angas, Upangas,** and the **Parikaranas** (See Chapter 5).

Classical Sanskrit Literature

The classical Sanskrit literature comprises a host of works ranging from poetry (such as epics *Mahabharata* and *Ramayana*) to dramas and prose. This form of literature flourished towards the end of the 1st millennium BCE and continued in the Gupta period. Notable literary figures like **Kalidasa** contributed richly to Indian literature. *The important writers/poets and salient pieces of work is given below.*

Author/Composer	Contribution and Important Works
Kalidasa (4th to 5th century CE)	• *Abhigyana Shakuntalam* (recognition of Shakuntala); a drama • *Malvikagnimitra* (a love story of Malvika and Agnimitra); a drama • *Vikramorvasiya* (a love story of Vikram and Urvashi); a drama • *Meghduta* (cloud messenger); a poem • *Raghuvamsa* (about kings of Raghu dynasty); a poem • *Kumar Sambhava* (birth of Kumara); a poem • *Ritu Samhara* (description of six seasons); a poem
Bhasa (4th century BCE to 2nd century CE) Date not fully certain	13 plays including *Swapanvasvadatta* (Vasvadatta in dream)
Sudraka (3rd century CE)	*Mricchakatika* (the Clay cart); a drama

Vishakadatta (from 4th century CE to 8th century CE) Date not fully certain	• *Mudraraksha* (a play describing rise of power of Chandragupta Maurya) • *Devi Chandra Guptam*
Bhavabhuti	*Uttar Ramcharitam* (the later portion of life of Sri Rama); a play
Bharavi (6th CE)	*Kiratarjuniya* (Kirat and Arjun); a poem
Magha (7th to 8th century CE)	*Sishupalavadha* (killing of Shishupala); a poem
Jayadeva (12th century CE)	*Gita Govinda* (song of Govinda)
Sri Harsha (7th century CE)	*Ratna Vali* (attributed to Indian emperor Harsha); a play
Dandin (7th– 8th century CE)	*Kavyadarsa* and *Dasakumaracharita*
Other Important Treatises	
• **Lagadha** (1400 to 1200 BCE)	*Vedanga Jyotisha* (astronomy)
• **Baudhyayana** (8th century BCE)	*Baudhayayana Sulabh Sutra* (a treatise on mathematics containing Pythagorean theorem statement)
• **Sushruta** (600 BCE)	*Sushruta Samhita* (treatise on medicine and surgery)
• **Charaka** (300 BCE)	*Charak Samhita* (treatise on medicine)
• **Vishnu Sharma** (date not exactly ascertained, around 3rd century BCE)	*Panchatantra* (compilation of stories dealing with practical wisdom in all fields of life)
• **Chanakya** (Vishnu Gupta) (2nd century BCE)	*Arthashashtra* (a treatise on economy statecraft, administration, etc.)
• **Kanada** (200 BCE)	*Vaisheshika* philosophy (matter composed of atom which are indivisible and eternal)
• **Bharata** (1st century BCE to 1st century CE)	*Natya Shashtra* (a treatise on dance and theatre and other performing arts)
• **Panini** (4th century BCE)	*Ashtadhyai* (treatise on Sanskrit grammar)
• **Vatsyayana** (2nd century CE)	*Kamasutra* (a treatise on love and sex)
• **Patanjali** (400 CE)	*Patanjali Yogasastra* and *Yoga Sutra* (196 aphorisms on Yoga)
• **Aryabhatta** (5th century CE)	*Aryabhatiya* (treatise on mathematics and astronomy)
• **Narayan Pandit** (9th century CE)	*Hitopadesh* (stories about animals, birds, and humans and of wisdom and benefit to individuals and society)
• **Varahamihira**	*Panch Siddhantika* and *Brihat Samhita* (astronomy and mathematics)

The Dravidian and the Sangam Literature

The literature composed in the southern part of India in the Tamil, Telugu, Kannada, and Malayalam languages is commonly referred as the Dravidian literature. A number of great literary works were composed in ancient India, particularly in the Tamil language which is believed to be the oldest amongst the Dravidian languages and closest to Sanskrit.

(a) Tamil literature: A vast body of Tamil literature was composed in the period 300 BCE to 300 CE and is referred to as **Sangam literature**. The literary work comprises poems and proses in 18 works (eight of prose and 10 of poems). This is a compilation of works of nearly 473 poets (of which 102 are unknown) including over 2381 poems. Among these 30 are believed to be women. This includes famous poet Avvaiyar.

During this period, *Tolkappiyam*, a work on the grammar of the Tamil language was also written. Another monumental Tamil work was the composition of the *Thirukkural* by the sage Thiruvalluvar which contains 1330 Kurals or couplets enunciating precepts to guide humanity to a noble living.

Tamil literature is also known for the twin epics—*Silappadhikaram* and *Manimekalai*. Further, it contains a rich body of works in the compositions of Alwars and Nayanars.

(b) Telugu literature: The Dravidian literature is also enriched by other notable works such as Nannaya's Mahabharatam (1030 CE), works of Lingayats (Virashaivas), and sage **Nachna Somanatha's** *Uttara Harivamsam.*

(c) Kannada literature: In Kannada, *Dharmanthapurana* is a famous text written by **Madhura** on the life of the 15th Tirthankara. Another famous literary work is *Kavirajamarga* written by **Nripatunga Amoghavarsha (10th century CE).**

Pampa is also referred to as Father of Kannada literature who composed *Adi Purana* and *Vikramarjuna Vijaya*. The three litterateurs Pampa, Ponna, and Ranna are also referred as *Ratnatraya* (or three gems) of Kannada literature.

(d) The Malayalam literature: The language and its literature developed in the latter half of the 1st millenia. It included works like *Kokasandisan* and *Bhasa Kautilya* (a commentary on *Arthashashtra*).

MUSIC AND DANCE IN ANCIENT INDIA

Music and dance are categorised as performing arts (along with puppetry and theatre). India has had a rich tradition of music and dance since ancient times, where it was considered as a part of *Natya*. Several ancient texts contain reference to music and dance of ancient times. Even Indian mythology attaches due importance and contains many references of these art forms.

The texts and treatises and the nature of music and dance in ancient India is discussed below.

References to Music and Dance in Ancient Texts

Reference in Samaveda and other texts: The most ancient reference to music is noted in Samaveda, which consisted of the hymns which were sung using notated melodies at the time of rituals. The Samveda is said to contain all the seven notes of the raga *Karaharapriya* in the descending order. The earliest raga is said to be *Samagana* or *Samaraga*. The Samaveda has two major parts (as discussed in an earlier chapter). It includes the melody collections in the first part (*Gana*) and the second part contains the verses (the *Archika* book). The melody in the first part thus corresponds to the verses in the second part. Thus, the roots of Indian music are contained in the Samaveda.

Reference to music is also obtained in Patanjali's *Mahabhasya* (500–400 BCE), *Kamasutra* of Vatsyayana, and even in some places in the Buddhist *Tripitakas* which mention the occasion for music. But the most important and relevant text is the *Natyashashtra* of Bharata (200 BCE to 200 CE). The other important texts are *Dathilan* which specifies the division of octave into 22 Srutis, *Brihedesi* written by **Matanga** (9th century CE), and *Sangeet Ratnakara* by **Saranga Deva** (13th century CE).

Natya Shastra: A Treatise on Music and Dance

The **Natya Shastra** is the most authoritative text of this period pertaining to the performing arts. Composed by sage **Bharata,** it is said to **contain more than 6000 shlokas**. It contains several chapters on music which delves on the octave and divides it into 22 keys or Srutis. However, **Natya Shastra** is not a book on music alone, but a comprehensive treatise on performing arts which included music, dance, and performance. The text in this treatise is in the form of a dialogue between sage Bharata and other *Munis* who seek knowledge from him about Natyaveda (*Natya* means performance or drama and *Veda* means knowledge). The replies are compiled in the form of a book.

Natya Shastra is thus a compilation of the knowledge of performing arts of a whole culture. In fact the work is not said to be the creation of a single person. The name Bharata is itself taken to be an acronym (Bha-Bhava, Ra-Raga, and Ta-Tal).

Music in Ancient India

The ancient and Vedic music was ritualistic and devotional. *Samagana* music was popular in the Vedic period which involved chanting of hymns as per the musical notations. Subsequently, for narration of epics, a form of music called *Jattigan* was evolved. Towards the latter half of the 1st millennia BCE, *Prabandh Sangeet* (written in Sanskrit) was in vogue from which originated a simpler form of music called *Dhruvpad*. It is believed that the medieval music Drupad had its origin in Dhruvpad.

Mythological Origin of Music and Dance

As per mythology, *Om* was the first word and the primordial sound of the universe. Thus from *Om* all music has originated. Music in the rudimentary form is said to be brought on the earth by Narada *Muni* who highlighted that the all pervading sound of the universe was *Naada Brahma* (or *Om*).

Lord Shiva who is also worshipped as *Nataraja* (the Lord of performers), is said to be the deity of music and dance. The famous *Tandava* dance shows Lord Shiva holding a *Damru* (from which celestial beats emanate) and performing a cosmic music. Some mythological accounts also consider Lord Brahma as the fountain head of music and dance.

Dances in Ancient India

Introduction

Ancient scriptures give common references to music and dance. Bharata's **Natya Shastra**, the most authoritative text on music and dance captures this art form right from ancient times. Referred to as the fifth Veda by sage Bharata, this treatise is said to take the **words** from *Rigveda*, **music** from *Samaveda*, **gestures** (Abhinaya) from *Yajurveda*, and **emotions** (Bhava) from *Atharvaveda*. Thus, Natya was a combination of all of the above— words, music, gesture, and emotion. Thus, in the classical tradition as formulated in **Natya Shastra,** dance and music were an integral part of performance referred to as Natya or drama. Further, in the classical dance form (as per **Natya Shastra**), the Natya can be said to comprise three elements which are *Natya*, *Nritya*, and *Nritta*. **Natya** refers to the elements of drama (not seen nowadays except in dance dramas). **Nritya** refers to the expression of the performer, while the **Nritta** refers to movement of the body as per rhythm.

Some Ancient Dance Forms

In ancient dance forms we get reference of *Tandava* and *Lasya*. The *Tandava* is a vigorous and energetic male dance form. Out of these, the **Shiva's Tandava** dance is more famous. This is said to be a cosmic dance in which Shiva is depicted with four hands and two legs balancing on a single leg in a specific dance posture. He holds a *Damaru* and carries a flame in his other hand while remaining two are in *Abhaya mudra* (Refer to the Nataraja statue and symbolism in the section on 'Bronze sculptures in medieval India'). The ***Laasya* is a soft, graceful, and feminine dance form**.

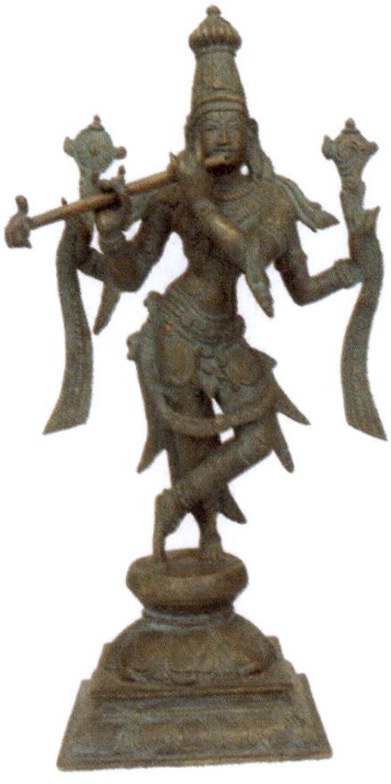

Tribhanga postured statue of Lord Krishna

Reference is also seen to the *Tribhanga* dance posture. The bronze statue of the dancing girl from Mohenjo-daro is an example of this posture (See Chapter 3). This posture has also been incorporated in several later sculptures and dances in medieval and modern times.

The *Tribhanga* (or bent thrice) is a body posture in which the performer is seen standing with the body bent {or seen to be breaking} at three positions, which are the neck, the waist, and the knee. The body is seen to be slightly but oppositely curved like an S and is considered to be a graceful and sensual posture. Paintings and sculptures also depict Krishna in this posture.

IMPORTANT TOPICS TO FOCUS ON

- Salient features of Mauryan art.
- Important stupas and pilliars, lion capital, chaityas, and their features.
- Important sculptures of the Mauryan period.
- Various dynasties in the Mauryan period and significant contribution to art.
- Important schools of art, salient points, and most important sculptures.
- Rock-cut architecture, important caves and salient points, most important being Ajanta and Ellora.
- Early ancient temples and their features, specially Dashavatara and Nachna Kuthara.
- Ancient universities and salient points about them particularly, Takshshila and Nalanda.
- Important literary works in ancient India.

PART 2

Art and Culture in Medieval India

CHAPTER 7

Temples and Architecture in Ancient and Medieval India

Temples are more than stone and mortar. They are filled with faith and fasting. They are built of trials and testimonies. They are sanctified by sacrifice and service.

Thomas S Monson

AN INTRODUCTION

The temples played an important role in the social and cultural life of people in ancient and medieval India. Many of these structures which were made in stone or bricks survive to this day and are a reflection of the architectural magnificence and the crucial role these temples had in the sociocultural space of the society. Though the temples and structures were largely of Hindu faith, many Buddhist and Jain temples were also constructed in this period that are an important source of information about their art and architecture.

TEMPLES AND THEIR FUNDAMENTAL ELEMENTS

The Hindu temples primarily had four important features, the ***garbhagriha, shikhar*** or ***vimana, mandapa,*** and the ***vahana***. In all these elements, a sense of proportion and geometry in form of shapes such as circles, square, or curves was visible. *Depending upon the shape and structure of the basic elements, the temples in India can be divided into three distinct categories:*

(i) the **Nagara** style or the **North Indian** temple architecture

(ii) the **Dravidian** style or the **South Indian** temple architecture

(iii) the **Vesara** style containing a **mix of both** the architectures

The Basic Features

The basic features of temples and the styles of architecture are briefly discussed below:

(a) The Garbhagriha Literally meaning the womb-chamber, the *garbhagriha* was the sanctum where the idol of the main deity was located. In earlier times, garbhagriha would be like a small cubicle. However, with the passage of time the size of the sanctum grew. The rituals pertaining to the worship of the deity are performed in the garbhagriha.

(b) The Shikhar and the Vimana Just above the *garbhagriha,* the temples have a large spire or a tower like structure. In **North Indian temples** these spires/towers are called ***shikhar*** and they have a curving shape. While in the **South Indian temples** (Dravidian style) these are called **vimanas**. These have a pyramidical shape and are a prominent feature in many Dravidian temples.

(c) Mandapa This refers to the colonnaded hall present before the *garbhagriha* just inside the entrance of the temple. This provides the space for the congregation of a large number of worshippers. *Mandapa* is a typical feature of temples in Dravidian style and it may be absent in some of the smaller North Indian temples which may have a smaller portico or a simple entrance to the temple.

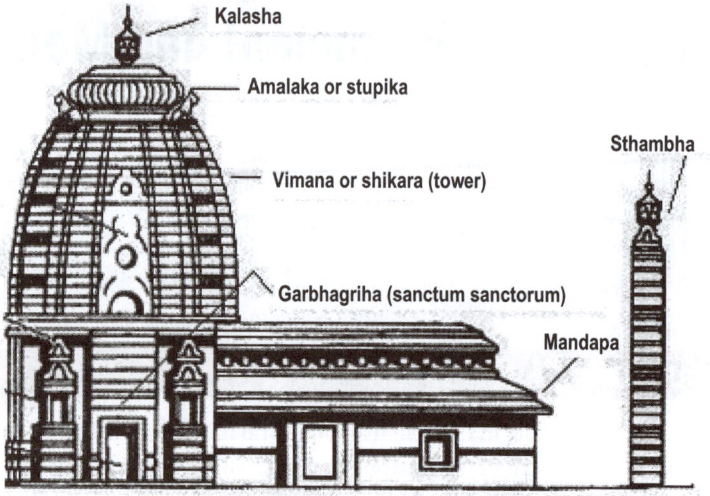

Basic Features of a Temple

(d) Vahana The *vahana* refers to the abode of the deity. The statue of the *vahana* is usually found atop a pillar (called Dhwaj) in front of the *garbhagriha.*

Apart from the above main features, the temples usually have a circumambulatory path or a *parikama-path* or *pradakshina-path* (referred as Nirandhara type temple). In some temples the *pradikshana-path* is absent (Sandhara type). Some temples could have access from all sides (Sarvatobhadhra type).

THE NAGARA TEMPLE ARCHITECTURE

This type of temple architecture was common in North Indian temples. Its specific features were:

- The temple was built on a raised stone platform called ***Jagati***. A flight of steps would lead to the level of **garbhagriha**. The *Jagati* would have another platform called ***Pithas*** over which a smaller platform called ***Adhisthana*** could be present on which the temple garbhagriha could be present.
- The temple would usually not have boundary wall around it. Further, a gateway at the entrance (called ***gopuram*** in South India) was also absent in the Nagara style temples.
- The temples would have a **singular tower** or spire above the *garbhagriha* (the spire resembled the peak of a mountain and hence called a *shikhar*). However, in later temples many such spires could be present. The tallest tower would however be present over the *garbhagriha* of the central deity.
- The *shikharas* could also be crowned (in some temples) by a stone disk called *amalaka*. Over the ***amlaka,*** a ***kalash*** could be present. This would be the topmost point of the temple.
- Depending on the type and shape of the *shikhara,* the Nagara temples are classified into
    - ❖ Latina or Rekha Prasada type
    - ❖ Phamsana type
    - ❖ Valabhi type

(a) **Latina or Rekha Prasada temple** In such type of temples, the *shikhara* has a square base. Its walls slope upwards or curve towards inside so as to meet at a point. It is the simplest type of temple structure.

(b) **Phamasana type temples** In these types of temples, the temple structure and the spire tend to be broader and shorter. The roofs of the temples consist of several slab-like structures. They rise to a single point, but the slope of the temple shikhar is not curved but inclined along a straight line.

(c) **Valabhi temples** In these types of temples, the ground plan is rectangular. There is a doorway on one of its longer sides. The *shikhar* is semicircular or resembling a vaulted chamber, the edge of which is rounded.

The temples of Nagara type further developed separate traits depending on the region they flourished in. These are broadly of the following categories.

(a) *Central Indian Temples* – Examples of this architecture is the **Dashavatara temple developed during the Gupta era** and **Khajuraho** temples developed under the Chandela rulers. These were marked by their ornate carvings. The latter contained erotic sculptures on their walls. The **Dashavatara temple** is of **Panchaytana** style where there is a main shrine at the centre and four other smaller shrines at the four corners (making a total of five shrines). The **Udayagiri temples** (Vidisha in Madhya Pradesh) is yet another example of this group of temples.

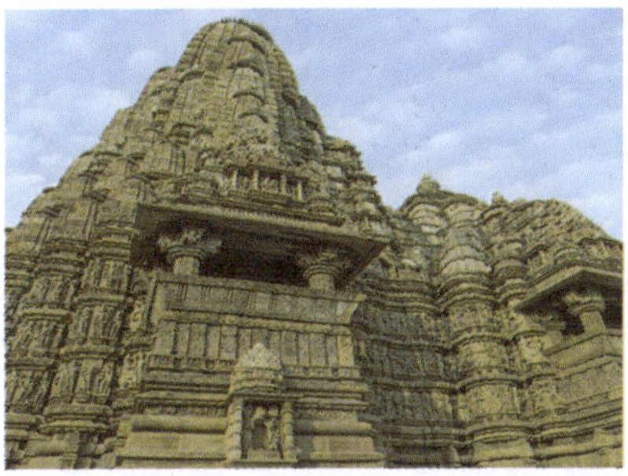

Khajuraho temple

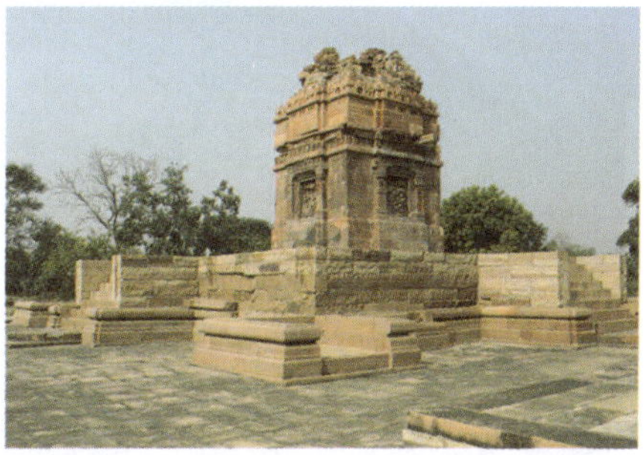

Dashavatara temple (Panchaytana style)

(b) ***The East Indian Temples*** – Examples of this architecture is the **Sun temple in Konark**, **Jagannath temple in Puri** and the **Lingraj temple at Bhubaneswar**. The interiors of these temples contain **exquisite carvings**. The *shikhar* is composed of several slabs placed one over the other. The important East Indian temples also includes the **Dev Parvatia temple** near Tezpur and **Sibsagar temple in Assam**. Further, in Bengal, the Terracotta temple at Bishnupur and **Siddheshwar Mahadev** temples in Burdwan are some fine examples of East Indian temple architecture.

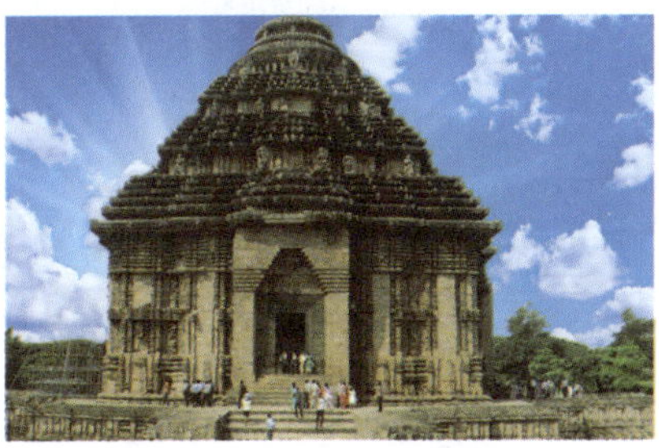

Konark Sun Temple

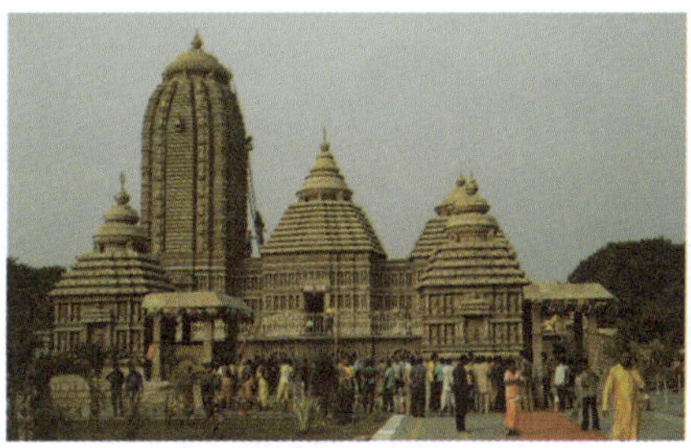

Jagannath Temple, Puri

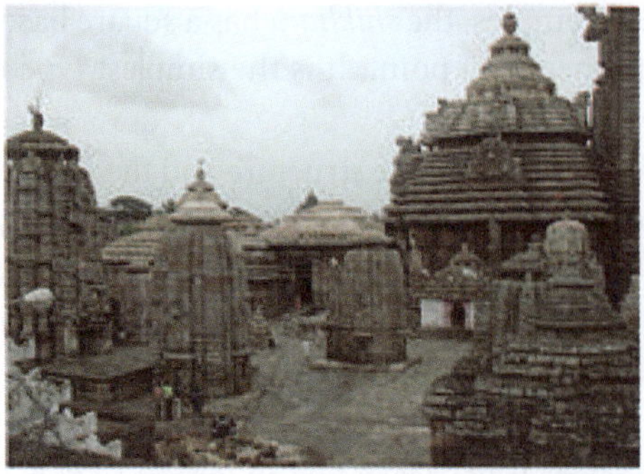

LIngaraj Temple, Bhubaneswar

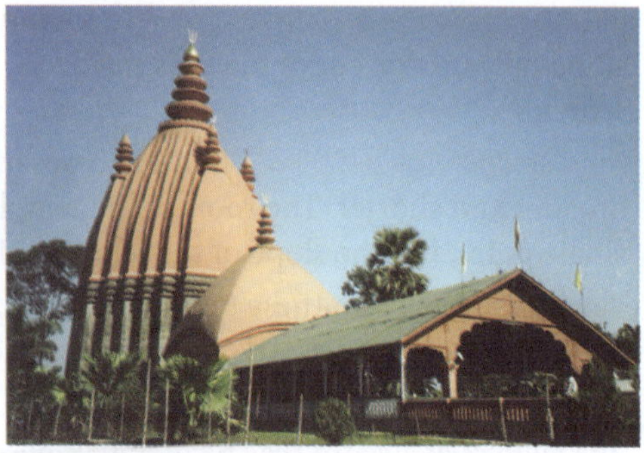

Sibsagar Temple, Assam

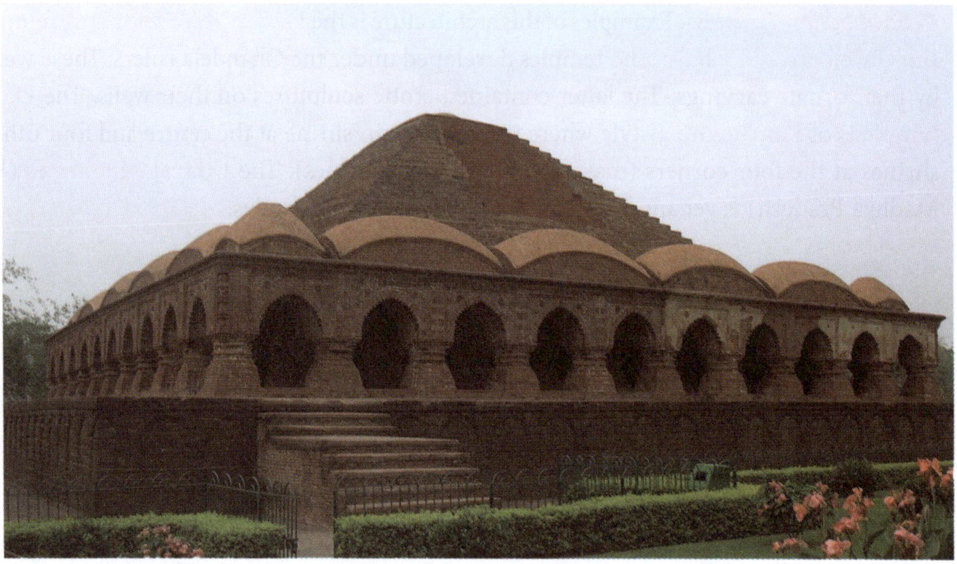

Bishnupur Temple

(c) ***The Temples in Western India*** – This group includes **Sun temple at Modhera** in Gujarat. This temple was built by **Solankis** (Western Chalukyas) in 11th century and is characterised by a massive **stepped rectangular tank**.

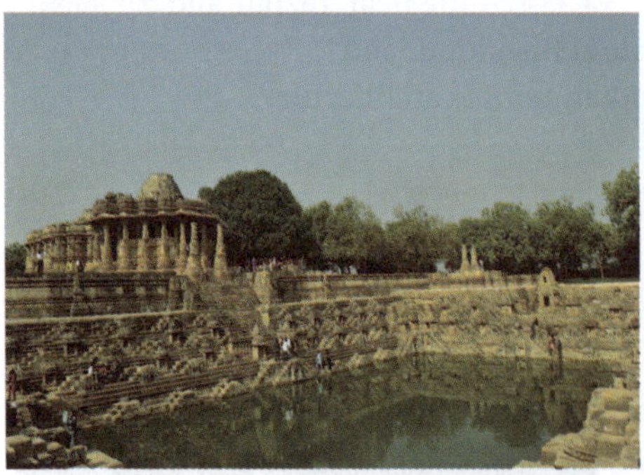

Sun Temple, Modhera

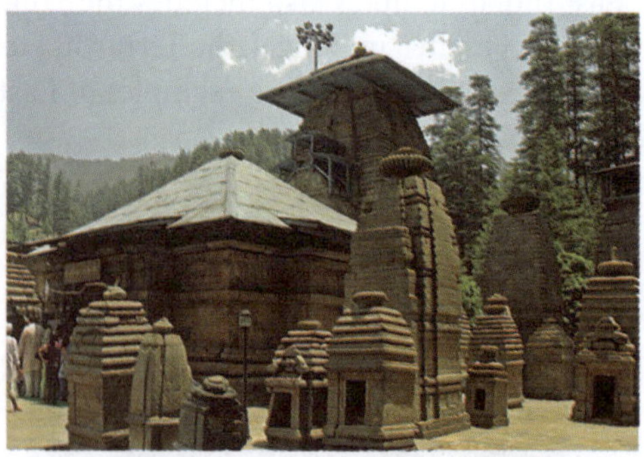

Jageshwar Temple, Almora

(d) ***Hill Temples*** – Hill Temples in Kumaon, Garhwal, Kashmir, and Himachal developed certain unique features of their own. The influence of various schools of architecture like the Mathura, Sarnath, and Gandhara had a blending influence on the temples in this region. Further, the indigenous architecture of wooden buildings with a pitched roof was also employed. The main **garbhagrihas** were made in Latina/Rekha Prasada type. The *mandapa* was of older form of wooden architecture. Important temples are **Laksna Devi Mandir** at Chamba (containing images of Mahisasura Mardini and Narsimha), **Jageshwar temple near Almora,** and **Champawat temple near Pithoragarh**.

DRAVIDIAN TEMPLE ARCHITECTURE

The Dravidian style of temple architecture was popular in South India and had certain distinct features as discussed below.

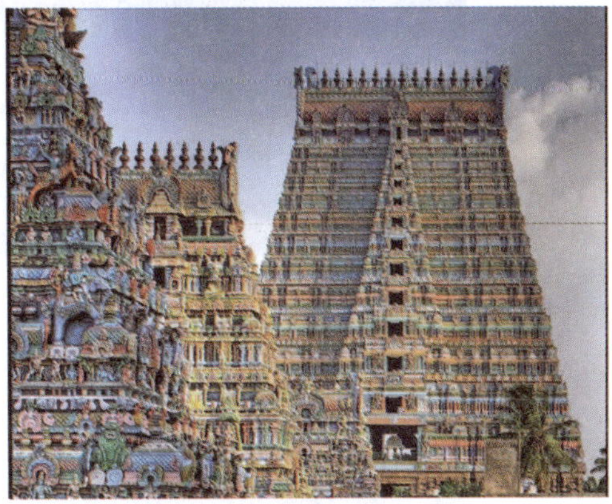

Srirangam Temple, Tiruchirapalli

- The entire temple complex was **enclosed in a compound wall**, which is not seen in the Nagara style.
- At the entrance of the temple are located gateways or ***gopurams*** which are often large and **highly decorated**. In the **Srirangam temple at Tiruchirapalli,** there are seven concentric walls rectangular in shape, each having a gopuram.
- The **Vimana** located above the *garbhagriha* is often like a stepped pyramid or geometrical in shape. It is not curving like the Nagara temples nor is the concept of multiple shikharas seen in the Dravidian temples.
- Above the ***vimana*** is the topmost portion which is shaped like a ***stupika***. In some temples, in place of the stupika an octagonal cupola like structure may be present. This is analogous to ***amalaka*** and ***kalash*** of the North Indian temples.
- A distinct feature of Dravidian temples was the presence of a water tank in the temple compound. These reservoirs, apart from serving ceremonial purposes would also be of practical utility as the Dravidian temples with large complexes would also be centres of sociocultural and religious activity.
- At the entrance of the temple, images or sculptures of fierce looking ***dwarpals*** (guards) would be present. This is in contrast to the images of Ganga and Yamuna, or *mithunas* found at the entrance of North Indian temples.
- In some temple complexes in South India where multiple *garbhagrihas* are found, the tower pertaining to the main deity may not be the largest one and rather it may even be the smallest one.

The important temples of this style are temples at Thanjavur, Madurai, Tiruchirapalli, Kanchipuram, Kumbakonam, and Mahabalipuram.

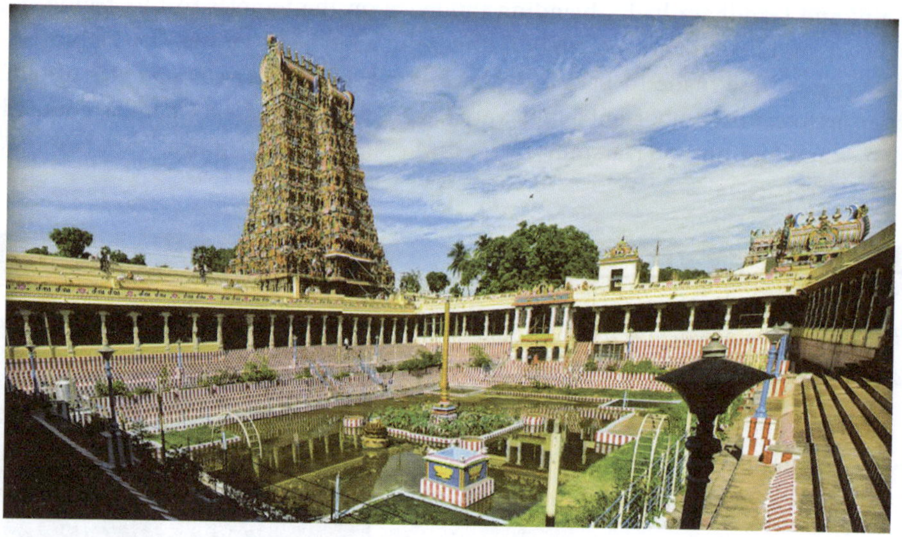

Madurai Meenakshi Temple

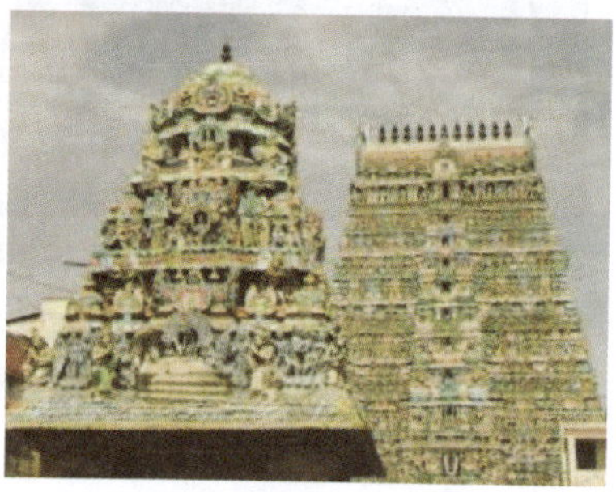

Kumbakonam Temple

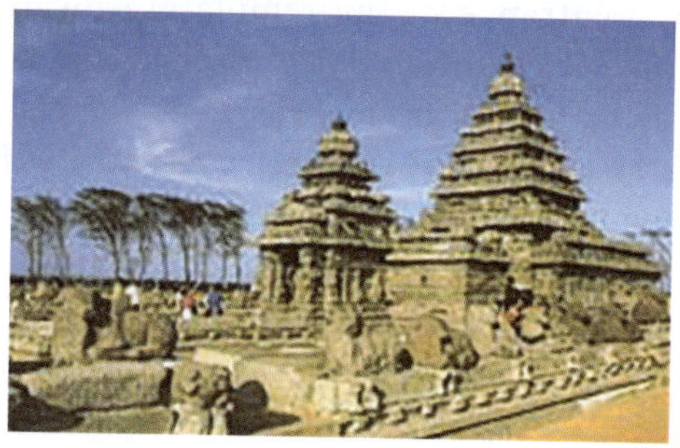

Mahabalipuram Temple

Sub-divisions of Dravidian Temple Architecture

The Dravidian temples can be further subdivided into different categories based on the shape of the temples. Further, they are also classified depending on the dynasty or the group of temples of which it is a part as they carried a distinct imprint of the art and architecture of the dynasty which built or patronised it.

Classification of Dravidian temple based on shape

- *Cuta* or *Katusara*; these were temples with square shape
- *Shala* or *Ayatsara*; these were rectangular in shape
- *Gaja-prishta* or *Vrittayata*; Gaja-prishta means 'elephant back', and it referred to temples shaped like an ellipse (vrittayata). These were similar to vaulted shapes of chaityas which have a horseshoe-shaped entrance.
- *Vritta*; or circular shaped temples
- *Ashtasara*; or octagonal shaped temples

Different Temple Groups in South India

(i) Pallava architecture – The Pallavas built a number of temples in the present Tamil Nadu region. The earlier ones were rock-cut while those in the later stages were structural temples. The most famous of them is the **'shore temple'** at **Mahabalipuram** (now Mammalapuram). The temple is built on the shore and is facing east. It is unique as it has three shrines, the east and the west ones are dedicated to Lord Shiva and middle one to Lord Vishnu. A structure of Nandi (bull), Lord Shiva's Mount lines the temple wall. Evidence of a water tank and *gopuram* is also found there.

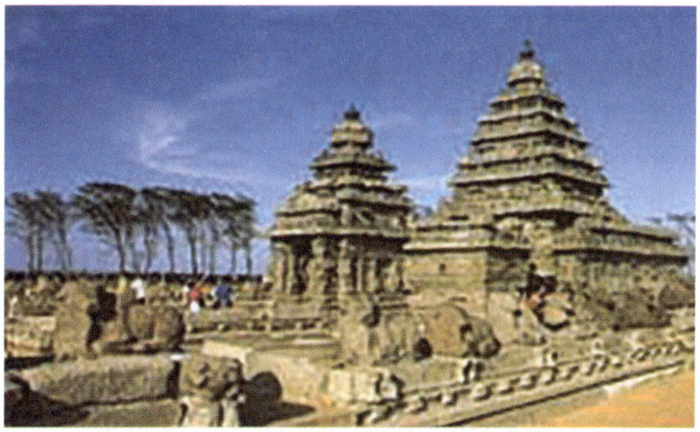

Shore Temple in Mahabalipuram

The Pallava temples are further classified as per the rulers and the features of temples. These subgroups are:

(a) ***Mahendraverman group*** – These were early rock-cut temples constructed during the reign of king Mahendraverman-1 (7th century CE), e.g. **Tiruchirapalli temple**.

(b) ***Narshima group*** – These temples marked the second stage of the Pallava architecture. The temples were carved out of monolithic rocks and also had intricately carved sculptures, e.g. *mandapa* and *panchrathas* of **Mahabalipuram**.

(c) ***Rajsimha group*** – Under Narasimhavarman II (also known as Rajsimha), structural temples were built. This was a marked departure from the construction of the rock-cut temples to real structural ones, e.g. **Kailashnath temple at Kanchi** and **shore temple at Mahabalipuram**.

(d) ***Nandiverman group*** – This style of architecture was common during the reign of Nandiverman Pallava. The temples were smaller but they were structural temples. E.g. Vaikunda Perumal temple at Tirunelveli and **Mukateshwara** temple.

(ii) Chola architecture – Like the Pallava architecture, the Chola architecture too is an important style of Dravidian temple construction. The most important temple of this group is the **Brihadeeshwara temple** at Thanjavur. Built by Raja Raja Chola in around 1009 CE (also called the **Rajarajeshwar temple**), this is the largest and also tallest temple in India. The *vimana* of the temple is 70m high and has a monolithic *shikhara* atop which is a massive 80 tonne stone, making the construction an engineering marvel. The temples of the Chola period were much grander than those of its predecessors, viz. the Pallavas, Chalukyas, and Pandyas.

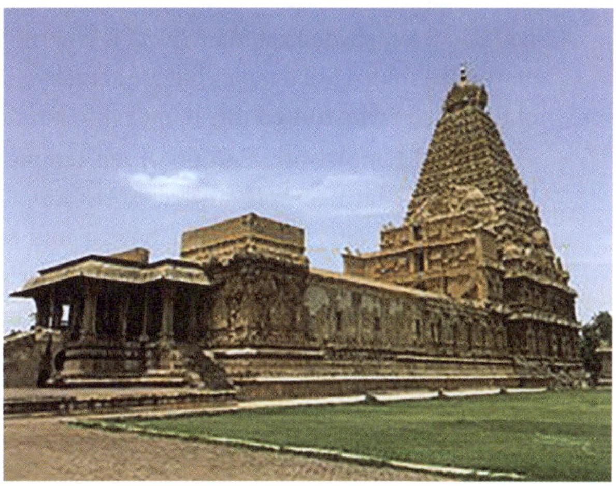

Brihadeeshwara Temple

VESARA STYLE AND DECCAN TEMPLE ARCHITECTURE

In the Deccan region of the country another style of temple architecture developed which contained elements from both the Nagara style and Dravidian style and was called **Vesara style.** Thus, a hybridised style of architecture could be seen in the Deccan region. However, not all temples of the Deccan region were of Vesara style and some are completely of Dravidian style.

Prominent temples of this style and others of the Deccan region are discussed here.

Chalukyan Architecture

The Chalukyan temple architecture gained prominence in the Karnataka region as early as the 6th century CE. While the early Chalukyan architecture was in the form of rock-cut caves, the later ones were structural temples. *Some notable points about them are:*

- These temples developed the unique **Vesara** style of architecture which can be seen in temples at **Ravan Phadi** cave, Lad Khan temple, **Durga temple** (all at Aihole in Karnataka), and **Paattadakal** temples (Karnataka).
- **Ravan Phadi** cave at Aihole is an earlier form of Chalukyan architecture. It is famous for the statue of **Nataraja** surrounded by *Saptamatrikas,* three of which are to right of the statue of Shiva and four are to its left. The figures have graceful and slim bodies and long oral faces and an extremely tall cylindrical crown.

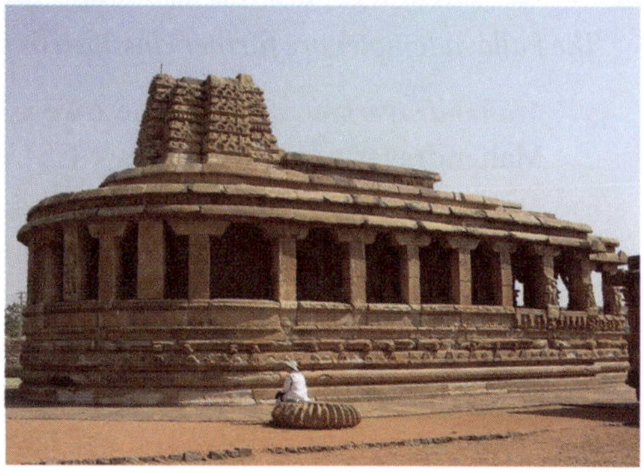

Durga Temple, Aihole

- **Durga temple** at Aihole has **features of Dravidian and Nagara architecture**. It also contains elements of earlier Buddhist shrines in the form of an apsidal shrine. It has a veranda and a shikhar that is similar to a Nagara one.
- **Lad Khan** temple dedicated to Shiva, is amongst the oldest of Hindu temples. It contains features of wooden roofed hill temples but are actually made in stone (believed to be known after the name of the person who turned this temple into a residence for a short period).
- **Pattadakal temples** are a group of ten temples including a Jain temple and is a UNESCO world heritage site. The temples have a mix of Dravidian and Nagara style. Some are exclusively in Dravidian and some are in Nagara style. The most famous temple is the **Virupaksha temple** also known as Sri Lokeshwar Maha Sila Prasad built by Lok Mahadevi, queen of Chalukya king Vikramaditya II (733–44 CE).

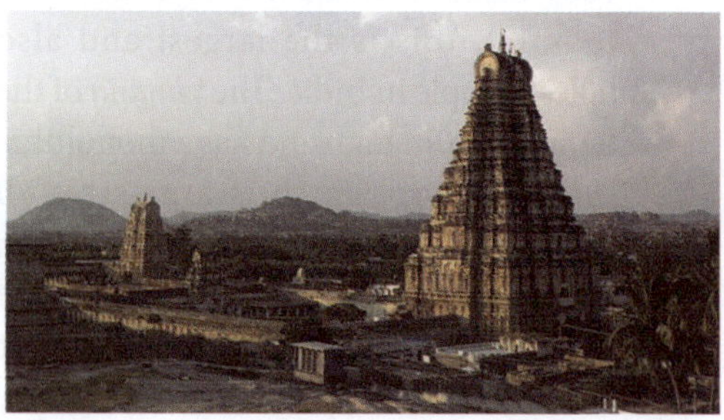

Virupaksha Temple

Rashtrakuta Architecture

- The Rashtrakutas came into prominence in the Deccan region in 750 CE. Their most important contribution was the **Kailashnath temple** of Ellora. The Jain temple at Pattadakal was also built by them.
- The Kailashnath temple, dedicated to Lord Shiva, is **carved out of a single piece of rock**. Thus, it is the largest monolithic temple structure. It has Dravidian architecture, with a gopuram, Nandi bull statue, a complete courtyard (carved from stone), an imposing vimana, subsidiary shrines, staircase, etc.

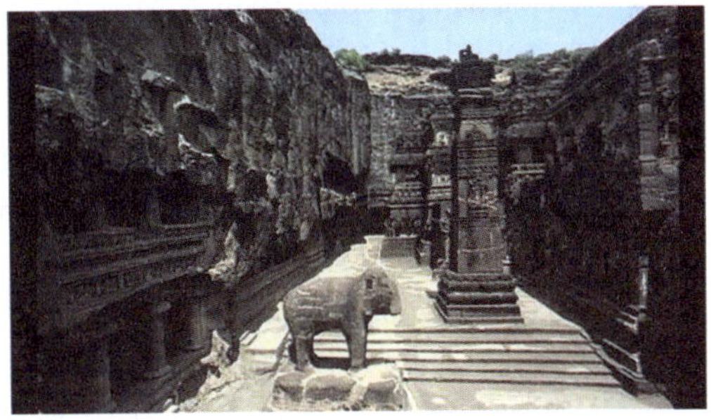

Kailashnath Temple

- It also houses the famous **sculpture of Ravana shaking mount Kailasa** which is considered as a masterpiece of Indian sculpture.

Hoysalas Architecture

The Hoysalas were in prominence in Karnataka around the Mysore region. Their reign contributed hundreds of temples, the remains of which have been found, but the most important being those at **Halebid**, Belur, and Somnathpuram.

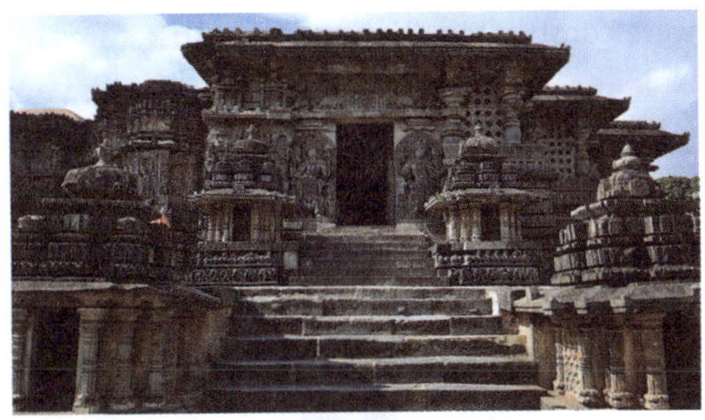

Hoysala Temple, Halebid

- The salient feature of temples of this dynasty's architecture was their increasing complexity owing to a number of projecting angles. Thus, the plan of these temples did not remain the simple square or the rectangle one **but became more like a star, which imparts it the name of stellate plan**. Another unique feature of these temples was their construction in soapstone, a relatively soft stone. This made it possible to carve intricate sculptures visible in the finesse of jewellery of the deities carved on the temple walls.
- The temple at **Halebid** (also called the **Hoysaleshvara** temple), built in around 1150 CE, was made of dark schist stone. It is of **Vesara style** and is dedicated to Lord Shiva who is depicted as **Nataraja**. A large *mandapa* hall is dedicated to music and dance. Singular projections have been cut out from the central square plan to give it a star like appearance. The carvings on the wall are highly intricate. The panel at the bottom which carries the image of a procession depicts hundreds of elephants, no two of which strike the same pose.

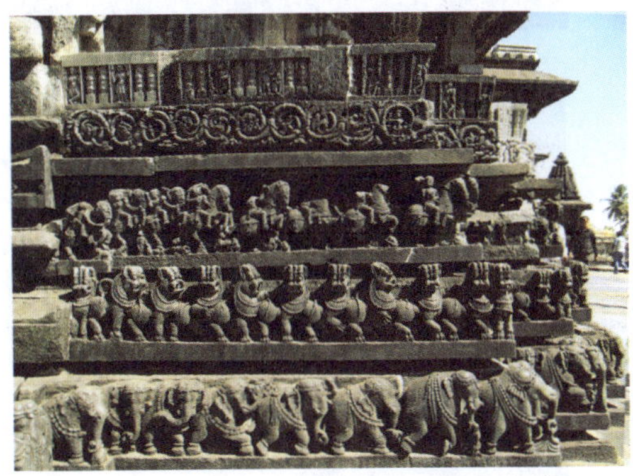

Elephant panel at Hoysaleshvara

Vijaynagar Architecture

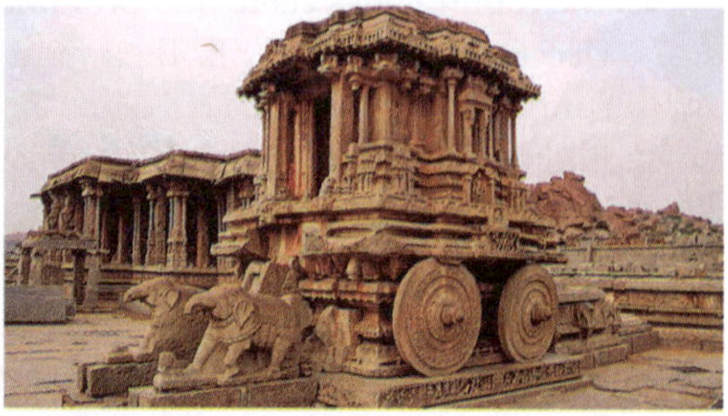

Stone Chariot, Vitthala temple, Hampi

- The Vijaynagar empire which came into prominence in around the 15th century CE had its capital at **Hampi** where ruins of a number of grand structures are still existing (UNESCO world heritage site).
- The architecture of Vijaynagar has influence of both the **Dravidian style** as well as the **Islamic style.**
- *Gopurams* which in other architectural style were usually in one side (front) were now built on all sides. Similarly, more than one mandapa was built. The temples walls were decorated with intricate carvings.
- Important structures at Hampi include the Vitthala temple, stone chariot (at Vittala temple), Virupaksha temple, Lotus Mahal, and Pushkarnis (water tanks).

BUDDHIST AND JAIN ARCHITECTURE

From the 5th century onwards, a number of prominent Buddhist and Jain temples and structures also were constructed. The Buddhist structures of significance are the **Mahabodhi temple** (Gaya in Bihar), **Nalanda university** (Bihar), **Vikaramshila university**, different Buddhist Maha Viharas, temple at Sirpur (Odisha), etc. Important Jain temples and structures can be seen at **Ellora, Aihole, Dilwara** (Mount Abu), **Ranakpur** (Rajasthan) **Khajuraho**, and **Gomateshwara** (where statue of Bahubali can be found).

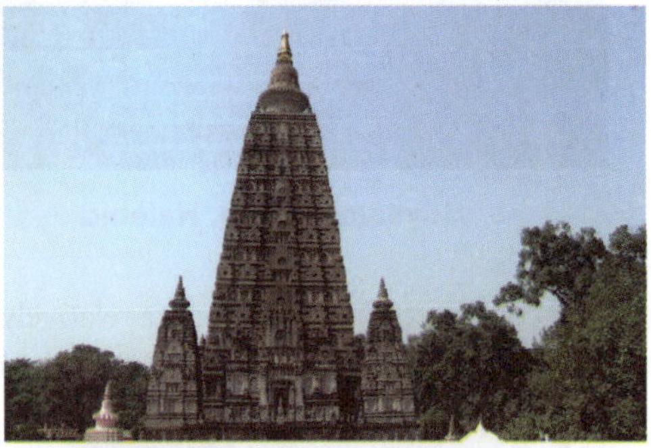

Mahabodhi Temple

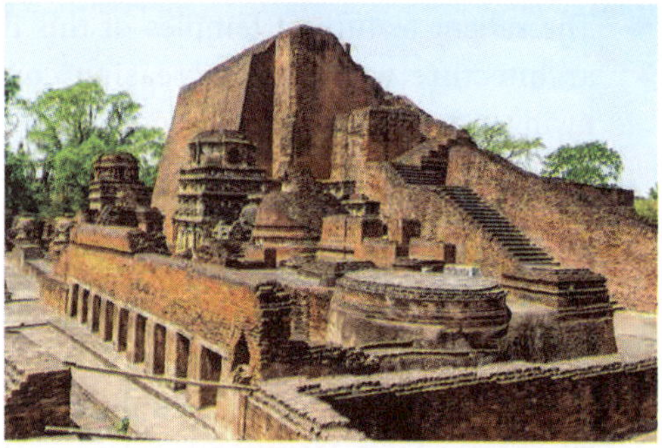

Nalanda University

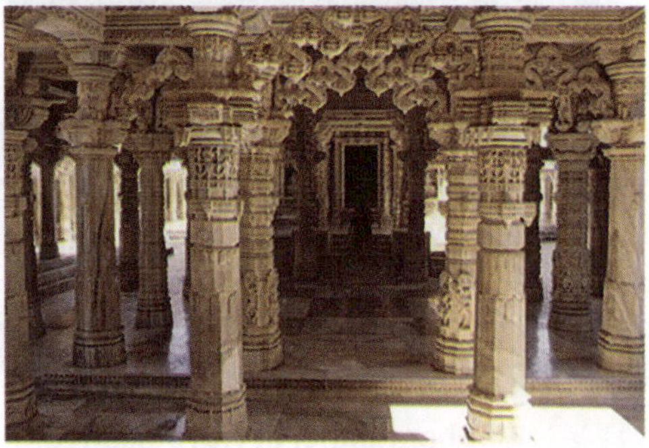

Dilwara Jain Temple, Mount Abu

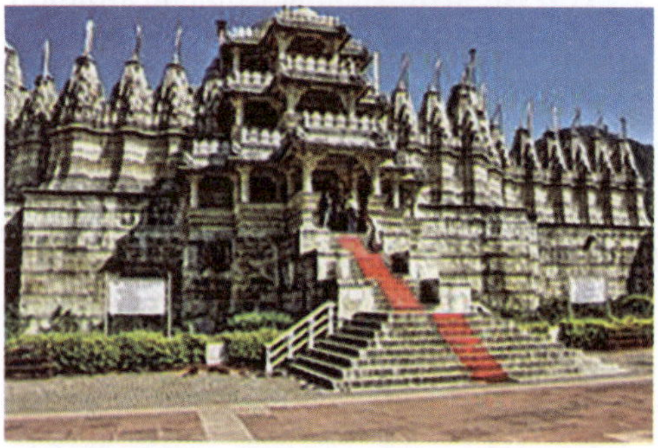

Ranakpur Jain Temple, Rajasthan

Some of these are briefly discussed here.

(a) Bodhgaya: It is an important Buddhist centre where Lord Buddha attained enlightenment. It has the Mahabodhi temple (located near Gaya in Bihar).

- The temple design is unique as its ***shikhar* is narrow like a Nagara** temple. However, it is **not curving** and rises along a straight line like the Dravidian structures. Thus, it is an amalgamation of both the styles.
- The **vedika** around the temple is of around 100 BCE while the main temple is a colonial reconstruction of the 7th century CE structure.

(b) Nalanda University: This was a Buddhist Mahavihara which flourished from 5th century CE to the 11th century CE. The university taught various disciplines including all forms of Buddhism, and had more than **10000** scholars from various parts of India, China, Southeast Asia, Tibet, Sri Lanka, etc.

- The monastery abounds with large structures several floors high, huge courtyards, and stupas built in brick.
- A number of sculptures and statues have been found which were mainly made in stucco stone and bronze.
- The art of this place can be termed as a distinct school **(Nalanda school)** which was influenced by Sarnath art. However, it had distinct features such as typical facial features, body form, and design of jewellery, clothing, etc. In 2016 it has been declared a UNESCO world heritage site.

(c) Gomateshwara: The statue of Bahubali, carved in granite stone is located at Shravanabelagola (Karnataka), an important **Jain** pilgrimage centre.

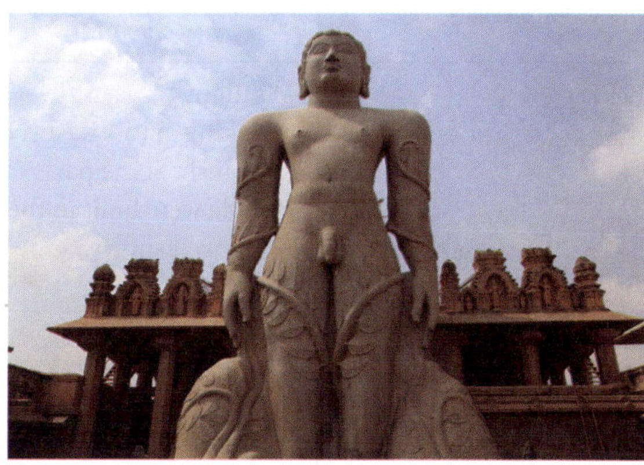

Shravanabelagola Bahubali

- The statue which is nearly 18m high is the **tallest monolithic free standing structure**.
- The statue was constructed by the **Ganga kings** (by Camundarya – Prime Minister of Ganga kings) in 10th century CE and is a reflection of the architectural marvel of the period.
- It is also famous for the *Mahamastakabhisheka* ceremony performed here after every twelve years.

(d) Dilwara temple in Mount Abu

- It was built in around 11th to 13th century CE and is an important Jain temple dedicated to Tirthankara Rishabhnath.
- It is famous for exquisite marble carvings and architecture.

IMPORTANT TEMPLES AND THEIR SALIENT FEATURES: A SUMMARY

Name of Temple & Location	Dynasty and Period of Construction	Style of Architecture, Salient Features, Important sculptures/Images
TEMPLES IN EASTERN INDIA		
(1) **Sun temple (Konark**, Odisha)	Built by Narasimha Deva-I of **East Ganga Dynasty** in **1255 AD**.	• Temple complex is in the form of a gigantic **chariot of Sun god**, Surya. • It has **12 pairs of stone wheels**, and pillars and walls have elaborate carvings, where some are erotic images of *Mithunas*. • The temple is oriented towards the **east** so that the first rays of the Sun enters the main entrance. • The wheels of the temple act as **sundials** which can calculate time to the accuracy of a minute. • It has Odisha or **Kalinga style architecture** (Nagara Phamsana shikhara). • A **UNESCO** world heritage site.
(2) **Lingaraja temple (Bhubaneswar**, Odisha)	Built in **11th century CE** by king Yayati Keshri of Somvansh. Some parts of the temple were built in the 7th century.	• Dedicated to Lord Shiva, it is the **largest temple of Odisha**. • It has **Kalinga style architecture**, its shikhar is of Nagara Phamsana type. • Built in sandstone and laterite, it is east facing. • It is built in **Deula style** and has four components, the *vimana* (which contains the garbhagriha), *jagmohana* (which is assembly hall), *nata-mandir* (hall for dance and festivals), and *bhoga-mandapa* (hall of offerings). • The *bhoga-mandir* hall has a pyramidical roof of several horizontal layers and has on top an inverted bell and *Kalasa*.

(3) Jagannath temple (Puri, Odisha)	Constructed in the 12th century CE by Anantvarma Chodganga Deva of Eastern Ganga dynasty	• Located on eastern coast of India at Puri, the temple is dedicated to Lord Jagannath (incarnation of Lord Vishnu). • The temple deities are unique as they are made of wood which are replaced every 12th year. • It is one of the four *dhamas* (four divine sites) associated with Hindu faith and is associated with the famous 'Rathyatra'. • The large temple complex contains over 120 temples and shrines. The main temple has four distinct structures: Deula (shikhar), *garbhagriha*, *mukhashala* (frontal porch), *nata-mandir*, and *bhoga mandap*.
(4) Siva Sagar Sivadol temple (Sibsagar district, Assam)	Built in 1734 by Ahom king Swargdeo Siba Singha	• It is a group of three temples—Sivadol, Vishnudol, and Devidol, located on the banks of the Sivasagar tank. • The temple has Ahom style of architecture. The spire of Sivadol is crowned with 8 high golden domes. • The Ahom style is also seen in Kamakhya temple (17th century) near Guwahati (Assam).
(5) Terracota temples of Bishnupur (Bankura district, West Bengal)	Built by different Malla kings in the 17th & 18th century CE	• These are a group of temples built by different kings of Malla dynasty, each having distinct features. • Rasmancha temple (1600 CE); dedicated to Radha Krishna has an unusually long pyramid shaped ***shikhar***. It has a number of adjoining turets which are hut shaped. • Jor Bangla temple (1655); dedicated to Lord Krishna, has Chala style of Bengal architecture. It has beautiful terracotta carvings set in walls and roofs with the shape of the roof being curving and sloping quite unlike other temples. • Panch Ratna temple; dedicated to Lord Krishna, has a low square plinth. It has an ambulatory pathway with a porch opened by three arches. It has a five shikhars, the central *shikhar* being octagonal and the remaining being square.

<table>
<tr>
<td>(6) Lakshmana temple
(Sirpur, Chhattisgarh)
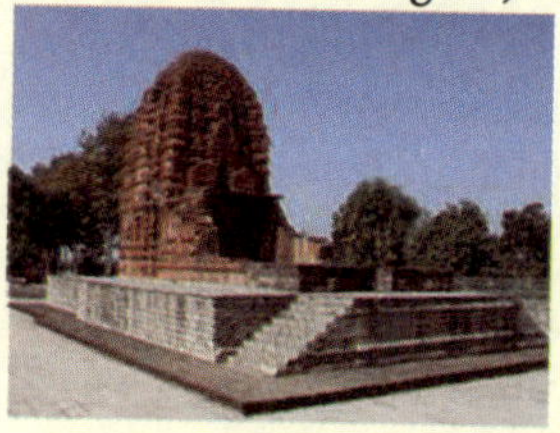
Lakshmana Temple</td>
<td>Built in 7th century CE</td>
<td>• Dedicated to Lord Vishnu, the Lakshmana temple is an excellent example of a brick temple.
• The temple is known for its unique symmetry and exquisite carvings on pillars.
• Images of Vishnu and Krishna Leela are found on its walls and pillars.
• The site has a number of Buddhist structures including viharas and statues of Buddha and Mahavira.</td>
</tr>
<tr>
<td colspan="3">TEMPLES IN CENTRAL INDIA</td>
</tr>
<tr>
<td>(7) Khajuraho temples
(Madhya Pradesh)</td>
<td>Built by Chandela kings 950 CE to 1050 CE</td>
<td>• The temple complex comprises a number of Hindu and Jain temples, the most famous being the Lakshmana temple (dedicated to Lord Vishnu, Kandariya Mahadeo temple (dedicated to Lord Shiva), the Chausath Yogini temple, and the Parsvanath Jain temple.
• Temples are of typical Nagara style of architecture. The Lakshmana temple has five shikhars (Panchayatana style) with four smaller temples in the centre. The towers rise high and are topped with a fluted disc (amlak) and a kalash.
• The walls are highly decorated with numerous erotic carvings signifying the importance attached to human experience in even spiritual pursuit.
• It is a UNESCO world heritage site.</td>
</tr>
<tr>
<td>(8) Dashavatara temple
(Deogarh District, UP)</td>
<td>Built in 500 CE in the late Gupta Period</td>
<td>• It is among the earliest Hindu temples.
• Dedicated to Lord Vishnu, it has the famous sculpture of Sheshayna Vishnu. Other important images are that of Nara-Narayan, and Gajendra Moksha Vishnu.
• It is a prototype of Sarvatobhadra temple.</td>
</tr>
</table>

(9) **Nachna Kuthara temple** (Panna District, Madhya Pradesh) 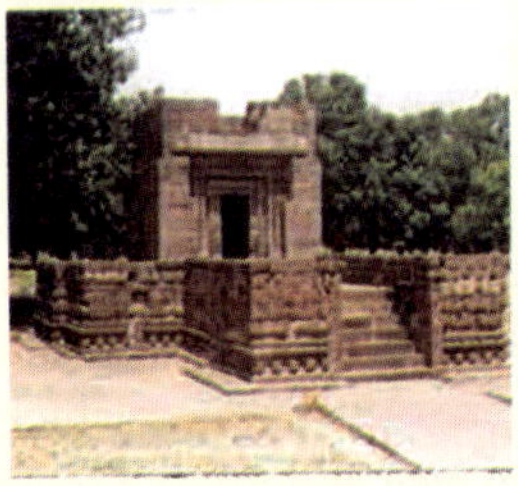 Nachna Kuthara Temple	Two temples built in **late Gupta period**	• It is among the earliest temple structures of ancient India. • The site is famous for two temples, the **Chaturmukhlinga temple** (it has Shivalinga with four faces) and the **Parvati temple.** • The Parvati temple built on a raised platform has walls over a metre thick and **faces west towards the setting sun**, making it unique.
	TEMPLES IN WESTERN INDIA	
(10) **Sun temple** (**Modhera**, Gujarat)	Built by **Raja Bhimdev** – I of Solanki dynasty in **1026 CE**	• Dedicated to **Sun god,** the temple faces east and at equinoxes, the rays of the sun shine directly on the main shrine. • It has a **large rectangular stepped tank (Surya Kund)** which is over 100 square meters and is the grandest temple tank with 108 miniature shrines carved in between the steps in the tank. • The architecture is unique as it has three axially aligned and integrated elements, viz. the **Surya kund** (temple tank), **Sabha mandap,** and **Guda mandap**.
(11) **Dilwara temple** (Mount Abu, Gujarat)	Built in **11th to 13th** century CE. The Vimal Vasahi temple of this group was built in 1031 CE by **Vimal Shah,** minister of Bhimadev-I, a Chalukya king	• It is a **Jain group of temples** which are world famous for **exquisite marble carvings.** • It comprises **five set of temples,** the most famous being Vimal Vasahi temple dedicated to Jain Tirthankara **Rishabhnath**.
(12) **Ranakpur temple** (**Pali** district, Rajasthan)	Built in **15th** century CE	• It is a **Jain temple** complex dedicated to the first Tirthankara **Adinath** (Rishabhnath). • The temple made in white marble is spectacular and has intricate carvings and statues. • Referred to as **Maru Gurjara architecture**, the temple is designed as *'chaumukh'* with four faces.

(13) **Kailash temple** (**Ellora,** Aurangabad district, Maharashtra)	Built by **Rashtrakuta king,** Krishna-I in 8th **century** CE	• It is the **largest rock-cut temple** carved from a single rock (monolithic structure) • Dedicated to Lord Shiva, the temple has a *mandapa, gopuram*, a courtyard, and a statue of Nandi carved out of stone. • It is a **UNESCO** world heritage site.
TEMPLES IN SOUTHERN INDIA		
(14) **Meenakshi temple** (Madurai, Tamil Nadu)	Built by Vishwanatha Nayakar, ruler of the **Nayak dynasty** in the **16th century** CE	• The temple is unique **as it has 14 *gopurams*** (towers of gateways) which **are *45–50 metre* *high*** and are the most visible structures of the temple complex. • It has **two golden sculptured vimanas** under which the garbhagrihas with the main deity is present. The ***vimanas* of the main deity are smaller in size** as compared to the **gopurams.**
(15) **Brihadeeshwara temple** (Thanjavur, Tamil Nadu)	Built by Raja Raja Chola I of Chola dynasty in 1009 CE	• Dedicated to Lord Shiva, it is also known as the Rajarajeshwar temple and is made of granite rock. • The vimana of the temple is nearly 70m high and one of the largest and tallest temple of India. It has the largest Shivlinga. • It has **Dravidian style architecture,** with a large vimana, mandapa hall, statue of Nandi, and gopuram (which is smaller than the vimana). • A **UNESCO** world heritage site.
(16) **Gangaikonda Cholapuram** temple (Thanjavur, Tamil Nadu)	Built by king **Rajendra Chola** (successor of Raja Raja Chola) in the 11th **century CE**	• Dedicated to Lord Shiva, it is a massive **temple, only next in size to Brihadeeshwara temple** but better than the latter in terms of quality of sculpture work. • A Dravidian architecture temple with *vimana* of 55m high which is nine storey high. • A huge Shiva linga 4m high is placed in the sanctum.

(17) **Shore temple (Mahabalipuram,** Tamil Nadu)	Built during the reign of **Pallava** dynasty ruler Narsimha Varman II in 8th century CE	• **Built onshore** facing east towards the ocean, it is a complex of **three temples**. Two of these are dedicated to Lord Shiva and one to Lord Vishnu. • Built with **sculpted granite rocks** it is a five storied **structural temple** (and not rock-cut). It is a pyramidical structure nearly 60ft high built on a raised platforms. • Along with other structures it forms a part of **UNESCO** world heritage site.
(18) **Pancha Rathas (Mahabalipuram,** Tamil Nadu)	Built in **7th century** CE during reign of **Mahendra Verman-1** and his son **Narsimha Verman** of **Pallava** dynasty	• It is located at a separate monument complex from the shore temple. • The pancharathas are **monolithic rock-cut temples**. • They **resemble and represent** the **five rathas of Pandavas,** the largest being the Dharmaraja-ratha and the smallest one was the Draupadi-ratha. The others were Arjuna-ratha, Bheema-ratha, and Nakula-Sachdeva-ratha. • The site is famous for the bas-relief or the **large sculptural panel** nearly thirty metres long and fifteen metres high. This tableau has a large number of images, the **most famous, being the image of Arjuna's penance.** 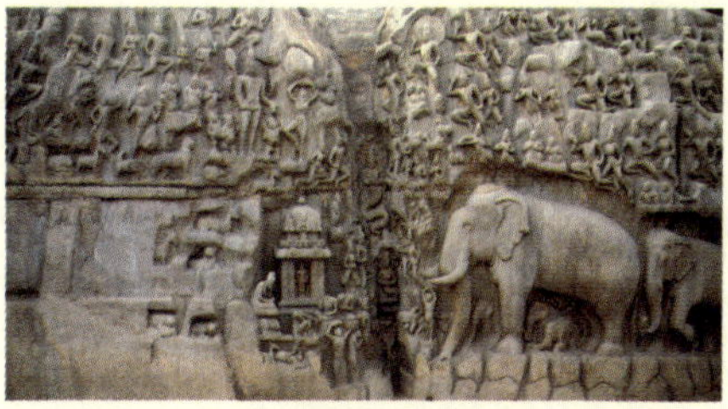 **Arjuna's Penance, Mahabalipuram** Some scholars interpret it is as the story of the descent of Ganga from heaven to earth and Bhagirath's penance for that. • Along with other monuments it is a **UNESCO** world heritage site.

(19) **Srirangam temple** (**Tiruchirapalli,** Tamil Nadu)	Built by **Chola** kings around **10th century** CE	• It is the **largest functioning temple complex in the world,** spread in 156 acres, second in size only to Angkar Vat complex (however the latter is not functioning as a temple). • It is a typical **Dravidian style temple.** It has 7 concentric walls (called *prakarmas*), 21 *gopurams*, 39 pavillions, fifty shrines, and several tanks/water bodies inside. • The vimana over the main deity (Ranganatha Swamy, an incarnation of Lord Vishnu) is shaped like Om and is **gold plated**. • It has a **1000 pillared hall**. The pillars have sculptures of various animals and other figures.
(20) **Durga temple** (**Aihole**, Karnataka)	Built in **7th & 8th century** CE by **Chalukyan** kings	• The temple is **unique as its plan is oblong or apsidal** and is similar to the earlier Buddhist chaitya halls. It employs **Gajprishta** architecture. • The temple is surrounded by a circum-ambulatory verandah and has a *shikhar* similar to Nagara architecture. Thus, **elements of Dravidian and Nagara style is incorporated**.
(21) **Virupaksha temple** (**Pattadakal**, Karnataka)	Built in **745 CE** by **Loka-Mahadevi,** queen of Vikramaditya-II of **Chalukya dynasty**	• This temple is the largest temple at Pattadakal group of monuments (a UNESCO world heritage site). • Dedicated to Lord Shiva, it has a typical Dravidian temple architecture and is famous for sculptures of **Lingobhava, Nataraja,** and **Ugra Narasimha.** • The Kailash temple at Ellora was modelled as per the Virupaksha temple.

(22) **Chennekeshva temple (Somnathpuram** district, Mysore, Karnataka)	Built in **1268** CE under **Hoysala** king Narasimha III	• Dedicated to Lord Vishnu, this temple is of **Dravidian style of architecture** and is unique as it has a **number of projecting angles appearing like stars** (**called stellate plan**). • The material used for construction is **soapstone** (green schist) which is a relatively soft stone, making the intricate sculpture possible (as seen in jewellery of deities). • Temple is built on *jagati* (a raised platform and is *trikuta* (triple shrine). The **vimanas** have a vestibutle connecting cach to the main *mandapa*. • The walls of the temple have scenes of Ramayana and Mahabharata depicted on them.
(23) **Hoysaleshwar temple** (**Halebid**, Karnataka)	Built by **Hoysala King** Vishnu Vardhan in **1150 CE**	• The temple architecture has a **mix of Dravidian and Nagara features**. Thus, it has a **Vesara temple architecture.** • Dedicated to Lord Shiva, who is depicted as Nataraja, the temple has two buildings (***Dvikutavimana***) which is a plan with two shrines and two superstructures. It has a long *mandapa* (hall) for music and dance. • It has a **stellate plan** with star like projections and fine carvings.
TEMPLES IN HILLS		
(24) **Jageshwar temples** (**Almora District,** Uttarakhand)	Temples built between **9th** century CE to **13th** century CE	• The temple complex comprises nearly **124 temples** of which **Mahamritunjay Mahadev is the oldest and largest** one and the **Tarun Jageshwar** is the principal temple. Both are dedicated to Lord Shiva. • It has **Nagara** style architecture.
(25) **Lakhsna Devi temple** (Chamba, Himachal Pradesh)	Constructed in **680 CE** by **Raja Meru Verman**	• It is famous for the image of **goddess Durga,** in four armed form of **Mahisasura Mardini**. • It has **Nagara style architecture** and has **features of old wooden architecture** with richly carved entrance.

CHAPTER

8

Bhakti Movement and Sufism

I searched for God and found only myself. I searched for myself and found only God.

Sufi Proverb

THE BHAKTI MOVEMENT

In the latter half of the first millennia, emerged a new devotional trend in the Hindu society which aimed to purge the religion of its Brahmanical orthodoxy, evils like untouchability, and loosen the grip of the caste system. Its tenets were **based on devotion to God** and **equality of mankind**. The movement reached its zenith in the 15th and 16th century and is referred to as the **Bhakti movement**.

The movement had its origin in the 6th century CE when the **Alvars** (Vaishnavites) and the **Nayanars** (Shaivites) had emerged in Southern India. The Bhakti movement emerged in Northern and Eastern India much later. Further, here it manifested in different forms; such as *Dvaitism* (dualism) or *Advaitism* (monism), *Saguna* and *Nirguna* schools, and different sects which were based on worship of different deities (such as *Vaishnavism, Shaivism, Shaktism, Smartism*, etc.).

REASONS FOR EMERGENCE OF THE BHAKTI MOVEMENT

The period of the 6th century CE onwards saw a varied influence on the Hindu religious thoughts. The Vedic traditions had started to give way to the Puranic culture. The Brahmanical ideas were getting disseminated in the society and at the same time local beliefs and practices were also influencing the broader Hindu thought. The influence of Buddhism and Jainism had started to stagnate and even decline. Amidst all the turbulence in society, there was emergence of the Bhakti movement which emphasised on devotion to God and reform of the religious belief and practices.

The key reasons for the growth of Bhakti movement are summarised as below:

- The Bhakti movement was partly a **response to the Brahmanical orthodoxy** and **rigidity in the caste system**.
- It provided an **inclusive platform** to the marginalised sections of society due to its emphasis on **equality of mankind**. It provided scope for salvation to all including women, artisans, weavers, cultivators, and untouchables. Thus, it appealed to a large underprivileged section of society where it gained popularity and emerged as a religious thought.
- The **stagnation and decline in Buddhism and Jainism** owing to pollution in their own thought (viz. emergence of tantric Buddhism (Vajrayana), etc.) led to disenchantment of masses from them. This enabled the emergence of a new religious thought based on devotion.

- **Political patronage** was another factor helping in its growth, (e.g., the support of Chola kings in Tamil Nadu to the Shaivite movement). While these movements sought the royal support for seeking land grants for construction of temples etc., the support of royalty to these movements helped the dynasties to be perceived as spiritual and religious. At times, they were also keen to seek the support of the eminent saints associated with the movement.

EARLY BHAKTI MOVEMENT—ALVARS, NAYANARS, AND VIRASHAIVAS

The emergence of Alvars and Nayanars in South India marked the beginning of the Bhakti movement. It was a departure from the Puranic religious thought process and was more egalitarian and inclusive.

The salient features of the twin movements are discussed below.

The Alvars

The word **Alvars** literally means, those immersed in devotion of Lord Vishnu. The Alvar movement began in the 6th century CE. Their Bhakti tradition was **characterised by penning of songs** and **poems in service and love of the God.** The saints and devotees would travel from place to place singing hymns in praise of Lord Vishnu or Krishna. There were 12 important Alvars who belonged to different social backgrounds, the best known being **Periyalvar** and his daughter **Andal**. Andal, a woman Alvar saint, wrote a number of compositions which are still sung to this day. The *Nalayira Divya Prabandham* is an important Alvar composition also revered as the Tamil Veda.

The Nayanars

These were devotees of Lord Shiva (literal meaning; leaders who are devotees of Shiva). Like Alvars, their mode of worship was singing hymns or devotional songs in praise of the deity and travel from place to place. **Karaikkal Ammaiyar** was a female Shiva devotee whose compositions are preserved to this day. The important Nayanars were **Sambandar, Sundarar**, and **Manikkavacakar**. The compilation of their songs is contained in *Tevaram* and *Tiruvackam*.

As a result of patronage of the Chola kings a number of temples of prominence dedicated to Lord Shiva were constructed at **Thanjavur, Chidamabaram,** and **Gangaikondacholapuram**. The Nayanar and Alwar traditions also inspired a number of splendid metal and stone sculptures (viz. the image of Shiva as Nataraja).

The Virashaivas or the Lingayats

The movement of **Virashaiva** (heroes of *Shiva*) or the **Lingayats** (wearers of the *Linga*) emerged in around 12th century in Karnataka. The movement was started by **Basavana** (a Brahmin) who was earlier a Jaina and a minister in the court of a Chalukyan king.

The Lingayats opposed the caste system and worked for the emancipation of women and the downtrodden in the society. They were opposed to ritualism and Brahmanical orthodoxy. They supported widow remarriage and post puberty marriage of girls. They did not believe in rebirths and believed in unification of the soul with Shiva on death. Hence, they did not cremate their dead but buried them. The teaching or the messages of the Lingayats is contained in ***Vachanas*** (literally meaning as sayings) which were composed in Kannada.

LATER BHAKTI MOVEMENT

While the first wave of Bhakti movement emerged from the southern part of India, it did not cover the entire country. Further, no such parallel movement was seen in northern part of India for centuries to come. This is attributed by the historians to the fact that Brahmins occupied important positions in the court of Rajput kings and discharged religious and secular functions. As such, challenge to their authority did not emerge from the non-Brahmanical background. Although some religious leaders did emerge from the non-Brahmanical background, viz. the **Naths,** the **Jogis,** and the **Siddhas,** it did not take the shape of a large scale movement.

The Impact of the Delhi Sultanate and the Advent of Islam

The advent of Islam and the establishment of Delhi sultanate had a profound impact on the Indian society in the following ways:

- The Islamic religion with its **concept of equality and egalitarianism** also influenced the Hindu society, particularly the marginalised section to whom the teachings of Islam appealed.
- The authority of the Rajputs and the socio-religious authority of the Brahmins waned under the Delhi Sultanate.
- The influence of Islam also brought into fore the **growth of Sufism**.
- There was a need for reform and consolidation of Hinduism in the midst of sweeping socio-religious political changes, religious conversions, and turmoil in the mainstream Hindu religion.

The above factors all led to the growth of the Bhakti movement. It is also noteworthy that the seeds of Bhakti movement were sowed in Upanishadic teachings and earlier revival in Hinduism brought about as a result of teachings and philosophy of Shankaracharya (*Advaita-Vedanta philosophy*), Ramanuja (*Vishisht-Advaita philosophy*), and Madhavacharya (*Dvaitavad philosophy*).

Thus, the later phase of Bhakti emerged in the 14th century CE and reached its peak in 15th and 16th century CE. It included many saints and preachers like **Ramananda, Kabir, Guru Nanak, Chaitanya, Mirabai**, etc.

Philosophies Characterising the Bhakti Movement

A number of philosophies are said to have influenced and characterised the Bhakti movement ranging from Vedantism to Sufism. Some of these are:

- **Vedantism** – The Upanishadic teaching particularly that of Shankaracharya, Madhavacharya, and Ramanuja had a salutory effect on reformation of the Hindu religion and reducing the influence of ritualism and orthodoxy. Thus, it paved the way for growth of Bhakti movement.
- **Dvaita and Adavaita Philosophy** – Bhakti movement incorporated in its fold both the *Advaita* philosophy or **monism** and the *Dvaita* philosophy or **dualism**. Elements of both philosophies can be found in teaching of Bhakti saints. While that of Nanak's and Kabir's philosophy were based on monism, many other Bhakti teachers preached the dualistic philosophy.

- **Nirguna and Saguna** – Bhakti movement also saw emergence of two distinct streams of devotion, the ***Nirguna;*** or those who believed in formless and attributeless God and ***Saguna;*** where God was perceived to be having attributes and was even personalised. While some preachers like **Kabir believed in a formless God** (*Nirguna Brahma*), the likes of Mirabai, Tulsidas, and Soordas were devotees of the *Saguna Brahma*.
- **Sufism** – This too had an important influence on Hindu society, particularly its emphasis on unity of God and equality of mankind. Sufism and its growth is also seen by scholars to be often parallel to the Bhakti movement.

Features of the Bhakti Tradition

- The movement emphasised on **Bhakti** (**or devotion to God**) as a means to attain salvation.
- The movement and most preachers emphasised on **monotheism** or existence of one God. However, the perception of God could be ***Nirguna*** (formless/attributeless) or ***Saguna*** (with attributes).
- The movement emphasised on **equality of mankind** and was inclusive. It professed **salvation to women** and the marginalised.
- It dispensed the need of rituals, attacked dogmas, Brahmanical superiority, and prescribed surrender to God through Bhakti as means of salvation.
- It preached mostly in local language and followed the ***guru-shishya* tradition**.

IMPORTANT PREACHERS IN THE BHAKTI MOVEMENT

Sl.no.	Preacher/Saint	Period, and region/ State in which preached	Salient features of teaching and important contributions, etc.
1.	**Shankaracharya**	8th century CE; Preached throughout India	• Also referred as **Adi Shankaracharya**, he was responsible for bringing **revival and reformation in Hinduism**. • His teachings are based on **Advaita philosophy** of Vedanta (monoism) emphasising on the unity of the creator and creation • **Founded the four 'mathas'** in different geographical locations of the country and thus unifying Hinduism • Laid the foundation of Bhakti movement with his compositions of devotional hymns in praise of Lord Vishnu, Lord Shiva, and goddess Shakti • Composed commentaries on the Vedas **(Brahma Sutras),** Upanishads, and the Gita

2.	**Ramanuja**	11th century CE; Tamil Nadu and South India	• He was the **propounder of the Vishishtadvaita philosophy**. Along with Advaita Philosophy (of Shankaracharaya) and Dvaita philosophy (of Madhavacharya), the three form the most important Vedantic philosophy • Follower of *Sri Vaishanavism* (worship of Vishnu and Lakshmi) • Teachings emphasised on Bhakti or devotion to a personal God
3.	**Basavanna**	12th century CE; Karnataka	• He was philosopher, a poet, a statesman, and a religious reformer • Laid the **foundation of Virashaiva or Lingayat sect** which emphasised on devotion to Lord Shiva (followers wore Shivlinga around neck). • Literary works are contained in '**Vachanas**' (sayings). Compilation of the Vachanas is called **Vachana Sahitya**
4.	**Madhavacharya**	13th century CE; Karnataka	• Propounded the **Dvaita philosophy** of Vedanta which emphasised on dualism or subtle but fundamental difference between the Brahman (creator) and Atman (soul) • Emphasised on attaining salvation through grace of God through the Bhakti tradition • Composed nearly 37 texts on ***Dvaita*** philosophy
5.	**Jnaneshwar**	Late 13th century CE; Maharashtra	• A saint poet in Maharashtra and early reformist. He was also a **philosopher** and a **yogi of the Nath tradition** • His commentary on Bhagvad Gita called *Jnaneshwari* and another work *Amrut-Anubhav* are important contributions in Marathi literature • Emphasised on 'Bhakti' and equality of all beings and condemned the caste system • Belonged to the **Varkari tradition** (A Bhakti tradition in Maharashtra and Karnataka where Lord Vishnu is worshipped in his incarnation as Vitthal or Vithoba)

6.	**Namdeva**	Late 13th and 14th century CE; Maharashtra, northern Karnataka	• He was a poet and saint of the *Varkari* tradition • He was a Vaishnavite and his preachings included the *Nirguna* as well as *Saguna* elements. • Preached and composed in local *Marathi* language
7.	**Ramananda**	Part of the 14th and 15th century CE; Varanasi region of Uttar Pradesh	• Founder of the **Ramanandi Sampraday**, one of the largest monastic Hindu order • Prominent preacher of Bhakti movement, a Vaishnava devotional poet and saint • **Initiated 12 disciples** (10 men and two women) which includes Kabirdas, Ravidas, Bhagat Pipa, and others • **First to preach in Hindi** (local language), author of *Gyanlila* and *Yoga Chintamani* (in Hindi) and other works like *Vaisanava-mata, Bhabhaskara,* and *Ramcharna Paddhati* in Sanskrit • Accepted both *Saguna* and *Nirguna* philosophies
8.	**Kabir**	15th century CE; Varanasi, Uttar Pradesh	• A prominent poet saint of Bhakti movement and a disciple of Ramananda • **Questioned dogmas and rituals** in both Hinduism and Islam, preached ***monism*** and ***Nirguna Brahma*** • Teachings are in the form of couplets *('dohas') compiled in works named Kabir-Bijak, Kabir-Parchai, and Kabir Granthawali.* • Some of Kabir's couplets also find place in the Sikh holy book *Adi Granth.*
9.	**Guru Nanak**	15th century CE; Punjab	• First of the ten Sikh gurus and **founder of Sikhism** • Teaching based on **monism**, **equality**, **love towards fellow beings, and devotion to God**. • Teaching contained in 974 verses in **Guru Granth Sahib** (holy text of Sikhism and compilation of teachings of various Sikh Gurus and also other preachers)

10.	**Chaitanya**	Late 15th and 16th century CE; Bengal, but travelled and preached throughout India	• Also referred as Chaitanya Mahaprabhu or Gaurang Mahaprabhu, he was the **founder of Gaudiya Vaishnavism** • Teachings were based on *Bhagvata Purana*, *Bhagvata Gita*, and Krishna Bhakti (devotion to Lord Krishna) • His teachings are recorded **Sikastakam** (which contains eight devotional prayers in Sanskrit).
11.	**Narsinh Mehta**	15th century CE; Gujarat	• A poet saint of Bhakti tradition who preached in Gujarat • Composed a number of Padas (verses) called *Aakhyan* and *Prabhatiya* • Well known for his poem/song '*Vaishno Jan to Tene re Kahiye*' sung by Mahatma Gandhi
12.	**Vallabhacharya**	15th and 16th century, born in South India. Preached throughout India. Died in Kashi, Uttar Pradesh	• Propounder of **Shuddhadvaita** and **Pushtimarg**. • Followers include *Pushti Sampradaya* and *Vishnu-Swami Sampradaya*
13.	**Surdas**	15th and 16th century; Vrindavan, Mathura, Uttar Pradesh	• Blind poet saint, dedicated in **devotion to Lord Krishna** • He is of the *Saguna* school of Bhakti movement where his devotion was to the 'Krishna' as he perceived • A disciple of Vallabhacharya • His verses are contained in famous works called *Sursagar, Sur-Saravali,* and *Sahitya Lahiri*
14.	**Raidas** or **Ravidas**	15th and early 16th century; Varanasi, Uttar Pradesh	• A **disciple of Ramananda,** Raidas, preached devotion to God, equality of mankind and removal of divides such as caste • Some of his verses included in Guru Granth Sahib

15.	**Shankardeva**	Mid 15th and 16th century CE; Assam	• He was a poet saint of **Assam** who started the **neo-Vaishnavite** movement, **'Ekasharna Dharma,** based on devotion to Lord Krishna • Made important contribution with his poem and plays and other works including *Kirtana Ghosha*, *Borgeets* and *Harischandra Upakhyana* • Teachings helped in social reformation of Hindu society in Assam
16.	**Mirabai**	16th century CE; Rajasthan	• She was a devotee poet seeped in Bhakti of Lord Krishna • A princess in Rajput dynasty, she considered Lord Krishna as her consort and composed many *'Padas'* to express her love and devotion
17.	**Tulsidas**	16th century CE; Varanasi, Uttar Pradesh	• Also referred as Goswami Tulsidas, he was a poet saint and a reformer; and belonged to the *Saguna* school. • Follower of **Ramanandi Sampradaya** (tradition of Ramananda) • Well known as the author of *Ramcharitamanas* (in Avadhi) and dedicated to the lineage of **devotion to Lord Rama** (an incarnation of Lord Vishnu) • Other works include *Vinay-Patrika*, *Hanuman-Chalisa*, (hymn) *Hanuman-Ashtak*, Tulsi-Satsai (in Braj)
18.	**Eknath**	16th century CE; Maharashtra	• Poet saint in Maharashtra • Belonged to the *Varkari* tradition preceded by **Jnaneshwara** and **Namdev** and succeeded by **Tukaram**
19.	**Dadu Dayal**	Late 16th century CE; Gujarat	• A poet saint in Gujarat whose teachings led to formation of **Dadu Panth** • 'Dadu' means brother and 'Dayal' a compassionate one. His teachings were based on devotion and compassion • Compositions recorded in **Dadu-Anubhav Vani** containing 5000 verses.
20.	**Tukaram**	Early 17th century CE; Maharashtra	• He was a poet saint of Bhakti movement belonging to the **Vaishnavite** sect (Varkari tradition) • His poetry (**Abhanga poetry tradition** and preachings were dedicated in devotion to Lord Vithala (an incarnation of Lord Vishnu)

SUFISM

Sufism refers to the teachings of the Sufi saints who emphasised on **monotheism and devotion to God** as opposed to the growing culture of materialism. It represents the mystical, esoteric, and spiritual aspect of Islamic faith.

The word Sufi is referred as *Tasawwuf* in Islamic texts that is interpreted differently by historians and scholars. Some believe that the word *Sufi* is derived from 'Sufi' meaning wool, thus referring to the coarse woolen clothes which were worn by the Sufis. However, others believe that the word owes its origin to 'Safa', meaning purity. Scholars also believe that it may have been derived from 'Suffa' which refers to the platform outside the Prophet's mosque where close followers assembled.

Sufism and Its Growth in India

India came in contact with the Islamic traditions first through the Arabic traders. Later in the 8th century, the Sind province was conquered by Muhammad Bin Qasim bringing it under the domain of the Caliph. The 11th century saw more invasions and finally in the 13th century, the Turks and Afghans established their rule in Delhi. The 16th century saw the rise of Mughal empire in India and subsequently the Deccan plateau region was also brought under the Muslim rule. Thus, the influence of Islam spread to large parts of India and along with it, the Sufi influence also permeated in the Indian society. Some scholars also believe that the Sufi influence on the society was a two-way process. It had impact on Hindu society but at the same time it was also influenced by the Vedantic philosophy and Buddhist thoughts (as seen particularly in the teachings of Kabir).

Sufism and Essence of Its Teaching

- Sufism **represented the spiritual and esoteric aspect of Islam**. It was opposed to the growing materialism and emphasised on mysticism and love for God. It was against any dogmatic interpretation of the Holy Quoran or the *Ahadith* (or *Sunna*; the traditions of the Prophet).
- It believed in **monotheism** or one God and preached that salvation lied in devotion to God and love for the fellow human beings.
- It emphasised on **inner purity, righteousness simplicity, austerity, piety, and love** as means to attain the almighty and was opposed to ritualism and orthodoxy. Devotional music and devotional songs formed an important part of the Sufi tradition.

Sufi Khanqahs and Silsilas

The entire **Sufi order was organised around the *Khanqahs* and the *Silsilas*.** Khanqahs were communities based in a hospice or a lodge, following the teaching of a master called *Shaikh* (in Arabic) or Pir or Murshid (in Persian). The rules of spiritual conduct were established by the master and the teachings were followed by the community. The master enrolled disciples called Murids and appointed successors called Khalifas. Thus, a chain of master and disciple was established which was called Silsilas. Thus, the Silsilas were the means by which religious teachings and spiritual powers were transmitted. The genealogy could extend to Prophet Muhammad himself.

They were several Silsilas in the Sufi order. The most important were the *Chistis* and the *Suhrawardis*. The other important ones were the *Qadriya Silsila, Naqshbandi Silsila*, the *Nimatullahi Silsila,* and the *Shattari Silsila.*

Some of the Silsilas, their important preachers, and teachings are highlighted here.

(a) The Chisti Silsila

S.No.	Important Sufi Preachers	Location of 'dargah'	Salient Features
1.	**Shaikh Moinud-din Chisti** (1141 CE to 1235 CE)	Ajmer	• One of the most renowned Sufi saints • Travelled to India from Iran and settled in Ajmer, had a large following • Teachings based on principles of monotheism, devotion to almighty, and love, fulfilling the needs of helpless and hungry • Also referred as Gharib Nawaj (benefactor of the poor) • Started the Chisti order in India
2.	**Qutubuddin-Bakhtiar Kaki** (1173 CE to 1235 CE)	Delhi	• Successor of Shaikh Moinnuddin Chisti • Spread the message of the master and helped in spreading the Chisti order in India
3.	**Sheikh-Faridud-dinGanj-e-Sha-kar** (1173 CE to 1265 CE)	Ajodhan, Pakistan	• Popularly known as Baba Farid, he spread the message of Chisti saints in the Punjab region • Used Punjabi language for writing verses and poetry.
4.	**Shaikh Nizamud-din Auliya** (1238–1325 CE)	Delhi (Nizam-muddin Dargah) (Ghiyaspur, now Southern Delhi)	• One of the **most famous Sufi saints** of the Chisti order (successor of Baba Farid) • His followers included Shaikh Naseruddin Muhammad Chirag-e-Delhi and **Amir Khusro** the famous musician and scholar of the Delhi court (whose grave is near that of Nizammudin Auliya)
5.	**Shaikh Nasirud-din Chirag-e-De-hlavi** (1274–1356 CE	Delhi (Chirag Delhi)	• A murid of Nizamuddin Auliya. He was also a poet in Persian language • His disciple included Bavala Nawaz Gezu Daraz who later moved to Daulatabad and further to Gulbarga (Karnataka), thus spreading the Sufi order

(b) Other important Sufi orders

(1) **Suhrawardi Silsila** – The Silsila was founded by Shaikh Sahabuddin Umar Suhrawadi in India. This order was represented by Sheikh Bahauddin Zakaria of Multan. Its area of influence was Kashmir, Punjab, Sind, and parts of Bengal.

(2) **Qadriya Silsila** – Popular in Punjab region, Shah Niamatullah (1430 CE) introduced the order in India.

HAGIOGRAPHY, NATH AND BHAKTI TRADITIONS

- **Hagiography** – These are the biographies of saints written by their followers which were often based on the teachings of the saint or their compositions. These may not be an accurate account of the life and times of the saint, but did give an account of as to how the followers perceived the saint.
- **Nathpanthis, Siddhas, and Yogis** – These were different religious groups and sects which emerged during the period of Bhakti movement (7th century to 16th century). They **advocated asceticism and renunciation of the world as a means to attain salvation.** They also preached that disciplining the mind and body through *pranayama* and *yoga* and performing meditation on the attributeless Brahma lead to the unification of the soul with the Brahma. They were opposed to ritualism and conventional religious orthodoxy and were inclusive in their outlook making them popular in the underprivileged and the ostracised sections of the society.

  The Nath tradition was developed by *Matsyendranath* and later popularised by Gorakhshanath. They were also referred as *'mahasiddhas'* or those having great spiritual powers. Their objective was attaining of salvation through renunciation and yogic asceticism. The *Nathsampradaya* are believed to have developed from earlier *Siddha* or *Avadhuta* traditions.
- **Bhakti tradition in Maharashtra** – **The region of Maharashtra saw a** number of poets saints (from 13th to 17th century CE) seeped in the Varkari Bhakti tradition. These included **Jnaneshwar, Namdev, Eknath, Tukaram,** and women saints **Sakhubai** and **Chokhamela**. The tradition involved devotion to Lord Vithala or Vithoba (incarnation of Lord Vishnu) worshipped in the temple at Pandharpur.

  The Varkari tradition emphasised on devotion and service to mankind while rejecting ritualism, casteism, and religious dogmas and orthodoxy. They did not even consider renunciation of world as a necessity for salvation and the poet saints continued to stay with their family.

IMPORTANT TOPICS TO FOCUS ON

- Reasons for emergence of the Bhakti movement
- Teachings and salient features of Bhakti movement
- Important Bhakti movements (viz. Alvars, Nayanars, and Virashaivas) and preachers
- Teachings and features of Sufism
- Important Sufi saints (particularly of Chisti Silsila)

CHAPTER 9

Architecture in Medieval Age Palaces, Forts, and Other Monuments

Architecture is inhabited sculpture

Constantin Brancusi

THE ISLAMIC INFLUENCE ON INDIAN ARCHITECTURE

The Islamic influence had a profound impact on the Indian society. Like many other facets of Indian life, the Indian architecture was also deeply influenced by the arrival of Islam in India. Although the Islamic influence began in the 7th and 8th century CE through the Arab traders and later increased after the conquest of Sind, it was only in the **early 13th century after the establishment of the Delhi sultanate** that the architectural and construction work started to bear the **Islamic imprint** on a larger scale.

However, the Islamic influence did not replace altogether the extant features of Indian architecture; rather it combined many features of the local traditions and cultures combining with its own architectural practice. Thus, what emerged was a mix of different architectural techniques and practices and has been referred by the historians and scholars as **Indo-Saracenic** or **Indo-Islamic** architecture.

FEATURES OF INDO-ISLAMIC ARCHITECTURE

- Indian architecture by 12th century had already accomplished some monumental structures. However, these structures were based on brackets, beams, and pillars to support the flat roofs or at times the vaults and small domes. Thus, Indian architecture was characterised by *trabeation* (i.e., use of beams as opposed to arches or vaulting). The deployment of arches if any, was neither as substantial weight bearing elements nor were large spacious domes incorporated in the construction.
- The Islamic influence ushered in an era of **use of arches to support large domes.** The arches were constructed with *voussoirs* (series of inter- locking blocks) and fitted with keystones. The domes rested on *pendentives* and *squinches* which enabled large spaces to be pillar free. (*Pendentive*; a construction feature in the shape of a curved triangle formed by the intersection of the dome with its supporting arches. *Squinch*; a construction filling the upper angels of a square room so as to form a base to receive an octagon or spherical dome)
- Thus, there was a **shift in the style of architecture from trabeate to arcuate** (based on arches and domes). The need for large spacious column free domed structure was a practical necessity for large congregations and community offering of prayers in Islam. The walls of the mosque would have a semi-circular niche called *Mihrab*. This would indicate the direction of *Kabba* in Mecca and the Muslims would pray facing the *Mihrab* which would have intricate designs and decorations.

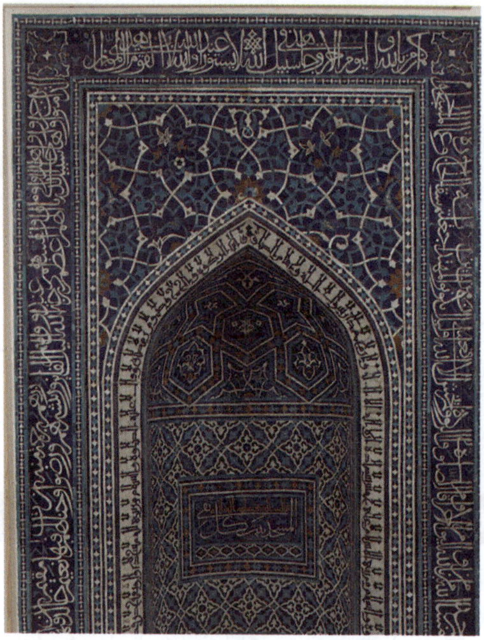

Mihrab

- In Hindu temples, the *garbhagrihas* were places where offering and religious ceremonies was performed. This was relatively small while the *mandapa* would be larger and spacious which would be used for congregation.
- Another notable feature incorporated by the Islamic architecture was use of ***minars* and minarets**. These were often deployed in the periphery or corners of the mosques and complimented the dome structure.
- The use of **lime mortar in construction** was also popularised. Further, lime was not only used as a plaster but as a base for decoration which was incised into the surface.
- Islamic influence was also visible in the **surface decoration** and finishing. While the walls of Hindu temples had images of Gods in different forms (or symbols), the Islamic structures were prohibited from carrying the images of living beings. As such, the surfaces of structures were covered with **calligraphy words**, geometrical patterns, some amount of **floral work,** and **Arabesque patterns** (these were patterns of scrolling and interlacing foliage tendrils or plain lines).

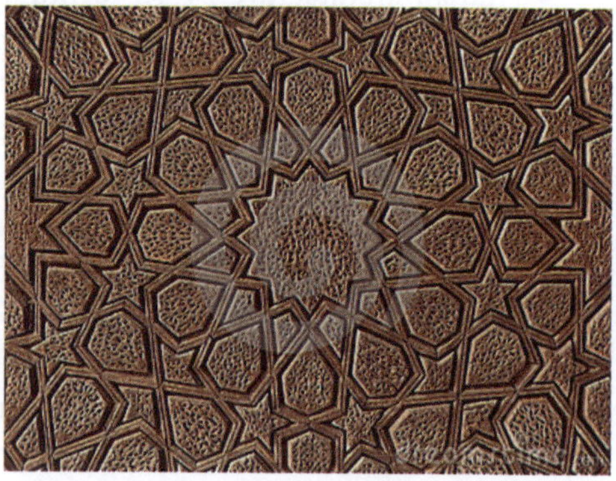

Islamic Surface Decoration

- A salient feature of Indo-Islamic architecture was use of intricate ***jali works***. They were perforated stones or latticed screens in the form of an ornamental pattern. Further, **'pietra dura'** which involved inlay work wherein precious/semi precious gems and stones were cut and inlaid in the walls, was another introduction to Indian art.

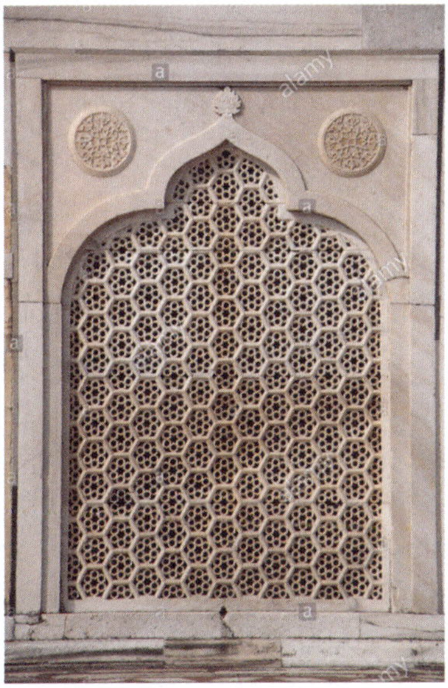

Jali work at Taj Mahal

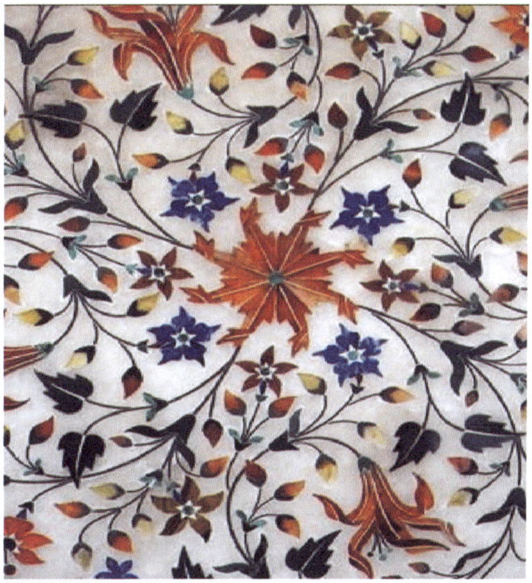

Pietra Dura

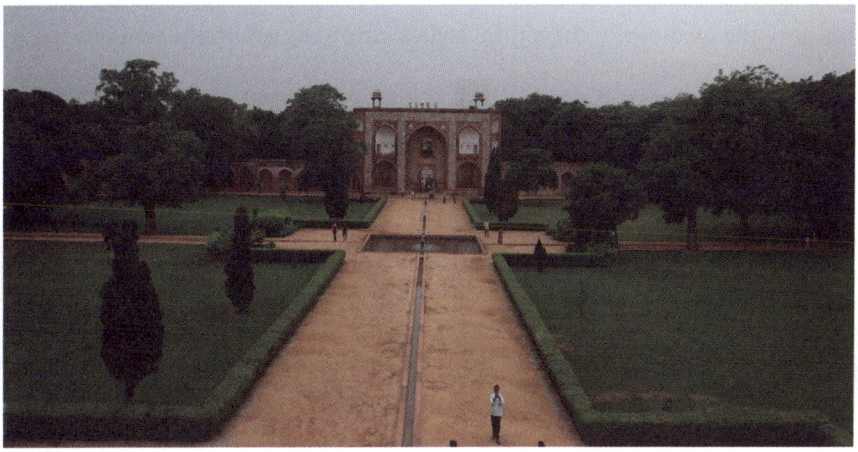

Charbagh style (Humayun's Tomb)

- Use of **gardens, fountains, and water works,** especially in later Mughal prominent monuments was another important feature. These would often be in ***charbagh*** style which is division of a garden into four parts by walkways.

INDO-ISLAMIC STRUCTURES AND ITS TYPES

A variety of new structures came up which were based on the socio-religious and political need. These included the **palaces** and **forts** (particularly in the Mughal period), the ***Jama Masjids*** (main mosques of cities and town where people congregate), **smaller mosques,** and **dargahs** (tombs of religious preachers and saints). Besides these, *minars, Kos Minars* (round pillars 30ft high serving as milestones), *sarais, caravan sararis* (roadside inns), *madarsas,* and *hamams* were also constructed.

CATEGORIES OF STYLES OF INDO-ISLAMIC ARCHITECTURE

The Indo-Islamic architectural style can broadly be categorised into the following major subtypes:

(a) The Imperial style (of Delhi sultanate)

(b) The Provincial style (of Mandu, Gujarat, and Bengal)

(c) The Mughal style (of Delhi, Agra, and Lahore)

(d) The Deccani style (of Bijapur, Golconda)

Besides the above, India also saw emergence of the **Rajput style** of architecture and in the 17th and 18th century of the **Sikh style** of architecture.

The initial styles of architecture particularly in the 13th and 14th century had only certain elements of the Islamic style. This is so as the initial conquerors did not come to India with the intention of settling here and hence their entourage was not accompanied by masons, craftsmen, etc. Thus, the Islamic structures borrowed a number of Indian features and relied on the local craftsmen. Such influences are seen in the imperial style of architecture in the early Delhi sultanate period, viz. *Quwwat-ul-Islam mosque* Delhi and *Adhai Din Ka Jhonpra,* Ajmer. However, with the **establishment of the Mughal dynasty in the 16th century, there was a substantial change in grandness, scale, and style of architecture** as seen in the structures of *Humayun's tomb*, *Agra Fort*, *Fatehpur Sikri*, *Red Fort*, and *Taj Mahal*. The Taj is considered to be the pinnacle of the medieval architectural style owing to its sublimity, proportions, and grandness.

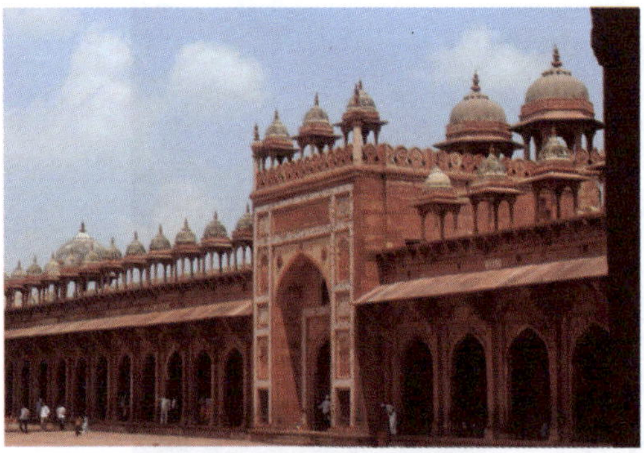

Fatehpur Sikri, Agra

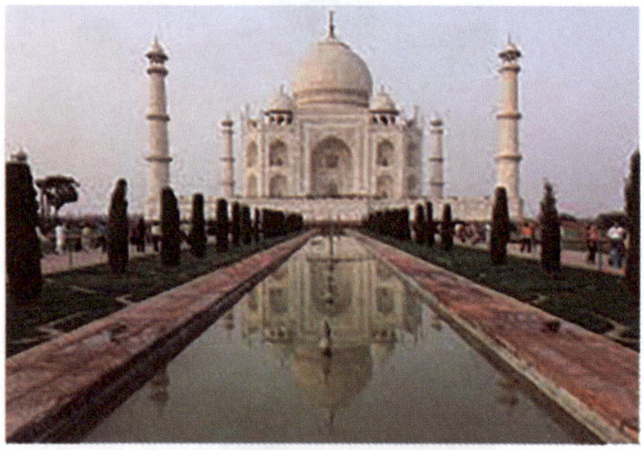

Taj Mahal, Agra

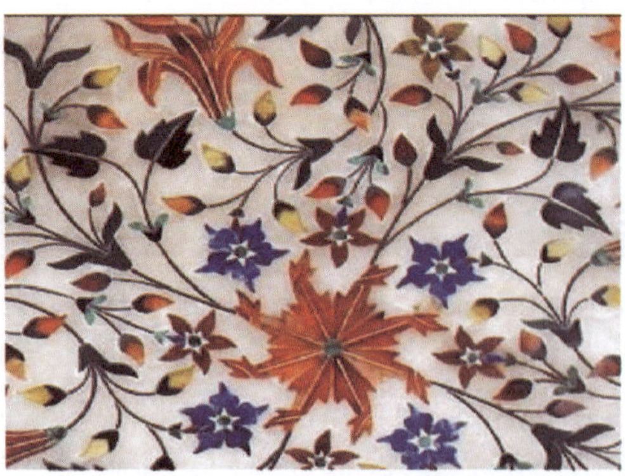

Pietra Dura at Taj Mahal

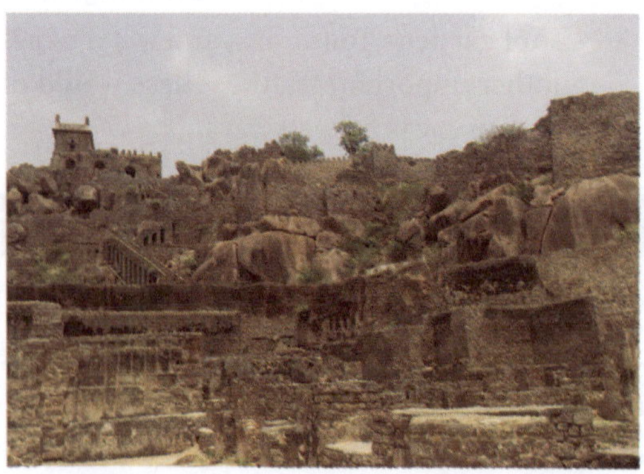

Golconda Fort, Hyderabad

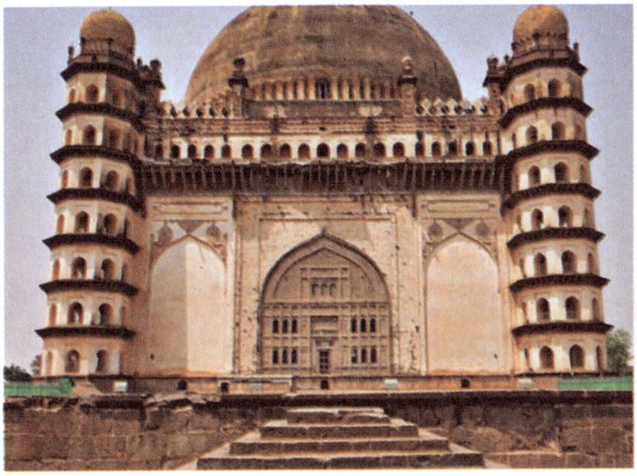

Gol Gumbaz, Bijapur

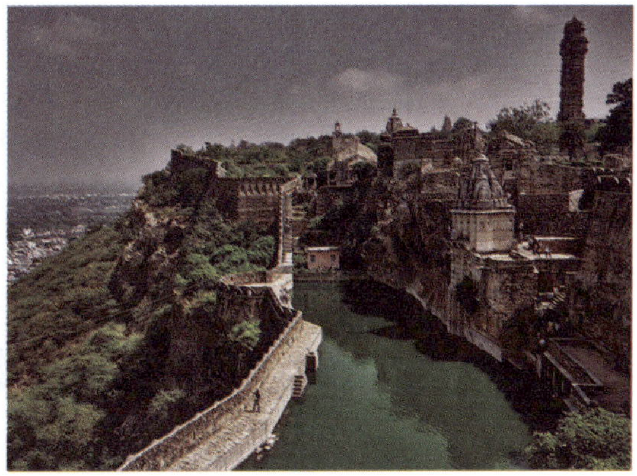

Chittorgarh Fort

Islamic architecture also flourished in the Deccan as seen in the **Bijapur School** (viz. *Golconda Fort* and *Gol Gumbaz (Bijapur)*. Besides, there were other regional schools as the **Bengal school** which was characterised by use of **bricks and** had a distinctive feature of **slanting roofs**. Many prominent structures also came up in the Rajasthan region in the medieval period. These were palaces and forts built in the **Rajput school style, viz. Chittorgarh Fort**, **Kumbhalgarh Fort**, **Amer Fort** (Jaipur), **Hawa Mahal** (Jaipur), many havelis, etc. The concept of balconies and chhatris was unique to this school of architecture.

DIFFERENT STYLES OF MEDIEVAL ARCHITECTURE AND IMPORTANT MONUMENTS

Imperial Style

Architectural Style	Important Monuments	Salient Points
(a) Slave dynasty (13th century CE)	**(i) Qutab Minar** (Delhi)	• It was started by Qutubuddin Aibak (1199 CE) and completed by Iltutmish, damaged by lightning in 1373, and two floors rebuilt by Feroz Shah Tughlaq.It is believed to be a **tower of victory** (marking the conquest over Rajput kings) • It is the **highest stone tower** in India with a height of 72.5 m. • Its unique features include projecting balconies and surface inscription.

	(ii) Quwwat-ul-Islam mosque, Delhi 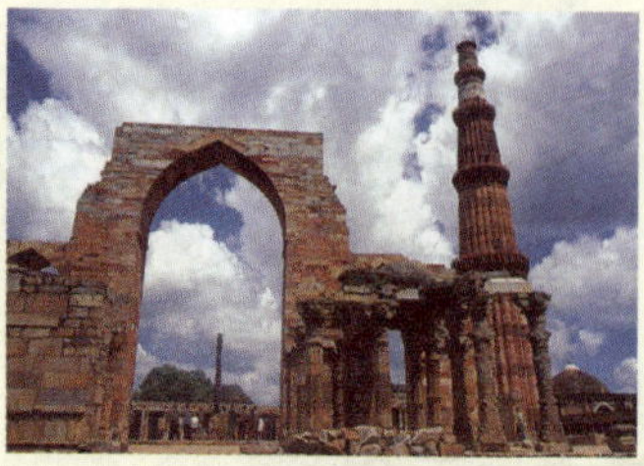	• It was constructed in 1197 AD by Qutubuddin Aibak (located in the vicinity of Qutab Minar).
	(iii) Adhai Din Ka Jhonpra (Ajmer) 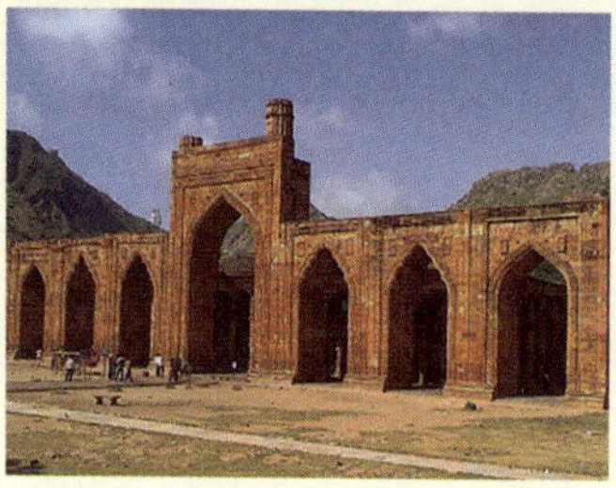	• It used the construction material by demolishing a number of Hindu and Jain temples within the Rajput citadel of Rajkot. • It was constructed in 1199 by Qutubuddin Aibak and completed by Iltutmish. • The mosque is an early example of Islamic architecture. It used construction material from destroyed Hindu and Jain temples. It is also believed by historians that a Sanskrit college was located at the site which was destroyed too. • It is the 2nd oldest mosque after Quwwat-ul-Islam mosque.
(b) Khilji Dynasty (1290 to 1320 CE)	**(i) Alai Darwaja** (Southern gateway at Qutub complex in New Delhi) and **Jamat Khana mosque**	• A dynasty of **Turkic origin** founded by Jalal-ud-din Firuz Khilji. The most prominent ruler of this dynasty was **Alauddin Khilji**. • Architecture features include use of **true arches and use of red sandstone** as construction material.
	(ii) Siri Fort, Delhi	• Built in 1303 CE during reign of Alauddin Khilji. Siri was the second amongst the seven cities of Delhi.
(c) Tughlaq Dynasty (1330 CE to 1413 CE)	(i) Tughlaqabad Fort	• Tughlaqabad was the **third city of Delhi** • Made of grey sandstone with thick walls and emphasis on defence
	(ii) Tomb of Ghiyasuddin Tughlaq	• Tomb of Ghiyasuddin Tughlaq is like a self-contained miniature fortress with sloping walls of circular bastions.

	(iii) Jahanpanah	• **Jahanpanah** was the **fourth city of Delhi**. This capital city got deserted due to the erratic policy of Mohammad Bin Tughlaq to shift capital to Daulatabad.
	(iv) Feroz Shah Kotla	• Feroz Shah Kotla was the **fifth city of Delhi** built by Feroz Shah Tughlaq.

Provincial Style

(a) Mandu or Malwa school	• Jahaz Mahal (Mandu) 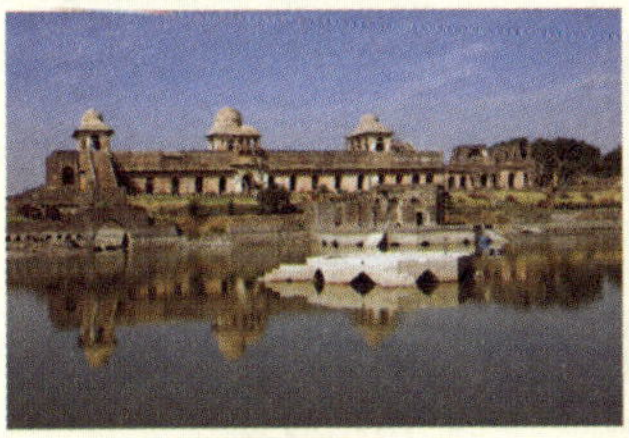 • Hindola Mahal • Taveli Mahal • Hoshang Shah's Ashrafi Mahal • Jama Masjid	• Dynasty of Malwa sultanate belonged to the Ghuri dynasty. Initial structures built by using remnants of destroyed Hindu temples. However, later its own Islamic style developed. • Number of important structures belonging to 15th and 18th century in the Mandu and Hoshangabad region. • Jahaz Mahal built by Sultan Ghiyasuddin Khilji. The Jahaz Mahal is unique as in the rainy season it would give the impression of a floating ship. • Hindola Mahal was built in Hoshang Shah's time. • Jama Masjid was built by Mahmud Shah Khilji.
(b) Gujarat School (1376–1479)	• **Jama Masjid** (Ahmedabad) 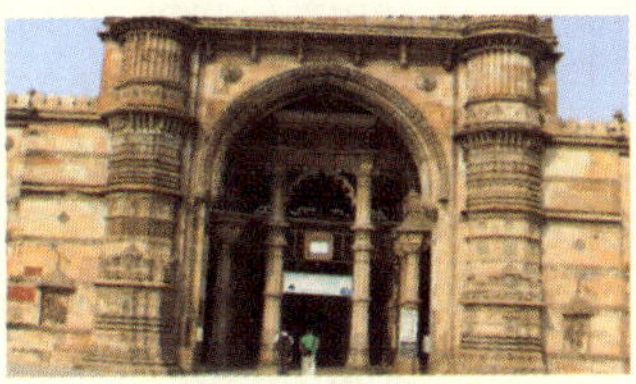 • **Jama Masjid (Champaner)** (UNESCO world heritage site)	• This school of art developed in fourteenth century during reign of Khilji dynasty which had placed its governor in Gujarat. • Jama Masjids at Ahmedabad and Champaner are the most notable contribution of this school. • Jama Masjid (Ahmedabad) is built in yellow sandstone on a large rectangular courtyard. It contains the famous shaking minarets which were partly destroyed in the earthquake. • Jama Masjid, Champaner with its elegant interiors incorporating many Hindu architectural features is considered the finest mosque in western India.

(c) Bengal School (1203 CE–1479 CE)	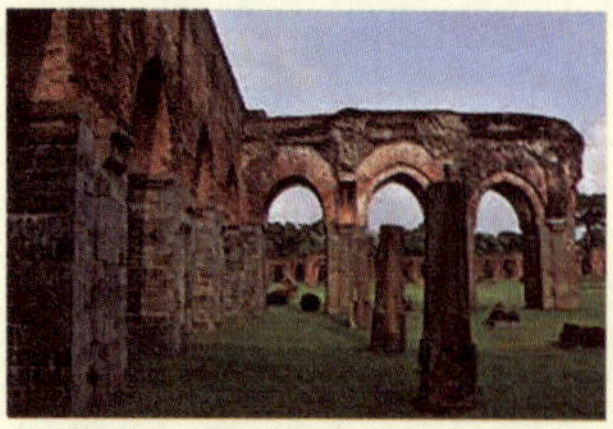 • **Adina Mosque** in Pandua • **Dakhil Darwaza**, Gaur (Malda)	• Local tradition merged with the Islamic influence to create the Bengal style. • Use of sloping roof with cornices which were analogous to the local bamboo construction. • Structures used bricks as chief building material and use of stone was limited to pillars only.
(d) Jaunpur School 1376 CE–1479 CE	• Jami Masjid, Jaunpur, Uttar Pradesh 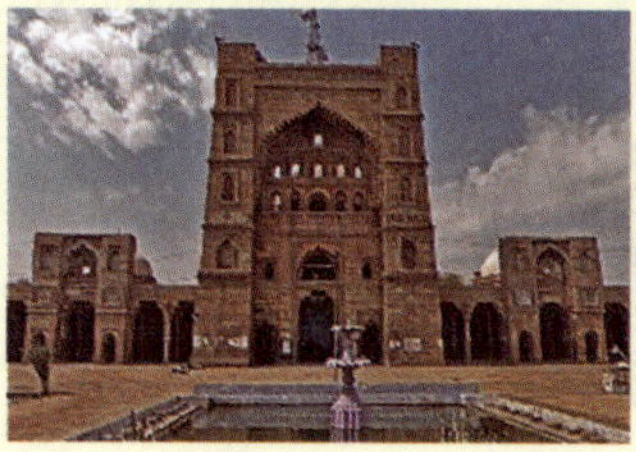 • **The Atala mosque,** Jaunpur • **Lal Darwaja Masjid, Jaunpur**	• Jama Masjid or Jami Masjid or Bari Masjid amongst the largest mosque of this region was built by Hussain Shah in 1470 CE. • The Atala Mosque was built by Sultan Ibrahim of Sharqi rulers. As such, architecture is also called the Sharqi style which is unique as it **did not contain any minars.**

The Deccani Style

(a) The Deccan school	• **Gol Gumbaz** Bijapur, Karnataka • Golconda Fort (Golconda) 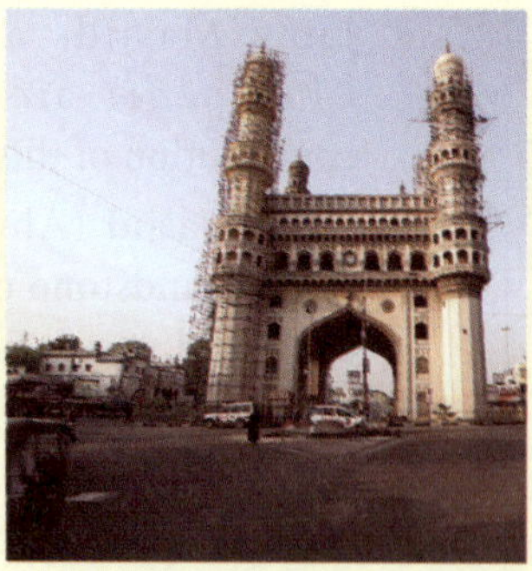 • Charminar (Hyderabad)	• Built by Muhammad Adil Shah (1626–1656) of the Adil Shahi dynasty, it is the largest masonry dome of the world. The central large dome is 57m high and 37m in diameter. Along the drum of the dome is a whispering gallery which is famous for echo and magnification of the sounds. • Built in 1525 by Mohammed Quli Qutub Shah, it was considered an impregnable fort of medieval times. • Built in 1591, it is considered an architectural marvel. The structure gets its name from the four towers (*minars*) which are intricately carved and has stucco decorations. The minars are built in granite and limestone and are 56m high.

MUGHAL ARCHITECTURE

During the rule of Mughals, the Indo-Islamic architecture acquired a new dimension and reached its zenith during the reign of Shah Jahan. The Mughals approached the country and its social ethos differently than the preceding regimes. They came here not as a transitory outsider but made an effort to merge and integrate with the society and rule as its own. This was particularly true for the reign of Akbar. As a result there was greater mingling of cultures. Further, with greater administrative unity, art and architecture also rose to greater heights and architectural marvels like Humanyun's tomb, Agra Fort, Fatehpur Sikri, Taj Mahal, Red Fort, and many other prominent structures emerged. The different rulers, their architectural contributions, and their salient features are being discussed in this section.

Mughal Architecture, Monuments, & Salient Features

Emperors	Important Monuments their and Salient Features
(1) **Babar** (1526–1530 CE)	• Short duration of reign in India • Built a number of gardens and mosques • Prominent mosques include those at **Panipat and Sambhal in Rohilkhand**
(2) **Humayun** (1530–1540 CE and 1550–1566 CE)	• Reign of Humayan was cut short by Sher Shah Suri. He could only regain his reign after the death of Sher Shah Suri. As such, he made no significant contribution to architecture. • **Humayun's Tomb** (Delhi) is a marvel of architecture. It was built after his death by his widow **Bega Begum**. Built on a raised platform in red sandstone with charbagh and water channels running, it **served as a prototype for the Taj Mahal**, which was built later. 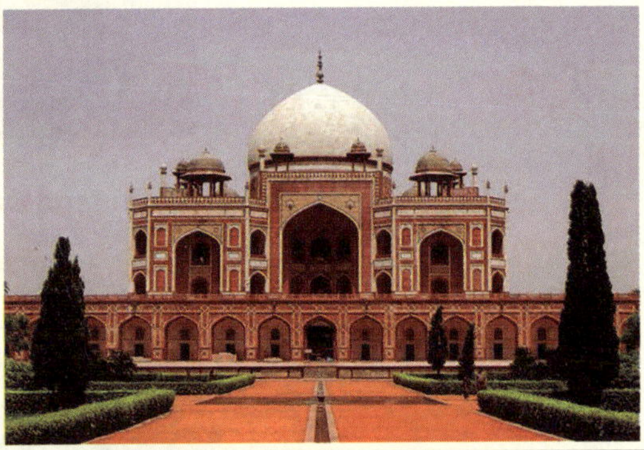
(3) **Sher Shah Suri**	• Although he was not of Mughal dynasty, his short reign left an indelible impact on many fields including architecture. • **Purana Quila** (New Delhi) and **Tomb of Sher Shah** (Sasaram, Bihar) were achievements of this period. • **Purana Quila** had strong and thick defensive walls with little ornamentation. • **Grand Trunk road** was constructed during this period.

(4) **Akbar** (1556–1605)	The nearly 50 year reign saw a number of important structures, viz. • **Agra Fort** – Built in red sandstone, the fort involved a number of Hindu and Islamic construction features. However, many components of this fort were built later during the reign of Shah Jahan. Amar Singh gate, Akbar's Baoli, etc. were built by Akbar, Diwan-i-Khas (Hall of Private audience), Diwan-i-Aam (Hall of Public audience), Moti Masjid (Pearl Mosque), Sheesh Mahal (Turkish Bath), and Khas Mahal (Resting apartment) were built during the reign of Shah Jahan. • **Fatehpur Sikri** (1569–1574) – This was a new capital built by Akbar made of red sandstone which deployed trabeated construction and limited ornamentation. *Some important structures in this complex are:* o **Buland Darwaza** – A massive 55 metres high gateway constructed to commemorate Akbar's successful Gujarat/Deccan campaign. 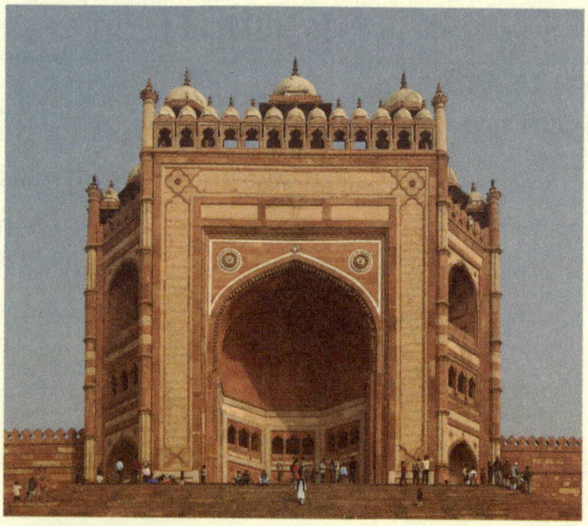 **Buland Darwaza, Fatehpur Sikri** o **Jama Masjid** – A congregational mosque with distinguishing feature of a row of chhatris. 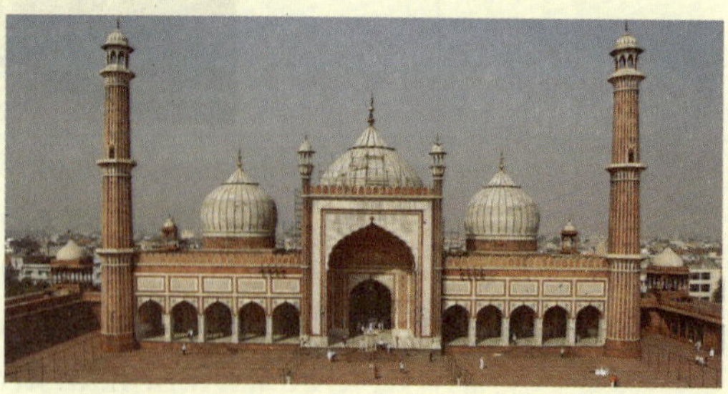 **Jama Masjid, Delhi**

<table>
<tr>
<td></td>
<td>
o Tomb of Salim Chisti – A white marble encased tomb of saint Salim Chisti (revered by Akbar).
o Diwan-i-Aam – Hall of public audience
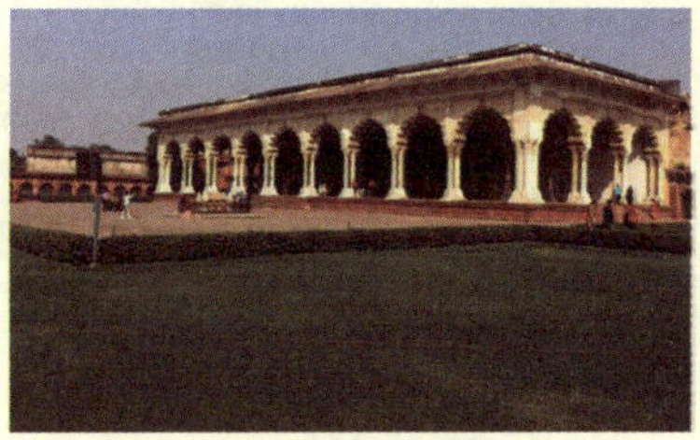
Diwan-i-Aam
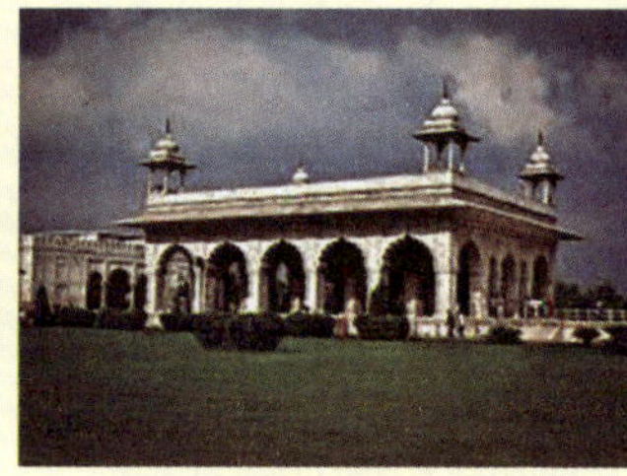
Diwan-i-Khas
o Diwan-i-Khas – Hall of private audience
o Ibadat Khana (House of worship) – Where Akbar laid foundations of Din-e-illahi and discussed religious matters with scholars
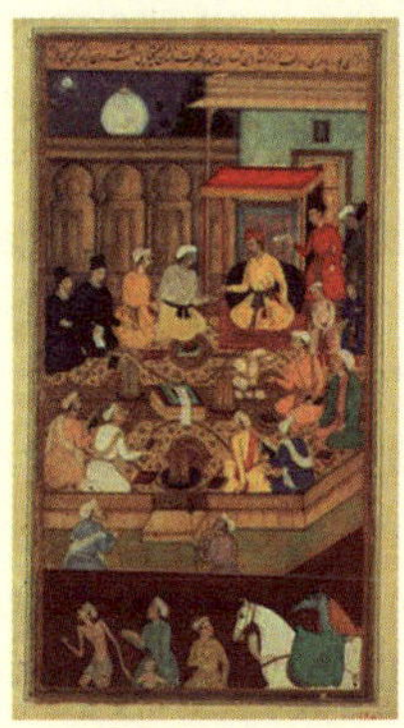
Ibadat Khana
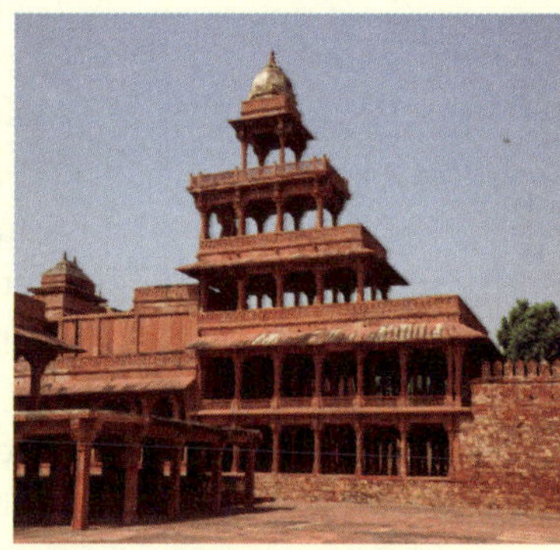
Panch Mahal
o Panch Mahal- A five storey palatial structure with gradually diminishing tiers and a chhatri atop it.
</td>
</tr>
<tr>
<td>(5) Jahangir (1605–1627)</td>
<td>
• Tomb of Akbar; Sikandra (Agra)
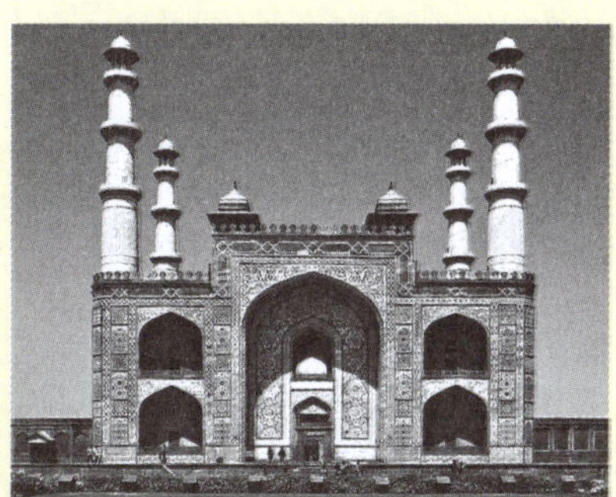
Sikandra, Agra
</td>
</tr>
</table>

<table>
<tr><td></td><td>

- Itmad-Ud-Daula; tomb of Mirza Ghiyas, Prime Minister of Jahangir and father of Noor Jahan (wife of Jahangir)

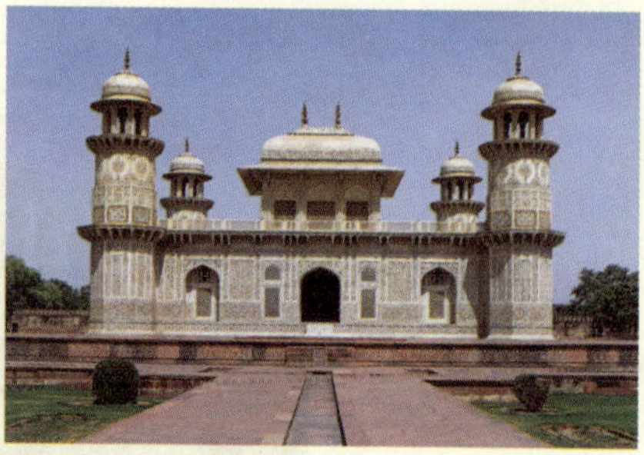

Tomb of Mirza Ghiyas

- **Shalimar Bagh**; Kashmir
- **Moti Masjid**; Lahore
</td></tr>
<tr><td>(6) Shah Jahan</td><td>

- Mughal architecture reached its pinnacle during the reign of Shah Jahan who built the most famous structure the Taj Mahal and many important ones like the Red Fort, Jama Masjid Delhi, city of Shahjahanabad, etc.
- Taj Mahal- Built in memory of Mumtaz Mahal, the Taj is an epitome of architecture owing to its exquisite beauty and proportions.
- Built in white marble with adjoining structures in red sandstone, it has a square structure with chamfered corners giving it an octagonal shape. The structure is recessed with deep arches. Four minarets at corners provide a sense of balance to the structure.
- The structure deploys pietra dura, technique with Arabesque designs, and calligraphy of Koranic verses. Further, the use of Jali works is exquisite.
</td></tr>
</table>

RAJPUT STYLE OF ARCHITECTURE

*The medieval period also saw a number of **palaces** and **forts** built by the Rajput kings. Some of these are described below.*

Forts

(i) **Jaisalmer Fort** – Built in 1156 CE by Rawal Jaisal, it is one of the largest forts with a golden hue in the Sam desert (Jaisalmer).

(ii) **Kumbhalgarh Fort** – Built in 15th century by Rana Kumbha, located in western Aravali, the fort has a massive 38 km long wall.

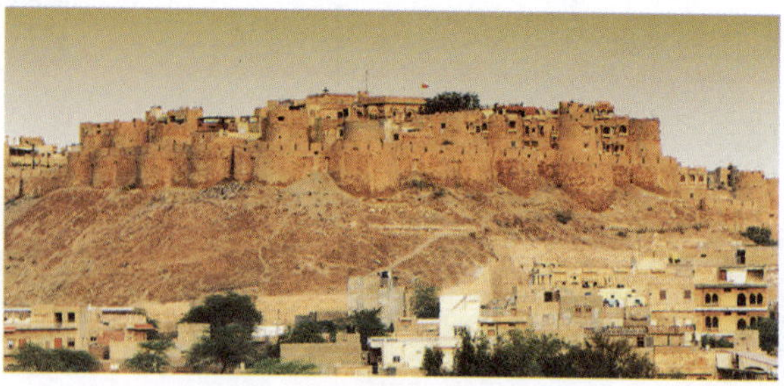

Jaisalmer Fort

(iii) **Chittorgarh Fort** – It is one of the **largest forts** in India, located on a hilltop the fort has a history of attacks and seizes, first by Alauddin Khilji and later by Akbar.

(iv) **Alwar Fort** – Another of the large forts nearly 5 km long and 1.5 km wide, built in 1550 by Hasan Khan Mewati.

(v) **Amer Fort** – Near Jaipur, located on a hilltop, covers an area of 4 km.

Palaces

A number of palaces were built by Rajput kings the most famous being those of **Udaipur** (Lake palace), **Jaipur** (Amer and City palace), and Jodhpur (Umaid Bhavan palace).

Other Structures

- **Hawa Mahal** – This was truly an experiment in architecture. The structure is more of a large façade or a giant screen wall of windows which are in the shape of slightly raised pavilions (over fifty in number). The objective was to allow the queens (and other women of the palace) a view of the royal processions and everyday street scenes without being themselves observed.

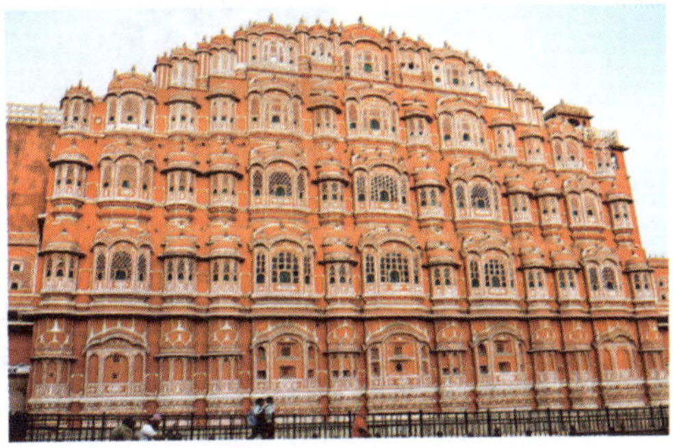

Hawa Mahal, Jaipur

- **Jantar Mantar** – The *Jantar Mantars* were five royal astronomical observatories built by **Raja Sawai Jai Singh** in the 18th century. They were built at **Jaipur, Delhi, Varanasi, Mathura, and Ujjain**. The ones at Delhi and Jaipur are much larger and well preserved. The observatories contain a number of giant sundials and other instruments for recording the movements and locations of sun, moon, and other planets. Indeed, these were an engineering and architectural marvel.

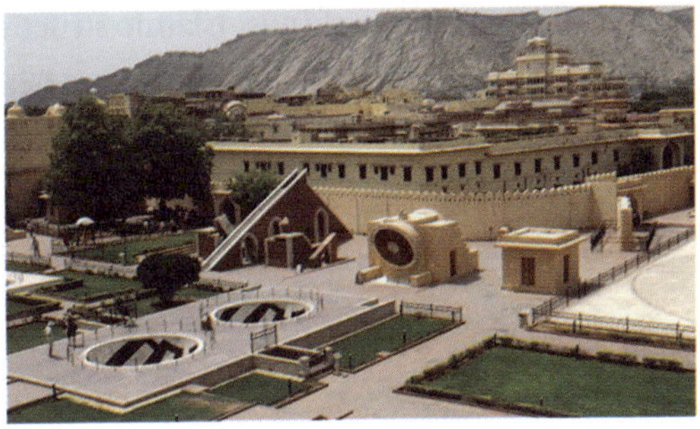

Jantar Mantar, Jaipur

SIKH ARCHITECTURE

With the growth of Sikhism, a number of Sikh structures, particularly the *gurudwaras* came up in the 17th century and later. They incorporated some features of the Indo-Islamic style but they were also progressive and evolving. Features like **use of chhatris, covering of domes by golden or brass plated copper sheets, or use of cupolas** at corners surrounding the main dome, is unique to the Sikh architecture. An example of Sikh style of architecture is the famous **Golden Temple at Amritsar** (the Harmandir Sahib) which was founded by the fourth Sikh Guru in 1577 (Guru Ramdas) but completed by Guru Arjan (the fifth Sikh Guru). Other important structures include **Gurdwara Janam Asthan Nankana Sahib** (Pakistan) and **Keshav Garh Sahib** (Anandpur Sahib, Punjab).

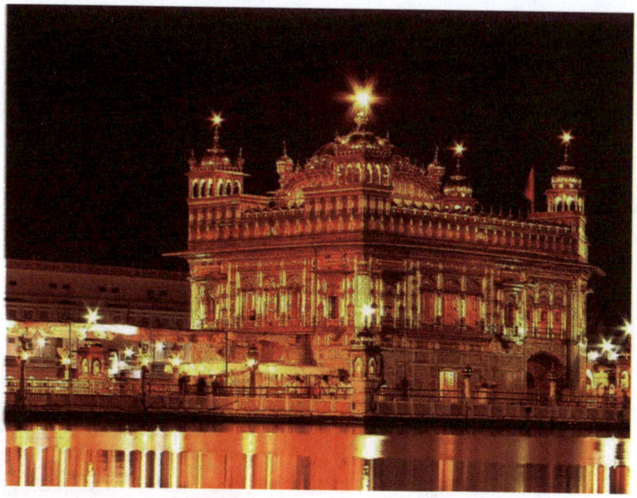

Golden Temple, Amritsar

IMPORTANT TOPICS TO FOCUS ON

- Reasons for emergence of a new form of architecture in India
- Type of structures built and their utility
- Salient features of Indo-Islamic structures and the regional schools
- Influence of Indian architecture on Islamic style of architecture and vice-versa
- Important monuments and their salient features

CHAPTER 10

Medieval India—Other Art Forms: Indian Paintings

Painting is silent poetry, and poetry is painting that speaks

—Plutarch

INTRODUCTION

The tradition of paintings in India has been an ancient one. It has also been as profound a medium of expression of human feelings, thoughts, and aesthetics as other art forms. Right from the days of prehistoric cave paintings to paintings on the walls of temples in South India, from miniature paintings on leaves and paper to the more contemporary on canvas, the story of Indian paintings has been that of continuous change and evolution.

INDIAN PAINTINGS AND THEIR ANTIQUITY

The **Bhimbetka cave paintings** (see box at end of the chapter) are an example of prehistoric cave paintings. Reference to painted palaces are also found in the *Ramayana* and the *Mahabharata*. Further, the Buddhist text *Vinay Pitaka*, gives reference to pleasure halls with walls adorned with pictures and halls painted with designs and figures. One of the most important centres and a veritable treasure trove of paintings is the **Ajanta caves**, which contains paintings on its walls dating from the 2nd century BCE to 7th century CE (see Chapter 6 on ancient Indian art).

This was followed by the cave paintings in **Ellora** (at the end of the first millenia and beginning of the second). While earlier, the location of paintings was restricted to the walls of caves, the medieval period saw adornment of the walls and ceilings of a number of temples in South India with paintings. Such murals are found in the **Pallava, Pandya, Chola, and Nayaka periods**, in the temples of Vijayanagar empire and even in temples in Kerala (in the 16th to 18th century).

The art of painting also saw emergence of a number of local schools such as the **Pala art, the Rajasthan school, the Himachal paintings, the Mughal miniatures,** etc. *These are briefly discussed here.*

ELLORA CAVE PAINTINGS

The Ellora caves are known not only for the **rock-cut caves and great sculptures, but also for mural paintings** found in the Hindu and Jain caves. These paintings date to 8th to 10th century and are found on the ceilings and in some cases on the walls of the Jain temples. *Salient points and features about them are:*

- These are found in five caves. They are somewhat **preserved in the Kailasa temple**.
- The features of the subjects are distinct from that of the earlier Ajanta paintings and is notable for sharp twists of head, sharp nose, elongated, open, and protruding eyes, angular bent of arms, etc.
- The paintings are contained in rectangular panels with wide borders. Thus, they do not have the large spread like the Ajanta paintings.
- Particularly notable paintings are that of the **'Flying Apsaras'** (cave xiii) and painted panel of **'Shiva as Nataraja'** (cave xix).

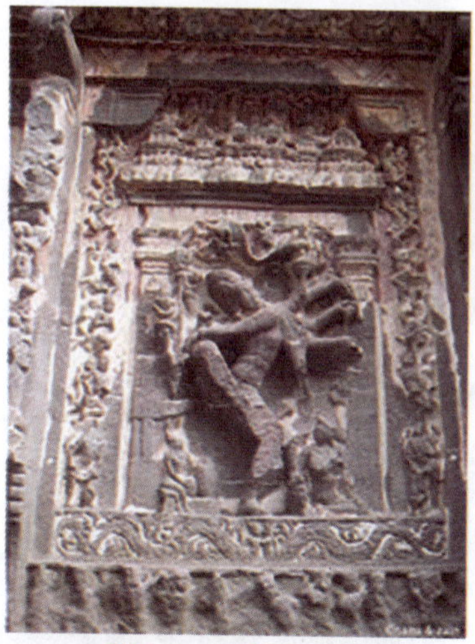

Shiva as Nataraja

MURALS IN SOUTH INDIA

A number of temples in South India came up with mural traditions during the reign of **Pallavas, Pandyas, Cholas, Nayaka period**, and in the Vijayanagar empire.

Important paintings and their salient features are discussed below.

(a) Badami Murals

- These murals were created in the 6th and 7th century CE.
- They are found on the walls of excavated caves in **Badami** (present Karnataka).
- They were patronised by **Chalukyan kings,** particularly **king Mangalesha**. The subjects were of Hindu Gods and deities.
- The walls of the mandapa of cave no. 4 contains the image of **Lord Vishnu**. Some other paintings depict a Chalukyan king watching a dance scene in a palace.

(b) Pallava Murals

- Pallavas who succeeded Chalukyas were patrons of art.
- **Mahendravarman** in the 7th century CE built temples in **Panamali** which contain mural paintings.
- The image at Panamali depicts a graceful image of a **female divinity**.
- Pallava king **Rajsimha** patronised the paintings at **Kanchipuram temple**. However, only traces of the paintings remain in this temple.

(c) Pandya Murals

- The **Tirumalapuram caves** (patronised during the Pandya rule) and **Jaina** caves at **Sittanavasal** contain some paintings of this period.

- The **Sittanavasal** paintings are depicted on ceilings and even on brackets.
- Subject of the paintings are dancing figures of celestial nymphs. The figures are painted in **yellow colour with red outline**. The expression on the face of the dancing figures is subtle and mellow and body postures are suggestive of motion and rhythm.

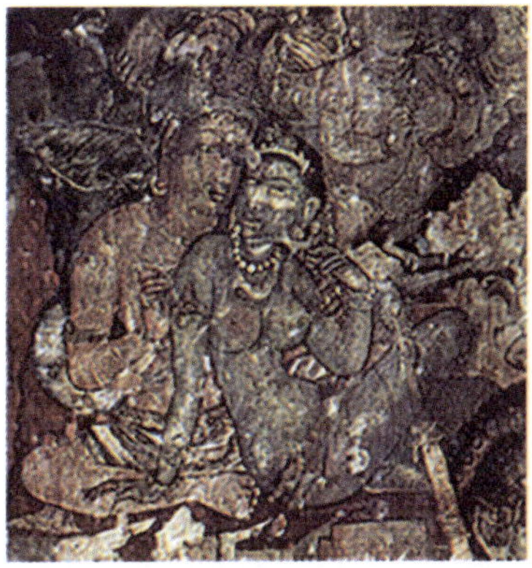

Celestial nymphs, Sittanavasal

(d) Chola Paintings

- Chola kings (9th to 13th century CE) built many great temples embellished with sculptures and paintings. These are Brihadeeswara temple (at Thanjavur), Gangaikondacholapuram, and Darasuram temples.
- The art of painting reached its zenith during the reigns of **Raja Raja Chola** and his son Rajendra Chola.
- **Brihadeeswara temple** contains paintings on walls in the narrow passage surrounding the shrine. Two layers of paint have been discovered. The outer layer pertains to the Nayaka period (16th century CE).
- Subjects of the paintings are those related to **Lord Shiva; Shiva as Nataraja, Shiva in mount Kailash,** etc. Some images are that of the patron king Raja Raja Chola and some are dancing figures.

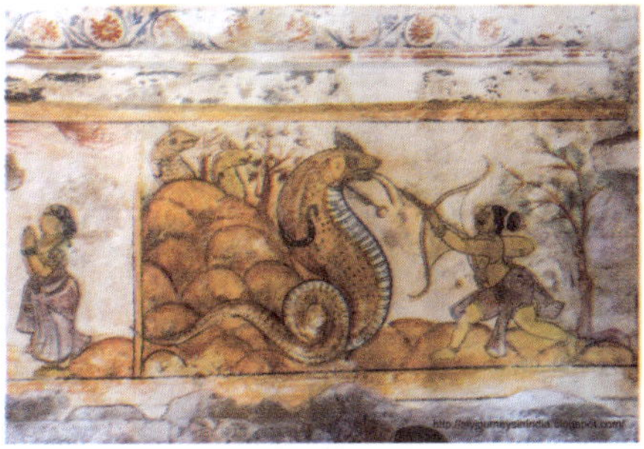

Thanjavur painting

- Paintings are mature in style with supple human figures and reflect the evolution of paintings over a period of lime.

(e) Vijayanagar Murals

- After the decline of the Chola period, the art of painting emerged only in the 16th century in the Vijayanagar empire.
- A number of paintings are found at **Tiruparakunram** (near Tiruchirapalli), **Virupaksha temple** at **Hampi,** and **Lepakshi temple near Hindurpur** in Andhra Pradesh.
- The paintings at **Tiruparakunram** pertain to the 14th century CE and represent the early phase of the Vijayanagar style.
- The paintings at **Virupaksha temple** are **depicted on the ceilings of the** temple. They contain images/scenes from Ramayana and Mahabharata.

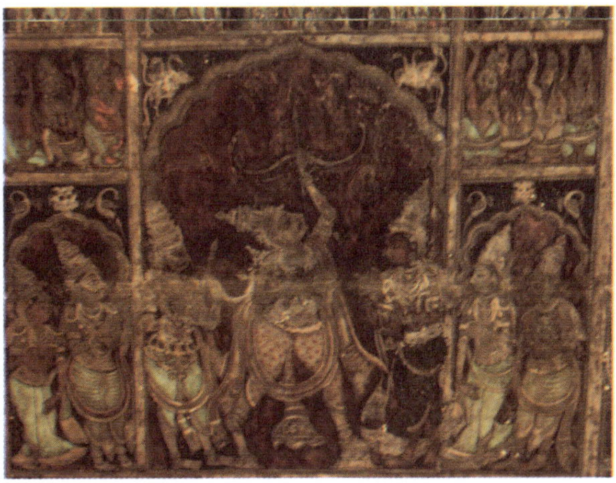

Painted Ceiling at Virupaksha Temple

- At **Lepakshi** the paintings are depicted **on the walls of the Shiva temple**.
- The paintings of the Vijayanagar period are evolved. The face and body figures are in proportion and objects and human figures are depicted in two dimensions.

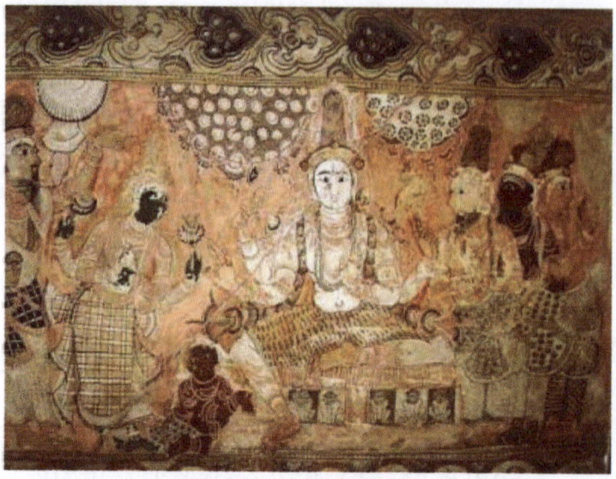

Lepakshi Paintings

(f) Nayaka Paintings

- The Nayaka paintings pertain to the 17th and 18th century and are found in **Thiruparakundram**, **Sreerangam**, **Tiruvarur**, and other places.
- The paintings at **Thiruparakundram** pertain to two distinct periods, the 14th century and the 17th century. The early paintings are depicting scenes from the **life of Vardhaman Mahavira**, while the latter ones depict scenes from *Ramayana*, *Mahabharata*, and even *Krishna Leela*.
- The paintings at Tiruvarur contain a panel which narrates the story of Muchukunda.
- In Chidambaram, there are panels depicting stories related to Lord Shiva and Lord Vishnu (as Mohini).
- At Chengam (Arcot district) the **Sri Krishna temple contains 60 panels** depicting scenes from the Ramayana. These represent the later phase of the Nayaka paintings.
- The Nayaka paintings are considered to be an extension of the Vijayanagar style with minor modifications and extensions.

(g) Kerala Murals

This style of painting evolved in Kerala in the 16th to the 18th century CE.

- The style of paintings can be said to have taken cues from the Nayaka and the Vijayanagar paintings, yet it incorporated the local traditions such as that of Kathakali and thus emerged as a distinct style.
- The figures are **depicted in three dimensions**. Luminous and vibrant colours are used to depict human figures.
- Paintings are depicted on walls of temples and subjects are from Hinduism. They depict the scenes from **local versions of** ***Ramayana*** and *Mahabharata*.

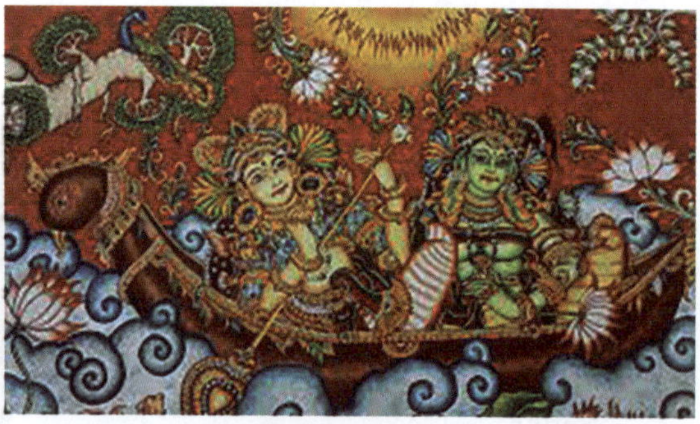

Kerala mural

- Nearly 60 sites have been found and these include:
  - Pundareekapuram Krishna temple, Thrissur Vadakkumnathan temple, and Triprayar Sri Rama temple.
  - Krishnapuram palace in Kayamkulam, Padamanabhapuram palace, and Dutch palace in Kochi.

MINIATURE PAINTINGS AND DIFFERENT SCHOOLS

Miniature paintings refer to the paintings which were **smaller in size but quite detailed in depiction.** These were in contrast to the murals which were painted on the walls and ceilings of caves and temples and provided a vast space for the artist to work upon. The miniatures would be painted on a **variety of surfaces including palm leaf, paper, cloth, etc.** and would be more perishable as compared to the murals. This art developed in around the 9th to the 10th century CE **in the Pala period,** who can be said to be the pioneers of this art. Later, miniatures also flourished in other school of arts, viz the **Mughal miniatures, Rajasthan school of painting, Pahari style of painting**, South Indian miniatures, and folk paintings.

The salient features of different styles and schools of painting are discussed briefly below.

PALA SCHOOL OF ART

- This is the **earliest example of Indian miniature painting** which flourished during the **Pala rule** in eastern part of India (750 CE to 1150 CE). The Pala art reached its peak in around the **9th and 11th century**.
- The subjects of these paintings were those related to **Buddhism,** viz. Lord Buddha, Bodhisattvas, or other characters from the Buddhist literature.
- The Buddhist Mahaviharas of Nalanda, Vikramshila, Odantpuri, and Somarupa were important centres of this art.
- The paintings were made usually on palm leaves. It was a naturalistic style of painting which had subdued tones of colour and employed curly and sinuous lines.
- Example of this style of painting is in the manuscript of *Astasahasrika Prajnaparamita* (executed in Nalanda monastery). The manuscript has illustration of six pages and on inside of wooden covers (Painting is located at Bodleian Library in Oxford, England).

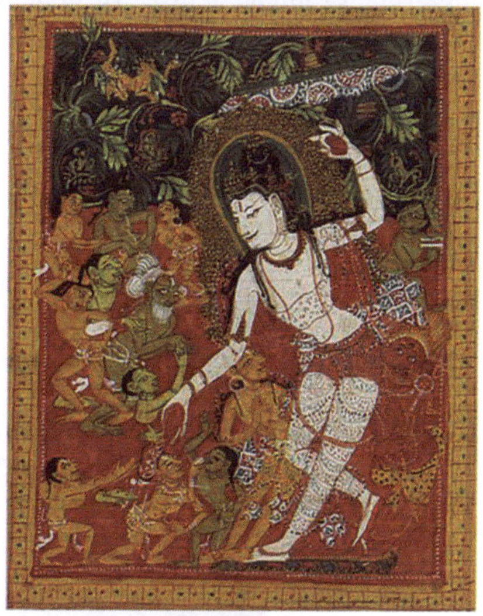

Pala painting

- This art form became almost extinct due to destruction of the Buddhist monasteries at the hands of Muslim invaders.

WESTERN INDIAN SCHOOL

- This school of painting was in vogue in the **Gujarat**, **Malwa,** and **Rajasthan** region under the reign of the **Chalukyan** kings from middle of the 10th century to 13th century CE.
- The subjects of paintings were taken from **Jain religious texts**. These were often commissioned by rich Jain merchants.
- These paintings were usually made on **palm leaf** (which was used for making manuscripts) and later paper was used.
- The paintings employed distortion of physical traits, such as protruding and elongated eyes, large hips, breasts, etc. Use of colours is vigorous and lends a vitality to the paintings.
- Examples of this school of painting are contained in two Jain texts: the *Kalpasutra* and the *Kalchakra Katha*.

MUGHAL SCHOOL

- The Mughal school of painting emerged during the reign of Akbar, who had an avid interest in this art form. This school flourished from **1560-1800** CE.
- The Mughal style was a synthesis of the **indigenous Indian style** of painting and the **Persian style of painting**.
- The paintings were high in aesthetics and accuracy of representation of human figures. **They were naturalistic** paintings based on observations. The paintings deployed **vibrant colours** (like gold, blue, etc.).

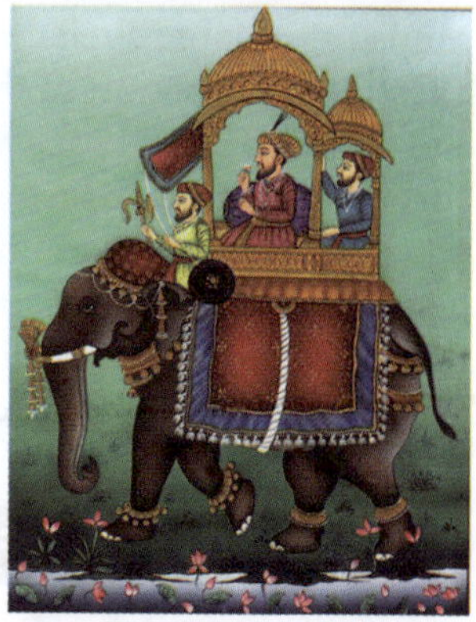

Persian Style Painting

Important examples of this style of paintings are contained in:

- *Tuti-nama*: It is a first work of Mughal school
- *Hamza-nama*: It contains illustration on cloth in seventeen volumes
- *Razm-nama*: It is a Persian translation of *Mahabharata*
- *Akbar-nama*: Written by Abul Fazal, this chronicle of Akbar's reign contains several paintings as illustration of the texts.

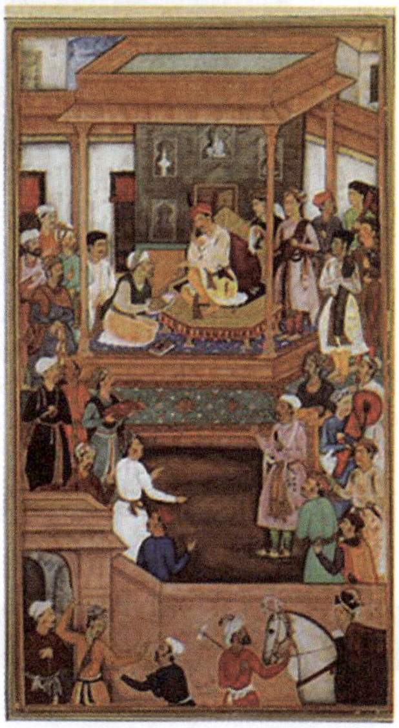

Akbarnama Painting

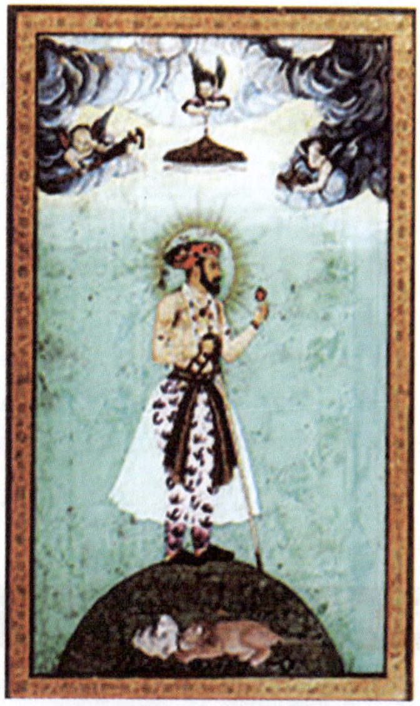

Shahjahan on Globe

- *Babar-nama*: It is an account/journal of Babar, translated in Persian during the reign of Akbar and also illustrated
- *Tarikh-e-Khandane Taimuria*: It recounts the history of Timurids (Timur and his successors) in an illustrated manuscript
- *Ayar-i-Danish*: An animal fable book
- *Portrait of Jahangir*
- *Portrait of Shahjahan* on a globe.

THE DECCANI SCHOOLS

Deccani schools flourished in the centres of Bijapur, Ahmedabad, and Golconda in the 16th and 17th century CE. Initially, the style of painting of these centres was independent of the Mughal style but later period paintings have increasing Mughal influence.

The important centres and styles of paintings are as below.

(a) Ahmednagar style: The volume of poems written by Hussain Nizam Shah I of Ahmednagar (1553–1565) is contained in a manuscript *Tarif-i-Hussain Shahi*. This is an illustrated manuscript and is the earliest example of this style of painting. The use of colours (such as golden sky) is rich and brilliant and has a distinct Persian influence.

(b) Bijapur style: This style of painting was patronised by **Adil Shah I** (1550–80 CE) and has successors. The document *Najum-Al-Ulum* (Stars of sciences) was illustrated by nearly 876 miniatures. The paintings have influences of the Lepakshi mural paintings (as seen in the dress and appearances of the ladies) as well as Persian influence (evident in the Arabesque design and use of golden colour).

(c) Golconda style: This style flourished during the reign of **Quli Qutab Shah** (1580–1611). The paintings usually contain court scenes. The style of painting absorbed the traditions of Vijayanagar style as well as the influences of the Mughal style.

(d) Hyderabad style: The painting style flourished during the reign of **Asaf-Jahi dynasty** (founded by Nizam-ul-Mulk in 1724 AD). The paintings included court scenes and portraits. They were rich in colour and appearance. Its distinctive features were observed in the treatment in paintings, of costumes, jewellery, colours, landscape, flora-fauna, etc.

(e) Tanjore style: This style flourished in the 18th and 19th CE. One example of this painting (presently in National museum) depicts the coronation of Rama. The typical feature of this style was the conical crown drawn in the paintings.

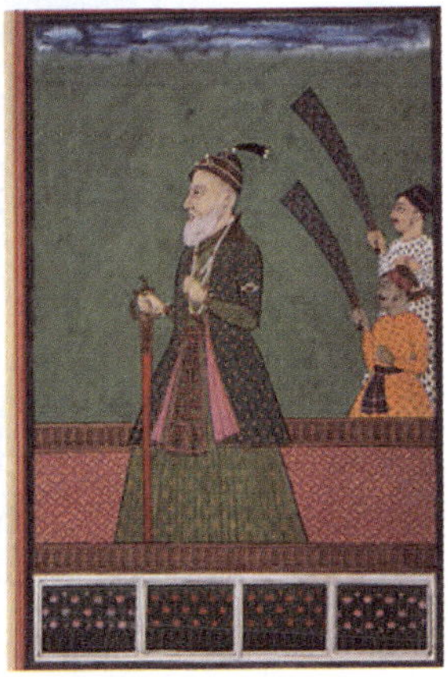

Hyderabad Paintings

CENTRAL INDIAN AND RAJASTHANI SCHOOLS

- These schools were rooted in the Indian Hindu traditions and had profound influence of the **Hindu texts and epics whose scenes were depicted**. Besides, the paintings were also influenced by the various sects of Vaishnavism, Shaivism, and Shaktism. The cult of Sri Krishna was quite popular in all these schools and paintings contained scenes from the Ramayana, Mahabharata, Bhagvata Purana, the Siva Purana, etc. Besides literary works such as *Gita Govinda* of Jayadeva, *Rasmanjari* of Bhanudatta, *Rasikpriya* of Kesavadasa, and *Ragmala* of Bihari were important subjects on which the paintings were based.
- Early paintings of these schools belong to the 16th century CE. The early paintings were based on the local style of western India and the *Chaurapanchasika* style—(A love poem written by Kashmiri Pandit Bilhana on which a series of paintings were based). However, the Mughal influence spread in the 17th and 18th century to these schools also.

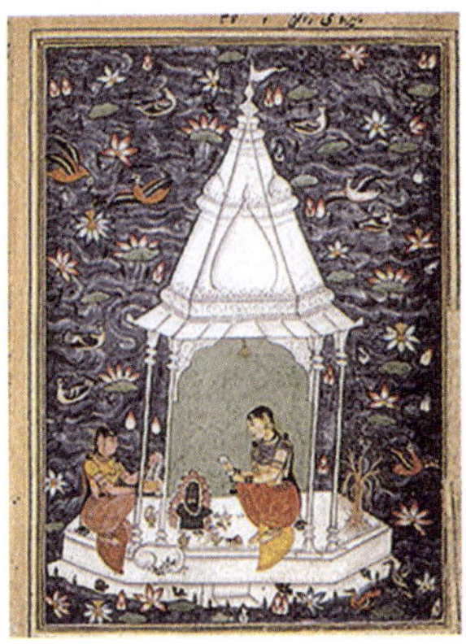

Ragmala

- The Rajasthani paintings are known for their bold drawing and contrasting colours. However, the figures drawn in these paintings are rather flat without being depicted in a natural manner and lacking perspective. The later influence of Mughal style brought in some elements of naturalism with the introduction of landscapes, trees, etc.
- The different centres/subschools of Rajasthani painting and important works of art are as below:
  (a) ***Mewar:*** Known for the *Ragmala* series painted in 1605 CE
  (b) ***Malwa:*** Known for the *Rasikpriya* series (1634 CE) and *Amarusataka* series (1652 CE).

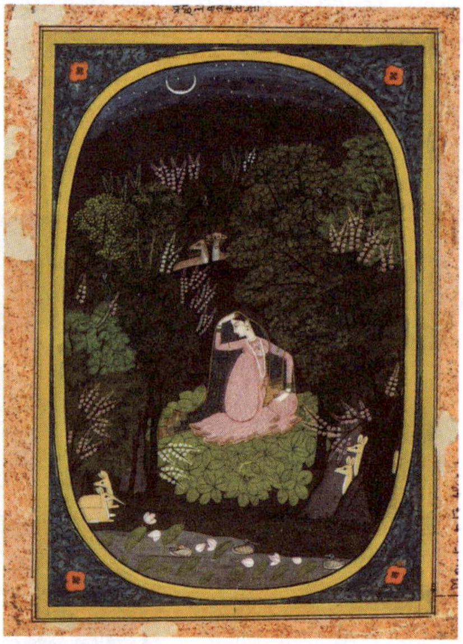

Rasikpriya Series

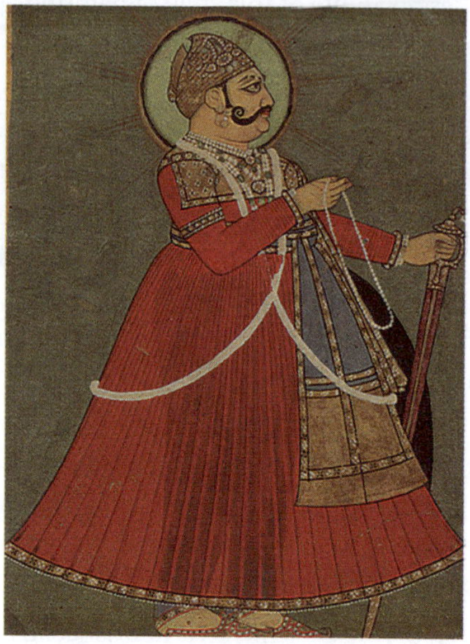

Jaipur Ruler

  (c) ***Bundi:*** Manuscript of *Bhagwat Purana* and *Rasikpriya* series of late 17th century.
  (d) ***Amer:*** Jaipur: Portraits of Jaipur rulers.
  (e) ***Bikaner:*** Painting of Krishna and Radha (18th century CE)
  (f) ***Marwar:*** *Ragmala* series (17th century CE)
  (g) ***Kota:*** Scenes of hunting in forests
  (h) ***Kishangarh:*** Paintings of Radha and Krishna (mid 18th century) by master painter Nihal Chand and also the famous painting of *Bani Thani* belong to this school.

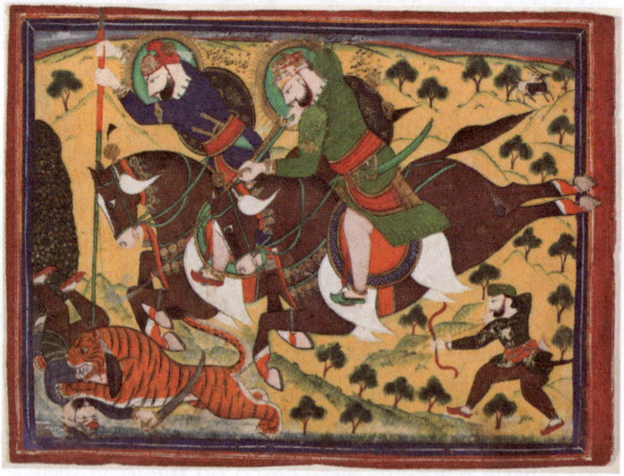

Kota Painting (Hunting)

PAHARI SCHOOLS

The Pahari school of painting refers to the indigenous style of painting developed in the states of Jammu and Kashmir, Himachal, and Almora region of Uttarakhand. The paintings can be classified into subgroups based on the centre of development. Like the Rajasthan schools they also drew their **subjects from the Hindu Epics**, Puranas, and literary works such as the *Gita Govinda* and *Satsai*.

- The painting style is **naturalistic** and the faces and human figures are well modelled. The paintings are seen to be using strong colours and facial appearances show variations from region to region.

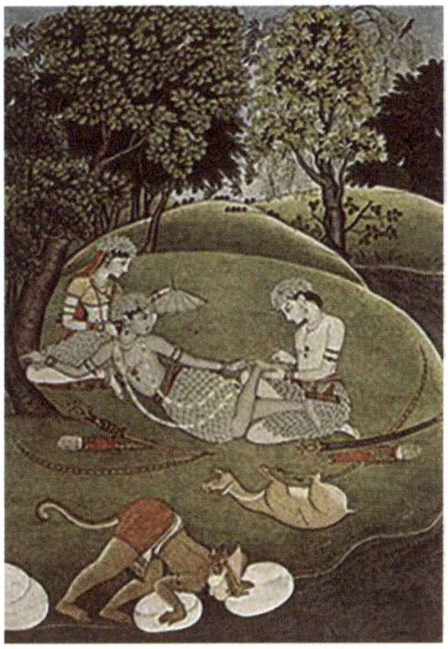

Kangra Painting

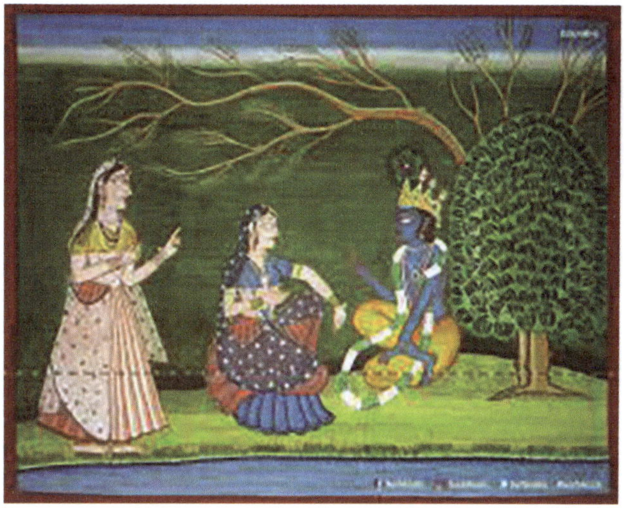

Basholi Painting

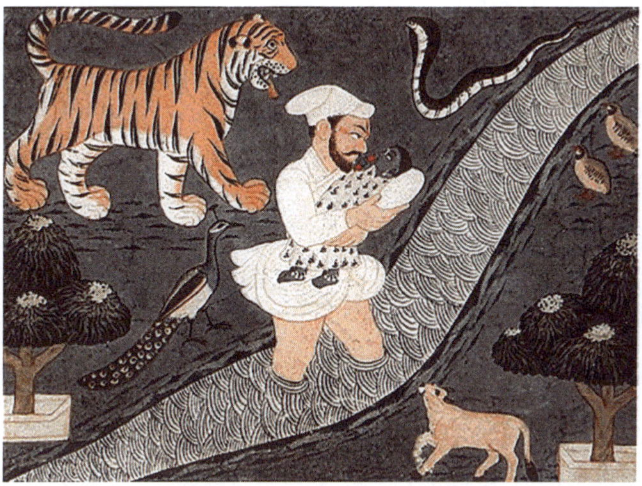

Kullu Mandi Painting

- Important centres/subschools are the **Kangra, Basholi, Guler, and Kullu-Mandi** style.

Prehistoric Cave Paintings

Prehistoric paintings refer to paintings and rock engravings which were found on the walls of caves and pertain to the prehistoric period (that period of human history which precedes the period for which the first written or documentary account appears. These include the Paleolithic, the Mesolithic, and Chalcolithic ages). In India, a number of sites have been discovered containing numerous prehistoric rock paintings. Most important of these are *Bhimbetka caves* (near Bhopal), *Lakhudiyar caves* in Kumaon (Uttarakhand), *Piklihal* and *Tekalakotta* in Karnataka, *Kupagallu in* Telangana, and Jogimara caves in Madhya Pradesh.

(a) **Bhimbetka caves:** Located nearly 55 kms from Bhopal in Vindhya ranges, Bhimbetka site **contains more than 800 shelters, five hundred of which bear such paintings.** The images depict events in daily life of prehistoric humans, including hunting, dancing, music, animals, elephant riders, and other household scenes. These paintings have been classified into seven historical periods, the most important of which are Period 1 or Upper Paleolithic; Period 2 or Mesolithic, and Period 3 or Chalcolithic.

- ***Upper Palaeolithic paintings:*** These are linear representations of animals like elephants, tigers, rhinos, bisons, etc. Humans are shown typically as stick-like figures. The different figures are usually painted in green and dark red. Some geometric patterns are also found.
- ***Mesolithic period paintings:*** Maximum number of paintings belong to this period (Period 2). The subjects are largely scenes of hunting or group hunting with a variety of weapons such as spears, bows, and arrows sticks, etc. A large number of animals, men, women, children and even the old have been depicted. Paintings also contain images of community dancing, gathering of honey, women preparing food, etc.
- ***Chalcolithic period:*** This period's (Period 3) paintings reflect further evolution of the society. They depict the exchange of the requirement of the dwellers of these caves with the agricultural communities in the Malwa plains.

  One rock of Bhimbetka is referred to as a **'Zoo rock'** due to depiction of a large number of animals together, viz. elephant, sambhar, bison, deer, peacock, snake, etc.

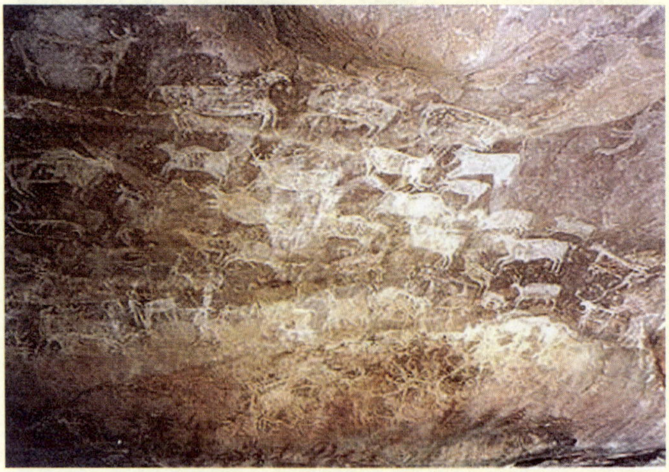

Bhimbetka Zoo Rock

(b) **Lakhudiyar caves in Uttarakhand:** *Lakhudiyar* literally means 'one lakh caves'. These are a group of rock caves/shelters in the Almora region. The paintings are divided into three distinct categories, those of human beings, of animals, and of geometric patterns. Humans are quite distinct as they are seen to be having a stick-like appearance. Images of long snouted fox and multiple legged lizard are many. Paintings here use red ochre, white, and black colours.

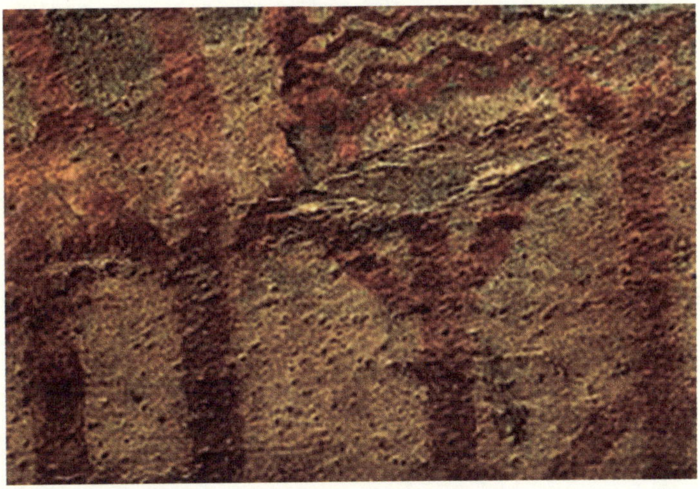

Lakhudiyar Paintings

IMPORTANT TOPICS TO FOCUS ON

- Important centre of murals and important works of art.
- Important centres of miniature painting/schools of painting in medieval time.
- Influence of Persian and Mughal school of art on the indigenous schools.
- Characteristic features of various important styles of painting.
- Prominent examples of the painting style/schools of painting.

CHAPTER 11

Medieval India—Other Art Forms: Bronze Sculptures

I saw the angel in the marble and carved until I set him free.

—Michelangelo

BRONZE SCULPTURE TRADITION

India has had a long tradition of making bronze sculptures right from ancient times. However, it was in the medieval period that making of bronze statues and sculptures reached its peak, particularly during the 9th to 14th century CE, **during the reign of the Pala kings** (in eastern part of India) and the **Chola kings** in the southern part of India. In this phase of history, the art of bronze sculptures not only flourished but even competed with other forms of sculpture, viz. terracotta and stone carving. Although the bronze sculptures would be usually smaller in size as compared to the stone sculptures, however they would be characterised by exquisite beauty and great aesthetic appeal. The bronze statues and sculptures would be produced by the traditional '**lost wax' process** (*See Box*). The subjects of these sculptures were mostly **Hindu gods and goddesses, Buddha, Bodhisattvas,** images from Buddhist scriptures, and life of Buddha.

Lost Wax Process

The bronze sculptures (bronze is an alloy of copper, zinc, and tin) were traditionally made by using the lost wax technique of casting. In this technique, first a wax model of the statue to be made is prepared. This is done using refined pure bees wax. The model is then coated with a mixture of wet clay, sand, and cow dung which is allowed to dry. This figure is heated allowing the molten wax to drain out through a tiny hole. The molten metal (which is nearly ten times in weight of the wax used) is poured and allowed to be solidified. Later, the cast is chiseled and polished.

IMPORTANT BRONZE SCULPTURES OF ANCIENT INDIA

- The bronze statue of **dancing girl** (*Tribhanga* posture) from **Mohenjo-daro** dating to 2500 BCE.
- Sculpture of a **bronze chariot** found at **Daimabad** (Maharashtra) dating to 1500 BCE.
- Several sculptures of **Jain Tirthankaras** discovered at **Chausa in Bihar** dating to the 2nd century CE (belonging to the Kushana period). Notable among

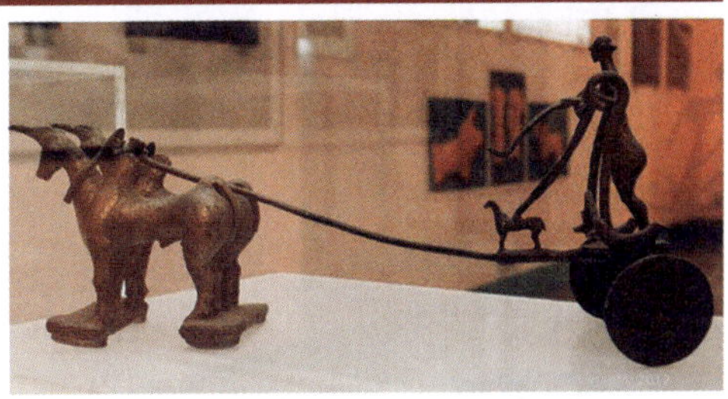

Bronze Statue, Daimabad

them is the image of **Rishabhnath** (first Tirthankara who is identifiable by his long hair (locks up till shoulder) unlike other Tirthankars who are shown having short hair).

- The bronze sculptures also include several images of Buddha (particularly in **Abhaya mudra**) made during the Gupta and post-Gupta periods. These are notable for the **serene and youthful appearance** of the Buddha **and the folds of transparent drapery**. Statues belonging to this period have been found at **Dhanesar Khera** (Uttar Pradesh) (which are similar to the images of Buddha in the **Mathura school**), **Sultanganj** in Bihar (similar to that of **Sarnath school**), and **Phopnar** in Maharashtra (similar to that of Amravati school).

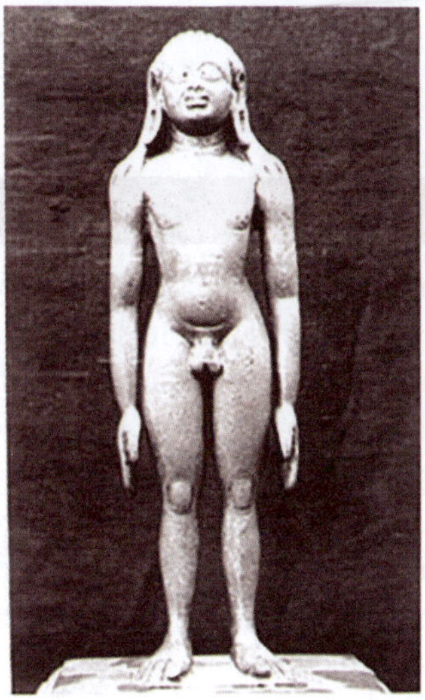

Rishabhnath

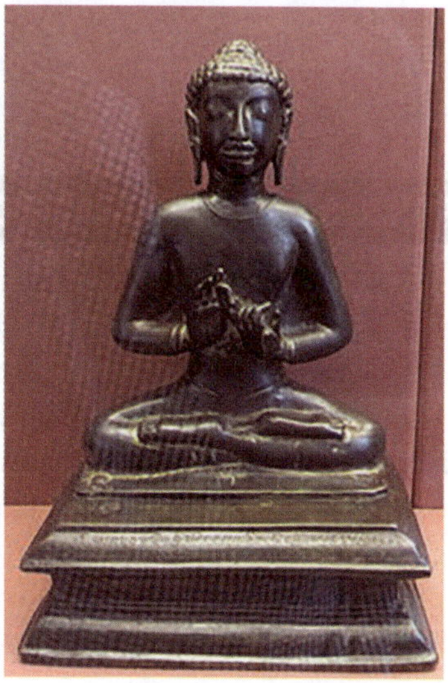

Danesar Khera Buddha

THE PALA ART OF BRONZE SCULPTURES

The Pala dynasty reigned in the eastern part of the country (present Bengal, Bihar, and Bangladesh) from the 8th to 12th century CE. The art in this period is captured in bronze sculptures and palm leaf paintings (miniatures). The subjects of the sculptures were **Buddha** or those **related to Buddhism** and at times Hindu deities. The Pala art carried forward the Gupta tradition (of the Sarnath School of Art) and is known for the **ornamental detail of the sculptures,** particularly the folds of the drapery. The centre of Pala art was **Kurkihar near Nalanda** (Bihar) and the art influenced far off centres even in Southeast Asia, Nepal, Tibet, etc.

Important specimens of this school of art are:

- Statue of four armed **Avalokitesvara in Tribhanga** posture.
- Statue of **Tara** seated on a throne in Abhaya mudra.
- Statue of **Buddha** in Abhaya mudra.
- Bronze figure of **Balarama**.

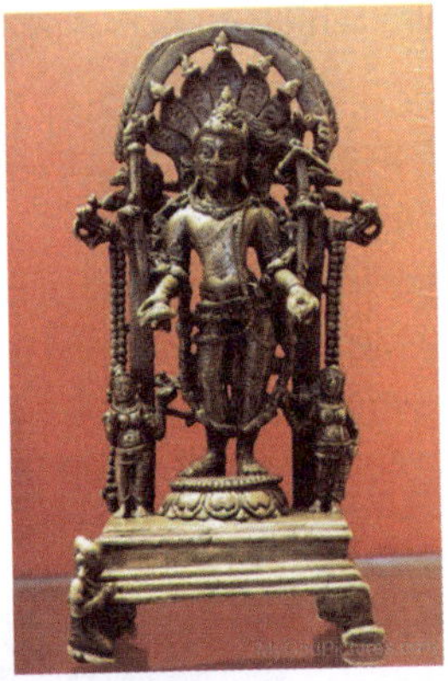

Bronze statue of Balarama

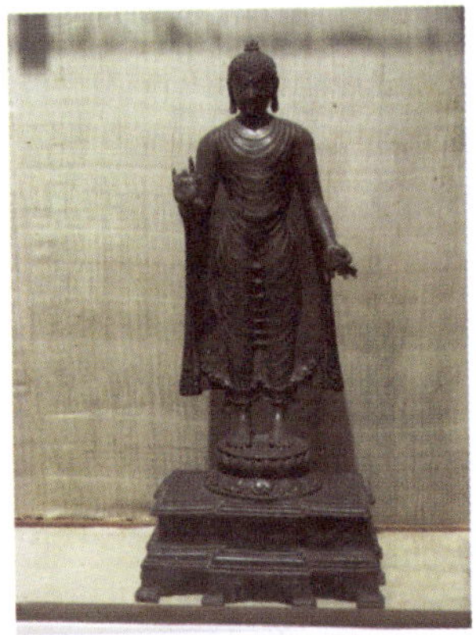

Kurkihar Buddha bronze statue

BRONZE ART IN SOUTH INDIA

South India had a rich tradition of bronze sculptures which was popular in the reign of the Pallavas, the Cholas, and the Vijayanagar empire. The technique used for casting the sculptures was the same as in North and East India which was the lost wax process but the sculptures were mostly of **Hindu gods and goddesses**, particularly of **Lord Shiva**.

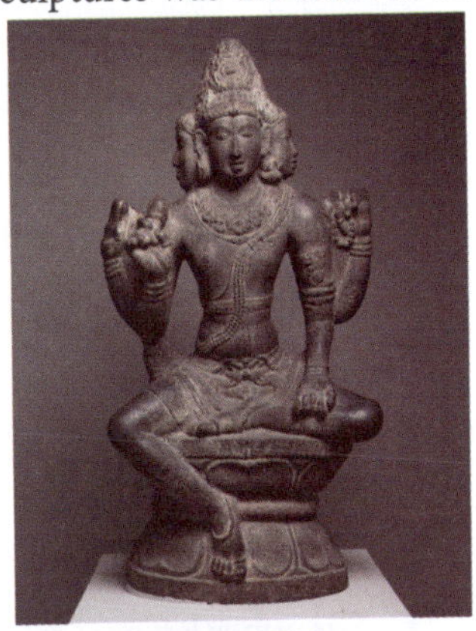

Pallava Shiva

(a) **The Pallava Bronze Sculpture:** This flourished during the 8th to 9th century CE. The most famous sculpture of this period is that of **Lord Shiva in a seated position** in *Ardhaparyanka asana* (with one leg kept dangling). His right hand is in the *Achamana mudra* indicating that he is about to drink poison).

(b) **Chola Bronze Art:** The period 10th to 12th century CE was a golden period of Chola bronze art. Chola queen **Sembiyan Mahadevi** was its important patron.

- The sculpture of **Shiva as Nataraja** is the **most famous Chola bronze art** which evolved during this period.

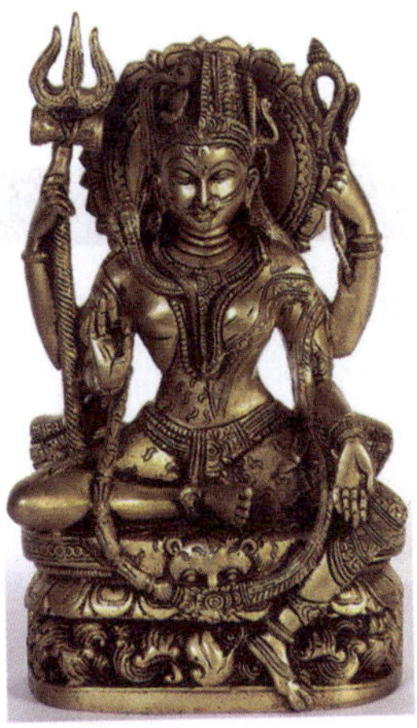

Ardhanarishvara statue

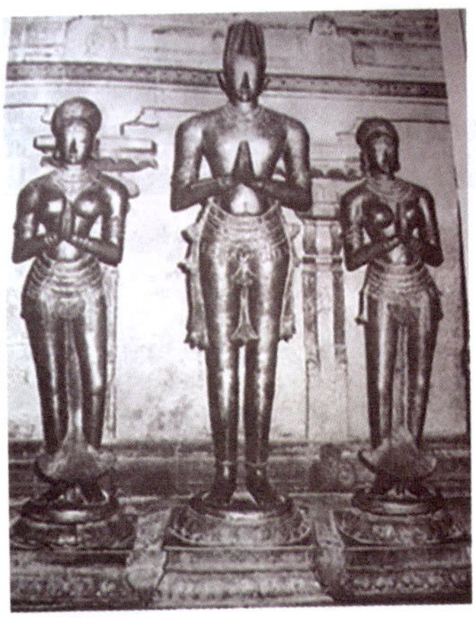

Krishnadevaraya and Two Queens, Tirupati

- Another remarkable bronze icon is the *Kalyansundaramurti* which depicts *Panigrahana* (marriage ceremony) of Shiva with Parvati.
- The *Ardhnarishvara* which is the union of Shiva and Parvati in a singular image, is another important icon depicting Parvati in the *Tribhanga posture*.

(c) **Vijayanagar Bronze Sculpture Art:** The bronze sculpture art dried up at the end of Chola period (early 14th century). However, the peace and prosperity of the Vijayanagar empire enabled the bronze sculpture art to flourish there, in the 16th century CE. The **life-size standing statue of king Krishnadevaraya and his two queens (at Tirupati)** is an example of the Vijayanagar bronze sculpture art.

The Nataraja Statue and its Symbolism

The Nataraja statue is a famous piece of bronze sculpture which depicts Lord Shiva performing the *Tandava. The following are its salient points and symbolic meaning:*

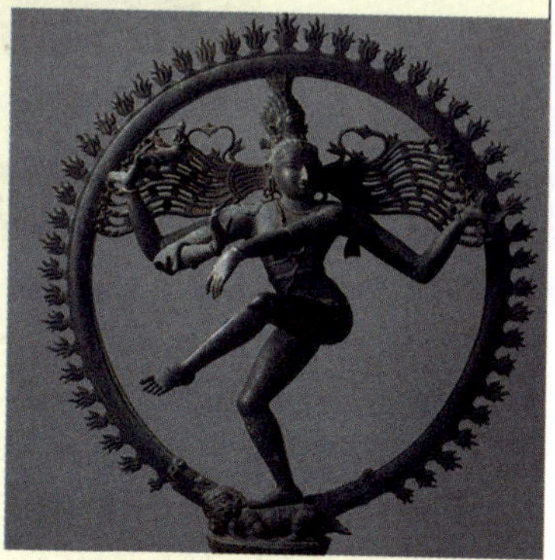

Shiva as Nataraja

- *Nataraja* means the Lord (king) of performers (dancers).
- The *Tandava* dance is a **cosmic dance** which symbolised the end of the physical world and the beginning of another.
- Lord Shiva is shown to be having **four hands** and **two legs** and balancing on a single leg in a specific dance posture.
- His right leg is seen to be **suppressing a demon** which symbolises ignorance. Thus, it implies **suppression of ignorance.**
- His left leg is raised and is seen to be kicking away (*Bhujangtrasita* stance). It symbolises **pushing away of the Maya** (illusion) from the mind of the devotees.
- His main right hand is in ***Abhaya mudra*** bestowing protection to devotees from ignorance and fear.
- His upper right hand holds *Damaru* from which cosmic beats emanates.
- His upper left arm carries a flame while the other left arm is held in *Dola hasta* and connects with right arm in Abhaya mudra (*Abhaya hasta*).
- The image is seen surrounded by a flame symbolising the entire universe.

IMPORTANT TOPICS TO FOCUS ON

- Important centres of bronze art and its features
- Important bronze sculptures and its features
- Lost wax process
- Nataraja figure and symbolism

12

CHAPTER

Literature in Medieval India

> Great literature is simply language charged with meaning to the utmost possible degree
>
> **—Ezra Pound**

EVOLUTION OF MEDIEVAL LITERATURE

The medieval period saw some major changes in the realm of languages and literature. With the establishment of the Delhi Sultanate and later the Mughal rule, quite like other art forms, the Persian influence on the Indian languages and literature was prominent. Further, the wave of Bhakti movement from 14th to 16th century had an indelible impact on the literary scene and led to many local languages coming in prominence and also to emergence of Hindi.

Some of the salient changes in this period are as below:

- The **emergence of Hindi and the local languages** took place. The compositions of the different Bhakti saints were **invariably in the local languages**. This led to the growth of local languages and dialects, many of which are recognised even today in the Constitution. Growth of *Apabhramsa* from *Prakrit* took place which **led to the evolution of modern Hindi**. The works of **Surdas** (in Brajbhasha) and Tulsidas (in Awadhi) were not in Sanskrit but in the local languages from which Hindi evolved.
- **Persian** was recognised as the **official language of the Delhi Courts** (in the Delhi Sultanate and Mughal empire). This led to a number of important works being composed in Persian such as that of the famous poet **Amir Khusrau**.
- The **emergence of a new language Urdu** took place which evolved under the influence of the *Apabhramsa and* other extant Indian languages, Persian and Arabic. While it retained the Persian script, the words and grammar were deeply influenced by the Indian languages. Many poets like Mirza Ghalib have richly contributed to the growth of this language. Even in the British period it was one of the languages of administration along with English in North India.
- A number of literary works were composed during this period which also richly contributed to philosophy, arts, science, etc. *The important developments in literature of this period are highlighted below.*

LITERATURE DURING THE BHAKTI MOVEMENT

The Bhakti movement had profound influence on the Indian literature. It led to the growth of literature in the vernacular language as opposed to its composition primarily in Sanskrit earlier. Thus, the literature of this period became truly accessible to the masses. Although the initial character of this literature was primarily religious and spiritual, at the end of the Bhakti period, the emergence of ***Ritikal*** poets also took place who dealt with subjects of love and beauty.

The prominent poets of this period and their salient works are discussed below.

S. No.	Author	Important Works
1.	**Jnaneshwar** (late 13th century)	*Jnaneshwari*; commentary on *Bhagvad Gita* and *Amrutanubhav* (in Marathi)
2.	**Ramananda** (14th & 15th century CE)	*Gyanlila, Yoga Chintamani* (in Hindi), *Vaisnava- mata, Bhavabhaskara, Ramcharan Padhati* (Sanskrit)
3.	**Kabir** (15th century CE)	*Kabir-Bijak, Kabir-Parachai, Kabir Granthawali*
4.	**Guru Nanak** (15th century CE)	*Guru Granth Sahib* (containing teachings in 974 verses)
5.	**Chaitanya** (15th & 16th century CE)	*Siksastakam* (eight devotional prayers in Sanskrit)
6.	**Narsinh Mehta** (15th century CE)	*Aakhyan* and *Prabhatiya* (in Gujarati) (considered *Adi Kavi* of Gujarati)
7.	**Surdas**	*Sur Sagar, Sur-Saravali, Sahitya-Lahiri* (Braj Bhasha)
8.	**Shankar Deva** (15th & 16th century CE)	*Kirtana Ghosha, Borgeets* (Sanskrit)
9.	**Mirabai** (16th century CE)	Devotional *Padas*
10.	**Tulsidas** (16th century CE)	*Ramcharitmanas* (Avadhi), *Vinay Patrika* (Brajbhasha)
11.	**Tukaram** (17th century CE)	*Abhanga* poetry

Besides the above, a number of literary works like *Prithviraj Raso* (an epic poem on the life of Prithviraj Chauhan) by **Chand Bardai**, *Rajatarangini* of **Kalhana** (written in Sanskrit and containing historical account of Kashmir kings and North-Western India) also existed. Further, poets like **Bihari** (*Bihari Satsai*), **Keshavadas,** and other poets of *Ritikal* enriched the Hindi literature.

PERSIAN AND URDU LITERATURE

The Islamic influence also led to growth of Arabic and Persian Literature in India. Urdu developed as a language as a result of the confluence of the vernacular language (*Apabhramsa* and its earlier forms) with Persian and Arabic. A rich body of literature in Urdu gradually developed.

The prominent authors and poets and their salient works are discussed below.

S.No.	Authors/Poets	Important works
1.	**Amir Khusrau Dehlavi**	**Diwans** (collection of poetry) which includes, *Tuhfat-us-Sighr*, *Wasat-ul-Hayat*, *Ghurrat-ul-Kamat*, etc. (in Persian)
2.	**Ziauddin Barani** (14th century CE)	• *Fatwa-i-Jahandari* (containing political ideas) • *Tarikh-ul-Firuz Shahi* (containing history of the Delhi Sultanate)
3.	**Babur** (16th century CE)	• *Tuzk-e-Babri*, also called *Baburnama*. It contains memoirs of Babar
4.	**Abul Fazal** (16th century CE)	*Akbar Nama* (official history of Akbar's reign) and *Ain-i-Akbari*
5.	**Malik Muhammad Jayas** (16th century CE)	*Padmavat* (in Avadhi) (It describes historic seize of Chittorgarh by Allaudin Khilji after hearing of beauty of Padmavati (queen of Chittor))
6.	**Work Commissioned by Akbar**	*Razmnama*; translation of Mahabharata in Persian
7.	**Work Commissioned by Akbar**	*Hamzanama*; exploits of Amir Hamza, an illustrated work

SOUTHERN INDIAN LITERATURE

The Vijayanagar empire saw the Golden age of Telugu literature, with poets like **Srinatha** and **Deva Raya II** of Vijayanagar contributing to literature. King **Krishnadevaraya** himself composed *Amuktamalyada* (poems). The period under Vijayanagar empire is also called **Prabandh** period in the field of literature.

Krishnadevaraya also patronised Tamil poet **Harihara** who wrote an exposition of Vaishnavism and Shaivism. Other important Tamil poets of this period were Arunagirinathar and Svarupananda Deshika.

IMPORTANT TOPICS TO FOCUS ON

- Impact of Islam, Sufism, and Bhakti movement on the Indian Literature
- Important literary works of the medieval period

CHAPTER 13

Music in Medieval India

Music fills the infinite between two souls

Rabindranath Tagore

INTRODUCTION

Music and dance along with theatre and puppetry, constitutes the performing arts. Thus, these are those art forms which are linked to the performance by the artist as contrasted with the visual arts (architecture, sculpture, and painting) and literary arts (poem, prose, and drama). India has an ancient and rich tradition of performing arts which has flourished under the patronage of kings and rulers as well as amongst the common masses as folk arts.

Reference, to music is obtained in ancient times as early as in the Vedic texts, particularly the *Samveda*. While the ancient music was ritualistic and devotional, **its character underwent a gradual change** in the medieval period and it assumed a character with which we are more familiar in modern times.

Some salient aspects of evolution of medieval music is as below.

EVOLUTION OF MEDIEVAL MUSIC

- Music in medieval times was deeply **influenced by the Islamic rule** which brought Arabic and Persian influence.
- There was **evolution of different kinds of music**. For instance, the **Dhruvpad** which was the traditional devotional music evolved into the **Dhrupad** style of singing. **Khayal**, **Thumri,** and other musical styles too emerged.
- **Classical music** evolved in this period (around 14th century CE) into two distinct styles, the **Hindustani music** and the **Carnatic music**. While the Hindustani music which evolved under the Persian-Arabic influence was popular in North India, the indigenous Carnatic music was common in the South. The Hindustani music emphasises on musical structures and gives more freedom for improvisation. The latter is more *Kriti* oriented.
- A **system of Gharanas** emerged in this phase, particularly in the North Indian music. The system referred to a **tradition of music identified with a family or a house of the origin of music.** The musicians owed allegiance to the particular style of music and had a lineage of apprenticeship (like the *guru* and *shishya*).

FUNDAMENTALS OF INDIAN MUSIC

Swara, Raga, and ***Taal*** are said to be the three fundamental elements of Indian music.

(a) **Swara:** This refers to the **pitch, notes, or scale degree** in a musical composition. Bharata's *Natya Shastra* identifies 22 notes scale. As per the Hindustani system of music, the 7 swaras are *Sadja* (Sa), *Risabha* (or Re), *Gandharva* (Ga), *Madhyama* (Ma), *Panchama* (Pa), *Dhaivata* (Dha), and *Nishada* (Ni).

(b) **Raga:** A combination of *Swaras* gives rise to *ragas* with their being at least five *Swaras* in a *raga*. The *Audava/Odava* raga contains five swaras, the *Shadava* raga contains six swaras, while *Sampurna raga* contains all seven *swaras*. In Hindustani music, there are six principal ragas which are specific to season, time of the day, mood etc. However in the Carnatic music, the number of ragas are much more. *The six principal ragas are*:

- **(i) *Hindola Raga:*** *Time* – dawn; *season* – spring; *mood* – romantic as of a young couple
- **(ii) *Deepak Raga:*** *Time* – night; *season* – summer; *mood* – compassion
- **(iii) *Megha Raga:*** *Time* – mid day; *season* – monsoon; *mood* – courage
- **(iv) *Sri Raga:*** *Time* – evening; *season* – winter; *mood* – happiness
- **(v) *Malkauns Raga:*** *Time* – midnight; *season* – winter; *mood* – youthful love
- **(vi) *Bhairavi:*** *Time* – morning; *season* – autumn; *mood* – peace and devotion

(c) **Taal:** *Taal* refers to the rhythmic arrangement of beats in a musical composition. The beats are arranged in a cyclical manner and can range from three beats to 108 beats. Nearly 32 types of *Taals* have been identified. The tempo of the beats which refers to the time span of the beats is referred as *Laya*. The Carnatic music is said to have 35 original *Talas* which are further split.

IMPORTANT MUSICAL STYLES, GHARANAS, AND EXPONENTS

The Medieval period saw emergence of a number of styles of music particularly in the Hindustani classical style. These included **Dhrupad, Dhamar, Khayal, Hori, Thumri, Dadra**, **Tappa, Tarana, Ghazal,** etc. Some features of the musical styles, *Gharanas* associated with them, and exponents of the style of music are briefly discussed here.

Hindustani Music		
(1)	**Dhrupad**	• It is the oldest form of Hindustani music believed to have originated from earlier forms of music like *Prabandha* and *Dhruvpad*. • It was patronised by emperor Akbar and exponents like Haridas, Tansen and Gopal Das were associated with it. • The style is a poetic one involving the use of Sanskrit syllables and is of temple origin. Usually it is sung with the accompaniment of *Tanpura* and *Pakhawaj*. • The famous Dagar Gharana with the last 18 generations of Dagars are considered to be the foremost exponents of this style.

(2)	**Khayal**	• Literally meaning a thought or an idea, this style is attributed to Amir Khusrau although other legends like Muhammad Shah Rangila and Hussein Shah Sharqi were also associated with it. • This music is more open to improvisation and its use of *Taans* distinguishes it from Dhrupad. • Six major Gharanas are associated with it, viz. the Gwalior, Kirana, Agra, Patiala, Delhi, and Atrauli-Jaipur.
(3)	**Thumri**	• This form of music is said to have originated in western Uttar Pradesh and was influenced by the Bhakti movement. A number of its compositions were in *Awadhi* or *Braj Bhasha*. • The subjects revolve around love (particularly love of a girl for Krishna) and at times the subject is separation and devotion. • Benaras and Lucknow Gharanas are the most famous ones associated with it and Begum Akhtar is its exponent.
(4)	**Dadara**	• It is similar to Thumri with texts being sensual, the difference between the two being the incorporation of more than one *Antara*. • Performed in Agra and Bundelkhand region.
(5)	**Tappa**	• This musical style is said to have originated from the folk songs of camel riders in North-Western India. • These are folklore of love and passion written in Punjabi. • The style developed in the court of Mughal emperor Muhammad Shah.
(6)	**Tarana**	• It is characterised by singing at a fast tempo in a rhythmical pattern. The main melody is usually short and repeated many times. • Amir Khusrau is said to have invented this style.
(7)	**Dhamar-Hori**	• The compositions are similar to Dhrupad but associated with the festival of Holi and compositions are sung in praise of Lord Krishna.
(8)	**Ghazal**	• It is said to be a poetic form of music which is said to have evolved from the Persian music form *Qasida*. • It became popular in India during Mughal period although Amir Khusrau is said to be among its first exponents. • Ghazals deal with a singular subject such as love, separation, etc. and have a specific form.

CARNATIC MUSIC AND STYLES

Introduction

The Carnatic music is referred to the form of music which is in vogue in the southern part of India. It is an **indigenous form of music** which was little influenced by the Arabian and Persian music. The recognition of Carnatic music as a separate form of music seems to have happened in the 14th century

CE as in Haripada's **'*Sangeet Sudhakara*',** the terms Carnatic music and Hindustani music are referred to for the first time. The Carnatic music further underwent refinement and systematisation in the late 15th century due to the efforts of **Purandaradasa,** also referred to as the *Carnatic Sangeet Pitamaha*. The **musical trinity** of **Tyagaraja, Muthuswami Dikshitar,** and **Syama Sastri** (in late 18th century) was another important milestone when Carnatic music is said to have reached its peak.

Some Features of Carnatic Music

- **Pallavi, Anupallavi, Charanam:** The Carnatic music compositions usually have three parts—**the *Pallavi*, the *Anupallavi*, and the *Charanam*.** The *Pallavi* refers to the thematic lines of the composition, usually the first two. This is followed by the next two lines referred to as the *Anupallavi*. The *Charanam* refers to the stanzas in the composition which is usually the end portion after the *Anupallavi*.
- **Varnam:** This refers to the composition played at the beginning of the recital indicating the form of the raga and comprises the *Purvanga* (former half) and *Uttaranga* (latter half).
- **Kirtanam:** It is a devotional form of music in simple form and is imbued with *Bhakti bhava*.
- **Kriti:** is said to be development of *Kirtana* and an evolved form of music. The *raga* and *bhava* are brought out in this form and the Kriti comprises a minimum of *Pallavi, Anupallavi,* and *Charanam*.
- **Pada:** These are compositions in Tamil and Telugu. Though mainly composed as dance forms, they are also sung in concerts.
- **Tanam:** This is a branch of raga *Alapana*. It is characterised by a perceptible rhythm.

DEVOTIONAL MUSICAL FORMS

(a) **Bhajan:** As a devotional music, bhajans became popular in the 15th and 16th centuries during the Bhakti movement. A number of Bhakti saints, like Surdas, Mirabai, Narsinh Mehta, Guru Nanak, and others conveyed their messages through bhajans. As a form of music, bhajans were simple melodies comprising one or two ragas. The lyrics would be in praise of god and at times stories/episodes from *Ramayana*, *Mahabharata*, other scriptures, or compositions would be sung.

(b) **Qawwali:** It is believed that Qawwali originated as a devotional form of music and became popular in India with the growth of Sufism. The music is simple and the lyrics are set in praise of Allah, Prophet Muhammad, and other saints. The Qawwali is usually sung in a group with one or two persons being the lead singers. Qawwali is believed to have originated form *Qaul*, a form of music and Amir Khusrau is said to have played an important role in its growth.

(c) **Shabad:** Shabad refers to the **devotional song** and music sung in the **gurudwaras** and **Sikh communities**. It is said to have originated in the 16th century. Guru Nanak's teachings were set in musical form which is said to be the origin of this devotional form of music.

(d) Kirtan: This is another devotional music associated with Bhakti movement. It became popular with the teachings of **Chaitanya** where it took the form of song and dance. Kirtans were of two types—***Nama-Kirtan*** involving the uttering of the name of god, and the ***Lila-Kirtan*** involving enactment of anecdotes from ***Bhagvatapurana*** or from stories of love of Radha and Krishna.

(e) Abhanga: These are devotional songs sung in Maharashtra in praise of lord Krishna/Vishnu in his incarnation as Vithoba or Vithal. It became popular during Bhakti movement with the **teachings of Gnaneshwar, Namdeva, Tukaram, Eknath etc**.

Basic Aspects of Dance

The *Natya Shastra* of Bharata classifies dance into two broad categories, *Tandava* and the *Lasya.*

The **Tandava** is the masculine dance form which is characterised with movement and energy along with rhythm. It is believed to have its origin in the Lord Shiva's cosmic Tandav dance which was seen and later communicated to the world by Tandu rishi; hence the name Tandav. This can be of different kinds, viz. Rudra Tandav, Anand Tandav, etc.

The **Lasya** is the feminine dance form which incorporates grace, beauty, happiness, and expressiveness (*bhavarasa).* It is believed that this dance was performed by goddess Uma /Parvati in response to lord Shiva's Tandava.

As per Nandikeshwara's *Abhinaya Darpana*, dance has three basic elements. These are **Nritta, Nritya,** and **Natya**.

Nritta refers to the pure dance implying the rhythmic and graceful body movements.

Nritya refers to the expressive part of the performance which includes mudras, gestures, mime, etc. through which the emotion and sentiments are expressed.

Natya refers to the dance drama aspect of the performance through which the message or the story is being conveyed. This includes the music, dialogue, costumes, symbolisms, stage effects, etc.

Rasa

The Indian musical system often refers to the *Navarasas.* A *rasa* essentially refers to a mental and an emotional state. Music is believed to have an inherent attribute of influencing our emotional state and thus, the type of music played should be in consonance with it. Therefore, Indian music, dance, dance-drama, and even poetry, all are invariably in accordance with one of the *navarasas* which reflect nine different emotional states. It is said that Bharata's *Natya Shastra* specifies eight of the *rasas* (some sources say all of the nine were identified in the *Natya Shastra*) and the ninth rasa '*Shantam*' was identified by sage Abhinavagupta.

Each of these *rasas* is associated not only with an emotional state but with a colour and presiding deity too. These are

S.No.	Rasa	Emotion	Colour
(a)	Sringaram	Love/attractiveness	Green
(b)	Hasyam	Laughter/Humour	White
(c)	Raudram	Fury/Anger	Red
(d)	Karunyam	Compassion	Dove coloured
(e)	Bibhatsam	Disgust	Blue
(f)	Bhayanakam	Horror/Terror	Black
(g)	Viram	Bravery	Wheatish brown
(h)	Adbhutam	Wonder	Yellow
(i)	Shantam	Peace/Tranquilly	White
In later years, two more *rasas* are further referred to which are *bhakti* (devotion) and *vatsalya* (motherly love).			

IMPORTANT TOPICS TO FOCUS ON

- The main two musical streams of India and their basic elements.
- Different musical styles in medieval India and their salient features.
- Main devotional musical styles and features.

PART 3

Art and Culture in Modern India

CHAPTER

14

Socio-Religious Reforms and Reformers in India

Arise, awake and stop not till the goal is reached

—Swami Vivekananda

SOCIO-RELIGIOUS MOVEMENTS AND THEIR OBJECTIVES

The 19th century saw the emergence of a number of socio-religious reform movements. The Brahmo Samaj spearheaded by Raja Ram Mohan Roy, the Young Bengal Movement, Arya Samaj, Prarthana Samaj, Theosophical Society, and Ramakrishna Mission were amongst the most prominent of them. The reforms in the socio-religious and spiritual realm ushered a change in Hindu society and at times, this entire movement is referred as the **Modern Hindu Renaissance**. Most of these reforms **opposed the caste system, Brahmanical orthodoxy, untouchability, evil practices like *Sati* and child marriages,** and **supported widow remarriages, education for women,** and emancipation of the downtrodden. Some of these also emphasised on the Vedantic philosophy and **spiritual regeneration** of the Hindu society. However, these reforms were not limited to Hinduism but also emerged as **Islamic movements** (e.g. Aligarh Movement and Deoband school), **Sikh reforms,** and **Parsi reforms**. Together they had a profound impact in preserving the strained socio-religious character of the Indian society and purging it of many evils plaguing it for centuries. *The important movements and their salient points are discussed here.*

IMPORTANT MOVEMENTS AND THEIR FOUNDERS

Brahmo Samaj

Established in 1828 by **Raja Ram Mohan Roy**, this was the earliest of the reform movements which worked against the practice of Sati, female infanticide, child marriage, caste system, and Brahmancail orthodoxy. Raja Ram Mohan Roy was himself an exponent of many languages including English, Sanskrit, Arabic, Persian, French, Latin, and Greek and was a modern thinking scholar. His efforts enabled William Bentinck to declare **Sati as a punishable offence in 1829** (vide the Abolition of the Sati Act of 1829). For his efforts, he is also referred as the **Father of Indian Renaissance**.

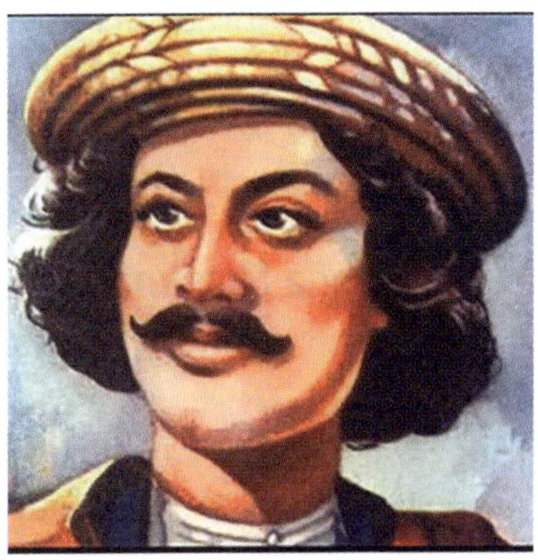

Raja Ram Mohan Roy

Raja Ram Mohan Roy established the **Brahmo Samaj**. After his death in 1833, the Brahmo Samaj divided into many sects. Adi Brahmo Samaj was established by Debendranath Tagore (father of Rabindranath Tagore), while Bharatiya Brahmo Samaj or Naba Bidhan Samaj was established by **Keshub Chandra Sen**. The Adi Brahmo Samaj focused on teachings from Upanishads. Keshub Chandra Sen tried incorporating Christian ideals and theology in the Hindu thoughts. In 1878, another split occurred in the Brahmo Samaj when **Pandit Shivnath Shastri** founded the **Sadharan Brahmo Samaj**. Later the sects were united in **Brahmo Samaj Milan.**

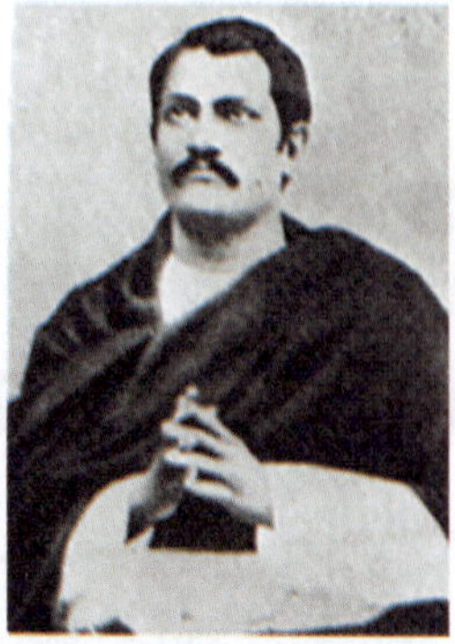

Keshub Chandra Sen

Important teachings and salient reforms brought by Brahmo Samaj:

- Believed in **monotheism** or one God who is supreme and in immortality of the human soul.
- Believed in goodness of different holy scriptures and **respect for other religions**.
- Emphasised on teachings of Upanishads and service to mankind.
- Opposed **idol worship, Sati, child marriages, girl infanticide, Brahmanical orthodoxy,** and **caste system**.

Young Bengal Movement

Founded by **Henry Vivian Derozio**, this movement comprised a **group of free thinkers who professed free spirit and thought,** questioned authority, and opposed the old traditions and decadent customs. Henry Vivian Derozio taught in the Hindu College in Calcutta. He died at an early age (24 years) due to cholera in 1833. The movement inspired by him also supported **rights and education of women,** and **opposed caste system, idol worship,** and **superstitions**.

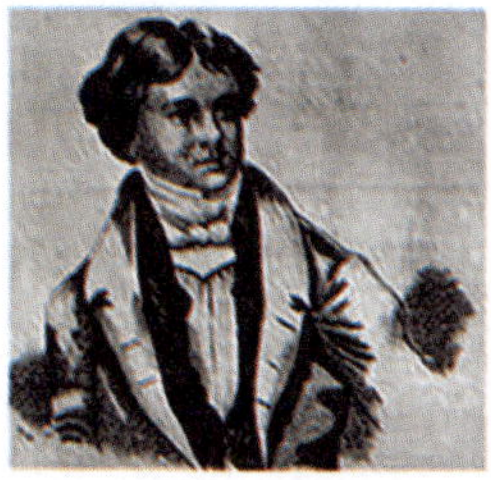

Henry Vivian Derozio

Prarthana Samaj

This movement was started in 1863 by **Atmaram Pandurang**. Later, **Justice M.G. Ranade** and **R.G. Bhandarkar** joined the movement. Justice Ranade also started the **Deccan Education Society**.

Prarthana Samaj (literal meaning, a prayer society), was a movement for bringing reforms within Hinduism. It advocated **belief in one God**. It opposed caste system and dominance of priests. Further, it promoted inter-dining and inter-marriage amongst different castes. It also **supported widow remarriage** and worked for the upliftment of women and the marginalised sections. Ranade was also the founder of the **Widow Remarriage Association** (1861).

Ramakrishna Mission

Swami Vivekananda founded the Ramakrishna Mission in 1897 in Belur (Howrah) to spread the teachings of Swami Ramakrishna Paramhansa. The philosophy of this movement was based on Vedanta which is also referred at times as *neo-Vedantism*. It aimed at **spiritual rejuvenation of the Indian society**. Swami Vivekananda himself came into prominence after his speech at 'Parliament of Religions' held in Chicago (USA) in 1893 and based his life's work on Vedantic thought and service to mankind. The movement in later years organised a number of schools, colleges, hospitals, and other charitable institutions.

Theosophical Society

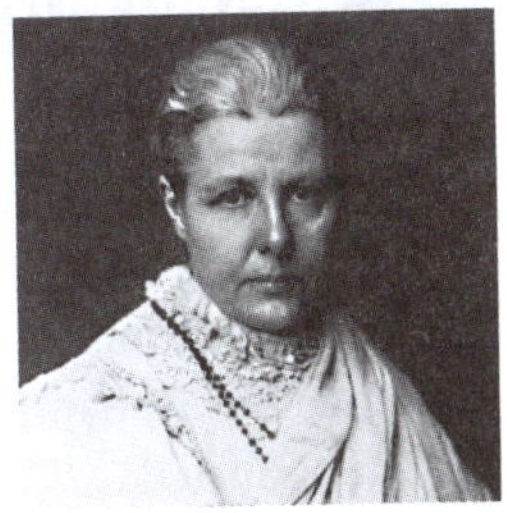

Annie Besant

It was founded by **Madam H.P. Blavatsky** (a Russian lady) and **Colonel Henry Olcott** (American) in 1875 (in USA). Later, the society came into prominence under the leadership of **Mrs. Annie Besant**. Its headquarters was Adyar near Madras (now Chennai).

The objective of the society was **attaining universal brotherhood** without distinction of race, colour, creed, etc. It also aimed to promote studies in ancient religions, science and philosophy, and strengthen and revive the glories of ancient India's religious and philosophical traditions.

Arya Samaj

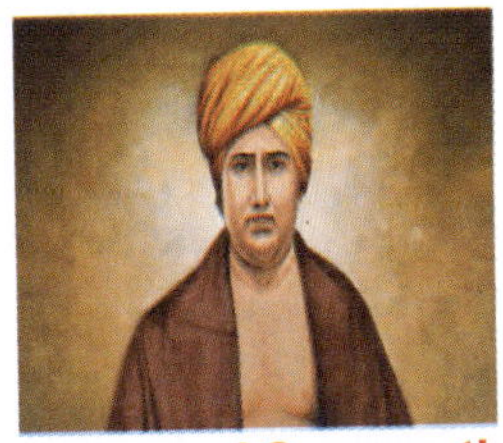

Dayanand Saraswati

Started by Swami Dayananda Saraswati in 1875, it based its teachings on the Vedas and opposed idolatry, caste system, ritualism, Brahmanical orthodoxy, child marriage, etc. It supported widow remarriages, inter-caste marriages, and began the *Shuddhi* Movement for bringing the Hindus who converted into other religions, back into the fold of Hinduism. It also started a number of educational institutions.

OTHER EMINENT REFORMISTS

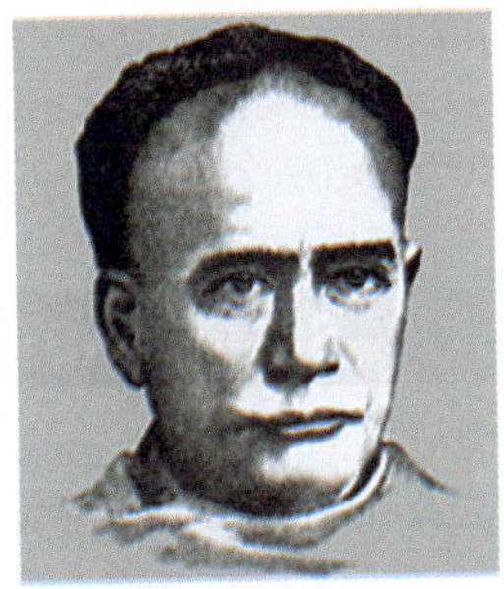

Ishwar Chandra Vidyasagar

(a) Ishwar Chandra Vidyasagar He was an **eminent educator and reformist** who firmly believed in education of the girl child and emancipation of women and started many schools for them. He opposed the child marriage and supported widow remarriage which was legalised by the Widow Remarriage Act of 1856.

(b) Jyotiba Phule He founded the **Satya Shodhak Samaj** in 1873 which opposed the caste system and Brahmanical supremacy. He also worked for education of women and spearheaded the widow remarriage movement in Maharashtra. He established the first girl's school in Pune in 1851 along with his wife.

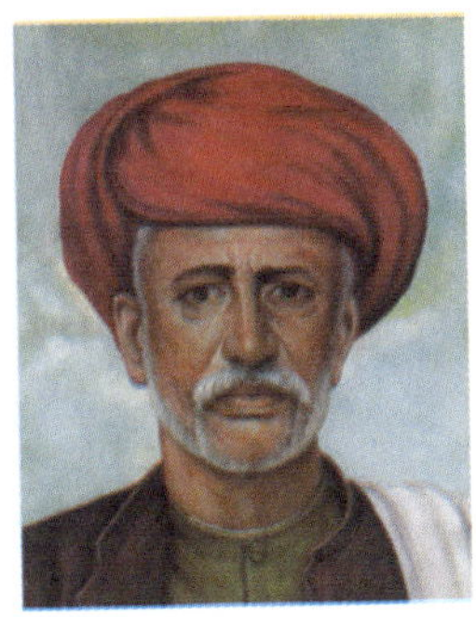

Jyotiba Phule

(c) Dhondo Keshav Karve Worked for women's education and remarriage of Hindu widows. He established in 1883 the **Widow Remarriage Association** and **Hindu Widows Home in 1896**. He also started a Women's University in 1916.

(d) E.V.R Periyar He started the **Self-Respect Movement** in the 1920s. Its objective was **upliftment of the Dravidians** and opposition to the caste system and suppression by the Brahmins. He also opposed child marriage and supported widow remarriage.

(e) Kandukuri Veeresalingam He pioneered **movement for girls' education in Andhra** and also widow remarriage. He founded the **Veda Samaj** in 1864 which opposed caste discrimination and supported widow remarriage.

REFORM MOVEMENT AMONGST OTHER RELIGIOUS COMMUNITIES

(a) Aligarh Movement This movement was started by Sir Syed Ahmad Khan which worked for **education and social upliftment of the Muslims**. He believed in imparting modern and scientific education to Muslims and asked them be broadminded and not to be secluded from the modern ideas. In 1866, he started the Muhammadan Educational Conference and in 1875 he founded the **Mohammedan Anglo-Oriental College at Aligarh**. He also worked for education of women and advocated removal of *purdah*.

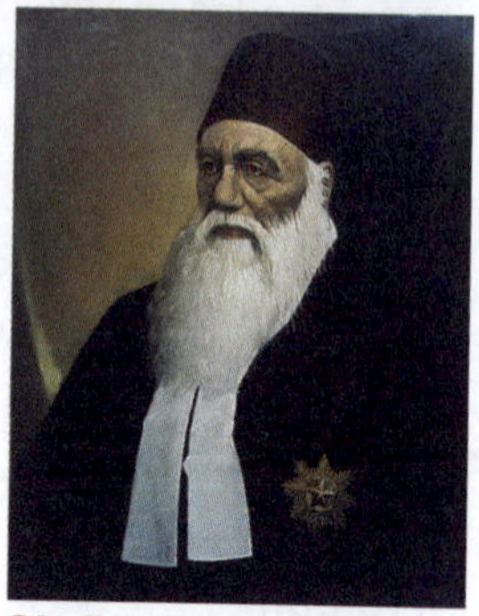

Sir Syed Ahmad Khan

(b) Ahmadiyya Movement This movement was started by **Mirza Ghulam Ahmad** and a number of schools and colleges were opened to impart modern education.

(c) Deoband Movement Also referred as the Deoband school, this movement emphasised on the **teachings of Quran and the Hadith** (traditions of the Prophet).

(d) Reform amongst Parsis In 1851, **Naoroji Furdoonji**, **Dadabhai Nauroji,** and **S.S. Bengalee** founded the Religious Reforms Association of the Parsis (*Rehnumai Maz'dayasan Sabha*). They also started a journal *Rast Goftar* for socio-religious messages. The movement strived to **remove orthodoxy** amongst Parsis and spread education, particularly amongst girls.

(e) Reforms amongst Sikhs The reform in Sikhs took place through several successive movements. The **Nirankari Movement** was started by Baba Ram Dayal Das which aimed at worshipping the God as a *nirankar* (formless entity). The **Namdhari Movement** was founded by Baba Ram Singh whose followers were encouraged to give up eating meat and wear white clothes. The **Akali movement started** in 1920s to improve the management of gurudwaras and Sikh shrines.

SOCIAL AND RELIGIOUS REFORMS AND THEIR IMPACT

The social and religious reforms had far reaching effect on the Indian society ranging from that on education and emancipation of women to loosening of the vice-like grip of caste on the society and its sanctions. Several legislations were passed by even the British government and later the social reforms became an integral part of the Indian National Movement and freedom struggle, particularly with the advent of Mahatma Gandhi on the national scene. *Some of the salient impacts of these reform movements are as below.*

- **Prohibition of Sati Act** was passed in 1829.
- Widow remarriage was legalised as per **Widow Remarriage Act of 1856**.
- Inter-caste and inter-communal marriages were sanctioned as per the Act of 1872 (**Special Marriages Act, 1872**)
- As per 1891 Law, child marriages were discouraged (**Age of Consent Act, 1891**). Further, as per the **Sharda Act of 1929**, marriage of girls below 14 and of boys below 18 was prohibited.
- Abolition of untouchability, education and emancipation of women, and communal harmony were specially emphasised upon by Mahatma Gandhi and were integral to the programmes of the Indian National Congress.
- Press, cinema, literature, and plays became an important medium for fight against untouchability, casteism, communalism, and for emancipation of women.

IMPORTANT REFORM MOVEMENTS AND REFORMS AT A GLANCE

Reform Movements	Founders and Prominent Reformists	Salient Contribution and Socio-Religious Issues Emphasised Upon
(1) **Brahmo Samaj** (Founded 1829) • Adi Brahmo Samaj • Bhartiya Brahmo Samaj (or Naba Bidhan Samaj) • Sadharan Brahmo Samaj	**Raja Ram Mohan Roy** (Founder) • Debendra Nath • Keshub Chandra • Pandit Shivnath Shastri	• Monotheism • Goodness of all scriptures and respect for all religions • Opposition to caste system and Brahmanical orthodoxy • Education and emancipation of women • Opposition to Sati and child marriages • Advocated service to mankind and teaching of Upanishads
(2) **Young Bengal Movement** (1830s)	**Henry Vivian Derozio**	• Emphasised modern and free thinking • Opposed orthodoxy and decadent customs • Advocated education for women
(3) **Prarthana Sabha** (1863)	Founded by **Atmaram Pandurang**. Important personalities associated with it were **Justice M.G. Ranade** and **R.G. Bhandarkar**	• A prayer association which advocated inter-caste dining, marriages, and mingling of people • Opposed child marriages and supported widow remarriages, education and emancipation of women
(4) **Arya Samaj** (1875)	**Swami Dayanand Saraswati**	• Advocated teachings of Vedas (particularly of Upanishadic teaching) • Opposed idolatry, ritualism, Brahmanical orthodoxy, caste system, child marriages, and supported widow remarriages and inter- caste marriages • Started Shuddhi movement for bringing converted Hindus back into the fold of Hinduism.
(5) **Theosophical Society** (1875)	Founded by **Madam H.P. Blavatsky** and **Col. H.S. Olcott**. Society came into prominence during leadership of Mrs. **Annie Besant**	• Aimed at universal brotherhood of man-kind • Promoted study of ancient Indian religion and philosophy and aimed to strengthen and revive the ancient religious and philosophical traditions

(6) **Ramakrishna Mission** (1897)	**Swami Vivekananda**	• Advocated the teachings of Vedanta (also referred as neo-Vedanta) • Spread the message of Ramakrishna Paramahamsa • Emphasised upon service to mankind and started schools and colleges and other charitable institutions. • Opposed caste systems, ritualism, and strived for moral and spiritual rejuvenation of the society
(7) **Aligarh Movement** (1875)	**Syed Ahmad Khan** (Foundation of Mohammedan Anglo-Oriental College at Aligarh laid in 1875)	• Aimed at providing education and bringing social upliftment of the Muslim community • Supported and worked for education of women and removal of *purdah*
(8) **Ahmadiyya Movement** (1899)	**Mirza Ghulam Ahmad**	• Opened a number of schools and colleges for providing modern education
(9) **Deoband Movement** (1867)	Inspired by scholar **Shah Waliullah Dehlavi** (1762)	• A movement for revival based on teachings of Quran and Hadith
(10) **Parsi Reforms**	**Naoroji Furdoonji, Dadabhai Nauroji,** and **S.S. Bengalee**	• Founded Rehnumai Maz' dayasan Sabha, 1851 • Spread of education, particularly amongst girls and removal of orthodoxy
(11) **Sikh reforms** • Nirankari Movement • Namdhari Movement • Akali Movement	 **Baba Ram Dayal** **Baba Ram Singh**	• Worship of God as a nirankar (formless entity) • Wearing of white clothes and giving up eating of meat • Reforms of the management of gurudwaras and Sikh shrines

IMPORTANT TOPICS TO FOCUS ON

- Important reform movements, their salient teachings, and significant contributions to the socio-religious reforms.
- Important reformists, the movements they were associated with, and salient contributions.

CHAPTER

15

Paintings in Modern India

I dream my painting and I paint my dream

—Vincent Van Gogh

GROWTH OF MODERN INDIAN PAINTINGS

The term 'modern Indian paintings' refer to the styles of Indian paintings emerging since the mid-nineteenth century. By this period, the style of miniature paintings as seen in the Mughal, Pahari, south Indian, and other schools of art had started to wane and increasing British influence was seen in the Indian paintings. These were commonly referred as the **Company Art**. However, the advent of the modern Indian paintings in a true sense only happened with the advent of **Raja Ravi Varma** whose subjects and ethos were uniquely Indian. This was followed by the **Bengal School of Art** which ushered a new era of revivalist nationalism in paintings. The famous **Progressive Artists' Group** (PAG) of Bombay (now Mumbai) of the post Independence was another important milestone which blended Indian art with more contemporary and abstract themes. Almost parallel to the growth of modern paintings has been the course of the folk paintings in India which includes traditional art forms such as the **Madhubani painting**, **Warli painting, Kalamkari art**, **Kalighat painting,** etc. These paintings included the subjects touching the everyday life of people, and reflected the life and style of the Indian villages and the hinterland of India.

A number of art movements and artists have contributed to the growth of Indian paintings. The salient ones are discussed below.

THE BRITISH ART AND THE COMPANY PAINTINGS

The British influence on the Indian paintings began with the advent of a number of prominent British painters in India such as Tilly Kettle, John Zoffany, George Chinnery, William Hodges, etc. Most of their paintings were in oil medium and the perspective was Western. However, **the mingling of the Indian art style with the British influence** brought out what was referred to as the **Company style of painting** (as it emerged during the influence of British East India Company). *The features of these paintings were:*

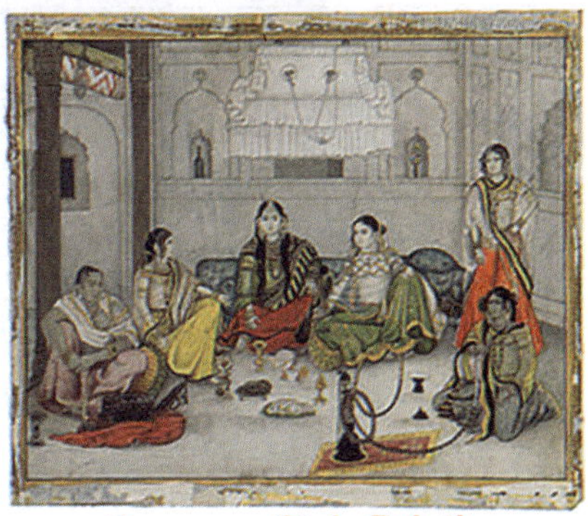

Company Style Painting

- There was **a blending of the European/British influence** with the **existing Mughal and Rajput styles** of painting.

- They were usually **water colours** mostly done on paper. They would reflect transparency of texture and soft tones.
- Subjects would include **Indian people, scenes of fairs and festivals, landscapes,** Indian flora and fauna, dancers, trades, etc. A series of paintings reflecting the marketplace scene was referred as the ***Bazaar paintings***.
- The paintings typically had a **mix of naturalistic representation** and the **features of the miniature Indian painting style**. However, they would also offer a close representation of visual reality with perspective, volume, and shading.
- These were first produced in the Madras presidency but spread to other centres in Calcutta (now Kolkata), Murshidabad, Patna, Benares, Agra, Lucknow, Delhi, and parts of western India.

PAINTINGS BY RAJA RAVI VARMA

Raja Ravi Varma can truly be described as the **first modern Indian painter and** *one of the greatest Indian painters. His paintings combined the Western/European technique with Indian sensibility and subjects.*

- The **subjects of his paintings were truly Indian,** inspired from characters and scenes of Indian epics of Ramayana and Mahabharata and Indian mythologies. In later years, they served as imagination of what gods and goddesses and other mythological characters would look like.
- He used oil and water colour technique of painting. His paintings involved employing the European style with **use of realism and perspective**. The use of light on skin and tonal effects added lifelike quality to them.
- Most famous of his paintings are *Shakuntala, Damyanti Hansa Samvad, Arjun and Subhadra, Rama Conquers Varuna, Jatayu Wars with Ravana, Ladies in Moon light,* and *Galaxy of Musicians* amongst many others.

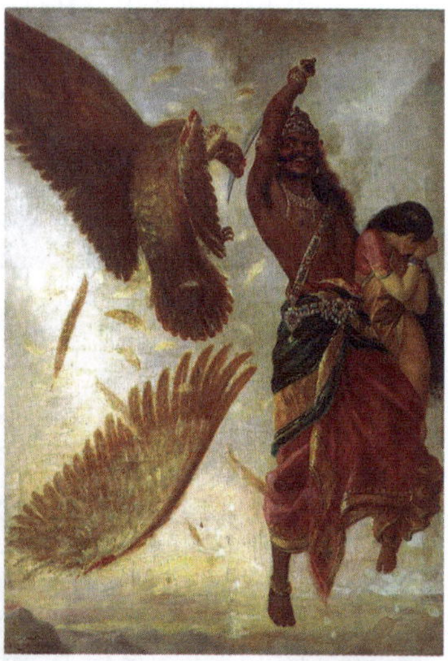

Ravana, Sita and Jatayu by Ravi Varma

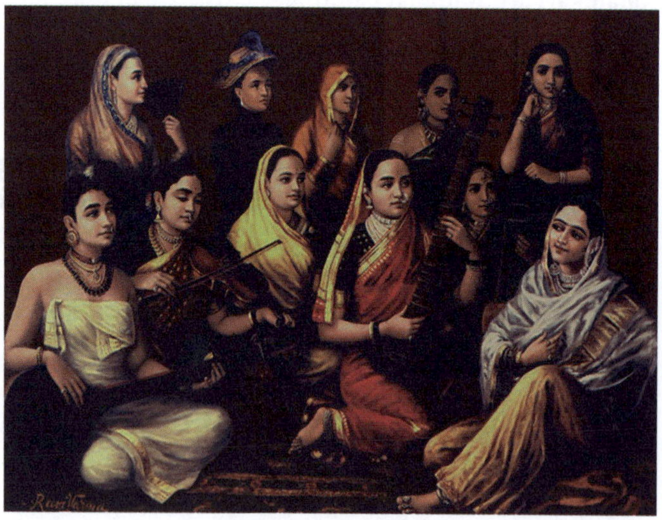

Galaxy of Musicians by Ravi Varma

BENGAL SCHOOL OF ART

The nationalistic fervour which was present in the early 20th century, influenced Indian paintings too and led to the emergence of what is known as the Bengal School of Art. This art movement was started by **Abanindranath Tagore** (nephew of Rabindranath Tagore) along with E.B. Havell (Principal of Government Art School, Calcutta) and Sister Nivedita (an associate of Swami Vivekananda). This art movement **emphasised on Indian subjects and indigenous material** such as tempera (rather than oil paintings). It drew inspiration from the murals of the ancient period and miniatures of the medieval period and developed a philosophy of pan-Indian Art.

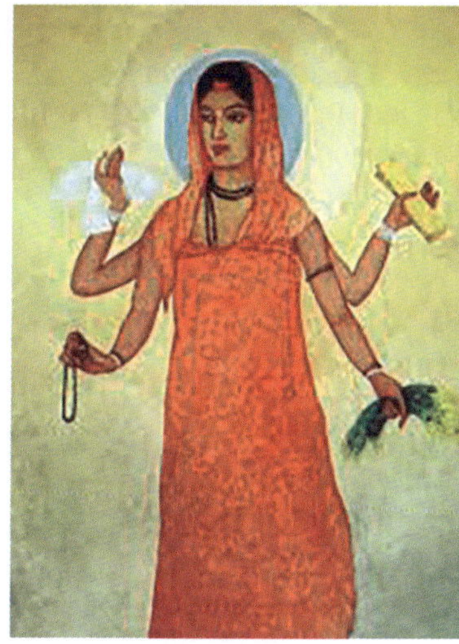

Bharat Mata by Abanindranath Tagore

Abanindranath Tagore was the pioneer of this School of art. His famous works include the *Arabian Nights series, Radha Krishna series, Bharat Mata, Krishna Leela, passing of Shah Jahan*, etc.

Salient points about this school of art are:

- It was truly an **Indian school of art** in technique, subjects, and character. It moved away from use of oil painting such as in western painting and popularised Indian paintings such as tempera and incorporated painting technique such as *washes*.
- It was **influenced by the murals and the miniature** style of paintings.
- **Subjects were indigenous.** It included the Indian landscapes, portraits, historical scenes, and anecdotes from daily life in the countryside.
- It led to the emergence of many new artists who developed their own style. Some of the notable painters associated with this movement were **Rabindranath Tagore, Gaganendranath Tagore, Nandalal Bose,** Asit Haldar, M.A.R. Chugtai, Kshitindranath Majumdar, Sarada Charan Ukil, and Sunayani Devi.

PROGRESSIVE ARTISTS' GROUP

Post independence, Indian art saw another significant leap; the formation of **Progressive Artists' Group of Bombay** took place with famous painters, **F.N. Souza, S.H. Raza, M.F. Hussain, K.H. Ara, H.A. Gade, and S.K. Bakre** (a sculptor) as its founder. Later, other eminent painters and artists such as Tyeb Mehta, Gaitonde, Manishi Dey, and Akbar Padamsee joined it.

The paintings of this movement broke away from the revivalist nationalism of Bengal Art movement and set the path for modern and abstract art which synthesised Indian art tradition with *European Modernism*.

IMPORTANT INDIAN PAINTERS

Painter	Salient points of painting style and important paintings
(1) **Raja Ravi Varma** (1848–1906)	• First modern Indian painter. • Combined western style with Indian ethos. • Subjects included characters from Ramayana, Mahabharata, and Indian mythology. • Most famous paintings include *Shakuntala, Damyanti Hansa Samvad, Rama Conquers Varuna, Jatayu Wars with Ravana, Ladies in Moonlight, Galaxy of Musicians, etc.*
(2) **Abanindranath Tagore** (1871–1951)	• Heralded the nationalistic fervour in painting and the Bengal School of Art movement. • Incorporated uses of Indian techniques and material such as tempera in the Indian paintings. • Famous paintings include, *Bharat Mata, Arabian Nights series,* and *Krishna Leela series,* amidst others.
(3) **Nandalal Bose** (1882–1966)	• One of the most prominent artists of modern India and a protégé of Abanindranath Tagore and Havell. • His uniqueness of paintings lied in synthesis, particularly of the historic artistic tradition and contemporary Indian art. • Subjects included painting of scenes from daily Indian life, villages, mythologies, etc. • Famous paintings include black and white *linocut of Dandi March and Mahatma Gandhi.* 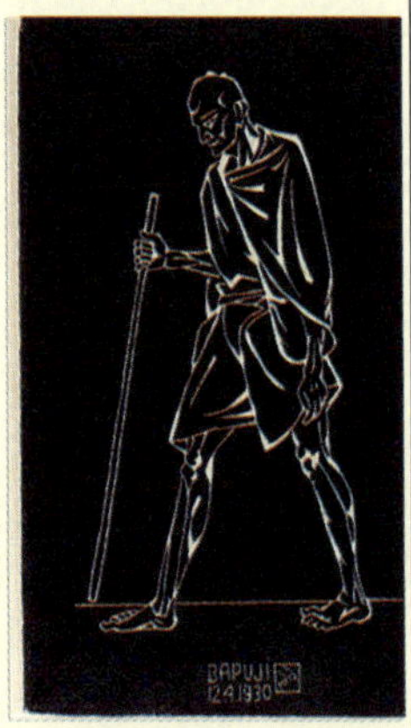 **Dandi March by Nandalal Bose**
(4) **Rabindranath Tagore** (1861–1994)	• Made foray in the world of paintings in his 60s and had no formal training in this art. • Had a highly imaginative and spontaneous style which would employ use of brush, rags, cotton, and even fingers. • His subjects would include a wide range from mysterious human faces to bizarre beasts, mystic landscapes to birds and flowers, etc.

(5) **Jamini Roy** (1887–1972)	• Renowned painter who in the 1920s ushered a new style incorporating the Kalighat style and the style of village Patua artists of Bengal. • His paintings involved use of inexpensive material as by folk artists (rather than oil and canvas) and painted ordinary men and women from the village. The use of colours was limited to seven earthy or mineral colours. • Famous paintings include, *Santhal Dance, Mother and Child, Gopini, Three Ladies*, etc. 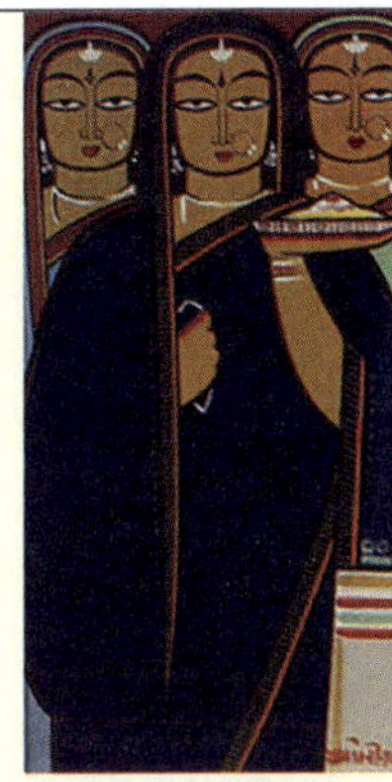 **Three Ladies by Jamini Roy**
(6) **Ramkinkar Baij** (1906–1980)	• He was a famous painter and sculpture of the Shanti Niketan School whose works were regarded to be a part of contextual modernism.
(7) **Amrita Shergil** (1913–1941)	• An **early modernist painter**, educated in France whose initial works were of Western style. Her style and subjects underwent a change on return to India in the 1930s. • Famous paintings include self portraits, *Brahmacharis, Bride's Toilet,* and *Three Girls.* 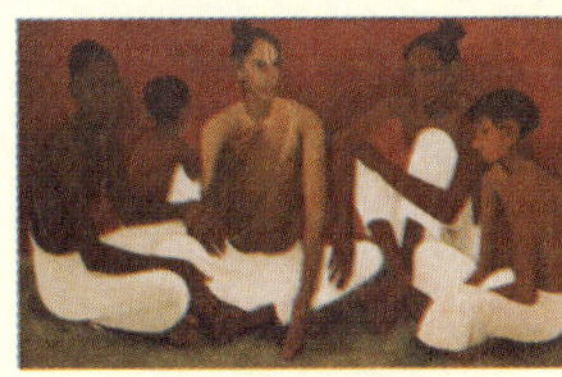 **Brahmacharis by Amrita Shergill**
(8) **F.N. Souza** (1924–2008)	• A modern artist who was the founding member of Progressive Artists' Group (PAG), Bombay. • His paintings were eclectic and are known for his inventive human forms. His well known paintings include, *The Mammon, Last Supper, Christ on Palm Sunday*, etc. 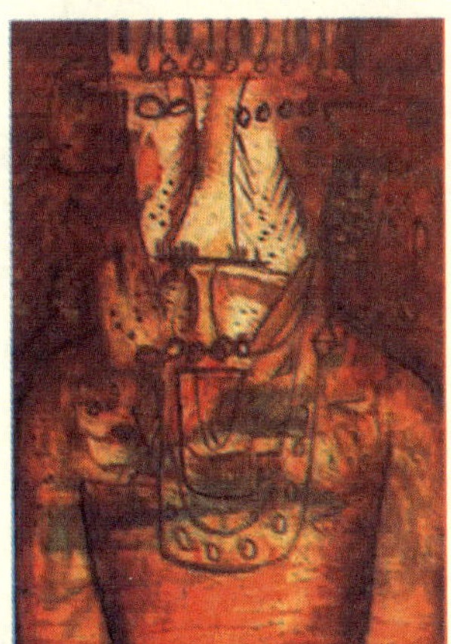 **Mammon by Francis Newton Souza**

(9) **Syed Haider Raza** (1922–2016)	• S. H. Raza, another founding member of the PAG was known for his abstract and expressionistic paintings which were done on acrylic and oil medium. • In later career, inspired by Indian philosophy, his paintings revolved around 'Bindu', (a dot) which symbolised source of energy. His paintings thus became thematic and abstract from expressionistic. 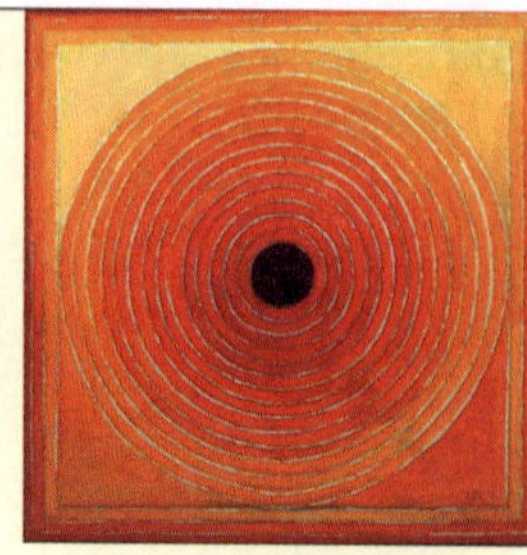 **Bindu Painting by S. H. Raza**
(10) **Maqbool Fida Husain** (1915–2011)	• Another founding member of the PAG, Hussain was a world acclaimed painter, often termed as the Picasso of India. His paintings were considered to be of modified Cubist style (an art movement of early 20th century where art objects are analysed, broken up, and reassembled in an abstract form). • His paintings were also famous for images of horses which represented free spirit and transition. • His famous paintings include, *Horses, Mother Teresa, Battle of Ganga Jamuna, Zameen,* etc. 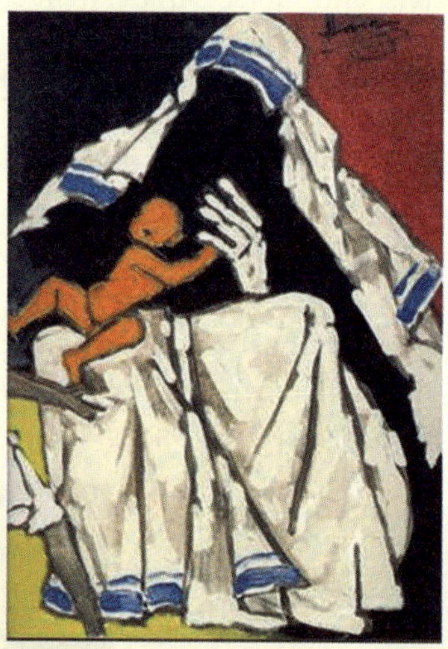 **Mother Teresa by M. F. Husain**
(11) **Satish Gujral** (1925)	• A famous painter, muralist, sculpture, architect, and writer of the PAG, Bombay. His style and technique involve modernism but are rooted in Indian ethos and traditions.
(12) **Tyeb Mehta** (1929–2001)	• A member of the PAG Bombay, Mehta's works were characterised by modernism and expressionistic styles. • His famous works include *'Kali', Falling Bull, Mahishasura,* etc.

<table>
<tr><td>(13) Vasudeo S. Gaitonde
(1924–2001)</td><td>• Foremost modern Indian abstract painter. A typical feature of his abstract paintings is translucent beams of light characterised by a meditative calm.
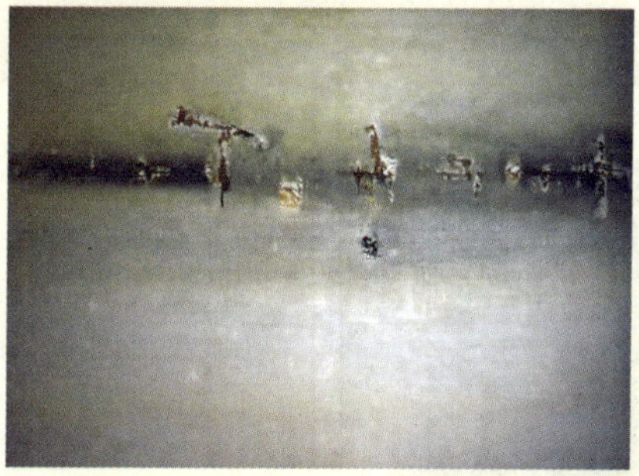
Translucent beams of light by Vasudeo Gaitonde</td></tr>
<tr><td>(14) Ganesh Pyne
(1937–2013)</td><td>• A contemporary artist of Bengal School of Art. His style is characterised by surrealism and dark imagery which revolve round subjects of Bengali folklore and mythology.
• His paintings include water colour, tempera, and mixed media.</td></tr>
<tr><td>(15) Manjit Bawa
(1941–2008)</td><td>• His paintings are noted for vibrant colours, which are traditionally Indian and for subjects from Indian mythology, spirituality, and culture.
• His famous paintings include 'Krishna and the Bull, Govardhan, Heer, After 84, etc.
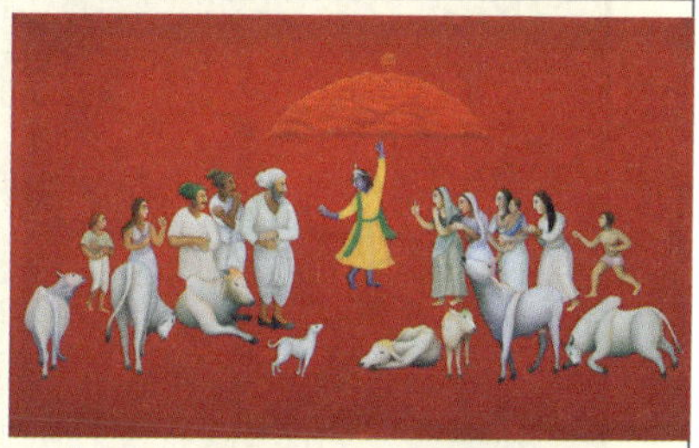
Govardhan by Manjit Bawa</td></tr>
</table>

Other important artists of modern times include **Gaganendranath Tagore** (1867–1938) **Gopal Rao** (1880–1945), **S.G. Thakur Singh** (1899–1976) **Anjolie Ela Menon** (1940), **Dhiraj Choudhary** (1930), **Jatin Das** (194), **Jogen Chowdhury**, etc.

FOLK PAINTINGS

India has had a rich tradition of folk paintings since ancient times. These paintings, whose style, technique, and subjects are diverse have prospered in different regions of the country and are drawn on the local culture and tradition. The subjects of these paintings have also been varied and include the scenes from community life (as in Warli paintings) to subjects of *Ramayana*, *Mahabharata*, and Indian mythology (Madhubani, Pattachitra, and Pichwai paintings), and from day-to-day happenings of rural life (Kalighat paintings) to rituals and ceremonies (Paitkar paintings).

These paintings would be done on walls, floor of house, paper, scrolls, and even fabric. Events like birth, marriage ceremony, festivals, rituals, etc. would often be the occasions for such paintings. Another feature of these traditional paintings would be use of natural and earthy colours available locally. Thus, these paintings were in consonance with the local environment and would reflect the indigenous ethos and culture.

Some important folk paintings and their features are highlighted below.

Folk Paintings and Region where practiced	Salient Features
(1) **Warli Paintings**; Maharasthra 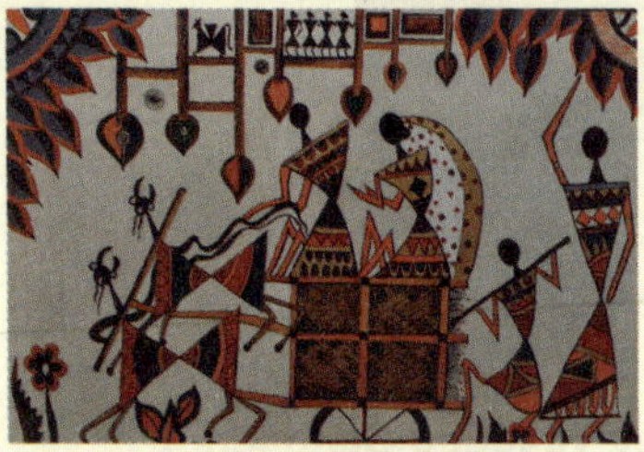 Warli Painting	• Practised by Warli tribals in Maharashtra. • Paintings usually done on home walls on ceremonial occasions • Rice paste with red ochre powder is used as painting material. • Scenes of daily community life including dancing, planting saplings, hunting, fishing, festivals, and rituals are depicted. • Human figures have a typical representation using triangles and straight lines, while white colour is predominant in a red ochre background.
(2) **Madhubani Paintings**; Madhubani, Mithila region of Bihar 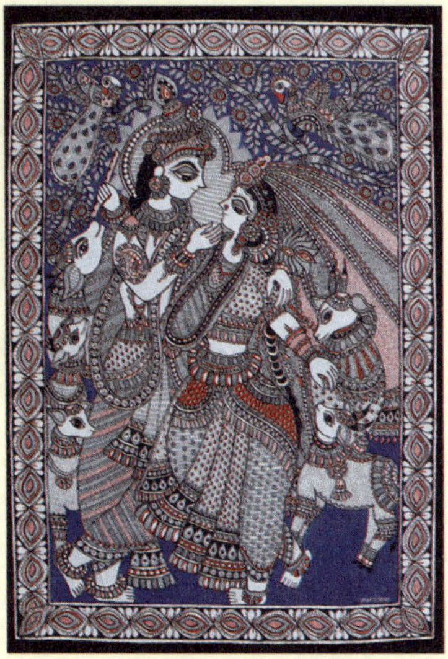 Madhubani Painting	• Also referred at times as Mithila paintings, this style of painting is said to have originated when king of Mithila, Janak asked the painters to draw the marital ceremony of Sita with Ram (the crown prince of Ayodhya). • The paintings are done on walls of houses and medium like canvas, cloth, etc. are used. These paintings are done particularly on occasions like birth, marriage, or festivals, etc. • Paintings depict scenes from Ramayana (particularly marriage of Rama and Sita or return of Rama from exile), or Krishna playing with gopis, or other events from mythologies/religious motifs. • Paintings often contain images of fish (considered auspicious) and snakes (which are propitiated). The features of subjects are usually exaggerated and are two-dimensional. The vacant spaces are decorated with designs and floral patterns. • Rice paste, cow dung, and vegetable colours are the materials used • Some famous painters include Ganga Devi, Sita Devi, Satya Narayan, Moti Karn, etc.
(3) **Kalighat Paintings**; Kolkata 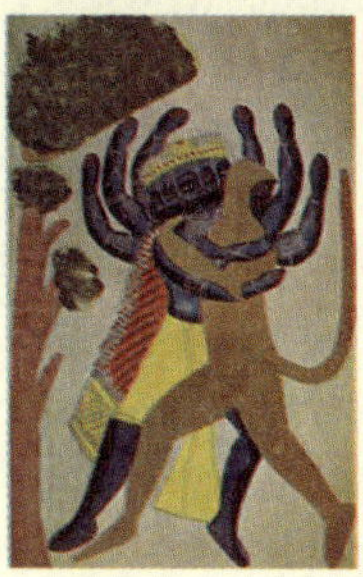 Kalighat Painting	• This style of paintings originated in the 19th century around Kalighat temple in present day Kolkata, where rural artists would prepare these paintings. • They contained originally images of Hindu gods and goddesses, but later diversified to scenes from rural life, and include images of birds, animals, snakes, and fishes. • Paintings are characterised by use of simplified figures, and bold colours. They were made on cloth, or patas or even on mill paper. • These paintings also inspired the artists like Jamini Roy of Bengal School of Art.

(4) **Pattachitra**; Orissa 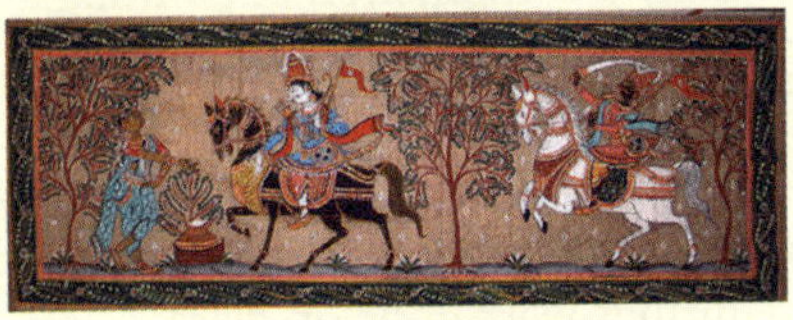 **Pattachitra Paintings**	• This folk art from Orissa (now Odisha), refers to paintings done on canvas or cloth (*Patta*-canvas/cloth; *Chitra*-painting) Earlier paintings were also done on palm leaf (referred as Tala Pattachitra). • The subjects of the paintings were religious in nature generally taken from imagery of Lord Jagannatha. Sometimes scenes from Geet Govinda and other devotional poems were also taken. • The paintings use colours such as deep red, ochre, black and blue which are obtained from organic sources, lac, shells, and minerals. • These paintings (called Pata) were earlier made as offerings to Lord Jagannatha in the temples.
(5) **Jharna Pattachitra** or **Patua Art;** West Bengal 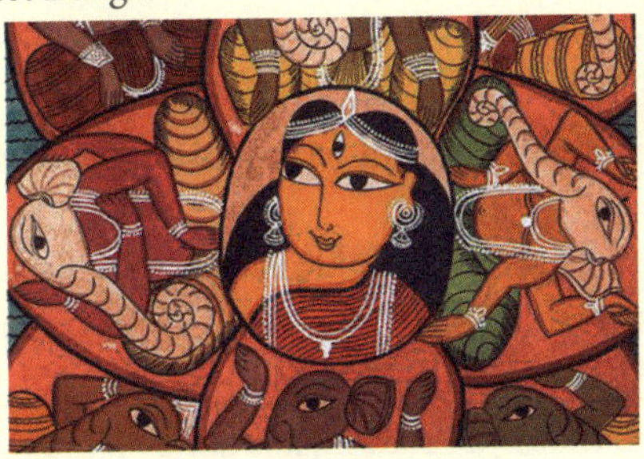 **Patua Painting**	• This folk art of West Bengal captured a series of paintings on a long vertical scroll of paper. The subjects of the paintings would be scenes from religious epics. • The artists would compose and sing songs from the epics and the relevant scene would be opened in the scroll before the audience. This art form is centuries old.
(6) **Kalamkari Paintings;** Andhra Pradesh	• Kalamkari or Vrathapani refers to paintings done on fabric by using Kalam (pen) which is made of pointed bamboo (*Kalam*-pen; *Kari*-craftsmanship). • Subjects were usually religious in character taken from the epics *Ramayana* and *Mahabharata*. • Two distinct styles: *Srikalahasti* style and *Machilipatnam style* are in vogue.
(7) **Phad Paintings**; Rajasthan	• This folk art popular in Rajasthan is done on long scrolls of fabric/cloth at the end of which bamboo shafts are tied for rolling the scrolls.
	• The *Bhopas* who are priest singers, carry the Phads which serves as temples of their folk deities.
(8) **Pichwai Paintings;** Udaipur, Rajasthan	• These are paintings done in cloth in Nathdwara temple in Rajasthan. • The subject of temple is Lord Srinathji and thus are of religious character.

(9) **Thanjavur or Tanjore Painting**; Thanjavur, Tamil Nadu 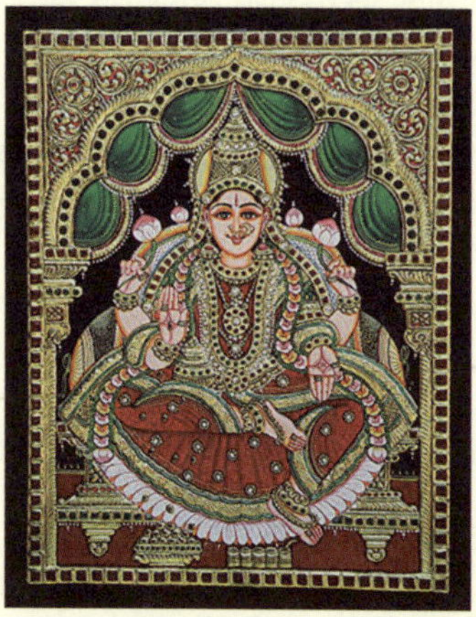 **Tanjore Painting**	• This art form is essentially a combination of painting and craft which flourished in Thanjavur (Tamil Nadu) during the Maratha rule. Thus, it is centuries old. • It is a panel based painting done on wood, with figures encrusted with semi-precious stones, overlaid with gold foils, etc. Later the paintings were done on glass. • The subjects are religious figures, deities, etc.
(10) **Manjusha Art**; Bhagalpur (Bihar)	• Popular in **Bhagalpur region,** it is also called Angika art (reference to Ang Pradesh, a Mahajanapada) and is centuries old • It originated and is based on the folklore of *Bihula-Bishari.* • The art form uses **only three colours—pink, green, and yellow** and is executed on boxes of jute and paper.
(11) **Tribal Art** (a) **Gond Paintings** (Madhya Pradesh) (b) Santhal Paintings (c) Paitkar Paintings 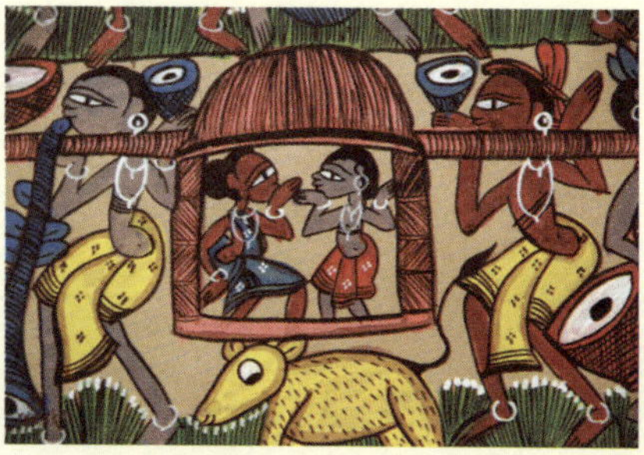 **Santhal Painting**	• Popular in Gonds of Madhya Pradesh, it is done on the walls of houses. Later it has been done on canvas and paper also. • Contains images from folk stories, flora and fauna, etc. • Santhal paintings are popular in Santhal tribes of Jharkhand and West Bengal. • The themes are taken from natural surroundings and objects of daily life. The images are simplistic and almost a diagrammatic representation. Colours are bright and natural pigments are used. • Popular in the state of Jharkhand, it is one of the oldest tribal paintings • The Paitkar paintings are scroll paintings (similar to Patua art) and are made on paper or palm leaves. It uses soil, glue, and colours extracted from natural sources, stones, vegetables, etc. • Subjects include scenes from daily life, stories of legends and mythologies, and even explores life after death.

IMPORTANT TOPICS TO FOCUS ON

- Important art movements of modern India, their features, and artists associated with it.
- Folk art, regions where popular, and unique features.

16

CHAPTER

Music In Modern India

Music is all about transporting people, speaking a language which languages fail to express

A. R. Rehman

MUSIC IN MODERN INDIA

Music in India has evolved through the ages. It was an intrinsic part of the Vedic traditions. Many elements of Indian music were compiled and structured in Bharata's *Natya Shastra*. In the medieval period, it absorbed the Persian and Arabic influences and emerged with altogether new features. Thus, modern Indian music has assimilated different features through centuries of evolution and today it manifests in varied forms ranging from Classical to 'Popular' and from Carnatic to Pop music. *The broad categories of music in vogue can be classified into the following*:

(i) **Hindustani Classical music**

(ii) **Carnatic music**

(iii) **Light classical music** which includes:

(a) Thumri, (b) Dadra, (c) Qawali, (d) Kajri, (e) Tappa, (f) Ghazal, (g) Khayal, etc.

(iv) **Devotional music:**

(a) Bhajan (b) Kirtan (c) Shabad, etc.

(v) **Folk music**

(vi) **Film and other popular music**

(vii) **Western music**

The Hindustani Classical, Carnatic, and different forms of light classical music and devotional music have already been discussed in the Chapter 13—'Music in Medieval India'. In this chapter, folk music, other forms of music in modern India, and famous personalities associated with them are described.

FOLK MUSIC

India has a rich tradition of regional and folk music. This form of music is deeply influenced by the regional and local culture, tradition, and language. *Some of the important forms of folk music prevalent today are discussed here.*

Folk Music	Salient Features
(i) **(a) Wanawan**	• Wanawan (also referred as Wanwun) is a traditional music and dance performed on **the occasion of marriage in Kashmir.**
(b) **Chakri**	• Chakri is another popular music of Jammu and Kashmir region which is **played with instruments like *harmonium, rabab, and sarangi.***
(ii) **Tappa**	A folk song of Punjab popular amongst camel riders. It is usually sung in Punjabi and Pashto language.
(iii) **Uttarakhand Folk Songs** (a) Bajuband (b) Basanti (c) Chhopati	These are folk songs of Uttarakhand which are sung in the Uttarakhandi language of Kumaoni and Garhwali. They are sung on various festivals, religious and other auspicious occasions, and subjects often include folk stories, religious traditions, etc. • Bajuband is a folk song of love and sacrifice. • Basanti is folk song of spring. • Chhopati is a folk song of love sung in Tehri and Garhwal region.
(iv) **Rajasthani Folk Songs** (a) Maand (b) Pankhida (c) Lotia (d) Panihore	Rajasthan has a rich folk singing tradition popular amongst communities of *Langhas, Saperas,* **Manganiars**, *Bhopas,* and *Jogis*. Some of these folk songs are: • Maand is a folk singing style of Rajasthan which is also recognised in the classical circles. However, it is not recognised as a true or a full-fledged **raga.** It is said to be **popular in the erstwhile royal courts of Rajasthan**. • Pankhida (literal meaning, lover) is **sung by peasants** while doing work in fields. It is sung to the accompaniment of *alghoza* and *manzira.* • Lotia is sung during festivals, particularly in the Chaitra month by the **womenfolk in Rajasthan**. The *lotas* (vessels) containing water filled from ponds and wells) are decorated with flowers with which the womenfolk return home. • Panihore are songs centered around **water and wells.**
(v) **Folk Songs of Uttar Pradesh** (a) Rasiyageet (b) Hori (c) Sohar	• Rasiyageet are folk songs of the **Braj region** of Uttar Pradesh which are sung in Braj Bhasha (a Hindi dialect). *Rasa* here refers to emotion and the songs have genesis to the singing in **praise of lord Krishna** describing his acts and antics. • Hori are songs sung on the occasion of festival of **Holi in Braj.** • Sohar are folk songs sung on the occasion of **child birth** particularly in the **Allahabad** region.

(vi) **Baul**	It is the folk music of **West Bengal** and is a kind of **religious music**. Baul is also a kind of religious sect, following Vaishnava and Sufi traditions. It is a centuries old musical tradition which is associated with mysticism. It is also said to have influenced Rabindra Sangeet.
(vii) **Rabindra Sangeet**	It refers to the **musical tradition of Rabindranath Tagore** and the repertoire of the music composed by him which is particularly popular in West Bengal. Over 2000 songs are said to have been composed by him that were influenced by Hindustani Classical, Carnatic, Baul, and other folk music of India.
(viii) **Pandavani**	It is a form of **folk music and folk theatre** which **involves narration of tales of Mahabharata**. Bhima is said to be the hero in the narrations. This form is popular in the regions of Chattisgarh, Odisha, Madhya Pradesh, and Andhra Pradesh.
(ix) **Bihu**	The word Bihu refers to the Bihu songs, dance, and Bihu festival of Assam. On the occasion of new year when the Bihu festival is celebrated, the Bihu songs are also sung. It is also a **song of joyfulness and love.**
(x) **Lai Haraoba**	It is a **Manipuri festival** with which a folk song is also associated.
(xi) **Alha**	It is a form of **ballad song** popular in Madhya Pradesh (Bundelkhand region). It is sung in praise of valour of Alha and Udal who fought against Prithviraj Chauhan (in 1182 CE).
(xii) **Lavani**	It is the folk music of **Maharashtra** which is a combination of **song and dance**. The dance form associated with it is called **Tamasha**. It is performed on the beat of *dholaki*, a drum like instrument.
(xiii) **Powada**	Powadas are a kind **ballad written in Maharashtra** describing a hero or a historical event, etc. The singers of these ballads are called **Shahirs**. Earliest known Powada was *Afzal Khancha Vadh* (killing of Afzal Khan) written by Agnidas (in 1659).
(xiv) **Burrakatha**	This is a **form of storytelling** popular in rural Andhra Pradesh often delivered in the form of songs. The subjects are mythological. At times, contemporary social issues are also taken.
(xv) **Mando**	This is a **Goan folk** song and music which has elements of both Indian and Western (Portuguese) culture.

Folk Singers in Rajasthan

Manganiars are folk singers in Rajasthan located in carvan towns, particularly in the desert area of Jaisalmer. They sing in praise of legendary kings of Rajasthan, battles, and also of Hindu gods. These are often Muslims of Rajput descent.

Langhas are **Muslim singing communities of Rajasthan** who are said to have descended from Jats and Rajputs. They play *shehnai* and *sarangi*. The *Langhas* stuck to the traditional musical audience while *Manganiyars* had a broader outlook. Other singing communities include the *Bhopas*, *Jogis*, and *Saperas*.

POPULAR MUSIC IN INDIA

Film Music

The film music is the most popular form of music in India providing for nearly 70% of all musical forms (in terms of sales volume). Churned out by the Bollywood (Hindi film industry), South Indian films, and regional film industries, this form of music has garnered an international appeal, particularly in Southeast Asia and also in those countries where Indian community has a sizeable presence.

The film songs and music are based on **light classical music, Hindustani Classical music, folk songs, Carnatic music,** and even **Western musical traditions.** Thus, it has provided a platform for amalgamation and evolution of music based on popular appeal and often transcending the rules and strict traditions of the respective forms.

Popular Western Musical Forms

Rock Music It refers to the genre of western music which became popular in the 1950s and 1960s in **America** and was called **Rock and Roll**. The music is fast paced and involves romantic songs to the accompaniment of instruments like electric guitar, base guitar, acoustics guitar, drums, keyboard, etc. A number of musical bands are associated with it. Its sub-genres include, **hard-rock, heavy-metal, psychedelic-rock, progressive-rock,** etc. In India, this music has become popular as **Indian rock** which is a music genre incorporating elements of mainstream rock music and Indian music.

Pop Music This form of music also became popular in the Western world in the 50s and 60s. However, it was softer as compared to the Rock music. Besides, it also borrows elements from other musical styles such as *Latin County*, *Urban*, etc. In India, it is popular as **Indipop** which is again a fusion of western pop and Indian elements. The film music and television music channels of 90s and 2000s substantially increased its popularity in India.

INDIAN MUSICAL INSTRUMENTS

A variety of Indian musical instruments have been used in the different forms of Indian music. They can be classified into (a) String instruments (b) Wind instruments (c) Percussion instruments (d) Non-drum percussion instruments.

- The **stringed instruments** (**chordophones**) are those having **single or multiple strings attached** and are played by plucking or bowing of the strings. They can be further categorised as (a) the plucked string instruments and (b) the bowed stringed instruments. The **former include** *sarod, sitar, tambura, rudra-veena, vichitra veena, ektara, gotuvadyam,* and *tumbi,* amidst others. The common Indian bowed string instruments include *dilruba, ektara,* violin, *sarangi, esraj, chikara,* etc. *Santoor* is a stringed instrument which does not fall in the above two categories as its strings are gently stuck with wooden mallets.

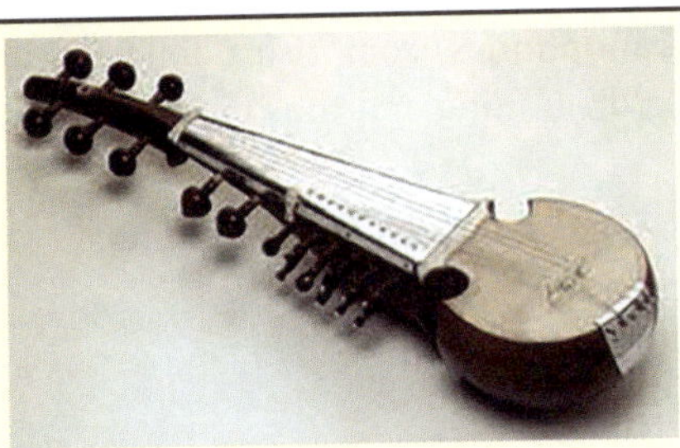

Sarod

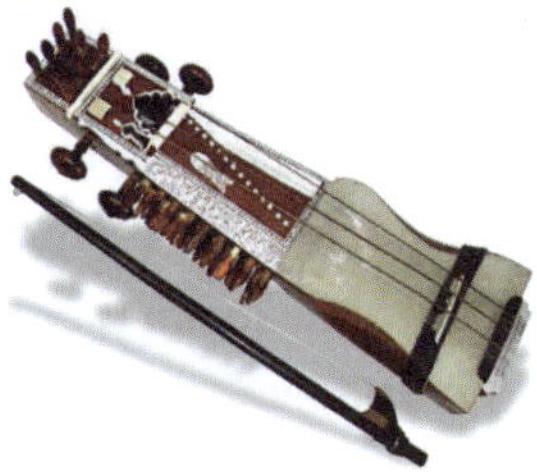

Sarangi

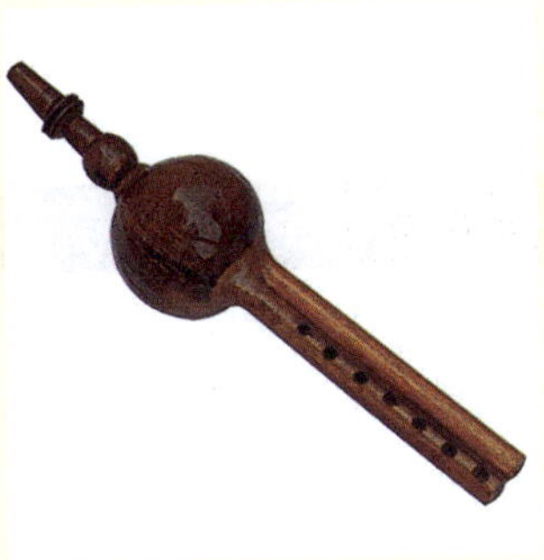

Pungi

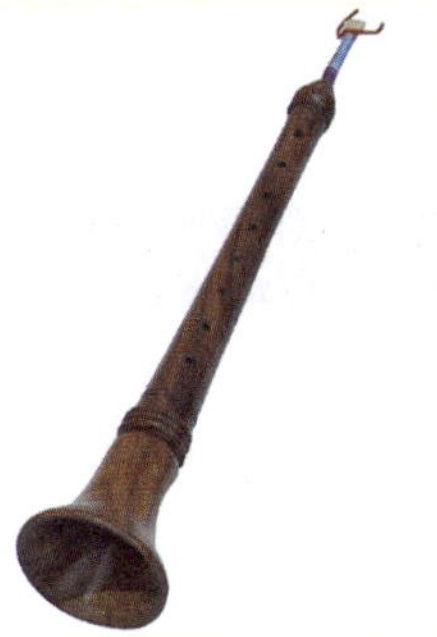

Shehnai

- **Wind instruments (aerophones)** are played by blowing air into them. These can be of single reed types such as ***pungi been*** or **double reed ones** such as ***shehnai*** *and* ***nadaswaram.*** *Flutes and bagpipes* and are also a category of wind instruments. India has various types of flutes such as the *bansuri, alghoza* (double flute), *venu* (Carnatic flute), etc. Indian bagpipes include *mashak* (North India) and *Titti* (Andhra Pradesh). *Harmonium* is a kind of musical wind instrument where wind is not blown but pushed/pumped by hand.

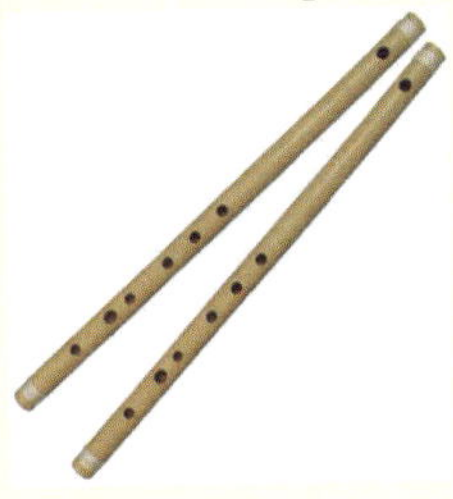

Algoza

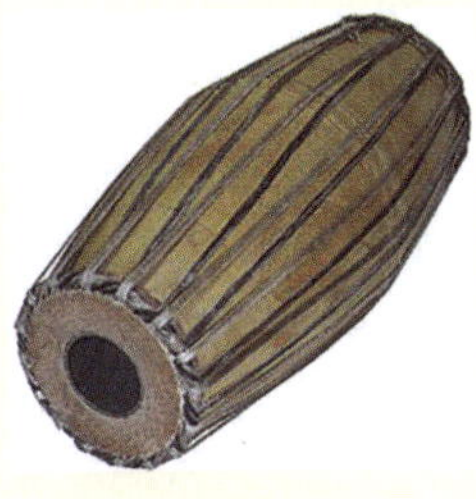

Mridangam

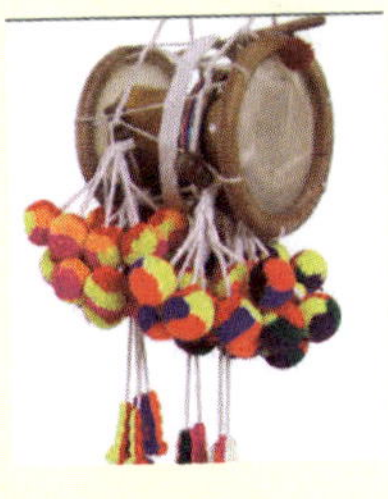

Idakka

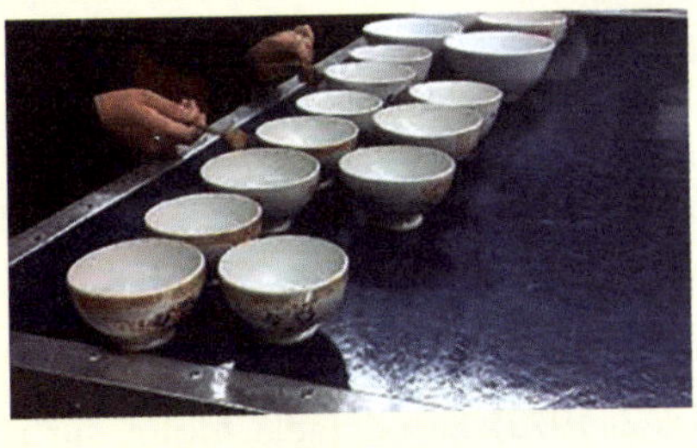

Jal Tarang

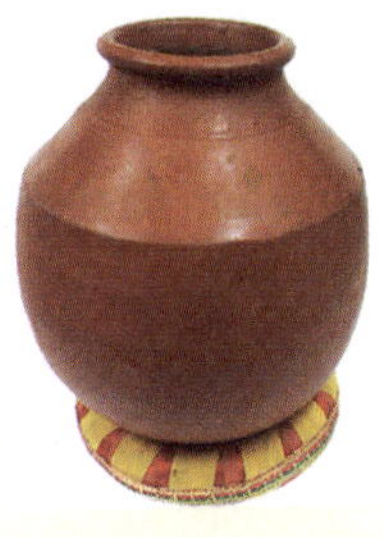

Ghatam

- The **membranous percussion instruments** (**membranophones**) comprise a hollow structure covered with a membrane which vibrates on beating/drumming and thus creates the desired sound. These can be classified as:
  - (a) **Hand-drums** such as *damru, dholak, mridangam, pakhavaj, tabla, dholaki,* etc.
  - (b) **Handframe drums** such as *kanjira, daf,* etc.
  - (c) **Stick and hand drums** such as *dhol, idakka, chenda,* etc.
  - (d) **Stick drums** including *nagara, pambaichandi,* etc.
- **Non-drum percussion instruments** (**idiophones**) are those which produce sound when struck but do not have any membrane stretched on the body. These include instruments like *jaltarang, ghatam* (earthen ware pot), *thali, manjeera, ghungroo, etc.*

EXPONENTS OF INDIAN CLASSICAL MUSIC

Indian classical music (Hindustani Classical and Carnatic) has produced a number of doyens both in the vocal and instrumental music traditions. *Some of the leading vocalists and instrumentalists are mentioned here.*

(a) Eminent Vocalists

(i) *Abdul Karim Khan* (1872–1937): (Kirana Gharana and expert of Carnatic music system)
(ii) *Alladiya Khan* (1855–1946): Hindustani Classical, Jaipur Atrauli Gharana
(iii) *Bade Ghulam Ali* (1902–1968): Khayal and Thumri, Patiala Kasur style
(iv) *Balamuralikrishna* (1930): Carnatic vocalist and multi-instrumentalist
(v) *Begum Akhtar* (1914–1974): Ghazal, Thumari, and Dadra
(vi) *Bhimsen Joshi* (1922–2011): Khayal, Thumri, Bhajan, etc. (**Bharat Ratna awardee)**
(vii) *D.K. Pattammal* (1919–2009): Carnatic vocal and film play back singing
(viii) *D.V. Paluskar* (1921–1955): Hindustani Classical
(ix) *Dagar Brothers:* Dhrupad singing
(x) *Gangubai Hangal* (1913–2009): Hindustani Classical, Kirana Gharana
(xi) *Mallikarjun Mansur* (1911–1992): Hindustani Vocal, Jaipur Gharana
(xii) *M.S. Subbulakshmi* (1916–2004): Carnatic vocalist (**Bharat Ratna awardee**)
(xiii) *M.L. Vasanthakumari* (1928–1990): Carnatic vocalist
(xiv) *Pandit Jasraj* (1930): Khayal singer, Hindustani Classical, Mewati Gharana
(xv) *Siddheshwari Devi* (1908–1976): Khayal, Thumri, and singing Hindustani Classical
(xvi) *Vishnu Digambar Paluskar* (1872–1931): Hindustani Classical

(b) Eminent Instrumentalists

(i) *Ali Akbar Khan* (1922–2009): Sarod, Maihar Gharana
(ii) *Alla Rakha* (1919–2000): Tabla, Hindustani Classical
(iii) *Amjad Ali Khan* (1945): Sarod, Hindustani Classical
(iv) *Baba Allaudin Khan* (1862–1972): Sarod, tabla, violin, surbahar
(v) *Bismillah Khan* (1916–2006): Shehnai, **Bharat Ratna awardee**

(vi) *Hariprasad Chaurasia* (1938): Flute, Hindustani Classical, and Film score
(vii) *Lalgudi Jayaraman* (1930–2013): Violin, Indian Classical, Jazz, and Fusion
(viii) *N. Ravikiran* (1967): Chitra Veena and Gotuvadhyam, Carnatic music
(ix) *Ravi Shankar* (1920–2012): Sitar, Hindustani Classical, **Bharat Ratna awardee**
(x) *Shiv Kumar Sharma* (1938): Santoor, Hindustani Classical
(xi) *L. Subramaniam* (1947):Violin, Carnatic, Classical, Jazz
(xii) *U. Srinivas* (1969–2014): Mandolin
(xiii) *V.G. Jog* (1922–2004):Violin
(xiv) *V. Doraiswamy Iyengar:* Veena, Carnatic music
(xv) *Vilayat Khan* (1928–2004): Sitar, Indian Classical
(xvi) *Zakir Hussain* (1951): Tabla, Hindustani Classic, Jazz, World music

Indian Music and Associated Institutions

Gandharva Mahavidyalaya: Established by V.D. Paluskar in early 20th century in Lahore, this institution aimed at spreading and enrichment of Indian music. The current institution in New Delhi was established in 1939.

Sangeet Natak Academy: As an institution of national eminence, it was established in 1952 by the Government of India. It is the apex institution of performing arts in India and aims to preserve and promote various arts including music, dance, and drama.

SPIC MACAY: (Society for the Promotion of Indian Classical Music and Culture Amongst Youth): It is a non-governmental organisation and a voluntary movement which aims to preserve and promote Indian classical music and culture amongst the younger generation. It has been successful in hosting a number of lecture-demonstrations and performances of eminent experts of music before lakhs of students in schools, colleges, and other educational institutions. It was established in 1977 by Dr. Kiran Seth.

IMPORTANT TOPICS TO FOCUS ON

- Folk music, regions associated with it, and its features
- Musical instruments, their classification, and type

CHAPTER 17

Dances in Modern India

> Everything in the universe has rhythm. Everything dances
>
> —Maya Angelou

CLASSIFICATION OF INDIAN DANCES

The majority of dances of India trace their origin to **Bharata's** *Natya Shastra*. However, over the centuries, this art form has tremendously evolved and diversified. The Islamic influence, the patronisation of dances by courts, the practice of temple dances, the different regions and their culture, all have cast their deep influence and created diverse dance forms in India. *The dances of India can broadly be categorised into two types:*

(a) **Classical dances**

(b) **Folk and tribal dances**

There are eight recognised classical dance forms. *These dances and their salient features and the region/ states in which they are popular are described herewith.*

(a) Kathak

The word Kathak is derived from *Katha,* meaning a story. Thus, the dance originated as a narrative form of storytelling, incorporating expressions and body movements. It became popular during the Bhakti movement (as a narrative of Radha-Krishna love) and later flourished in the Mughal courts. In the present day, it is particularly **popular in Uttar Pradesh** and other parts of northern India.

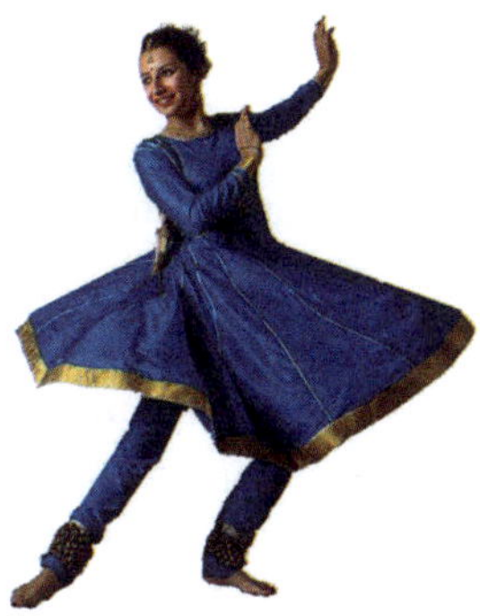

Kathak dance

- It has three distinct **Gharanas**—the **Lucknow Gharana** which emphasises on *bhava*, the **Jaipur Gharana** which stresses on *laya* (rhythm), and the **Benaras Gharana.**
- The dance is characterised by its circular pirouettes and dexterous footwork and is performed to the accompaniment of Hindustani classical music. Use of *ghungroos* is an important feature of this dance form.
- The important elements of dance include *Amad* (entry), *Salami* (salutation), *Thaat* (soft gliding movements), *Tukada,* and *Tora* or cadences (which are fast rhythmic but small pieces of performance). This is followed by a *Nritta* performed on a *nagma.*
- Its exponents include **Shambhu Maharaj, Sitara Devi, Pt. Birju Maharaj, Shovna Narayan, Prerana Shrimali,** etc.

(b) Odissi

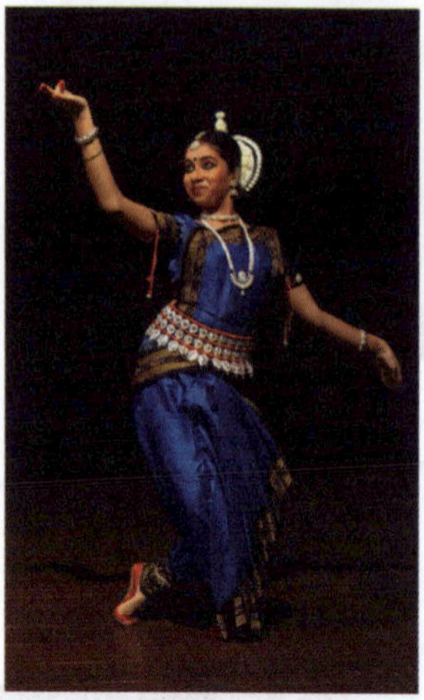

Odissi

This classical dance form is of **Orissa (now Odisha)** and is centuries old. Reference to it is also found in Udayagiri and Khandagiri caves of 2nd century BCE, in the ancient text *Natya Shastra,* and in the hall of dance (*nata mandap*) at Sun temple at Konark built in the 13th century CE.

- The dance was initially performed by the ***Maharis*** or the ***Devadasis*** in the temples. But later they came to be employed in the royal courts leading to the degeneration of the art form. Later, a class of boys called ***Gotipuas*** were trained in this art.
- Odissi is primarily **a dance of love and passion**. The facial expressions *(bhava)*, the hand gestures, and the body movements are together channelised by the performer to depict the *rasa*.
- The body movements are built around the postures, called **Chowk** and ***Tribhanga***. While ***Chowk* is a masculine stance** which is imitating a square, the *Tribhanga* **is a feminine** and more graceful stance. Here, the **body is bent at three positions** at the neck, torso, and knee (Tri-bhanga: thrice-bent).
- Its important constituents can be said to be (a) *Mangala Charan* (entry of dancer on stage), (b) Invocation of deity (c) *Nritta* (involving salutation to God and guru), (d) *Batu* (the performance of basic steps), (e) *Abhinaya* (main feature of performance), and (g) *Pallavi* (one or more such items based on *abhinaya*)
- The dance is performed to the accompaniment of instruments like *pakhawaj, sitar, manjira, flute,* etc.
- Its famous exponents include **Kelucharan Mohapatra, Sanjukta Panigrahi,** and **Sonal Mansingh** amongst others.

(c) Manipuri

It is a famous dance form of Manipur (a state in Northeastern India). This art is centuries old and has a **religious character**.

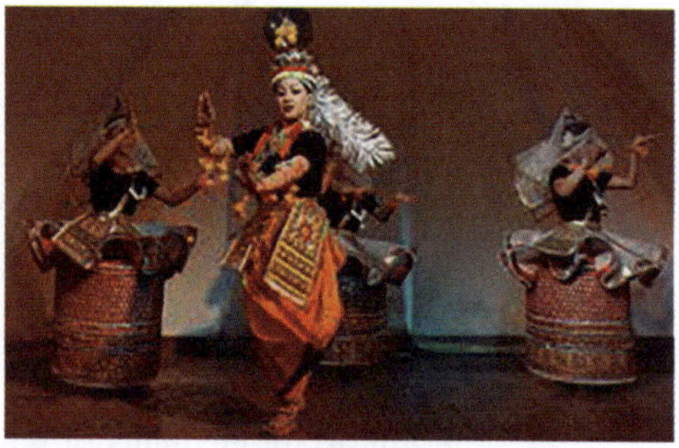

Manipuri

- The dance is particularly performed during the **Manipuri festival of Lai-Haraoba.** Priests and priestesses enact creation of the universe. The dance has a strong **Vaishnavite influence.** However, dances pertaining to *Shaivism* (worship of Lord Shiva) and *Shaktism* are also integrated. A common form of this dance also depicts *Krishna Leelas.*
- The Manipuri dance incorporates three dance forms:
  - (i) **Rasa** or *Raslila* – This depicts the **love of Radha and Krishna**
  - (ii) **Sankirtan** – This is a **devotional Kirtan** form of dance.
  - (iii) **Thang Ta** (also called **Thang Pah**) – This is a **martial art form** of dance.

- The dancing technique involves depiction of the *rasa* using the **entire movement of the body** and there is no undue emphasis on facial expression or the *bhava* to express the *Rasa*.
- Further, **there is no use of ankle-bells** (ghungroo) in this dance form. Instruments like *pung* (barrel drum), *kartals* (cymbals), harmonium, flute, etc. are used.
- Its constituent elements are (a) *Alarippu* – invocatory pure dance (b) *Jatiswaram* – a short pure dance (c) *Shabdam* – a dance performance in adoration of God (d) *Varnam* – the main performance (e) *Padams* and *Javalis* – performed usually on the theme of love (g) *Tillana* – the final performance at the end (g) *Mangalam* – or invocation of God.
- Its exponents include **Elam Endira Devi, Darshana Jhaveri, Y. Gambhini Devi, Guru Bipin Singh, etc.**

(d) Bharatnatyam

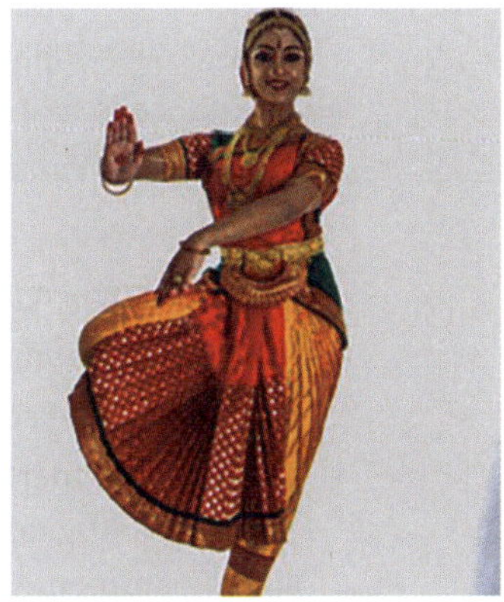

Bharatanatyam

Popular in **Tamil Nadu** and adjoining regions, Bharatnatyam is among the most ancient of Indian classical dance forms. Its origin can be traced to **Bharata's** *Natya Shastra*. Reference to it is also noted in **Nandikeshwara's** *Abhinaya Darpana*. Besides, elements of this art is also seen in sculptures in the Chidambaram temple.

- This was essentially a **temple dance** art and the dance form survived through the **Devadasi system**. These were women dedicated to the temple and married to the God. But after the Devadasi system ended (in the 19th century) the art form declined till its revival in the 20th century.
- The dance form involves all the three elements of dance, viz. **Nritta** (pure dance), **Nritya** (solo and expressive dance), and **Natya** (dance-drama). It is traditionally performed by women where a dancer performs many roles.
- The dance involves **emphasis on *abhinaya*** (mime). This includes gestures, movement of hands, and expression of eyes and facial muscles. **The bending of knee** with equal distribution of weight on both legs is a typical posture. There is emphasis also on **rhythmic footwork.**
- The **subjects of dance are the mythological legends and spiritual ideas** of Hindu texts and scriptures.
- It is performed to the accompaniment of **Carnatic music** along with instruments like *mridangam* (drum), *nadaswaram* (a long pipe), *nattuvangam* (cymbals), *veena*, *flute*, etc.
- The exponents of this dance form are Rukmini Devi, Meenakshi Sundaram Pillai, Balasubramaniam, Mrinalini Sarabhai, Mallika Sarabhai, Sonal Mansingh, and S. Kanaka amongst others.

(e) Kuchipudi

This classical dance form is popular in Andhra Pradesh, Telangana, and adjoining regions. It is said to have originated in a village Kuchipudi in the Krishna district in the 17th century under the aegis of a Vaishnava saint **Siddhendra Yogi**. Originally, this art form was a **dance drama** where themes from Krishna Leela and other Vaishnava traditions were performed. Later, solo tradition also developed in this art form.

- Kuchipudi involves all the three elements of dance viz. **Nritta, Nritya, and Natya.** It involves substantial stage movement and dexterous footwork. The style is quite expressive with use of gestures of hand, and expressions of eyes and face.
- Some features of the dance form are similar to that of Bharatnatyam such as ***ardhamandala*** which is a partial squat with legs bent. However, while Bharatnatyam is a dance of temple tradition, where emphasis on geometric perfection and spiritual aspect is more, **Kuchipudi is more sensuous** with more supple body movements.
- Some performances exhibit dancing with several pots on their head or dancing on the rim of a brass plate.
- The dance is said to be comprising
  (a) *Ganesha Vandana* or invocation
  (b) *Jatiswaram* – a *nritta* performance
  (c) *Shabdam* – a narrative performance
  (d) *Nrityaabhinaya* – based on literary cum musical forms such as *Padam, Jaavli,* etc.
  (e) *Tarangam* – concluding performance.

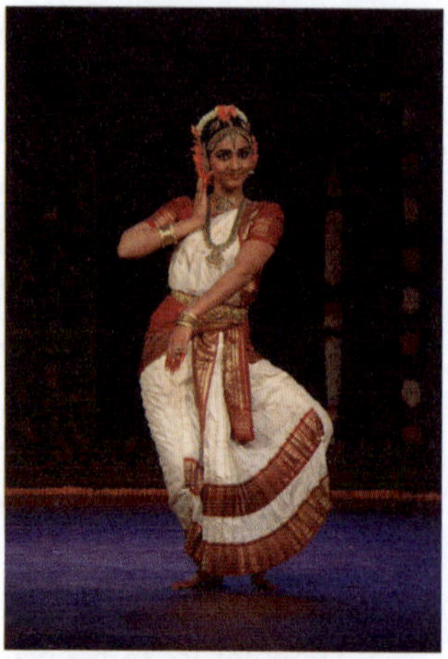

Kuchipudi

- The dance is performed to the **accompaniment of Carnatic music** where the vocals are in Telugu language. Instruments like *mridanga*, *veena*, cymbal, flute, etc. are also used as accompaniment.
- The well-known exponents of Kuchipudi are **Raja and Radha Reddy** and **Yamini Krishnamurthy,** amongst others.

(f) Kathakali

It is one of the major classical dance forms of India which is **popular in Kerala.** As a form of **dance-drama** as in vogue today, it was revived in the 1930s by the Malayali poet **V.N. Menon.** This dance form also draws from many other local dance forms of Kerala, viz. **Koodiyattam, Krishnanattam, Ramanattam,** and **Chakyar Koothu.** Some scholars suggest that even the martial art form of Kerala, Kalaripayattu has contributed to it.

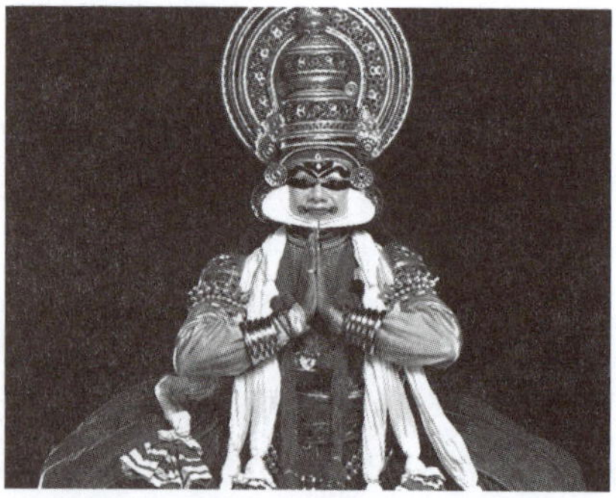

Kathakali

- Kathakali is a form of a dance-drama where there is harmonious blend of dance, music, and acting. It dramatises stories which have been adopted from the Indian epics like *Ramayana, Mahabharata,* Krishna Leela, etc.
- As a dance it combines all the three elements of dance, viz. **Nritta, Nritya,** and **Natya.** It also incorporates elements of ***Abhinaya*** (acting), viz. which are (a) ***Angika*** (physical aspect of acting through gesturing and movement of body and limbs), (b) ***Aharya*** (costume and makeup), (c) ***Vachika*** (oral aspect of acting), and (d) ***Satvika*** (emotional aspect of acting).

- The **costume and makeup of the artists is the most elaborate amongst all dance forms**. The face makeup is quite detailed and deeply painted, appearing as if the performer is wearing a mask. Headgear, costumes, and other makeup are done as per the characters. This includes seven basic makeups, viz. **Pacca** (green), **Payuppu** (ripe), **Katti** (knife), **Kari**, **Tati**, **Minukku,** and **Teppu**. The lips, eyebrows, eyelashes are all made to look prominent through makeup.
- The characters are **Satvik** (the heroes), **Rajsik** (kings and warriors), and **Tamsik** (devilish antiheroes) and different colours of the face represent different characters, viz. **green face with red lips represents Satvik characters** such as Rama, Krishna, Yudhisthira, Arjuna, etc.
- The **use of entire body in the dance, that of facial muscles, and movement of eyebrows and eyeballs** (which depict a range of emotions) are unique features of this dance form. It incorporates all nine *rasas* and 24 major *mudras* in its repertoire.
- A Kathakali begins with *Kelikottu* - calling attention of the audience (b) *Thodayama* - a devotional invocatory performance (c) *Purappadu* - pure *nritta* (d) *Melappadam* - performance by musicians (e) *Tiranokku* - debut of characters on stage (f) Main performance.
- The dance is performed to the accompaniment of **Sopana Sangeet** of Kerala, with musical instruments like *mandalam* (barrel shaped drums), *centa* (cylindrical drums), *idakka* (hourglass shaped drums), and other instruments.
- Exponents of this art form include, **Kalamandalam Gopi, K. Sivaraman, K.R Nair, K.C Panicker**, etc.

(g) Mohiniattam

Mohiniattam is another **classical dance form popular in Kerala**. The dance is said to have been structured by the Travancore kings. But in the 19th and the early 20th century owing to the Devadasi system, it declined, till it was revived by the Malayali poet **V.N. Menon** in the 1940s.

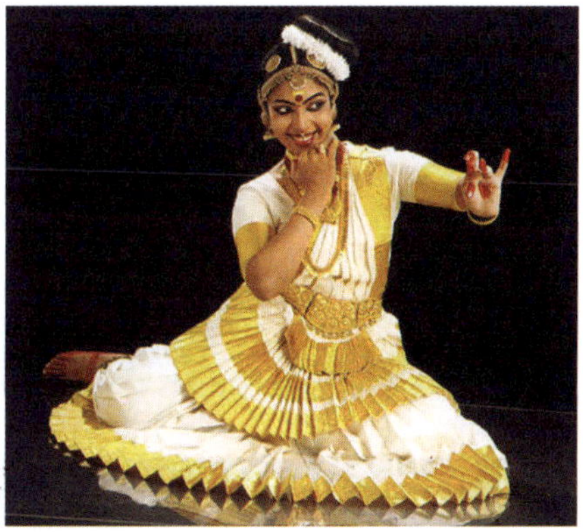

Mohiniattam

- The word Mohiniattam is derived from two words: Mohini, a mythological enchantress and Attam (rhythmic motion or dance). Thus, the **dance of Mohini is the inspiration of this art**. Mohini is referred in Hindu mythology as an incarnation of Lord Vishnu, a celestial enchantress who emerges during the distribution of nectar between the *Asuras* and *Devas* after the churning of the ocean. Also, the character is a central figure in the story of defeat of *Bhasmasura*.
- It is a **feminine and Lasya form of dance which incorporates graceful and swaying body movement** (akin to swinging palm leaves and gentle undulation of ocean waves). It does not involve abrupt body motion, sudden jerks, or even leaps. The footwork is soft and not terse and the whole demeanour is graceful and sensuous.
- The dance lays emphasis on abhinaya and expression of the emotion of the character with which the performer identifies.
- The costume includes white, off-white, cream coloured saris with golden or coloured embroidery and borders.

- The dance is performed to the accompaniment of vocal song (a mix of Malayalam and Sanskrit) and instruments like *mridangam* (barrel drum), *idakka* (hourglass drum), *kuzhitalam* or *elathalam* (cymbals), etc.
- Famous exponents include Dr. Kanak Rele, Bharati Shivaji, Sunanda Nair, etc.

(h) Sattriya Dance

It is a **classical dance of Assam** which has its origin in Krishna Bhakti Vaishnavism. This dance is also attributed to the 15th century Bhakti saint Sri Sankardev, who propagated the Vaishnava faith through it.

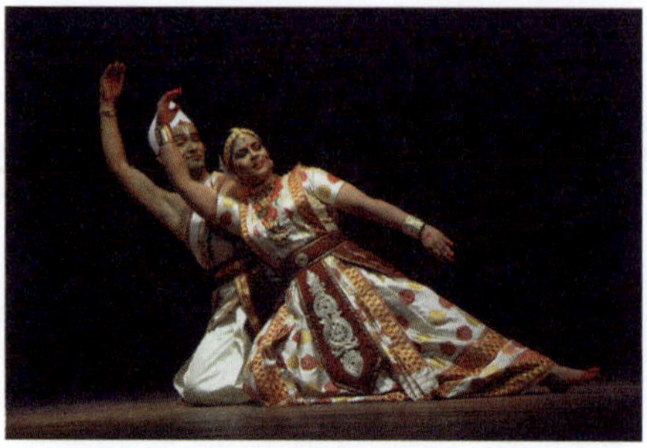

Sattriya Dance

- The word *Sattriya* originated from *Sattara* which were the monasteries or temples. The dances were performed by the Vaishnava monks, hence the dance form is **ritualistic and has temple origin**.
- The dance also incorporates one act plays which are called **Ankiya-Nat** which is a **ballad form of dance drama** combining the religious as well as aesthetic elements. The themes are often related to Lord Krishna or other avatars of Lord Vishnu and is performed usually by **male monks** in groups.
- The dance has principles strictly laid down with respect to *Aharyas*, music, footwork, *hast mudras,* and other aspects of dance.
- It is evolved in two streams—the ***Gayan-Bhayanar Nach*** and the ***Kharmanar Nach***.
- The dance is performed to the accompaniment of *Borgeets* (composed by Sri Sankardev and other saints). *Khols* (two faced asymmetrical drums), flute, harmonium, and violin are instruments which are a part of the performance.
- Its exponents include **Ghanakanta Bora Barbayan** and **Dr. Anwesa Mahanta** amongst others.

FOLK AND TRIBAL DANCES

India being a land of great diversity in terms of geographical regions, flora-fauna, weather, language, culture, and festivals, has a large number of folk and tribal dances which are rich and varied. These dances are performed for a variety of reasons including, on occasion of festivals, to mark onset of a season, to celebrate agricultural produce, on occasions of birth, marriages, or other rituals, as an expression of joy, as a means of propagation of a story/a message, or simply as a form of community entertainment.

These dances were usually performed with accompaniment of songs and some basic instruments. The use of **bright dresses, head gears, and even masks** (in some tribal dances) is a common practice. These dances are **performed by common folks as a community dance** ensuring wide social participation. Further, these are characterised by easier steps and movements and less of rules and formal rigour as compared to the classical dance forms.

Some of the popular folk and tribal dances are discussed below:

State/Region and Important Folk/ Tribal Dances	Characteristic Features
(1) **Jammu and Kashmir** (a) Dumhal (b) Rouf	• Dumhal is performed using **long colourful robes** and conical caps and Rouf dance is usually performed by men of **Rauf tribe**
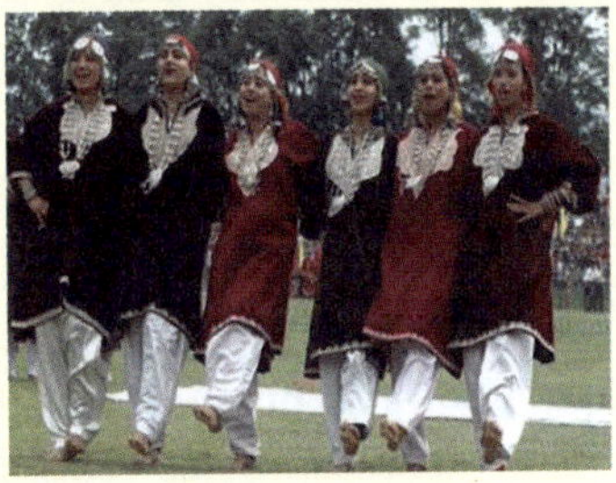 Dumhal Dance	• Rouf dance is a popular dance of Kashmir region performed by **girls/women** facing each other
(2) **Himachal Pradesh** (a) Kullu Nati (b) Chham (c) Rakshasa	• Himachal Pradesh has a number of folk dances amongst which Kullu Nati is the most popular. It is performed in the **Kullu region** • Chham is a very colourful dance performed by **Buddhist monks in monasteries** • Rakshasa dance is **performed in Kinnaur** wearing demon masks. It is believed to propitiate the good forces and ward off evil
(3) **Punjab** (a) Bhangra 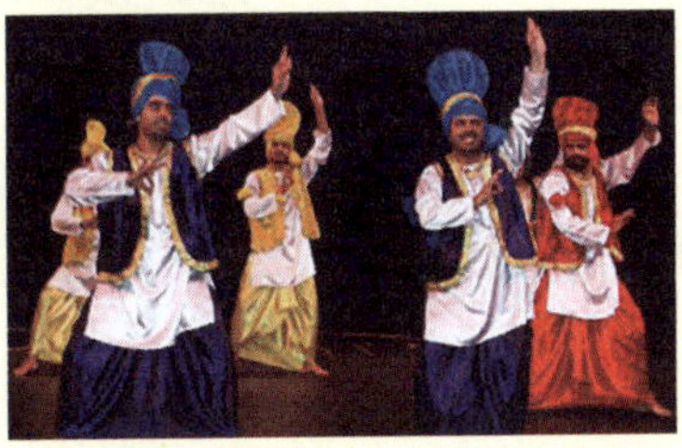 (b) Giddha	• The two dance forms Bhangara and Giddha are performed in Punjab on occasion of harvest festivals of Lohri, Baisakhi, and on occasion of other festivals • **Bhangra** is performed by men to the fast beats of drums. It is an **energetic dance** performed usually with arms raised and with the formation of a circle • **Giddha** is performed by womenfolk wearing clothes of wide variety of colours and traditional ornaments. It is similar to Bhangra
(4) **Rajasthan** (a) Ghoomar 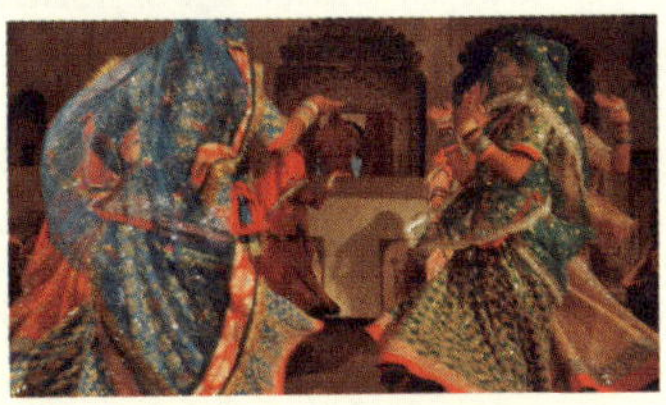 Ghoomar Dance (b) Kalbelia	• Ghoomar is a traditional dance **performed by women wearing coloured dresses** with face covered with a veil. The dance involves pirouetting with swirl of ghagras (long skirts), at the accompaniment of beats, with graceful movement of body • Kalbelia dance is performed by ***Kalbelia*** or *sapera* community (snake charmers). The women dance to the tune of *been* or *pungi* (a wood wind musical instrument) Other folk dances of this region include the *chakri* dance, *drum* dance, fire dance, etc.

(5) **Uttar Pradesh** (a) Rasleela (b) Dadra	• Popular in **Braj region** (Western Uttar Pradesh), Rasleela is a form of **theatrical dance-drama** based on stories of Lord Krishna, particularly of love of Radha and Krishna • Dadra is another folk dance which is performed to the accompaniment **of Dadra music** Other folk dances and folk theatres of this region include **Swang, Khyal, Ramleela,** while **Nautanki** is a folk theatre
(6) **Gujarat** (a) Garba, (b) Dandiya 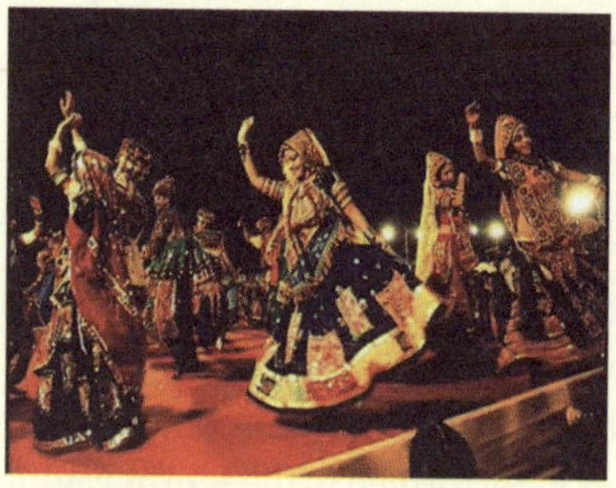 **Dandiya Dance**	• Garba is a dance **performed on the occasion of** *Navratri*. The dance was said to be originally performed in the Garbhagriha or sanctum of the temple of Goddess Durga in front of an earthen lamp; hence its name • The dance, Dandiya or Dandiya Raas is performed using sticks and traditionally by men in **leaping and twirling patterns**. It symbolises the battle of Durga and Mahisasura. This dance is also performed on the occasion of **Navratri** and has immense popularity in Gujarat and even abroad
(7) **Madhya Pradesh** (a) Matki Dance 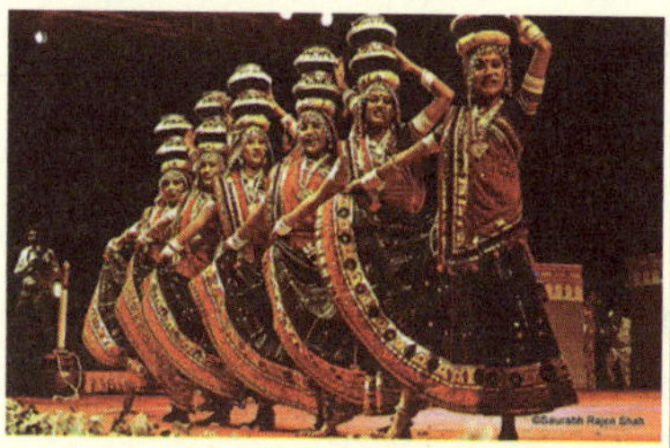 **Matki Dance** (b) Jawara dance	• Matki is a **community dance of Malwa region performed by women** who dance to the beat of a drum called matki • Jawara is a dance **associated with agricultural harvest** and is performed by both men and women. The latter **balance a basket full of Jawar on their head**. It is popular in the Bundelkhand region Other dances of Madhya Pradesh include **Rai** (where men dress as women), **Badhai** (performed on occasion of birth, marriage), **Gangaur** (on festival of Gangaur), etc.
(8) **Chattishgarh** (a) Raut Nacha (b) Gaur Maria	• Raut Nacha folk dance is performed by the community of ***Yadavas* or** who consider themselves as descendants of Lord Krishna. It is performed on the occasion of the **festival Devudni Ekadashi** (for a week after Diwali) and the dance incorporates anecdotes of **Krishna Leela,** specially the *rasa* aspect of it • Gaur Maria dance form is performed by **Bison Horn Maria tribes of Bastar district**. It imitates the movement of bisons and is usually performed on the occasion of marriages, both by men and women Another important dance of Chattisgarh is **Panthi** (of Satnami community)

(9) **Jharkhand** (a) Jhumar	• Jhumar is a **harvest dance performed by the tribal people.** This is also popular in Odisha. The performers dance in a circle wearing colourful costumes.
(b) Chhau 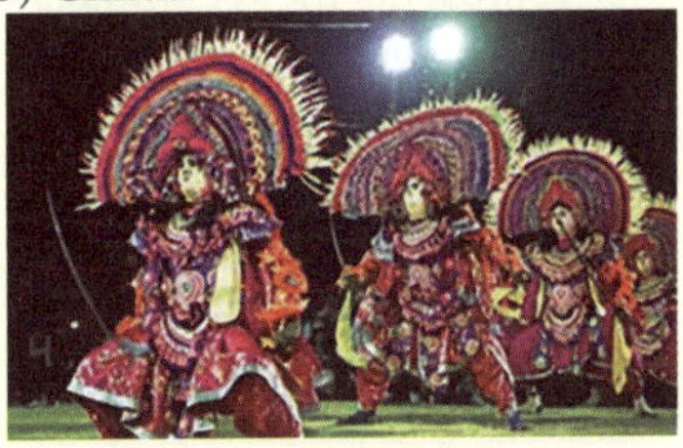 Chhau Dance	• Chhau dance is **popular in Jharkhand, West Bengal, and Odisha**. It has three different forms; Seraikela Chhau of Jharkhand, Purulia Chau of West Bengal, and Mayurbhanj Chhau of Odisha • The dance is usually **performed wearing a mask using vigorous movements and martial art features**. Themes of dances are taken from the mythological stories of *Ramayana*, *Mahabharata*, and other scriptures Other dance forms of Jharkhand include **Santhal** (performed by the Santhal tribes)
(10) **Bihar** (a) Jat-Jatin (b) Jhijhiya dance (c) Jhumeri	• Jat-Jatin is a popular folk dance of north Bihar of Mithila and Kosi region which is **performed by a man and a woman**. It depicts an emigrant husband and wife, their love, poverty, and sorrow • Jhijhiya is performed to invoke Indra, the God of Thunder for good rains • Jhumeri is similar to Garba of Gujarat but performed by **married women**. Kajari dance is another folk dance of Bihar
(11) **West Bengal** (a) Gambhira (b) Alkap	• Gambhira is popular in **Malda district** of West Bengal. It is also popular in the Muslim community. Gambhira is performed using various **wooden masks** • Alkap is a **mix of dance with music and theatre**. The subjects dwell on various socio-economic issues of rural areas Another famous dance is **Chhau** of Purulia district
(12) **Assam** (a) Bihu 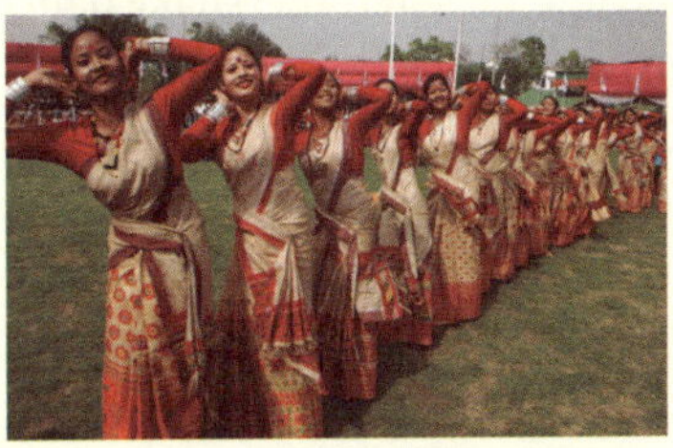 Bihu Dance	• Bihu is amongst the most famous of the Assam folk dances which is performed on the occasion of **Bihu festival** • Adorned in traditional and colourful clothing, **both men and women perform the dance to the beat of drums** with brisk steps with flipping of hands and swaying of hips Others important dances include **Bodo dance** (performed on festivals and rituals)

<table>
<tr><td>(13) Manipur
(a) Khamba Thoibi
(b) Thang Ta
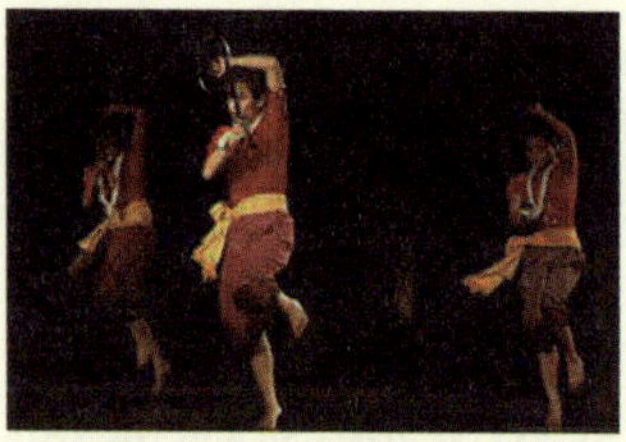
Thang Ta</td><td>• Khamba Thoibi is a duet dance performed by a male and female partner which depicts the love of Khamba and Thoibi, characters of the regional folklore
• Thang Ta is a martial art dance form. Thang means sword and Ta means spear and the dance represents the techniques of fighting with sword and spear incorporated in a form of a dance
Other folk dances of Manipur include Maibi dance, Nupa Pala, etc.</td></tr>
<tr><td>(14) Odisha
(a) Ghumura Dance</td><td>• Although Chhau dance of Odisha (Mayurbhanj) is the most known among the folk dances, Ghumura is the most sought and among the leading folk dances. It is also depicted in the sun temple at Konark
• It resembles a war dance while its steps and actions resemble a classical dance
Other folk dances of Odisha include Paika (a martial dance), Chaitighoda (a dummy horse dance), and Changu and Karma (tribal dances)</td></tr>
<tr><td>(15) Andhra Pradesh
(a) Burrakatha</td><td>• Burrakatha is a form of a ballad dance and singing in which a story or a message is conveyed by the dance to the audience. The earlier stories were from Hindu mythology/scriptures while contemporary and social issues are also now being taken up
Other folk dances of this region are Gobbi (performed in Sankranti festival), Bathukamma (a ceremonial dance of Siddis), and Veeranatyam (ritualistic dance)</td></tr>
<tr><td>(16) Tamil Nadu
(a) Karakattam
(b) Mayilattam
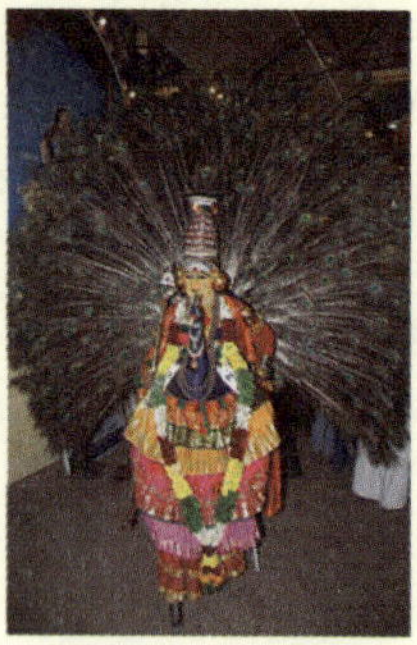
Mayillatam</td><td>• Karakattam is a folk dance in which dancers balance a water pot on their head. It is performed in praise of/propitiation of rain Goddess Mariamman
• Mayilattam is performed in temples by female dancers who are dressed as a peacock
Other dancers of this region include Pampattam (snake dance) and Oyilattam (dance by men)</td></tr>
</table>

(17) Maharashtra (a) Lavani	• Lavani word is derived from Lavanya, which means beauty. It is a sensous dance which is **performed to the rhythmic beats of the dholaki** Other folk dances of this region include Dindi, Kala (religious folk dances), and Pavri Nach (by Kokna tribals)
(18) Goa (a) Dekhni (b) Tarangmel	• Dekhni dance is a **mix of different cultural traditions** which is usually performed on Western music by Christian girls adorned in a fully Indian dress with dance steps seemingly taken from classical dances such as Bharatnatyam and Kathak • Tarangmel is an energetic and youthful dance performed with colourful dresses, flags, etc. on the occasion of Dussehra and Holi Other dances include **Dhalo, Fugdi,** etc.
(19) **Karnataka** (a) Kunitha Dances	• Kunitha are ritual dances of Karnataka • **Dollu Kunitha** is a dance which is accompanied by beating of drums and singing • **Pata Kunitha** is another dance form popular in Mysore region which involves dancing with bamboo poles with ribbons (*pata*)
(20) Kerala (a) Theyyam (b) Padayani	• Also called Kaliyattam, Theyyam is a sacred ritual dance performed before Goddess Kali • Padayani is a **martial art dance performed with masks in Kerala**. This is altogether different from **Kalaripayattu,** a martial art form of Kerala which is not a dance.

FOLK THEATRE

Many forms of folk theatre are popular in India. Some prominent ones include Ramlila, Nautanki, Jatra, Tamasha, Bhavai, Yakshagana, Bhand Pather, and Swang. They have been in vogue for centuries and have been an important means of spreading religious and social messages, as well as entertainment. Folk theatre invariably involves substantial elements of music and dance. *They are categorised as a separate performing art popular for theatres and their salient features are as below:*

(i) **Ramlila:** This is popular in Uttar Pradesh, Bihar, Madhya Pradesh, and other parts of India. It is performed particularly during the festivals of Navratri and Dussehra. Similarly, *Krishna Leela* and *Raas Leela* (story of Lord Krishna) is also performed in different parts, particularly in Braj region of western Uttar Pradesh.

(ii) **Nautanki:** This is a folk theatre associated with Uttar Pradesh and some parts of northern India. Performance is based on folk themes, mythologies, romantic tales, stories of local heroes, etc.

(iii) **Jatra:** This is popular in West Bengal and Odisha, and it literally means, a procession. It is a musical form of a theatre in which stories from epics, mythologies, historical stories, and even topical, social and political issues are depicted. It played an important role during freedom struggle in spread of messages of non-violence and against untouchability.

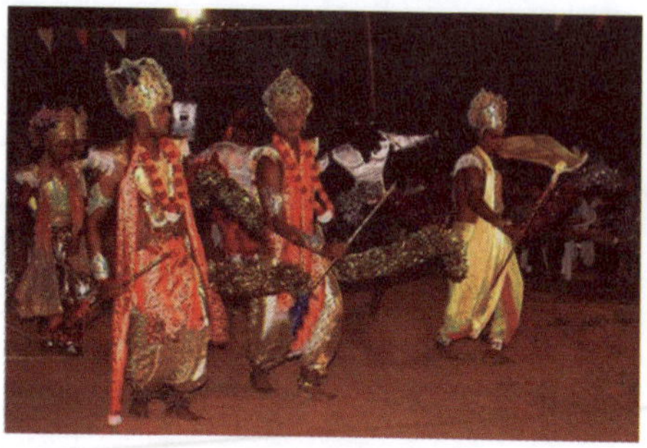

Jatra

(iv) **Bhand Pather:** This is a folk theatre of Kashmir which involves dances, music, and acting. It is characterised by the use of satire and wit to evoke laughter.

(v) **Swang:** This is popular in Haryana and western part of Uttar Pradesh. It was originally a music-based theatre but evolved to include prose also.

(vi) **Maach:** This is a traditional theatre of Madhya Pradesh. It is characterised by prominence of songs between dialogues.

(vii) **Bhaona:** It is popular in Assam, Bengal and Odisha. A form of it is seen in Uttar Pradesh (Vrindavan in Mathura). The story is first narrated by the *sutradhar* followed by the performance.

(viii) **Yakshagana:** It is the folk theatre of Karnataka where stories of Ramayana, Mahabharata, and other mythological stories are performed.

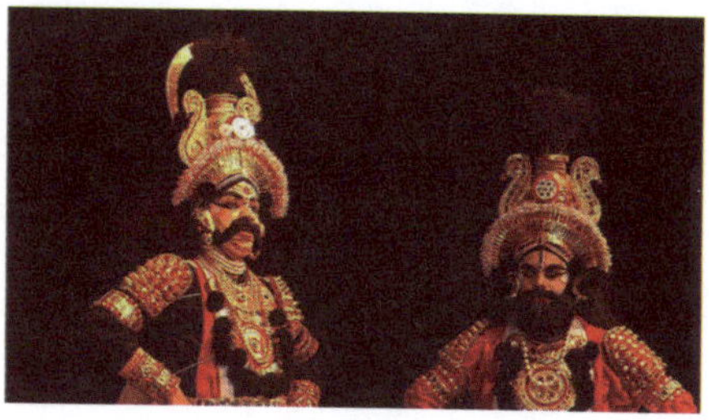

Yakshagana

(ix) **Tamasha:** It is the traditional theatre of Maharashtra where the female actress is the chief exponent of dance movement in the play.

(x) **Therukoothu:** This is performed in temples of Tamil Nadu to propitiate Goddess Mariamman for good rainfall and rich harvest.

(xi) **Koodiyattam:** It is one of the oldest folk theatres and popular in Kerala (based on Sanskrit theatre traditions). The *sutradhar* or the narrator and the *vidushak* are the main protagonists.

(xii) **Krishnanattam:** This is another traditional theatre of Kerala where eight plays are performed in eight days.

- Other folk/traditional theatres include *Mudiyettu* (Kerala), *Bhavai* (Gujarat), *Akhyana* (narration of religious/historical stories in Sanskrit, popular in Gujarat), and *Dashavatar* (Goa in Maharashtra).

IMPORTANT TOPICS TO FOCUS ON

- Various classical dance forms, the regions where they are popular, and salient features.
- Important folk dances and regions where popular.
- Various folk theatres and regions where popular.

18
CHAPTER

Indian Textiles

> The notion of education through handicrafts rises from the contemplation of truth and love permeating life's activities
>
> **Mahatma Gandhi**

INDIAN TEXTILES AND RELATED HANDICRAFTS

A Brief History

The story of Indian textiles is thousands of years old. Fabrics and cloths have been an important means of fulfillment of human need as well as a medium of expression of individual choices and art of the times. Indian textiles and handloom products have also been a part of world market since time immemorial. There were flourishing exports to ancient Egypt, Rome, and Greece and they have been found even in the tombs of the pharaohs. The Indus Valley civilisation and the Harappan culture reveal the cultivation of cotton and preparation of its fabric.

Coming to the later period and to the medieval ages, Indian handicraft expanded its repertoire to new materials, mixes, and artwork like *zardozi* under the Islamic influence. Thus, the story of Indian fabric grew from strength to strength. It reached new heights in terms of colour, design, and fashion, particularly during the Mughal period. The 18th and 19th century saw the suppression of the Indian handloom by cheaper products of Manchester mills. This was an important economic and political ploy of the British regime, which successfully trounced India as an exporter of cloth to a producer of raw materials and a net importer of machine-made fabric.

Our freedom struggle has also been marked with revolts opposing the forced indigo cultivation and calls for supporting the Indian Khadi/handmade fabric. Even Mahatma Gandhi's dream of a village republic envisaged production of yarn/hand spinning of Khadi as a village/household industry.

TRADITION OF WEAVING AND WEAVERS

The tradition of weaving and weavers has been an ancient one. This has been passed on as a family tradition and also as a community tradition from generation to generation. As a result, it has grown over the centuries into a specialised art form which is replete in colour, design, embroidery, fabric, etc. Be it the Kanjeevaram silk, the brocade work of Varanasi, the zari work of Surat, the embroidery of Kutch, or the Chikan work of Lucknow, they have essentially been a traditional craft for a long time in the weaving communities who have taken it to the level of an art form. A number of such weaving communities are known for their skills. These include *Vunkars* in Gujarat, *Mehers* in Orissa (now Odisha), *Ansaris* in Uttar Pradesh, *Devangas* and *Padmashalis* in south India, *Saliyas* in Kerala, and *Khatris* in Kutch among others.

Although the weavers were financially flourishing communities till the medieval period, today they are on the economic and social fringes. Weaving is no more an economically remunerative craft. They have to compete with machine-made fabrics which are cheaper and mass produced at a much quicker pace, albeit not as intricate as the handloom products. Thus, the communities and artisans engaged in weaving, dying, embroidery, hand printing, and applique work are all now being pushed to the margins, although they are upholders of a living craft tradition.

POPULAR FABRICS IN TEXTILE WEAVING

Cotton, silk, wool, a mixture of these, and gold and silver have been traditionally used in India as fibre for weaving. *The traditional products of these fabrics are being discussed below.*

Cotton

Cotton has been a popular fabric for thousands of years. Indian muslin (a fine cotton fabric) was used in the shrouds of the Egyptian kings and also in garments of the Mughal emperors. As a fabric which could absorb moisture and allow aeration (in summers) and yet retain heat in winters, it was ideally suited for the Indian conditions. The popular ***Khadi*** industry is largely based on handspun cotton. The famous embroidery ***Chikan*** work of Lucknow is done on cotton. The traditional ***Dhaniakhali*** saree of West Bengal which has been accorded Geographical Indication (GI) tag, is also made of cotton.

The Geographical Indication (GI) Tag

The GI tag indicates that the product corresponds to a specific geographical location or origin. The tag is granted by the Government of India (as a member of WTO) under the Geographical Indication of Goods (Registration & Protection) Act. It ensures that none other than those registered as the authorised user(s) or those falling under the geographical territory are able to use the tag.

Silk

- The art of silk-making came to India from China, although as per some historians, archaeological discoveries in Harappa and Chanhudaro suggest use of silk threads and existence of sericulture.
- Owing to it softness, lustre, and tensile strength, silk is amongst the most prized of fabric materials. Over the years, weaving of silk fabric, particularly silk sarees, has become quite popular. The **Kanjeevaram silk sarees** (of Kancheepuram, Tamil Nadu) and the **Banarasi silk sarees** with brocade work (of Varanasi, Uttar Pradesh) are amongst the most famous. The latter are usually a part of bridal trousseau.

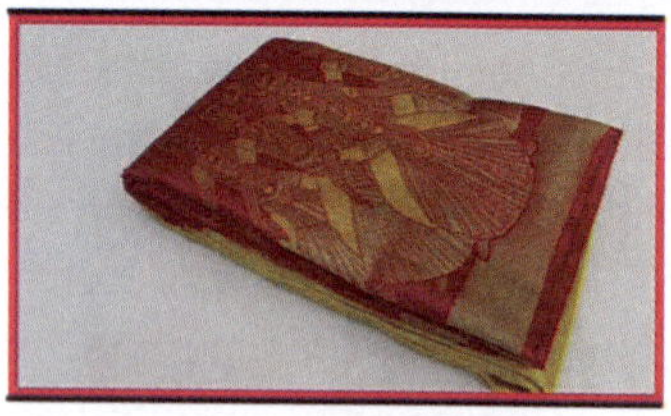

Kanjeevaram silks

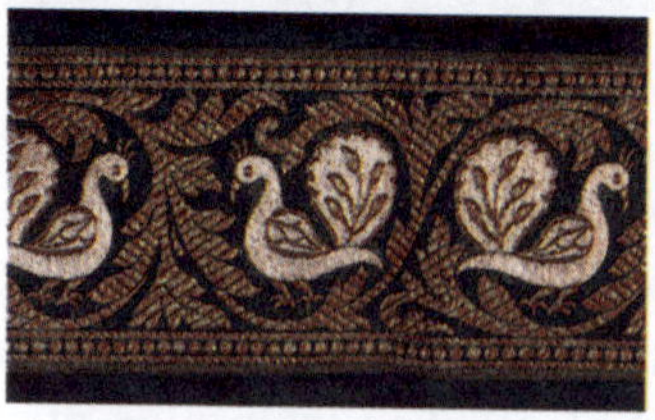

Brocade work of Varanasi Silk

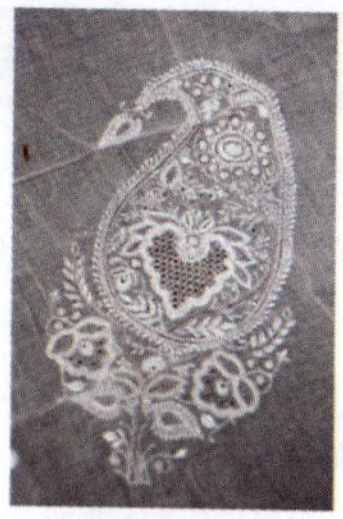

Chikan embroidery of Lucknow

- Assam is an important centre of silk production where different varieties of silk is produced which include, **Golden Muga**, **White Pat (Mulberry silk),** and **Eri silk**. Other centres of silk production are in the states of Jharkhand, Chhattisgarh, Bihar, Madhya Pradesh, etc. where **Tussar silk** is produced which has coarse and uneven texture. The bulk of Indian silk is of the variety **Mulberry silk** which is produced in the states of Karnataka, Andhra Pradesh, and Tamil Nadu.
- Silk fabric has been used for creating a variety of specialised products, specially sarees, by using different weaving and dying techniques such as **tie and dye, resist dye** and others. These specialised works include the brocade work of Banarasi sarees, Tanchois of Gujarat, the resist dye technique of Patola sarees of Gujarat, Ikats of Odisha (includes, Sambalpuri, Balangir, Sonepur, and other Ikats of Odisha), tie and dye technique of Bandhej of Rajasthan and Gujarat, and Pochampally Ikats of Telangana.
- The **Mysore silk, Kancheepuram silk**, and **Salem silk** have been given the **Geographical Indication Tag.** Crafts and products such as Banarasi brocade sarees, Ikats of Odisha, Patola sarees of Gujarat, Paithani sarees of Aurangabad (Maharashtra), and Baluchari sarees of West Bengal have also acquired the GI tag. These products are usually made of rich silk fabric.

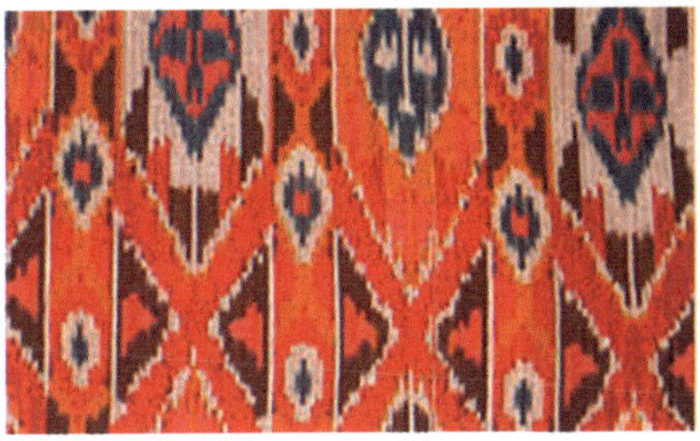

Ikat of Odisha

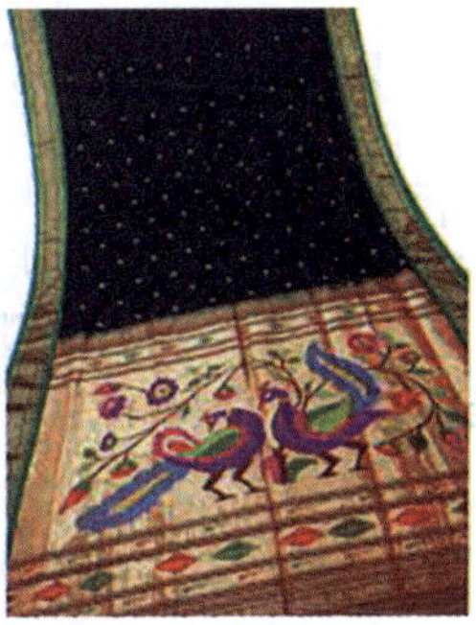

Paithani Saree

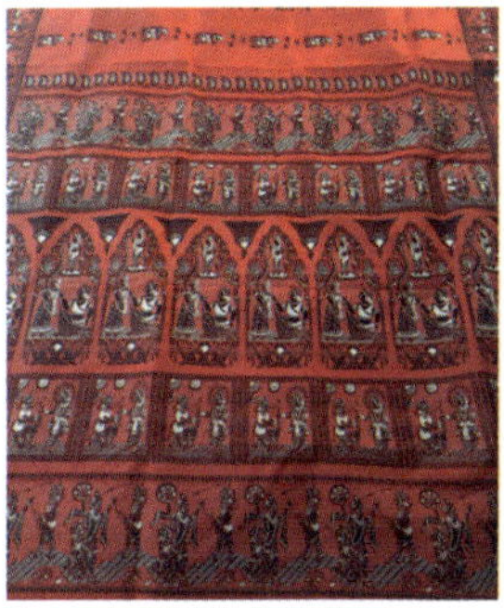

Baluchari Saree

Types of Silk

There are four types of natural silk which are produced commercially. These include the **Mulberry Silk** which is commercially the most important, the **Eri silk, Tussar silk (or Kosa Silk),** and **Muga Silk**. Silk is produced by silkworm which feeds on specific type of leaves. The caterpillar of the moth then spins a cocoon of the fine silk fibre. The cocoons are small and oval, generally the size of a pigeon's egg. The cocoons are boiled, and the silk is then extracted, reeled, twisted, dried, and polished. Depending on the type of worm employed and the type of leave it feeds on, different categories of silk is produced.

The **Mulberry silk** comprising nearly 90% of the entire silk production is produced by the Mulberry silkworm, which feeds only on the mulberry leaves. The **Tussar** silkworm feeds on a variety of plants such as *som, wali, arjun, jamun, oak, sakhua,* etc. This variety is coarser than the Mulberry silk.

Eri silk is produced by the castor silkworm which feeds on the leaves of the castor oil plant and produces white or brick red threads. The **Moga silk** is produced only in Assam in India and produces golden yellow silk threads. It feeds on *Ashoka* tree leaves. The traditional costumes of Assam, ***Mekhela Chadar*** are produced from it.

Silk and Cotton and Other Mix

A mix of silk with other fibres is used to produce a variety of fabrics. **Himru is a mix of silk and cotton while Mashru can use silk with cotton or wool.** It can even be a mix of cotton with wool. Generally, the warp of the cloth is of one type of fabric while weft is of another type. The ***Chanderi sarees*** (which has GI tag) manufactured in Chanderi, Madhya Pradesh are made of a mix of silk and cotton. They can also be of pure silk or pure cotton. They are known for the beautiful geometric patterns, images of flora, fauna, etc. woven into the fabric.

Wool

Wool is a fabric prepared from the hair of animals. Generally, the hair of sheep is used for production of wool but that of other animals is also occasionally used. The hair of the Angora rabbit is used to produce **Angora wool** which is fine, soft, and silky. Similarly, ***shahtoosh*** is the fabric produced from the hair of the **Himalayan Ibex** which is so fine that an entire ***pashmina*** shawl (which has GI tag) is said to pass through a ring. Its production and sale is banned as Ibex is an endangered species.

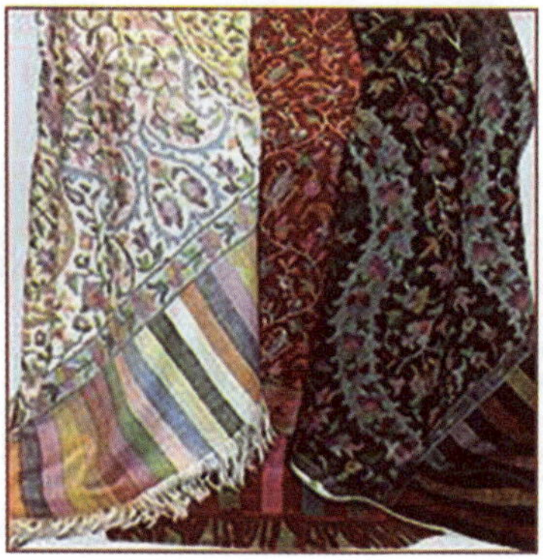

Jamawar Shawl

Wool has been used for thousands of years and thus this craft has developed many famous products. These include the ***Jamawar*** shawls of Kashmir (which could contain as many as 50 colours), the ***Dhabalas*** (of rough goat wool) of Kutch, ***Pheran*** (traditional Kashmiri dress), the **blankets and Pashmina** shawls (GI tag) **of Nubra** valley of Ladakh, **headgear of Kullu** (Himachal Pradesh), and a variety of woolen products of *Bhotias* and *Garhwals* of Uttarkhand. The **Kani shawl** (of Kanimora, Kashmir) and **Tangaliya shawl** (of Saurashtra, Gujarat) are some other handicraft woolen products which have the GI tag.

TEXTILE TECHNIQUES AND HANDICRAFTS

Textile techniques and handicraft have been used traditionally to bring out a variety of artistic products. Textile techniques refer to **loom decorated** and **post loom decorated** processes and techniques. Both these techniques are employed to add pattern, texture, and design to the fabric.

Loom Decorated Processes and Techniques

These techniques **impart artistic treatment** to the fabric while it is on the loom itself. In this technique, the texture is produced by varying the count of warp thread and by weaving them tightly or loosely. Further, by using different colours of warp and weft threads, different patterns are produced.

What is Weft and Warp?

Weft and Warp are the transverse and longitudinal/lengthwise thread employed in weaving. Thus, the warp threads are strung vertically on the loom and the weft threads move across them, usually once over the warp and then under the next warp, and so on.

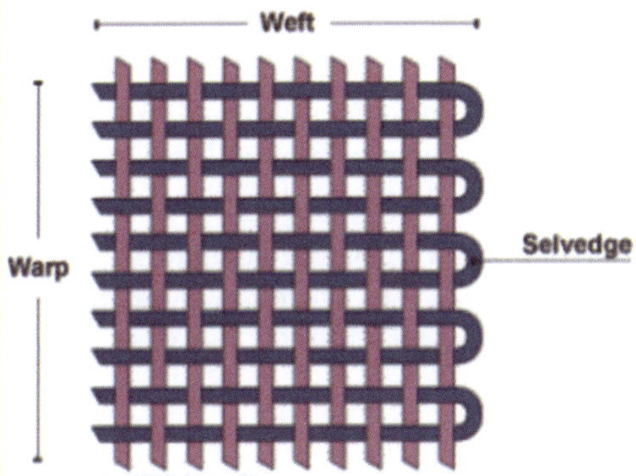

Weft and Warp

Loom decorated techniques are used in the Northeast to weave cotton shawls bearing different images. The women here use narrow loin looms which they attach to their waists.

Post Loom Decorated Processes and Techniques

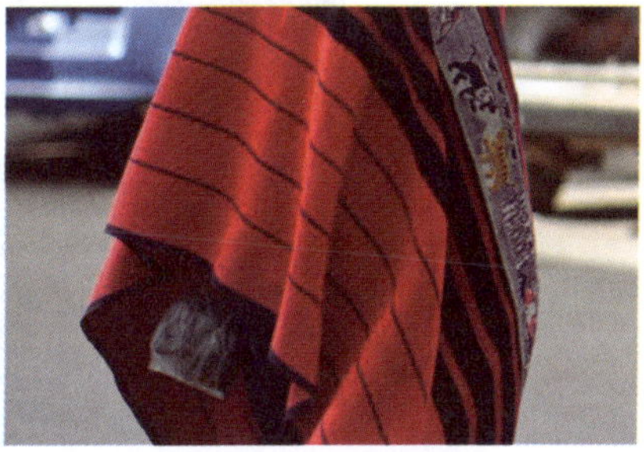

Northeast Shawl

The post loom decorated fabrics involved several techniques such as:

- Dyeing and tie dyeing
- Hand printing, and hand painting
- Embroidery
- Applique and patchwork

(a) **Dyeing and tie dyeing:** Dyeing refers to the process of colouring of fabric and that of fibre and yarn. Traditionally in India, yarn and fabric have been given a variety of colours generally by using vegetable and mineral colours. Pomegranate, lac, and madder were used for pink red and brown colours. Yellow was generated from flower petals (particularly myrobalan) and black from iron castings. Similarly, pistachio shells produced green, onion skins produced reddish brown, and concentrated cow urine, a deep yellow. Dyeing a fabric fully (or partly) has been employed as a technique to add colours and designs to clothes.

In tie dyeing, the cloth/fabric is tied into small dots at several places using thread and then the dye is applied to create beautiful patterns wherever the fabric has been tied. Resist dyeing is another form of dyeing where a substance such as wax or mud is applied to certain portions of the cloth to prevent the portion from getting dyed, thus creating a pattern. *Bandhej* of Rajasthan and *Bandhini* of Gujarat are examples of tie dyeing.

(b) **Hand printing and hand painting**

(i) ***Hand printing:*** This is done by means of blocks and is also referred as block or hand block printing. Usually, blocks of wood or of metal are prepared with intricate design. These are dipped in dyes/liquid colour prepared using vegetable colours. These are pressed on the fabric at desired places to create the required pattern. Different regions of country have their unique block printing style. Some of the famous block prints are **Bagh Prints of Madhya Pradesh** (from the tribal town of Bagh) which has GI tag, **Dhamadka of Kutch** (Gujarat), **floral butis design of Sanganer** (Rajasthan), **Bagru** (Rajasthan) **hand block print** (has GI tag), and **paisley design** of Farrukhabad (Uttar Pradesh) (has GI tag).

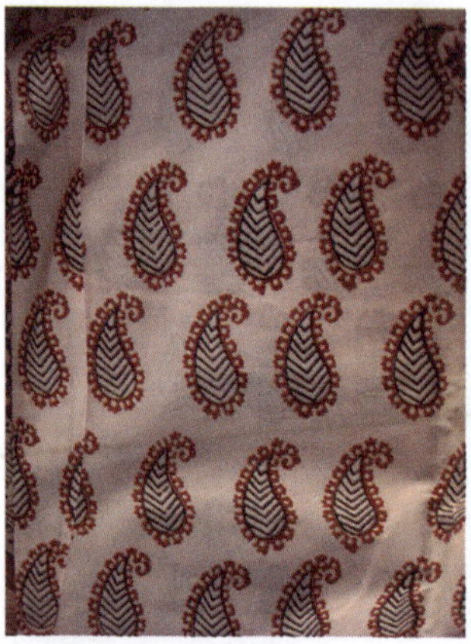

Bagh Prints

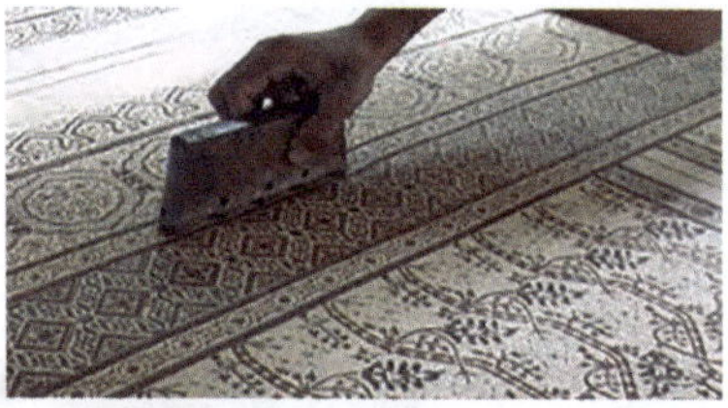

Dhamadka of Kutch

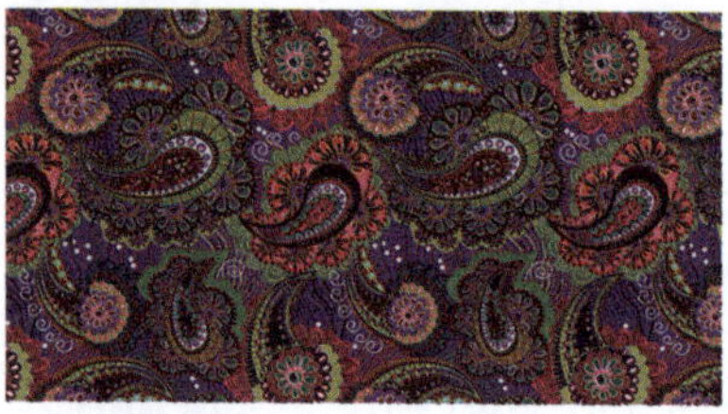

Paisley Pattern Design

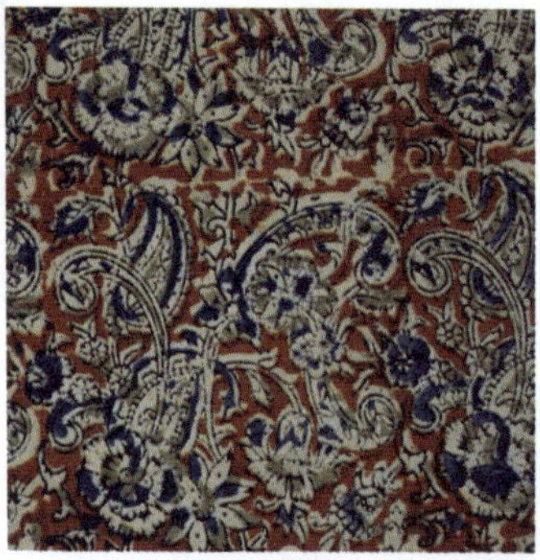

Kalamkari

(ii) ***Hand painting:*** Fabric is also painted by hand to produce intricate and beautiful designs, particularly on sarees. One such craft is ***Kalamkari* of Andhra Pradesh**. This is of two types, the **Srikalahasti and Machilipatnam style,** both of which have a GI tag. In the former, a *Kalam* (a pen) is used for drawing the pattern or the design on the cloth. Generally, religious motifs were earlier painted. Kalamkari can also be of block printing style. Machilipatnam Kalamkari falls in this category.

In different regions nowadays, regional and folk art like **Madhubani paintings, Warli paintings,** etc. are also painted on silk and cotton fabric, particularly on sarees.

(c) **Embroidery:** Embroidery refers to the art of creating patterns and designs on a fabric by means of needle and thread (or yarn). Thus, it can said to be decorating a fabric by stitching various designs. In India, embroidery has been popular for centuries. Marco Polo, the famous traveller in the 13th century, had referred to the Indian embroidery as one of the best in the world. Today, embroidery is a flourishing art popular in different parts of the country. From the *'Dorukha'* shawl of Kashmir, to the mirror work embroidery of Kutch, from *Chikan* work on cotton of Lucknow, to *Kantha* work of West Bengal, India has a large gamut of embroidery work. *Some of the well known embroidery arts are described below.*

Embroidery	Features and Region in which Popular
(1) **Aari**	• Practised in **Kashmir and Kutch** (Gujarat) • Employs the use of **beads with sharp edged needle** to create chain stitch type of designs. It is known for delicate and fine thread work
(2) **Banjara Embroidery**	• Popular with *banjaras* (gypsies) of **Andhra Pradesh and Madhya Pradesh** • It is a mix of **bead work, embroidery, and applique work** and characterised by rich colours and geometric patterns and designs
(3) **Chamba Rumal** 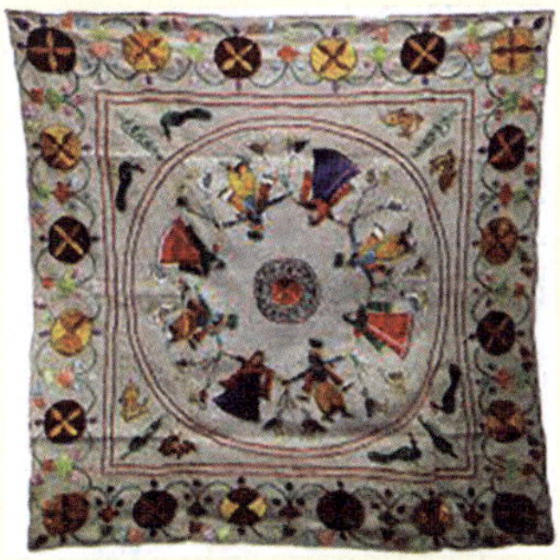	• It is an embroidery done on ***rumals*** (handkerchiefs) **in Chamba region** (Himachal Pradesh) (has GI tag) • It is characterised by **intricate needle work** with designs of animal, birds, trees, geometrical patterns, and articles of everyday use
(4) **Chikan** 	• A famous work of **Lucknow** (Uttar Pradesh), Chikan work (has GI tag) is believed to have originated in the medieval period when empress Noorjahan was making a cap for her husband Jahangir • Involves **creation of intricate designs** of flower, paisleys, stars, etc. on cotton/muslin cloth or fine fabric (usually white or of light colour). More than **22 different types of stitches** are practiced and the art is famous for beauty and dexterity

(5) **Kantha** 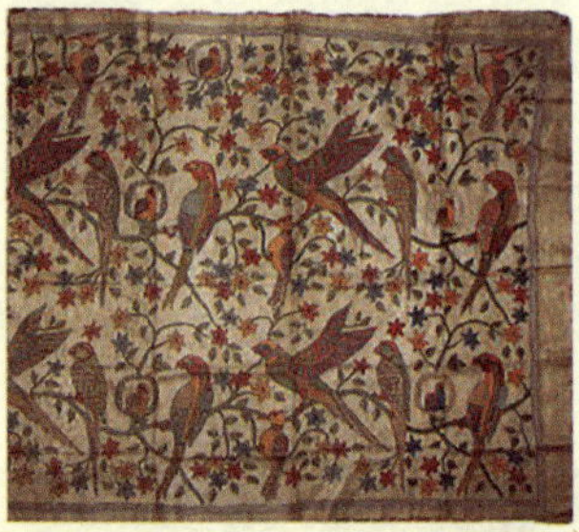	• This embroidery technique is popular in **West Bengal** • It involves **thousands of stitches on the fabric** giving it a puckered quilted look. Traditionally, it is done on quilts, *dhotis, and sarees*. Nowadays, it is even found on *dupattas*, shawls, pillow covers, etc. • **Nakshi Kantha** is a type of traditional quilt made of old clothes (**has a GI tag**)
(6) **Kasuti** 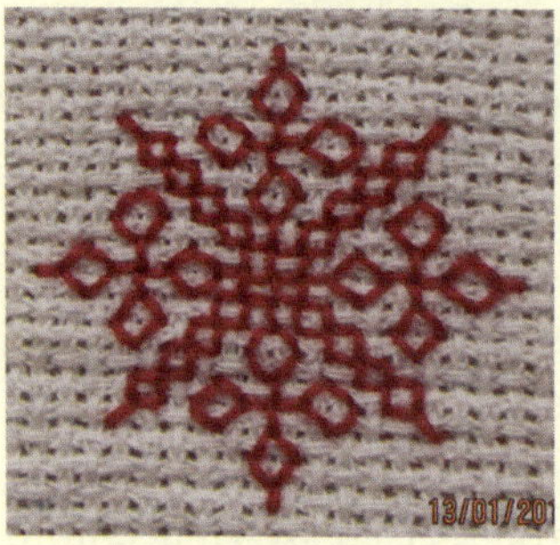	• It is popular in **northern part of Karnataka** (has a GI tag). • Involves **creation of designs which are pictorial** in character, such as eight pointed stars, parrots, peacocks, Tulsi plant, temple chariots, etc.
(7) **Kashida** or **Kashmiri Embroidery**	• It is an ancient art popular in **Kashmir** which is done on a variety of products like woolen rugs and woolen *Kurtas (phirans)*, bed spreads, pillow covers, etc. • The designs include natural motifs like trees, flowers, birds, trees, chinar leaves, etc.
(8) **Kutchi Embroidery**	• Also called *Kutchi kadhai*, this artwork is famous in the Kutch region of Gujarat and is made on a variety of clothing, such as skirts, veils, cholis (blouse), quilts, etc. (has GI tag) • It is characterised by bright and varied colour **mirror work and designs** of flowers, peacocks, parrots, elephants, etc.
(9) **Mukaish** or **Kamdani**	• Also referred as **Mukeish**, this work is done in **Lucknow**. It involves **twisting of thin metallic threads** on fabric to create a variety of designs. Owing to there being only a few craftsmen of this work, it is said to be a dying art • In another variant of this art, the wire is attached to a small length of thread. This helps to make the work easier and is called **Kamdani**

(10) **Phulkari** 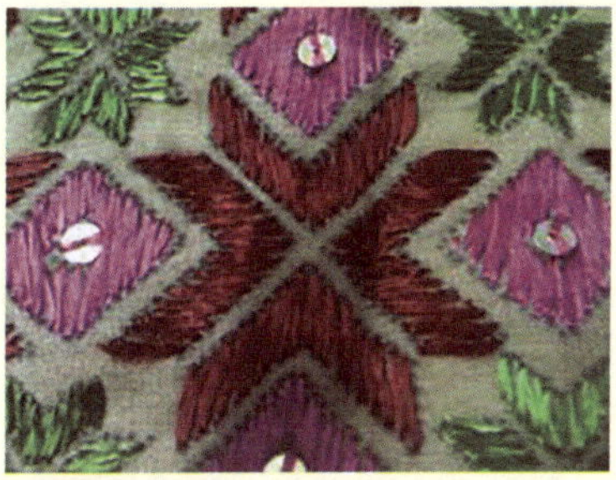	• This embroidery is popular in Punjab. It literally implies **flower work** (has GI tag) • The base cloth used is handspun Khadi. Bright coloured threads are used and reverse satin stitch is done. A whole *dupatta* with embroidery may appear like a *bagh* (a garden of flowers)
(11) **Sozani Tilla**	• Sozani is an embroidery of **Kashmir** which is done on a **variety of shawls**. Designs involve motifs of flora and fauna (has GI tag) • **Tilla** embroidery is done using **gold and silver thread**
(12) **Sujini** 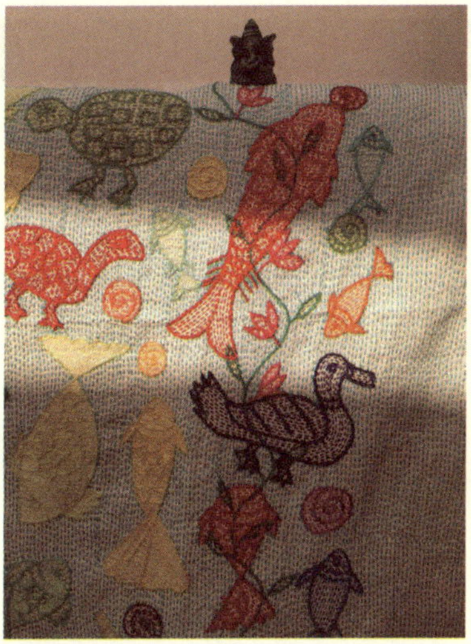	• Popular in **Bihar,** it is a form of **embroidery** employed for making quilts and bedspreads (has GI tag) • Earlier, it was used to be done on **old clothes** with two layers of clothes with simple stitches. The designs include narrative themes and stories
(13) **Zardozi**	• It is a form of **Zari work** popular in **Uttar Pradesh**. The design is quite elaborate and uses even gold, silver, and silk threads. The Lucknow Zardozi has a GI tag.
(14) **Zari Work**	• It refers to **intricate traditional work of weaving threads** made of gold and silver into fabric, primarily of silk, to create beautiful designs on fabrics. Earlier, such fabric was associated with aristocracy. The **Surat Zari** is a famous work which has GI tag

(d) **Applique and patchwork:** Both of these are other techniques of post loom decoration of fabric. **Applique is a technique in which designs or patterns are** created by stitching smaller pieces of fabric to a larger piece of fabric which is generally of contrasting colour and texture. **Patchwork involves sewing of smaller pieces of fabric** together to create a large piece of fabric and thus, creating a design. India has a rich tradition of both the art forms. *Some of the well known crafts of* **applique/patchwork** *are:*

(i) ***Gota work of Rampur, Lucknow:*** **Here, small pieces of zari ribbon are applied to the fabric to create intricate designs.** Even strips of gold and silver ribbons (or other coloured ones) are used in bridal trousseau work. **Gota work is also famous in Rajasthan.**

(ii) ***Pipli:*** This is another famous applique work of **Odisha** (**has GI tag**). **Brightly coloured fabric pieces** are sewn together to include images of human forms, animals, etc. This technique was practised to prepare hangings for Rathyatra processions.

(iii) ***Khatwa:*** This is the applique and patchwork of **Bihar** (has **GI tag**) which is often seen in *shamianas* (decorative tents), wall hangings, and now even in table cloths, cushions covers, *saris,* and *dupattas.* This work is also done by **Rabari community in Gujarat** (Kutch) and in some communities of Rajasthan.

IMPORTANT TOPICS TO FOCUS ON

- Different types of fabrics and traditional weaving art practised on them.
- Different textile techniques and important regional crafts associated with them, particularly those accorded GI tag.
- Find if any new regional fabric/weaving technique or handicraft product has been accorded GI tag recently.

CHAPTER 19

Handicrafts in India

Magnificence is hand crafted

Anonymous

HANDICRAFTS AND ITS TRADITION IN INDIA

Handicrafts refer to a wide variety of traditional products or works which are made by craftsmen by hand or by means of ordinary tools. They invariably involve skill and adroitness usually acquired over generations by practicing the work in local communities, tribes, or regional pockets. The article produced may vary from relatively inexpensive objects of daily use to rich works of art and decoration, but all are valued for the dexterity of work and aesthetic appeal.

India has a rich and diverse tradition of handicrafts. Right from the Indus Valley civilisation to the medieval period and further, even in the present day, the Indian handicrafts have been an important export of the country. The domain of Indian handicrafts is quite diverse and includes **gems and jewellery, pottery, leather products, glassware, terracotta crafts, wooden products, brass, bronze,** and other **metal products,** to name a few, apart from the textiles and carpets. *Some well known Indian handicrafts are discussed below.*

GEMS AND JEWELLERY

Since time immemorial gems and jewellery have been an important means of expression of Indian art and in the present day, they are valuable items of export too. Jewellery handicraft includes many areas of specialisation such as antique jewellery, *kundan* work, *minakari*, silver jewellery, *bidri*, *filigree* work, etc.

(a) **Traditional and antique jewellery:** The work of manufacture of gold jewellery by the traditional artisans (*karigars*) is recognised by the Government of India (since July 2015) as a work of handicraft. These works involve making of traditional gold jewellery or antique gold jewellery (which has an old and ethnic appearance). *The craft incorporates different techniques and traditional art forms which include the following:*

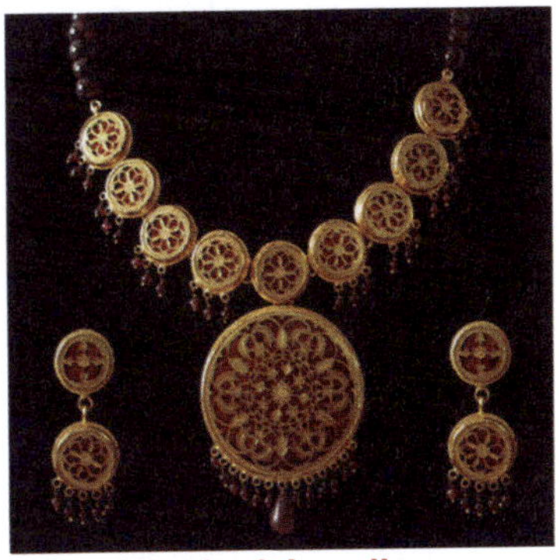

Minakari Jewellery

(i) ***Kundan work:*** This includes making of traditional Indian gemstone jewellery with gems set in a gold/gold silver mix base.

(ii) ***Minakari:*** This refers to enamelling and decorating the surface of jewellery by attaching or fusing pieces of different mineral substance. Famous *minakari* works are that of Delhi, Jaipur, and Varanasi. The **Gulabi** *Minakari* of Varanasi is also accorded a GI tag.

(b) **Silver jewellery:** *This work is also known for many specialised handicraft techniques such as:*

(i) ***Filigree work:*** This involves making of jewellery involving delicate metal work. Usually silver (and at times gold) metals wires are used to form intricate jewellery designs. The well known filigree works include that of **Cuttack** (Odisha) known as **Tarakasi** and that of **Karimnagar** (Telangana). The latter has acquired a GI tag.

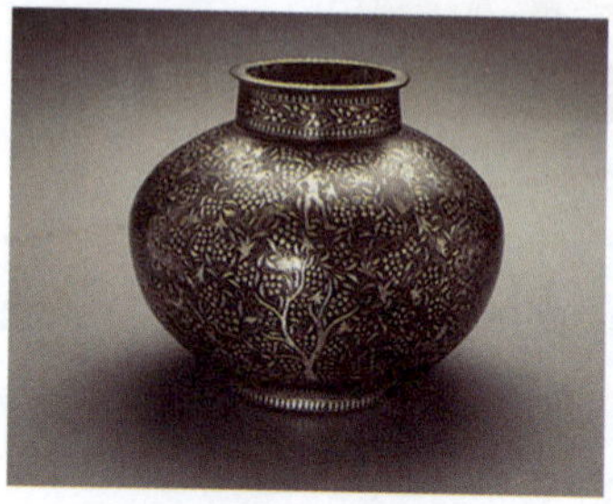

Bidri Work

(ii) ***Bidri work:*** This refers to the manufacture of metalware (usually of silver) with beautiful inlay work. It originated from **Bidar** (Karnataka) and hence the name. It too has a GI tag.

POTTERY WORK

Indian pottery has an ancient history which goes back thousands of years and predates even the Indus Valley civilisation. While earlier pottery making was limited to clay and terracotta potteries, in modern days, apart from the above categories of potteries, glazed and unglazed pottery are also prepared. There are many important centres and styles of pottery making, some of which have even been accorded a GI tag.

(i) **Glazed pottery of Chunar (Uttar Pradesh):** This place is famous for **glazed and red terracotta** pottery manufactured in this region for centuries.

(ii) **Blue pottery of Jaipur:** This glazed pottery of Jaipur is known for its blue colour (obtained by adding dye). Some of the pottery is semi-transparent bearing designs of animals, birds, etc. It has been accorded GI tag.

(iii) **Black pottery of Manipur and of Azamgarh (Nizamabad in Uttar Pradesh):** The black pottery of Manipur is a traditional craft called **Longpi** produced from a special variety of rock called serpentine rock. The black Nizamabad pottery is made of fired local clay which is decorated with floral motifs and designs. **Nizamabad pottery** has been accorded GI tag.

(iv) **Dal Gate pottery (glazed pottery of Kashmir):** This is a type of glazed pottery which is available in a variety of colours such as deep blue, green, brown, ochre, etc. It is made in Srinagar and adjoining regions in Kashmir.

(v) **Kagzi pottery of Alwar:** This pottery popular in the Alwar region is paper thin and hence acquired its name. It comes in variety of shapes, colours, and engravings and its origin is of the medieval period.

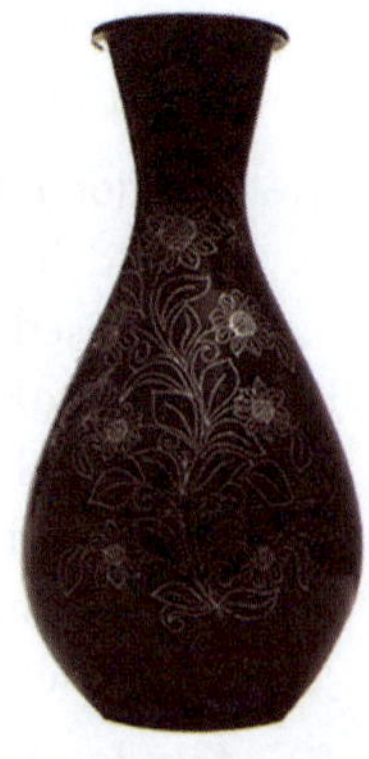

Nizamabad Pottery

TERRACOTTA HANDICRAFTS

Terracotta refers to clay-based ceramic which has been prepared by firing of the earth (clay). It may be glazed or unglazed. Usually, the terracotta crafts have a porous surface.

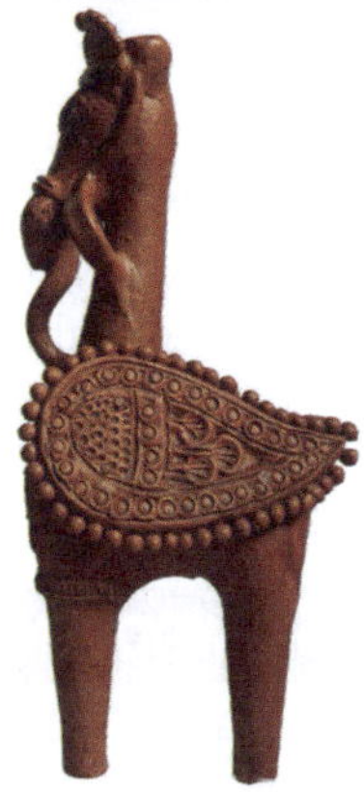

Bankura Horse

In West Bengal where the terracotta temples were made, there continues the tradition of making terracotta art and crafts. The most famous of these is the **Bankura horse** or the **Panchmura horse** (Panchmura is a gram panchayat in Bankura district in West Bengal). This handicraft has been accorded GI tag.

Also famous is the **Villianur** (Pondicherry) terracotta products made of fine green clay and it has been accorded GI tag.

Another unique terracotta handicraft is the **Molela clay work** (of Molela, Rajsamand district Rajasthan). The local artists of the village prepare **terracotta plaques** which are bought by tribals (of as far as Madhya Pradesh) for ritual purposes. This product too has a GI tag.

LEATHER PRODUCTS

Manufacture of leather products in India is thousands of years old. In the present day, leather products are also an important item in India's basket of exports. *Among the many leather products being commercially produced the traditional and handicraft oriented products include:*

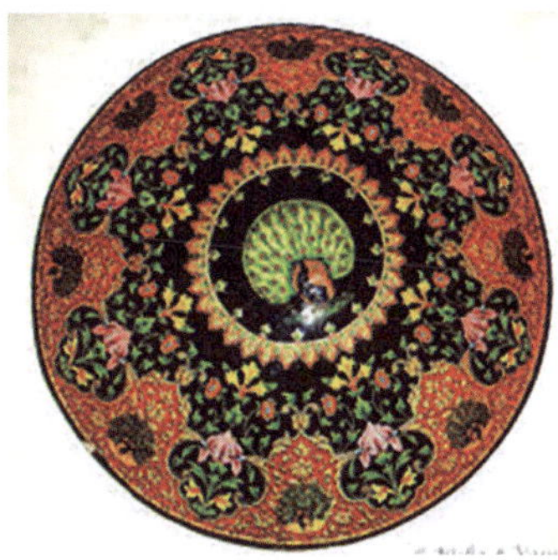

Usta Art

- **Juttis:** These are **traditional shoes** with extensive embroidery and beautiful designs. These are quite popular in the Punjab region and other parts of northern India.
- **Mojaris:** These are also **leather footwear** (a type of traditional shoe) which is beautifully handcrafted. It is popular in Jaipur and Jodhpur region (Rajasthan).
- **Kolhapuri Chappal:** These are **leather slipper footwear** which are popular and manufactured in Kolhapur (Maharashtra). The slippers are made of tanned leather and are given a colour using vegetable dyes. These are beautifully handcrafted.
- **Usta and Manoti art:** Popular in Bikaner district (Rajasthan), this is an art combination performed on camel leather to produce a variety of products of leather. This art is also performed on walls, ceilings, glass, wood, etc. Usta art refers to art of *naqqashi* and *manoti* performed by Usta artisans.
- The **stuffed leather toys of Indore** are another famous handicrafts work. It has been accorded GI tag.

GLASS HANDICRAFTS

India has a long history of glass product manufacturing. Reference to glass products is noted in the epics, particularly *Mahabharata*. This art received great impetus during the medieval period, especially during the Mughal rule. Today, a wide range of glass products are manufactured ranging from glass beads, bangles, and toys to utility and decoration items like chandeliers, lamps crockery, bottles, etched and stained glass, etc. *The famous glass handicrafts products include:*

- **Glass bangles:** Although manufactured in different parts of the country, the most famous glass bangles are those of **Hyderabad** where a whole market (*Chudi bazaar* or *Laad baazar*) deals in a variety of glass bangles.
- **Glass toys:** Firozabad (Uttar Pradesh) is famous for manufacturing of glass bangles and other glass products such as chandeliers, *Itra* bottles, utility bottles, flower vases, decorative lights, bulbs, candle stands, etc. of different varieties and colours. The glass products of Firozabad have also been accorded GI tag.
- **Glass beads:** These are manufactured in Varanasi where very thin glass is used to make *Tikulis* for women.

WOODEN HANDICRAFTS

The tradition of wooden handicraft is quiet rich and diverse. *The famous Indian wooden handicrafts include:*

- **Bastar wooden craft:** This craft is very popular in **Bastar** region (Chhattisgarh) amongst **Muria**, **Badhai** and other tribes who manufacture a variety of traditional wooden craft products of bamboo. This art is also accorded GI tag.

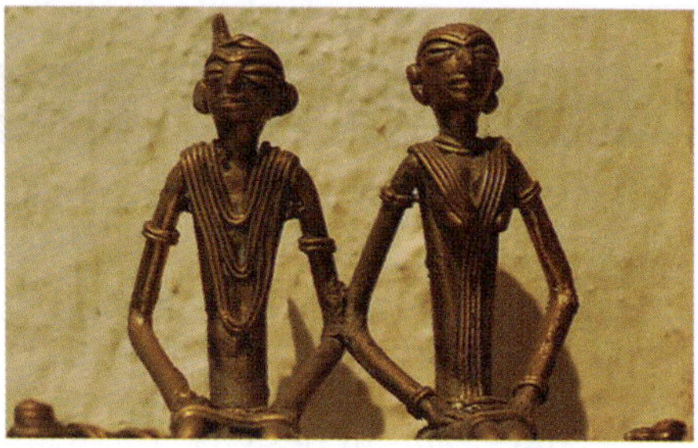

Bastar Wooden Craft

- **Cane handicrafts:** Such handicrafts are prepared in the Northeastern states. Cane handicrafts products, particularly of Tripura are quite famous.
- **Sandalwood articles:** Beautiful handcrafted sandalwood products of **Mysore** are well known.
- **Mysore rosewood inlay:** This craft involves making of various items of rosewood in which decorative pieces of mother of pearl, sandalwood, ivory, etc. are fixed in excavated depressions in the wood. It has been accorded GI tag.
- **Sankheda furniture:** These are famous teak wood furniture manufactured in the **Sankheda** village in Gujarat. These are made in traditional design with maroon and gold polish. It has been accorded GI tag.
- **Kashmir walnut wood carving:** These are intricately carved walnut wood products manufactured in Kashmir. It has been accorded GI tag.
- **Screw pine craft:** The famous craft of Kerala involves making of mats, wall hangings, and other utility products by artisans using leaves of screw pine plant. It has been accorded GI tag.

BRASS, BRONZE, WROUGHT IRON AND OTHER METAL HANDICRAFTS

India has a very ancient tradition of metal craft and rich knowledge of metallurgy. The bronze dancing girl statue of Mohenjo-daro, the iron pillar of Mehrauli, the bronze statue of Nataraja of the Chola period, and many bronze works of Pala period are a testimony to it.

The important metal craft products of modern times are:

- **Moradabad (Uttar Pradesh) metal craft:** It is famous for **brassware** with exquisite *naqqashi* (engraving). It has a GI tag too.
- **Bastar Dhokra art:** Bastar (Chhattisgarh) is famous for non-ferrous metal castings (done by lost wax process) as well as iron castings. It is popular in the various tribes of this region. It has been accorded a GI tag.
- **Bell metal of Datia/Tikamgarh:** A variety of handcrafted articles are manufactured at Datia/Tikamgarh made of bell metal (a hard alloy). This is a tribal craft and has been accorded a GI tag.
- **Tarkashi and Koftagari works of Jaipur:** Tarkashi is **inlaying of brass copper or silver in wood** to form beautiful patterns. It is a famous handicraft work of **Jaipur** and other areas in Rajasthan. Another ornamental work of this region is **Koftagari**, which involves inlaying of steel with gold which is a form of etching or damascening (an art of inlaying of different metals into one another, typically of gold or silver into a steel background).
- **Swamimalai bronze icons:** These are bronze icons and statues manufactured in Swamimalai (Tamil Nadu). It has a GI tag.

STONEWARE AND CRAFT

The famous stoneware and craft products of India are:

- **Makrana marble works:** Makrana (Rajasthan) is famous not only for its marble, but also for marble work, carvings and inlays, sculptures, and a variety of handicraft items. These include the famous inlay work (pietra dura) and the *jali* work in marble. It has been accorded a GI tag.
- **Konark stone carving:** It is an important handicraft of Odisha and a centre for production of numerous statues and carvings in stones. The products are known for their skillful craftsmanship. These products are carved in different kinds of stone ranging from hard black granite to soft soapstone.

TOYS AND PUPPETS

Indian handicrafts are also known for a variety of toys and puppets. Earlier, these were play items for children but now they are also known for their craftsmanship. Many of these are wooden products and have been accorded GI tag. These include:

- **The shadow puppets of Andhra Pradesh**
- **The Thanjavur dolls** of Tamil Nadu
- **The Channapatna toys** of rural Bengaluru which are made of wood. These have a GI tag.
- **Kunnal** (Karnataka) **wooden toys**. These have a GI tag.

- **Kondapalli Bommalu** which are handcrafted wooden toys of Andhra Pradesh (of Kondapalli). These have a GI tag.
- **Nirmal toys** and crafts made up of wood is another traditional product (protected under GI tag).
- The stuffed **leather toys of Indore** which is a unique product in this category. These have a GI tag.
- **Varanasi toys** made of wood and lacquerware. These have a GI tag.

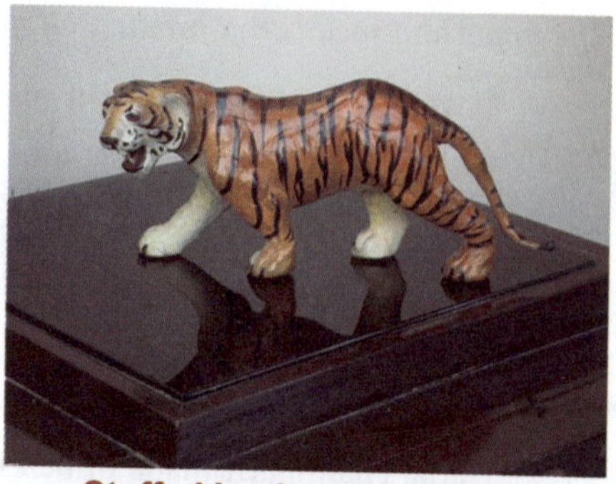

Stuffed leather toy, Indore

PAPIER MACHE

Also referred to as chewed paper, it is a mixture of paper and glue, or paper, pulp, water, etc. The mixture is moulded in a variety of shapes and gradually becomes hard, thus retaining the shape it has been given. The traditional papier mache crafts of India include:

- **Tirukanur papier mache:** This traditional art is popular in Puducherry. A variety of dolls, idols, etc. are made.
- **Kashmir papier mache:** This handicraft of Kashmir is more than 500 years old. A variety of artefacts such as cups, bowls, vases, boxes, and lamp bases are made from papier mache in bright colours with beautiful decorations.

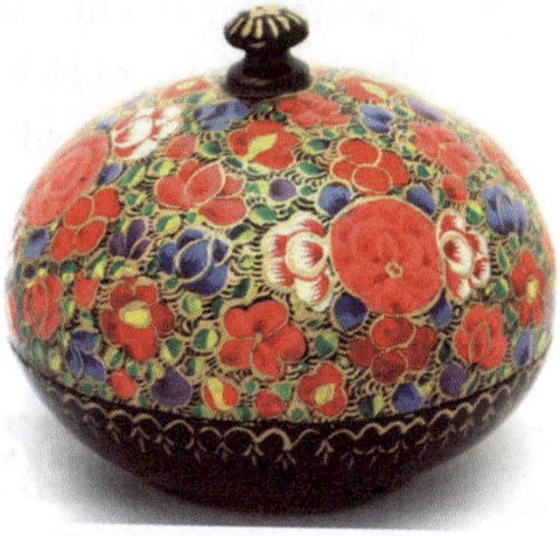

Kashmir Papier Mache

IMPORTANT TOPICS TO FOCUS ON

- Handicrafts techniques
- Important handicrafts
- Important centres of production of handicrafts

CHAPTER 20

Languages and Literature of Modern India

A country that does not take pride in its language and literature can never progress

Dr. Rajendra Prasad

EVOLUTION OF INDIAN LANGUAGES AND LITERATURE

Languages and literature are salient elements of the cultural mosaic of any society. The diversity of languages and the richness of their literature are truly a reflection of the extent of evolution of the culture of its people. The Indian languages and literature can rightly be said to be the most ancient in the world. The *Vedas* and in particular the *Rigveda* is said to be nearly 3500 (or more) years old. The *Vedas* along with other ancient texts, the *Puranas*, the *Dharmasutras*, the *Buddhist Pitakas*, and other Buddhist and Jain canonical texts, are a part of a great heritage of ancient language and literature. Over the period of several centuries, Indian languages and literature have diversified and evolved. They have assimilated the Buddhist and Jain influences in the ancient times as well as the Arabic and Persian influences of the medieval period. With the passage of centuries, while many ancient languages like *Prakrit* have not remained in vogue, new languages like Urdu have originated and those like Hindi (*Khariboli*) have evolved from the extant ones. These new languages too have evolved with a distinct and a large literature of their own. Thus, the story of Indian languages and their literature is indeed a saga of continuous change and evolution.

The diversity of Indian languages is also reflected in the fact that **22 languages are recognised** in the **Eighth Schedule of the Indian Constitution**. Besides them, there are nearly **122 major languages** and nearly 1599 minor languages or dialects in vogue in the country. Many of these major languages also boast of their own literature which reflects the vastness of culture and the life of people of different regions.

INDIAN LANGUAGES AND THEIR CLASSIFICATION

The Indian languages can broadly be classified into the following types:

(a) **Indo-Aryan group**

(b) **Dravidian group**

(c) **Austric or Austroasiatic group**

(d) **Sino-Tibetan group**

(e) **Others**

(a) Indo-Aryan Group

- The Indo-Aryan group of languages is the largest family of modern Indian languages and comprises all of the major languages of northern, western, and eastern parts of India. These include Sanskrit, Hindi, Bengali, Oriya, Urdu, Punjabi, Marathi, Gujarati, Sindhi, Assamese, Dogri, Kashmiri, Konkani, Maithali, and Nepali (from amongst the languages in the Eighth Schedule of the Constitution).
- Besides, a number of other languages of these regions which are major or minor dialects are also a part of this family (although they are not recognised in the Eighth Schedule). As per the 2001 Census of India, nearly 790 million speakers or **75% of the population spoke languages of Indo-Aryan group** with Hindi being the language spoken by the maximum number of people and in the largest area of the country.
- Amongst all of these languages, **Sanskrit is the oldest**. Its antiquity is traced to the Vedic texts which were composed in the earliest form of Sanskrit referred as the **Vedic Sanskrit**. Considering that the period of composition of Rigveda is accepted to be around 2000–1500 BCE, the development of the language Sanskrit—which expressed the rich Vedic philosophy—would surely have taken place much earlier. Thus, Sanskrit as a language is in existence at least for the last five thousand years. The **Classical Sanskrit** was laid out in the grammar of **Panini** in the 5th century BCE. As a language, Sanskrit has had a profound influence on other Indian languages including some of the Dravidian languages.
- **Hindi** as a language is spoken in central and northern India by more than 420 million people. Besides, it also serves as a link language or *lingua franca* in other parts of the country. Modern Hindi is said to have originated from *Khariboli* in the last 200 years. Today, it is recognised as one of the major Indian languages in the Eighth Schedule of the Constitution and it is also recognised as the **official language** of the country as per the Official Languages Act. (The Constitution, however does not specify Hindi/or any other language as the national language). Hindi has the same script **Devanagari** as that of Sanskrit which is also the script of many other Indo-Aryan languages. Besides, it also shares a number of words with Urdu. Different variations and dialects of Hindi are popular in different parts of northern and central India.
- The Indo-Aryan group of languages is said to be a branch of **Indo-Iranian language** family which itself is a branch of subfamily of the Indo-European language family.

(b) Dravidian Group

This is the second largest group of languages in India. These languages are said to have **evolved indigenously** and not to have been influenced by Indo-Iranian/Indo-European languages. The Dravidian languages are spoken largely in the southern part of India and some parts of central and eastern India. **Tamil, Telugu, Kannada,** and **Malayalam** are the most important of the Dravidian languages (those included in the Eighth Schedule of the Constitution). As per the 2001 Census, nearly 215 million people or nearly 20% of the Indian population speaks the Dravidian languages.

(c) Other Languages

The other language groups include **Austric, Sino-Tibetan, Negroid, and Tai-Kadai** languages and others. The Sino-Tibetan languages are spoken across the Himalayas, in Ladakh, Himachal Pradesh, Arunachal Pradesh, Meghalaya, Nagaland, Tripura, etc. The **Tai-Kadai** language includes Kamrupi language (ancient language of Assam), and some other languages spoken in Arunachal Pradesh and Assam. The Austric includes those spoken by Mundas and Kols and some other tribes in central, eastern, and north eastern parts of India.

SCHEDULED LANGUAGES AND OFFICIAL LANGUAGES IN INDIA

(a) Scheduled Languages: The Eighth Schedule of the Constitution includes 22 Indian languages. At the time of the enactment of Constitution, there were 14 scheduled languages including *Assamese, Bengali, Gujarati, Hindi, Kannada, Kashmiri, Malayalam, Marathi, Oriya, Punjabi, Sanskrit, Tamil, Telugu, and Urdu.* Later, through constitutional amendments, eight languages were added. These include **Sindhi** (added by the 21st Amendment of the Constitution), **Konkani, Manipuri, Nepali** (added by the 71st Amendment), **Bodo, Dogri, Maithali, and Santhali** (added by the by 92nd Amendment).

These Scheduled languages are entitled to representation in the Official Languages Commission. The Government is also required to take measures for development of these languages.

(b) Official language: As per the Official Languages Act 1963, **Hindi in Devanagri script** has been accorded the status of the **Official language** of the Union, while English has been given the status of subsidiary official language of the Union. Thus, Hindi and English continue to be used for official purpose in the Central Government and for communication between the Centre and the States. However, the states can conduct official business in a language as chosen by them and they may choose any of the scheduled languages for this purpose.

CLASSICAL LANGUAGE STATUS

The Government of India decided (in 2004) to select some languages as classical languages which fulfill certain required criteria, which are:

(a) **Antiquity** of texts
(b) Existence of a body of **valuable ancient literature**
(c) **Originality** of literary tradition
(d) **Distinctness** of the classical language and literature from its modern forms/offshoots

The objective was to preserve the literary heritage of such languages and to recognise and promote modern work in them. Till now, **six Indian languages have been identified as classical languages**. These are **Tamil** (recognised in 2004), **Sanskrit** (2005), **Telugu** (2008), **Kannada** (2008), **Malayalam** (2013) and **Odia** (2014), which is the last language to be accorded that status.

As per Government of India's decision (vide Resolution dated 1.11.2014) such languages would be liable for the following benefits:

- Two major annual **awards to scholars** of eminence in these languages
- Establishment of a **centre of excellence** for studies in them
- Request to University Grants Commission (UGC) to start a certain number of **professional chairs** in these languages at least in the central universities

MODERN INDIAN LITERATURE AND ITS EVOLUTION

From the perspective of Indian literature, the phase of modern literature covers the period of 19th century onwards, particularly the period of 1850 and later. This was a phase of change and turmoil in the Indian political and social setup and that reflected in the growth of Indian literature too. By the 19th century, the British rule had become firmly established in India and after 1858 it came directly under the British crown. At this juncture, a number of socio-religious reforms were also sweeping the Indian society. The Brahmo Samaj, Prarthana Sabha, the Deccan Education Society, the Arya Samaj, and others, all opposed the centuries old decadent practices like *sati*, child marriage, and caste system and worked for spread of education amongst the masses, particularly amongst the women. Thus, they had an important influence on the growth of literature in different regions.

Some of the important milestones in this phase of evolution of Indian literature can be said to be the following:

Growth of prose: The growth of prose, particularly in the regional languages in the early 19th century heralded the advent of modern literature. There was a break from the poetry tradition of the medieval period. The subject of literature could become more diverse unlike that of the medieval literature which was focused on spiritualism, socio-religious poetry (*Bhaktikal*), and the later genre to love and romance (*Ritikal*).

Printing press: The establishment of the first printing press in Serampore in Bengal (1800) by William Carey was a landmark event which enabled printing and distribution of books in India. It is said that between 1800 and 1832, more than 2,00,000 books were published.

Newspapers: The growth of newspapers and periodicals proved to be a watershed in the Indian literary and social landscape. It marked the beginning of expression of Indian thought and led to the growth of **nationalistic fervour** in the years to come. It also led to growth of **regional literature** and provided a platform for literary work and people's expression.

Nationalistic growth: The period post 1857, was marked by a nationalistic, reformistic, and revivalistic fervour. This was equally reflected in Indian literature. **Bhartendu Harishchandra's** works in Hindi (*Bharat Durdasha*, and *Andher Nagari*), **Bankim Chandra Chatterjee's** *Anand Math* and *Durgesh Nandini* (in Bengali), and the writings of **Gokhale** and **Tilak**, marked the generation of a pan-India consciousness and nationalistic fervour.

English education and its impact: The above was aided by the emergence of a new class of Indians who were educated in the British law and system. This was partly possible due to growth of English education and which also led to the growth of English press and English literature in India.

Advent of Rabindranath Tagore: In the 20th century, Indian literature reached great heights with the advent of **Rabindranath Tagore** who was also awarded the Nobel Prize in literature. He wrote in Bengali and translated his works in English. His writings were also influenced by the nationalistic fervour and reflected the unity in diversity and other Indian ethos.

Realism in literature: In the late 1920's and 1930's, Indian literature acquired a new hue. While the writings continued to reflect the rise of Indian nationalism, the works of the likes of **Premchand** (Hindi), **Sarat Chandra Chatterjee** (Bengali), **V.S. Khandekar** (Marathi) and others, expressed numerous social and moral issues plaguing the society. Thus, it reflected more closely, the life of Indian villages and the life and perspective of the common people.

Nationalism and reformism: This phase of literature also saw the emergence of a variety of literary forms and genre. Novels of Bankim Chandra, Sarat Chandra, Rabindranath Tagore, Bhartendu Harishchandra, Premchand, Hari Narayan Apte (Marathi), and Samuel V. Pillai (Tamil), not only created a national consciousness but also spoke against social evils like casteism, child marriages, untouchability, etc. Thus, the literature was nationalistic as well as reformistic. Poems, prose, plays, essays, and articles (in newspapers) were other means of literary expression.

Spiritualism and romanticism: The literary evolution also encompassed spiritualism and romanticism. These were reflected in the works of **Aurobindo** (The Life Divine) and in the writings of **Vivekananda**. Even some of the works of **Tagore** emphasised on humanism and democratic values and touched upon the above traits.

Chhayavad literature: A new genre of Hindi romantic poetry called *Chhayavad* emerged with stalwarts like Nirala, Jaishankar Prasad, Mahadevi Verma, and Sumitra Nandan Pant (in Hindi). Similar genre also emerged in regional poetry with **Vallathol, Kumaran Asan** (Malayalam), Puttappa, B.M. Srikantaiah, Bendre (Kannada), Vishwanatha Satyanarayana (Telugu), Kalindi Charan Panigrahi (Oriya), and Uma Shankar Joshi (Gujarati).

Progressive literature: The next milestone of Indian literature was the growth of progressive literature. The influence of Marxism and more importantly of Gandhism (as opposed to imperialism) was profound on the Indian literature. This led to the growth of ***Pragativad*** (in Hindi literature) replacing the *Chhayavad*. Example of this genre was Nagarjun. This social realism was also seen in the works of regional literature like of **Fakir Mohana Senapati** (Oriya), **Vaikom Muhammad Basheer** (Malayalam), **T.S. Pillai** (Malayalam), **Faiz Ahmed Faiz** (Urdu), **Abdul Malik** (Assamese), and **Subhash Mukhopadhyay** (Bengali).

Post Independence and experimentalism: Post independence, Indian literature turned a new leaf. It ushered in an age of experimentalism. Literature was deeply influenced by the new hope of freedom, grief of blood bath of partition, and despair of the unfulfilled hopes after years of independence. This resulted in emergence of litterateurs who believed in Western values as well as those who believed in traditional Indian values. Thus, a crisis of identity along with an experimentation was reflected in the works of **S.H. Vatsyayan Agyeya**, (Hindi), V.K. **Gokak** (Kannada), **Navkanta Baruah** (Assamese), **Harbhajan Singh** (Punjabi), and **Bheeshma Sahni**. This phase also saw writings supporting the cause of marginalised and downtrodden sections.

Contemporary literature: The contemporary literature is said to be characterised by its proximity to the life of a common man. It endeavours to reflect this without the baggage of any ideology or social prejudices and is referred as **post-modernism**.

English literature: The growth of English literature too is a crucial part of the story of India's literature. It has contributed many celebrated authors like Salman Rushdie, Vikram Seth, Naipaul, Ruskin Bond, Khushwant Singh, R.K Narayan. Nayantara Sahgal, Arundhati Roy, Anita Desai, Kiran Desai, Amitav Ghosh, and Aravind Adiga amongst others.

HINDI LITERATURE

The history of Hindi literature is divided into four phases: the **Adikal**, the **Bhaktikal**, the **Ritikal,** and the **Adhunik kal.**

(a) Adikal: The **Adikal** or the early/foremost period of Hindi literature spans a period of nearly four hundred years from the middle of 10th century till the end of the 14th century. The works (usually in the form of poems) eulogised the heroic deeds of Rajput kings and warriors, such as *Prithviraj Raso* by **Chand Bardai** and **Narpati Nalha's** *Visaldev Raso*. Hence, it is also referred as the *Veergatha-kal* (age of valour) in Hindi literature. Besides, this period also saw literary works of *Siddhas* and *Nathpanthis* which brought out the religious ideologies (such as works of Gorakhnath).

(b) Bhaktikal: The next phase of Hindi literature, **Bhaktikal** (15th to 17th century) saw saint poets such as **Surdas, Kabirdas, Tulsidas, Nanak, Meerabai, Rahim**, and others whose works were inspired by the spirit of devotion to God. These compositions were mostly in Avadhi or Braj Bhasha and were largely composed in *Dohas* (two liners), *Chaupais* (four liners), etc. The poets and literary works of this period are classified into ***Nirguna***—or believers of a formless and attributeless God (such as Kabir, Nanak, etc.) and ***Saguna***—or believers of God with attribute/form (such as Surdas, Tulsidas, Mirabai, etc).

(c) Ritikal: The next phase, **Ritikal** comprised poets whose works were largely in *Sringara-rasa* (as opposed to *Bhakti-rasa* of Bhaktikal or *Veer-rasa* of Adikal). The emphasis in this phase shifted to the description of the physical beauty of Lord Krishna and his consort Radha rather than on devotion and spiritual values. Thus, sensuousness, physical beauty, and romance became primary attributes of the works. Poets like **Biharidas** and **Keshavdas** were leading poets of this genre.

(d) Adhunik kal and modern Hindi Literature: The *Adhunik kal* is said to begin in the middle of the 19th century with the phase **Bhartendu Yug** (1869–1893) which was followed by **Dwivedi Yug** (1813–1937). The period post 1937 has been referred as **Adhunik Yug** or the contemporary period.

- The advent of **Bhartendu Harishchandra** in the literary scene in the mid 19th century heralded the modern period of Hindi literature and thus it is quiet appropriate that he is referred as the Father of modern Hindi literature. His works included prose, poetry, collection of plays, and translations. *Bharat Durdasha* and *Andher Nagari* were acclaimed plays which aroused the national consciousness. *Prem Madhuri* and *Raag Sangraah* were amongst many of his collection of poems while *Bhartendu Granthavali* is the collection of essays written by him.
- **Mahavir Prasad Dwivedi** who ushered the **Dwivedi Yug** played a very significant role in establishing the modern Hindi literature, particularly the style of writing prose. His critical works include *Sahitya Sandarbh* and *Vichar Vimarsh*. He was also the editor of *Saraswati* magazine (1903).

Another stalwart of this age was **Maithili Sharan Gupt** who was the author of poems of the epic tradition like *Saket, Jayadrath-Vadh,* and *Yashodhara*. He popularised the use of Khariboli in Hindi literature. For his famous book *Bharat Bharti*, he was given the title of 'Rashtrakavi' by Mahatma Gandhi.

- The next phase of Hindi literature saw the emergence of a number of poets of the ***Chhayavad*** genre; a style of poetry built on romanticism which had deeper and symbolic meaning other than the literal meaning. This phase included many eminent poets like **Jayashankar Prasad** (his works include *Kamayani, Chandragupta, Skandagupta, Dhruvswamini, Janmejayka Yagya, etc.*); **Suryakant Tripathi Nirala** (*Ram Ki Shaakti Puja, Parimal, etc.*); **Sumitranandan Pant** (*Chidambara*) (Sahitya Akademi, Jnanpith, and Padma Vibhushan awardee); **Mahadevi Verma** (*Mere Bachpan Ke Din, Neerja, Sandhya Geet, etc.*) (Sahitya Akademi, Jnanpith, and Padma Vibhushan awardee). This phase also saw another stalwart of Hindi poetry, **Ramdhari Singh Dinkar** (Rashtrakavi)(Sahitya Akademi, Jnanpith, and Padma Bhushan awardee), whose works contained elements of *Chhayavad* as well as of next genre of progressive literature (*Kurukshetra, Rashmirathi, Urvashi, Parshuram ki Prateeksha, Sanskriti ke Chaar Adhyay, etc.*).
- The period after *Chhayavad* called *Adhunik Yug* or contemporary literature saw emergence of new genres of literature. The first was the ***Pragativada*** or the **progressive movement**. This movement, which also was seen in the regional literature focused on the social realism. It emphasised on rootedness to the soil, brought out the plight and misery of the underprivileged, and explored the life of ordinary people. It was also inspired and influenced by the Gandhian and the Marxist philosophies. Eminent litterateurs of progressivism were **Premchand** (*Godan, Nirmala, Seva-Sadan,* etc.), **Nagarjun** (*Patarheen Nagna Gach* and *Kal Aur Aaj*) (Sahitya Akademi awardee), **Dinkar**, **Bhagwati Charan Verma** (*Chitralekha* and *Bhoole Bisre Chitra*) (Sahitya Akademi and Padma Bhushan awardee)
- *Pragativad* was followed by **Prayogavad** or experimentalism which could also be said to be a reaction to the earlier genres of *Chhayavad* and *Pragativad*. Thus, the poems of this phase experimented with new themes and unexplored areas of literature. **S.H. Vatsyayan Ajneya** (Sahitya Akademi and Jnanpith awardee), **Shiv Mangal Singh Suman** (Sahitya Akademi and Padma Bhushan awardee), **Nirmal Verma,** and **Dharmaveer Bharti** (Padma Shri awardee) were prominent litterateurs of this phase.
- Apart from the growth of poetry in the above phases, prose writing in Hindi literature also evolved substantially. This comprised the writing of novels, plays, short stories, essays etc. **Pt. Devki Nandan Khatri** was the earliest writers of novels (*Chandrakanta, Chandrakanta Santati*), while the greatest litterateur of Hindi prose was **Munshi Premchand.**
- The post-independence literature was characterised by the occurrences which marked the Indian socio-political scene, viz. independence, partition, etc. It reflected the hopes and despair of people who were caught between the Indian ideals and Western values. This phase is referred to as the phase of realism in Hindi literature.
- Like other regional literature, the next phase of Hindi literature is called **post-modernism**. It deals with issues of the common man and life as it is without the prejudices and ideologies of the previous literary genres.

REGIONAL LITERATURE

The regional literature of India is quite diverse and vast. There are 22 scheduled languages and many other major languages, each of which has a rich literature with a history ranging from hundreds to thousands of years. Here, a snapshot and salient elements of the prominent regional literatures are being captured.

Regional Literature	Salient Elements And Important Literary Works
(1) **Assamese literature**	• **The earliest literary works of Assamese literature include** the *Charyapadas* (Buddhist songs) of 8th to 12th century CE; the *Prahlada Charita* of **Hema Saraswati** (14th century CE) • **Medieval literature**—post Vaishnavite period—these include works of **Shankar Deva** (*Kirtana-ghosha, Harishchandra-Upakhyana*, etc.). Other important litterateurs of this period include **Madhavdev, Damodardev,** etc. • **Modern literature: Hemchandra Barua, Lakshminath Bezbaruah,** and **Hemchandra Goswami** were important contributors to modern Assamese literature. Other prominent litterateurs of the 20th century are **Rajnikanta Bordoloi** (novelist and journalist), **Birendra Kumar Bhattacharya, Syed Abdul Malik** (Sahitya Akademi and Padma Bhushan awardee), **Navakanta Barua** (Sahitya Akademi and Padma Bhushan awardee), amongst others
(2) **Bengali literature**	**Earliest Bengali literature** can be traced to the *Charyapads/Charyageet* of the 8th century CE and later to the *Panchali* and *Mangal-kavya* of the 12th and 13th century CE • *Geet Govinda* by **Jayadeva** (12th century CE) was another great literary work of this region • Vaishnava texts of **Chaitanya** are examples of Bhakti literature in the medieval period • In modern times, the greatest literary figure was **Rabindranath Tagore** who received Nobel Prize for literature (1913) for his collection of poems '*Geetanjali*'. He also composed the songs adopted as national anthems of India and of Bangladesh • Amongst other great litterateurs are **Sharat Chandra** (composed novels *Durgesh Nandini* and *Anand Math*), **Michael Madhusudan Dutta** (composed literary epics like *Tilottama Sambhav Kavya*), **Kazi Nazrul Islam, Sunil Gangopadhyay,** and **Subhash Mukhopadhyay** (poet) (Sahitya Akademi and Jnanpith awardee) amongst others

(3) **Gujarati literature**	• Gujarati literature is divided into three parts—the *Pracheen Sahitya* (early literature), *Madhyakalin Sahitya* (medieval literature, and *Arvachhin Sahitya* (modern literature) • The **early literature** (up to 1450 CE) comprised Gujarati writing by Jain authors which were in form of *Rasas*, *Phagus*, and *Vilasas*. *Bharteshvara Bahubali-rasa* by **Salibhadra Suri** and **Vijaysena's** *Revanagiri-rasa* were important works of this time • **Medieval literature** comprised the Bhakti literature of saint poets like **Narsinh Mehta** (*Surata Sangrama*, *Sringar Mala*, *Sudama Charit*, and *Govind Gaman*) • **Akshaydas** (or Akh.), **Syamaldasa Bhatt,** and **Premananda Bhatta** were other great poets of the 17th and 18th century. • Among the modern Gujarati litterateurs, the most important are **Dalpatram**, **Narmadashankar** (composed Rajrang, Gujarati dictionary), **K.M. Munshi**, Mahatma Gandhi (wrote *Satyana Prayogoor* (My Experiments with Truth) and Satyagraha in South Africa), and **Umashankar Joshi** (Sahitya Akademi and Jnanpith awardee)
(4) **Kannada literature**	• The Kannada literature can be divided into three phases, **old** (450–1200 CE), **middle** (1200 to 1700 CE), and **modern** (1700 CE onwards) • Early and middle phase literature were largely of religious origin which were of Jaina, Virashaiva, or Vaishnava tradition • *Kavirajamarga* (850 CE) written by Rashtrakuta king **Amoghavarsha** is the earliest known Kannada text. **Pampa** (9th century CE) and **Ponna** (10th century CE) were great poets of this phase • *Kumaravyasa Bharata* written by **Kumar Vyasa** contained the first ten *parvas* of Mahabharata. It was an important Kannada text of the middle period. • **Nijaguna Sivayogi** (15th century), a poet saint of Virashaiva tradition compiled *Viveka Chintamani*, an encyclopedic treatise on astronomy, medicine, poetry, musicology, dance-drama, etc. • Among the important modern litterateurs are **Kempu Narayana** of 19th century (composed *Mudramanjusa*) and L. Lakshminarayanappa (composed *Rama Pattabhishekam*) • Among the post modern Kannada writers of acclaim are **Vinayaka Krishna Gokak** (Jnanpith and Padma Shri awardee), **U.R. Anantamurthy** (Sahitya Akademi, Jnanpith, and Padma Bhushan awardee), **D.R. Bendre** (*Sahitya Akademi, Jnanpith and Padma Shri awardee*), **K.V.P Kuvempu** (Sahitya Akademi and Padma Vibhushan awardee), and **M.V. Iyengar** (Jnanpith awardee)

(5) **Kashmiri literature**	• Kashmiri is among the oldest languages of India tracing its origin to as early as the 5th to 6th century CE. In the course of evolution, it has been influenced by a variety of languages such as Sanskrit, Tibetan, Hindi, Persian, Dogri, etc. • **Kalhana's** *Rajatarangini* is the oldest Kashmiri literature (12th century CE). *Mahanaya Prakasha* of **Rajanaka Shitikantha** is another important composition of the 14th century. • In the medieval period, **Habba Khatoon** (poet and ascetic) composed Lol (poems on love and romance). She is also called the Nightingale of Kashmir. In the medieval period, Kashmiri adaptation of Ramayana was also brought out by Divakar Prakasa Phatta. • Important modern Kashmiri poets and litterateurs include **Rahman Rahi** (poet), (Sahitya Akademi, Jnanpith, and Padma Shri awardee), **Dinanath Nadim** (poet), and **Motilal Kemmu** (dramatist)
(6) **Malayalam literature**	• Malayalam traces its origin to the 9th century CE. Earlier forms of Malayalam literature could be an admixture of Malayalam and Tamil, Malayalam and Sanskrit, or pure Malayalam • *Ramacharitam* by **Cheeramakavi** (8th century) is among the oldest, Malayalam literature. *Bhasa Kautaliyam* (12th century) is a commentary on Arthashastra. • **C. Namboothri's** *Krishnagatha* is an important treatise of the medieval period • **T. Ramanujam Ezhuthachan** (17th century) is considered as Father of modern Malayalam language. His works include *Adhyatma Ramayanam*, *Srima Bharatam*, *Bhagwatam*, *Uttara Ramayanam*, etc. • *Kundalata* (1887) by T.M., is considered the first Malayalam novel. • Important modern Malayali litterateurs include **O. Chandu Menon** (novel writer), **P. Kesava Dev**, **T.S. Pillai, Vaikom Mohammed Basheer** (Sahitya Akademi and Padma Shri awardee), **G. Sankara Kurup** (Sahitya Akademi, Jnanpith, and Padma Bhushan awardee), **S.K. Pottekkatt** (Sahitya Akademi and Jnanpith awardee), and **M.T. Vasudevan Nair** (Sahitya Akademi, Jnanpith, and Padma Bhushan awardee), amongst others.
(7) **Manipuri literature**	• The earliest Manipuri literature can be traced to 10th century CE) • **Govindram Nunganba** (18th century) is considered a prominent modern Manipuri litterateur. • **Lamabam Kamal Singh** (composition; *Madhavi*) and **H. Guno Singh** (prose and short stories) are other important modern writers.

(8) **Marathi literature**	• The literature in Marathi is around a thousand years old and is divided into **old/ancient literature** (1000 CE to 1800 CE) and **modern literature** (1800 CE onwards) • The first major work in Marathi is considered to be *Viveka Sindhu* by Mukund Raj (12th century CE) • The Bhakti saints too made immense contribution to Marathi literature. This includes **Dyaneshwar's** (13th century) *Dnyaneshwari* and *Amrutanubhav*, **Namdev's** (14th century) Bhakti poetry, *Eknath's* (16th century) *Eknathi Bhagwat*, **Tukaram's** (17th century) over 3000 *Abhanga* poetry, and **Samarth Ramdas's** (17th century) *Dasabodha* • **Keshavsuta** (19th century) can be said to be the first modern Marathi poet. **Madhav Julian** was another prominent poet who formed the *Ravikiran Mandal* which comprised poets who wrote romantic and Victorian poetry. **Hari Narayan Apte's** *Madhali Sthiti* is considered the first Marathi novel. • With the beginning of journalism in the 19th century, a number of personalities associated with social reforms and freedom movement contributed to the national cause through Marathi journalism and literature. This includes **Jyotiba Phule** (*Deenbandhu*; a journal), **Balgangadhar Tilak** (newspaper; *Kesari*), and **Gopal Krishna Gokhale** (newspaper; *Sudharak*) • Post-independence, prominent Marathi litterateurs include **Vijay Tendulkar** (playwright; Padma Bhushan awardee and Saraswati Samman), **Vishnu S. Khandekar** (Sahitya Akademi, Jnanpith, and Padma Bhushan awardee) (novelist), **Vishnu Vaman Shirwadkar** (poet, playwright, and novelist; Jnanpith and Padma Bhushan awardee), **Vinda Karandikar** (poet, writer, and critic; Jnanpith awardee), **Bhalchandra Nemade** (novelist and critic; Jnanpith and Padma Shri awardee)
(9) **Mizo literature**	• This literature is written in **Mizo tawng** language (the main language of Mizo people. It has undergone major evolution in the 19th and 20th century with Mizo alphabets being created in 1894 and the first Mizo language book published in 1896 (Mizo Zir Tir Bu: A Mizo primer) • The early Mizo literature was brought out by Christian missionaries. Prominent writers of the 20th century include **Liangkhaia** who published a number of articles in the monthly *Kristian Tlangau* and also authored *Mizo chanchin* • Other prominent litterateurs were **Awithangpa** (poet) and **Pu Rokunga** (poet). **Nuchhungi Renthlei** and **Laithangfala Sailo** (prose and short stories), were also recipients of Padma Shri award.

(10) **Oriya literature**	• The Oriya literature can be traced to the *Charyapadas* written in the 8th century CE. The earliest important Oriya literary work can be said to be *Chandi Purana*, *Vilanka Ramayana*, and *Mahabharata* written by **Sarala Das** (14th century). *Rama-Bibah* written by **Arjuna Dasa** was another important literary work in the nature of an epic poem. • The medieval Oriya literature was inspired by Bhakti movement, particularly Chaitanya's Vaishnavism. • **Ramchandra Patnayak's** *Harvali* was a novel of the 17th century. The 19th century saw three great Oriya poets in **Rai Bahadur Radhanatha Ray, Madhusudan Rao,** and **Phakiramohana Senapati.** Phakiramohana Senapati was a novelist and poet who contributed significantly to Odia literature in the 19th century. • Important Oriya litterateurs of the 20th century include **Gopal Chandra Praharaj** (compiled *Purnachandra Odia Bhashakosha),* **Annada Shankar Ray** (poet and essayist; Sahitya Akademi and Padma awardee), **Kalindi Charan Panigrahi** (poet and novelist), **Ramakanta Rath** (poet; Sahitya Akademi, Saraswati Samman, and Padma Bhushan awardee), **Sitakant Mahapatra** (poet and critic; Sahitya Akademi, Jnanpith, and Padma Vibhushan awardee)
(11) **Punjabi literature**	• The tradition of Punjabi literature can be traced to the Sufi saint Fariduddin Ganjshakar (Sufi saint and poet) (12th and 13th century CE). • The teachings and composition of the 10 Sikh gurus and other related religious literature form the bulk of the Punjabi literature of the medieval period. This includes the *Janam-sakhis* (biographies of gurus), *Bachnas* (sayings), *Paramarthas* (commentary on scriptures), *Gurbani,* etc. • *Heer-Ranjha* by **Waris Shah** and *Sohni-Mahiwal* by **Fazal Shah** were romantic, non-religious stories of this period • Heroic poetry of Punjabi literature includes *'Vaar'* which are Punjabi ballads. Guru Gobind Singh's *Chandi di Vaar* (depicting battles of Goddess Durga with demons) is also an example of epic heroic poetry • Litterateurs of modern period include **Amrita Pritam** (writer and poet; Sahitya Akademi, Jnanipath, and Padma Vibhushan awardee), **Jaswant Singh Rahi** (poet; designated as Rashtrakavi by Government of India), **Pash, Kulwant Singh Virk** (Sahitya Akademi awardee), **Balwant Gargi** (playwright, novelist; Sahitya Akademi, and Padma Shri awardee), **Harbhajan Singh** (poet; Sahitya Akademi and Saraswati Samman) among others.

(12) **Sindhi literature**	• Earliest reference to Sindhi literature is found in references of Arab historians. Records of Sindhi literature is noted in the heroic ballads of **Shah Abdul Karim** (16th century). But the most important contribution of the medieval period is poetic compendium *Shah-Jo-Risalo* by **Shah Abdul Latif** (a Sufi poet). • The important contributors to modern Sindhi literature are **Kishanchand Bevas** (poet), **Dayaram Gidumal** (poet) **Hyder Bakhsh Jatoi** (poet), and **Kauromal Chandanmal Khilnani** (prose). • The post-independence renowned contributors to Sindhi literature are **Ram Panjwani** (Padma Shri awardee), **Sundri Uttamchandani, Prof M.U. Malkani** (all Sahitya Akademi awardees) amongst others
(13) **Tamil literature**	• Tamil literature is one of the oldest literatures of India after the Sanskrit literature. Its history is traced to the Sangam period (3rd century BCE to 4th century CE). The *Tolkappiyam* (commentary on grammar, phonetics, etc.) and ***Thirukkural*** or ***Kural*** by **Thiruvalluvar** are great masterpieces of this period. • The subsequent period saw a mass of religious literature of the Alvars, Nayanars, and Virashaivas. • The period of Cholas saw great literary works such as *Kamba Ramayana* (adaptation of Valmiki Ramayana, also called Ramavataram) by Kamban. • In modern period, **Samuel Vedanayagam Pillai** was the first Tamil novelist. **Subramanya Bharathi** was a renowned litterateur who wrote inspirational and patriotic poems and songs. **U.V. Swaminatha Iyer** (poet) worked for revival of interest in Sangam literature. • Other prominent Tamil litterateurs of the modern period are **Akilan** (novelist and short story writer; Jnanpith awardee) and **Jayakanthan** (writer and journalist; Sahitya Akademi, Jnanpith, and Padma Bhushan awardee) amongst others.
(14) **Telugu literature**	• The earliest account of Telugu literature is noted in translation of Mahabharata in Telugu from Sanskrit by **Nannaya**. • Telugu literature was subsequently influenced by Lingayat movement (Virashaivism). • The medieval period of Telugu literature (14th and 15th century) is referred as the age of **Srinatha**. During this period, evolution of the **Prabandha style** composition took place. Srinatha was a court poet and composed *Salivahana Saptshati, Shivaratri Mahatyam, Harivilasa*, etc.

	• The Vijayanagara empire period (14th to 17th century) was the golden period of Telugu literature and it is said that eight Telugu luminaries called the *Ashtadiggajas* were a part of the king Krishnadevaraya's court. • In the modern period, **K. Viresalingam Pantulu** is considered as the Father of Telugu literature and credited to have written over a 100 books. He also played a prominent role in the development of Telugu journalism • Other important litterateurs of modern Telugu are **R. Subba Rao** (poet), **G. Appa Rao** (poet), **K. Venkateswara Rao**, **Vishwanatha Satyanarayan** (Sahitya Akademi, Jnanpith, and Padma Bhushan awardee), C. Narayan Reddy (Jnanpith and Padma Bhushan awardee), and **Ravuri Bharadwaja** (Sahitya Akademi and Jnanpith awardee)
(15) **Urdu literature**	• Urdu as a language developed in around 14th century CE as a result of the confluence of the Hindu and Islamic cultures. The language derived its vocabulary from Arabic and Persian and also from the Sanskrit based Prakrit. • **Amir Khusro** was one of the earliest and the greatest influence on the growth of its literature. It also gained from the teachings and compositions of Sufi saints such as **Khwaja Banda Nawaz Gesu Daraz**. • Muhammad Quli Qutb Shah, ruler of Golconda and a distinguished poet brought secular context to Urdu literature • In the 19th century, **Bahadur Shah Zafar,** the last Mughal emperor was a prominent Urdu poet, while **Mirza Asadullah Khan Ghalib** is considered to be the greatest of Urdu poets • The Aligarh movement by **Syed Ahmad Khan** (19th century) was a prominent influence on Urdu literature too. **Muhammad Iqbal** (poet) **Munshi Premchand** (novelist), **Krishna Chander** (novelist), **Rajinder Singh Bedi** (writer, screen writer), **Saadat Hasan Manto** (short stories), and **Faiz Ahmed Faiz** (poet) are prominent Urdu writers of pre-Independence India. The partition of India had its impact on Urdu literature too. • During the post independence period, the prominent Urdu litterateurs were **Ismat Chugtai, Qurratulain Hyder** (Jnanpith, Sahitya Akademi and Padma Bhushan awardee), **Rashid Jahan** (short stories and plays), **Firaq Gorakhpuri** (Jnanpith, Sahitya Akademi, and Padma Bhushan awardee), and **Qazi Abdul Sattar** (novelist)

Literary Awards in India

Sahitya Akademi Award – Incepted in 1954, these awards are given annually by the **Sahitya Akademi of India** for the most outstanding books of literary merit published in any and each of the major Indian languages. The Sahitya Akademi confers these awards for 24 Indian languages including 22 of those in the Eighth Schedule of the Constitution as well as English and Rajasthani. The award consists of a cash award (Rs. 1 lakh and a citation plaque) and is the foremost literary honor in the respective Indian languages. The Sahitya Akademi also awards **Bhasha Samman** for significant literary contribution to languages other than the 24 Indian languages, a prize for translation, Bal Sahitya Puraskar (award for children book, and a Yuva Puraskar for young Indian authors.

Jnanpith award – This is another prestigious literary award conferred by Bharitya Jnanpith since 1965 for outstanding contribution towards literature. Every year only one Jnanpith award (comprising cash prize of Rs. 11 lakh, a citation plaque, and a statue of Goddess Saraswati) is awarded to an Indian writer for writing in any of the Indian languages included in the Eighth Schedule to the Constitution and in English. The Bharitya Jnanpith is a research and cultural institute founded in 1944 by Sahu Shanti Prasad Jain (an industrialist).

Moortidevi award – This award is granted by Bhartiya Jnanipth for a work which emphasises on Indian culture and philosophy.

Saraswati Samman – This is another prestigious award for contribution to prose or poetry in any of the 22 languages in the Eighth Schedule of the Constitution. Instituted in 1991 by the K.K. Birla foundation, it covers a cash award (of Rs.10 lakhs), a citation, and a plaque.

IMPORTANT TOPICS TO FOCUS ON

- Classical and scheduled Indian languages
- Modern Indian literature and its evolution
- Salient elements of Hindi and regional literature in modern times

CHAPTER 21

Religions in Modern India

> The essence of all religions is one. Only their approaches are different.
>
> **Mahatma Gandhi**

DIVERSITY OF RELIGIOUS FAITH IN INDIA

India is home to numerous religions and faiths. For thousands of years, different religious communities have coexisted in peace and harmony imbued in the spirit of tolerance and universal acceptance. Thus, the uniqueness of India's religious character lies in the fact that the Indian society has afforded space and acceptance to all religious faiths, irrespective of the differences in their beliefs and practices, and irrespective of whether they originated in the Indian subcontinent (as in cases of Hinduism, Buddhism, Jainism, and Sikhism) or whether they came to India through religious preachers and missionaries (viz. Christianity and Islam). Even communities which came to India seeking shelter from persecution like the Zoroasters and Jews have found social acceptance and space in the Indian society. Thus, tolerance, pluralism, and harmony have been the integral characteristics of socio-religious elements of the Indian culture.

While Hinduism is the oldest living religion of India (and of the world), Sikhism which is nearly 500 years old can be said to be the youngest of the established and recognised religions of India. The salient aspects of Hinduism, Buddhism, and Jainism have already been discussed in chapters 2, 3, and 4 of this book. *In this chapter, the salient aspects of other important religious faiths of India are discussed.*

CHRISTIANITY

Christianity originated 2000 years ago in Jerusalem and is based on the life and teachings of Jesus Christ. Today, it is the largest religion of the world with over 2.4 billion followers or roughly a third of the world's population. In India there are around 28 million Christians.

Christian Faith and Fundamental Beliefs

Christianity is a **monotheistic religion** believing in the existence of only one God. They believe in the **Holy Trinity, the Father, the Son, and the Holy Spirit** (Holy Ghost). **Jesus Christ** is considered as the messenger or the Son of the God. He is considered to be a prophet in human form who spread the message of God and was a saviour of mankind. He endured suffering and crucifixion to save mankind from sin and to grant salvation to those who believed in him. Christians also consider God to be omniscient, omnipotent, omnipresent, just, loving, eternal, holy, and sinless and that He is knowable through His Son Jesus Christ.

Scriptures in Christianity

The **Holy Bible** is the sacred text of Christians which comprises the **Old Testament** and the **New Testament**, the two major sections. The Old Testament written in Hebrew text is considered to contain information about the creation of the World. It is sacred to both Jews and Christians alike. **The life and teachings of Jesus Christ is contained in the New Testament and forms the core of the Christian faith.** The teachings of Jesus Christ are compiled from the **Gospels** (or written accounts of Jesus's life and teachings). There are four Gospels which are considered canonical and are included in the Bible. These are Gospels of **Mathew, Mark, Luke,** and **John**.

Sects in Christianity

Christianity is divided into several sects, the most important of which are the **Roman Catholic** and the **Protestants**. Originally, the Christian religion was referred to as the Catholic religion with the Roman Pope as its head. However, differences amongst the Christians lead to splitting of the Church into the **Western Roman Catholic** and **Eastern Orthodox** groups. Further, in the 16th century, owing to the numerous reforms advocated by **Martin Luther King,** the emergence of the **Protestant School** of Christianity took place.

Christianity in India

With nearly 28 million followers (as per 2011 Census), Christianity has the third largest following in India after Hinduism and Islam. As per a particular set of scholars, Christianity came to India in the 1st century CE itself. It is believed that **Thomas the Apostle** came to India in the Malabar coast in Kerala in 52 CE. However, scholars generally believe that Christianity was fully established in India by the 6th century CE.

Concerted Christian missionary activities started in India only after the arrival of **St. Francis Xavier** (mid 16th century) followed by other Christian missionaries. Substantial spread of Christianity eventually took place during the British rule, particularly in the 19th and 20th centuries.

Christians in India are followers of different sects and churches. These include the followers of the **Roman Catholic Church** (in Goa, Malabar coast, and other parts), **Syrian Church** (mostly in South India), the **Protestant Missions** (parts of South India), **Church of North India,** and **Church of South India,** etc.

ISLAM

The Islamic religion has the second largest following in the world (1.7 billion followers). It has its origin in the teachings of **Quran** revealed by God (Allah) to the **Prophet Muhammad** (570 CE to 632 CE) who is also considered the last Prophet of the God. The religion had its origin in **Mecca** in the 7th century CE. By the 8th century it had spread to the entire Arabian peninsula and from the Iberian peninsula in the west (covering Portugal and Spain) to the Indus river in the east.

Islamic Faith and Fundamental Beliefs

- Islam is a **monotheistic** religion which believes in only **one God** or Allah (the incomparable one) with **Prophet Muhammad as his last messenger**.
- It advocates **universal brotherhood, love, and equality of mankind**; as key tenets of Islamic teachings and prohibits idolism and deity worship.
- The five pillars of Islam are at the core of Islamic religious beliefs. These include:

  Shahda – or belief in one God or Allah with Muhammad as his messenger and the last Prophet.

  Namaz – or offering of prayer to the God five times a day.

  Roza – keeping of compulsory fast in the holy month of Ramadan.

  Zakat – Giving charity as an obligation to the extent of 2.5% of one's yearly savings to the needy.

  Hajj – To take the pilgrimage to **Mecca** once in a person's lifetime for those who can afford to do so physically as well as financially.
- Islam also believes in earlier Prophets, viz. **Abraham, Moses**, and **Jesus** but believes that Prophet Muhammad was the last messenger or Prophet of God.
- It believes in the faith that the world will come to an end on the Last Day or the *Qiyamah*, when everybody will be accountable for their deeds.

Scriptures in Islam

The Islamic faith is based on the **Holy Quran** which is believed to contain the revelations of God to the Prophet Muhammad. It contains 114 verses or *Surahs* which cover varied subjects.

The next important source of Islamic belief is the ***Hadith*** or the ***Sunnah***. These are the traditions of the Prophet as to what he did or said or approved regarding various subjects, which were compiled by his companions. Thus, *Sunnah* plays an important role in the interpretation of the Quran.

Sects in Islam

The **Shias** and the **Sunnis** are the two main sects of Muslims with the Sunnis comprising the majority (85%–90%). The Shias consider Ali who was the son-in- law of Prophet Muhammad as the rightful Khalifah (Caliph) and do not believe in Abu Bakr, Umar, and Usman who were the first three Caliphs in which the Sunnis believe.

Islam in India

Islam is believed to have first come to India in the 7th century CE along with the Arab traders who came to the Malabar coast. Islam also spread to Sindh and parts of Gujarat through the Arabic traders. However, large scale Islamic influence and presence only happened after the Turkic invasion and establishment of the Delhi Sultanate in the 12th century CE. With the establishment of the Mughal dynasty in the 16th century in large parts of India, Islamic influence too spread in India.

Today, there are 172 million Muslims in India (2011 Census) and constitute the second largest religious group after the Hindus. The Indian Muslims are largely the followers of *Hanafi Madhab* which is one of the four Sunni Orthodox schools. Some Muslims in Kerala are also the followers of the *Shafi Madhab*.

SIKHISM

Amongst the major religions of the world, Sikhism is the youngest and only 500 years old. It originated in the Punjab region in the teachings of Guru Nanak (in the 15th century CE) and in that of the subsequent other nine Gurus. Today, it has nearly 28–30 million followers the world over.

Faith and Fundamental Beliefs

Sikhism is a **monotheistic** religion which believes in **one God**, who is considered to be *Saguna* (with attributes) as well as *Nirguna* (without attributes). It is also a **monistic religion** where the world is considered to be a reflection of the creator and hence, not an entity separate from it. It considers God to be *Sat* (or truth), *Sat Guru* (true guru), *Kartar* (creator), *Nirankar* (without form), *Akal Purakh* (timeless being), and *Wahe Guru* (praise to guru). Thus, God is omnipresent (*Sarv Vyapak*), infinite, and is signified by *Ik-Onkar* which represents the divine melody of the one Supreme Being.

Sikhism emphasises on **realisation of truth as the highest ideal**. But it does not prescribe the path of ascetism and self mortification for this. It professes one to be *Gurmukh* (or God conscious) and to follow the path of *Japa* (recitation of the name of God), *Kirtana* (devotional prayer), and *Naam-Simran* (singing the names of God). It also emphasises on humans to be wary of the five thieves in the path of salvation which are **ego, anger, greed, attachment,** and **lust**.

Scriptures in Sikhism

Sri Guru Granth Sahib or the **Adi Granth** is the Holy Book of the Sikhs. It comprises 3384 verses composed by the 10 Sikh gurus and many other saints of the Bhakti period such as Kabir, Namdev, Ramanand, Pipa, Ravidas, Sheikh Farid, and others. Guru Nanak (the first guru) contributed 974 hymns while guru Arjan Dev contributed 2218 hymns. After the tenth and last guru; Guru Gobind Singh, the Guru Granth Sahib has been the guiding light of Sikhism.

The Khalsa

Although the initial development of Sikhism was influenced by the devotion to God and the *Bhakti* movement, the persecution of Guru Arjan and Guru Teg Bahadur at the hands of Mughal Emperors (Jahangir and Aurangzeb) led to the birth of a military order within Sikhism. The Khalsa, literally meaning *the pure*, was introduced by Guru Gobind Singh (the tenth and the last Guru) as the *Sant-Sipahi* (a saint soldier) to protect the freedom of conscience and religion. It sought to bring purity and strength in its followers through knowledge of *shastra* (scriptures) and power of *shastra* (weapons) through *Jnana* and *Kriya Shakti*. It exhorted its followers to wear the five symbols of *kesh, kangha* (comb), *kada* (steel bracelet), *kaccha* (short drawers), and *kirpan* (sword).

ZOROASTRIANISM

The faith of Zoroastrianism had its origin in Persia in the teachings of Zoroaster (or Zarathustra) in around 500–600 BCE. The followers of this faith are less than three million in number and are largely concentrated in Iran. Some followers are also in India where they are referred to as the **Parsis**. The teachings of Parsis are contained in their Holy Book **Zenda Avestha**.

The Zoroaster faith believes in a single God or **Ahura Mazda**. However, it also believes in a concept of duality based on constant strife between the forces of good (represented by Ahura Mazda) and of the evil **Angra Mainyu** (or **Ahriman**). Human beings have the choice to follow the good forces or the evil one, but on the **Day of the Judgment,** they have to account for their deeds and will go to heaven or hell depending on their deeds.

The Zoroasters' place of worship is the **Fire Temple,** as fire is considered to be the Son of Ahura Mazda. A unique practice of this faith is disposing the dead by excarnation (neither by cremation nor by burial). It involves placing the dead in stone enclosed circular structures called *Dakhma* (*tower of silence*) for the corpse to be eaten by vultures or other such carrion birds.

As a religion, Zoroastrianism is among the oldest of religions and their faith also influenced the other religious thoughts, particularly of Christianity as seen from the teachings in the Old Testament.

Zoroastrianism in India

Due to persecution of Zoroasters in the 7th and 8th century CE, pursuant to Arab conquest of Islam, there was a migration of Zoroasters to India. They migrated in the region around Gujarat and are referred to as **Parsis**. Today, they are less than 50,000 in number and their population is believed to be dwindling further.

JUDAISM

Judaism is an ancient **monotheistic religion** which is nearly 3000 (or more) years old. It traces its origin to the Abrahamic religion of the Middle East which also influenced the religious thought of Christianity, and later Islam. However, Judaism in the present form owes its origin to **teachings as revealed to Moses by God on Mount Sinai, referred to as the Ten Commandments**. Today there are 14–15 million followers of Judaism, mostly in Israel.

Jewish Faith and Salient Aspects of Religion

As a monotheistic religion, Judaism believes in only one God called **Yahweh**. Its basic tenets of faith are based on the **Ten Commandments** which are considered the Word of God and are sacrosanct. The ***Torah*** is the religious text of the Jewish people which is also a part of the larger text called **Tanakh** or the Hebrew Bible.

The Jews also believe in the concept of the **Day of Judgment,** when the world comes to an end and when everybody will be answerable for one's deeds. The Jewish place of worship is called the **Synagogue**.

Sects in Judaism

There are three main sects of Judaism—the **Orthodox Judaism**, **the Conservative Judaism,** and the **Reform Judaism**. The Orthodox Judaism believes that **Torah** and Jewish laws are divine and must be followed. The Reform and Conservative Judaism are more liberal than Orthodox Judaism. The Conservative Judaism follows a more traditional path than the Reform Judaism, and is a sort of middle position between Orthodox and Reform groups.

Judaism in India

Jews are believed to be in India for nearly 2500 years. These include five sects of Jews which are:

- **The Cochin Jews** who are said to have arrived with the merchants of King Solomon.
- The **Bene Israel** (or Children of Israel) are the most numerous. These are Marathi speaking Jews. They are said to have come to India from Pakistan after partition.
- The **Baghdadis** are Jews who came to India from Baghdad nearly 250 years ago and settled around Mumbai and Pune.
- The **Bnei Menashe** are communities of Mizo and Kuki tribesmen in Manipur and Mizoram. They claim to be the descendants of one of the 10 lost tribes of the Jews.
- **Bene Ephraim** is a small community of Telugu speaking Jews (Telugu Jews).

IMPORTANT TOPICS TO FOCUS ON

- Salient teachings of different faith
- Scriptures and sects of different religions

22

CHAPTER

Modern Indian Architecture

> Architecture is sculpture with gestures of human occupation
>
> **Charles Correa**

EVOLUTION OF MODERN ARCHITECTURE IN INDIA

The period of Indian history of late 18th century onwards, saw a steady decline in the power of the Mughal dynasty and other Indian rulers. In different parts of the country, European colonial powers established their political authority. As a result, it brought an end to the Islamic rule and with it, the Indo-Islamic architecture. It also marked the beginning of what is referred as the **Colonial architecture**.

Although the British authority vested over the largest part of the Indian territory, the Portuguese, French, Dutch, and Danish too had smaller regions of stronghold. Thus, the period of the last 250–300 years saw varied influences on the Indian architecture in different parts of the country. This could be the **Neo classical, the Romanesque, the Victorian, or the Gothic influence** as in British structures, **the Iberian and the Baroque influences** in the Portuguese structures (of Goa), or the **Cartesian grid plan architectural influences** of the French (Pondicherry, now Puducherry).

Post-independence Indian architecture initially suffered from a hangover of the colonial era. Later, it was inspired by the modern architecture movements in Europe and America. However, growth of modern cities like Chandigarh gave opportunity for development of modern architectural style based on the indigenous need and ethics. They were examples of modern architecture which is still evolving. In the present context, utility, cost, energy consumption, and green architecture of modern structures have been important considerations influencing the architecture apart from the aesthetics of structures.

COLONIAL ARCHITECTURE

A brief account of the different architectural style, poignant features, and important buildings in the colonial period are discussed here.

Architecture Type	Region/City in which prominent	Salient features and prominent examples
(1) **French architecture in India**	**Pondicherry** (Puducherry)	• The city layout was characterised by **Cartesian grid plan** and urban design of settlements

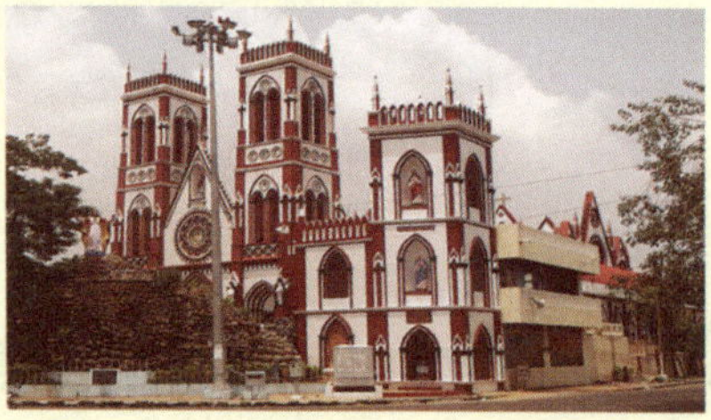 **Church of Sacred Heart, Pondicherry**		• Structures had **classical** architectural plan • Prominent examples include, the **Church of Sacred Heart of Jesus, Eglise de Notre Dame de Anges,** and **Eglise de Notre Dame de Lourdes**
(2) **Portuguese architecture in India**	**Goa** and **Kochi**	• The Portuguese arrived in India as merchants in 1498 and remained till the next 400 years in Goa • Portuguese architecture is seen in Churches and houses of Goa which are of **Iberian** style. The Churches typically depicted the **Baroque architecture** style (Renaissance architecture of Europe) • **Basilica of Bom Jesus** (old Goa) built in 1606 which holds mortal remains of St. Francis Xavier is the best example of this style 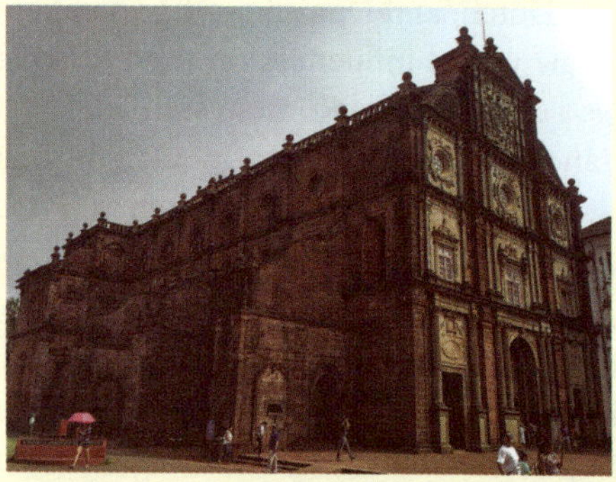 **Basilica of Bom Jesus, Goa** • Other prominent structures include Se Cathedral, Church of St. Francis of Assisi, Our lady of Immaculate Conception Church, Reis Magos Fort in Goa, and St. Francis Church of Kochi
(3) **Dutch architectural influence**	**Surat, Ahmedabad,** and **Kochi**	• The Dutch started trading in India in the early 17th century and remained in India for nearly 200 years. They colonised areas in Ahmedabad, Surat, Bharuch, and Kochi which they took over from the Portuguese

		• The Dutch architecture is visible in a variety of surviving structures which include **Dutch Factory** (built in 1630 in Bharuch), cemetry in Ahmedabad, **Mattancherry Palace** in Kochi (originally built by Portuguese), David Hall (former residence of Dutch commanders in Kochi), and Fort at Kochi beach
(4) **British architectural influence**	**Calcutta** (now Kolkata), **New Delhi**, **Madras** (now Chennai)	• The British came to India in the early 16th century and remained in India for nearly 400 years. The British regime extended to large parts of India and influenced the Indian architecture the most • British architecture brought with itself different architectural styles referred as the **Gothic**, **Imperial**, **Victorian, Renaissance,** etc. which also incorporated the indigenous architectural features or some elements of it • The style and architecture are reflected in a variety of structures ranging from forts, palatial structures, residences, official buildings, churches, commemorative structures, to ordinary residences, dak-bungalows, etc. • **Victorian style** which is also referred as the **Indo-Gothic style** and **Indo-Saracenic** style incorporated elements of Gothic, Persian, and the indigenous Indian style. • It included features like **pointed arches**, **large windows**, **thinner walls** (than Islamic style), **domed roofs,** etc. in rather large sized structures. It incorporated use of modern construction techniques such as iron and steel, bricks along with stones, and later concrete

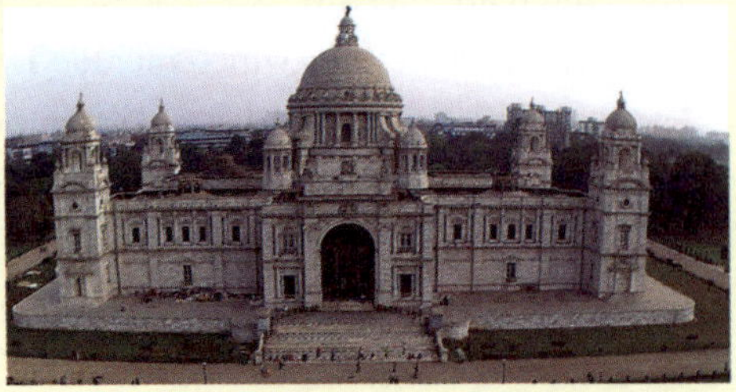

Victoria Memorial, Kolkata

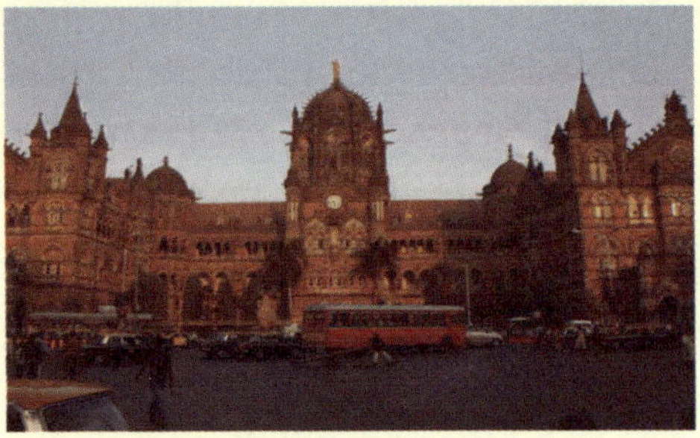

Victoria Terminus, Mumbai

- Prominent examples include the Victoria Memorial, Fort William and Raj Bhavan in Kolkata, Victoria Terminus and Gateway of India in Mumbai, Secretariat complex in Delhi, All Saints Cathedral in Allahabad, and St. Michael's Cathedral in Shimla

- **New Delhi** and the neo-Roman architecture: In 1911, the capital of British India shifted from Kolkata to New Delhi where the construction of the city of New Delhi was done. Designed primarily by architect **Edwin Lutyens** who was responsible for the overall layout and also for the architecture of the Viceroy's house, India Gate, etc. The new city was said to have **Neo-Roman** or **Neo-classical** architecture.
- The structures employed elements of Roman architecture, viz. columns, arches, and domes but also added a number of indigenous elements such as *chattris, jaalis,* and *chajjas*
- Another prominent architect, **Herbert Baker** designed the **North and South Blocks** adjoining the Viceroy's House (now Rashtrapati Bhavan), **the Parliament House,** etc.; while **Robert Tor Russell** built the **Connaught Place** and the Eastern and Western Courts.

POST INDEPENDENCE ARCHITECTURE

For years to come post independence, the Indian architecture did not evolve much. Rather, it was caught between two architectural schools of thought, the **Revivalists** and the **Modernists**. While the Revivalists believed in continuing the past architectural tradition, the Modernists wanted to emulate the modern European and American architectural movement. However, their architectural vision was also without consideration of the indigenous elements.

ARCHITECTURE OF CHANDIGARH

An important leap in Indian architecture took place in the design of the capital city of Punjab (Chandigarh) by **Le Corbusier** (a Swiss French architect). Pierre Jeanneret, Jane Drew, and Maxwell Fry were other associate architects. The city of Chandigarh was divided into three sections. The topmost or head contained the capitol complex comprising the political, judicial, and administrative buildings. The middle portion or the body housed the residential, educational, and commercial complexes with the commercial complex being at the metaphorical heart and arms which were perpendicular to the main axis had academic and leisure facilities. The lower portion or feet consisted of the industrial complex and the railway station. The city had an overall rectangular shape with gridiron pattern.

- In July 2016, **the capitol complex of Chandigarh** was declared as the **UNESCO World Heritage site** under the inscription of '*Architectural work of Le Corbusier, an outstanding contribution to the modern movement*'.
- Other important architectural efforts have been that of Laurie Baker who significantly contributed to the mass housing concept in Kerala and the designs of Charles Mark Correa and D.V. Joshi.

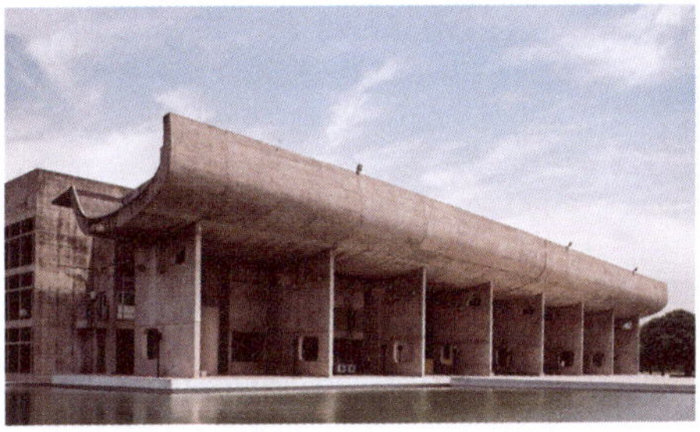

Capitol Complex, Chandigarh

IMPORTANT TOPICS TO FOCUS ON

- Colonial architecture, important architectural styles, their features, and examples
- Chandigarh Capitol Complex and its recognition as a UNESCO World Heritage site

23

CHAPTER

Indian Theatre And Cinema

> Cinema's characteristic forte is its ability to capture and communicate the intimacies of human mind
>
> **Satyajit Ray**

INDIAN THEATRE AND ITS ORIGIN

The tradition of theatre in India has a history of thousands of years. The earliest reference to Sanskrit drama is found in the works of **Panini** in the 4th–5th century BCE and later in *Mahabhashya* of **Patanjali** in the 2nd–1st century BCE. Theatre and its various forms are also documented in the ***Natya Shastra* by Bharata** (200 BCE to 200 CE), which considered theatre to be composed of dance, music, and acting. The *Natya Shastra* describes the various types of theatre and also documents various aspects of theatre such as acting, dance, music, dramatic construction, costumes, makeup, props, etc.

CLASSICAL SANSKRIT THEATRE AND ITS FEATURES

The ancient Indian literature is replete with a wide variety of Sanskrit plays written by eminent dramatists such as **Ashvaghosha, Kalidasa, Bhasa, Sudraka, Bhavabhuti,** and others. Traditionally, 10 different types of Sanskrit plays or *Rupaks* were identified. Amongst these, the *Nataka* and *Prakarana* were two play types which were emphasised upon, particularly in the Natya Shastra.

Natya Shastra

Bharata's *Natya Shastra* identifies 10 types of dramas or Rupaks which are *Nataka, Prakarana, Samavakra, Ithamagra, Dima, Vyayoga, Anka, Prahasana, Bhana,* and *Vithi*. The *Natakas* were often based on epics/epic material while *Prakaranas* were authors' own creation. As per **Bharata,** the central character in the *Nataka* was to be virtuous, of striking abilities, glorious, and preserver of the Dharma and the Vedas, while in the *Prakarana,* the characters could have all sorts of *vrittis* (viz. attributes).

The Sanskrit theatre was traditionally performed on sacred grounds such as in temples and its courtyards and later on in palaces. Its objective was to educate as well as entertain the people. As a form of art, it was bound by certain rules and traditions. For example, a *sutradhar* (holder of strings) who was like a stage manager/director was considered integral to the play. Invocation of God and pre-play rituals (*purvaranga,* comprising music and dance) at the beginning of the theatrical performance was another salient element. The theatre itself could employ male as well as female actors or both. But certain types of sentiments and characters were considered better suited for either male or female and hence, there was a typecasting of roles to a certain degree.

Decline of the Sanskrit Theatre

Sanskrit theatre though quite popular in the 1st millennia, suffered a decline thereafter. This was due to lack of royal patronage, diminishing significance of Sanskrit as a mass language, and languages like *Prakrit* becoming popular. Further, the orthodoxy of the Sanskrit theatre also restricted the creative maneuverability of the playwrights. With the advent of the Islamic regime, Sanskrit theatre suffered a further decline and remained alive only in a few pockets of the country.

IMPORTANT SANSKRIT PLAYS AND PLAYWRIGHTS

	Important playwrights	Salient features and plays composed
1.	**Ashvaghosha** (80 CE to 150 CE)	• Considered the first Sanskrit dramatist • Composed *Sariputra-Prakarana* in nine acts (better known for his work *Buddha Charita*)
2.	**Bhasa** (2nd century BCE to 2nd century CE)	• Credited with having written 13 plays which were lost for centuries and discovered later (which were being used in *Koodiyattam* performances) • **Kalidasa** (5th century CE) in *Malavikagnimitram* refers to Bhasa as a celebrated dramatist and so does **Rajashekhara,** the famous poet of 9th century CE. • Composed *Swapna-Vasvadatta* (the dream of *Vasvadatta*), a romantic drama of Vatsa king *Udayana* and *Vasvadatta,* the daughter of the ruler of Avanti.
3.	**Sudraka** 2nd century BCE to 5th century CE	• His most famous play being *Mricchakatika* (The Little Clay Cart), the story of *Charudatta,* an impoverished Brahmin who falls in love with a courtesan *Vasant Sena* who is being pursued by somebody else. The play explores various emotions of love, humour, villainy, deceit, and intrigue.
4.	**Kalidasa** (4th century CE)	• One of the most famous playwright and litterateur whose works *Abhijnana-Shakuntalam, Malvikagnimitram,* and *Vikramorvasiyam* are considered to be masterpieces and the best examples of Sanskrit plays. His *Meghdutam* (poem), *Raghuvamsa* (epic poem), and *Kumar Sambhava* (epic poem) are some of his other exemplary works. • While *Malavikagnimitram* is the story of King *Agnimitra's* love with exiled servant *Malavika*, *Vikramorvasiyam* is another love story of mortal king *Pururva* with celestial nymph *Urvasi. Abhijnana-Shakuntalam* is a story of King *Dushyant's* marriage to *Shakuntala*, daughter of a sage, their separation, and later the king forgetting about her, and how he eventually recalls her and accepts her as his wife. • Kalidasa was also a court poet in the court of Gupta kings.
5.	**Bhavabhuṭi** (8th century CE)	• Composed *Mahavira-charita* (early life of Rama) and *Uttar-Ramacharita* (later life of Rama). Another of his famous play is *Malati-Madhava* (based on the romance of *Malati* and *Madhava)* • He was a court poet in the court of King *Yashovarman* of Kannauj.

6.	**Vishakhadatta** (4th century CE to 8th century CE)	• A famous poet and playwright who composed the famous plays *Mudrarakshasa* (about ascent of Chandra Gupta Maurya) and *Devi Chandraguptam* (story of defeat of King Rama Gupta by a Saka king and its avenging by Chandragupta II).
7.	**Harsha-vardhana** (590 to 647 CE)	• The great India emperor is credited with having written the plays *Ratnavali*, *Priyadarsika,* and the Buddhist drama *Nagananda.*
8.	**Rajashekhara** (880 CE to 920 CE)	• An eminent poet and playwright who was also a court poet of Gurjara Pratiharas. • Wrote famous play *Karpuramanjari.*

FOLK THEATRE

Introduction

Many forms of folk theatre are popular in India. Some prominent ones include **Ramlila, Nautanki**, **Jatra**, **Tamasha, Bhavai**, **Yakshagana, Bhand Pather,** and **Swang**. These forms of folk theatre have been in vogue for centuries and have been an important means of social religious communication as well as entertainment. Folk theatre invariably involves substantial elements of music and dance and is categorised as a separate performing art distinct from the classical theatre forms.

Popular forms of folk theatres in India and their salient features are as given here:

(i) **Ramlila** – Popular in **Uttar Pradesh, Bihar, Madhya Pradesh,** and other parts of India. It is performed specially during the festivals of *Navratra* and *Dussehra.* Similarly, *Krishna Leela* and *Raaslila* (story of Lord Krishna) is also performed in different regions, particularly in the Braj region of Western Uttar Pradesh. *Ramlila* and *Raaslila* are also considered a part of ritual theatre (which depict religious themes). Ramlila is also **recognised as an intangible cultural heritage by UNESCO.**

(ii) **Nautanki –** Nautanki is a folk theatre popular in Uttar Pradesh and also in some parts of northern India. Performance is based on folk themes, mythologies, romantic tales, stories of local heroes, etc.

(iii) **Jatra –** Popular in **West Bengal**, it literally means a procession. It is a musical form of a theatre in which stories from epics, mythologies, historical stories, and even topical social and political issues are depicted. It played an important role in freedom struggle in the spread of messages of non-violence and against untouchability.

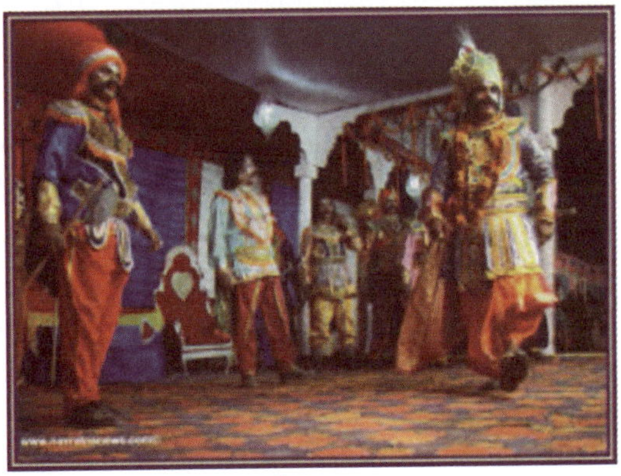

Jatra

(iv) **Bhand Pather –** It is the folk theatre of **Kashmir** which involves dance, music, and acting. It is characterised by use of satire and wit to evoke laughter.

(v) **Swang** – Popular in **Haryana** and **Western Uttar Pradesh**, it was originally a music-based theatre but evolved to include prose also.

(vi) **Maach** – A traditional theatre of **Madhya Pradesh**, it is characterised by prominence of songs between dialogues.

(vii) **Bhaona** – It is popular in **Assam, Bengal,** and **Orissa (now Odisha)**. A form of it is seen in Uttar Pradesh (in Mathura and Brindaban). The story is first narrated by the *sutradhar* followed by the performance.

(viii) **Yakshagana** – It is the folk theatre of **Karnataka** where stories of Ramayana, Mahabharata, and other mythological tales are performed.

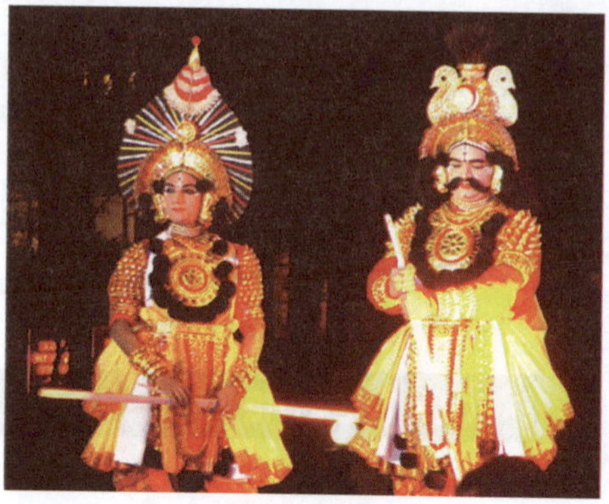

Yakshagana

(ix) **Tamasha** – It is the traditional theatre of **Maharashtra** where the female actress is the chief exponent of dance movement in the play.

(x) **Therukoothu** – It is performed in temples of **Tamil Nadu** to propitiate Goddess *Mariamman* for good rainfall and rich harvest.

(xi) **Koodiyattam** – It is one of the oldest folk theatres and popular in **Kerala** (based on Sanskrit theatre traditions). The *sutradhar* or the narrator and the *vidushak* are the main protagonists. It is also recognised as an intangible cultural heritage by the UNESCO.

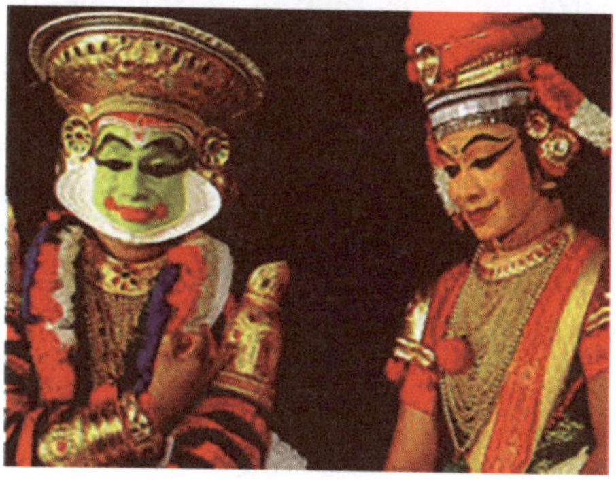

Koodiyattam

(xii) **Krishnanattam** – This is another traditional theatre of **Kerala** where eight plays are performed in eight days.

Other folk/traditional theatres include *Ankia Naat* (ritual theatre of Assam), *Mudiyettu* (Kerala), *Bhavai* (narration of religious/historical stories in Sanskrit, popular in Gujarat), *Akhyana* (Kerala), *Dashavatar* (Maharashtra and Goa), *Kariyila* (Himachal Pradesh), and *Bayalata* (open air theatre of Karnataka).

PUPPETS

Puppetry has been a prominent form of entertainment theatre for centuries. The earliest reference to puppets is found in the Tamil classic **Silappadikaram** (considered to be written in around 1st century BCE or 2nd century BCE). Thus, puppets have a history of more than 2000 years. In the past, puppetry has been based mostly on stories in epics and legends but later, it also diversified into local folklore. Puppetry has different traditions and forms in different parts of the country. This is based on styles of puppetry, painting, sculpture, and presentation craft. *Broadly, puppets in India are categorised as given here:*

(a) **String puppets**

(b) **Glove puppets**

(c) **Rod puppets** and

(d) **Shadow puppets**.

The salient features of these art forms and their regional characteristics are described below.

	Type of puppetry and regional variations	Salient characteristics
1.	**String puppets**	• Also referred as marionettes, these are of the size of a doll. The limbs of the puppets are controlled by strings. These allow greater flexibility of movement and are the most versatile of all puppet forms.
	(a) Kathputli (Rajasthan) 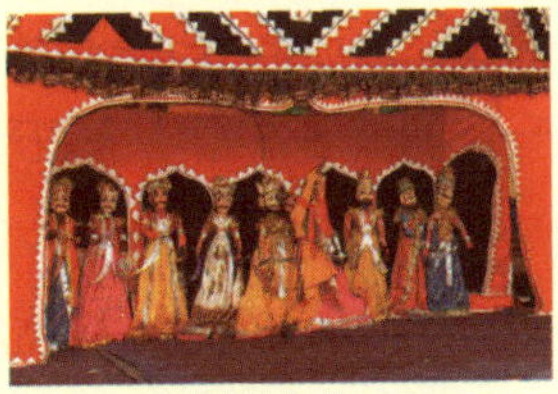 **Kathputli, (Rajasthan)**	• These stringed puppets are carved from a single piece of wood and are of the size of dolls. They are covered in colourful Rajasthani costumes with exaggerated features such as large eyes, oval faces, arched eyebrows, and large lips. The performance is done to the accompaniment of dramatised version of regional music. The strings control the puppets which are tied to the fingers of the puppeteers.
	(b) Kandhei Nacha (Odisha)	• These are stringed puppets. They too are made of light wood which are covered in long flowing skirts. However, they have more joints enabling greater manipulation and versatility of movement. The costumes have resemblance to those of the *Jatra* procession. Puppeteers also use a triangular wooden prop to which the strings are attached which enables the manipulation of puppets.
	(c) Gombeyata (Karnataka)	• These string puppets are designed like characters from *Yakshagana* and *prasangas* (anecdotes) of *Yakshaganas* are enacted in them. The puppets have joints in arms, legs, and hips which enable better manipulation. This is done by using props by two to three puppeteers at a time.
	(d) Bommalattam (Tamil Nadu)	• These puppets combine techniques of string as well as rod puppets. These are the heaviest and largest of puppets (as high as 4.5 feet) and most articulate of the puppet forms.
2.	**Rod Puppets**	• Popular mostly in West Bengal and Odisha, rod puppets are much larger and are supported as well as manipulated by rods from below.

	(a) Putul Nach 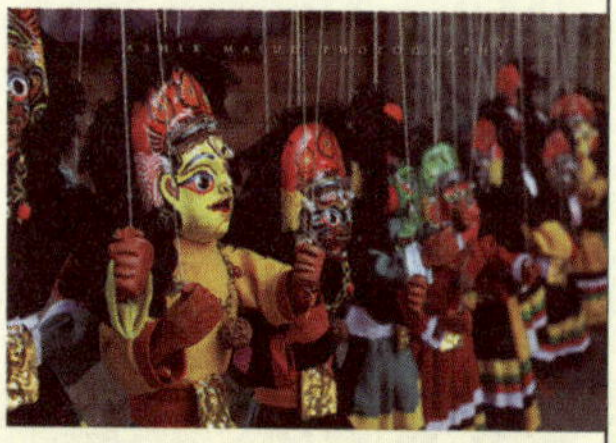 **Putul Nach** **(b) Yampuri (Bihar)**	• The rod puppets of West Bengal earlier could be of human size, now they are usually of 3–4 feet. A rod supports the frame of the puppet with the neck, shoulders, and both hands of the puppet joined to the rod. This rod is placed in a bamboo made hub which in turn is tied to the waist of the puppeteer. Thus, the puppeteer by dancing and by moving his body imparts movement to the puppets. • The Odisha rod puppets are smaller in size and their hands are joined by strings. Thus, the elements of rod and string puppets are combined. • These rod puppets are made of a single piece of wood with no joints, making the manipulation more complicated.
3.	**Glove puppets** **(a) Pavakoothu (Kerala)** 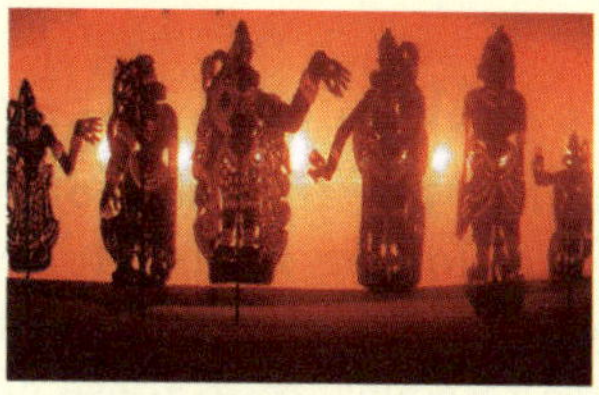 **Pavakoothu, (Kerala)**	• In this form of puppetry, the puppets are small and are worn on the hand. These are also called hand, palm, or sleeve puppets. The manipulation of the puppets is done by movement of fingers and palm. • This glove puppet came into origin as a result of influence of *Kathakali* dance in the 18th century. The puppets of size 1–2 feet are worn on the hand and manipulated. They are decorated with colourful costumes, face paint, head gear, etc. which are similar to that of a Kathakali performer. • Glove puppets are also popular in Uttar Pradesh, Odisha, and West Bengal. In Uttar Pradesh, they incorporate social themes, while in Odisha they are based on anecdotes/stories revolving around love of Radha and Krishna.
4.	**Shadow puppets** **(a) Togalu Gombeyaata (Karnataka)**	• Shadow puppetry involves casting of shadow of cutout figures (of puppets) on screens and conveying the story or the message through the movement of these shadows. The puppets are flat figures cut out of leather, which is treated to make it translucent. These puppets are pressed against a screen with a strong light source enabling the formation of colourful shadows. • Popular in Karnataka, the puppets are small in size. However, their size varies according to the social status; viz. kings are depicted with large size puppets.

	(b) Tholu Bommalata (Andhra Pradesh) 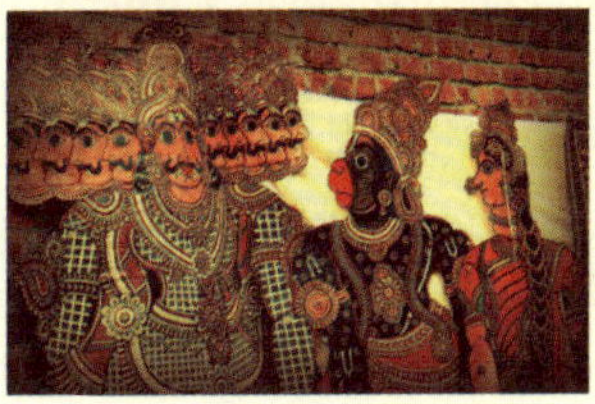 Tholu Bommalata	• These puppets are large in size and coloured on both the sides, thus throwing coloured shadows on the screen
	(c) Ravana-chhaya (Odisha)	• It is considered as one of the most theatrical shadow puppetry. The puppets are of one piece and have no joints. They are not coloured and throw opaque shadows on screens. Literally, this art form means shadow of Ravana. It depicts the story of Ramayana based on *Vichitra Ramayana* (of Oriya poet Vishwanath Khuntia)

MODERN THEATRE

Modern theatre emerged in India in the 18th century during the British rule. Earlier, Indian theatre was confined to the different forms of folk theatre or to the theatre performed in the palaces of kings and royalty. However, during the British rule it emulated the model of the London theatre. The first of these theatres emerged in Bengal, Maharashtra, and Tamil Nadu where the metropolis cities of Calcutta (now Kolkata), Bombay (now Mumbai), and Madras (now Chennai) existed. Later, the regional theatre also emerged in other languages like Gujarati, Kannada, Oriya, Urdu, and Hindi. However, Bengali and Marathi theatre have been at the forefront of theatre movement in India.

A brief description of the salient aspects of these theatres is given.

Bengali Theatre

- The origin of Bengali theatre can be traced to the **Calcutta Theatre** (1779) which had Warren Hastings as its patron. Among the early plays staged were those by **Goloknath Das** (1795), **Prasanna Kumar Thakur** (established *Hindu Rangamancha* 1831), **Nabin Chandra Basu** (*Jorasanko Theatre* 1854), **Dwarkanath Tagore** and **Jyotirindranath Tagore** (*Jorasanko theatre*), **Girish Chandra Ghosh** (*National Theatre* 1872), and **Michael Madhusudan Dutta** (playwright of *Meghanad Badh Kavya*).
- Advent of **Rabindranath Tagore** was an important milestone in Bengali theatre. His plays included *Valmiki Pratibha* (first play), *Dak Ghar*, *Visarjan*, *Chandalika* (untouchable girl), *Raktakarabi* (Blood Orleanders), *Raja*, *Chitrangada*, and *Shyama*. The plays of Rabindranath Tagore explored different manifestations of human values and heralded a theatre movement which is also referred as ***Rabindra Nritya Natya***.

- Bengali theatre was not merely a means of entertainment but soon became a means of bringing **social reform** and also creating **national awakening.** Plays like *Naba Natak* and *Kulnakulasarbasa* opposed polygamy while *Nil Darpan* brought out the plight and exploitation of the local farmers at the hand of the planters. Perceiving its potential, the **Dramatic Performances Control Act of 1876** was enacted so as to regulate this art form.
- The formation of the **Indian People's Theatre Association** in 1943 (as a Cultural wing of the Communist Party of India) was a landmark event in the field of theatre. Stalwarts of theatre were associated with this movement and included the likes of **Bijon Chakraborty, Balraj Sahni, Prithviraj Kapoor, Utpal Dutt, Ritwik Ghatak, Salil Chaudhary, Shambhu Mitra, Bijon Bhattacharya,** etc. It staged plays in *Nabanna* (folk cultural festival of Bengal) which portrayed the Bengal famine of 1943, the plight of people, and their neglect by the British and the upper class.
- In the post-independence period, Bengal also saw many eminent theatre personalities like **Badal Sarkar** (produced plays like *Basi Khabar, Sari Raat, Pratap, Juloos,* etc), **Bijon Bhattacharya** (produced plays like *Nabanna, Dharti Ke Lal,* etc.), Mohit Chattopadhyay, etc.

Marathi Theatre

- The Marathi theatre started in the middle of the nineteenth century with great playwrights being associated with it; like **Vishnudas Bhave** (*Sita Swayamvar*) and **Anna Saheb Kirloskar** (who started *Abhigyan Shakuntalam* theatre).
- The later phase of Marathi theatre saw emergence of many theatre personalities like **K. Prabhakar Khadilkar** (writer), **Bal Gandharva** (singer and actor), and **Deenanath Mangeshkar** (singer, actor, and father of Lata Mangeshkar and Asha Bhonsle).
- In the post-independence phase too, many eminent personalities contributed to Marathi theatre. These included **Vijay Tendulkar** (his famous plays include *Ghashiram Kotwal, Shanta, Court Chalu Aahe,* and *Sakharam Binder*), **Vijaya Mehta** (founder of Mumbai-based theatre group *Rangayan* along with Vijay Tendulkar), **Sriram Lagoo,** etc.

Hindi Theatre

The dawn of modern Hindi Theatre can be traced to **Bhartendu Harishchandra** (1850–1885) who composed the famous plays *Andher Nagari* (a satire on the British rule), *Bharat Durdasha, Satya Harishchandra, Neel Devi,* etc. He was also an actor, director, and manager apart from being a playwright.

- After Bhartendu, the important Hindi playwrights were **Jaishankar Prasad** (*Skandagupta, Chandragupta,* and *Dhruvaswamini*) and others. However, the staging of plays and the Hindi theatre movement was not as active as compared to the Bengali and Marathi theatre.
- The emergence of IPTA in 1943 gave a fillip to the Hindi theatre with eminent playwrights, artistes, and actors getting associated with it. These included the likes of **Prithviraj Kapoor, Balraj Sahni, Durga Khote, Dina Pathak, Kaifi Azmi,** and **Krishan Chander**. The Prithvi theatre founded by Prithviraj Kapoor in 1944 was a travelling theatre troupe which helped in popularising the Hindi theatre.
- Post-independence, the formation of **Sangeet Natak Akademy** (1952) to promote the performing arts and **National School of Drama** (NSD) (1959), a theatre training institute, were very important

milestones in the theatre movement. The latter became an independent school in 1975 and a deemed university in 2011. The NSD heralded in a new phase of creativity to the theatre movement with trainers like **Ebrahim Alkazi**. Veteran actors like **Om Puri, Naseeruddin Shah, Om Shivpuri, Vijaya Mehta** (director and actor), and **Rohini Hattangadi** were associated with it. Several plays of eminent directors have been staged by NSD over the years. These include *Tughlaq* of **Girish Karnad**, *Andha Yug* of **Dharmaveer Bharati**, *Asadh Ka Ek Din* of **Mohan Rakesh**, besides classics like **Abhigyan Shakuntalam** and many others.

- Hindi and Urdu theatre also saw emergence of eminent theatre personalities like **Safdar Hashmi** who popularised street theatre (he was the founder of **Jana Natya Manch** and was associated with the IPTA) and **Habib Tanvir** (a playwright, actor, director, and poet) who enacted famous plays like *Charandas Chor, Kamdev Ka Apna Basant Ritu Ka Sapna, Agra Bazar,* etc.

Other Regional Theatres

- The Kannada theatre too underwent substantial evolution since the early 20th century. In the 1930s, **A.N. Krishna Rao** and **K.S. Karanth** were important playwrights. Post-independence, **Girish Karnad** wrote several plays such as *Tughlaq, Hayavadana, Naga-Mandala,* etc.
- Other important regional theatres include Gujarati, Urdu, Telugu, and Malayalam theatre. A number of celebrated playwrights too emerged in the country in the post-independence period, which include **Sharad Joshi** (*Andhon Ka Haathi* and *Ek Tha Gadha Urf Aladad Khan*), Mohan Rakesh (*Aadhe-Adhure, Ashadh Ka Ek Din*, and *Leheron Ke Raj Hans*), and **Bhisham Sahni** (*Kabira Khada Baazar Mein, Madhavi, Hanush,* and *Muavze*).

Sangeet Natak Puraskar and Kalidas Samman

Sangeet Natak Akademi Puraskar – This award is conferred by the Sangeet Natak Akademi of India (see Chapter 16), for significant contribution in the fields of **music, dance, theatre, other traditional arts, and puppetry**. It is the highest award given to practicing artists in these fields of art and comprises a citation, a brass plaque, and a cash award. The award has been given since 1952 for various crafts associated with theatre, viz. acting, direction, play writing, etc. The award for acting is conferred for different regional theatres, viz. Assamese, Bengali, Hindi, etc.

Kalidas Samman – This award instituted and given by the Madhya Pradesh Government (since 1980) is conferred for contribution in the fields of **classical dance, classical music, theatre, and plastic arts**.

CINEMA IN INDIA

The art of film making is only 120 years old in the world and marginally less in India. However, today it is one of the most popular and profound social mediums of artistic expression. As an art, it shares many skills and attributes essential to theatre, viz. acting, direction, script writing, etc. and therefore, in a way, theatre was a precursor to cinema. But over a period of time, it has emerged as a distinct art form substantially overtaking theatre in popularity, reach, and versatility of artistic expression.

In about 100 years, the **Indian cinema has emerged to be the largest film industry in the world** (in terms of movie production volume) with over 1700 feature films (in 2013) produced in different languages generating revenues of nearly $2 billion. While the Mumbai-based Hindi film industry (colloquially referred as the Bollywood) is the biggest, many regional film industries, such as Tamil, Malayalam, Kannada and Telugu (South Indian Film Industry), Marathi, Bengali, and Bhojpuri are also large and popular.

History of Indian Cinema

The First Exhibition

- The first exhibition of motion picture in India took place in 1898. This was done by the Lumiere Brothers, the inventors of the cinematograph.

Silent films

- *Pundalik* was the first silent feature film made by N.G. Chitre and R.G. Torney (1912). However, it was a not a complete Indian effort.
- The eminent filmmaker **Dadasaheb Phalke** produced *Raja Harishchandra* **in 1913, the first Indian feature film of the silent era**. Interestingly, the female roles in this film were played by male actors. This film was followed by other films like *Mohini-Bhasmasur, Satyavan Savitri* (1919), and *Lanka Dahan*. Some of the other noteworthy films of the silent era were; *Nala Damayanti* (1921), *Gopal Krishna* (1929), and *Achhut Kanya* (1936).

The First Talkie film

- ***Alam Ara*** was the first Indian talkie film directed by **Ardeshir Irani**. *Kalidas* (1931) was first talkie film of south India in Tamil language. It was released around seven months after *Alam Ara*.

Pre-independence producers and movies

- Although movie making was in nascent stages in this period, yet, it saw many eminent filmmakers and productions. **V. Shantaram** (*Manoos, Dr. Kotnis Ki Amar Kahani,* and *Duniya Na Mane*) was one such cinematographer whose films focussed on social issues. Other filmmakers of great repute were **Sohrab Modi** (*Khoon Ka Khoon, Jailor,* and *Sikander*), **P.C. Barua** (*Devdas*), **Bimal Roy** (*Udayer Pathey*), and **Mehboob Khan** (*Aurat* and *Ek Hi Raasta*).

The 1930s and 1940s

While the films of the earlier genre were often based on religious and mythological characters (*Raja Harischandra, Nala Damayanti, Sant Tukaram, etc.*), the movies of late 1930s and 1940s also brought to the fore issues like emancipation of women (*Achhut Kanya, Manoos, Duniya Na Mane*) and other social issues. But movies of the entertainment genre were also popular in this period. Amongst many others it included the movies produced by Wadia & Wadia like *Hunterwali, Toofan Mail, Punjab Mail, Flying Rani,* etc. which featured the Australian actress Mary Evans, nicknamed the fearless Nadia.

- This phase also saw the emergence of eminent actors and the very first stars of the silver screen such as **Ashok Kumar, Durga Khote, Devika Rani, Prithviraj Kapoor** (actor and producer), and **K.L. Saigal** (actor and singer).

Cinema in post-independence

- In the post-independence period and particularly in the 1950s, the Indian cinema made notable advances. The Government set up the **Central Board of Film Certification** to regulate the content of the movies. This period also saw the first technicolour movie *Jhansi Ki Rani* by **Sohrab Modi.**

International Recognition

- The Indian movies gained substantial international recognition too. *Do Beegha Zameen* (1953) by Bimal Roy was the first Indian movie to win an award at the **Cannes Film Festival**. It was a movie succinctly reflecting some of the existing harsh social realities and is considered a part of **Indo Neorealist movement;** often dubbed as the beginning of the **Parallel Cinema**. Earlier, *Neecha Nagar* (1946) shared the *Palme D'or* award at the Cannes Film Festival. Another eminent filmmaker **Satyajit Ray** was awarded at the Cannes Film Festival in 1956 for the film *Pather Panchali*. Ray's other two films of the trilogy, *Aparajito* and *Apur Sansar,* also reflected social realism.
- Another landmark movie of this genre was *Mother India* which was directed by **Mehboob Khan**. It won an **Oscar nomination** in 1958 in the category of 'Best Foreign Language Film'.

Popular movies of post-independence phase

- The popular and entertainment genre of movies saw many memorable and melodious ones, like *Aawara, Barsaat, Shree 420* of Raj Kapoor, *and Pyaasa, Chaudavi Ka Chaand,* and *Kagaj Ke Phool* of Guru Dutt. Other popular movies included *Baiju Bawara* (1952, Vijay Bhatt), *Parineeta* (1953, Bimal Roy), *Boot Polish* (1954), *Mirza Ghalib* (1954), *Devdas* (1955, Bimal Roy), *Do Aankhen Barah Haath* (1957, V. Shantaram), etc.

The Golden Age of the 60s

- The period of 1960s has been termed as a Golden Age of Indian cinema. It was also an era of transition in Indian cinema. The films of 60s started to depart from the concept of social realism and rural fixation to exotic foreign locales. They depicted plush lifestyles, urban settings, and were known for their melodious songs. Thus, **focus on entertainment** of the masses was a key feature of the movies. Actors of this decade got immense popularity and became stars and household names. These included actors of eminence such as Dilip Kumar, Dev Anand, Raj Kapoor, and later Rajesh Khanna.
- The 60s also saw the setting up of the **Film and Television Institute of India** in Pune (an autonomous body conducting various certificate courses pertaining to various faculties of film and television production).
- The Government of India also instituted the **Dadasaheb Phalke Award** (1969) to commemorate the contribution of Dadasaheb Phalke, often regarded as the **Father of Indian Cinema.**

Cinema in the 70s and 80s

- The 70s saw the emergence of **Amitabh Bachchan** essaying the role of 'an angry young man', in various popular movies such as *Zanjeer, Sholay, Namak Haram, Deewar, Trishul, Muqaddar Ka Sikandar,* etc. Movies of a similar genre were also very popular in the early 80s. These movies depicted **the hope and despair of the middle and the lower middle class of the society**. The protagonist/ hero would be depicted either to be operating outside the system or emerging victorious despite the social ills and system failures. Thus, these movies often portrayed characters who were against the system which was riddled with inefficiency and corruption.

Movies in 1990s and 2000s

- The 1990s and 2000s saw movies with a mixed genre becoming successful. There were many romantic movies (*Dilwale Dulhaniya Le Jayenge*), family drama (*Hum Aapke Hain Kaun, Lagaan*), comedy (*Andaz Apna Apna, Munna Bhai MBBS*), anti-hero (*Darr, Bazigaar*), and action (*Agneepath, Border*).
- This was a phase of transition in Indian cinema, not only in the context of the subject and genre, but also in terms of popularity of cinema as a means of mass entertainment.
- With the policy of liberalisation, the Indian movies received a huge challenge from video and television, particularly from the cable television. The family audience to the theatres substantially dwindled.
- Further, with economic prosperity reaching the middle class, there was a change in the aspirations and celluloid tastes of the people. The background of the movies started to become more urbane. Further, a variety of themes and genres were experimented by the filmmakers in a bid to win the audience back to the theatres.

Parallel Cinema

The term parallel cinema refers to the genre of so called art movies, depicting the social and national issues of significance and challenge. These movies were influenced with the wave of cinematographic realism and naturalism; i.e., depicting the reality of society as it is, even though it may seemingly be bitter or harsh. Thus, the focus of these movies was not merely popular entertainment, but more on the theme and the social reality or the message it endeavoured to convey.

In the 1930s and 1940s, the movies like *Acchut Kanya* (Franz Osten*), Neecha Nagar* (K.A. Abbas), and *Manoos* (V. Shantaram) fell in this category. They depicted issues related to women, untouchability, and other social challenges. This movement was also influenced by the *French New Wave* and the *Japanese New Wave* in cinema.

The early pioneers of social realism and parallel cinema were Bengali filmmakers which included stalwarts like **Satyajit Ray** (Appu trilogy; *Pather Panchali, Aparajito, Apur Sansar*), **Ritwik Ghatak** (*Jukti Takko Aar Gappo, Meghe Dhaka Tara*), **Shyam Benegal** (*Ankur, Manthan, Nishant*). Some movies of 1950s such as *Do Bigha Zameen* of Bimal Roy, *Mother India* of Mehboob Khan, and *Do Aankhen Barah Haath* of **V. Shantaram** also belong to the same genre, albeit they tasted commercial success also.

However, in the 1970s and early 80s, the divide between the parallel and popular cinema became sharper, with not many parallel movies being a large commercial success or becoming popular as movies of general entertainment. However, they would invariably win critical acclaim. *Ankur* (1973) and *Bhumika* (1977) by Shyam Benegal, and *Bhuvan Shome* (1969) and *Mrigayaa* (1976) by Mrinal Sen, were some movies of this category. They have also been referred as middle cinema. Many regional movies like those by Adoor Gopalakrishnan also fall in this category.

In the 1990s and 2000s, the focus was again on popular entertainment. Although movies highlighting social issues and realism were made, the element of entertainment too was incorporated in them. Thus, social realism or parallel cinema as a distinct stream of movies did not flourish in this period.

Parallel Cinema: Its Emergence and Decline

Many reasons are attributed to the emergence of parallel cinema. These include influence of social realism as also reflected in other art forms such as theatre and literature. Further, the period of post-independence was a period of transition, hope, and despair. The parallel movies endeavoured to capture these very emotions of the people. Recognition of such movies in international and national award functions too encouraged their production.

The opening of the economy and the shifting of social focus and taste of masses in 1990s and 2000s brought a shift to the movies of popular entertainment. The commerce of parallel cinema started becoming unviable resulting in amalgamation of social themes with entertainment, bringing decline of this distinct genre of movies.

Indian Cinema and Its Significance

Indian cinema emerged as a mass media in the early part of 20th century. As a means of entertainment and a tool for social communication, it occupied initially the same social space as the theatre. However, owing to its versatility of depiction of a vast range of subjects, depth of reach, and comparative lower entertainment cost, it gained in popularity tremendously and made a deep impact, not only as a means of entertainment, but also as a means of spreading awareness on social issues. As a means of entertainment it provided a temporary escape and at times, a hope to the impoverished and marginalised in their mundane existence. As a means of mass communication it has highlighted numerous issues ranging from social evils to national causes, and plight of women to rural life and its challenges. In modern times, as the challenges are changing, so are the issues of modern cinema which is experimenting and keeping abreast with times.

Indian cinema, which has now become the biggest film Industry in the world reaching a turnover of US $2 billion has also played a vital role in the economy and generated thousands of employment in different crafts and trades. As an industry, its reach has been wide covering large parts of South and South East Asia and different parts of the world where the Indian population is in sizeable numbers. Even countries like Russia (and erstwhile USSR countries) have also been an important market of the Indian films. In fact, in all these countries, Indian films have been an unofficial ambassador of Indian culture and ethos.

Over the years, Indian films have also got intertwined with art forms like music, singing, dancing, acting, etc. and have been an important platform for cultural expression on the whole.

Film Awards

National Film Awards

Instituted by the Government of India (1954), the National Film Awards are the most important awards given for **film production and different art and crafts associated with it**. The awards are conferred in three categories—**feature films, non-feature films,** and the **best writing on cinema**. The *Swarna Kamal* (or the Golden Lotus Awards) is given for the *best feature film, best director, best popular film for wholesome entertainment, best children film, best first film of a director, and best animated film*. The Rajat Kamal (Silver Lotus Awards) are conferred for the categories *best actor, best actress, best music direction, best male and female playback singing,* etc. The awards are conferred by the President of India on the occasion of National Film Festival and include a medallion, cash prize, and a certificate of merit.

Dadasaheb Phalke Award

Instituted and given since 1969 along with other National Film Awards, this award is conferred to an eminent film personality for outstanding contribution to the growth and development of Indian cinema. **Devika Rani** was the first recipient of this award.

Film Television Institute of India (FTII)

Set up in 1960, FTII is an autonomous institute under the Ministry of Information and Broadcasting of Government of India. The institute was set up in Pune at the premises of the Prabhat Film Company. It has been running a number of post-graduation courses in film direction, acting, art direction, editing, cinematography, audiography, etc. It has played an important role over the years in imparting trained personnel and artistes needed for various faculties of film production. It is a premier institution of the country in this field.

IMPORTANT TOPICS TO FOCUS ON

- Elements of classical Sanskrit theatre
- Important Sanskrit plays and playwrights
- Important folk theatre forms and regions where they are practiced
- Significant contributors to modern theatre
- Milestones of Indian cinema, important contributors, and parallel cinema movement.

24

CHAPTER

Other Elements of Indian Culture

Culture is the widening of the mind and the spirit

Jawaharlal Nehru

INSTITUTIONS OF CULTURAL INTEREST

A number of institutions of our country are engaged in promotion and preservation of different facets of our national culture. While many of them are governmental institutions established and functioning within different Ministries, some are non-governmental organisations too which are rendering yeoman's service. Together, these institutions are enabling preservation as well as promotion of different elements of Indian culture. *The institutions of national repute and the salient aspects of their work are discussed here.*

	Cultural Institutions	Salient Aspects of Their Work
1.	**Anthropological Survey of India** (www.ansi.gov.in)	• Established in 1945 as a scientific research organisation, it presently functions under the Ministry of Culture. • Acts as a **nodal organisation of scientific research in anthropology**. It also conducts bio-cultural research, pertaining to human evolution in the country and salient traits of various Indian tribes.
2.	**Archaeological Survey of India** (www.asi.nic.in)	• Functions under the Ministry of Culture as the **apex national institution for** conducting **researches in the field of archaeology in India**. • Its activities include: (a) **conservation and maintenance of centrally protected monuments** and sites (b) **conducting archaeological expeditions, explorations,** and **excavations** (c) bringing out archaeological publications. • Nearly **3600 monuments** have been declared as **centrally protected** including several world heritage monuments. • It also administers the laws—*Archaeological Sites and Remains Act 1958* and *Antiquities and Art Treasures Act 1972*—for protection and conservation of various monuments.

3.	**All India Radio** (AIR) (www.allindiaradio.gov.in)	• AIR is the **national broadcaster of India** (instituted in 1936). Its objective is to **inform, educate, and entertain** the **masses**. It functions under the Ministry of Information and Broadcasting and is one of the largest broadcasters of the world covering more than 99% of the Indian population. • Over the years it has rendered valuable service in the field of broadcasting with some very popular programmes such as *Vividh Bharti*, providing a mix of music, songs, skits, short plays, and interactive programmes. It also airs regional programmes in 24 different languages.
4.	**Asiatic Society** (www.asiaticsocietycal.com)	• Founded in 1784 by indologist **William Jones** for inquiring into history, science, and literature of Asia, it was declared an institution of national importance in 1984 by the Government of India. • It maintains a museum in Kolkata which has a large library and collection of books and journals and has undertaken several Asiatic researches and their publication.
5.	**Centre for Cultural Resource and Training** (CCRT) (www.ccrtindia.gov.in)	• CCRT functions as an **autonomous organisation under the Ministry of Culture**. It was founded in 1979 at the behest of **Kamaladevi Chattopadhyay** and **Kapila Vatsyayan**. • Its objective is **widespread dissemination of Indian art and culture**. It conducts **training programmes** for in-service teachers to enable them to get a deeper understanding of the Indian culture. It also organises **academic programmes** for students and a **'Cultural Talent Scholarship'** scheme. It publishes relevant material on different facets of Indian culture.
6.	**Directorate of Film Festival** (www.dff.nic.in)	• The Directorate, set up in 1973, is a part of the Ministry of Information and Broadcasting. It organises the **National and International Film festivals of India**. It also presents the **National Film Awards** including the **Dadasaheb Phalke Award**.
7.	**Film and Television Institute of India** (www.ftiindia.com)	**Refer to Chapter 23**

8.	**Indian Council for Cultural Relations** (ICCR) (www.iccr.gov.in)	• ICCR is an **autonomous organisation functioning under the Ministry of Culture**. Founded in 1950, its objective is to **promote Indian culture on international platforms**. It works for formulation and implementation of policies and programmes pertaining to cultural relations of India vis-à-vis other countries. • It sponsors various cultural programmes and awards sponsorship to numerous international students studying various artistic and cultural disciplines. It empanels various performing artists and also brings out publications in different languages.
9.	**Indian Council of Historical Research** (ICHR) (www.ichr.ac.in)	• ICHR is an autonomous body (established in 1972) functioning under the Ministry of Human Resource Development. Its objective is to **promote and preserve Indian History**. • It **formulates and implements a national policy** for conducting writing of historical research and scientific history. For this, it also gives fellowships and grants besides bringing out journals (*Indian Historical Review* and *Itihaas*), and other publications.
10.	**Indian National Centre for Art and Cultural Heritage (INTACH)** (www.intach.org)	• INTACH is a non-profit NGO formed and registered in 1984. Its objective is **conservation and protection of India's cultural and natural heritage**. It has over 170 chapters in different Indian cities as well as in U.K. and Belgium. • INTACH **undertakes restoration of historical monuments which fall outside the purview of the Archaeological Survey of India**. It also conducts programmes to spread awareness amongst the masses and brings out various publications.
11.	**Indira Gandhi National Centre for Art (IGNCA)** (www.ignca.nic.in)	• This autonomous institution was established in 1985 in the memory of late Prime Minister Smt. Indira Gandhi. Its objective **is research, conservation, display, and dissemination of various art forms**. It has six important units: (a) *Kalanidhi*: The multiform library (b) *Kalakosa*: The research and publication division (c) *Janapada Sampada*: Division of lifestyle studies (d) *Kaladarsana*: Units transforming researches and studies into visible form through exhibitions (e) *Cultural Informatics Laboratory*: Applies technology tools for cultural preservation and propagation (f) *Sutradhara*: Administrative section for coordination The Diaspora Cultural Resource Centre of IGNCA builds a cross cultural inter-disciplinary dialogue.

12.	**Lalit Kala Akademi** (www.lalitkala.gov.in)	• Also referred as the **National Academy** of **Fine Arts**, it functions as an autonomous body under the Ministry of Culture. Its objective is to **promote and propagate understanding of Indian art** both within and outside the country. It also organises a National exhibition. • Its focus is more on visual art. It also conducts research, brings out publications, and confers the '**National Art Awards**'.
13.	**National Archives of India** (www.nationalarchives.nic.in)	• Established in 1891, National Archives of India was created as a **repository of official records**. Today, it functions as an attached office of the Ministry of Culture and is engaged in **collection and scientific preservation of non-current records of the Government of India.** Its objective is to hold them in trust for administrators and scholars.
14.	**National Mission for Manuscripts** (www.namami.org)	• Established in 2003, this mission operates under the **Ministry of Culture** and its objective is to **unearth and preserve the wealth of manuscripts of India**. • There are estimated to be over 5 million manuscripts in India which is probably the largest collection in the world. The mission would entail **locating, documenting, preserving** (physical as well as digital preservation), **and enabling access to the documents.**
15.	**National Book Trust (NBT)** (www.nbtindia.gov.in)	• NBT was established in 1957 as an autonomous organisation to encourage **production of good books and literature for availability at a low cost, and wider dissemination** amongst educational institutions, libraries, students, etc. Its activities include **publishing, promotion of books and reading**, assistance to authors and publishers, publication of children's literature, and promotion of books abroad.
16.	**National Gallery of Modern Art** (www.ngmaindia.gov.in)	• It is a premier institution of the country (established in 1954) functioning under the Ministry of Culture, whose objective is **preservation and promotion of contemporary Indian art**. • It has a collection of 14000 works including those of Raja Ravi Varma, Abanindranath Tagore, Rabindranath Tagore, Gaganendranath Tagore, Nandalal Bose, Jamini Roy, Amrita Shergill, Thomas Daniell, etc. It also houses prestigious sculpture works.
17.	**National School of Drama (NSD)** (www.nsd.gov.in)	**Refer to Chapter 23**

18.	**Sahitya Akademi** (www.sahitya-akademi.gov.in)	• The Sahitya Akademi or India's 'National Academy of Letters' was established in 1954. Its objective is **promotion of Indian literature and languages** throughout the world. For this, it recognises 24 Indian languages, including English. • It organises workshops and seminars, provides research grants, and publishes books and journals including Encyclopedia of Indian literature. Besides, it confers various awards including the prestigious **Sahitya Akademi Award** and Sahitya Akademi Fellowship (for lifetime achievement) (see Chapter 20 for Sahitya Akademi Awards).
19.	**Sangeet Natak Akademy** (www.sangeetnatak.gov.in)	**Refer to Chapter 16**
20.	**SPIC MACAY** (www.spicmacay.com)	**Refer to Chapter 16**

Besides the above, there are many other cultural organisations of eminence which too play an important role in preservation and promotion of Indian culture. These would include Nehru Memorial Museum & library, Bharat Bhavan (Bhopal), Central Institute of Indian Languages, Doordarshan, Indian Institute of Islamic Studies, Central Institute of Buddhist Studies, Indira Gandhi Rashtriya Manav Sangrahalaya, Kalakshetra, and National Centre for Performing Arts.

FAIRS AND FESTIVALS IN INDIA

Fairs and festivals have been an integral part of Indian society since time immemorial. Today, a wide variety of festivals are celebrated in different parts of the country, amongst different communities, and for varied reasons. While many have religious character, some are related to societal activities such as agriculture or are even related to occasions like marriage, births, etc. While festivals like Deepawali, Dussehra, Holi, etc. are celebrated in large parts of the country, others like Pongal, Baisakhi, etc. are common within a specific community or a region. All have their own significance and reasons for celebration but all add colour and gaiety to the social life.

India being a pluralistic society has had a very healthy tradition of inter-community celebration of festivals. Those festivals like Deepawali, Holi, Christmas, and Eid see participation across the various religious communities. Thus, over the years, festivals have helped in creating social cohesion and a unique bond amongst the masses. *Some of the important fairs and festivals and their salient aspects are highlighted herewith.*

Festivals of India

Name of Festival	Salient Aspects of The Festival
1. **Deepawali**	• Also known as Diwali or the Festival of lights, it is a major Hindu festival celebrated across communities throughout India and now in many parts of the world. • It falls on the day of new moon (*Amavasya*) in the month of *Kartik* (October–November). Lighting of lamps, bursting of crackers, exchange of gifts, and worship of Goddess Lakshmi (as an endower of good fortune and wealth) are common forms of celebration. It also marks the return of Lord Rama to Ayodhya after vanquishing Ravana and completing his exile.
2. **Holi**	• Holi is another Hindu festival which transcends communities and is celebrated in different parts of the country, symbolising a feeling a communal unity and brotherhood amongst people. • The festival of colours is celebrated in the month of *Phalgun* (March). It incorporates smearing various colours on each other. It also marks the death of Holika and survival of **Prahlad** (a devotee), thus symbolising the victory of good over evil.
3. **Dussehra** and **Durga Puja**	• This is another major Hindu festival which has pan-India celebrations. It falls on the 10th day of *Ashvin* month (September–October). The festival marks the victory of Lord Rama over Ravana, symbolising the victory of good over evil. The festival is preceded by nine days of worship of Goddess *Durga* who vanquished the demon *Mahishasura* and many others, thus symbolic of victory of good over evil. • Apart from traditional worship, the festival is marked by music and dance (like *Garba* and *Dandiya* in Gujarat) and organisation of traditional fairs in different parts of the country.
4. ***Harvest Festivals***	
(a) **Makar Sankranti**	• It is a Hindu festival related to worship of the Sun God. It marks the beginning of the journey of the Sun in the northern hemisphere/ (*Uttarayan*) as it enters the constellation *Makar* (Capricorn). It is also a festival of celebration of the winter harvest and usually falls on the 14th of January.
(b) **Pongal**	• The festival of Pongal is also celebrated around the 14th of January. This is another harvest festival popular in **Tamil Nadu** which is a form of thanksgiving to the nature for its bounties. It marks the beginning of the third Tamil month of *Thai.*
(c) **Lohri**	• This is a harvest festival of Punjab celebrated on the 14th of January marking the end of winter solstice and beginning of the Sun's northern journey. The festival involves lighting of bonfire in the night, offering of harvest/ produce, and performance of traditional songs and dance.

(d) **Magh Bihu**	• The Magh Bihu is celebrated in Assam around the 14th–15th January. It is also a harvest festival which also marks the winter solstice. It is celebrated by people of all religions, castes, and all tribes of the region. The **Bohag (Baisakh)** Bihu is celebrated in April while **Kati Bihu** (Kartik Bihu) is celebrated in October.
(e) **Baisakhi**	• Celebrated on the 1st day of Punjabi new year (13th to 14th April), Baisakhi is another important harvest festival of Punjab.
(f) **Onam**	• Onam is a harvest festival which is popular in Kerala and celebrated in August–September. It also involves worship of lord **Padmanabhan** and celebration of the return of mythical king Bali from the nether world.
5. Festivals associated with birth of deities/prophets/religious leaders	
(a) **Ramanavami**	• It is a Hindu festival celebrating the **birth of Lord Rama**. It falls on the ninth day of *Chaitra* month (March–April). The festival is also preceded in many parts of India by the celebration of the *Chaitra Navratri* which incorporates worship of Goddess Durga for nine days.
(b) **Janamashtami**	• It is the celebration of **birth of Lord Krishna**, which falls on the eighth day of *Krishna-paksha* (dark fortnight) of the month of *Shravana* (August–September). The celebrations of the Braj region are particularly famous, so are the *Dahi-Handi* celebrations of Maharashtra.
(c) **Ganesh-Chaturthi**	• It marks the birth of **Lord Ganesh** and is celebrated on the fourth day of the 2nd fortnight (*Shukla-paksha*) in the month of *Bhadrapada* (August–September). The *puja* and immersion of the Ganesh idol is particularly famous in Maharashtra, Telangana, Andhra Pradesh, and Karnataka.
(d) **Maha-Shivratri**	• This is a Hindu festival observed usually on the 14th day of *Magha* (in the month of February–March). Literally meaning, the great night of Shiva, it is a celebration to venerate Lord Shiva. The festival is associated with performance of fast, worship of Lord Shiva, performance of yoga, meditation, etc.
(e) **Buddha-Purnima**	• It is a celebration of birth of **Lord Buddha**. This is done on the full moon day (**Purnima**) of the month of *Vaisakha* (April–May).
(f) **Mahavir Jayanti**	• Celebrated by the Jain community, this day marks the **birth of Lord Mahavira**, the 24th Tirthankara of the Jains. It is celebrated on the 1st day of the month of *Bhadrapada*.
(g) **Christmas**	• Christmas is the birth anniversary of **Jesus Christ** which is celebrated on the 25th December. The celebration begins with a midnight mass held in churches on the 24th–25th December. At midnight, singing of Christmas carols and other festivities are also organised. Though the celebrations happen throughout the country, they are particularly marked with colourful and long festivity in the states of Goa, Kerala, and Pondicherry.

(h) **Milad Un-Nabi**	• This is the day of birth of **Prophet Muhammad** and is celebrated on the 12th day of the **Rabi-al-awwal** (third month of the Islamic calendar). It is also referred as **Mawlid** or **Maulid-Nabi.**
(i) **Guruparab**	• Guruparab refers to the celebration of the **anniversary of the Sikh Gurus**. The most important Guruparabs are the birth anniversary of **Guru Nanak,** the first guru, and **Guru Gobind Singh,** the tenth and last guru. The martyrdom of Guru Arjan Dev and Guru Teg Bahadur, installation of Guru Granth Sahib in Harmandir Sahib at Amritsar, and formation of **Khalsa Panth** on the day of Baisakhi are other important Guruparabs.
6. ***Other Important Religious Festivals***	
(a) **Basant Panchami**	• Celebrated on the fifth day of *Magh* (on the onset of the spring season). This is a Hindu festival pertaining to worship of Goddess Saraswati (Goddess of learning).
(b) **Gangaur**	• It a popular festival of **Rajasthan** dedicated to **Goddess Gauri** (a form of Goddess Parvati). It is also a festival celebrating spring harvest and marital well-being.
(c) **Rath Yatra**	• It is a famous chariot festival of Puri in Odisha. It involves moving of the idols of Lord Jagannath, Balabhadra and Subhadra in large chariots.
(d) **Raksha Bandhan**	• It is celebrated on the full moon day of the month of *Sravana* (August–September). It is a festival celebrating the love between a brother and a sister, where the sister prays for the well-being of the brother while the latter avows to protect her.
(e) **Chhath**	• Chhath is a Hindu Vedic festival dedicated to the Sun God as the sustainer of life on Earth. It is observed on the 6th day of *Shukla Paksha* of *Kartika* month and involves fasting and paying obeisance to the Sun God. It is popular in Uttar Pradesh, Bihar, and Jharkhand.
(f) **Eid-ul-Fitr**	• It is celebrated among the Muslims after the end of holy month of *Ramadan* (ninth month of the Islamic calendar). It also marks the end of the month long fasting. The festival is held on the first day of the month of *Shawwal*, once the new moon has been sighted. It involves offering of community prayers (*Namaz*). Holding of traditional fairs and community feasting is also common.
(g) **Eid-ul-Zuha**	• Also referred as Bakrid, this festival involves the sacrifice of a goat. It signifies the devotion of prophet **Ibrahim** to God, who even showed willingness to sacrifice his own son at the command of God, but God instead accepted the sacrifice of a ram.

(h) **Muharram**	• This is a festival of mourning amongst Muslims, where the martyrdom of **Hussain-ibn-Ali** in the battle of **Karbala** is remembered and respected (61 A.H. of the Islamic calendar or 680 CE).
(i) **Easter and Good Friday**	• Good Friday marks the occasion of **crucifixion of Jesus Christ**. It usually occurs in the month of March and April. As per the Biblical belief, three days after Jesus was crucified, he was again resurrected. This day is celebrated as the day of Easter. The entire week before the day of Easter is referred to as the Holy Week.
7. New Year Festivals	
(a) **Ugadi**	• It is the new year day of **Kannada and Telugu communities**. It is celebrated on the 1st day of *Chaitra* (as per *Saka* calendar). This coincides usually with March 21/March 22.
(b) **Gudi Padwa**	• This is the new year festival of **Maharashtra, Goa,** and **Konkan** region. This is also celebrated on the 1st day of *Chaitra*.
(c) **Rongali Bihu**	• Amidst the three Bihu festivals of **Assam,** the Rongali Bihu is celebrated in mid April as the new year day.
(d) **Navroz/Nowruz**	• This is the new year day of the ***Parsi*** community.
(e) **Vishu**	• Vishu is celebrated in **Kerala** as the beginning of the new harvest year. It usually falls in mid-April (13th/14th April).
(f) **Puthandu**	• This is the new year day in **Tamil Nadu** which is celebrated in mid-April (13th/14th April).
(g) **Poila Baisakh or Naba Barsha**	• This is the new year day in Bengal and also in some parts of North East. It is celebrated in mid-April usually around 13th or 14th April (as festivals of Vishu and Puthandu are celebrated).
(h) **Vaisakhi**	• Vaisakhi, the harvest festival of Punjab, is the Punjabi new year falling on the first solar month of the Punjabi calendar and celebrated on 13th/14th April.
8. Other Festivals	
(a) **Phoolwalon Ki Sair or Sair-e-Gul-Faroshan**	It is the annual **Festival of flowers** which is held in the **Old Delhi** region.
(b) **Beating of Retreat**	Beating of Retreat is a **military ceremony held on 29th of January which marks the end of the Republic day festivities**. The bands of all the three wings of the armed forces perform on this day.
(c) **Batkama or Bathukamma**	It is a **floral festival** usually celebrated by **Hindu women** in the **Telangana region**.
(d) **Desert Festival**	Celebrated in Jaisalmer in February, this festival is a mix of cultural events, camel races, and various other competitions.

9. *Fairs*	
(a) **Kumbh Mela**	Kumbh refers to the mass Hindu pilgrimage for bathing in a sacred river on certain very auspicious occasions. There are four widely recognised Kumbhs (a) **Haridwar Kumbh** (b) **Prayag-Allahabad Kumbh** (c) **Nashik Trimbakeshwar Simhastha** and (d) **Ujjain Simhasta**. The four kumbhs are held in rotation usually after three years and once in 12 years in a place.
(b) **Ganga Sagar Mela**	This fair is held on the **Ganga Sagar island** on the day of **Makar Sankranti** (14th January). On this day, a large number of Hindu pilgrims gather on this island to take a holy dip at the **confluence of river Ganga with the Bay of Bengal**.
(c) **Pushkar Mela**	Held in **Pushkar in Rajasthan**, it is a **fair of camels and other livestock**. The event is held annually for a period of five days in the month of *Kartik* (October–November). Hindu devotees also take a holy dip in the Pushkar lake and pay obeisance to Lord Brahma (the creator among the Holy Trinity).
(d) **Sonepur Mela**	It is the **largest cattle fair of Asia**, which is held in Sonepur, Bihar on the confluence of river Ganga and Gandak. The festival takes place in the month of *Kartik* (usually in November) and continues for nearly a month.
(e) **Nagaur Mela**	Held in **Nagaur in Rajasthan**, this is a **fair of cattle** and other animals. It is celebrated over a span of 4 days.

CALENDARS IN INDIA

The word 'calendar' has its origin in the Roman word *calends/kalends* which means a method of distributing time into certain periods. Thus, a calendar is understood to be a measure/reckoning of time which keeps its record in terms of divisions called years, months, weeks, and days. Since ancient time, different civilisations have adopted different methodologies for tracking this time. Usually, it has been based on the movement of the earth and the moon. A year has been taken as the time for one revolution of the earth around the sun while the month is usually taken as the time for one revolution of the moon around the earth. A day is the period of rotation of the earth on its axis. Thus, year, month, and days are natural units or measures of time, while further subdivisions of time as hours, minutes, and seconds are artificial/man-made. However, many variations in these systems of measurement exist which are manifested in the different calendar systems.

In India, the most common calendar systems used are:

(a) The **Gregorian** calendar

(b) The **Saka** calendar and

(c) The **Vikram Samvat** calendar

Besides these, regional variations such as the Bengali calendar, Tamil calendar, etc. also exist.

The Gregorian Calendar

This is a solar calendar with a year comprising **365 days**. The entire year is divided into **twelve months of 30/31 days** (except February). Hence, the months are longer than the lunar months of 28 days. The calendar is said to commence from the year of the birth of Jesus Christ, also referred as Anno Domini (the year of Christ) (AD) which is now referred to as the Common Era (CE).

This calendar was introduced in 1582 CE by **Pope Gregory XIII** who made modification to the then in vogue **Julian calendar** and brought about a .002% correction in the length of the year. Its objective was to bring the calendar in consonance with the equinoxes and the solstices. The Gregorian calendar is the most widely used calendar worldwide and followed in India too, although it is not the designated official calendar.

Gregorian Calendar: Facts of Interest

A solar year comprises 365 days, 5 hours, 49 minutes, and 12 seconds or 365. 2425 days. The earlier Julian calendar which was commonly used prior to 1582 CE (the year of introduction of Gregorian calendar) took the length of the year to be 365.25 days. This difference meant that in every 400 years, the Julian calendar calculated 3 more days to have occurred. As a result, the solstices and equinoxes were not in synchronisation with the days of the calendar. Pope Gregory XIII's reform reduced the number of leap years in 400 years from the earlier 100 to 97. Thus, every year divisible by 4 was to be a leap year, but the centuries were not leap years, except those divisible by 400. Thus, year 1900 was not a leap year but year 2000 was. When the new calendar was introduced in 1582, it had been in vogue for the last 1300 years (since the council of Nicaea of the Church). As a result, there were 10 days extra in the Julian calendar. These 10 days were skipped in the year 1582 which did not have dates October 5 to October 14.

The Saka Calendar

The Saka calendar is the **national calendar of India**. It starts in **78 CE** and is a **luni-solar calendar**. While the year is solar consisting of 365 days, the months are lunar. The calendar begins on the **22nd March** which coincides with the 1st day of the first month *Chaitra* of the Saka calendar (the leap year begins on the 21st March). The months of the year are (i) *Chaitra* (ii) *Vaisakha* (iii) *Jyeshtha* (iv) *Asadha* (v) *Shravana* (vi) *Bhadrapada* (*Bhadra/Bhado*) (vii) *Ashwin* (viii) *Kartika* (ix) *Agrahayana/Marghasirsa* (x) *Pausha* (xi) *Magha* and (xii) *Phalguna.*

The months of *Vaisakha* to *Bhadrapad* have 31 days each, while in the leap year, *Chaitra* month too has 31 days. The remaining six months have 30 days each. Months are also divided into two lunar phases of *Shukla Paksha* (phase of ascendency of the moon) and *Krishna Paksha* (phase of descendency of the moon).

The Saka calendar was adopted as the national calendar in 1957 by the Government of India. It is used alongside the Gregorian calendar in various official works.

The Vikram Samvat Calendar

This calendar is based on **Vikram Samvat** which commences in 56 BCE. It is a lunar calendar. The year is of 354 days while the 12 months are lunar. The deficit of 11 days is made up by adding an extra month called '*Adhika Masa*' after a cycle of 2.71 years (approximately 32.5 months).

The name of months is the same as in the Saka calendar. The year begins on the first day of new moon in the month of *Chaitra*, which is in March–April.

MARTIAL ART FORMS IN INDIA

A variety of martial arts exist in India, each with its unique features and regional variations. The entire gamut of Indian martial arts covers different armed as well as unarmed combats. The most important of these are described here.

- **Kalaripayattu** – It is one of the **oldest fighting systems** which is from **Kerala**. It involves both **unarmed and armed combat** techniques. The latter involves use of traditional weapons like swords, spears, shields, etc.
- **Silambam** – It is a **weapon-based martial art** form of **Tamil Nadu.**
- **Gatka** – It is a **martial art of the Punjab** region involving **fighting with sticks** which mimic a sword.
- **Thang Ta** – It is a martial art form of **Manipur** (as well as dance) which involves **fighting with swords and spears**.
- **Musti Yuddha** – It is an **unarmed martial art** involving **fist fights** and boxing (unarmed). This is a traditional fight in **Varanasi**. *Loh Musti*, a variant of it, is from Punjab.
- **Kathi Samu** – It is a martial art form of **Andhra Pradesh** popular in erstwhile royal armies involving **fighting with swords**.
- **Pari-khanda** – It is a martial art form of **Bihar** involving fighting with **swords and shields.**
- **Mardani Khel** – This is a **weapon-based martial art** from **Maharashtra**.
- **Lathi Khela** – It is a **stick fighting** martial art popular in **Bengal** and **Punjab**.

IMPORTANT TOPICS TO FOCUS ON

- Know about the important cultural institutions and their area of work.
- Know about important festivals, their purpose of celebration, and the region/community in which celebrated.
- Calendars, their types, and salient features.
- Important martial arts of India and their features.

CHAPTER 25

Cultural Heritage and UNESCO

> No culture can live if it attempts to be exclusive
>
> **Mahatma Gandhi**

WHAT IS CULTURAL HERITAGE?

The term 'cultural heritage' has been defined by United Nations Educational and Scientific Cultural Organisation (**UNESCO**) as the **legacy of physical artefacts and intangible attributes of a group or a society, that are inherited from the past generations, maintained in the present, and bestowed for the benefit of future generations.** *The cultural heritage of the country or a society can be classified as comprising*:

(a) tangible heritage
(b) intangible heritage, and
(c) natural heritage

TANGIBLE CULTURAL HERITAGE

The objects and items of cultural heritage which are physically perceptible are referred to as tangible cultural heritage. These include **artefacts, monuments, and historic places.** As they are a reflection on the culture of the people, they are considered appropriate to be conserved. Such objects, artefacts, or monuments may also be of significance from the perspective of archaeological history, science, art, and architecture besides being of cultural significance.

Article 1 of "**Convention Concerning the Protection of World Cultural and Natural Heritage**" of 1972 defines cultural heritage as below:

For the purpose of this Convention, the following shall be considered as "cultural heritage":

(a) ***Monuments:*** *architectural works, works of monumental sculpture and painting, elements or structures of an archaeological nature, inscriptions, cave dwellings and combinations of features, which are of outstanding universal value from the point of view of history, art or science;*

(b) ***Groups of buildings:*** *groups of separate or connected buildings which, because of their architecture, their homogeneity or their place in the landscape, are of outstanding universal value from the point of view of history, art or science;*

(c) ***Sites:*** *works of man or the combined works of nature and man, and areas including archaeological sites which are of outstanding universal value from the historical, aesthetic, ethnological or anthropological point of view.*

Tangible cultural heritage can further be subdivided into **movable and immovable heritage**. *Historic places, monuments, etc.* are immovable elements of cultural heritage which have to be conserved *in-situ*, while artwork like *paintings, sculptures, pottery, minor installations*, and other artefacts are the parts of movable cultural heritage.

INTANGIBLE CULTURAL HERITAGE

This comprises those aspects of cultural heritage of a society which are not physically perceptible. These would include **performing arts** (like music, dance, and drama), **oral traditions and language, rituals, festive events, spiritual beliefs, social practices, knowledge and skills to produce traditional crafts,** and **knowledge and practices concerning nature and the universe**.

The significance of intangible cultural heritage is not merely in the cultural expression of these elements but in the knowledge and skills which is passed on in the society from generation to generation. Such heritage should not merely be traditional but **living and contemporary**. Besides, it should be **inclusive, representative, and community-based.** Understandably, the conservation of the intangible elements of cultural heritage is far more challenging than that of the tangible elements.

NATURAL HERITAGE

The UNESCO has also considered the natural heritage as an important aspect of societies' cultural heritage. This would include the natural environment, its flora and fauna (biodiversity), its geological elements including mineralogical, geomorphological, and paleontological (geodiversity), as well as countryside and cultural landscapes (natural features which may have cultural attributes).

Article 2 of **Convention Concerning the Protection of World Cultural and Natural Heritage,** of 1972 defines natural heritage as below:

For the purposes of this Convention, the following shall be considered as "natural heritage":

(a) *natural features consisting of physical and biological formations or groups of such formations, which are of outstanding universal value from the aesthetic or scientific point of view;*

(b) *geological and physiographical formations and precisely delineated areas which constitute the habitat of threatened species of animals and plants of outstanding universal value from the point of view of science or conservation;*

(c) *natural sites or precisely delineated natural areas of outstanding universal value from the point of view of science, conservation or natural beauty.*

Conservation of the above is significant from the societies' cultural, economic (tourist attraction), ecological, and other perspectives.

UNESCO AND CONSERVATION OF CULTURAL AND NATURAL HERITAGE

Over the last 45 years, UNESCO has adopted several conventions for protecting the world's cultural and natural heritage, the most important of these being the ***UNESCO World Heritage Convention of 1972.*** Besides it, the other relevant and important convention includes ***UNESCO Convention on Protection of Underwater Cultural Heritage***.

UNESCO also designates masterpieces of oral and intangible heritage of Humanity. It has further constituted a committee on Economic, Social, and Cultural Rights.

As a result of the above efforts, UNESCO has so far declared **936 World Heritage** sites in 153 countries (725 cultural, 183 natural, and 28 mixed). The basic ethos of UNESCO is that these are the **heritage from the past** and need to be conserved for the future. As a world heritage, these sites belong to the entire humanity irrespective of the territory on which they are located.

LEGAL PROTECTION TO WORLD HERITAGE SITES

A site declared as a World Heritage site is considered to be culturally sensitive and important. It is accorded legal protection under **Geneva Convention; Law of War** (Article 53) along with other international treaties and conventions (including the 'Hague convention for the protection of cultural property in the event of armed conflict and international law'). Thus, the conventions prohibit the destruction or damage to such property in the event of armed conflict, war, etc.

CONSERVATION OF WORLD HERITAGE SITES

The UNESCO, as per its World Heritage Mission, undertakes the following measures.

- Encourages countries to sign the World Heritage convention and to ensure the protection of natural and cultural heritage.
- Encourages States parties to **establish management plans** and set up reporting systems on the state of conservation of World Heritage Sites (WHS)
- Provides **emergency assistance** for the World Heritage Sites in immediate danger.
- Encourages **participation of the local population** in the preservation of the cultural and natural heritage.
- Encourages States parties to the convention to **nominate sites** within their national territory **for inclusion in the World Heritage list**.
- Helps States parties safeguard World Heritage properties by providing **technical assistance and professional training**.
- Supports States parties' public awareness building activities for World Heritage convention.
- Encourages **international co-operation** in the conservation of our world's natural and cultural heritage.

For the purposes of nomination of sites as UNESCO World Heritage Sites, the UNESCO follows certain criteria which are briefly discussed below.

Criteria for Cultural and Natural Sites

(i) It represents a masterpiece of human creative genius.

(ii) It exhibits an important interchange of human value over a span of time, or within a culture area of the world, on developments in architecture of technology, monumental arts, town-planning, or landscape design.

(iii) It bears a unique or exceptional testimony to a cultural tradition or to a civilisation which is living or which has disappeared.

(iv) It is an outstanding example of a type of building, architecture, or technology ensemble or landscape which illustrates a significant stage(s) in human history.

(v) It is an outstanding example of a traditional human settlement, land-use, or sea-use which is representative of a culture or human interaction with the environment especially when it has become vulnerable under the impact of irreversible change.

(vi) It is directly or tangibly associated with events or living traditions, with ideas or with beliefs, with artistic and literary works of outstanding universal significance.

(vii) It contains superlative natural phenomena or areas of exceptional natural beauty and aesthetic importance.

(viii) It is an outstanding example representing major stages of the Earth's history including the record of life, significant on-going geological processes in the development of landforms, or significant geomorphic or physiographic features.

(ix) It is an outstanding example representing significant on-going ecological and biological processes in the evolution and development of terrestrial, fresh water, coastal and marine ecosystems, and communities of plants and animals.

(x) It contains the most important and significant natural habitats for in-situ conservation of biological diversity, including those containing threatened species of outstanding universal values from the point of view of science or conservation.

Criteria for Intangible Cultural Heritage

As per UNESCO, the following are the features of intangible cultural heritage.

Intangible Cultural heritage is:

- ***Traditional, contemporary, and living at the same time:*** Intangible cultural heritage represents not only inherited traditions from the past but also contemporary rural and urban practices in which diverse cultural groups take part.
- ***Inclusive:*** We may share expressions of intangible cultural heritage that are similar to those practiced by others. Whether they are from the neighbouring village, from a city on the opposite side of the world, or have been adapted by people who have migrated and settled in a different region, they all are intangible cultural heritage: they have been passed from **one generation to another**, have evolved in response to their environments, and they contribute to giving us a sense of identity and continuity, providing a link from our past, through the present, and into our future. Intangible cultural heritage does not give rise to questions of whether or not certain practices are specific to a culture. It contributes to social cohesion, encouraging a sense of identity and responsibility which helps individuals to feel part of one or different communities, and to feel part of the society at large.
- ***Representative:*** Intangible cultural heritage is not merely valued as a cultural good, on a comparative basis, for its exclusive or its exceptional value. It thrives on its basis in communities and depends on those whose knowledge of traditions, skills, and customs are passed on to the rest of the community, from generation to generation, or to other communities.

- ***Community-based:*** Intangible cultural heritage can only be a heritage when it is recognised as such by the communities, groups, or individuals that create, maintain, and transmit it—without their recognition, nobody else can decide for them that a given expression or practice is their heritage.

WORLD HERITAGE SITES IN INDIA

UNESCO has recognised **35 sites of India as World Heritage sites**. These include 27 cultural, 7 natural, and one mixed site. India also has a tentative list of 43 sites for consideration as World Heritage sites.

In July 2016, **three new sites of India** were included in the list of World Heritage sites. These include:

(i) The archaeological site of **Nalanda Mahavihara** (Nalanda University) at Nalanda in Bihar.

(ii) The **Capitol Building Complex**; the Architectural work of Le Corbusier in Chandigarh.

(iii) The **Khangchendzonga National park** in Sikkim.

The list of World Heritage sites in India is as below:

(a) UNESCO Tangible Cultural, Natural, and Mixed Heritage in India

No.	Name	Region	Period
01	**Kaziranga Wildlife Sanctuary**	Assam	20th century
02	**Manas Wildlife Sanctuary**	Assam	20th century
03	**Mahabodhi Temple Complex at Bodh Gaya**	Bihar	3rd century BC, 5th and 6th century AD, and 19th century
04	**Humayun's Tomb**	Delhi	1572
05	**Qutab Minar and its Monuments**	Delhi	Late 12th century
06	**Red Fort Complex**	Delhi	1648
07	**Churches and Convents of Goa**	Velha Goa (Old Goa), Goa	16th and 18th centuries
08	**Champaner-Pavagadh Archaeological Park**	Gujarat	Prehistoric and 8th to 14th centuries
09	**Group of Monuments at Hampi**	Ballari district, Karnataka	14th and 16th centuries
10	**Group of Monuments at Pattadakal**	Bagalkot District, Karnataka	8th century
11	**Buddhist Monuments at Sanchi**	Madhya Pradesh	2nd and 1st centuries BC to the 12th century AD
12	**Rock Shelters of Bhimbetka**	Madhya Pradesh	30,000 years

No.	Name	Region	Period
13	Khajuraho Group of Monuments	Madhya Pradesh	950 AD to 1050 AD
14	Ajanta Caves	Maharashtra	2nd century BC to 6th century
15	Ellora Caves	Maharashtra	600 to 1000 AD
16	Elephanta Caves	Maharashtra	5th to 8th centuries
17	Chhatrapati Shivaji Terminus (formerly Victoria Terminus)	Maharashtra	1887–1888
18	Sun Temple, Konark	Puri District, Odisha	13th century
19	Keoladeo National Park	Bharatpur, Rajasthan,	1981
20	Jantar Mantar	Jaipur, Rajasthan	1727 and 1734
21	Great Living Chola Temples	Brihadeeswarar temple, Gangaikonda Cholapuram, Tamil Nadu	11th and 12th century
		Airavateshwarar Temple, Darasuram, Tamil Nadu	12th century
		Brihadeeswarar Temple, Thanjavur, Tamil Nadu	10th century
22	Group of Monuments at Mahabalipuram	Mahabalipuram, Tamil Nadu	7th and 8th centuries
23	Agra Fort, Agra	Uttar Pradesh	16th century
24	Fatehpur Sikri, Agra	Uttar Pradesh	16th century
25	Taj Mahal, Agra	Uttar Pradesh	17th century
26	Mountain Railways of India	Darjeeling Himalayan Railway (1999), Darjeeling, West Bengal	19th and early 20th centuries
		Nilgiri Mountain Railway (2005), Ooty, Tamil Nadu	
		Kalka-Shimla Railway, Himachal Pradesh (2008)	

No.	Name	Region	Period
27	Nanda Devi and Valley of Flowers National Parks	Chamoli District, Uttarakhand	1939 and 1982
28	Sundarbans National Park	West Bengal	1939 and 1982
29	Western Ghats	Agasthyamalai Sub-Cluster	
		Periyar Sub-Cluster	
		Anamalai Sub-Cluster	
		Nilgiri Sub-Cluster	
		Talakaveri Sub-Cluster (five properties)	
		Kudremukh Sub-Cluster (five properties)	
		Sahyadri Sub-Cluster	
30	Hill Forts of Rajasthan	Chittorgarh	5th to 17th centuries AD
		Kumbhalgarh	
		Ranthambhore	
		Amber Sub-Cluster	
		Jaisalmer	
		Gagron	
31	Rani ki vav (The Queen's Stepwell)	Patan, Gujarat	11th century AD
32	Great Himalayan National Park	Himachal Pradesh	
33	Nalanda	Bihar	5th to 12th centuries AD
34	Khangchendzonga National Park	Sikkim	
35	The Architectural Work Of Le Corbusier	Chandigarh	20th century AD

(b) UNESCO Intangible Cultural Heritage in India

S.No.	Element of Intangible Cultural Heritage	Year in which designated
1	Koodiyattam: Sanskrit theatre, Kerala	2008
2	Mudiyett: A ritual theatre of Kerala	2010
3	The Tradition of Vedic Chanting	2008
4	Ramlila: The Traditional Performance of the Ramayana	2008
5	Ramman: Religious festival and ritual theatre of the Garhwal Himalayas	2009
6	Novruz/ Nowrouz/ Nooruz/ Navruz/ Nauroz/Nevruz : Parsi New Year	2009
7	Kalbelia: Folk songs and dances of Rajasthan	2010
8	Chhau dance: A tradition from eastern India	2010
9	Buddhist chanting of Ladakh: Recitation of sacred Buddhist texts in the trans-Himalayan Ladakh region, Jammu and Kashmir, India	2012
10	Sankirtana: Ritual singing, drumming, and dancing of Manipur	2014
11	Traditional brass and copper craft of utensil making among the Thatheras of Jandiala Guru, Punjab	2014

IMPORTANT TOPICS TO FOCUS ON

- What is tangible heritage, intangible heritage, cultural heritage, and natural heritage?
- Why it is important to conserve the cultural heritage?
- Efforts of UNESCO to conserve the cultural heritage
- Important cultural heritage sites and intangible heritage of India, especially sites or elements designated in the current year

PART 4

Appendices

APPENDIX 1

Practice Questions for Preliminary Examination

The following questions on Indian art and culture have been carefully selected and prepared based on the trend of questions asked in the Civil Services Preliminary examination

1. Which of the following pairs is **not** correct about the Indus Valley Civilisation?
   (i) Town planning – grid pattern
   (ii) Great Bath-- irrigation
   (iii) Indus script – hieroglyphic
   (a) (iii) (b) (ii) & (iii)
   (c) (i), (ii) & (iii) (d) (ii)

2. Which amongst the following is **not** a part of the six systems of ancient Hindu philosophy?
   (1) Yoga (2) Samkhya
   (3) Vaisheshika (4) Charvaka
   (5) Purana
   (a) 3, 4, 5 (b) 4, 5
   (c) only 4 (d) 2, 4, 5

3. Which amongst the following pairs are correct?
   (1) *Jatakas*–The stories from the previous births of Buddha
   (2) *Gahpati*–The head of a clan of Buddhist monks.
   (a) Only 1 (b) Only 2
   (c) Both 1 & 2 (d) Neither 1 nor 2

4. Which amongst the following are correctly matched?
   (1) *Agamas* – Jain scriptures containing Jain philosophies and teachings of Tirthankaras
   (2) *Anekantavada* – The Jain philosophy that truth is one but owing to different perspectives, different people perceive it differently
   (a) Only 1 (b) only 2
   (c) Both 1 & 2 (d) Neither 1 nor 2

5. Which amongst the following is **not** a part of the Lion Capital of Sarnath?
   (1) An image of a Yakshini engraved on the back of the capital.
   (2) An inverted bell shaped base covered with a lotus.
   (3) An abacus with a figure of horse, bull, lion and elephant on it.
   (4) Four chakras
   (a) 1, 2 (b) 1, 2
   (c) 1 (d) 3

6. Which amongst the following is **not** correct?
   (a) Nirandhara temples were early temple shrines which had *Pradakshina-path* built around it.
   (b) Vedika was the outer railing of a stupa enclosing a *pradakshina* path inside it
   (c) Nachna Kuthara temple and Deogarh temples represent the early phase of temple construction in India.
   (d) None of the above

7. In which amongst the following places one would expect to find murals?
   (1) Lepakshi temple
   (2) Ajanta caves
   (3) Udayagiri and Khandagiri caves
   (a) 2 only (b) 1 & 2
   (c) 2 & 3 (d) 1, 2 & 3

8. The famous image of 'Ravana shaking mount Kailash', can be found in
   (a) Mahabalipuram
   (b) Kailashnath temple, Ellora
   (c) Meenakshi temple, Madurai
   (d) Gangaikondacholapuram temple

9. Which amongst the following is a correct match?
   (1) Alwars (a) Vaishnavites
   (2) Nayanars (b) Shaivites
   (3) Virashaivas (c) Lingayats
   (a) 1-a 2-b 3-c (b) 1-a 2-c 3-b
   (c) 1-b 2-a 3-c (d) 1-b 2-c 3-a

10. The term *Khanqah* referred to
   (a) A hospice or a building designed for gathering of a Sufi brotherhood.
   (b) A lineage of Sufi order.
   (c) The award of equivalent of sainthood in Sufi order.
   (d) A spiritual state of enlightenment of a Sufi saint.

11. The Indo-Sarcenic style of architecture with archuate features emerged in the Indian subcontinent in the
   (a) 7th and 8th century as a result of the influence of the Arab traders.
   (b) 8th century after the conquest of Sindh by Muhammad Bin Qasim.
   (c) After the establishment of Delhi Sultanate, post Turkic invasion in the thirteenth century.
   (d) After the establishment of Mughal dynasty in the 16th century.

12. Which amongst the following contain cave paintings?
   (1) Bhimbetka caves in Madhya Pradesh
   (2) Lakhudiyar caves in Kumaon (Uttarakhand)
   (3) Piklihal and Tekalakota in Karnataka
   (4) Kupgallu in Telangana
   (a) 1 only (b) 1 & 2
   (c) 1, 2, 3 (d) 1, 2, 3, 4

13. Lost wax process refers to,
   (a) The technique of casting of bronze sculptures in medieval and ancient India.
   (b) The technique of forging of iron weapons in medieval India.
   (c) The technique of preparing wax models based on which intricate stone sculptures were carved
   (d) All of the above.

14. Which amongst the following was **not** an area of emphasis of *Prarthana Samaj* which advocated socio-religious reforms in the 19th century?
   (1) Belief in one god
   (2) Belief in infallibility of Vedas
   (3) Promotion of inter-caste marriages and widow remarriage
   (a) 1, 2 & 3 (b) 1 & 2
   (c) 2 (d) 3

15. Which amongst the following is **not** a correct description of the terms given below?
   (1) *Tappa* – A folk song of Punjab popular amongst camel riders
   (2) *Langhas* – Muslim singing communities of Rajasthan
   (3) *Manganiars* – Tribal community of Rajasthan which perform folk theatre
   (a) 1, 3
   (b) 2, 3
   (c) 3
   (d) 1

16. Which amongst the following statements can be said to be correct about Sattriya dance?

(1) The dance is of temple origin and followed Vaishanava traditions.

(2) It incorporates one act plays called *Ankiya-Nat* a ballad form of dance.

(3) It is performed to the accompaniment of Borgeets.

(a) 1, 2, 3 (b) 1, 2

(c) 2, 3 (d) 1 only

17. Which amongst the following are correct?

(1) Bidri work refers to the manufacture of metalware (usually of silver) with beautiful inlay work. It originated in Karnataka.

(2) Bankura horse refers to a tribal craft of carving of wooden horses.

(a) Only 1 is correct

(b) Only 2 is correct

(c) Both 1 & 2 are correct

(d) Neither 1 nor 2 are correct

18. Which amongst the following are correct about the recognition of a language as a Classical language of India?

(1) Antiquity of text and existence of valuable ancient literature are amongst the parameters for considering a language as a classical language.

(2) Hindi is one of the six languages recognised as a classical language.

(a) Only 1 is correct

(b) Only 2 is correct

(c) Both 1 & 2 are correct

(d) Neither 1 nor 2 is correct

19. Which of the following statements are correct?

(1) *Dakhma* or the 'towers of silence' are places of disposal of the bodies of dead by excarnation in the Zoroaster faith.

(2) *Torah* is the religious text of the Jewish people.

(a) Only 1 is correct

(b) Only 2 is correct

(c) Both 1 & 2 are correct

(d) Neither 1 nor 2 is correct

20. Which amongst the following are correct about India's national calendar?

(1) Saka calendar is the national calendar of India.

(2) It started in 56 BCE.

(3) Its new year falls on 1st of April.

(a) 1 only (b) 1 & 2

(c) 1 & 3 (d) 1, 2 & 3

21. Which of the following statements is/are correct?

(i) Mohenjo-daro was built in two distinct parts, the higher town or the citadel and the larger lower town.

(ii) The citadel was built on a raised platform of mud and brick and had a wall all around it.

(iii) The lower town was of much larger area but did not have any wall around it.

(a) (i), (ii) & (iii) (b) (i) & (iii)

(c) (i) & (ii) (d) (ii) & (iii)

22. Which amongst the following is a correct match?

(1) Smritis	(a) Vedanga
(2) Vedas	(b) Scriptures containing all knowledge of people
(3) Ramayana	(c) Scriptures of human origin
(4) Jyotisha	(d) Itihasa

(a) 1-d 2-b 3-c 4-a

(b) 1-c 2-b 3-a 4-d

(c) 1-c 2-a 3-b 4-d

(d) 1-c 2-b 3-d 4-a

23. Which amongst the following is a correct match?

(1)	1st Buddhist Council	(a)	Vaishali
(2)	2nd Buddhist Council	(b)	Ajatashatru
(3)	3rd Buddhist Council	(c)	Hinayana–Mahayana
(4)	4th Buddhist Council	(d)	Ashoka

(a) 1-a 2-b 3-d 4-c
(b) 1-b 2-a 3-c 4-d
(c) 1-b 2-c 3-a 4-d
(d) 1-b 2-a 3-d 4-c

24. Which amongst the following are integral to the teachings and philosophy of Jainism?

(1) To attain freedom from the cycle of birth and death or to attain *Kaivalya* one must practise right Karma
(2) The whole world is animated (has life) and this would include even the non living things such as water and stones etc.
(3) To attain nirvana one must follow the four noble truths and the eightfold path

(a) 1, 2, 3 (b) 1, 2
(c) 1, 3 (d) 1

25. Which amongst the following is a correct description?

(1) Barabar caves – Oldest rock cut caves also known as Lomush Rishi caves
(2) Elephant figure at Dhauli – It bears Ashokan rock edict

(a) only 1 (b) only 2
(c) both 1 & 2 (d) neither 1 nor 2

26. Examine the following two statements.

(1) *Tribhanga* meaning thrice bent, was a female body posture often depicted in sculptures and statues particularly in ancient India.
(2) The rock cut caves of Ellora are world famous for its miniature paintings.

(a) Only 1 is correct
(b) only 2 is correct
(c) both 1 & 2 are correct
(d) neither 1 nor 2 is correct

27. Which amongst the following represents a correct match?

(1)	Sudraka	(a)	Swapnavasavadatta
(2)	Bhasa	(b)	Uttara-Ramacharitam
(3)	Bhavabhuti	(c)	Mricchakatika

(a) 1-a 2-b 3-c
(b) 1-c 2-b 3-a
(c) 1-c 2-a 3-b
(d) 1-b 2-a 3-c

28. Which amongst the following are features of Brihadeeswarar temple at Thanjavur?

(1) It is shaped like a ratha.
(2) It is the largest and tallest of all Indian temples.
(3) It is dedicated to Lord Vishnu.

(a) 1, 2, 3 (b) 1, 2
(c) 2, 3 (d) 2

29. Vachanas contained the teachings/message of

(a) Siddhas (b) Lingayats
(c) Alwars (d) Naths

30. Pietra-dura refers to

(a) Creation of floral and arabesque patterns on the walls of monuments.
(b) Creation of perforated stones or latticed screens in form of ornamental pattern in the walls of monuments.
(c) Inlay work involving precious and semi precious jewels inlayed in walls of monuments.
(d) None of these.

31. The Pala School of Art was famous for

(a) Bronze sculptures
(b) Miniature paintings
(c) Both (a) & (b)
(d) Neither (a) nor (b)

32. Tyagaraja, Muthuswami Dikshitar and Syama Sastri were
   (a) Renowned musical trinity of Carnatic music in the 18th century.
   (b) Great exponents of Bharatanatyam of the early 19th century.
   (c) Eminent poets in the court of Raja Krishnadeva Raya in the 16th century.
   (d) None of the above

33. Which category of musical instrument is Idakka?
   (a) A bowed string instrument
   (b) A single reed wind instrument
   (c) A membranous percussion instrument
   (d) A non-drum percussion instrument

34. Which amongst the following is category of traditional silk sarees?
   (1) Ikat of Orissa
   (2) Chikan of Lucknow
   (3) Kanjeevaram of Tamil Nadu
   (4) Jamawar of Kashmir
   (a) 1, 2 (b) 1, 3
   (c) 2, 3, 4 (d) 1, 2, 3, 4

35. Which amongst the following are correct about the modern Hindi literature?
   (1) Hazari Prasad Dwivedi is usually considered as the father of modern Hindi literature.
   (2) *Chhayawad* was a genre of Hindi poetry which described the physical or transient beauty of the characters.
   (a) Only 1 is correct
   (b) Only 2 is correct
   (c) Both 1 & 2 are correct
   (d) Neither 1 nor 2 is correct

36. Which one of the following is a correct match?

(i) Pashupati seal	(a) Dholavira
(ii) Bronze dancing girl statue	(b) Proto Shiva
(iii) Signboard	(c) Mohenjo-daro
(iv) Great granary	(d) Harappa

   (a) (i) (b) (ii) (c) (iii) (d) (iv) (a)
   (b) (i) (b) (ii) (d) (iii) (c) (iv) (a)
   (c) (i) (a) (ii) (b) (iii) (c) (iv) (d)
   (d) (i) (b) (ii) (c) (iii) (a) (iv) (d)

37. Consider the following two statements.
   (1) The *Atharvaveda* contained knowledge having application in daily life ranging from medicine to other physical sciences.
   (2) *Aranyakas* were the third layer of Vedas which contained philosophical and metaphysical thoughts.
   (a) Only statement 1 is correct
   (b) Only statement 2 is correct
   (c) Both statement 1 & 2 are correct
   (d) Neither statement 1 nor 2 is correct

38. Which amongst the following teachings do **not** constitute a part of the Buddhist philosophy and teachings?
   (1) Non-violence and not hurting other living beings
   (2) Worship of idols
   (3) Asceticism and penance
   (a) 3
   (b) 2
   (c) none of the above
   (d) 2, 3

39. Which amongst the following is correct about the symbolic significance of the lion capital at Sarnath?
   (1) It marked the suzerainty of emperor Ashoka as an undisputed king.
   (2) It symbolised the first sermon of Buddha and the turning of the wheel of law.
   (a) 1 only
   (b) 2 only
   (c) Both 1 & 2
   (d) Neither 1 nor 2

40. Which amongst the following represents a correct match?

(1) The flying Apsara — (a) Ajanta caves
(2) The Kailasha temple — (b) Ellora caves
(3) Trimurti/Maheshmurti sculpture — (c) Kanaheri caves
(4) Avlokiteshwar image — (d) Elephanta caves

(a) 1-a 2-b 3-c 4-d
(b) 1-a 2-b 3-d 4-c
(c) 1-a 2-c 3-d 4-b
(d) 1-b 2-c 3-a 4-d

41. Jivak, Panini, Charak and Vishnu Sharma are said to be associated with

(a) Nalanda university
(b) Takshshila university
(c) Vikramshila university
(d) Not associated with any single university

42. Which amongst the following are common to the teachings and philosophy of Buddhism and Jainism?

(1) Both were opposed to ritualism, animal sacrifices, etc.
(2) Both emphasised on asceticism for attainment of Nirvana
(3) Both believed in rebirth and Karmic cycle

(a) 1, 2, 3 (b) 1, 2
(c) 1, 3 (d) 2, 3

43. Which amongst the following was the North Indian temple style?

(a) Nagara (b) Dravida
(c) Vesara (d) None of the above

44. Which amongst the following were features of the teachings/practices of *Nath-panthis*, *Siddhas* and *Yogis*?

(1) They advocated asceticism and renunciation of the world as a means to attain salvation.
(2) They believed in a personal god with attributes or *Saguna Brahma*.
(3) They believed in disciplining of mind through *Pranayama* and *Yoga*.
(4) They discarded ritualism and religious orthodoxy.

(a) 1, 2, 3, 4 (b) 1, 3, 4
(c) 2, 3, 4 (d) 1, 3

45. Which amongst the following represents a correct match?

(1) Sikandara — (a) Tomb of Adil Shah
(2) Gol Gumbaz of Bijapur — (b) Qutubbudin Aibak
(3) Quwwatul Islam Mosque — (c) Ghiasuddin Khilji
(4) Jahaz Mahal Mandu — (d) Tomb of Akbar

(a) 1-d 2-a 3-b 4-c
(b) 1-d 2-b 3-a 4-c
(c) 1-c 2-a 3-d 4-b
(d) 1-a 2-b 3-c 4-d

46. Which amongst the following were the characteristics of Mughal School of painting?

(1) They were known for accuracy of representation of human figures.
(2) The paintings were naturalistic and incorporated perspective and depth.
(3) It used vibrant colours like blue and gold.
(4) Subjects were often taken from Persian mythology.

(a) 1 (b) 1 & 2
(c) 1, 2, 3 (d) 1, 2, 3, 4

47. Which amongst the following is correct?

(a) *Shabad* was a form of devotional music and song which was sung in the Gurudwaras and Sikh religious communities and originated in the medieval period.
(b) Qawwali originated as a devotional form of music and became popular in India with growth of Sufism.
(c) Both (a) & (b)
(d) Neither (a) nor (b)

48. With which field of art are Nandalal Bose and Jamini Roy associated?
   (a) Rabindra Sangeet
   (b) Bengal movement of Painting
   (c) Bengali literature of early 20th century
   (d) Bengal theatre movement

49. Which amongst the following statements is correct about the dance form Odissi?
   (a) It is dance which was earlier associated with *Devadasis.*
   (b) *Tribhanga* and *Chowk* are two basic postures associated with it.
   (c) Both (a) & (b) are correct
   (d) Neither (a) nor (b) is correct

50. Dhokra art refers to
   (a) Non metal ferrous casting and iron castings of Bastar
   (b) Preparation of traditional wooden toys by tribals
   (c) Preparation of traditional painting by using earthy colours by tribals
   (d) None of the above

51. Which of the following can be said to be true about the Indus Valley Civilisation?
   (i) It was an urban civilisation.
   (ii) It was a predominantly Hindu civilisation as seen from the seal of Pashupati.
   (a) (i) only (b) (ii) only
   (c) Both (i) & (ii) (d) Neither (i) nor (ii)

52. Which amongst the following is a correct match?

(1) Shwetambaras	(a) Eight auspicious Jain symbols
(2) Ashtamangala	(b) Right conduct
(3) Triratna	(c) Clad in white clothes
(4) Samyak Charitra	(d) Core values to be adopted for attaining Kaivalya

   (a) 1-c 2-a 3-d 4-b
   (b) 1-c 2-b 3-a 4-d
   (c) 1-c 2-a 3-b 4-d
   (d) 1-a 2-c 3-b 4-d

53. The image of Yakshini of Didarganj was a famous sculpture of
   (a) Gupta period
   (b) Mauryan period
   (c) Chalukya dynasty
   (d) None of the above

54. *Vimana, Shikhar* and *Vahana* are terms associated with
   (a) Elements of a temple structure
   (b) Elements of a stupa structure
   (c) Both (a) & (b)
   (d) Neither (a) nor (b)

55. Which among the following statements is **not** correct?
   (a) Dharmashastras were texts which prescribed laws and religious duties pertaining to righteous conduct in the society.
   (b) Rigveda is the oldest of the Vedas.
   (c) Sankhya is not a part of the *Shad-Darshana.*
   (d) Yajurveda was a compilation of verses or mantras invoked or chanted in various rituals/offerings by the priests.

56. Examine which of the following statements are correct?
   (1) The famous Brihadeeswarar temple at Thanjavur was built during the reign of King Mahendravarman of the Pallava dynasty.
   (2) The Shore Temple of Mahabalipuram is an example of Vesara architecture.
   (a) Only 1 is correct
   (b) Only 2 is correct
   (c) Both 1 & 2 are correct
   (d) Neither 1 nor 2 is correct

57. Which amongst the following was **not** a feature of Bhakti movement and its teachings?
(1) It was an inclusive movement which rejected Brahmanism and caste distinction.
(2) It preached asceticism and renunciation as a means for salvation.
(3) It used Sanskrit as a means for preaching and compilation of teachings in the religious text.
(4) It integrated Pranayama, Meditation and Bhakti tradition.
(a) 2, 3, 4 (b) 1, 2
(c) 3, 4 (d) 2, 4

58. Examine whether the following descriptions are correct.
(1) *Abhidhama-Pitaka* – Contains teachings of Jainism and Jain Philosophy
(2) *Theravada* – The doctrine of elders in Buddhism which emphasised on attaining of individual *nirvana*
(a) Only 1 (b) Only 2
(c) Both 1 & 2 (d) Neither 1 nor 2

59. The Buland Darwaza at Fatehpur Sikri was constructed to
(a) Commemorate Akbar's successful military expedition.
(b) Fulfill a practical need of movement of Akbar's large ceremonial procession.
(c) A monument of ode to Salim Chisti who was revered by Akbar.
(d) Both (a) & (b)

60. Which amongst the following can be said to be correct about the bronze sculpture of the Chola period depicting Lord Shiva performing the *Tandava*?
(1) Lord Shiva is depicted having six hands in which two arms are depicted in Abhay a mudra, one is carrying a Damaru and another, a flame, and another two are striking a posture of dance.
(2) In the Tandava pose, he is balancing himself on one leg on the body of a demon referred as *Apasmara* symbolising ignorance.
(a) Only 1 is correct
(b) Only 2 is correct
(c) Both 1 & 2 are correct
(d) Neither 1 nor 2 is correct

61. Which amongst the following represent a correct match?

(1) Jyotiba Phule	(a) Widow Remarriage Association
(2) Dhondo Keshav Karve	(b) Aligarh movement
(3) EVR Periyar	(c) Satya Sodhak Samaj
(4) Syed Ahmad Khan	(d) Self Respect movement

(a) 1-c 2-a 3-d 4-b
(b) 1-c 2-d 3-a 4-b
(c) 1-a 2-c 3-d 4-b
(d) 1-a 2-b 3-c 4-d

62. Which amongst the following were important features of Bengal School of Art of the early 20th century?
(a) It emphasised on use of indigenous subjects and materials.
(b) It incorporated the western painting technique with Indian subjects.
(c) It incorporated both indigenous and western techniques
(d) None of the above

63. Which amongst the following are considered to be a classical form of dance?
(1) Sattriya
(2) Rouf
(3) Mohiniattam
(a) 1, 2, 3 (b) 2 & 3
(c) 1 & 2 (d) 1 & 3

64. Which amongst the following are fully correct with respect to the Geographical Indication tag (G.I tag)?

(1) The G.I tag corresponds to a specific geographical location or origin.

(2) This tag is given so as to identify a good or a service to a specific geographical location.

(a) Only 1 is correct

(b) Only 2 is correct

(c) Both 1 & 2 are correct

(d) Neither 1 nor 2 is correct

65. Jnanpith award is conferred for:

(a) Outstanding contribution to Hindi literature.

(b) Outstanding contribution to the literature of an Indian language included in the Eighth Schedule of the Constitution.

(c) Outstanding contribution to the literature of an Indian language included in the Eighth Schedule of the Constitution as well as for English.

(d) None of the above

66. Which of the following are correctly matched?

(i) Lothal - Dockyard

(ii) Chanuhodaro - Craft production

(iii) Black Harappan Pottery - Omani copper

(iv) Weights - Chert

(a) (i), (ii), (iii), (iv) (b) (i), (ii), (iii)

(c) (i), (ii), (iv) (d) (i) & (ii)

67. Which amongst the following represent the difference in Northern and Southern Indian temple architecture?

(1) North Indian temples did not usually have a gopuram or a gateway in a boundary wall. This was present in the Dravida temples.

(2) The Dravida temples did not have multiple Shikharas while the North Indian temples could have multiple shikharas.

(a) Only 1 is correct

(b) Only 2 is correct

(c) Both 1 & 2 are correct

(d) Neither 1 nor 2 is correct

68. Consider the following systems of philosophy.

	System	Description
(1)	Nyaya	Deals with formal reasoning logic, theology, metaphysics
(2)	Samkhya	It deals with the concept of *Purush* and *Prakriti*

(a) Only (1) is correctly described

(b) Only (2) is correctly described

(c) Both (1) & (2) are correctly described

(d) Neither (1) nor (2) correctly described

69. Who amongst the following Bhakti saints was/were a part of Warkari Bhakti tradition?

(1) Dadu Dayal (2) Sakhubai

(3) Tukaram (4) Kabir

(a) 1, 2, 3, 4 (b) 2, 3, 4

(c) 2, 3 (d) 2, 4

70. The *Shraman Mudra* of Buddha is symbolic of

(a) Buddha's renunciation of the worldly pleasures.

(b) Buddhist's victory over Mara (the demon trying to entice Buddha into worldly pleasures).

(c) Buddha being in deep meditation.

(d) Buddha being in a pose of benediction.

71. In which amongst the following, mural paintings can be found?

(1) Ellora Caves

(2) Badami

(3) Sittanavasal caves

(4) Virupaksha temple

(a) 4 only (b) 2 & 4

(c) 2, 3, 4 (d) 1, 2, 3, 4

72. Which amongst the following represent a correct match?

(1)	Borgeets	(a)	Chaitanya
(2)	*Siksastakam*	(b)	Tulsidas
(3)	Vinaya Patrika	(c)	Shankar Deva
(4)	Abhanga Poetry	(d)	Tukaram

(a) 1-a 2-c 3-d 4-b
(b) 1-c 2-a 3-d 4-b
(c) 1-a 2-c 3-b 4-d
(d) 1-c 2-a 3-b 4-d

73. Which amongst the following is a correct description of the terms given below?

(1) *Gotuvadhyam* – This is a plucked stringed instrument
(2) *Burra-Katha* – This is form of story telling popular in rural Andhra Pradesh often delivered in form of songs.

(a) Only (1) is correct
(b) Only (2) is correct
(c) Both (1) & (2) are correct
(d) Neither (1) nor (2) is correct

74. Which of the following can be said to be correct about the Harappan culture?

(i) People believed in life after death as seen from their burial practices.
(ii) Barley and wheat were the major crops cultivated.

(a) Only (i) (b) Only (ii)
(c) Both (i) & (ii) (d) Neither (i) nor (ii)

75. Which amongst the following is **not** correct?

(a) M.S. Subbalakshmi was a Carnatic vocalist
(b) F.N. Souza was a famous painter and a founding member of the Progressive Artists' Group of Bombay.
(c) Sonal Mansingh is a famous Odissi and Bharatanatyam classical dancer.
(d) None of the above

76. Which amongst the following statements is/are correct?

(1) *Satyameva Jayate* is contained in Manduka Upanishad
(2) Upanishads describe the various rituals required to be performed to propitiate the elements of nature.

(a) Only 1 is correct
(b) Only 2 is correct
(c) Both 1 & 2 are correct
(d) Neither 1 nor 2 are correct

77. Which amongst the following dances are correctly matched against the region they pertain to?

(1) Koodiyattam – Kerala
(2) Mohiniattam – Kerala
(3) Bharatanatyam – Tamil Nadu
(4) Bihu – Assam

(a) 1, 2, 3, 4 (b) 1, 2, 3
(c) 1, 2, 4 (d) 1, 3, 4

78. Which amongst the following is correct about the art of Kalamkari?

(1) It is a traditional art of fabric weaving.
(2) It is a traditional art of hand painting of designs on sarees.
(3) It is practised in Tamil Nadu region.
(4) It is practised in Andhra Pradesh region.

(a) 1, 3 (b) 1, 4
(c) 2, 3 (d) 2, 4

79. Consider the following statements.

(1) In July 2016, the Capital Complex of Chandigarh was declared as a UNESCO World heritage site.
(2) Le Corbusier was another important architect who along with Edward Lutyens designed the modern capital of New Delhi.

(a) Only 1 is correct
(b) Only 2 is correct
(c) Both 1 & 2 are correct
(d) Neither 1 nor 2 is correct

80. Which amongst the following are correct?

(1) *Phoolwalon ki sair* is a festival of flowers held in old Delhi region.

(2) Sonepur mela is one of the largest cattle fairs of Asia.

(3) Gudi Padwa is the new year festival of Maharashtra and Goa region.

(a) 1, 2, 3 (b) 1, 2

(c) 1, 3 (d) 2, 3

81. In which among the following *Janapadas* did Buddha preach in his lifetime?

(1) Magadha (2) Kosala

(3) Kuru (4) Chedi

(a) 1, 2, 3, 4 (b) 1, 2, 3

(c) 1, 2 (d) 1

82. Which amongst the following is correct about the term *Shalabhanjika*?

(a) It was the image of a mythical woman adorning the gate of Sanchi Stupa whose touch was supposed to cause trees to flower.

(b) It was the image of a *Yakshini* whose statue was found at Paraksham.

(c) It refers to a Buddhist *Bhikshuni* who had denounced the world and attained a high spiritual state.

(d) None of the above

83. In which of the following places one would find a chaitya hall?

(1) Karla (2) Bhaja

(3) Ajanta

(a) 1, 2, 3 (b) 1 & 2

(c) 1 & 3 (d) 2 & 3

84. Which amongst the following represent a correct match?

(1)	Shesh Narayana Vishnu	(a)	Sun temple, Modhera
(2)	Massive rectangular stepped tank	(b)	Kailasanath temple, Ellora
(3)	Panch-rathas	(c)	Dashavatara temple, Deogarh
(4)	Rock cut temple	(d)	Mahabalipuram

(a) 1-c 2-d 3-a 4-b

(b) 1-a 2-b 3-c 4-d

(c) 1-b 2-a 3-d 4-c

(d) 1-c 2-a 3-d 4-b

85. Which amongst the following would be the correct chronology of the following saints?

(1) Shankaracharya

(2) Ramanuja

(3) Tulsidas

(4) Ramananda

(a) 1, 2, 3, 4 (b) 2, 1, 3, 4

(c) 2, 1, 4, 3 (d) 1, 2, 4, 3

86. Which amongst the following is correct?

(1) The origin of the form of music called *Khayal* is attributed to Amir Khusro.

(2) Carnatic music evolved indigenously without being much influenced by the Arabian and Persian music.

(a) Only (1) is correct

(b) Only (2) is correct

(c) Both 1 & 2 are correct

(d) Neither 1 nor 2 is correct

87. Which of the following artefacts/ archaeological finds pertain to the Indus Valley Civilisation?

(i) Terracotta figurines of mother goddess

(ii) Coins of gold and silver carrying various inscriptions

(iii) Weights and ivory scale

(a) (i), (ii), (iii) (b) (i) & (ii)

(c) (i) & (iii) (d) (ii) & (iii)

88. Which amongst the following are a traditional community of weavers?

(1) Vankars of Gujarat

(2) Mehers of Orissa

(3) Manganiyars of Rajasthan

(4) Muria of Bastar

(a) 1, 2, 3, 4 (b) 1, 2, 3

(c) 1, 2 (d) 2, 3

89. *Vasudhaiva Kutumbakam*, the Sanskrit phrase which means, 'the world is one family', is contained in which of the following Upanishads?
    (a) Mahopanishad
    (b) Kathopanishad
    (c) Mundaka Upanishad
    (d) None of the above

90. Which of the following folk theatres are correctly matched with the places/regions where they are popular?
    (1) Jatra – West Bengal
    (2) Bhand Pather – Rajasthan
    (3) Tamasha – Madhya Pradesh
    (a) 1, 2, 3 (b) 1, 2
    (c) 1, 3 (d) 2, 3

91. Which amongst the following statements are correct in respect of Buddhist symbols?
    (1) **Wheel** – Represents the first sermon by Buddha at Sarnath or Dharma Chakra Pravartana
    (2) **Lotus** – Represents the birth of Buddha
    (a) Only (1) (b) Only 2
    (c) Both (1) & (2) (d) Neither (1) nor (2)

92. Which amongst the following were a part of the Sufi traditions and practices?
    (1) It believed in monoism.
    (2) Devotional music and song were a part of sufi traditions.
    (3) It advocated an orthodoxical interpretation of Quran.
    (a) 1, 2, 3 (b) 1, 2
    (c) 1, 3 (d) 2, 3

93. *Kandhei* and *Gombeyeta* are
    (a) Forms of stringed puppets.
    (b) Forms of folk dances.
    (c) Forms of folk paintings.
    (d) None of the above

94. Karaikkal Ammaiyar was a
    (a) Court poet of Krishnadeva Raya's court.
    (b) Female Nayanar saint.
    (c) Protagonist in South Indian classical literature of Sangam period.
    (d) None of the above

95. Which among the following are the sects of Jains?
    (1) Shwetambar (2) Vajrayan
    (3) Digambar (4) Stharvadins
    (a) 1, 2, 3, 4 (b) 1, 2, 3
    (c) 1, 3 (d) 1, 2, 4

96. Determine the correct match.

(1) Mathura School of Art	(a) Greek Hellinistic features
(2) Gandhara School of Art	(b) Little ornamentation around the halo of Buddha
(3) Amravati School of Art	(c) Stupa drum slab
(4) Sarnath School of Art	(d) Buddha with decorated halo

    (a) 1-a 2-d 3-c 4-b
    (b) 1-d 2-a 3-b 4-c
    (c) 1-d 2-b 3-c 4-a
    (d) 1-d 2-a 3-c 4-b

97. *Nalayira Divya Prabandham is a*
    (a) Compilation of composition of Alwars.
    (b) Historical account of the administration during the reign of king Raja Chola.
    (c) Sanskrit treatise capturing the love story of Nala and Damayanti.
    (d) None of these

98. Consider the following statements.
    (1) Harmika was the balcony above the semi-circular structure of a stupa. It represented the abode of gods.
    (2) Vedika was the gateway to the stupa.

(a) Only 1 is correct
(b) Only 2 is correct
(c) Both 1 & 2 are correct
(d) Neither 1 nor 2 is correct

99. Who amongst the following were associated with the Theosophical Society?

(1) Madam H.P Blavatsky
(2) Colonel Henry Olcott
(3) Mrs Annie Besant
(4) Henry Vivian Derozio

(a) 1, 2, 3, 4
(b) 1, 2, 3
(c) 1, 2
(d) 1, 3

100. Which among the following are a part of Jain philosophy?

(1) Syadavada (2) Ajivika
(3) Vaisheshika

(a) 1, 2, 3 (b) 1, 2
(c) 1 (d) 3

101. Consider the following statements regarding Indian culture:

1. *Gita Govinda* is a work composed by Jayadeva.
2. Ananda Tandava is one of the seven basic types of Tandava.
3. Lasya is a dance in response to the male energy of the cosmic dance of Tandava.

Choose the correct answer using code given below:

(a) 1 only (b) 1 and 2 only
(c) 2 and 3 only (d) 1, 2 and 3

102. Consider the following statements regarding Indian art:

1. The character of Indian art is best described as plastic, organic and sculptural.
2. Indian art is deeply rooted in religion and it conduces to fulfilling the ultimate aim of life.
3. The earliest examples of miniature painting in India exist in the form of illustrations to the religious texts on Buddhism executed under the Palas.

Which of the above statement(s) is/are correct?

(a) 1 and 2 only (b) 2 only
(c) 2 and 3 only (d) All of the above

103. Which of the following statements is NOT correct regarding puppetry in India?

(a) The earliest reference to the art of puppetry is found in the Tamil classic *Silappadikaaram*.
(b) The string puppets of Orissa are known as Kundhei.
(c) The string puppets of Karnataka are called Gombeyatta.
(d) Puppets from Kerala are known as Bommalattam.

104. With reference to Andal consider the following statements;

(i) She was a female Alwar saint.
(ii) She was the proponent of Dhamar form of music
(iii) She composed the *Nalayera Divya Prabandham* also revered as Tamil Veda.

(a) only I is correct
(b) only II is correct
(c) only I & III are correct
(d) None of the above are correct

105. Consider the following statements regarding Khajuraho temple:

1. It is a group of Hindu and Buddhist temples in Madhya Pradesh.
2. These temples were built by the Chola dyanasty.
3. It is a UNESCO World Heritage site.

Which of the above statements is/are correct?

(a) 1 only (b) 1 and 3 only
(c) 3 only (d) 2 and 3 only

106. Consider the following statements with reference to undesired and unhealthy practice of forcing girls to serve as Devadasis:

1. It is a religious practice whereby parents marry a daughter to a deity or a temple.
2. The marriage usually occurs after the girl reaches puberty.

Which of the above statements is/are correct?

(a) 1 only (b) 2 only
(c) Both 1 and 2 (d) Neither 1 nor 2

107. The *Abhinaya Darpana* by Nandikesvara is one of the main sources of textual material for the study of the technique and grammar of body movement in which of the following classical dances of India?

(a) Bharatanatyam dance
(b) Kathakali dance
(c) Kuchipudi dance
(d) Sattriya dance

108. In the *Natya Shastra* compiled by Bharata Muni, musical instruments have been divided into four main categories on the basis of how sound is produced. In this regard which of the following is incorrect?

(a) The Tata Vadya— Wooden instruments
(b) The Sushira Vadya— Wind instruments
(c) The Avanaddha Vadya—Percussion instruments
(d) The Ghana Vadya— Solid instruments which do not require tuning.

109. Which of the following statement is incorrect with reference to Indian art and architecture?

(a) The beginning of Indian architecture can be traced back to the advent of Buddhism in India.
(b) In central India, the Paramara rulers built a magnificent temple complex at Khajuraho.
(c) The most notable achievements of the Pallava rulers were the rock-cut temples of Mahabalipuram and the temples of Kanchipuram.
(d) The Indo-Saracenic architecture combined the features of Hindu, Islamic and western elements.

110. With reference to Chanhudaro which of the following statements are correct?

(i) It was a small settlement in Harappan civilization involving bead making.
(ii) It is a Harrappan settlement which is known for discovery of burial site.
(iii) It is an important port city in the Harappan civilisation.

(a) Only I is correct
(b) only II is correct
(c) Only III is correct
(d) Both I and III are correct

111. Consider the following matches

(i) Discovery site of canal irrigation in Harappan civilisation	(a) Vajji
(ii) An early Janapada	(b) Silappadikaram
(iii) A Tamil epic	(c) Shortugai

Which one of the above is correctly matched?

(a) (i)- a (ii)-b (iii)-c
(b) (i)-c (ii)-b (iii)-a
(c) (i)-a (ii)-c (iii)-b
(d) (i)-c (ii)-a (iii)-b

112. Consider the following statements regarding social and cultural awakening movements in India:

1. They were motivated by doctrines of reason and humanism.
2. They addressed both social and religious issues.
3. The modern and reformative ideas spread among common Indians primarily through Indian languages.

Which of the statements given above is/are correct?

(a) 1 only (b) 1 and 2 only
(c) 2 and 3 only (d) 1, 2 and 3

113. Consider the following pairs.

(Dance)	(States)
1. Padayani	Kerala
2. Ghode Mudni	Goa
3. Dindi	Rajasthan
4. Karma	Bihar

Which of the above pairs is/are correctly matched?

(a) 1 only (b) 1 and 2 only
(c) 1, 2 and 4 only (d) 1, 2, 3 and 4

114. Daskathia is a form of ballad singing prevalent in:

(a) Assam (b) Odisha
(c) Kerala (d) Rajasthan

115. Amongst the following, which have been included as UNESCO World Heritage Site

(1) The Victorian Gothic art Deco ensembles of Mumbai
(2) Rani ka Vav, Patan, Gujarat

(a) Only 1 (b) Only 2
(c) Both 1 & 2 (d) Neither 1 or 2

116. Consider the following pairs:

(Architecture)		(Location)
1. Kadam Rasul Mosque	:	Gaur
2. Gol Gumbaz	:	Bijapur
3. Chand Minar	:	Gulbarga

Which of the above pairs is/are correctly matched?

(a) 1 only (b) 1 and 2 only
(c) 2 and 3 only (d) 1 and 3 only

117. 'Koodiyattam' is a unique theatre tradition survived from ancient past. It deals with the plays of eminent Sanskrit dramatists such as Bhasa, Harsha, Kalidasa, Mahendra Vikrama and Saktibhadra. It belongs to:

(a) Assam (b) Kerala
(c) Odisha (d) Tamil Nadu

118. Consider the following statements regarding the Bharatanatyam Dance:

1. Abhinaya Darpana is one of the main sources for the study of the technique and grammar of body movement in Bharatanatyam Dance.
2. Ekaharya is an essential feature of this dance.
3. The first item in this dance is the Alarippu, literally meaning - to adorn with flowers.

Which of the statements given above is/are correct?

(a) 1 only (b) 2 only
(c) 1 and 3 only (d) 1, 2 and 3

119. The earliest examples of miniature painting in India exist in the form of illustrations to the religious texts executed under the Palas of the eastern India and western India during the 11th-12th centuries A.D. It was/were related to which of the following religions?

(a) Buddhism (b) Jainism
(c) Islamism (d) Both (a) and (b)

120. With reference to Indo - Islamic Architecture, consider the following pairs:

Architecture	Built By
1. Adhai din-ka-jhonpra	Qutub-ud-Din-Aibak
2. Sidi Sayyid Mosque	Muzaffar Shah III
3. Gol Gumbaz	Muhammad Adil Shah

Which of the above pairs is/are correctly matched?

(a) 1 and 3 only
(b) 1 only
(c) 3 only
(d) 1, 2 and 3

121. In ancient India thottavariyam, panchavariyam and ponvariyam were:
   (a) Names of different varnas during ancient times.
   (b) Titles of different functions of village administration.
   (c) Titles of military officers.
   (d) Titles of land revenue officers.

122. The national calendar based on the Saka Era, with Chaitra as its first month and a normal year of 365 days was adopted from:
   (a) 22nd March 1949 (b) 22nd March 1957
   (c) 22nd March 1952 (d) 1st April 1957

123. Which of the following is NOT matched correctly?
   (a) Trimurti : Elephanta caves
   (b) Ravananugraha : Kailash Temple
   (c) Descent of the Ganges : Mahabalipuram
   (d) Panchapandava Ratha : Pattadakal

124. Consider the following statements regarding spread of Indian culture:
   1. The cultural contact between India and Burma dates back to the Ashoka period.
   2. Java was part of the Sailendra Empire.
   3. Under the early rulers in Cambodia, Shaivism and Vaishnavism made steady progress.

   Which of the statements given above is/are correct?
   (a) 1 and 2 only (b) 2 only
   (c) 2 and 3 only (d) 1, 2 and 3

125. Ajmer has earned the epithet of "Madinatul Hind or the Madina of India". Each year the devotees of all sects and faiths congregate here from all parts of the world on the occasion of the annual festival of Urs. It is famous for its rich architecture/ architectures of which of the following?
   1. Indo-Islamic 2. Royal Rajasthani
   3. Indo-Saracenic 4. Jain styles

   Select the correct answer using the code given below.
   (a) 1, 3 and 4 only (b) 1 and 4 only
   (c) 1 only (d) 1, 2, 3 and 4

126. Consider the following pairs:

	Temple	Location
1.	Chennakeshava	: Gujarat
2.	Meenakshi Sundareshvara	: Karnataka
3.	Surya Mandir	: Odisha

   Which of the pairs given above is/are correctly matched?
   (a) 1 and 2 only (b) 3 only
   (c) 2 and 3 only (d) 1, 2 and 3

127. Consider the following statements with regard to Mohiniyattam Dance:
   1. It is characterized by graceful, swaying body movements with abrupt jerks or sudden leaps.
   2. It belongs to the lasya style.
   3. The hand gestures, 24 in number, are mainly adopted from *Hasta Lakshana Deepika*, a text followed by Kathakali.

   Which of the statements given above is/are correct?
   (a) 2 and 3 only
   (b) 1 and 3 only
   (c) 2 only
   (d) 1, 2 and 3

128. With reference to the Cave Architecture which of the following statement is NOT correct?
   (a) The Ajanta caves depict the story of Buddhism.
   (b) Some of the caves at Ajanta depict stories from the Jatakas.
   (c) Monasteries of Buddhists are examples of cave architecture.
   (d) Maharashtra is home to the spectacular and amazing Ajanta and Ellora group of caves.

129. Consider the following statements regarding the Kuchipudi Dance:

1. Kuchipudi is a dance-drama performance art that originated in a village of Krishna district of Andhra Pradesh.
2. This ancient dance form finds place in the 10th century copper inscriptions and in 15th century texts like *Machupalli Kaifat*.
3. Similar to all leading Indian classical dance forms, Kuchipudi too evolved as a religious art rooting back to the age-old Hindu Sanskrit text 'Natya Shastra'.

Which of the statements given above is/are correct?

(a) 1 and 2 only (b) 2 and 3 only
(c) 3 only (d) 1, 2 and 3

130. The mural paintings of Ajantha mostly illustrate the life of the person as depicted in the Jataka stories. Who among the following could be that person?

(a) Lord Buddha
(b) Lord Mahavira
(c) Ashoka
(d) Chandragupta Maurya

131. The Kailasanatha temple at Kanchi and the Shore temple at Mamallapuram remain the finest examples of the early structural temples of the:

(a) Satavahanas (b) Rashtrakutas
(c) Pallavas (d) Chalukyas

132. Consider the following statements regarding the Tillana:

1. It is corresponding to the Tarana of Carnatic music.
2. It is mainly a dance form, but on account of its brisk and attractive music, it sometimes finds a place in music concerts as a conclusion piece.
3. It usually begins with jatis.

Which of the statements given above is/are correct?

(a) 2 and 3 only (b) 1 and 3 only
(c) 2 only (d) 1, 2 and 3

133. Consider the following statements regarding the Odissi Dance:

1. The Natya Shastra mentions many regional varieties, such as the south-eastern style known as the Odhra Magadha which can be identified as the earliest precursor of present day Odissi.
2. The techniques of movement are built around the two basic postures of the Chowk and the Tribhanga.
3. The torso movement is very important and is an unique feature of the Odissi style.

Which of the statements given above is/are correct?

(a) 1 and 3 only (b) 1 only
(c) 2 only (d) 1, 2 and 3

134. The temple at Deogarh near Jhansi and the sculptures in the temple at Garhwa near Allahabad remain important specimen of the

(a) Gupta art (b) Rashtrakuta art
(c) Mauryan art (d) Pallava art

135. Which of the following dances do Pandanallur and Thanjavur styles belong to?

(a) Kuchipudi (b) Bharatanatyam
(c) Kathakali (d) Odissi

136. Consider the following statements about Sankhya School of Philosophy:

1. Its foundation is attributed to Kapila.
2. It mentions god as the super power.

Which of the statements given above is/are correct?

(a) 1 only (b) 2 only
(c) Both 1 and 2 (d) Neither 1 nor 2

137. Consider the following statements regarding Bhimbetka paintings:

1. White and red colors have been used most commonly in these paintings.
2. Most of the paintings belong to the Neolithic period.

Which of the statements given above is/are correct?

(a) 1 only (b) 2 only
(c) Both 1 and 2 (d) Neither 1 nor 2

138. Consider the following statements about Ghoomar:

1. It is the traditional folk dance of Rajasthan.
2. It was developed by Gond tribe.

Which of the statements given above is/are correct?

(a) 1 only (b) 2 only
(c) Both 1 and 2 (d) Neither 1 nor 2

139. Consider the following statements about Nagara styled temples:

1. The amalaka was placed at the top of shikhar.
2. The kalash was placed below amalaka.
3. The flag was erected at the top of kalash.

Which of the statements given above is/are incorrect?

(a) 1 only (b) 2 only
(c) 1 and 3 only (d) 1 and 2 only

140. Consider the following statements about the Provida style of temples:

1. They evolved during the Vijaynagar rule.
2. The presence of a large number of pillars is an important feature.
3. The pillars have images mostly of cows.

Which of the statements given above is/are correct?

(a) 1 and 2 only (b) 2 and 3 only
(c) 1 and 3 only (d) 1, 2 and 3

141. Consider the following statements regarding 'Stupa':

1. There is no reference of Stupa in any of the Vedas.
2. The Buddhist Stupa building activities were at their peak during post Mauryan age.

Which of the statements given above is/are correct?

(a) 1 only (b) 2 only
(c) Both 1 and 2 (d) Neither 1 nor 2

142. Consider the following statements regarding the paintings of Ellora Caves:

1. The theme of the paintings is religious only.
2. The earlier paintings show Lord Vishnu and Lakshmi borne through the clouds by Garuda.
3. Paintings of the flying Apsaras are also found.

Which of the statements given above are correct?

(a) 1 and 2 only (b) 1 and 3 only
(c) 2 and 3 only (d) 1, 2 and 3

143. Which of the following paintings was/were prevalent in India during Delhi Sultanate?

1. Mural painting
2. Miniature painting
3. Painting on cloths

Select the correct answer using the codes given below:

(a) 1 and 2 only (b) 2 and 3 only
(c) 3 only (d) 1, 2 and 3

144. Consider the following statements regarding dances in India:

1. The Rig Veda mentions dance.
2. Women performed dances during the Harappan period.

Which of the statements given above is/are correct?

(a) 1 only (b) 2 only
(c) Both 1 and 2 (d) Neither 1 nor 2

145. Which of the following are stringed instruments?

1. Sitar
2. Pakhawaj
3. Santoor
4. Mridangam
5. Sarangi

Select the correct answer using the codes given below:

(a) 1, 2 and 3 only
(b) 1, 3, 4 and 5 only
(c) 2, 3, 4 and 5 only
(d) 1, 3 and 5 only

146. Consider the following statements regarding Urdu language:

1. It was court language during Delhi Sultanate.
2. It was used to write accounts of later Mughals.
3. It is second official language of Uttar Pradesh and Bihar.

Which of the statements given above are correct?

(a) 1 and 2 only
(b) 2 and 3 only
(c) 1 and 3 only
(d) 1, 2 and 3

147. Consider the following statements:

1. Nritya corresponds to pure dancing where the movements of the body do not express any mood and do not convey any meaning.
2. Nritta corresponds to dancing with miming and gesticulation.
3. Natya corresponds to a drama.

Which of the statements given above is/are correct?

(a) 1 and 2 only
(b) 3 only
(c) 1 and 3 only
(d) 1, 2 and 3

148. The distinguished use of spotted red sandstone for sculptures is found in which of the following sculpture schools of India?

(a) Sarnath
(b) Gandhara
(c) Mathura
(d) Amravati

149. Consider the following statements about Ajanta paintings:

1. The Ajanta caves show two clear-cut phases of paintings with depiction of Buddha.
2. All the paintings in Ajanta caves are frescoes.

Which of the above statements is/are correct?

(a) 1 only
(b) 2 only
(c) Both 1 and 2
(d) Neither 1 nor 2

150. Which of the following statements is *not* correct about 'Raga'?

(a) A raga must contain at least five swaras starting with 'sa'.
(b) Most of the ragas have their own stipulated time.
(c) Each raga has its own speed of singing which could be slow, medium or fast.
(d) A raga is divided into units, the smallest being called '*matra*'

151. 'Natya Shastra', an ancient Indian treatise on the performing arts, contains commentaries on which of the following performing arts?

1. Theatre
2. Puppetry
3. Music
4. Dance

Select the correct answer using the codes given below:

(a) 1, 3 and 4 only
(b) 1, 2 and 3 only
(c) 2, 3 and 4 only
(d) 1, 2, 3 and 4

152. With reference to the art and culture of ancient India, which of the following statements is/ are true about Amaravati style of sculpture?

1. More importance was given to corporal aestheticism.
2. Idols were primarily made of bright marble.
3. Pallava dynasty patronized this style of sculpture.

Select the correct answer using the codes given below:

(a) 1 only (b) 1 and 2 only
(c) 2 and 3 only (d) 1, 2 and 3

153. The demon '*Apasmara*' lying under the foot of the dancing Nataraja symbolizes:

(a) Ignorance (b) Darkness
(c) Evil (d) Sorrows

154. Consider the following statements regarding the Alvar poet-saints:

1. They were considered devotees of Lord Vishnu.
2. Their songs of love and devotion ar compiled in a book known as Nalayira Divya Prabandham.
3. They were all Brahmins.

Which of the statements given above is/are correct?

(a) 1 only (b) 1 and 2 only
(c) 2 and 3 only (d) 1, 2 and 3

155. Which of the following are not limbs of Ashtanga Yoga?

1. Dharana 2. Dhyana
3. Jnana 4. Bhakti

Select the correct answer using the codes given below:

(a) 1 and 2 only (b) 2 and 3 only
(c) 3 and 4 only (d) 1 and 4 only

156. Which of the following temples depict Nagara style of temple architecture?

1. Sun temples at Konark and Modhera.
2. Dashavatara Temple at Deogarh.
3. Durga temple at Aihole.
4. Kailashnath Temple at Ellora.

Select the correct answer using the codes given below:

(a) 1 and 2 only (b) 2 and 3 only
(c) 3 and 4 only (d) 1, 2, 3 and 4

157. Consider the following statements about Indian music:

1. Carnatic music was highly influenced by Persian and Sufism traditions.
2. Classical genres of Carnatic music are dhrupad, dhamar, khyal, tarana and sadra.

Which of the statements given above is/are correct?

(a) 1 only (b) 2 only
(c) 1 and 2 only (d) Neither 1 nor 2

158. Which of the following are associated with Mauryan era?

1. Stupas of Sanchi and Sarnath
2. Rock-cut caves at Barabar
3. Mathura school of sculpture
4. Rock-cut temples in western Deccan

Select the correct answer using the codes given below:

(a) 1 and 2 only (b) 2 and 3 only
(c) 1 and 3 only (d) 2 and 4 only

159. Consider the following statements regarding bead art in India:

1. It was prevalent in the era of Harappan Civilization.
2. Only precious stones are used to make beads.

Which of the statements given above is/are correct?

(a) 1 only (b) 2 only
(c) Both 1 and 2 (d) Neither 1 nor 2

160. Which of the following statements in regard to the features of the Vesara style of temple architecture in India is/are true?

1. It is a combination of Dravida and Nagara styles.
2. It was prevalent in Eastern India.

Select the correct answer using the codes given below:

(a) 1 only (b) 2 only
(c) Both 1 and 2 (d) Neither 1 nor 2

161. Which of the following statements regarding cultural activities in India in the 18th century are correct?

1. Decline in the Mughal architecture and painting.
2. Decline in music.
3. Vigorous growth in Urdu poetry.

Select the correct answer using the codes given below:

(a) 1 and 2 only (b) 2 and 3 only
(c) 1 and 3 only (d) 1, 2, and 3

162. Which of the following statement is not correct about the 'Mathura School of Sculpture' during the pre-Gupta age in India?

(a) Mathura was primarily a centre of indigenous art.
(b) There was an influence of Gandhara School of Art on it.
(c) Several stone images of Vardhamana Mahavira were created under this school.
(d) Several stone images of Krishna were created under this school.

163. Consider the following statements about the 'Temple architecture' of India:

1. Originally Nagara style was practised in North India while Dravida style was practised in South India.
2. Vesara style of temple architecture was predominant in the territory between the Vindhyas and the Krishna river.
3. While Dravidian form flourished regionally, the Nagara style on the other hand, developed dynastically.
4. The temple at Bhitargaon is the first to have a shrine with a Shikhara.

Which of the following statements given above are correct?

(a) 1, 2 and 3 only (b) 2, 3 and 4 only
(c) 1, 3 and 4 only (d) 1, 2 and 4 only

164. In the Indian performing arts, a rasa is an emotion inspired in an audience by a performer. Consider the following statements in this regard:

1. Rasas are created by bhavas: the gestures and facial expressions of the actors.
2. Expressing Rasa in classical Indian dance form is referred to as Rasa-abhinaya.
3. The Melattur style of Bharatanatyam dance was developed largely out of the devadasi traditions

Which of the statements given above is/are correct?

(a) 1 and 2 only
(b) 2 and 3 only
(c) 1 and 3 only
(d) 1, 2 and 3

165. Consider the following statements:

1. The process of the construction of Viharas and Chaityas in the north-western Deccan in India, was started in second century B.C.
2. Viharas were Buddhist temples and Chaityas were monasteries.

Which of the statements given above is/are correct?

(a) 1 only
(b) 2 only
(c) Both 1 and 2
(d) Neither 1 nor 2

ANSWER KEY

S.No.		S.No.		S.No.		S.No.		S.No.	
1	b	34	b	67	c	100	c	133	d
2	b	35	d	68	c	101	d	134	a
3	a	36	d	69	c	102	d	135	b
4	c	37	c	70	a	103	d	136	a
5	c	38	d	71	d	104	a	137	a
6	d	39	b	72	d	105	c	138	a
7	b	40	b	73	c	106	a	139	b
8	b	41	b	74	c	107	a	140	a
9	a	42	c	75	d	108	a	141	b
10	a	43	a	76	a	109	b	142	b
11	c	44	b	77	a	110	a	143	d
12	d	45	a	78	d	111	d	144	c
13	a	46	c	79	a	112	d	145	d
14	c	47	c	80	a	113	c	146	b
15	c	48	b	81	c	114	b	147	b
16	a	49	c	82	a	115	c	148	c
17	a	50	a	83	a	116	b	149	a
18	a	51	a	84	a	117	b	150	d
19	c	52	a	85	d	118	d	151	a
20	a	53	b	86	c	119	d	152	b
21	c	54	a	87	c	120	a	153	a
22	d	55	c	88	c	121	b	154	b
23	d	56	d	89	a	122	b	155	c
24	b	57	a	90	c	123	d	156	a
25	c	58	b	91	c	124	d	157	d
26	a	59	a	92	b	125	d	158	a
27	c	60	b	93	a	126	b	159	a
28	d	61	a	94	b	127	a	160	a
29	b	62	a	95	c	128	c	161	c
30	c	63	d	96	d	129	d	162	d
31	c	64	a	97	a	130	a	163	d
32	a	65	c	98	a	131	c	164	d
33	c	66	a	99	b	132	a	165	a

Selected Explanation

103. Puppets from Tamil Nadu are known as Bommalattam.

105. Khajuraho temple is a group of Hindu and Jain temples in Madhya Pradesh build by Chandela dynasty between 950 and 1050 AD. They are UNESCO World Heritage sites.

106. The marriage under Devadasi system usually occurs before the girl reaches puberty.

107. The *Abhinaya Darpana* by Nandikesvara is one of the main sources of textual material for the study of the technique and grammar of body movement in Bharatanatyam dance.

108. In the *Natya Shastra*, compiled by Bharata Muni, musical instruments have been divided into four main categories on the basis of how sound is produced.

    (i) The Tata Vadya or Chordophones— Stringed instruments

    (ii The Sushira Vadya or Aerophones— Wind instruments

    (iii) The Avanaddha Vadya or Membrano-phones— Percussion instruments

    (iv) The Ghana Vadya or Idiophone— Solid instruments which do not require tuning.

109. In central India the Chandela rulers built a magnificent temple complex at Khajuraho.

113. Maharashtra is famous for devotional dances on the Krishna theme which are called "dindi" and "Kalaa". A vocalist sings to the accompaniment of the mridanga. Around them men and women dance, and this takes place usually during the Ekadasi day of Karthik.

114. Daskathia is a form of ballad singing prevalent in Odisha. Daskathia is a name derived from a unique musical instrument called "Kathi" or "Ram Tali", which are wooden clappers used during the presentation. The performance is a form of worship and offering on behalf of the "Das", the devotee.

116. Kadam Rasul mosque is situated at Gaur. Chand Minar is situated at Daulatabad and the Gol Gumbaz, the mausoleum of Muhammad Adil Shah is situated at Bijapur.

117. *Koodiyattam*, the Sanskrit theatre tradition of Kerala, India, has been declared as among the 'Masterpiece of the Oral and Intangible Heritage of Humanity' by UNESCO.

118. The *Abhinaya Darpana* by Nandikesvara is one of the main sources of textual material, for the study of the technique and grammar of body movement in Bharatanatyam dance. Bharatanatyam dance is known to be ekaharya, where one dancer takes on many roles in a single performance. The first dance item is the alarippu, literally means ` to adorn with flowers'.

120. Adhai din-ka-jhonpra is actually a masjid built by Qutub-ud-Din-Aibak. Sidi Sayyid mosque was built in the year 1572-73 by an Abyssinian known as Sidi Saeed or Sidi Saiyyed. He built this magnificent monument during the reign of Sultan Muzaffar Shah III, the last ruler of Gujarat. The Gol Gumbaz of Bijapur is the mausoleum of Muhammad Adil Shah (1627-57).

122. The national calendar based on the Saka Era, with Chaitra as its first month and a normal year of 365 days was adopted from 22 March 1957 along with the Gregorian calendar for official purposes. Dates of the national calendar have a permanent correspondence with dates of the Gregorian calendar, 1 Chaitra falling on 22 March normally and on 21 March in leap year.

125. Ajmer has earned the epithet of "Madinatul Hind or the Madina of India". Each year, the devotees of all sects and faiths ongregate here from all parts of the world on the occasion of the annual festival of Urs to pay their obeisance to seek the Saint's blessings for fulfillment of wishes. Thus, the festival

presents a unique picture of harmony and universal brotherhood. Ajmer is a centre of culture and education. It is famous for its rich Indo-Islamic, Royal Rajasthani, Indo-Saracenic and Jain styles of architecture.

126. Chennakeshava temple is located in Karnataka. Meenakshi Sundareshvara is located in Tamil Nadu.

127. Mohiniyattam dance is characterised by graceful, swaying body movements with no abrupt jerks or sudden leaps.

128. Monasteries are examples of rock cut architecture.

129. All the given statements are correct with reference to 'Kuchipudi dance'.

30. The mural paintings of Ajantha mostly illustrate the life of the Buddha as depicted in the Jataka stories.

131. The Kailasanatha temple at Kanchi and the Shore temple at Mamallapuram remain the finest examples of the early structural temples of the Pallavas.

132. The Tillana, corresponding to the Tarana of Hindustani music, is a short and crisp form. It is mainly a dance form, but on account of its brisk and attractive music, it sometimes finds a place in music concerts as a conclusion piece. It usually begins with jatis.

133. All the given statements are correct regarding Odissi dance.

134. The temple at Deogarh near Jhansi and the sculptures in the temple at Garhwa near Allahabad remain important specimen of the Gupta art.

136. Sankhya School of Philosophy doesn't mention anything about god.

137. The paintings mostly use white and red colors, though yellow and green colors have also been used. But most of the paintings belong to the Mesolithic period and not the Neolithic period.

138. Ghoomar was developed by Bhil tribe of Rajasthan.

139. In Nagara style temple, kalash was placed over the amalak. At the top of kalash, the flag was erected.

140. The Provida style evolved during the Vijayanagar dynasty rule. The pillars have the images of horses. Rajarajeshwara temple is the evolution of Dravidian style during the Cholas.

141. The earliest reference of Stupa is found in Rigveda, where it is used to refer to fire coming out of sacrificial alter. The stupa building activities were at their peak during post Mauryan age, eg. The Sungas, Kanavas, Satavahanas constructed a number of Stupas.

142. The theme of the paintings is both religious as well as day to day life.

145. Sitar, Santoor and Sarangi are stringed instruments, whereas Pakhawaj and Mridangam are percussion instruments.

146. The court language of Delhi Sultanate was Persian.

147. Nritya corresponds to dancing with miming and gesticulation. Nritta corresponds to pure dancing where the movements of the body do not express any mood and do not convey any meaning.

149. For many years Ajanta paintings were called frescoes, but this is an erroneous term in this case, and they are now referred to as murals, due to the fact that they were painted on a dry surface and not on a wet surface. The monument of Ajanta has 31 caves, which were excavated in the horse-shoe shaped gorge of the Waghora River in two phases. Ajanta caves can be classified into two phases namely the Hinayana phase and the Mahayana phase.

150. Each tala is divided into units, the smallest being called 'matra'.

152. Amravati Style of sculpture flourished in the Andhra region of southeastern India from about the 2nd century BC to the end of the 3rd century AD, during the rule of the Satavahana dynasty.

153. The dance of Shiv symbolizes the cosmic cycle of creation and destruction along with the daily rhythm of birth and death, which is the basis of all existences. The dwarf lying under Shiva's foot is the demon 'Apasmara', which symbolizes Shiva's victory over 'ignorance'.

154. The Alvar poet-saints had different origins and belonged to different castes. As per tradition, the first three Alvars, Poigai, Bhutha and Pei were born miraculously. Thirumazhisai was the son of a sage, Thondaraddi, Mathurakavi, Periaalvar and Andal were from brahmin community, Kulasekhara from Kshaytria community, Namm was from a cultivator family, Tirupana from Panar community and Tirumangai from Kazhwar community.

155. The eight limbs of Ashtanga Yoga of Patanjali Yoga are: Yama, Niyama, Asana, Pranayama, Pratyahara, Dharana, Dhyana and Samadhi.

156. Durga temple and Kailashnath temple are example of Vesara and Cave temple architecture respectively.

157. In contrast to Carnatic music, Hindustani music was not only influenced by ancient Hindustani musical traditions, historical Vedic philosophy and native Indian sounds but also enriched by the Persian performance practices of the Mughals. Dhrupad, dhamar, khyal, tarana and sadra are classical genres of Hindustani music.

158. Mathura school of sculpture flourished from the 2nd century BC to the 12th century AD. Rock-cut temples, in western Deccan, were excavated in the early years of the Christian era.

159. Metals, clay, ivory and even wood also are used to make beads from the very beginning of this art.

60. Vesara style of temple architecture was prevalent in Deccan and it is a combination of Dravida and Nagara styles.

161. Music continued to develop and flourish in the 18th century in India.

162. The Mathura School of Sculpture ignored the images of Krishna during the pre-Gupta age in India.

163. Dravidian form flourished dynastically while the Nagara style, on account of much wider area of distribution, developed regionally, each region manifesting its own particular qualities.

165. Chaityas were Buddhist temples and Viharas were monasteries.

APPENDIX 2

Previous Years Preliminary Examination Questions on Indian Heritage and Culture

2001

1. In which one of the following cities is the Lingaraja temple located?

(a) Bhubaneswar (b) Bijapur
(c) Kolkata (d) Shravanabelagola.

2. Consider the following statements

1. Arya Samaj was founded in 1835.
2. Lala Lajpat Rai opposed the appeal of Arya Samaj to the authority of Vedas in support of its social reform programme.
3. Under Keshab Chandra Sen, the Brahmo Samaj campaigned for women's education.
4. Vinoba Bhave founded the Sarvodya Samaj to work among refugees.

Which of these statements are correct?

(a) 1 and 2 (b) 2 and 3
(e) 2 and 4 (d) 3 and 4

3. Who amongst the following Englishmen first translated the Bhagavad Gita into English?

(a) William Jones
(b) Charles Wilkins
(c) Alexander Cunningham
(d) John Marshall

4. Hoysala monuments are found in

(a) Hampi and Hosper
(b) Halebid and Belur
(c) Mysore and Bangalore
(d) Sringeri and Dharwar

5. Match List I with List II and select the correct answer using the codes given below the lists.

List I (Dance)	List II (Dance)
A. Kalamandalam Kshemavaty	1. Kathakali
B. Kottakkal Sivaraman	2. Manipuri
C. Lakshmi Viswanathan	3. Mohiniattam
D. N Madhabi Devi	4. Bharatanatyam

Codes

	A	B	C	D
(a)	1	3	2	4
(b)	3	1	4	2
(c)	1	3	4	2
(d)	3	1	2	4

6. Which one of the following animals was not represented on seals and terracotta art of Harappan culture?

(a) Cow (b) Elephant
(c) Rhinoceros (d) Tiger

7. Which one of the following pairs is correctly matched?

(a) Harappan Civilisation — Painted Grey Ware
(b) The Kushans — Gandhara School of Art
(c) The Mughals — Ajanta Paintings
(d) The Marathas — Pahari School of Painting

8. Who among the following presided over the Buddhist Council held during the reign of Kanishka at Kashmir?

(a) Parsva (b) Nagarjuna
(c) Sudraka (d) Vasumitra

Directions *The following item consist of two statements. One labelled the 'Assertion A' and the other as 'Reason R'. You are to examine these two statements carefully and decide if the 'Assertion A' and the 'Reason R' are individually true and if so, whether the 'Reason R' is the correct explanation of the given 'Assertion A'. Select your answer¬sheet accordingly.*

Codes

(a) Both A and R are individually true and R is the correct explanation of A
(b) Both A and R are individually true, but R is not a correct explanation of A
(c) A is true, but R is false
(d) A is false, but R is true

9. Assertion (A) Harshavardhana convened the Prayag Assembly.

Reason (R) He wanted to popularise only the Mahayana form of Buddhism.

2002

1. The ancient Indian play *Mudrarakshasa* of Visakhadutta has its subject on

(a) a conflict between gods and demons of ancient Hindu lore
(b) a romantic story of an Aryan prince and a tribal woman
(c) the story of the power struggle between two Aryan princes
(d) the court intrigues at the time of Chandragupta

2. In ancient Indian 'Buddhist monasteries, a ceremony called Pavarana used to be held. It was the

(a) occasion to elect the Sanghparinayaka and two speakers, one on Dhamma and the other Vinaya
(b) confession by monks of their offences committed during their stay in the monasteries during the rainy season
(c) ceremony of initiation of new person into the Buddhist Sangha when the head is shaved and when yellow robes are offered
(d) gathering of Buddhist monks on the day to the full Moon day of Ashadha when they take up a fixed abode for the next months of rainy season

3. Which one of the following statements is not correct?

(a) The statue of Gomateshwara at Shravana-belagola represents the last Tirthankara of Jains
(b) India's largest Buddhist monastery is in Sikkim.
(c) The Khajuraho temples were built under the Chandela kings
(d) The Hoysaleswara temple is dedicated to Lord Shiva

4. Who among the following was the first Bhakti saint to use Hindi for the propagation of his message?

(a) Dadu
(b) Kabir
(c) Ramananda
(d) Tulsidas

5. Match List I (Ancient site) with List II (Archaeological finding) and select the correct answer using the codes given below the lists.

List I (Ancient site)	List II (Archaeological finding)
A. Lothal	1. Ploughed field
B. Kalibangan	2. Dockyard
C. Dholavira	3. Terracotta replica of a plough
D. Banawali	4. An inscription comprising ten large sized signs of the Harappan script

Codes

	A	B	C	D
(a)	1	2	3	4
(b)	2	1	4	3
(c)	1	2	4	3
(d)	2	1	3	4

2003

1. Consider the following statements

1. Kitab-i-Nauras, a collection of songs in praise of Hindu deities and Muslim saints, was written by Ibrahim Adil Shah II.
2. Amir Khusrau was the originator in India of the early form of the musical style known as Qawali.

Which of these statements is/are correct?

(a) Only 1 (b) Only 2
(c) Both 1 and 2 (d) Neither 1 nor 2

2. 'Mrichchhakatika', an ancient Indian book written by Sudraka deals with

(a) the love affair of a brahmin with the daughter of a courtesan
(b) the victory of Chandragupta II over the Shaka Kshatrapas of Western India
(c) the military expeditions and exploits of Samudragupta
(d) the love affairs between a Gupta king and a princess of Kamarupa

2004

1. Which one of the following four Vedas contains an account of magical charms and spells?

(a) Rigveda
(b) Yajurveda
(c) Atharvaveda
(d) Samaveda

2005

1. Consider the following statements

1. Ishwar Chandra Vidyasagar founded the Bethune School at Calcutta with the main aim of encouraging education for women.
2. Bankim Chandra Chattopadhyay was a the graduate of the Calcutta University.
3. Keshav Chandra Sen's campaign against *Sati* led to the enactment of a law to ban *sati* by the then Governor General.

Which of the statements given above is/ are correct?

(a) Only 1 (b) 1 and 2
(c) 2 and 3 (d) 1, 2 and 3

2006

1. Which one of the following pairs is not correctly matched?

	Monastery	State
(a)	Dhankar Monastery	Himachal Pradesh
(b)	Rumtek monastery	Sikkim
(c)	Tabo Monastery	Himachal Pradesh
(d)	Kye Monastery	Arunachal Pradesh

2. The initial design and construction of which massive temple took place during the reign of Suryavarman II?

(a) Sri Mariamman temple
(b) Angkor Vat temple
(c) Batu Caves temple
(d) Kamakhya temple

3. Which one of the following pairs is correctly matched?

(a) Vikramshila Monastery : Uttar Pradesh
(b) Hemkund Gurudwara : Himachal Pradesh
(c) Udayagiri Caves : Maharashtra
(d) Amaravati Buddhist Stupa : Andhra Pradesh

4. The Allahabad pillar inscription is associated with which one of the following?

(a) Mahapadma Nanda
(b) Chandragupta Maurya
(c) Ashoka
(d) Samudragupta

2007

1. Where is the famous Vijaya Vittala Temple, having its 56 carved pillars emitting musical notes located?

(a) Belur (b) Bhadrachalam
(c) Hampi (d) Srirangam

2009

1. Anekantavada is a core theory and philosophy of which one of the following?

(a) Buddhism (b) Jainism
(c) Sikhism (d) Vaishnavism

2. Where is the famous Virupaksha temple located?

(a) Bhadrachalam (b) Chidambaram
(c) Hampi (d) Srikalahasti

3. Consider the following pairs

Tradition	State
1. Gatka, a traditional martial art	Kerala
2. Madhubani, a traditional painting	Bihar
3. Singhey Khababs Sindhu Darshan festival	Jammu and Kashmir

Which of the pair(s) given above is/are correctly matched?

(a) 1 and 2 (b) Only 3
(c) 2 and 3 (d) 1, 2 and 3

4. There are only two known examples of cave paintings of the Gupta period in ancient India. One of these is the paintings of Ajanta caves. Where is the other surviving example of Gupta paintings?

(a) Bagh caves
(b) Ellora caves
(c) Lomas Rishi caves
(d) Nasik caves

2010

1. Why did Buddhism start declining in India in the early medieval times?

1. Buddha was by that time considered as one of the incarnations of Vishnu and thus became a part of Vaishnavism.
2. The invading tribes from Central Asia till the time of the last Gupta king adopted Hinduism and persecuted Buddhists.
3. The Kings of Gupta dynasty were strongly opposed to Buddhism.

Which of the statements given above is/are correct?

(a) 1 only (b) 1 and 3 only
(c) 2 and 3 only (d) 1, 2 and 3

2. Among the following, who was not a proponent of bhakti cult?

(a) Nagarjuna (b) Tukaram
(c) Tyagraja (d) Vallabhacharya

2011

1. Regarding the Indus valley civilisation, consider the following statements

1. It was predominantly a secular civilisation and the religious element, though present, did not dominate the scene.
2. During this period, cotton was used for manufacturing textiles in India.

Which of the statements given above is/are correct?

(a) Only 1 (b) Only 2
(c) Both 1 and 2 (d) Neither 1 nor 2

2. The 'Dharma' and 'Rita' depict a central idea of ancient Vedic civilisation of India. In this context, consider the following statements

1. 'Dharma' was a conception of obligations and of the discharge of one's duties to oneself and to others.
2. 'Rita' was the fundamental moral law governing the functioning of the universe and all it contained.

Which of the statements given above is I are correct?

(a) Only 1 (b) Only2
(c) Both 1 and 2 (d) Neither 1 nor 2

2012

1. How do you distinguish between Kuchipudi and Bharatanatyam dances?

1. Dancers occasionally speaking dialogues in Kuchipudi dance, but not in Bharatanatyam.
2. Dancing on the brass plate by keeping the feet on its edges is a feature of Bharatanatyam, but Kuchipudi dance does not have such a form of movement.

Which of the statement(s) given above is/are correct?

(a) Only 1
(b) Only 2
(c) Both 1 and 2
(d) Neither 1 nor 2

2. The Nagara, the Dravida and the Vesara are the

(a) three main racial groups of the Indian subcontinent
(b) three main linguistic divisions into which the languages of India can be classified
(c) three main styles of Indian temple architecture
(d) three main musical gharanas prevalent in India

3. With reference to the history of ancient India, which of the following was/were common to both Buddhism and Jainism?

1. Avoidance of extremities of penance and enjoyment.
2. Indifference to the authority of the Vedas.
3. Denial of efficacy of rituals.

Select the correct answer using the codes given below

(a) Only 1 (b) 2 and 3
(c) 1 and 3 (d) 1, 2 and 3

4. With reference to Dhrupad, one of the major traditions of India that has been kept alive for centuries, which of the following statements are correct?

1. Dhrupad originated and developed in the Rajput kingdoms during the Mughal period.
2. Dhrupad is primarily a devotional and spiritual music.
3. Dhrupad Alap uses Sanskrit syllables from mantras.

Select the correct answer using the codes given below

(a) 1 and 2 (b) 2 and 3
(c) 1, 2 and 3 (d) None of the above

5. Which of the following statements is/are correct regarding Brahmo Samaj?

1. It opposed idolatry.
2. It denied the need for a priestly class for interpreting the religious texts.
3. It popularised the doctrine that the Vedas are infallible.

Select the correct answer using the codes given below

(a) Only 1
(b) 1 and 2
(c) Only 3
(d) 1, 2 and 3

6. Lord Buddha's image is sometimes shown with the hand gesture called 'Bhumisparsha Mudra'. It symbolises

(a) Buddha's calling of the Earth to watch over Mara and to prevent Mara from disturbing his meditation
(b) Buddha's calling of the Earth to witness his purity and chastity despite the temptations of Mara
(c) Buddha's reminder to his followers that they all arise from the Earth and finally dissolve into the Earth and thus this life is transitory
(d) Both the statements (a) and (b) are correct in this context

2013

1. Some Buddhist rockcut caves are called Chaityas, while the others are called Viharas. What is the difference between the two?

(a) Vihara is a place of worship, while Chaitya is the dwelling place of the monks
(b) Chaitya is a place of worship, while Vihara is the dwelling place of the monks
(c) Chaitya is the stupa at the far end of the cave, while Vihara is the hall axial to it
(d) There is no material difference between the two

2. Which of the following characterises/ characterise the people of Indus civilisation?

1. They possessed great palaces and temples.
2. They worshipped both male and female deities.
3. They employed horse-drawn chariots in warfare.

Select the correct answer using the codes given below

(a) 1 and 2 (b) Only 2
(c) All of these (d) None of these

3. With reference to the history of philosophical thought in India, consider the following statements regarding Samkhya School

1. Samkhya does not accept the theory of rebirth or transmigration of soul.
2. Samkhya holds that it is the self-knowledge that leads to liberation and not any exterior influence or agent.

Which of the statements given above is/are correct?

(a) Only 1 (b) Only 2
(c) Both 1 and 2 (d) Neither 1 nor 2

4. Consider the following historical places

1. Ajanta caves.
2. Lepakshi temple.
3. Sanchi stupa.

Which of the above places is / are also known for mural paintings?

(a) Only 1
(b) 1 and 2
(c) All of these
(d) None of these

5. In the context of cultural history of India, a pose in dance and dramatics called Tribhanga has been a favourite of Indian artists from ancient times till today. Which one of the following statements best describes this pose?

(a) One leg is bent and the body is slightly but, oppositely curved at waist and neck
(b) Facial expressions, hand gestures and make up are combined to symbolise certain epic or historic characters
(c) Movements of body, face and hands are used to express oneself or to tell a story
(d) A little smile, slightly curved waist and certain hand gestures are emphasised to express the feelings of love or eroticism

6. With reference to the history of Indian rock-cut architecture, consider the following statements

1. The caves at Badami are the oldest surviving rock-cut caves in India.
2. The Barabar rock-cut caves were originally made for Ajivikas by Emperor Chandragupta Maurya.
3. At Ellora, caves were made for different faiths.

Which of the statement(s) given above is/are correct?

(a) Only 1 (b) 2 and 3
(c) Only 3 (d) All of these

7. Which one of the following describes best the concept of Nirvana in Buddhism?

(a) The extinction of the flame of desire
(b) The complete annihilation of self
(c) A state of bliss and rest
(d) A mental stage beyond all comprehension

8. Consider the following Bhakti Saints:

1. Dadu Dayal 2. Guru Nanak
3. Tyagaraja

Who among the above was/were preaching when the Lodi dynasty fell and Babur took over?

(a) 1 and 3 (b) 2 only
(c) 2 and 3 (d) 1 and 2

9. Which of the following statements is/are applicable to Jain doctrine?

1. The surest way of annihilating Karma is to practice penance.
2. Every object, even the smallest particle has a soul.
3. Karma is the bane of the soul and must be ended.

Select the correct answer using the codes given below.

(a) 1 only (b) 2 and 3 only
(c) 1 and 3 only (d) 1, 2 and 3

2014

1. Ibadat Khana at Fatehpur Sikri was

(a) the mosque for the use of royal family
(b) Akbar's private chamber prayer
(c) the hall in which Akbar held discussions with scholars of various religions
(d) the room in which the nobles belonging to different religions gathered to discuss religious affairs

2. With reference to the cultural history of India, the term 'Panchayatan' refers to

(a) an assembly of village elders
(b) a religious sect
(c) a style of temple construction
(d) an administrative functionary

3. With reference to the Indian history of art and culture, which of the following pairs is/are correctly matched?

Famous Work of Sculpture	Site
1. A grand image of Buddha's Mahaparinirvana with numerous celestial musicians above and the sorrowful figures of his followers below	: Ajanta
2. A huge image of Varaha avatar (boar incarnation) of Vishnu, as he rescues Goddess Earth from the deep and chaotic waters, sculpted on rock	: Mount Abu
3. 'Arjuna's Penance' / Descent of Ganga sculpted on the surface of huge boulders	: Mamallapuram

Codes

(a) 1 and 2 (b) Only 3
(c) 1 and 3 (d) All of these

4. With reference to the famous Sattriya dance, consider the following statements

1. Sattriya is a combination of music, dance and drama.
2. It is a centuries-old living tradition of Vaishnavites of Assam.
3. It is based on classical Ragas and Talas of devotional songs composed by Tulsidas, Kabir and Mirabai.

Which of the statement(s) given above is / are correct?

(a) Only 1 (b) 1 and 2
(c) 2 and 3 (d) All of these

5. Which of the following pairs is/are correctly matched?

1. Garba : Gujarat
2. Mohiniattam : Odisha
3. Yakshagana : Karnataka

Codes

(a) Only 1 (b) 2 and 3
(c) 1 and 3 (d) All of these

6. With reference to India's culture and tradition, what is 'Kalaripayattu'?

(a) It is an ancient Bhakti cult of Shaivism still prevalent in some parts of South India
(b) It is an ancient style bronze and brass work still found in southern part of Coromandel area
(c) It is an ancient form of dance, drama and a living tradition in the northern part of Malabar
(d) It is an ancient martial art and a living tradition in some parts of South India

7. Consider the following statements

1. 'Bijak' is a composition of the teachings of saint Dadu Dayal.
2. The philosophy of Pushti Marg was propounded by Madhavacharya.

Which of the statement(s) given above is / are correct?

(a) Only 1 (b) Only 2
(c) Both 1 and 2 (d) Neither 1 nor 2

8. A community of people called Manganiyars is well known for their

(a) martial arts in North-East India
(b) musical tradition in North-West India
(c) classical vocal music in South India
(d) pietra dura tradition in Central India

9. With reference to Buddhist history, tradition and culture in India, which of the following pairs is/are correctly matched?

Famous Shrine		Location
1. Tabo monastery and temple complex	:	Spiti valley
2. Lhotsava Lhakhang temple, Nako	:	Zanskar valley
3. Alchi temple complex	:	Ladakh

Codes

(a) Only 1 (b) 2 and 3
(c) 1 and 3 (d) All of these

10. Which one of the following pairs does not form part of the six systems of Indian Philosophy?

(a) Mimamsa and Vedanta
(b) Nyaya and Vaisheshika
(c) Lokayata and Kapalika
(d) Sankhya and Yoga

11. The national motto of India, 'Satyameva Jayate' inscribed below the Emblem of India is taken from

(a) Katha Upanishad
(b) Chandogya Upanishad
(c) Aitareya Upanishad
(d) Mundaka Upanishad

12. Which of the following Kingdoms were associated with the life of the Buddha?

1. Avanti   2. Gandhara
3. Kosala   4. Magadha

Select the correct answer using the code given below.

(a) 1, 2 and 3   (b) 2 and 4
(c) 3 and 4 only   (d) 1, 3 and 4

13. Consider the following languages:

1. Gujarati
2. Kannada
3. Telugu

Which of the above has/have been declared as 'Classical Language/Languages' by the Government?

(a) 1 and 2 only   (b) 3 only
(c) 2 and 3 only   (d) 1, 2 and 3

14. Consider the following towns of India:

1. Bhadrachalam
2. Chanderi
3. Kancheepuram
4. Karnal

Which of the above are famous for the production of traditional sarees/fabric?

(a) 1 and 2 only   (b) 2 and 3 only
(c) 1, 2 and 3   (d) 1, 3 and 4

2015

1. Kalamkari painting refers to

(a) a hand-painted cotton textile in South India
(b) a handmade drawing on bamboo handicrafts in North-East India
(c) a block-painted woollen cloth in Western Himalayan region of India
(d) a hand-painted decorative silk cloth in North-Western India

2. Which of the following has/have been accorded 'Geographical Indication' status?

1. Banaras Brocades and Sarees
2. Rajasthani Daal-Bati-Churma
3. Tirupathi Laddu

Select the correct answer using the code given below.

(a) 1 only   (b) 2 and 3 only
(c) 1 and 3 only   (d) 1, 2 and 3

3. Which one of the following kingdoms were associated with the life of the Buddha?

1. Avanti   2. Gandhara
3. Kosala   4. Magadha

Select the correct answer using the code given below.

(a) 1, 2 and 3   (b) 2 and 3 only
(c) 1, 3 and 4   (d) 3 and 4 only

4. With reference to the art and archaeological history of India, which one among the following was made earliest?

(a) Lingaraja temple at Bhubaneswar
(b) Rock-cut Elephant at Dhauli
(c) Rock-cut monuments at Mahabalipuram
(d) Varaha Image at Udayagiri

5. Which one of the following was given classical language status recently?

(a) Odia   (b) Konkani
(c) Bhojpuri   (d) Assamese

6. Which of the following kingdoms were associated with the life of the Buddha?

1. Avanti   2. Gandhara
3. Kosala   4. Magadha

Select the correct answer using the code given below.

(a) 1, 2 and 3   (b) 2 and 3 only
(c) 1, 3 and 4   (d) 3 and 4 only

7. Consider the following:

The arrival of Babur into India led to the

1. Introduction of gunpowder in the subcontinent
2. Introduction of the arch and dome in the region's architecture
3. Establishment of Timurid dynasty in the region

Select the correct answer using the code given below.

(a) 1 and 2 only (b) 3 only
(c) 1 and 3 only (d) 1, 2 and 3

2016

1. Which one of the following books of ancient India has the love story of the son of the founder of Sunga dynasty?

(a) Swapnavasavadatta
(b) Malavikagnimitra
(c) Meghadoota
(d) Ratnavali

2. With reference to the cultural history of medieval India, consider the following statements:

1. Siddhas (Sittars) of Tamil region were monotheistic and condemned idolatry.
2. Lingayats of Kannada region questioned the theory of rebirth and rejected the caste hierarchy.

Which of the statements given above is/are correct?

(a) 1 only (b) 2 only
(c) Both 1 and 2 (d) Neither 1 nor 2

3. With reference to the religious history of India, consider the following statements:

1. The concept of Bodhisattva is central to Hinayana sect of Buddhism.
2. Bodhisattva is a compassionate one on his way to enlightenment.
3. Bodhisattva delays achieving his own salvation to help all sentient beings on their path to it.

Which of the statements given above is/are correct?

(a) 1 only
(b) 2 and 3 only
(c) 2 only
(d) 1, 2 and 3

4. Satya Shodhak Samaj organized

(a) a movement for upliftment of tribals in Bihar
(b) a temple-entry movement in Gujarat
(c) an anti-caste movement in Maharashtra
(d) a peasant movement in Punja

5. What is/are common to the two historical places known as Ajanta and Mahabalipuram?

1. Both were built in the same period.
2. Both belong to the same religious denomination.
3. Both have rock-cut monuments.

Select the correct answer using the code given below.

(a) 1 and 2 only
(b) 3 only
(c) 1 and 3 only
(d) None of the statements given above is correct

6. With reference to the cultural history of India, the memorising of chronicles, dynastic histories and epic tales was the profession of who of the following?

(a) Shramana
(b) Parivraajaka
(c) Agrahaarika
(d) Maagadha

2017

1. With reference to the religious history of India, consider the following statements:

1. Sautrantika and Sammitiya were the sects of Jainism.
2. Sarvastivadin held that the constituents of phenomena were not wholly momentary, but existed forever in a latent form.

Which of the statements given above is/are correct?

(a) 1 only (b) 2 only
(c) Both 1 and 2 (d) Neither 1 nor 2

2. The painting of Bodhisattva Padmapani is one of the most famous and oft-illustrated paintings at

(a) Ajanta (b) Badami
(c) Bagh (d) Ellora

3. Consider the following pairs:

Traditions		Communities
1. Chaliha Sahib Festival	–	Sindhis
2. Nanda Raj Jaat Yatra	–	Gonds
3. Wari-Warkari	–	Santhals

Which of the pairs given above is/are correctly matched?

(a) 1 only (b) 2 and 3 only
(c) 1 and 3 only (d) None of the above

4. Which of the following is/are famous for Sun temples?

1. Arasavalli
2. Amarakantak
3. Omkareshwar

Select the correct answer using the code given below:

(a) 1 only
(b) 2 and 3 only
(c) 1 and 3 only
(d) 1, 2 and 3

5. With reference to Manipuri Sankirtana, consider the following statements:

1. It is a song and dance performance.
2. Cymbals are the only musical instruments used in the performance.
3. It is performed to narrate the life and deeds of Lord Krishna.

Which of the statements given above is/are correct?

(a) 1,2 and 3 (b) 1 and 3 only
(c) 2 and 3 only (d) 1 only

2018

1. With reference to the religious practices in India, the "Sthanakvasi" sect belongs to

(a) Buddhism (b) Jainism
(c) Vaishnavism (d) Shaivism

2. With reference to the cultural history of India, consider the following statements :

1. White marble was used in making Buland Darwaza and Khankah at Fatehpur Sikri.
2. Red sandstone and marble were used in making Bara Imambara and Rumi Darwaza at Lucknow.

Which of the statements given above is/are correct?

(a) 1 only (b) 2 only
(c) Both 1 and 2 (d) Neither 1 nor 2

3. With reference to Indian history, who among the following is a future Buddha, yet to come to save the world?

(a) Avalokiteshvara (b) Lokesvara
(c) Maitreya (d) Padmapani

4. Consider the following pairs:

Craft		**Heritage of**
1. Puthukkuli shawls	—	Tamil Nadu
2. Sujni embroidery	—	Maharashtra
3. Uppada Jamdani saris	—	Karnataka

Which of the pairs given above is/are correct?

(a) 1 only
(b) 1 and 2
(c) 3 only
(d) 2 and 3

5. Consider the following pairs :

	Tradition	State
1.	Chapchar Kut festival	- Mizoram
2.	Khongjom Parba ballad	- Manipur
3.	Thang-Ta dance	- Sikkim

Which of the pairs given above is/are correct ?

(a) 1 only
(b) 1 and 2
(c) 3 only
(d) 2 and 3

6. The well-known painting "Bani Thani" belongs to the

(a) Bundi school
(b) Jaipur school
(c) Kangra school
(d) Kishangarh school

7. With reference to cultural history of India, consider the following statements :

1. Most of the Tyagaraja Kritis are devotional songs in praise of Lord Krishna.
2. Tyagaraja created several new ragas.
3. Annamacharya and Tyagaraja are contemporaries.
4. Annamacharya kirtanas are devotional songs in praise of Lord Venkateshwara.

Which of the statements given above are correct?

(a) 1 and 3 only
(b) 2 and 4 only
(c) 1, 2 and 3
(d) 2, 3 and 4

2019

1. Building 'Kalyaana Mandapas' was a notable feature in the temple construction in the kingdom of

(a) Chalukya (b) Chandela
(c) Rashtrakuta (d) Vijayanagara

2. Which one of the following is not a Harappan site?

(a) Chanhudaro (b) Kot Diji
(c) Sohgaura (d) Desalpur

3. In which of the following relief sculpture inscriptions is 'Ranyo Ashoka' (King Ashoka) mentioned along with the stone portrait of Ashoka?

(a) Kanganahalli (b) Sanchi
(c) Shahbazgarhi (d) Sohgaura

4. Consider the following:

1. Deification of the Buddha
2. Treading the path of Bodhisattvas
3. Image worship and rituals

Which of the above is/are the feature/ features of Mahayana Buddhism?

(a) 1 only (b) 1 and 2 only
(c) 2 and 3 only (d) 1, 2 and 3

5. With reference to forced labour (Vishti) in India during the Gupta period, which one of the following statements is correct?

(a) It was considered a source of income for the State, a sort of tax paid by the people.
(b) It was totally absent in the Madhya Pradesh and Kathiawar regions of the Gupta Empire.
(c) The forced labourer was entitled to weekly wages.
(d) The eldest son of the labourer was sent as the forced labourer.

Answer Key

2001	2002	2003	2004	2006	2006	2007	2009	2010
1. (a)	1. (d)	1. (c)	1. (c)	1. (b)	1. (d)	1. (c)	1. (b)	1. (a)
2. (d)	2. (b)	2. (a)			2. (b)		2. (c)	2. (a)
3. (b)	3. (b)				3. (d)		3. (c)	
4. (b)	4. (c)				4. (d)		4. (a)	
5. (d)	5. (b)							
6. (a)								
7. (b)								
8. (d)								
9. (b)								

2011	2012	2013	2014	2015	2016	2017	2018	2019
1. (c)	1. (a)	1. (b)	1. (c)	1. (a)	1. (b)	1. (b)	1. (b)	1. (d)
2. (c)	2. (c)	2. (b)	2. (c)	2. (c)	2. (b)	2. (a)	2. (d)	2. (c)
	3. (b)	3. (b)	3. (c)	3. (d)	3. (b)	3. (a)	3. (c)	3. (a)
	4. (b)	4. (b)	4. (b)	4. (b)	4. (c)	4. (a)	4. (a)	4. (d)
	5. (b)	5. (a)	5. (c)	5. (a)	5. (b)	5. (b)	5. (b)	5. (a)
	6. (b)	6. (c)	6. (d)	6. (d)	6. (c)		6. (d)	
		7. (a)	7. (d)	7. (c)			7. (b)	
		8. (d)	8. (b)					
		9. (d)	9. (c)					
			10. (c)					
			11. (d)					
			12. (c)					
			13. (c)					
			14. (b)					

Selected Explanation

2002

3.(b) The statue of Bahubali/Gomateshwara was the son of Rishashnath the first Jain Tirthankara.Rumtek in Sikkim is the second largest Buddhist monastery while Tawang monastery in Arunachal Pradesh is considered the largest monastery in India.

2003

2.(a) The play is about a young Brahmin Charudatta who falls in love with a wealthy courtesan Vasantasena.

2006

1.(d) Kye Monastery is situated in Himachal Pradesh.

2.(b) Angkor Vat temple built in (1113-1150) by Suryavarman II in Cambodia is dedicated to Lord Vishnu and is a world heritage site.

4.(d) The pillar carries Asokan edict but it is noted for containing later inscriptions attributed to king Samudragupta.

2009

1.(b) The meaning of Anekantavada is that there are several aspects of truth.

2.(c) Now it is called Presidency College.

3.(c) Gatka is a martial art form of Punjab region in which wooden sticks are used to mimic swords in sparring matches.

2012

1.(a) A feature of the Kuchipudi is Tara, in which the performer dances on edges of a brass plate.

4.(b) Dhrupad is the oldest surviving form of Indian classical music and starts with the Alap.

2013

3.(b) The Samkhya School is part of the six orthodox schools of Indian philosophy. The sage Kapila was the founder of the Samkhya School.

2014

4.(b) Recognised as one of the eight classical dance forms of India, the Sattriya a dance–drama evolved in AD 15th century. It was created by the great Vaishnava saint Mahapurusha Sankaradeva.

2015

2.(c) A Geographical Indication (G1) is the name or sign used on certain products which correspond to a specific geographical location or origin (e.g. a town, region or country).

2016

4.(c) The main aim was to liberate the shudra (untouchable) castes from exploitation and oppression.

2017

1.(b) Sautrantika and Sammitiya are related to Tibetan Buddhism.

2.(a) The painting of Bodhisattva Padmapani from cave I is one of the masterpieces of Ajanta painting executed in the late 6th century A.D.

3.(a) Nanda Raj Jaat Yatra is a festival of Uttarakhand while Gonds are tribals of Central India. Wari-Warkari is related to Maharashtra while Santhals belong to eastern India.

4.(a) Arasavalli Sun temple is a 7th-century AD Sun Temple at Arasavalli in Andhra Pradesh, India. It is believed that the temple was built by king Devendra Varma, ruler of the Kalinga Dynasty.

5.(b) Sankirtana which is a ritual of singing, drumming and dancing of Manipur is among the 14 elements inscribed on the Representative List of the UNESCO Intangible Cultural Heritage of Humanity.

It is practised at the centre of a temple, where performers narrate the lives and deeds of Krishna through songs and dance.

The musical accompaniment for Manipuri dances comes from a percussion instrument called the Pung (a barrel drum), small kartals (cymbals), sembong, harmonium, a stringed instrument called the pena and wind instrument such as a flute

2018

1.(b) Sthanakvasi is a sect of Jainism founded by a merchant named Lavaji in 1653 AD. It believes that idol worship is not essential in the path of soul purification and attainment of Nirvana or Moksha.

2.(d) Statement 1 is incorrect, because, Buland Darwaza is made up of the red and buff sandstone. Statement 2 is also incorrect, because, neither Red sandstone nor marble were used in making Bara Imambara and Rumi Darwaza at Lucknow. The material used for the Rumi Darwaza is bricks and it's then coated with lime.

3.(c) Maitreya Buddha is considered as the 5th Buddha that is believed to appear in this Kalpa or era. Thus, Maitreya Buddha is considered as the Future Buddha that is yet to appear in this age.

4.(a) Option 1 is correct, because, Toda tribe of Tamil Nadu do the intricate Pithukuli work on cream coloured shawls. The colours are always red and black, and the shawl can be used both sides. A worked- on shawl costs Rs 800. Option 2 is incorrect, because, Sujani (also known as Sujini) is a form of embroidery originating from the Bhusura village of Bihar in India. Option 3 is incorrect, because, Uppada jamdani sarees are diaphanous silk saree that trace its origin to Uppada in Andhra Pradesh.

5.(b) Option 1 and 2 are correct, because, Chapchar Kut is a festival of Mizoram, India. It is celebrated during March after completion of their most arduous task of Jhum operation i.e., jungle-clearing (clearing of the remnants of burning). In Manipur's context, the ballad 'Khongjom Parba' is a narrative on the heroic deeds of Manipuri warriors who fought the imperialistic British forces in 1891 A.D. in safeguarding the freedom of the then Manipur kingdom. Option 3 is incorrect, because, The Thang Ta dance form has originated from the north eastern state of Manipur. This dance is an Indian martial art form that involves the use of weapons for the performance.

6.(d) Bani Thani is an Indian miniature painting painted by Nihâl Chand from the Marwar school of Kishangarh. It is a painting by Nihal Chand and portrays a woman who is elegant and graceful. Bani Thani, was a singer and poet in Kishangarh in the time of king Sawant Singh. This form of painting is characterized by features like arched eyebrows, lotus-like elongated eyes and pointed chin.

7.(b) Tyagaraja Kritis are generally in praise of Lord Rama. Annamacharya lived between 1408 and 1503, while Thyagaraja lived between 1767 and 1847. They were not contemporaries.

2019

1.(d) Vijayanagara architecture has kalyanamandapas.

2.(c) The Sohgaura site was related to copper plate inscription written in Prakrit in the Brahmi script. It was discovered in Sohgaura, a village on the banks of the Rapti River, about 20km south-east of Gorakhpur, in the Gorakhpur District, Uttar Pradesh.

3.(a) An Inscription in Brahmi read "Ranyo Ashoka"(King Ashoka) was found at site Kanganahall, Sannati.

4.(d) All statements are correct. The emergence of Bodhisattva is central to Mahayana sect of Buddhism, which emerged during the fourth council of Buddhism held in 1st century A.D at Kashmir during the reign of Kanishka. Bodhisattvas were perceived as deeply compassionate beings who accumulated merit through their efforts but used this not to attain Nibbana and thereby abandon the world but to help others. The worship of images of the Buddha and Bodhisattvas became an important part of this tradition. Hence all the statements are correct.

5.(a) Forced labour (vishti) is a forced labour which became more common than before in 300-600C. It is mentioned along with taxes in land grant inscriptions which suggests that it was considered as a source of income for the state, a sort of tax paid by the people.

3

APPENDIX

Model Questions for the Main Examination

This section contains a collection of 30 model questions with solutions that have been carefully prepared based on the pattern of the main examination followed by an additional 20 unsolved questions with hints and references to pages in this book.

A thorough study of all these questions will enable the reader to get a proper perspective of the type of questions that are expected to be asked in the actual examination and how to approach the answers. It covers a wide range of topics which further supplements the contents of the previous chapters and will impart the aspirant with appropriate knowledge and confidence to tackle any question in the actual examination.

It is hoped that readers will find this section a valuable tool in their overall strategy for preparation.

1. What do you understand by the term `culture'. Do you consider it as the same as civilisation? Is culture a part of religion or is it a wider term inclusive of culture?

Points to be included

- The connotation of the word `culture' is vast and cannot be restricted to a singular definition. However, it can be understood as the collective values of a society, manifested through its numerous institutions as well as, in the disposition, attitudes and manners of its individual members. Those in turn find expression in various material objects, abstract ideas and beliefs of individuals and society.
- Thus, culture includes certain aspects of collective institutions, such as morality, religion, spirituality, law, customs, art etc. which are not restricted to an individual and which are handed over from generation to generation. Evidently the institutional elements of culture are evolutionary and dynamic.
- Culture also includes intellectual and knowledge elements pertaining to languages, literature, human learning, social norms, customs and behaviour.
- Human and social aesthetics are another aspect of culture, encompassing within it the numerous manifestation of tangible and intangible art forms, viz, music, dance, sculpture, painting and architecture etc.
- Civilisation on the other hand, refers to a fairly advanced stage of human development of a people which encompasses social, urban, technological as well as cultural development. Thus cultural growth is an important but not the only factor to be reckoned for charcterisation of a society as a civilisation. Therefore, neither the two terms mean the same nor they are analogous, although a developed culture may be considered a sine-qua-non for an advanced civilisation.

- Religion refers to a particular system of faith, belief and worship which is usually integrated with a belief in god(s). Neither religion nor culture can be said to be a sub-part of the other although there remains a profound interconnect between them. From the perspective of religion, elements of culture are manifested often in form of ceremonies, rituals or other material and non-material religious practices. Thus, along with spirituality, morality, philosophy and other canonical beliefs, culture also aids the religion in its objective which is to find the real meaning and purpose of life. But culture also influences these elements of religion such as its philosophy, its religious text and even moral beliefs.
- From the perspective of culture, the religious aspect of culture is one amongst many elements defining it but indeed a vital one. Thus, the aspect of religion which is bereft of the external trappings and is the soul of religion can also be said to be the soul of culture; for culture without that element which defines the real purpose of life, is akin to only a body bereft of life.
- To conclude, religion and culture can be said to be distinct elements of human civilisation albeit all having a deep interconnect.

2. What do you understand by the term nation and what are its elements? Do you consider culture to be an essential element of nationhood? Discuss in the context of modern nations and particularly in the Indian context.

Points to be included

- The modern concept of a nation and nationhood is only a few centuries old. Nationhood is usually understood as a large group of people domiciled in a geographical unit and united by a common political/administrative order, law, culture, common history, economic order and language. Other uniting characteristics could be commonality of race, religion, ethnicity etc.
- From the modern perspective, the intermingling of races and freedom of faith and belief has rendered, race, religion and ethnicity meaningless as defining factors for nationhood. Similarly, the multitude of spoken languages in many modern nations does not make commonality of spoken/official language as a necessary condition for nationhood.
- Thus modern day nations can be recognised by its people domiciled in a geographical area, united by legal/political order, culture, history and economic activity. However, exceptions and marginal variations would exist and a watertight definition may not be possible. Thus, while in countries like U.S.A., European nations, Japan, etc language has been a common factor, for many South Asian nations and India in particular, the same cannot be true.
- Further, while countries like India, China, Japan, Egypt and Turkey boast of a long and a common history, the national state of Singapore or of Australia does not have this vital element to define its nationhood. Even U.S.A has a relatively lesser history of only a few centuries.
- In the Indian context, India is a well-defined geographical entity with partly natural boundaries. The Constitution, the common history, economic singularity and its culture are the factors uniting the people which are otherwise characterised by different religions, languages, race, ethnicity etc. Thus, Indian culture plays an important role in defining Indian nationhood. However, Indian culture has its own regional, social, linguistic and other variations too. Thus, pluralism and unity in diversity remain the cornerstone of Indian culture which is also the hallmark of Indian nationhood.

3. The town planning and drainage system of the Indus Valley Civilisation was reflective of an evolved urban culture. Discuss.

Points to be included

- Archaeological discoveries indicate existence of a number of urban centres viz. Harrappa, Mohenjodaro, Dholavira, Ganeriwala, Rakhigarhi, Lothal, Kalibangan etc.
- Well preserved **city of Mohenjodaro** is reflective of an advanced town planning.
- Division of town into **upper town or citadel** and a larger lower town is indicative of division of urban society into two parts. The citadel was built on raised platform with high walls. Lower town was built on lower ground but walled to keep flood water away.
- The entire town was well planned with streets running north-south and east- west in **grid like pattern**. The corners of roads were rounded to enable movement of heavy vehicles.
- An advanced drainage system was found with houses having private wells, bathrooms etc. The drains were underground running from houses to main drain, with sumps at regular intervals to enable their cleaning, indicating substantial municipal advances.
- Town planning and architecture is also evident in domestic houses which centred around a courtyard with rooms built around it.
- The existence of **great bath, great granary, dockyard at Lothal, a script, several types of seals** indicating flourishing trade, weights, and measures (in binary nature) pottery, artifacts etc all indicate the existence of an advanced and flourishing urban culture.

4. Did the Indus Valley Civilisation have kingship as a form of government? Support your answer by citing appropriate archaeological evidences.

Points to be included

- Archaeological discoveries of the Indus Valley Civilisation show **existence of uniformity in town planning**, viz, Upper town (citadel) and lower town, arrangement of streets etc is noted to be similar in different excavations.
- Further, it is noted that there is **uniformity in Harappan bricks** which had same ratio of length, breadth and height and uniformity in seals and weights,s although they were found in different places/not produced in the same centre.
- The existence of town planning and establishment of settlements near the source of raw material, is also noted in various excavations.
- All of the above point to existence of **some kind of central authority** and some form of governance.
- Lack of discovery of large and distinct structures such as palaces as found in Egypt and Mesopotamia suggest that the central authority may not have been a monarch or a king. However the discovery of the statue of a bearded man named as the priest king suggest to the contrary.
- As such existence of central authority or some form of governance can be assumed but its exact form cannot be concluded.

5. The Vedic philosophy of the Aryans was ritualistic in nature involving propitiation of the elements of nature. Discuss.

Points to be included

- The Vedas are said have been composed in the period 1500 BCE to 600 BCE with the *Rig Veda* being the earliest. The other Vedas being the *Yajur Veda, Sama Veda* and *Atharva Veda.* Each of the Vedas are said to comprise four layer or parts which were the Samhitas, the Brahmanas, the Aranyakas and the Upanishads.
- The Rigveda contained hymns or Suktas (around 1028 in number) for **propitiation of various deities**. The earliest deities were elements of nature viz. Agni, (god of fire), Indra (god of thunder and rain), Varuna (god of celestial oceans) Soma etc. Similiarly, *Yajur Veda* is a compilation of verses or mantras chanted in various rituals/offerings by priests. It prescribed modalities for conduct of different Yajnas and rituals. The *Sama Veda* was a book of chants and hymns notated as melodies.
- **Thus early Vedic texts contained shuktas and hymns which were ritualistic in nature meant for sacrifices and yajnas for propitiation of elements** of nature. These ritualistic hymns are contained in the initial layers of Vedas which are Samhitas and Brahmanas. Together they comprise the *Karma Kanda* or the ritualistic portion of the Vedas.
- However, the later layers of Vedas viz. Aranyakas and Upanishads which were also referred as *Jnana Kanda* or knowledge portion of the Vedas contain philosophical and metaphysical questions. It deals with questions such as nature of god, origin of universe, Brahma, Atma etc. The Upanishads in particular are considered to be revelatory of truth or knowledge and are also referred as *Ved-Shirsha* or *Vedanta* (end of the Vedas).They often contain the philosophical and metaphysical issues in form of a dialogue between a guru and *shishya.*
- Thus while the *Karma Kanda* or action portion of the Vedas contains the ritualistic aspect of Vedas (also referred as *Poovra-Mimansa* or former inquiry) the latter portion of the Vedas or (Uttara Mimansa – latter enquiry) referred as *Jnanakand* or knowledge portion is a repository of philosophical and metaphysical knowledge.

6. The Buddhist thoughts and philosophy were a marked departure from the Vedic Hindu philosophy. Critically examine the statement.

Points to be included

- The Buddha's teaching emerged as a separate religion called Buddhism as distinct from Vedic Hinduism. Both vied for the same social space, till Buddhism was gradually pushed out from the Indian society.
- The following of **middle path** of neither indulgence nor extreme asceticism along with the four noble truths and the eightfold path form the core of the Buddhist philosophy. It rejected the orthodox Brahmanism, idol worship and ritualism which tended to symbolise the early Vedic culture. Its concept of **Ahimsa** particularly, **rejection of animal sacrifices,** was different from the extant practices of the Vedic societies.

- Although Vedic philosophy and Buddhism were in agreement over certain metaphysical concepts, viz. cycle of birth and death and rebirth, *karmic* philosophy and practising good *karma* to free the soul from the cycle of rebirth (viz. to attain Nirvana), it propounded different means to attain it. While ritualism and sacrifices were considered essential by a school of Hinduism and asceticism by another school, Buddhism rejected both and emphasised on the middle path.
- Further, the Vedic philosophy propounds the existence of god as Brahma in different schools of thought. However, Buddhism does not believe in god as a creator of universe or an eternal or unchanging soul. However, Buddhist texts and teaching do not contain any express denial of god.
- However, some philosophical similarities can be noted in Vedanta and Samkhya philosophy with Buddhism. The former schools of philosophy reject the ritualistic path and emphasise on right knowledge for attaining salvation.
- Thus, except for some basic elements of philosophy, Buddhism was different from Vedic philosophy in its approach, particularly on issues of ritualism, idolatry, Brahmancial, orthodoxy asceticism and its approach of middle path for salvation.

7. The Jain and Buddhist teachings lead to emancipation of downtrodden and spread education, art and culture amongst the masses. Discuss.

Points to be included

- Both Jainism and Buddhism preached non-violence and equality of all beings. They were opposed to varnashram dharma and Brahmanical supremacy. They admitted **bhikshus (monks) in their order without any caste distinction** and as such provided a means for emancipation of the down trodden. While the *shudras* did not have religious and educational rights in the fold of Hinduism which did not prescribe for them any means and had no hope of attaining salvation, no such distinction was made in Buddhism and Jainism.
- With the emphasis on non-violence and opposition to ritualistic sacrifices, Buddhism and Jainism in particular, influenced Hindu thoughts and social practices, thus reducing killings of animals and also reducing the significance of *Yajnas*/rituals. The focus of Hindu thoughts was brought back on core values such as the Vedantic thoughts and Samkhya philosophy, which otherwise were mired in ritualism and orthodoxy.
- Buddhism and Jainism **spread their teaching in the language ofthe masses** which was in Pali and Prakrit (respectively.). This enabled the spread of religious philosophy which otherwise was restricted to Brahmans and select sections of the society.
- **Teachings in vernacular language, reading of religious scriptures and education thus spread** to non Brahmanical order also. While earlier contribution to literature arts, crafts etc. came from the Brahmanical section of the society, the Buddhist and Jain contribution was inclusive of all sections as seen from the works of Ajanta.

  Thus it can be concluded that Buddhism and Jainism did provide for emancipation of the masses. They also were instrumental in reducing the emphases on idolatry ritualism and animal sacrifices. Further, they helped in bringing back the emphasis of Hindu religious thoughts on Vedantic philosophy. But it did not alter the Varnashram structure or purge Hinduism of the above practices altogether.

8. Rock-cut architecture in ancient India was the epitome of Indian art and architecture and reflected the religious thought and philosophy. Do you agree?

Points to be included

- Rock cut architecture refers to the creation of structures and objects of art by cutting and removal of stone from solid natural rock. Over 1500 rock cut architectures/structures survive today from ancient times most of which are of religious origin. The Barabar caves (near Gaya) pertaining to the 3rd century BCE (of Mauryan period) is the oldest example of rock-cut architecture while the Kailasa temple at Ellora (built by Rashtrakutas in the 8th& 29th century) was among the last and grandest of rock cut structure representing the culmination of a millennia long expertise. The other important rock cut structures were the Ajanta caves, Elephanta caves, Kanaheri caves, Guantapalle caves, Nasik caves, Bhaja caves, Mahabalipuram rock cut *rathas* amongst many others.
- The subjects of the architecture ranged from Buddhist chaityas and viharas to images of Buddha, Boddhisatvas, Hindu gods and goddesses and Jain Tirthankaras. Thus these architecture represented different religious thoughts and incorporated different art forms.
- The **Ajanta caves** which contained Buddhist motifs contains the world famous mural paintings in cave no. 12, 16 & 17. The most famous being the images of Buddha with Rahul and Yashodhara, the image of an apsara and the image of *Padmapani* Boddhisatva. The paintings use natural tones and limited colours and reflect the grandeur of ancient art of paintings of murals. Further the carving of image of Buddha's *Mahaparinibbana* is another masterpiece.
- The **Ellora caves** built from 5th to 11th century CE represented a confluence of Buddhist, Brahmanical and Jain subjects. They represented different styles of architecture and craftsmanship. The Buddhist caves contain images of Buddha guarded by *Vajrapani* and *Padmapani* and images of Boddhisatvas. The image of Gajasur Shiva and images of Vishnu are found in the Hindu Dashavtara cave
- The **Kailashnatha temple** (cave no. 16) cut out of a single piece of rock is the largest monolithic temple representing engineering and architecture at its best and its confluence with the religious philosophy. Some of the caves at Ellora also contained Jain structures.
- The **Elephanta** caves originally believed to be a Buddhist site but its latter images are of Shaivite faith. Its most famous sculpture being the large *Trimurti* or *Maheshmurti* image. The sculptures show slenderness with a unique light and dark effect. The **Kanaheri caves** contained 108 rock cut Buddhist structure mostly viharas. The image of *Avlokiteshwar* is quite prominent.
- Besides, a number of other rock cut structures exist which were constructed on religious lines and reflected the religious thought. They depicted the dexterity and craftsmanship of painting and sculpture skills. There were great engineering feats too, as in the case of the Kailashnath temple.

9. Do you consider the Gupta age as the golden age of art, architecture and sculpture in ancient India? Give reasons in support of your answer.

Points to be included

- From the perspective of art, architecture and sculpture the ancient Indian history can be divided into four broad phases:

  (a) The Mauryan period

  (b) The post Mauryan period

  (c) The Gupta period and

  (d) the post Gupta period.

The Gupta period which extended from the 3rd century CE to the 6th century CE ushered in a new phase of growth and development in all walks of life. Historians have termed it as a golden age of Indian history as not only did art, architecture and sculpture but other areas of human knowledge like science, technology, astronomy, philosophy flourished along with rapid growth in agriculture, commerce and trade. A sound administrative/political regime ensured peace and development, taking Indian culture to great heights. The salient achievements in different fields of culture is as below.

- Art and architecture reached its zenith during this period and included Hindu, Buddhist and Jain art. The Dashavatara temple at Deogarh containing the reclining image of Lord Vishnu is a grand example of the sculpture of this age. During this period, both Gandhara and Mathura school of art flourished. The image of Vishnu at Mathura and the seated image of Buddha at Sarnath are the finest examples of sculpture. The sculpture of Varaha at Udayagiri caves is another example of great craftsmanship. The standing image of Buddha at Mathura and Buddha's bronze statue, are other art works which exemplify the artistic excellence of this period.
- Temple architecture too evolved by leaps as seen from the *Dashavatara* stone temple at Deogarh and *Chaturmukhlinga* Shiva temple at Nachna (Madhya Pradesh). Cave and rock cut sculpture flourished as evident from the Udayagiri caves and early works of the Elephanta caves.
- The ancient university of Nalanda was founded during the Gupta period. The university at its peak had over 10000 scholars from all over India and Asia. Glorious description of this university is obtained in the writings of Faxian and Xuan Zang (Chinese travellers)
- Eminent litterateurs like Kalidasa, who composed all times classics like *Abhigyana Shakuntalam, Meghadootam, Raghuvamsam* etc. belonged to this period. Other great playwrights and poets who enriched Sanskrit literature include Vishakadata, Bharavi, Magha. The great names of Patanjali (who composed Yogasastra) and astronomer and mathematician Aryabhatta and Varahmihira were also a product of this age. Other eminent personalities of this period also include Vishnu Sharma and Vatsyayana who excelled in their respective fields.
- The art of music too reached great heights in this period. King Samudragupta was himself a poet and a musician and is depicted playing a Veena in one of the coins.

10. The Greek and Roman art had a profound influence on the Indian art and sculpture in the ancient India. Discuss.

Points to be included

- The ancient Indian art and architecture developed and flourished in different regions of the country in the form of different schools of Art. The most prominent of these were the (a) Gandhara School of Art (in North Western region) (b) the Mathura school of art (c) The Sarnath school of Art and (d) The Amravati School of Art.
- The **Gandhara school of Art** which developed in the first century CE during the reign of Kushana ruler Kanishka and exhibited profound Graeco-Roman influence. While the **subjects were Buddhist** including images from the life of Buddha and Bodhisatvas, the **features of the images were Hellinistic**. It was also referred as the Graeco-Buddhist School of art.

- The sculpture included many images of Buddha such as the famous Bamyan Buddha of Afghanistan. The images of Buddha are standing or seated depicting different *mudras*. The expression is serene. Curly hair, sharp features of eyes, ears, lips and absence of fleshy heaviness are typical features of these sculptures. The drapery of folds of cloth create an image of transparency. A high degree of craftsmanship is depicted in these figures which have a strong resemblance to Greek sculptures.
- The images of Gandhara Buddha was influenced by Hellenistic realism which bears the influence of Persians, Sycthians and Parthians models. These influences are seen in depiction of Buddha as a man-god, with wavy hair, extensive drapery, sandals, which were common features of Greek-god sculptures. Even materials such as stucco and plaster commonly observed in Greek art was seen in the Gandhara Art.
- However, such Graeco Roman influence was limited to the Gandhara School of Art. The Mathura, Amravati and Sarnath Schools of Art were indigenous schools and did not have Hellinistic influence.
- The Mathura images of Buddha were distinct from that of Gandhara. They had typical boldness, images were large with faces round and smiling. Besides, Vaishnavite and Shaivite images were also made later. The Sarnath Buddha had transparent drapery with halo around Buddha being less ornamental. The Amravati school too had images of Buddha as well as that of Hindu gods and goddesses. However these lacked the Graeco Roman influence.
- Over the period of time the images of the indigenous schools too evolved. The images of the 3rd and 4th century CE showing reduction in fleshiness, refinement of features, greater transparent quality of drapery etc. Thus these refinements suggest incorporation of some features of Hellinistic art.

11. The Dravidian literature reached great heights in ancient India. Discuss by citing appropriate examples.

Points to be included

- The Dravidian literature refers to the compositions in Southern India in Tamil, Telugu, Kannada and Malayalam languages. Each has a large body of literary compositions pertaining to ancient India.
- The Tamil language is considered to be the oldest among the Dravidian languages and closest to Sanskrit. A vast body of Tamil literature was composed in the period 300 BCE to 300 CE referred to as the Sangam literature. This is a compilation of 18 works, including eight of prose, 12 of poems. The latter are a compilation of works nearly 473 poets including the famous poet Avvaiyar.
- This period also referred as the Sangam age, saw the composition of Tamil grammar *Tolkapiyyam* and composition of the *Thirukural* by Thiruvalluvar. These include 1330 Kurals which enunciate precepts to guide humanity to a noble living.
- Besides, Tamil literature is known for the twin epics *Sillapadhikaram* and *Manimekalai* and also for the rich body of works of Alwars and Nayanars.
- The Telugu literature comprised some notable works. These include Nannaya's *Mahabharatam*(1030 CE), works of Lingayats (Virashaivas), sages Nachna Somanathas' *Uttarhari Vamsam*.

- In Kannada, *Dharmanathapurana* is a famous text on the life of the15[th] Tirthankara. Another famous literary work is *Kavirajamarga* written by Nriputanga Amoghvarsha (10 century CE). Pampa also referred as Father of Kannada literature, composed *Adi Purana* and *Vikramarjuna-Vijaya*. The three litterateurs Pampa, Ponna and Ranna are also referred as *Ratnatraya* (or three gems) of Kannada literature.
- The Malayalam language and its literature developed in the latter half of the first millenia. It included works like *Kokasandisan* and *Bhasa Kautilya* (a commentary on *Arthashashtra*)

12. Temple architecture in ancient India was an evolved science. Discuss.

Points to be included

- In ancient India the free standing temple structures began to emerge only around the fifth century C.E. These included temples like NachnaKuthara and Deogarh temple. These initial temples were simple structures consisting of a veranda, a hall and a shrine in the rear. However in the next 500-600 years the science of temple architecture evolved considerably. This period saw the construction of architectural and engineering masterpieces like the Brihadeeswarar temple of Thanjavur, the tallest and the largest temple and the Kailashnath temple at Ellora-the largest monolithic temple in the world.
- These later temples were constructed out of rock and often had complex geometrical shapes. This required indepth knowledge of architecture. Besides, these heavy structures required a solid and strong foundation. The trabeate style of construction with beams and columns also required sound engineering knowledge and skills.
- The temple design and architecture of construction was also a documented science with well established features including the *garbha-griha, shikhar or vimana, mandapa and the vahana.* In all these elements, a sense of proportion and geometry in form of shapes such as circles, square or curves was visible. Depending upon the shape and structure of the basic elements, the temples in ancient India could be divided into three distinct categories; (a) the **Nagara** style of the **North India**. (b) the **Dravidian** style of the **South India** temple architecture. (c) the **Vesara** style containing a **mix of both** the architectures.

  The temples also had certain intrinsic, or basic architectural features which were:

  The Garbha-griha: Literally meaning the womb-chamber, the *garbhagriha* was the sanctum where the idol of the main deity was located.
- **The Shikhar and the Vimana** – Just above the *garbha-griha,* the temples had a large spire or a tower like structure. In **North Indian temples** these spires/towers were called ***shikhar*** and they had a curving shape. While in the **South Indian temples** (Dravida style) these are called **Vimanas**. These had a pyramid-like shape. Construction of such shapes and large size structures required sound knowledge of geometry and civil constructional science as well.
- **The Mandapa** –or the colonnaded hall was present before the *garbha- griha* just inside the entrance of the temple. This was a typical feature of temples in Dravida style. It often contained a large number of pillars required to it. Another feature was the *vahana* which refers to the abode of the deity.

- The temples of Brihadeeswara was an epitome of engineering feat. This had the tallest vimana 70m high and had a monolithic shikhar atop which is a massive 80 tonne stone. Similarly the Kailashnath temple was a monolithic structure carved from a single mountain following the top down approach requiring great engineering skills and precision. Such knowledge of geometry and construction science was also evident in many rock cut temples such as Kailashnath, Pancharathas of Mahabalipuram, Buddhist structures such as chaityas and viharas.
- Thus ancient temple construction was an evolved engineering and architectural science incorporating with it elements of sculpture and religion.

13. The Bhakti movement was a reaction to the Brahmanical orthodoxy and rigidity in caste system. Do you agree?

Points to be included

- The emergence of Bhakti movement first took place in southern India where the Alwars and Nayanars preached devotion and began the Vaishanavite and Shaivite movements respectively. However, a larger scale Bhakti movement began to spread to northern and western India and other parts of India only in the 13th century and later.
- The general characteristic of Bhakti movement was devotion to God as a means to attain salvation. It emphasised on equality of mankind and was inclusive. It also professed salvation to women and the marginalized. It dispensed the need for rituals, attacked dogmas, brahmancial superiority and prescribed surrender to god by Bhakti for attaining salvation. The need for elaborate rituals and sacrifice was all dispensed with. Thus, it provided an **inclusive platform** to the marginalised sections of society due to its emphasis on **equality of mankind**. It also **provided scope for salvation to all** including women, artisans, weavers, cultivators and untouchables. Thus, **it appealed to a large underprivileged section of society** where it gained popularity and emerged as a religious thought.
- Thus the Bhakti movement was indeed opposed to the extant orthodoxical religion, particularly the caste hierarchy and Brahmanical order. This socio-religious ferment provided the appropriate ground for it to emerge as a movement for reform of the Hindu society. Thus the Bhakti movement was partly a **response to the Brahmancial orthodoxy and rigidity in the caste system** as several factors led to its emergence and spread.
- The **stagnation and decline in Buddhism and Jainism** owing to pollution in their own thought (viz. emergence of tantric Buddhism-Vajrayana etc) **led to disenchantment of masses from them**. This enabled the emergence of a new religious thought based on devotion.
- Further, the earlier reforms in Hindu society brought about by Vedantic saints and thinkers like Shankaracharya (Advaitism) Ramanuja (Vishisht Advaita) and Madhavacharya (Dvaitavad) also prepared the ground for emergence of the Bhakti movement. **Political patronage** was another factor helping in its growth, (eg. the support of Chola kings in Tamil Nadu to the Shaivite movement). While these movements sought the royal support for seeking land grants for construction of temples etc, the support of royalty to these movements helped the dynasties to be perceived as spiritual and religious. At times, they were also keen to seek the support of the eminent saints associated with the movement.
- Thus a mix of factors led to emergence of Bhakti movement with Brahmanical orthodoxy and caste rigidity being among the most important reasons.

14. The Indo Sarcenic or Indo-Islamic architecture was substantially different from the ancient Indian architecture in terms of aesthetics, structural features and practical utility of structures. Discuss.

Points to be covered

- The glimpses of ancient Indian architecture is seen in the grand temples, chaityas, viharas and rock cut structures which survive to this day. However, these structures were based on brackets, beams and pillars to support the flat roofs or at times the vaults and small domes. Thus the ancient Indian architecture was characterised by trabeation (i.e use of beams as opposed to arches or vaulting).
- The Islamic influence ushered in an era of use of arches to support large domes. The arches were constructed with *voussoirs* (series of interlocking blocks) and fitted with keystones. The domes rested on pendentives and squinches which enabled large spaces to be pillar free. Thus in Indo-Islamic or Indo-Sarcenic architecture, there was a shift in style from trabeate to archuate (based on arches & domes). The need for large spacious column-free domed structure was a practical necessity for large congregation and community offering of prayers in Islam.
- Other notable features were use of Minars and Minarets, use of lime-mortar in construction which was not only used as a plaster but as a base for decoration which was incised into the surface.
- Islamic influence was also visible in the surface decoration and finishing, Jalli works and Pietra dura. The surfaces of structures were covered with calligraphy works, geometrical patterns, some amount of floral work and Arabesque patterns. The Jalli works were perforated stones or latticed screens in the form of an ornamental pattern. '**Pietra dura** involved inlay work wherein precious/ semi-precious gems and stones were cut and inlaid in the walls.
- Use of **gardens, fountains and water works** especially in later Mughal prominent monuments was another feature. These would often be in *charbagh* style.
- A variety of new structure too came up which were based on the socio religious and political need. These included the palaces and forts the Jama Masjids (main mosques of cities and town where people congregate), smaller mosques, dargahs. Besides Minars, Kos Minars, sarais, caravan sararismadarsas and hamams were also constructed.

15. Murals were a pan-India art form which were a true reflection of the religion and culture of the ancient Indian society. Discuss.

Points to be included

- India has a rich and ancient tradition of murals painted on walls and ceilings of caves, temples and palaces. They date from 2nd century BCE as in case of Ajanta murals (2nd century BCE to 7th CE) to 18th century as in case of Kerala murals (16th to 18th Century CE). Thus they span a period of two millennia.
- Murals have been discovered in several places. These include Ajanta and Ellora in Central India in Badami caves, Kanchipuram temple, Tirumalapuram temple, Virupaksha temple, Lepakshi temple and in several temples and palaces in Southern India. Thus murals had a large geographic presence if not a pan-India one.

- The subjects of the murals varied. The most famous Ajanta murals were predominantly Buddhist in nature and included the images of Buddha and Boddhistavas, scenes from *Jatakas* and *Avadanas*. These include the famous paintings of Buddha with Yashodhara and Rahul and that of Padmapani and Vajrapani. However, scenes of dancing girls, an *apsara;* a lady doing her makeup, mythical birds, animals, geometrical patterns etc. were also painted. Thus, the images were not only Buddhist but secular in nature too and depicted a wide variety of subjects.
- Murals at Ellora caves were found in Hindu and Jain caves. The better preserved ones are in the Kailasa temple. The painting of Shiva as Nataraja and that of the flying *apsaras* are the most famous.
- The murals in South India pertain to different regimes and dynasties. viz. Pallavas, Pandyas, Cholas, Nayaka period, Vijaynagar and the Kerala murals. In these murals predominantly the subjects were Hindu gods and goodness, anecdotes from the epics mythologies etc. Some of the prominent murals are that of Lord Vishnu, in Badami caves, female divinity in Panamali, Nataraja-Shiva of Chola murals in Brihadeeswara temple, scenes and paintings of life of Mahavira at Thiruparakunram, scenes from *Krishna-leela* at Chengam. Thus, the subjects of these murals were largely taken from the socio religious landscape.
- The style of painting of murals was also quite varied, while the Ajanta paintings are notable for their large spread, use of limited colours and natural tones, the Ellora paintings were characterised by rectangular panels with wide borders, sharp and elongated features, angular bent of arms, protruding eyes. Similarly, each style of the painting had its own uniqueness reflective of the region and the culture of the times.

16. The Vijayanagara empire saw the golden age of literature and art in Southern India. Elucidate with appropriate examples.

Points to be included

- The Vijayanagara empire established by Harihara1 and Bukka-Raya flourished from the 14th century to the early 17th century. It reached its zenith during the reign of Krishnadevaraya when it covered the whole of southern India peninsula and was truly a golden age for literature and art in Southern India.
- This period saw eminent poets like Srinatha (Telugu), Chamarasa (Kannada) Kumar Vyasa (Kannada), Gunda Dimdima (Sanskrit) who were patronized by king Deva Raya II (1424-1446). The latter himself was an eminent litterateur who composed works like. *Sobagina Sone* and *Amruka* (in Kannada) and *Mahanataka Sudhanidhi* (Sanskrit). This period is also referred as the *Prabadh* period in literature of Southern India and literature of Tamil, Telugu, Kannada and Sanskrit all flourished.
- King Krishnadevaraya (1509-1529) was also an accomplished poet and composed *Amukata Malayada* an epic poem in Telugu, considered a master piece, besides other works such as *Madalasa Charita, Satyavadu Parinaya, Rasmanjari* and *Jambavati Kalyana*.
- In the period the famous Tamil poet Harihara who wrote an exposition on Vaishnavism and Shaivism. Arunagirinathar, a Tamil saint poet composed *Thiruppugazh*. Other prominent poets include Allasani Pedanna (also known as *Andhra Kavita Pitamah*), Nandi Thimmana (composed *Paryatha Paharanam*) Mallana (composed *Raja Shekhara*)

- The architecture too reached great heights as evident from the structures of its capital in Hampi (now a UNESCO World Heritage site). The architecture had influence of both the Dravida style as well as the Islamic style. Gopurams which in other architectural styles were usually in one side (front), were built in all sides and similarly, more than one *mandapa* was built. The temples, walls and pillars were decorated with intricate carvings.
- Many splendid structures were erected in Hampi which include the Vittala temple, the stone chariot (at Vittala temple), Virupaksha temple, lotus palaces, *Pushakarnis* (water tanks etc). Other famous temple structures include those of Kolar, Sringeri (in Karnataka) Lepakshi, Tirumala, Venkateshwara and Srikalahasti (in Andhra Pradesh), Kumbakonam, Kanchi and Srirangam (in Tamil Nadu).
- Another significant achievement was the construction of a great cosmopolitan city of Hampi including many secular structures which included Islamic features such as arches, domes and vaults.
- Paintings of this period too were evolved with face and body figures being in proportion and objects and human figures depicted in two dimension. These include images of *Ramayana* and *Mahabharata* adorning the ceiling of Virupaksha temple, the Dashavtara painting and scenes depicting marriage of Parvati and Shiva at Virupaksha Temple (Hampi), *Shivapurana* murals at Lepakshi temple and a number of murals at Tiruparakunram temple (near Tiruchirappalli).
- The patronage of Vijaynagara empire also enabled Carnatic music to evolve. Further, the art of making bronze sculptures (as seen in Devi statues of Vijaynagara), and stone sculptures (as evident in the numerous sculptures of Hampi) too reached great heights during this period.

17. The Mughal regime brought about the integration of Hindu and Islamic culture and ushered the Hindustani culture. Do you agree?

Points to be included

- The Islamic influence on the Indian culture began with the establishment of the Delhi Sultanate in the 13th century CE. This influence is seen in architecture such as Quwwat-Ul-Islam mosque. Qutab Minar, Adhai Din Ka Jhopra etc. However they bore primarily an Islamic influence and little integration with it of the extant local art and architecture was made.
- Some assimilation of the Islamic and Indian culture took place in the development of Hindi or Urdu as an admixture of Persian and local western Hindi dialect. Similarly, spiritual integration in the Bhakti and Sufi movements was also seen. Musicians like Amir Khusaru brought about some evolution of new forms of music such as Khayal. However, none of these had any institutional support or an administrative push.
- Substantial and institutional integration of the two cultures began during the Mughal regime. Its rulers who approached the country and its social ethos differently than the previous regimes. They came in India not as a transitory outsider but made an effort to merge and integrate with the society and rule as its own. This was particularly true about the reign of Akbar which led to the intermingling of cultures and emergence of the Hindustani culture.
- This fusion of culture was evident in numerous aspects of art, architecture language and literature. In architecture the Mughal architecture emerged which was influenced by the Hindu style and assimilated many local elements such as *chatris* and *chajjas*. These are evident in Jama Masjid and Panch Mahal at Fatehpur Sikri (capital of Akbar). The Jama Masjid at Champaner, Gujarat,

is another excellent example of integration of the Hindu and Islamic architecture. It contains numerous artwork and ornamentation of the mosque and tomb with motifs of Sun, diamonds, lotus, pots and vines etc. Similarly, the Hindu architecture too incorporated the arches and domes in its structure. This is best seen in the Vijaynagara empire structure at Hampi, the Sikh structures such as Golden Temple (which had prominent domes) and even some Rajput palaces and forts.

- In language and literature, the influence of Persian as a language of administration became established. This led to a substantial spread of knowledge of Persian among the Hindu subjects, many of whom became prominent Persian writers. Translation of Hindu texts such as *Ramayana* and *Mahabharata* into Persian also took place. Dara Shikoh who was deeply interested in Hindu philosophy had translated in Persian, The Gita, Upanishads and Yoga Vashishtha. He himself authored *Majma Ul-Bahram* (meeting place of two oceans) which was a comparative study of Hindu Muslim mystic philosophy.
- Many forms of music such as Dhrupad, Dhamar, Dadra etc. emerged or became popular during the Mughal period. Dhrupad is said to have emerged from Dhruvpad, an earlier form of music. Its exponents the Dagars were partronised by Mughals. Akbar himself partronised exponents like Haridas, Tansen and Gopal Das.
- A new form of painting of Mughal school emerged which influenced the extant Rajput schools with its technique, use of vibrant colours and perspective.
- But the most important cultural confluence was brought about by Akbar's effort to integrate the two faiths. He removed the *Jaziya* tax on Hindus, appointed many Hindu kings like Raja Todar Mal (revenue system head) and Raja Man Singh (general of Akbar) and married a Hindu princess. He even propounded the faith of Din-e-Ellahi as a synthesis of the best elements of different faiths. Thus in a true sense the Mughal regime and in particular the reign of Akbar, led to elimination/ reduction of the feeling of alienation of the subjects of majority faith vis-à-vis the ruler who was of a different faith. This enabled building of bridges across the two communities, intermingling of cultures and emergence of the Hindustani culture. However, this confluence began to disintegrate with the divisive policies of Aurangzeb.

18. The socio-religious reforms of the nineteenth century ushered a renaissance in the Indian society and particularly in Hinduism. Do you agree?

Points to be included

- The 19th century saw the emergence of a number of socio-religious reform movements. These included the Brahmo Samaj, Young Bengal movement, Prarthana Samaj, Arya Samaj, Theosophical Society which brought sweeping changes in the Hindu society.
- However the reforms were not limited to Hinduism alone. The Aligarh Movement, Ahamadiya Movement and Deobandi Movement amongst Muslims, the Sikh reforms and Parsi reforms were also aimed at spread of education and targeted numerous social evils and religious orthodoxy.
- The Brahmo Samaj (founded in 1828), spearheaded by Raja Ram Mohan Roy was the earliest of these movements. It targeted social evils like *sati,* female infanticide, child marriage, caste systems and Brahmanical orthodoxy. As a result of the persistent efforts of Raja Ram Mohan Roy and the Brahmo Samaj, *sati* was declared as a punishable offence and Abolition of Sati Act of 1829 was passed.

- The Young Bengal movement founded by Henry Vivian Derozio emphasised on free thinking and supported the rights and education of women. It opposed caste system, idol worship and superstitions. Similarly, the Prathana Samaj supported and worked for widow remarriage. The Arya Samaj movement emphasized on Vedantic philosophy and teachings, while the Ramakrishna Mission aimed at spiritual rejuvenation, spread of education and Vedantic thought and service to mankind.
- Thus the various reform movements targeted social evils, supported the cause of women (like abolition of *sati*, child marriage, support of widow remarriage, opposed the Brahmanical orthodoxy and caste system. Further they emphasised on essence of Hinduism and Vedantic thoughts. Their efforts also led to enactment of numerous legislations which supported the movement and targeted the social evils. These included, 'The Abolition of Sati Act', legalisation of widow remarriage via 'The Widow Remarriage Act of 1856', inter-caste and inter-communal marriages getting the sanction of law as per 'The Special Marriages Act 1872', child marriages being deterred due to enactment of 'Age of Consent Act 1891' and 'Sharda Act of 1929' (which prohibited marriage of girls below 14 and of boys below 18).
- The caste system too became less stringent with movements such as 'Self Respect Movement' opposing it. Besides stalwarts like Ishwar Chandra Vidyasagar (who relentlessly supported the education of girl child) Jyotiba Phule (who opposed caste system and supported widow remarriage) too brought reforms in the Hindu society in different regions.
- Amongst the Muslims, the Aligarh Movement pioneered by Sir Syed Ahmed Khan was the most important one. It aimed at imparting modern and scientific education to Muslims, to embrace modern ideas and be broad minded. He founded the Mohammedan Anglo Oriental College of Aligarh and worked for education of women and removal of *purdah*.
- A century of reforms indeed brought sweeping changes in the Hindu society and other religious faiths. Thus these can truly be referred to as a socio-religious renaissance.

19. Many of the classical dances of India were a means of propitiation of deities or an expression of human devotion as a form of an art. Do you agree?

Points to be included

- The majority of Indian classical dances trace their origin to Bharata's *Natyashashtra*. Over the centuries they have evolved and diversified tremendously. Nevertheless most of these dances retain their devotional character and temple origin in some form of artistic expression, be it beginning with invocation of deity or the very subject of dance being based on religious or mythological anecdotes and characters.

  This is evident from the following features of the classical dances.
- **Sattariya dance :** This classical dance form of Assam has its origin in Krishna Bhakti Vaishnavism. It is attributed to the 15th century Bhakti saint Sri Sankardev who propagated the Vaishanava faith through it. The very word Sattariya originated from *Sattara* which were monasteries or temples. The dances were performed by the Vaishnava monks. Thus Sattariya is indeed a ritualistic dance having temple origin.

- **Manipuri dance** : This dance too has a strong Vaishnavite influence. It also includes performances which are based on Shaivism, Shaktism and Krishna Leelas. The Manipuri dance involves three elements. The Sankirtan; which is a pure devotional form of dance; the Rasa or Rasalila depicting the love of Radha and Krishna and the Thang Ta, a martial art form of dance. Thus, devotional as well as mythological elements are deeply integrated in this dance.
- **Bharatanatyam** : This was essentially a temple dance which was earlier performed by the *Devadasis* in temples in the region of present day Tamil Nadu. Many temple sculptures particularly in Chidambaram temple depict this dance. The subjects of the dances are mythological, legends and spiritual ideas of Hindu texts and scriptures.
- **Kuchipudi:** This dance originated under the aegis of 17th century Vaishnava saint Siddhendra Yogi. It originated and evolved as a form of dance-drama where themes from Krishnaleela and other Vaishnava traditions are performed.
- **Odissi:** This is another dance form of temple origin. Reference to it is seen in the Bharata's *Natyashashtra* and even in the Natya-mandap(dance-hall) of Konark temple (13 century CE). The dance was performed in the temples by the *Maharis* or the *Devadasis*. Even in its modern form the *Mangal-Charan* (entry) is always followed by invocation of the deity.
- **Kathakali:** A form of dance-drama, it often includes stories from Indian epics like Ramayana, Mahabharata, Krishna Leela. It too begins with an devotional invocatory performance called *Thodayam*.
- **Kathak:** The name Kathak derived from the word *katha* or story telling became popular during Bhakti movement as a narrative of Radha-Krishna love.
- **Mohiniattam:** The dance draws its name from the mythological enchantress Mohini.

  Thus all of the classical dance forms had devotional or temple origin or were means for spreading of religious and spiritual messages or veneration of the deity. Today also they incorporate several elements of this socio-religious character as evident from the features specified above.

20. In the context of continuity of Indian culture, discuss the various cultural phases and cultural confluences of Indian society. Also bring out their poignant features.

Points to be included

- Over a period of 5000 years, Indian society has witnessed several phases of cultural evolution. Each of these phase had its own distinct features. Many of these cultural phases overlapped with each other resulting in cultural confluence and leading to emergence of new cultural traits. These cultural phases were the Indus valley culture, the Vedic culture, the Buddhist and Jain cultural influence, the Puranic culture, the Islamic influence and the Hindustani Culture, and finally European influence and the modern India culture.
- The Indus Valley culture often referred to as the fountain head of India culture was a distinct urban culture, which flourished from 3500 BCE to 2000 CE. Its unique features included an evolved town planning, modern cities, with grid like streets, efficient drainage system, walled citadel, extensive trade, evolved science and technology, flourishing arts of lead making, sculpture pottery etc. However, this culture did not have any cultural confluence with the Vedic culture which emerged around 1500 BCE.

- The Vedic culture phase lasted from 1500 BCE to 500 BCE. It could be categorised into the early and later Vedic phases. It was marked by the composition of four Vedas. Performance of the Vedic rites, propitiation of elements of nature (viz. Indra, Agni Varun etc.) characterised this culture. In the later Vedic phase, greater development of the Upanishadic philosophy took place which explored the relationship of Atma, Brahma and other metaphysical aspects.
- With the emergence of Buddhism and Jainism in the 6th century CE, a cultural confluence of the Vedic and Buddhist and Jain culture emerged. The latter were opposed to Vedic rituals, Brahmanical order, Varnashram system, idol worship and animal sacrifices which characterised the Vedic culture. Thus, a culture of equality and egalitarianism emerged in Indian society. This period from 600 BCE to 200 BCE was not only a phase of cultural confluence but also of socio-culture upheaval, as each faith vied for capturing the socio religious space.
- The next cultural phase saw the emergence of Puranic culture and the coming 700-800 years were referred as the golden phase of Hindu culture. This also coincided with the emergence of the Gupta empire. The six systems of India philosophy (Nyaya Vaishesika, Samkhya, Yoga, Poorva Mimansa and Uttar Mimansa) emerged in this phase. Compositions of Puranas also took place. The religious emphasis shifted from the Vedic gods who were elements of nature to the Trinity of Brahma, Vishnu and Mahesh. This was the second cultural confluence.
- The next cultural phase (beyond 700 AD) was marked by emergence of a wave of Bhakti in Southern India in the Alwars and Nayanars. Later the teachings of Shankaracharya, Ramanuja and Madhavarcharya led to the reformation in Hinduism, thus pushing Buddhism and Jainism out of the mainstream Indian society. It also paved the way for the emergence of the Bhakti culture.
- The Islamic influence post establishment of Delhi Sultanate created the next cultural wave. The influence of Islam was seen in different walks of life, ranging from personal faith, administration, literature, language, architecture and art. It ushered in a new cultural confluence or the Indo-Islamic phase. Development of new language Urdu took place. Use of arches and domes emerged in Indian architecture with many new structures also getting built. But the most significant was the emergence of Sufism which for the next few hundred years along with Bhakti movement had a profound influence on the socio religious and spiritual aspects of culture.
- The Bhakti movement which swept the Indian society from the 13th to 17th century created a new religious-cultural path for the Indian society. It reformed the Hindu society and shifted the spiritual emphasis on devotion. At the same time, it provided a religious alternative to Buddhism and Jainism which were on decline.
- With the advent of Mughal empire in the 16th century and particularly during the reign of Akbar, the foundations were laid for the next cultural confluence, the emergence of the Hindustani culture. This assimilated several features of Indian and Islamic culture to give shape to a relatively pan-Indian culture. The confluence was evident in architecture which included Islamic as well as Indian features, language and literature, where translations of epics like Ramayana and Mahabharata and other religious scriptures into Parsi took place. The Mughal school of painting emerged which influenced the Rajasthani and other schools. New forms of music like Dhrupad emerged under the patronage of Mughal emperors. Most importantly, a social fabric of peaceful co-existence emerged during this period which enabled the cultural confluence and Hindustani culture to take shape. However, this culture began to decline during the reign of Aurangzeb to be later over shadowed by the colonial culture.

- The next wave of cultural influence swept the country in the 18th and the 19th century owing to the colonization of India at the hands of British and other European powers. It greatly influenced the administration and law and order to begin with and brought a large part of nation under a singular authority for the first time after the reign of Akbar. The British and European culture did influence a large part of the country territorially. However, it could not permeate within the masses, as largely people did not accept it or integrate with it. Its influence was nevertheless prominent in the field of modern education, railways, post and telegraph etc. This imbibed a modern and scientific approach at least in a section of Indian society. In the cultural field the influence was indeed visible in areas like architecture, painting, literature and language etc. Thus, this was another phase of cultural confluence for India.

  The Independence ushered in a new phase of cultural regeneration. India now had the occasion to consider its continuous cultural legacy of over 5000 years. It also had the freedom to change and evolve as per the need of time and sound of its soul, which would succinctly characterise the evolution of emerging modern culture.

21. Folk art of Modern India defines the cultural landscape of the hinterland of India. Discuss citing prominent examples of folk paintings music and dances.

Points to be included

- Folk art usually refers to the traditional and indigenous cultural art forms popular in rural and non- urban areas, practised by common folk, as contrasted with elite or professional artists of the mainstream society.These art forms incorporate hand tools and techniques rather than mechanical facilities, and lay greater emphasis on utilitarian and decorative aspects of art rather than on pure aesthetics.
- The Indian folk art encompasses,folk paintings,folk music,folk dances and theatre and handicrafts inter alia other art forms. All of the above art forms have diverse styles, techniques and subjects and have prospered in different regions of the country drawing from the regional and local social life, festivals, traditions values, myths etc. They are truly reflective of the cultural landscape of the Indian hinterland.
- The most popular of Indian folk paintings include the Madhubani, Warli, Kalighat, Pattachitra, Jharna, Kalamkari, Phad, Pichwai, Manjusha, Thanjavur and tribal art paintings. Each of these paintings is from a different region, incorporate different subjects and involve different painting techniques. Thus, while community life is the recurrent theme of Warlipaintings practised by the Warlitribals of Maharashtra, subjects of Ramayana and Mahabharata and Indian mythology are themes of Madhubani paintings(of Mithila region of Bihar) and Pichwai paintings (of Udaipur Rajasthan).Day to day happenings of rural life, rituals and ceremonies are captured respectively in Kalighat paintings (Kolkata) and Paitkar paintings (tribals of Jharkhand)
- Folk music has flourished in India along with the Hindustani Classical, Carnatic, light classical and popular music forms. It includes Chakri, Tappa, Hori, Wanawan, Choppati, Maand, Baul, Bihu, Pandavani, Lai Haroba, Alha, Burrakatha, Powada and Mandu amongst many others. Each of these are characterised by the style,subject and region where its practised. While Tappa is a folk song of Punjab popular amongst camel riders,Hori is sung in Uttar Pradesh on occasion of Holi. Baul is the religious folk music of West Bengal. Pandvani is the folk music and theatre narrating tales of Mahabharata and popular in Odisha, Madhya Pradesh, Andhra Pradesh and Chhattisgarh region. Bihu is the song and dance practised on the occasion of New Year in Assam when Bihu festival is celebrated. Rasiageet are sung in praise of Lord Krishna in Braj region.

- Folk and tribal dances (as contrasted with the classical dances) also encompass a great diversity in terms of regions,subjects,techniques,songs,dresses and gears of accompaniment.Raas-Leela is a theatrical dance drama of Braj region of Uttar Pradesh based on stories of Lord Krishna and his love for Radha. Bhangraand Giddaare performed in Punjab on the occasion of harvest festivals of Lohri and Baisakhi. Dumhalis performed by men of Rauf tribe in Jammu and Kashmir region wearing long colourful robes. Garba and Dandiya are dances of Gujarat practised during Navratara. Important folk dances of other regions include Raut Nacha (Chhattisgarh),Jhumar (Jharkhand),KulluNati (Himachal Pradesh),Chhau (tribals of Jharkhand,West Bengal and Odisha), Ghumar (Rajasthan),Bihu (Assam), Gambhira (West Bengal),Chhau (Odisha), Burrakatha (Andhra Pradesh), Ghumura (Odisha), Lavani (Maharashtra) Jat-Jatin (Bihar), Kunitha (Karnataka), Theyyam (Kerala), Dhekni (Goa).
- Thus folk art forms encompass varied elements of community and social life reflecting the indigenous cultural elements.

22. From company style paintings to abstracts, modern Indian paintings not only evolved in technique but absorbed and reflected the national ethos in style and subject. Discuss.

Points to be included

- The term `modern Indian painting' denotes the painting style which emerged since the mid-nineteenth century. By this period the style of miniature paintings as seen in the Mughal, Pahari, South Indian and other schools of art had started to wane and increasing British influence was seen in the Indian paintings. These were commonly referred to as the Company art.
- The mingling of the Indian style with the British influence brought out the Company style of painting. The subjects of the paintings would include Indian people, scenes of festivals and fairs, Indian flora and fauna, dancers, traders etc. A series of such paintings reflecting the market place scene was referred as Bazaar paintings. The paintings were usually water colours on paper and had a mix of naturalistic representation and the features of miniature Indian painting style.
- The advent of Raja Ravi Varma ushered in a style of painting with Indian sensibility and subjects while combining the Western/European technique. The subjects of his paintings were inspired by the characters and scenes from Indian epics of Ramayana and Mahabharata and other Indian mythologies.He used oil and water colour technique of painting and incorporated use of realism and perspective. The use of techniques like light on skin and tonal effects added to life- like quality. His most famous paintings include *Shakuntala, Hans Damayanti Samvad, Rama Conquers Varuna, Ladies in Moonlight, Jatayu Wars with Ravana* etc.
- The nationalistic fervour which was present in the early 20th century influenced the Indian paintings too and led to the emergence of what is known as the Bengal School of Art. This movement was started by Abanindranath Tagore along with E.B.Havell and Sister Nivedita. The movement emphasised on Indian subjects as well as Indian material such as tempera (rather than oil paintings) and drew inspiration from murals of ancient period and miniatures of the medieval period. Rabindranath Tagore, Gaganendranath Tagore, Nandalal Bose, Asit Haldar, M.A.R Chugtai, Kshitindranath Majumdar, Sarda Charan Ukil and Sunayni Devi were some of the notable painters associated with this movement.

- Post-independence, Indian art saw the formation of the 'Progressive Artists Group of Bombay 'with famous painters like F.N Souza, S.H Raza, M.F Hussain, K.H Ara, H.A Gade and S.K Bakre (a sculptor) as its founders. Later, eminent painters like Tyeb Mehta, Gaitonde, Manishi Dey, and Akbar Padmasee joined it. The paintings of this genre broke away from the revivalist nationalism of Bengal Art movement and set the path for medium and abstract art which synthesised Indian art tradition with Europeanmodernism.

23. Describe how folk theatre integrated different cultural elements of music, dance and drama with religious and social beliefs, mythology and history. Give examples to substantiate.

Points to be included

- Folk theatres for centuries have reflected the popular local traditions, social and religious messages, mythological and historical tales, anecdotes from epics etc in form of theatre while also involving the elements of music and dance.
- *Ram-leela* one of the most popular folk theatre forms depicts the story of Ramayana and has been practised for ages throughout the country particularly in North India during Dussehra period. *Krishna-leela* and *Raas-Leela* are popular in Braj region of Uttar Pradesh and draw anecdotes or stories from life of lord Krishna. Thus they incorporate elements of mythology and religion.
- *Nautanki* is another folk theatre of Uttar Pradesh based on folk themes, mythologies, romantic tales of local heroes etc. *Jatra* practised in West Bengal and Orissa is a musical theatre form depicting stories from epics, mythologies, historical stories and even social and political issues. *Tamasha* is the traditional theatre of Maharashtra where female actresses are the chief exponent of the dance movement in play.
- *Koodiyattam* and *Krishnattam* are popular folk theatres of Kerala. The former is based on Sanskrit theatre tradition and one is of the oldest folk theatres. It is recognised by UNESCO as intangible cultural heritage. *Therukoothu* is performed in temples of Tamil Nadu to propitiate goddess Mariamman for good harvest and rainfall.
- Other important folk theatres forms include; *Bhand Pather* (Kashmir) which involves dance, music and acting. *Swang* - (Haryana) a music based theatre, *Maach* (Madhya Pradesh), characterised by performance of song between dialogues, *Bhaona* (Assam,Bengal and Odisha) in it the story is first narrated by the sutradhar followed by the performance, *Yakshaganga* (Karnataka) stories of Ramayana and Mahabharata and other mythological are incorporated.
- Thus folk theatres combined elements of songs and dance with drama to capture anecdotes and stories from epics, mythologies, historical accounts, or even local folklore.

24. Colonial architecture was a mishmash of several styles of architecture but incorporated little of indigenous Indian elements. Do you agree with the statement? Discuss with suitable examples.

Points to be included

- The period of late 18th century onwards saw the emergence of European colonial powers and the decline of the Islamic rule and with it of the Indo-Islamic architecture. This phase also marked the beginning of what is referred as the Colonial architecture. Although the British authority had control over the largest partof Indian territory, the Portugeese, the French, the Dutch and the Danish too had smaller regions of stronghold. Thus this period saw varied influences on the Indian architecture in different parts of the country.

- The British architecture the most predominant of all can be seen in the cities of Calcutta (Kolkata) New Delhi, Madras (Chennai). It brought with itself different architectural styles referred as the Gothic, Imperial, Victorian and Renaissance etc which also incorporated the indigenous architectural features or some elements of it. The style and architecture are reflected in a variety of structures ranging from forts, palatial structures, residences, official building, churches, commemorative structures to ordinary residences,dak-bungalows etc. Victorian style- also referred as the Indo-Gothic style and Indo-Sarcenic style, incorporated elements of Gothic, Persian and some of the indigenous Indian style.
- Prominent examples include the Victoria Memorial, Fort William and Raj Bhavan in Kolkata, Victoria Terminus and Gateway of India in Mumbai, Secretariat complex in Delhi, All Saints Cathedral in Allahabad, St. Michael's Cathedral in Shimla, the city of New Delhi with the Viceroy's house, India Gate etc. (neo-Roman or neo-classical architecture.) North and South Blocks adjoining the Viceroy's House (now Rashtrapati Bhavan), the Parliament House and the Connaught Place.
- The city of Pondicherry (Puducherry) is the best example of French Architecture. The city layout was characterized by cartesian grid plan. Prominent examples include the Church of Sacred Heart of Jesus,Eglise de Notre Dame de Agnes and Eglise the Notre Dame de Lourdes.
- Portuguese architecture is seen in churches and houses of Goa which are of Iberian style. The churches typically depicted the Baroque architecture style (Renaissance architecture of Europe). Bassilica of Bom Jesus (Old Goa) is the best example of this style.
- The Dutch architecture is visible in a variety of surviving structures which include Dutch factory (in Bharuch), cemetery in Ahmedabad, Mattancherry palace in Kochi (originally built by Portuguese), David Hall residence of Dutch commander in Kochi, Fort at Kochi beach.
- Thus, colonial architecture refers to different styles of architecture flourishing in different regions and pockets and not to a distinct or singular style. While the Victorian style incorporated elements of indigenous architecture, the other styles were patently and exclusively European.

25. What do you understand by the term cultural heritage? Distinguish between tangible and intangible heritage. Why conservation of natural heritage is important?

Points to be included

- The term `cultural heritage' has been defined by United Nations Educational and Scientific Cultural Organisation (UNESCO) as the legacy of physical artefacts and intangible attributes of a group or a society that are inherited from the past generations, maintained in the present, and bestowed for the benefit of future generations. The cultural heritage can be classified as comprising(a) tangible heritage (b) intangible heritage and (c) natural heritage.
- The objects and items of cultural heritage which are physically perceptible are referred to as tangible cultural heritage. These include artefacts, monuments and historic places. As they are a reflection on the culture of the people, they are considered appropriate to be conserved. Such objects, artefacts or monuments may also be of significance from the perspective of archaeology, history, science, art and architecture, besides being of cultural significance. Tangible cultural heritage can further be subdivided into moveable and immovable heritage. Historic places, monuments etc. are immoveable elements of cultural heritage which have to be conservedin-situ, while art work, like paintings, sculptures, pottery, minor installations and other artefacts are the parts of moveable cultural heritage.

- Intangible Cultural Heritage comprises those aspects of cultural heritage which are not physically perceptible. These would include performing arts (like music, dance and drama), oral traditions and language, rituals, festive events, spiritual beliefs, social practices, knowledge and skills to produce traditional crafts, knowledge and practices concerning nature and the universe. The significance of intangible cultural heritage is not merely in the cultural expression of these elements but in the knowledge and skills which is passed on in the society from generation to generation. Such heritage is not merely traditional but often living and contemporary. Besides it may also be inclusive, representative and community based.
- Natural heritage is an important aspect of a society's cultural heritage and includes the natural environment, its flora and fauna (bio-diversity), its geological elements including mineralogical, geomorphological and paleontological (geodiversity), as well as countryside and cultural landscapes (natural features which may have cultural attributes).
- Conservation of natural heritage is important as their being representative of (i) a superlative natural phenomena or areas of exceptional natural beauty and aesthetic importance (ii) an outstanding example representing major stages of the Earth's history including the record of life, significant on-going geological processes in the development of landforms, or significant geomorphic or physiographic features.(iii) an outstanding example representing significant on-going ecological and biological processes in the evolution and development of terrestrial, fresh water, coastal and marine ecosystems, and communities of plants and animals (iv) an important and significant natural habitat for in-situ conservation of biological diversity, including those containing threatened species of outstanding universal values from the point of view of science or conservation.

26. Trace the genesis of modern Indian theatre movement, highlighting the growth and contribution of Bengali and Marathi theatre.

Points to be included

- Modern Theatre emerged in India in the 18th century during the British rule. Earlier, Indian theatre was confined to the different forms of folk theatre or to the theatre performed in the palaces of kings and royalty. However, during the British rule it emulated the model of London theatre. The first of these theatres emerged in Bengal, Maharashtra and Tamil Nadu where the metropolis cities of Calcutta, Bombay and Madras existed. Later, the regional theatre also emerged in other languages like Gujarati, Kannada, Oriya, Urdu and Hindi. However, Bengali and Marathi theatre have been at the forefront of theatre movement in India.
- The origin of Bengali theatre can be traced to the **Calcutta Theatre** (1779) which had Warren Hastings as its patron. Among the early plays staged were those by **Goloknath Das** (1795), **Prasanna Kumar Thakur** (established Hindu Rangamancha 1831) **Nabin Chandra Basu** (Jorasanko Theatre 1854) and **Dwarkanath Tagore** and **Jyotirindranath Tagore** (Jorasanko theatre), **Girish Chandra Ghosh** (1872- National Theatre), **Michael Madhusudan Dutta** (playwright of –*Meghanad Bodh Kavya*)
- Advent of **Rabindranath Tagore** was an important milestone in Bengali theatre. His plays included *Valmiki Pratibha* (first play) *Dak-Ghar, Visarjan, Chandalika* (untouchable girl) *Raktakarabi* (Blood Orleanders), *Raja, Chitrangadaand Shyama*. The plays of Rabindranath Tagore explored different manifestations of human values and heralded a theatre movement which is also referred as **Rabindra Nritya Natya**.

- Bengali theatre was not merely a means of entertainment but soon became a means of bringing **social reform** and also creating **national awakening**. Plays like Naba-Natak and Kulakulasarbasa opposed polygamy while Nil Darpan brought out the plight and exploitation of the local farmers at the hand of the planters.
- The formation of the **Indian People's Theatre Association** in 1943 (as a cultural wing of Communist Party of India) was a landmark event in the field of theatre. Stalwarts of theatre were associated with this movement and included the likes of **Bijon Chakraborty, Balraj Sahni, Prithviraj Kapoor, Utpal Dutt, Ritwik Ghatak, Salil Chaudhary Shambhu Mitra, Bijon Bhattacharya** etc. It staged plays in Nabanna (folk cultural festival of Bengal) which portrayed the Bengal famine of 1943 the plight of people and their neglect by the British and the upper class.
- In the post-independence period, Bengal also saw many eminent theatre personalities like **Badal Sarkar** (produced plays like *Basi Khabar, Sari Raat, Pratap, Juloos* etc.) **Bijon Bhattacharya** (Plays : *Nabanna, DhartiKe Lal*), Mohit Chattopadhyay etc.
- The Marathi theatre started in the middle of the nineteenth century with great playwrights being associated with it; like Vishnu **Das Bhave** (*Sita Swaymvar*) and **Anna Saheb Kirloskar** (who started AbhigyanShakuntalam theatre).The later phase of Marathi theatre saw emergence of many theatre personalities like **K. Prabhakar Khadilkar** (writer) **Bal Gandharva** (singer& actor) **Deenanath Mangeshkar**.
- In the post-independence phase too, many eminent personalities contributed to Marathi theatre. These included; **Vijay Tendulkar** (his famous plays include *Ghasiram Kotwal, Shanta Court Chalu Aahe, Sakharam Binder*), **Vijaya Mehta** (founder of Mumbai based theatre group Rangaayan along with Vijay Tendulkar), **Sriram Lagoo etc.**

27. Grant of classical language status has more to do with the antiquity, literary heritage of the language than its popularity or spread in modern times. Explain the above in context of the criteria for selection of a classical language.

Points to be included

- A policy decision was taken by the Government of India (in 2004) to select some languages as classical languages with the objective to preserve the literary heritage of such languages and to recognize and promote modern work in them. The selected languages were required to fulfill certain criterias which are:
- High antiquity of its early texts/ recorded history over a period of 1500-2000 years.
- A body of ancient literature/ texts which is considered a valuable heritage by generations of speakers.
- The literary tradition should be original and not borrowed from another speech community.
- The classical language and literature being distinct from modern, there may also be a discontinuity between the classical language and its later forms or its offshoots.
- Thus the emphasis of the policy is on the antiquity, literary heritage & tradition and distinctness of the language and literary tradition rather than on the geographical spread or even popular usage of the language .
- Till now **six Indian languages have been identified as classical languages**. These are **Tamil** (recognized in 2004), **Sanskrit** (2005), **Telugu** (2008) **Kannada** (2008) **Malayalam** (2013). **Odia** (2014) is the last language to be accorded that status.

28. What was Parallel Cinema? Trace its growth in India. Highlight their contribution in identifying social issues and in evolving the art of film making. What eventually led to the decline of this movement?

Points to be included

- The term `parallel cinema' refers to the genre of so called art movies, depicting the social and national issues of significance and challenge. These movies were influenced with the wave of cinematographic realism and naturalism; i.e depicting the reality of society as it is, even though it may seemingly be bitter or harsh. Thus, the focus of these movies was not merely popular entertainment but more on the theme and the social reality or the message it endeavoured to convey.
- In the 1930s and 1940s the movies like, *Acchut Kanya* (Franz Osten), *Neecha Nagar* (K.A Abbas), *Manoos* (V. Shantaram) fell in this category. They depicted issues related to women, untouchability and other social challenges. This movement was also influenced by the French New wave and the Japanese new wave in cinema.
- The early pioneers of social realism and parallel cinema were Bengali film makers which included stalwarts like **Satyajit Ray** (Appu trilogy; P*ather Panchali, Aparajito, Apur Sansar*), **Ritwik Ghatak** (*Jukti Tako Aar Gappo, Megha Dhaka Tara*), **Shyam Bengal** (*Ankur, Manthan, Nishant*). Some movies of 1950s such as, *Do Bigha Zameen* of Bimal Roy, *Mother India* of Mehboob Khan, *Do Aankhen Barah Haath* of **V. Shantaram** also belong the same genre albeit they tasted commercial success also.
- However, in the 1970s and early 80s the divide between the parallel and popular cinema became sharper, with not many parallel movies being a large commercial success or becoming popular as movies of general entertainment. However, they would invariably win critical acclaim. *Ankur* (1973) and *Bhumika* (1977) by Shyam Bengal, *Bhuvan Shome* (1969) and *Mrigya* (1976) and by Mrinal Sen, were some movies of this category. They have also been referred as middle cinema. Many regional movies like those by Adoor Gopalakrishanan in Malayalam also fall in this category.
- In the 1990s and 2000s the focus was again on popular entertainment. Although movies highlighting social issues and realism were made, the element of entertainment too was incorporated in them. Thus, social realism or parallel cinema as a distinct stream of movies did not flourish in this period.

Parallel cinema: Its emergence and decline

Many reasons are attributed to the emergence of parallel cinema. These include influence of social realism as also reflected in other art forms such as theatre and literature. Further, the period of post-independence was a period of transition, hope and despair. The parallel movies endeavoured to capturethese very emotions of the people. Recognition of such movies in international and national award functions too encouraged their production.

The opening of the Indian economy and the shifting of social focus and taste of masses in 1990s and 2000s brought a shift to movies of popular entertainment. The commerce of parallel cinema started becoming unviable resulting in amalgamation of social themes with entertainment and thereby bringing decline of this distinct genre of movies.

29. Weaving is a community based art form which is dying a slow death in modern times. Do you agree?

Points to be included

- The tradition of weaving and weavers has been an ancient one. This has been passed on as a family tradition and also as a community tradition from generation to generation. As a result it has grown over the centuries into a specialized community art form which is replete in colour, design, embroidery fabric etc. Be it the Kanjeevaram silk the brocade work of Varanasi, the zari work of Surat, the embroidery of Kutch or the Chikanwork of Lucknow, they have essentially been a traditional craft for a long time in the weaving communities who have taken it to the level of an art form.
- A number of such weaving communities are known for their skills. The Julahas are a weaving community found in North India, particularly in Punjab, Himachal, Jammu and Kashmir, Uttarakhand, Delhi, Rajasthan and also in Uttar Pradesh, Bihar and Jharkhand. Artisans of the Koshta community are spread over north and Deccan India, in the states of Uttar Pradesh, Bihar, Madhya Pradesh, Chhattisgarh, Maharashtra and Andhra Pradesh. Other weaving communities include Vankars in Gujarat, Salvis in Rajasthan & Gujarat, Panikas in Chhattisgarh, Jharkhand, Madhya Pradesh, Odisha and Uttar Pradesh, Mehers in Orissa, Ansaris in Uttar Pradesh, Devangas and Padmashalis in South India, Saliyas in Kerala, Khatris in Kutch among others. Thus weaving has been, and is still practised, as a community trade in almost all parts of India.
- Although the weavers were financially flourishing communities till the medieval period, today they are on the economic and social fringes. Weaving is no more an economically remunerative craft. They have to compete with machine made fabrics which are cheaper and mass produced at a much quicker pace, albeit not as intricate as the handloom products. Thus the communities and artisans engaged in weaving, dying, embroidery, hand printing and applique work are all know being pushed to the margins, although they are upholders of a living craft tradition.

30. What are the various forms of puppets in India and what are their specific features? Give example of string puppets.

Points to be included

- Puppetry has been a prominent form of entertainment theatre for centuries and even finds reference in the Tamil classic the *Silappadikaram* (1st or 2nd century BCE). Based on styles of puppetry, painting, sculpture and presentation craft, it has different traditions and forms in different parts of country which are categorized as below.
- (a) **String puppets** also referred as marionettes, are of the size of a doll. The limbs of puppets are controlled by strings. These allow greater flexibility of movement and are the most versatile of all puppet forms. String Puppets include the following;
  - (i) **Kathputli (Rajasthan) :** These stringed puppets are carved from a single piece of wood. They are covered in colourful Rajasthani costumes with exaggerated features such as large eyes, oval faces, arched eyebrows and large lips. The performance is done to the accompaniment of exaggerated version of regional music. The strings control the puppets which are tied to the fingers of the puppeteers.

(ii) **Kundhei (Orissa) :** They are made of light wood which are covered in long flowing skirts. However, they have more joints enabling greater manipulation and versatility of movement. The costumes have resemblance to those of Jatraprocession. Puppeteers also use a triangular wooden prop to which the strings are attached which enables the manipulation of puppets.

(iii) **Gombeyata (Karnataka) :** These string puppets are designed like characters from Yakshagana and prasangas (anecdotes) of Yakshaganas are enacted in them. The puppets have joints in arms, legs and hips which enable better manipulation. This is done by using props by two to three puppeteers at a time.

(iv) **Bommalattam (Tamil Nadu) :** These Puppets combine techniques of string as well as rod puppets. These are the heaviest and largest of puppets (as high as 4.5 feet) and most articulate of puppet forms.

(b) **Glove puppets :** In this form the puppets are small and are worn on hand. These are also called hand, palm or sleeve puppets. The manipulation of the puppets is done by movement of fingers and palm. Eg. *Pavakoothu* (Kerala)

(c) **Rod puppets :** Popular mostly in West Bengal and Orissa, rod puppets are much larger and are supported as well as manipulated by rods from below. Eg *Putul Natch* of West Bengal and *Yampuri* of Bihar.

(d) **Shadow puppets** involves casting of shadow of cut-out figures (of puppets) on screens and conveying the story or the message through the movement of these shadows. The puppets are flat figures cut-outs of leather, which is treated to make it translucent. These puppets are pressed against a screen with a strong light source enabling the formation of colourful shadows. Eg. *Ravan Chhaya* (Orissa), *Togalu Gombeyetta* (Karnataka)

ADDITIONAL QUESTIONS WITH HINTS

Given below are 20 more questions carefully handpicked for the Main examination. Hints to answers have been provided in form of relevant points and also as references to specific pages of this book where the topic has been dealt in detail.

1. **The principal events of the life of Buddha have been a recurring theme in Buddhist art, right from the Ashokan capital at Sarnath to the stupas of Sanchi and Amravati, and paintings in Ajanta. Discuss.**

   Hint: See pages 6.2, 6.3 of Chapter 6.

   The principal events include:

   (a) The birth (represented by elephant)

   (b) the great renunciation (represented by a horse)

   (c) enlightenment (represented by Pipal/Bodhi tree)

   (d) *Dharma Chakra Prabartana* or the first sermon (represented by a wheel or the lion-signifying a roar of truth)

(e) *Mahaparnirvana* (represented by a stupa)

- The Sarnath lion capital represents the *Dharma Chakra Prabartana*, symbolised by the four lions (roar of truth) and four wheels. Animals on the abacus also represent events in Buddha's life. The elephant represents birth of Buddha; the horse represents great renunciation, the lion – (roar of truth), represents first sermon; while the Bull symbolises strength and power of truth.
- Sanchi stupa contains many engravings/sculptures particularly on the gateway which show symbolic representation of these events such as horse, foot-prints representing Buddha, canopy under the Bodhi tree representing enlightenment stupa image representing Mahaparinibanna, Chakra-wheel representing Buddha's first sermon elephant and trees representing the birth of Buddha etc.
- Similar images are present at Amravati Stupa, which includes that of the horse, stupa, the demon Mara's assault on Buddha, and also Buddha preaching (in human form). Such images are also found at the Bharhut stupa. The Ajanta caves also depicts the famous sculpture of Buddha's Mahaparnirvana.

2. A number of Harappan seals have been discovered. What information can be gathered and inferences drawn from them about the culture of Indus Valley civilisation, particularly about the religious aspect?

Hint: See page 2.7 'Seals pottery and other artefacts' of Chapter 2.

3. The *Shaddarshanas* or the six systems of ancient Indian philosophy, although different in form, had a common underlying theme connecting the philosophies. Do you agree?

Hint: See page 3.7 'Shaddarshanas' of Chapter 3 that describes the specific features of these philosophies.

- The six philosophies viz, Nyaya, Vaishesika, Samkhya Yoga, Purvamimansa and Vedanta all endeavoured to discover and construct the true meaning of life and the path to salvation, although their approach and understanding was different.

4. Discuss the four noble truths and eightfold paths of the Buddhist philosophy and its significance.

Hint: See page 4.3 of Chapter 4 on Buddhism.

- The 'four noble truths' represent Buddha's quest for truth and meaning of life. The 'eight fold path' prescribes the means for attaining salvation which are further exemplified in the Buddhist philosophies of *ahimsa*, nobility and co-existence.

5. What aspects/discoveries at various sites of Indus Valley Civilisation show that advanced trade and commerce was an integral part of the Harrappan culture?

Hint: See page 2.11 'Trade & Commerce of Chapter 2 .

6. What were the factors which led to the spread of Buddhism and Jainism? Discuss the significance of royal patronage and support to them.

Hint: See pages 4.2 and 5.1 'Spread of Buddhism' of Chapter 4.

- Similar teachings of Jainism, its philosophy, opposition to Varnashram Dharma, inclusive approach, opposition to Brahmanical orthodoxy, caste system, idol worship etc enabled the spread of Jainism. Jainism too was supported by kings and nobles. However, its spread was lesser as compared to Buddhism owing to its strict emphasis on Ahimsa while the latter recommended following a 'middle path'.

7. Pre-historic rock paintings reflected the life and society of the cave dwellers. Discuss citing specific examples.

Hint: See page 10.1 'Prehistoric cave paintings' of Chapter 10.

8. Discuss the evolution of free standing early temples and their architecture in the first half of the first millennia. Bring out the features of these temples.

Hint: See page 6.1 'Early temple architecture' of Chapter 6.

9. The Ajanta paintings were a culmination of Indian art over centuries and signify maturity in the art form of painting. Comment on the statement.

Hint: See page 6.2 Rock cut architecture Ajanta caves of Chapter 6.

- Mural paintings of Ajanta were characterised by naturalism, use of limited colours and no over stylization. The images were clearly defined and there was use of natural tones for body colours which merge with outerline creating volume effect.
- Images from the life of Buddha, (eg. image of Buddha, Yashodara and Rahul), Boddhistavas (Avalokiteshwara Padmapani & Vajrapani) *Jatakas* and *Avadanas*, and non canonical images (apsara, dancing girl) are masterpieces.
- The paintings itself were done over a period of several centuries and all these examples and style represent maturity of the art of painting.

10. Comment on the growth of classical Sanskrit literature in ancient India. Cite specific examples to substantiate your answer.

Hint: See page 6.20 'Classical Sanskrit literature' of Chapter 6.

11. Although separated by centuries and despite originating in different parts of the country the essence of the teachings of Alwar saints of South India and Varkari saints of Maharashtra was the same.

Hint: See pages 8.2 and 8.11 'Bhakti traditions in Maharashtra' of Chapter 8.

- The Alwars (6th-7th century CE) as well as the Varkari Saints (13th to 17th century which included Jnaneshwar, Namdev, Eknath,Tukaram etc.) believed in Bhakti traditions and were worshippers of Lord Vishnu. The former composed and sang in praise of Lord Vishnu/Krishna while the latter worshipped and composed songs in devotion to Vithala or Vithoba, an incarnation of Vishnu. Thus they all can be said to be a part of Vaishnava tradition.

- More importantly, both prescribed devotion as the path to salvation rejecting casteism, Brahmancial superiority and ritualism.

12. The Chola temples were the grandest in the realm of temple architecture in ancient India. Do you agree?

Hint: See page 7.9 of Chapter 7.

You may also include following points

- The Brihadeeshwar temple at Thanjavur with a 70m high pyramidical *vimana* and a 80 tonne stone Stupika atop was the tallest and biggest of all temples and bigger than those built by its predecessor the Pallavas, Chalukyas or Pandyas. It is indeed an engineering marvel.
- The temple included two large gateway towers (gopuras) with elaborate sculptures. Such a feature is noted for the first time in temple architecture.
- Large Nandi figures found in Shikhara and hundreds of stucco figures decorate the Vimana.
- Walls around the sanctum contains paintings/murals of mythological anecdotes. The temple has been declared a UNESCO World Heritage site.
- Other great Chola temples include the Gangaikondacholapuram temple, and the Aairavateshwara temple at Darasuram. All were dedicated to Lord Shiva. The other two were smaller than the Thanjavur temple but equally intricate in design, architecture and sculpture.
- Over a 100 Chola temples survive even to this day.

13. Ancient India was renowned for its knowledge and learning systems. Comment in the light of the universities of ancient India discovered in various parts of India.

Hint: See page 6.18 'Ancient universities' of Chapter 6

14. Analyse the reasons for adoption of local languages by the Bhakti and Sufi preachers for spreading their messages.

Hint:

- Objective of the Bhakti preachers was to reach the masses through their teachings which common folk could understand.
- The teachings were also based on principles of equality and inclusiveness. This could be achieved not through Sanskritised sermons but by messages which ordinary people could understand.
- Further, the preachers were also opposed to orthodoxy and restriction of canonical Sanskrit education to a select few. Thus the above objective could be fulfilled only if the sermons were delivered in local language.
- Eg. Ramananda, Kabir, Nanak, Chaitanya, Narsinh Mehta, Surdas, Tulsidas, Shankardev etc who preached in local languages.

15. Why are the Vijayanagar temple architecture considered unique and a departure from the traditional Dravida architecture style?

Hint: See page 7.11 of Chapter 7 for 'Vijayanagar architecture' and also question no. 16 (page AP. 3.13) of this section.

16. The essence the teachings of the Bhakti and Sufi preachers was the same. Do you agree?

Hint : See page 8.4 'Features of Bhakti traditions' and page 8.9 Sufism and essence of its teachings' in chapter 8.

17. What were the major categories of Indo Islamic architecture? Discuss the salient characteristics and examples of these.

Hint: See page 9.4 of Chapter 9 'Categories of styles of Indo-Islamic Architecture'

Different styles of medieval architecture and important monuments.

18. Discuss the art of making bronze sculpture in medieval period, citing specific examples of it.

Hint: See Chapter 11.

- Highlight the Pala Art and Chola art of bronze sculptures. Indicate important specimens of their art and their features viz. Shiva as Nataraja (Chola Bronze sculpture) statue of Buddha (Pala bronze sculpture)

19. The Mughal style of miniature paintings and its integration with manuscripts heralded a new form of artwork, quite close to the production of books today. It also influenced the other painting styles. Comment.

Hint: See page 10.6 'Mughal School' of Chapter 10

- Mughal style of painting was a synthesis of Persian style and Indian elements of painting. It was naturalistic with emphasis on aesthetic and accuracy of representation of figures. The concept of depth (perspective/3rd dimension in a picture) emerged with this school. The use of gold borders, vibrant colours and calligraphy in paintings were other features of Mughal miniatures which influenced the technique of other schools of painting as well.
- Miniature paintings were also incorporated as illustrations in manuscripts. These contained scenes of court, portraits of kings, battlefield and hunting scenes, etc., which added to the textual description given in the manuscripts. Thus their style was akin to modern books with illustrations. Akbarnama, Badshahnama were examples of such manuscripts which contained nearly 150 full page or double page illustrations.

20. Discuss the features of any four traditional textile and related handicraft. What purpose does a Geographical Indication tag serve?

Hint : See Chapter 18

You may also discuss features of silk, cotton, wool and mix textiles and prominent handicrafts related with these textile forms.

APPENDIX

4 The Essence of Indian Culture and the Phases of Cultural Evolution in Ancient India

The term **culture** is varyingly understood, often as encompassing different manifestations of human intellectual and other expressions, particularly of ideas, beliefs, customs and social behaviour. At a more granular level this conception incorporates different art forms, languages and literature, traditions and values and even religious expressions and practices. At times, even urbane lifestyles and discerning tastes of material subjects are considered archetypal of what culture embodies.

India, with its near continuous history of more than 5000 years as an evolving civilisation, has a dynamic and living culture. It is justifiably proud of this unique heritage which is often considered a key element of its own national identity. However, there are questions as to what is the true Indian culture and which hue in this multitude of cultural-chroma can be said to be quintessential representative of the Indian civilisation. But this begets some more queries as to, what is civilisation, what is the wider domain of culture, how has it evolved in India, how inextricably is it linked to our religious thoughts and practices and most importantly what is nationhood itself. A brief perusal of these concepts would help in better appreciation of the domain of culture and in capturing a glimpse of the vibrant Indian culture, the endeavour of this work.

Culture: A Mosaic of Collective Institutions, Intellectual and Human Knowledge Elements

The connotation of the word culture is vast and cannot be restricted to a singular definition. However, it can be understood as the collective values of a society, manifested through its numerous institutions as well as, in the disposition, attitudes, manners of its individual members. Those in turn find expression in various material objects, abstract ideas and beliefs of individuals and society.

Thus, culture includes certain aspects of **collective institutions**, such as morality, religion, spirituality, law, custom, art etc. which are not restricted to an individual and which are handed over from generation to generation. Evidently the **institutional elements** of culture are evolutionary and dynamic.

Culture also includes **intellectual and knowledge elements** pertaining to languages, literature, human learning, social norms, customs and behaviour. **Human and social aesthetics** are another key aspect of culture, encompassing within it the numerous manifestations of **tangible and intangible** art forms, viz, music, dance, sculpture, painting and architecture etc.

The new-age theatre and cinema are as much a reflection of the modern culture as are the cave paintings of a prehistoric society, of which we know so less. The Bhakti and Sufi movements were the embodiment of the **spiritual elements** of the medieval culture, as were the imposing forts and grand palaces of this age a reflection of its societal and corporeal cultural constituents. The Sangam literature was the manifestation of the **human intellectual and socio–ethical** elements of a culture at its zenith nearly two millennia ago. Folk art and traditional lifestyles are also as much indicative of the culture of a society as is urbane lifestyle and transient tastes. Thus, our habitat, cuisine, costumes, physical objects, apart from performing arts and architecture, are all reflective of the **material or tangible elements of culture**, as are religions, customs, festivals, traditions, social practices and ethics, philosophy and law, reflective of **non-material or intangible elements.**

Civilisation: A Milestone of Human Evolution

At times used synonymously with culture, the word civilisation is said to have its origin in the Latin word *Civitas,* meaning a city. Thus, it was originally meant to distinguish the human settlements particularly the more complex urban settlements from the nomadic, transitory or rootless people or those with a rudimentary society and negligible form of institutional governance. In modern context, civilisation refers to a fairly advanced stage of human development of a people, which encompasses social, urban, technological as well as cultural development.

The presence of organised urban settlements, with diversity of human activity hierarchical society, distinct form of governance, social stratification, development of economic systems, technological growth, evolution of ethical traits and cultural elements, all can be said to be distinct features ascribable to an evolved civilisation.

Thus, cultural growth is an important albeit not the only factor to be reckoned for characterisation of a society as a civilisation. Therefore, neither the two terms are analogous, nor mean even closely the same, although a developed culture may be considered a sine-qua-non for an advanced civilisation.

Religion and its Interconnect with Culture and Civilisation

Religion generally refers to a **socio-cultural system of faith, belief and worship** which is usually integrated with a belief in god(s). Although, there may not be any universally accepted definition of religion, there are indeed some identifiable features. Its core elements are invariably, spiritualism, morality and ethics with outward layers of customs, rituals, practices, sermons and other systems of veneration. Canonical texts, metaphysics, mythologies, rules of social and individual conduct such as at births, matrimony and funerary etc. are its other distinctive features. Existence of religious bodies and orders, priests and monks, sects and cults, festivals and ceremonies, along with associated cultural elements of literature, art forms music and dance, are other visible elements of religion. In the **Indian context,** the **seeking of truth and quest for eternal knowledge, along with righteous social and individual conduct are the cornerstones of religion.**

Neither religion nor culture can be said to be a sub-part of the other, although there remains a profound interconnect between them. From the perspective of religion, elements of culture are manifested often in form of ceremonies, rituals, religious literature, art forms or other material and non-material religious practices. Thus, along with spirituality, morality, philosophy and other canonical beliefs, culture also aids the religion in its objective which is to find the real meaning and purpose of life. But culture also influences these elements of religion such as its philosophy, its religious text and even moral beliefs.

From the perspective of culture, the religious aspect of culture is one amongst many elements enriching it and indeed an extremely vital one. Thus, that aspect of religion which is bereft of the external trappings and truly be characterised as its soul, can also be said to be the very soul of culture; for culture without that element which defines the '**real purpose of life**', is akin to only a body bereft of life.

Put albeit simplistically, **religion as well as culture are indeed distinct elements of human civilisation** albeit all **having a deep interconnect.**

Nationhood, its Elements and Culture Interconnect in the Indian Context

We often deliberate as to what is our true national culture and how has it evolved through the ages. A prerequisite to this discussion would be, to understand, what is nationhood and what are its elements. Are race, religion, language and history essential elements of nationhood? Does culture have a significant bearing on the concept of nationality? How is Indian nationhood distinct and unique?

The modern concept of a nation and nationhood is only a few centuries old. Nationhood is usually understood as a large group of people domiciled in a geographical unit and united by a common political/administrative order, law, culture, common history, economic order and language. Other uniting characteristics could be commonality of race, religion, ethnicity etc.

From the modern perspective, the intermingling of races and freedom of faith and belief has rendered, race, religion and ethnicity meaningless as defining factors of nationhood. Similarly, multitude of spoken languages in many modern nations does not make commonality of a spoken/official language as a necessary condition for nationhood.

Thus, modern day nations can be recognised by its people domiciled out of free will, in a geographical area, united by legal/political order, culture, history and economic activity. However, exceptions and marginal variations would exist and a watertight definition may not be possible. Whereas in countries like United States of America, European nations and Japan, language has been a common factor, for many South Asian nations and India in particular, the same cannot be true.

Further, while countries like India, China, Japan, Egypt and Turkey boast of a long and a common history, the nation state of Singapore or of Australia does not have this vital element to define its nationhood. Even the United States of America has a relatively lesser history of only a few centuries. In the Indian context, India is a well-defined geographical entity with partly natural boundaries. The democratic Constitution, the common history, economic singularity and its culture are the factors uniting the people which are otherwise characterised by different religions, languages, race, ethnicity etc.

Thus, Indian culture plays an important role in defining Indian nationhood. However, it has its own regional, social, linguistic and other variations too. Besides, Indian culture itself has never been static or an isolated silo of homogenous attributes. It has always been pervious, dynamic and evolving. Different waves of socio-cultural influences encompassed the Indian landscape leading to emergence of diverse cultural milieus, though unique to a time and space, but never singular and always sprouting.

Thus, any singular culture no matter how brilliant and seemingly comprehensive, only offers a partial perspective of the national culture. For it to appropriate the legacy of national culture would be akin to a part endeavouring to represent the whole. Indeed, pluralism, vibrancy, evolution and co-existence remain the cornerstone of Indian culture which is also the hallmark of Indian nationhood.

Phases of Cultural Evolution and Confluences

Over a period of 5000 years Indian society has witnessed several phases of cultural evolution. Each of these had its own distinct features. Many of these cultural phases overlapped with each other, resulting in a cultural confluence and leading to emergence of new cultural traits. These cultural phases were, the Indus Valley culture, the Vedic and the Dravidian culture, the Buddhist and Jain cultural influences, the Puranic culture, the Bhakti movement, the Islamic influence and the Hindustani culture, the European influence and finally the modern Indian culture. A snap shot of these phases and cultural confluences is captured below.

THE INDUS VALLEY CIVILISATION: THE FIRST PHASE OF CULTURAL EVOLUTION

Often referred to as the **harbinger of cultural evolution** in India, the Indus Valley Civilisation was a distinct and foremost urban culture which flourished from 3500 BCE to 1800 BCE (early and mature Harappan phases). Its unique features included; **an evolved town planning, modern cities, elaborate drainage system, walled citadel, extensive trade, developed script, evolved science and technology, growth of cotton and development of textiles, flourishing arts; of sculpture, bead and jewellery making, making of pottery, utensils, instruments and even weapons**. According to Sir John Marshall (who oversaw the early excavations at Harappa and Mohenjodaro), standards of civilised life attained by people living in the theses cities was higher than that of Egyptians and ancient Babylonians and equivalent to that of Sumerians. Spread over a large of present North and North-West India, Pakistan and parts of Afghanistan at its zenith, this advanced civilisation had a distinct and evolved culture. Further, the recent researches and discoveries in India have revealed some unique aspects of this civilisation also throwing light also on their cultural practices.

The larger settlements of Mohenjodaro, Harappa and others reveal the extensive town planning, large and efficient drainage systems, network of streets and roads with iron grid layout, existence of walled citadels and lower towns built on burnt/sundried bricks, presence of sizable granaries, great baths and other public places, besides innumerable seals, potteries, weights, cherts and other artefacts. All of these are truly indicative of an efficient governance structure and municipal functions, organised labour and social stratification and well-defined rules of social intercourse and conduct. Besides, flourishing commerce and trade, knowledge of engineering and sciences, belief in socio-religious rituals, their art and aesthetics are also clearly evident from the findings over here and newly discovered settlements of this civilisation.

The existence of a tidal dockyard **at Lothal** (in Gujarat) with its bead making industry has revealed flourishing trade through sea. The city was not only an important centre of production but also of overseas trade with far of cities in Persian Gulf region. The channel-based **docking system,** with a large man-made basin and a unique locking system, is a reflection of advanced knowledge of hydraulics and engineering, besides that of the extensive trade and commerce. Also known as the seafarers of Meluha in far of Sumer, these people had extensive knowledge of seas, navigational astronomy and even winds and ocean currents to guide them over thousands of kilometres of perilous journeys.

Recent discoveries at **Dholavira** (Kutch, Gujarat), reveal extensive water conservation systems including rock cut channels and reservoirs for storage and efficient utilisation of water from nearby streams and rain water. Researches also indicate change in the cropping pattern, to a low water requiring cereal such as millets, in response to the changing and drying weather system.

Agricultural practices are also evident at **Kalibangan** (Rajasthan) where discovery has been of a ploughed field which has cross grid of furrows. Further, at Shortughai (Afghanistan) discovery of dry land farming has been made. Excavations here have also revealed an irrigation canal for fetching water.

Discovery at **Rakhigarhi** (Haryana) and **Kalibangan** of **fire altars**, are indicative of emergence of rituals and sacrificial practices. The cemetery and burial sites of Rakhigarhi where skeletons of dead have been found with pottery and other items of daily use, are indicative of existence in belief in after-life and other funerary practices.

Apart from the above, **bronze statue of dancing girl, the bearded priest king bust, the Pashupati seal, the Mother Goddess figurines** and a number of seals with animal and other inscriptions have been found. These succinctly reveal tangible elements of their culture, art and aesthetics, besides the existence of at least a rudimentary religious culture. The inscription on numerous seals and on the Dholaveera signboard point to the evolution of a written script. Although undeciphered as yet, the script is believed to be pictographic or logographic, implying that individual symbols represent things and concepts.

Thus, it is amply evident that the Harappan culture attained great heights and it truly rivalled the cultures of Mespotamia and Egyptian civilisations of this age. It engendered an **unparalleled urban culture.** As a civilisation lasting nearly two millennium, it can truly be said to be usherers of a cultural wave heralding a neo-culture hitherto unknown to the human race. But an important question is, as to **why this civilisation did not survive, what was its enduring cultural legacy** (if any). Did it have any material impact on the ensuing society or did the subsequent cultural phase remained totally disconnected from this first cultural wave?

It is believed that Harappan culture did not have any perceivable cultural confluence with the Vedic culture which is said to have emerged around 1500 BCE. Experts earlier accepted the **'Aryan invasion theory'** (by Mortime Wheeler) as the root cause of decline of this civilisation. As such, a cultural disconnect between the Harappan culture and the succeeding Aryan culture, was a natural corollary and a foregone conclusion. However, latest researches reveal varying and largely **environmental factors as the cause for decline** of many of these once bustling cities. The Aryan invasion hypothesis, as a cause of their destruction is largely discarded. While Mohenjodaro and Lothal were ravaged by floods, the changing weather pattern and the great **Meghalayan drought** which is believed to have lasted nearly 300 years (around 2000 BCE) and affected the global weather, was the root cause of decline of Dholaveera, Rakhigarhi and some other sites around this very period. The changing weather and dearth of water made such large city systems unviable and eventually leading to their gradual abandonment. **But what happened to the people and their knowledge?**

The current researches do not shed any conclusive light into the post decline aspect of this great civilisation. Some theories suggest their being pushed eastwards due Aryan migration or because of environmental factors and resettlement in villages/ rural set up. Some hypotheses also suggest their moving southwards and **gradual merger and evolution of the Dravidian culture**. An archaeological finding in Tamil Nadu (Melaperumpallam near Poompuhar) in May 2007, shows pots with arrow head symbols similar to that found on seals of Mohenjodaro. Similarly, a 2014 discovery in a cave in Kerala is believed to show 19 pictograph symbols similar to Indus writing. A deeper connect is believed to seen in the Indus script with the Dravidian languages. Prof. Asko Parpola, of university of Helsinki, Finland (who worked on deciphering the scripts since 1968) believes that the script may have been similar to the family of Dravidian languages (or its proto languages). A stone celt (axe like structure) belonging to 2nd millenium BCE, found in Mayiladuthurai (Tamil Nadu), had many more Indus period symbols. According to Prof Iravatham Mahadevan, these represented a connect between the Indus script and early Dravidian languages. Whether these evidences are indicative of resettlement or contact due to trading for gold, is not fully established. But a semblance of cultural influence is quite noticeable.

A **cultural connect with the Vedic civilisation** is also seen in the numerous figurines of a female figure, adorned in jewellery and imposing fan shaped headgear.This is believed to be similar to that of **Mother Goddess** of the subsequent Vedic culture. Similarly, a connect is also established by the seal depicting a figure seated cross legged in a yogic posture with a horned head dress. The figure is surrounded by a number of animals and is considered to be a proto-Shiva or early form of **Pashupati/Rudra**. Seal of the **Swastika symbol** found in Harappa and other seals with animal motifs such as bull, elephant and tiger (vahana of celestial deities) which are revered in the Vedic culture, also indicate the cultural and religious influence.

At Lothal, one of the painted terracotta jars found was seen to be bearing the **image of 'the crow and the fox'**, believed to be depicting the story of the crow and the cunning fox, of the well-known fable. (This jar is on display at the onsite Archaeological Survey Museum at Lothal). Another jar is said to be carrying the image of the 'thirsty crow' dropping the pebbles. The discoveries though seemingly innocuous, suggest that the fables have continued to be a part of folklore in the subsequent culture(s) and are popular even till this day. Could it be a reflection of a moderate intermingling and continuity of some folk cultural elements?

But as of now experts generally agree that the Harappan culture did not have any substantial cultural confluence with the Vedic culture, which emerged as the next phase of cultural evolution in India.

THE VEDIC CULTURE: A NEW CULTURAL WAVE

The **Vedic age,** the next wave of cultural evolution, emerged around 1500 BCE, post the decline of the Indus valley civilisation. The new civilisation and society it created, dominated the Indian landscape for nearly 1000 years and continued to profoundly influence it even beyond this period. It is generally believed that the advent of the Aryans from central Asia to northern part of India and later to eastern portion in the Ganga-Yamuna doab region, heralded this cultural phase. However, there is no unanimity of experts as to the origin of Aryans or even to Aryan migration theory.

This period was characterised by the composition of four Vedas. These remain the chief source of information about this civilisation and its cultural practices and hence the name, the *Vedic culture*. The Vedic phase is further divided into the early Vedic (1500 BCE to 1000 BCE) and later Vedic phases (1000 BCE to 600 BCE). From an archaeological perspective, this period coincides with the **Black and red ware culture** period (1450 BCE to 1200 BCE) prevalent in western Gangetic plain. The pottery found in this period were typical black and red coloured and fall in the period of late Bronze Age and early Iron Age. It was succeeded with the **Painted Grey ware** culture period, an iron-age culture which was prevalent in the Ghagra–Hakra valley and western Gangetic plain. (BRW culture is believed to be from 1500 BCE to 700 BCE or 1300 BCE to 500 BCE).

Organisation of the Vedic society: The early Vedic society was largely agrarian, with dependence on agriculture as well as pastoralism. Larger cities like that of Indus Valley civilisation were absent in this phase. The administrative order was based on kingship (***rajya*** and ***rajan***) with ***sabhas*** and ***samitis*** as representative bodies being unique features of socio-political setup in this age. The ***Jana*** (tribe) the ***Grama*** (village) and ***Kula*** (clan or family) were the fundamental units social orders. Pastoral lifestyle and cattle rearing (specially cows and bulls) were in vogue. Wheat and barley and later rice, were the chief cultivated crops. Cotton and woollen fabrics were common. Copper, bronze and later iron were actively used in manufacturing of day-to-day items, utensils and weapons. Use of horses and chariots was known well in this age.

The **Varna system** provided the socio-economic order and division of labour and divided the society into four working classes. To begin with, it imparted an egalitarian social order with appropriate social mobility. Reference in Vedic texts is also seen of ***Daas*** and ***Dasyus***, who were referred as people outside the Aryan society and belief system (viz. not performing sacrifices and believing the commandment of the gods).Perhaps these were non-Aryan or aboriginal tribes (as believed by some historians). Vedic texts also indicate a greater respect for women as seen from the accounts of certain women poets and sages (Lopamudra, Viswavara, Apala, Ghosha, Kadru, Savitri, Vak Ambhrini, etc mentioned in Rigveda). Child marriages were unheard, *swayasmvara* as the right of women to select a groom was common and monogamy was the order of the day with polygamy being largely restricted to the nobility and royalty classes. Widow remarriages were also permitted.

Performance of ***Soma*** **sacrifice** and other yagnas/rituals by the king under the chief priest/ *raj-purohit* was another significant custom/religious belief based cultural element of the society. Numerous references to it are received particularly in the Vedic texts.

The political orders based on the kingship and clan/tribal identities was not bereft of conflicts and disputes. This is also evident from the Rigvedic account of '**Battle of 'ten kings'**. As per historians, this battle led to the eventual emergence of the earliest of the Vedic states, the 'Kuru dynasty' .The performance of ***Ashwamedha yagna***, sanctioned by the Vedas to the 'powerful and noble kings', was another means by which kingship could be expanded to regions where the sacrificial horse wandered. This could lead to battles and conflicts or acceptance of the over-lordship and political hegemony. But it definitely lead to consolidation and emergence of larger political units.

The Battle of Ten Kings : The Emergence of Kuru Dynasty

The Rigveda also contains the account of the 'Battle of ten kings' which took place on the banks of river Parushini (modern Ravi). Historians describe this as battle amongst the different Vedic tribes. The tribe of Bharatas was led by their king/ chief Sudas, which entered into a battle against ten tribes. The Bharatas lived in the upper regions of river Saraswati while another tribe of Purus, their western neighbour, lived in the lower regions, the remaining tribes lived northwest of Bharatas. In the ensuing battle, the Bharatas emerged victorious while the Puru chief Purukutsa was killed. Post war the two tribes, the Bharats and the Purus merged into a new tribe, the Kurus.*(Rigveda, mandal, hymns 18.33.83)*

The Vedas: the text defining a cultural age: The word Veda is derived from the root word *'vid'* or knowledge or wisdom. Thus, the Vedas were considered as the scriptures containing the sum total of the knowledge of the people. Further, the word *'vid'* also refers to the knowledge which could illuminate the path in the darkness (of ignorance), eventually leading to salvation. The Vedic texts comprise the **Rigveda,** the **Yajurveda,** the **Samveda** and the **Atharvaveda**. The Rigveda is oldest of all the Vedas and the most ancient of scriptures. Each of the Vedas further consists of and includes the **Samhitas,** the **Brahmanas** (both together comprising the Poorva Mimansa) and the **Aranyakas** and the **Upanishads** as separate parts or layers of the Vedas. (Both comprise the **Uttara Mimansa** or **Vedanta**, the latter literally meaning *the end of the Vedas*)

The socio-religious and philosophical elements of culture of the early Vedic age is reflected in the philosophy of **Poorva Mimansa** (literally meaning *former enquiry*) as contained in the teachings of Samhitas and Brahmanas. It considers the Vedas to be eternal and infallible and emphasizes on *mantras* and rituals as prescribed therein in Vedas, as being of primary importance. This cultural philosophy concerns more with **dharma** and **duties** of a person or 'Karya' or *Karmakand* rather than metaphysical knowledge.

Thus, a defining cultural practice emanating in this period was performance the Vedic rites and *soma* sacrifices. Propitiation of elements of nature was an integral practice. These include rain, fire earth, water, wind and the the associated deities viz. **Indra, Agni, Prithvi, Mitra, Varun, Maruts** etc. As a religious-cultural practice, it was indicative of the very close integration of the daily lives of the people with the nature and profound connect with its constituent elements.

Indra, as the god or rain, was one of the most important early Vedic deity. Nearly 250 Vedic hymns are dedicated to him and his propitiation was critical, for an agrarian society dependent on the vagaries of rainfall. He was also the king of *devas*, who was also referred as *Purandara* or the breaker of forts. Thus, he also epitomised valour in wars and his propitiation was perhaps seen as crucial for victory of the Aryans in their onward spread.

Agni was a deity whose propitiation was essential in performance of the numerous Vedic rites and *yagnas* and nearly 200 hymns in his praise are contained in the Vedic texts. **Varuna**, the next important deity, symbolised water and the mighty oceans. He was the upholder of the natural order of the world. The **Marut** personified storms and the power of wind.

Veneration of Rivers: A Culture of Embodiment of Divinity in Nature

The Vedic culture flourished on the banks of mighty rivers and reference to the *Sapt-sindhu* (seven rivers in the Indian subcontinent) and others is often contained in the Vedas. The rivers were the givers of life and nurtured the civilisation and thus venerated as a living deity. One such composition in the Rigveda refers to the prayer of sage Vishwamitra to grant a passage through them.

Vishwamitra : *O' rivers, who come down from the mountains like two swift horses like, two shining cows that lick their calves .You move like chariots to the sea through the power of Indra. You are full of water and wish to unite with one another.*

The rivers: *We who are full of water move along the path, the Gods have made for us. Once we start flowing we cannot be stopped. Why do you pray to us o' sage?*

Vishwamitra : *O' sisters please listen to me, the singer who has come from a distance with his chariots and carts, let your your water not rise above our axles so that we can cross safely.*

The rivers: *We will listen to your prayers so that you can cross safely.*

In the later Vedic period, the conception of universe is seen to have become more profound. We find reference to Gods such a Prajapati (identified later as Brahma of the Puranic age), who is not merely an element of nature, but perceived as the very creator of the universe. *Vishnu* as one of the Adityas (who in the Puranic period is identified as the preserver of universe) and *Rudra* or *Pashupati* (later identified as Shiva or Mahadeva) are also referred to. Veneration of these deities is seen in some of the Shlokas of this age.

The most significant aspect of this cultural phase was the conception of the **Upanishadic philosophy**. This philosophy emphasized on *Jnana* (or knowledge) and explored metaphysical subjects like ***brahman, atman***. **While the former was equated with** the cosmic being, the supreme creator, the primeval being and the infinite consciousness the latter was described as true self or the soul of the sentient being. This doctrine laid greater stress on acquisition of true knowledge and spiritual development rather on rituals and sacrifices. It eventually propounded the enduring philosophy of unitism or monism as a part of the Vedantic thought **emphasising on the unity of the Brahman and the Atman.** This was also hailed as the very objective of life which was the ultimate **realisation of Brahman.**

Thus, emerged in this age, the **doctrine of Vedanta**. This philosophy is very succinctly described by Dr Radhakrishnan in the book, 'The Hindu view of Life'. He states," *Vedanta is not a religion but a religion in the most universal and deepest significance."* The emergence of this profound and all-encompassing thought was indeed a marked departure from the early Vedic philosophy and led to evolution of a totally new dimension and perspective of culture in India.

Varnashrama Dharma : A New Socio-Cultural and Philosophical Order

The Vedic period also saw the emergence of the philosophy of the **Varnashrama dharma**. This philosophy enunciated and integrated the concepts of social order and socio-economic concept of division of labour, with socio-cultural and ethical obligations and duties. These in turn were determined as per the stage and calling of life. The concept is said to be traceable to the *Purushasukta* of the Rigveda (hymn 10.90). This *sukta* attributes the creation of the different varnas to the various parts of the body of the *Purusa*; the all- pervading cosmic being. Thus, this *sukta* brings out the cosmic connect between all the *varnas*. The different parts only symbolise their having different social duties. The concept itself finds elaboration in the *Manusmriti* and the other Dharmashastras.

The word *Varnashrama Dharma* is composed of three distinct words. ***Varna*** (here referred to as the class), ***ashrama*** (or stage/station in life) and ***dharma*** (duty or obligation). Thus, based on *varna* (class) and *ashrama* (station) a person was obliged to discharge his duties. The shastras identified four Varnas and four Ashrams. The four varnas are **brahmans** (priests, preachers, teachers), **kshatriyas** (kings, soldiers, warriors), **vaishyas** (merchants, agriculturists, artisans etc) **shudras** (labourers/service providers).

The four ashramas were ***brahmacharya, grihastha, vanprastha and sanyasa. Brahmacharya*** was the first stage of the life where the objective was to acquire knowledge and lead a life of discipline and celibacy. ***Grihastha*** or the stage of house-holder, was the next, where one was to choose his occupation as per varna, marry and raise a family. ***Vanaprastha*** was the third stage literally meaning proceeding to the forest. After fulfilling the duties of a house holder, with the onset of age, a person could retire from worldly matters and spend more time in spiritual pursuits. ***Sanyasa*** was the final stage where a person was to detach himself from the society and fully pursue attainment of salvation or *moksha*. Depending on the varna and ashram a person was required to discharge his dharma as enunciated duty.

Thus, this cultural philososphy was to serve as the lodestar of the seeker through the journey of life and beyond. The *atman* in its physical embodiment was to pass through the numerous stages of life. It would acquire the various attributes including knowledge and material wealth. It would also undergo the experience of the worldly pleasures and sufferings. A seeker was not to remain mired in the worldly pursuits but the true purpose of life was to seek the salvation through integration of the *Atman* with *Brahma*. The virtuous pursuit of appropriate worldly duties or the right *karma* was the key to emancipation in this eternal cycle.

Varnashrama Dharma and Social Mobility

As a basis for socio-economic order and division of labour, the varnashrama system was egalitarian and flexible to begin with. The *Purushsukta* hymn sites the common origin of all varnas from the same cosmic entity the *Purusha*. Further, social mobility within the varnas was permitted as a matter of individual choice of occupation. The co-existence of different varnas in the same family is evident from the Rigvedic hymn;

I am a poet my father is a physcian, my mother is a grinder; earning livelihood through different means we live together(Rigveda IX.112)

Another rigvedic hymn which elucidates existence of social mobility is hymn 3.44-45 .

O, Indra, fond of soma, would you make me the protector of people, or would you make me a king, would you make me a sage who has drunk soma, would you impart to me endless wealth.

Thus, the rigidities of birth based *varna* does not seem to be existent as an early Vedic practice. But over a period of centuries, the **varna system** seems to have metamorphosed into a more stringent and rigid social-system or the **caste system**. Varna was now determined by birth with individual's choice in its determination altogether ceasing. Adding to it, there was emergence of a dominant Brahmanical order of the priestly class, with emphasis on rituals and sacrifices. Finally, with the marginalisation of the shudras in this socio-economic order, this system had ceased to be socially and culturally inclusive. The time was now ripe for a new thought to emerge and another cultural wave to sweep the land. This was provided by the Buddhism and Jainism and its more inclusive philosophy.

Unitism and Vedanta an enduring legacy of the Vedic age: From the perspective of cultural evolution, the Vedic age does not seem to have engendered an urban civilisation akin to the erstwhile Indus Valley Civilisation. It is only in the last phase of this period around 600 BCE that we see the emergence of bigger cities in *Mahajanapadas*. But the evolution of other tangible and intangible elements of culture, particularly of music and medicine, is indeed noticeable in the verses of Samaveda and Atharvaveda. Similarly, growth of disciplines of mathematics, astronomy, metallurgy and other fields, can be traced to developments in this period. However, the **Vedantic philosophy** and the concept **of unitism** are truly unique and enduring cultural heritages of this age. If the highest perspective of culture is it's that element, which seeks to understand the true meaning and purpose of life, then the **Vedantic philosophy was the pinnacle of cultural evolution** and which indeed left an enduring legacy for all ages and cultures which ensued.

THE DRAVIDIAN CULTURE

The word *Dravida* in the Sanskrit language usually refers to the region in the southern part of India or the peninsular India. Thus, the culture of this region and people domiciled therein is referred by historians as the Dravidian culture. As experts dwell on the elements of Dravidian culture and endeavour to define its contours, they invariably strive to identify, as to whether this culture was distinct from the Vedic-culture? If yes, what were its unique features? Whether there was any confluence of these two streams? But the search for answer to the above queries also begets the question as to who were the Dravidian people.

The Dravidian People and Origin

The origin of Dravidian people remains a subject of research and debate with many theories being proposed. The first being, that the Dravidians were the Harappan people who were pushed back to the eastern and southern parts of India because of the Aryan invasion. But with the Aryan invasion theory itself being discarded by experts, this notion too stands repudiated. Another hypothesis is that the Dravidians were the aboriginal settlers, who over the centuries, were pushed to the peninsular India, owing to the expansion of the Aryans. The contact between the two led to the each influencing the language and culture of others. Historians and linguists point to existence of many words in the Vedic texts which are supposedly having origin in Dravidian languages.

Another theory is that the Dravidians people could have indeed been the Indus Valley settlers, who eventually abandoned the collapsing cities owing to the flooding of some of them and later because droughts of several centuries (the Meghalayan drought 2000BCE to 1800 BCE) and eventually moved eastwards and later southwards. Prof Asko Parpola and Iravatham Mahadevan are proponents of this theory and believe, of there being strong evidences for a proto-Dravidian origin of the ancient Indus Valley civilisation. The existence of a stone celt found in Tamil Nadu having markings similar to Indus signs and other evidences are adduced to support this hypothesis. Recent studies of the DNA samples, of a female skeletal-remains, found from Rakhigarhi (of 2500BCE) suggest, that it had DNA which is largely in common with the current South Asian population (see chapter 2). Thus, the genetic connect of the Indus people with current South Asian population is intact. This has led further credence to the migration of Harappan people and their later being identified as *Dravidas*. Some theories also suggest their west/central Asian origin hypothesis. However, there seems to be no consensus as to any of these above theories and question of origin of Dravidian people still remains shrouded in mystery.

Dravidian Culture and its connect with Indus Valley civilisation: Whether the Dravidian people were the Indus valley settlers or not, remains not fully established, but the close contact between the two and existence of the Dravidian civilisation prior to the Aryan culture establishing itself in North India, is duly accepted by the experts. Archaeological evidences, which suggest a close contact, are discovery of; **pots in Tamil Nadu with arrow head symbols** similar to that found on seals of Mohenjodaro; **pictograph symbols similar to Indus writing in a cave in Kerala, a stone celt** belonging to 2nd millenium BCE, found in Mayiladuthurai (Tamil Nadu) which is having many more Indus period symbols. The gold ornaments found in the Indus valley were having origin in the gold mines in southern India which suggest a possible trade between the two regions and cultural links. Discoveries at Adichanallur (in Thoothukudi district, Tamil Nadu), of an **ancient burial site**, indicate close similarity in practices of burial in urns and pots as found in some Indus valley sites. Further, the Brauhi language spoken in parts of Baluchistan has a lot of words common with the Dravidian languages.

Mutual influence of Dravidian and Aryan cultures: Whether the Dravidas got pushed because of an advancing Aryan culture, or whether they abandoned the Indus Valley Civilisation (IVC) cities due to extreme vagaries of nature, irrespective of above, experts do agree that both cultures did come in contact with each other and the marks of this cultural influence on both is apparent.

The *Sangam* period literature remains one of the most important sources of information about the Dravidian culture and society. This literature also talks about the three *Sangams* or academies of seers and experts of different fields which took place in the ancient city of Madurai. These academies or *Sangams* took place in different periods and are variously dated. Some experts believe the oldest Sangam to be held around 2500 BCE or even earlier. But is generally believed that the last occurred around 300BCE to 250 BCE. One of these academies is said to have been led by sage Agastya who was a prominent Aryan preacher from the northern India. Agastya is said to have spent a substantial period in the Dravida region preaching the Aryan philosophy and other disciplines. His work *Agathiyan* is said to have been an earliest treatise on Tamil grammar. Further, his twelves disciples are said to have composed a number of treatises on literature, grammar, music and dance which are themselves considered salient works of Sangam period. One such treatise, *Tolkappiyam,* is purported to have been composed around 1000BCE, by his disciple Tolkappiyar, after the loss of *Agathian* in a great deluge (flood). *Tolkappiyam*, extant even today, lays the foundation of Tamil grammar and reveals about the culture and society. The dates of its composition and authorship remain disputed. However, from cultural perspective, what is relevant is that sage Agastya, who finds mentions in Rigveda, is believed to be the first composer of Tamil grammar and is largely venerated in the Dravidian culture and his disciples authored seminal works of this culture.

The **Dravidian influence on the Aryan culture** is evident in the number of words incorporated in Rigveda from the Dravidian languages. These words and their usage become more in the subsequent Vedic layers after the *Samhitas*. The worship of Shakti (or mother goddess) is believed to have permeated in the Vedic culture apparently from the Dravidian worship of the mother goddess which is also evident from the Dravidian practice of worship of *Sapt Matrikas*. This concept in the puranic phase finds expression in the tradition of Shaktism and development of Puranic legends related to the different forms of the deity. The concept of Rudra and Pashupati in vogue in the Dravidian culture also seems to have merged into Aryan god of Shiva/Mahadeva in the Later Vedic period. Thus, the two cultures influenced each other over centuries and tended to have a greater confluence towards a culture which eventually emerged in the Later Vedic period.

The Sangams and the Dravidian culture: Some of the literary works of the Sangam period which survive to this day, reveal a wealth of information about the people, society, the cultural evolution and the great height the Dravidian civilisation attained. Sangams usually refer to the three academies or Sangams, the first of which is said to have taken place in the ancient city of Madurai. The three Sangams include, the head Sangam, the middle Sangam and the last Sangam. However, the first two Sangams are usually considered only legendary and it is only the last Sangam which is accepted as a historical fact and said to have occurred in the present Madurai. The Sangam period referred to by experts spans 6th century BCE to 3rd century CE. The most important treatises of this period extant today are the ***Tolkappiam***, the ***Pathupattu*** and the ***Ettutokai***. The original manuscripts of these treatises were lost for centuries and were rediscovered in a Shaiva monastery in Kumbakonam only in the 19th century.

The *Tolkappiam*, oldest surviving literary work is the most ancient work on Tamil grammar and also the oldest non-Sanskrit text. Some experts believe this to be a work from second Sangam or around 1st millennium BCE. However, most scholars do agree to a date of 2nd to 1st century BCE for its creation/compilation. The entire work is divided into three sections or books (*atikaram*). It has nearly 1612 sutras which provide the rules of etymology, phonology, orthography, sentence structure, semantics, prosody etc.

The *Pattupattu* which is a collection of 10 long poems can be said to be the earliest work of Tamil literature. The poems in the anthology range between 100 to 800 lines and are thus truly a substantive literary work. The most important of this collection is *the Nakkirar's Tirumurukatruppadai* (a guide to lord Murugan).

Ettutokai or the 'collection of eight' is another poetic literary work from this period, which along with the Pathupattu/*Pattupattu* forms the compilation of 18 ancient great literary works. These eight anthologies are a compilation of 2371 poems, each with 3 to 40 lines. These poems are attributed to nearly 470 poets whose names can be arrived at from their works. Among these nearly 30 are believed to be women. These poets in themselves were from different parts of the region and engaged in different occupations. However, in nearly100 stanzas the names of their authors cannot be worked out.

The poems of the Sangam period are broadly classified as *Akam* or *Agam or Aham*, meaning, 'inner' or 'love' and *Puram*, meaning 'outer' or 'public life'. These poems are of varied themes including love and emotion, worship of deities, veneration of king and his works and even themed on war. Thus, these grand literary works were truly a reflection of the intellectual and institutional elements of the society and its culture.

Dravidian Society and Culture; its Salient Elements

The Dravidian society like the early societies had agriculture as the substratum of socio-economic activity. As evident from the period's literature and archaeological findings, that industry of weaving and dyeing of cotton and woollen cloth, shipping was in vogue. Making of gold silver and other jewellery with stone inlays, ivory products making, metal working, making of leather products was well known. Trade with land and sea was established, the latter particularly with many southeast Asian regions in Malaya peninsula and even with far of Egypt and Roman empire the coins of which have been found.

The society was centred around kingship with the king, a monarch (also called *Mannam, Ko, Vendan, Korravan Iraivan* etc) being the centre of administration. Social division of labour and different classes existed and were partly based on birth and choice of occupation. A rigid caste system does not seem to have been the order of the day. Many Dravidian societies were matriarchal and social standing and respect of woman was much higher.

The religious believe and practices seem to be of an early form of *Shaktism* and *Shaivism*. The reverence to mother goddess and *Saptmatrikas* is believed to have existed in this period. Shiva was worshipped as *Rudra* or *Pashupati*. Murugan, (also know a Skanda, Karthikeya and Subrahmanya), the warrior lord, was another revered deity of this period.

The Dravidian culture seems to have flourished into larger settlements and cities. Reference to ancient city of Madurai is received where the first Sangam was held while the second in Kaptapuram and third in present Madurai after the earlier two cities were lost in deluge. There was substantial growth in scientific disciplines as seen in irrigational practices and building of dams etc. A system of calendar is known to be developed. A well-developed script and language with defined grammar and many literary works existed out of which only a few have survived. These are evident in works of *Tolkappiyam*, *Pathupattu* and *Ettutokai*, whose manuscripts are existing even today. The subjects and its depth are reflective of a literary and cultural evolution spanning multiple disciplines. Most importantly, the authors of these works were not a handful of seers, but many scholars including women distributed in the region, with works itself being reflective of the intellectual achievements of a society. Further, the **very conduct of these Sangams is reflective of a highly evolved culture** with excellence in different disciplines and great social respect for them.

EMERGENCE OF JAINISM, BUDDHISM AND SRAMANA TRADITIONS: THE AGE OF PLURALISM

With the emergence of **Buddhism and Jainism and other Sramana traditions** in the 6th century CE, a cultural confluence of the Vedic and Buddhist and Jain culture emerged. The latter were opposed to Vedic rituals, Brahmanical order, Varnashrama system, idol worship and animal sacrifices, which were some of the key features the Vedic system. This period from 600 BCE to 200 BCE was not only a phase of cultural confluence but also of socio-culture upheaval, as each faith vied for permeating the socio-religious space. But what emerged from this social churning was a pluralistic and syncretic culture not bound by the dogma and capable of assimilating new thoughts and practices. Thus, **socio-cultural evolution and co-existence of multiple faiths** can truly be said to the characteristic of this age.

The doctrine of ahimsa or non-violence or non-injury to any sentient being was a defining socio-cultural and spiritual influence of this age. Although in vogue in the earlier Vedic systems too, the Jain doctrine followed by the Buddhist thought, brought the concept of ahimsa in centre stage of the religious and social life. The principle of ahimsa was the corner stone of the Jain metaphysics, spiritual doctrine and its ethical conduct. It believed in the essence of life or soul to be existent in all sentient beings and thus there being a universal interconnect. Killing or injury to any such being meant further entrenchment of the soul-body bondage and further spiritual decay. Both Jainism and Buddhism strongly believed in the precept of Ahimsa and this meant **opposition to the Vedic sacrifices of animals**, a ritual accepted and practiced for centuries and even hallowed.

But most importantly, ahimsa was not just limited to the prohibitory precept of non-injury of any sentient being, but to the positive attribute of boundless and loving **compassion** for all. Termed as ***metta*** (*maitri* in sankrit), it was this attribute, which endowed **universalism** to the **doctrine of ahimsa**. This in turn was an integral element of ***Panchamahavrat*** in Jainism and ***Triratna*** in Buddhism and thus it cast a profound social influence in this phase of cultural history. A few centuries down the chronology of time, we see building of the colossal Mauryan empire by emperor Ashoka on the very foundation of ahimsa and universalism; an empire which in terms of the spread of political boundary had reached its zenith for centuries to come. But more significantly, the essence of this philosophy and the socio-cultural- religious influence, spread much beyond the vast boundaries to a significant part of the world influencing it for the next two millennia and more.

Karma as the basis of salvation, was also another spiritual concept emphasised upon by the two faiths. Although similar theories of *karma* were also propounded in the Upanishadic philosophy, what was significant was the singular emphasis by Buddhism and Jainism on *karma* and rejection of ritualism as the basis of spiritual evolution. Even the concept of a **personal god,** as the creator and the sustainer of the universe, on whose grace the emancipation of the human soul was dependent or whose wrath was to befall on the vile, was completely rejected. The *karma* of the being was the basis of its salvation and its providence. The 'laws of universe' were the sustainers of the cosmos. Thus, ritualism of appeasement or the rites borne out of fear had no role in liberation of the soul and were summarily rejected, thus shifting the complete onus of spiritual gain on the being and his/her endeavour.

Henceforth emerged heterodox schools of thought which rejected the concept of a **personal god**, the infallibility of the **ritualism in Vedas,** which decried the **animal sacrifices** and emphasized on **universalism and ethical conduct**.

A new **inclusive social order** was clearly in the offing. The **Brahmanical supremacy** and orthodoxy was rejected. They were not to be the only interpreters of the holy scriptures, neither the spiritual education was to remain the exclusive preserve of a specific *varna*. The common folk irrespective of their birth and *varna* were all eligible to be a part of the religious order which included the Brahmins and Shudras alike. Thus, every being could strive and hope for salvation and spiritual evolution. The sangha of Buddhism and the order of monkhood of the Jainism made no class or varna distinction in admittance of people in its fold. The only requisite was the believe in its doctrine and acceptance of its practice. Further, the concept of particular *ashram* (stage of life) for renunciation was not necessary in the two faiths and a person could adopt the life of monkhood at any stage.

While the members of the royal household like Rahul (son of Buddha) were accepted in the Sangha, so were Amrapali (a courtesan) and Angulimal (the reformed dacoit). While Sariputta the chief disciple of Buddha and Mahakashyap, another venerated disciple, were from the Brahmanical order, Upali, a barber, was entrusted the responsibility as the chief disciple in matters of Vinaya and Sunita a scavenger, later on became an Arahant.

Even women whose social status had been ebbing over the centuries were admitted in the monkhood being called the *sadhvis* (in Jainism) and *theris* (in Buddhism). Mahaprajapati Gautami was the first woman to be admitted in the Buddhist Sangha. They made significant contribution to the spiritual cause.

Therigatha, a class of scripture which was a part of the *Khudakka Nikaya* of *Sutta Pitaka*, was composed by the elder *bhikhhunis* and *theris*. Thus, also emerged a formal and inclusive **order of monks** which steered the evolution of *dharma* and conduct of the monks and laity over centuries.

The **spiritual discourses were in the Prakrit languages** (Pali, Ardha-magadhi etc) and not limited to Sanskrit, enabling the common folk to comprehend the message and be integrated in this quest for socio-spiritual elevation. Further, the followers of the Buddhism, Jainism and other Sramana traditions were not restricted to the monks who had denounced the house-hold but also included the house-holders and laity, for whom a more benign social-spiritual conduct was acceptable rather than the strict codes of monkhood. The reliance on the spoken language of the masses also gave a fillip to **education of the common folk** in the Jain, Buddhist and other traditions, thus creating a more inclusive social order, a far cry from the social segmentation of the *varna* system.

A rational approach to spiritual and epistemological inquiry was another seminal contribution of this age. The basic premise of Jain and Buddhist doctrines was the theory of cause and effect. This is best captured in the words of Buddha in Dhammapada where he states:

"Everything has a cause and produces an effect. This simple principle governs the whole universe, gods and men, heaven and earth. It is applicable not only to this vast universe stretching through boundless space, with its dazzling world systems and endless series of alternations of growth and decay, but also to the events of human life and affairs of history. If we can detect and eliminate the cause of suffering, suffering itself will disappear."

A similar approach is adopted by the Jain doctrine which considers the interplay of *karma* in the framework of the governing laws to be squarely responsible for our lives and its events. Further, both the schools decried blind faith and emphasised on the understanding of the reasoning to be essential in appropriate adoption of the doctrine and its practice.

The conception of the Jain theological fundamentals is best exemplified in **Tattvartha Sutra** an authoritative Jain scripture containing its philosophy. The spiritual discourse displays a unique scientific enquiry wherein it explains the fundamentals, not just of the theory of *karmic* causation of the soul-matter bondage (*bandha*), *samvara* (its prevention) and *nirjara* (its elimination) from the province of the soul, but also elucidates the basics of the material world. It conceives matter (*pudgal*) to be composed of *paramanu* (atoms or the primary building blocks of matter) which aggregate together two or more *paramanus* in bonds called *skandhas* (akin to a molecule) and eventually build the simplest of matters to the *panch-bhoot* (the five elements) to the whole of universe. Indeed, it's a sterling scientific theory which could withstand the test of modern scientific knowledge and enquiry. The theory further considers matter (*pudgal*) to undergo change in its characteristics (transformation) but the fundamental substance (*paramanu*) remains the same and is indestructible.

The Jain treatises like the **Agamas** further dwell on a variety of topics ranging from the **philosophy to mathematics to logic** etc. displaying an abiding **scientific and rational outlook to the spiritual conception**. This scientific and rational approach was further tempered with a sense of individual inquiry, thus eschewing any dogmatism and blind faith. This is best exemplified in the following words of Buddha to his disciples in the Anguttara Nikaya (fourth *nikaya* of the Sutta Pitaka).

"This I have said to you O' Kalamas: but you may accept it not because it is the report, not because it is a tradition, not because it is so said in the past, not because it is given from the scripture, not for the sake of discussion, not for the sake of a particular method, not for the sake of careful consideration, not for the

sake of forbearing with wrong views, not because it appears to be suitable, not because your preceptor is a recluse; ***but if you yourself understand that this is so meritorious and blameless, and when accepted, it is for benefit and happiness, then you may accept it.***

The emergence of the **many Sramana traditions** and **the plurality of faith** and belief systems was another salient aspect of this cultural phase. Literally the word Sramana refers to 'labour and toil'. Thus, it implied the spiritual-toil of the class of seekers and ascetics. This phase oversaw the emergence of a number of faiths which professed its distinct philosophies at times radically different from the mainstream Vedic thought. Thus, the Sramana tradition began to refer to those schools of philosophy and spiritualism which were **non-Vedic and did not accept the infallibility of the Vedas.** They were also referred to as *nastik* or **heterodox schools** for rejecting the Vedic epistemology.

While Jainism with its emphasis on Ahimsa and ethical conduct and Buddhism eulogising the middle path and *Dhamma*, soon rose to prominence and had greater social acceptance than the rest, schools like the Ajivika, the Charvaka, the Ajnana etc. also arose around this time. Some of these existed even prior to Mahavira and Buddha and had good following. But down the centuries they did not enjoy the same social acceptance as the other two faiths. However, they did contribute their unique philosophies to this age of spiritual seeking.

The ***Ajivikas*** led by Makkhali Ghosal, were a school of fatalists, believing in the soul and consequences of nature and its laws. They professed ascetism akin to Jainism. However, they denied the existence of free will and role of karma in altering the predetermined course of our lives.

Ajita Kesakambli of the ***Lokayata- Charvaka*** school believed in materialism, denied the philosophy of *karma*, after-life or rebirth etc. It believed that with death, the humans disintegrated to the constituent elements and thus there was no fruits of good or evil deeds.

Ajnana school led by Sanjaya Bellathiputta was agnostic and sceptic disbelieving in existence or non-existence of afterlife, good, evil, karma, soul etc. The school of amoralism propagated by **Purana Kasyapa** did not believe in inherent morality or immorality of any act.

However, the most important aspect of this phase was the **questioning of the extant theology and breaking away from the dogma.** The support these faiths enjoyed particularly Jainism and Buddhism, is a clear indication of their social acceptance. Thus, there was the emergence of numerous doctrines which struck root in the socio-cultural soil and sprouted the saplings of **pluralism.**

Coexistence and tolerance of different faiths and their believers is another salient characteristic of this cultural age. Each of these traditions sincerely believed in its own correctness and at times was critical of the other, but all coexisted and competed for social and political acceptance. **Anekantvada**, a fundamental doctrine of Jainism on non-absolutism talked of relative perspectives and coexistence of multiple aspects of the same truth. Thus, it was non-critical and accommodative of differing perspectives. Buddha himself preached his disciples to be tolerant of critics.

Although political patronage was extended to these theologies, the professing of others was never prohibited or discourage by the royalty or its administration. Bimbisara, a contemporary of Mahavira and Buddha is believed to have supported both the faiths. Ashoka, one of the most important patrons of Buddhism, respected and supported other sects too. The Barabara caves were built by him for the Ajivikas as well as the Buddhist. But the respect for all faiths is best exemplified in his rock edicts where he exhorts all to respect one's own as well as other faiths, thus proclaiming one of the greatest gospels of **peaceful coexistence based on *Dhamma*.**

The mutual influence and confluence: The mainstream theological belief systems and the Vedic culture though remained intact and flourished in this age but did not remain uninfluenced by these new thoughts. The concept of ahimsa permeated deep in the Vedic society too. The emphasis on ethics and spiritualism was reignited. Thus, *dharma* and *moksha* started to receive due significance as compared to *artha* and *kama* and the Upanishadic ideals too came into prominence as compared to the oft emphasised ritualistic practices.

Down the centuries, new philosophical schools of thought emerged within the Vedic system viz. the Samkhya, Yoga and others which assimilated some of the views of the Sramana traditions. Rather, the emergence of these thoughts and the changes in the Vedic system brought a palpable influence on the Buddhism too. The religion which decried idol worship became an inspiration of Gandhara School of Art which later saw sublime statues of Buddha. This influence was not limited to merely art and other tangible elements. Several aspects of the Vedic thoughts and the belief in personal god, were soon imbibed in the mainstream Buddhism which is believed to have later given rise to Mahayana Buddhism. Soon Buddha, the heterodox was to become the divinity he decried.

The **conception of the Shad-darshanas** also took place in this period. These were the six branches of Hindu philosophy—*Nyaya, Vaisheshika, Samkhya, Yoga, Purva Mimansa* and *Vedanta.* Some scholars also hold that the development of some of these philosophies took in the period of 200 BCE to 200CE. These six philosophies are also referred as the *astika* philosophies or the orthodox school as they accepted the authority of the Vedas and believed in validity of its doctrines unlike the *nastika* or unorthodox schools of Buddhism, Jainism and others.

The **Samkhya** was **rationalist** school of whose philosophy revolved around the dualistic concepts of *Purusha* and *Prakriti.* While *Purusha* was the Supreme Consciousness, *Prakriti* implied the nature whose bond with the *Purusha* created the *jiva* (the living being). Its belief system of the true knowledge being an emancipator of the *jiva*, is considered a combination of rationalism and spiritualism. While **Nyaya** a **realist** school of philosophy dealt with formal reasoning and logic, **Vaisheshika** a **naturalist** school postulated the composition and functioning of the physical universe to the fundamental units called *paramanu* (atom). Thus, a spirit of logic, metaphysics and even other sciences were combined with the spiritual seeking. The **Yoga** system of philosophy, propounded rationalism, analogous to the Samkhya but also expounded the virtues of **karma** (righteous action) as a means of salvation.

The other two schools comprised the **Vedic** philosophy. The former emphasised on the rituals and practices and thus was a form of school of **philosophical realism**. The latter emphasised on the right knowledge of *Advaita* philosophy or **non-dualistic monism** for salvation. Thus, these diverse schools embodied a **liberalist and rational perspective of religious culture**, eventually laying the foundation of a pluralistic approach to the seeking of the Divine.

Over all this was an **age of diverse thoughts and liberation from orthodoxy**, where numerous competing faiths emerged. At times these multiple faiths exercised mutual influence, however they did not converge to a singular belief system. Nor did it see the emergence of a predominant theology which could annihilate or subsume the others.

The tangible and non-theological cultural elements of this age were a marked departure from the erstwhile Vedic age. The socio-political administration saw the emergence of the 16 Janapadas with Magadha amongst the most powerful of all. The **concept of a republic** also saw its birth in the Vajji Sangha of the Licchavis. But **kingship** remained the main form of political administration. The emergence of Chandragupta Maurya who vanquished the Greeks and the Nandas, led to the emergence of a strong political establishment hitherto unseen. By the time Ashokan regime ended, the **largest empire ever** whose boundaries covered the entire Indian subcontinent and even beyond was founded. This influenced all elements of the socio-cultural life.

The emergence of **large human settlement and cities** were seen for the first time in more than a millennium. Agriculture trade and commerce were much better organised and expanded. Political administration was diversified as seen from the appointment of officers/administrators for specific fields of work. This is best evident in Ashokan rock-edicts where he proclaims appointment of *mahamatras* (officers in-charge for administration and justice) for *dhamma*, welfare of women, family, animals etc.

Stone as a building material gained prominence along with wood, with exquisite palaces such as of Ashoka being built. New architecture was flourishing in chaitya, viharas and stupas. The stone pillars carrying Ashokan edicts with large capitals atop, weighing several tons and having mirror like finish, and dexterous carving of petals, were **engineering and sculptural wonders** of this age. One such pillar at Sarnath with a lion capital, has bequeathed an enduring legacy to the modern Indian republic in form of its **national symbol**.

Literature and other intellectual elements too had a fair share of evolution. Seminal works such as; *Shushruta Samhita*, a treatise on medicine and surgery; Panini's *Ashtadhyayi*, the earliest of works Sanskrit grammar; *Arthashastra* of Kautilya which laid the rules of political-economic administration; *Panchatantra* by Vishnu Sharma and *Charak Samhita*, another fundamental work on medicine, all had birth in this phase. A range of non- canonical literature of Buddhist and Jains in form of *Jatakas* and others emerged. Schools of logic, mathematics and other sciences and important works in them developed. But most importantly, the emergence of the ancient university of Taxila was truly the crowning glory of this **age of lore and reason**, reflecting the yearning for knowledge and education, of its people.

THE PURANIC AGE

The next cultural phase saw the emergence of **Puranic culture**. The ensuing 800-900 years are referred as the golden phase of Hindu religion. This also coincided with the emergence of the Gupta empire. **Composition of Puranas** the seminal canonical literature defining this age took place. The Absolute or the Brahman which was God without attributes continued to be the core of the Vedantic philosophy, but there was also the emergence of the personal god who was the supreme manifest with attributes. The religious emphasis shifted from the Vedic gods who were elements of nature to the trinity of Brahma, Vishnu and Mahesh. Cults of Vishnu, Shiva and Shakti emerged. Brahmanism saw a revival. *Dharmashastras* or the various schools of personal law and of social code and ethics emerged. This was also the **Classical age** and the next **cultural confluence.**

The texts defining an age: The word *Purana* literally means, old or ancient or historical. The Puranas are a part of the Smriti texts and cover a vast repository of canonical literature. Reference to Puranas is also seen in some Vedic texts such as Atharvaveda where the word *Itihasa-Purana* is referred to in Shatapatha Brahmana, thereby reflecting their antiquity. However, it was only in this age (200 BCE to 700 CE) that they attained popularity and were compiled in the present form (around 400CE) thus ushering the Puranic age. Overall, 18 Puranas are said to have been composed, which are often recognised as the *Mahapuranas* (main Puranas) besides 18 other Up-Puranas are also recognised. The *Mahapuranas* are categorised into six main groups in terms of the central deity around which the anthology of tales or the narration of eulogy is built. Thus emerged an age of polytheism.

From profound monotheism to vibrant polytheism: While the Advaita philosophy and Vedic dharma continued to remain the cornerstone of the canonical belief, over a period of time there was a gradual assimilation of the popular beliefs, regional traditions and even local conception of the divinity. The notion of the *Brahman* without attributes remained the pinnacle of the conception of the Supreme, but now the religion also recognised the personal god or the conditioned Brahman. Thus, the belief in divinity as Supreme consciousness expanded to include its physical manifestation. God with attributes became the mainstream thought. This God was perceived varyingly, as Vishnu, Shiva, Shakti etc. Further the emergence of the divine trinity took place which posited the three cosmological roles of the Supreme in the three physical manifestations of **Brahma, Vishnu and Mahesh.** The Vedic Gods like Indra, Agni, Varun, Mitra, Soma etc. remained to be significant albeit with the status of demi-gods and not that of the cosmological creators. Hence emerged a religious tradition which harboured a **profound monism as well as a vibrant polytheism.**

A syncretic and assimilative culture: The Puranic tradition was not only assimilative of divergent philosophical traditions which perceived the Supreme as that with or without attributes, but also imparted a vast firmament under which the numerous sectarian traditions flourished and even integrated. The *Mahapuranas* were classified as per a central deity such as Brahma, Vishnu, Shiva, Shakti, Surya, Agni, Ganesh, Skanda etc. Thus, it clearly recognised the extant traditions revolving around the different personal gods and accepted them as a part of the vast Puranic pantheon. Though the sectarian tradition of devotion as seen in Vaishnavism, Shaivism, Shaktism etc. found consonance in them, the Puranas in themselves were pluralistic. The union of Shiva-Shakti brought out in the Puranas, is incomplete without the cardinal conception of the female divinity. Thus, this very notion emphasises on integration and harmony of the seemingly diverse forces of the cosmos. Similarly, lord Shiva and lord Vishnu the godheads around which two distinct traditions flourished are considered often the manifestation of the same deity. Even the **trinity of Brahma, Vishnu and Mahesh** find a merger in one singular deity referred often as **Mahavishnu** or **Mahashiva** thus converging the pantheon of Gods and believes to monism and Unity.

The Puranas were encompassing of the multitude of beliefs, seeing the Divine in all Its grand manifestation. They were not exclusionary or prescriptive as to corral the belief systems into a singular perspective or a dominant doctrine. As **Dr Radhakrishnan** puts in the book, *The Hindu View of life*, '*The Puranic Hinduism accepted the significance of different institutions of reality and the different scriptures of the peoples living in India, **(sarvagama pramanya).***' Thus, it engendered a theistic pluralism and accommodative culture.

The cult and believe in the Dravidian conception of the ***Saptmatrikas*** and the pre-Vedic mother Goddess finds reflection in the worship of **Shakti** and her numerous manifestations. The concept of **Pashupati** of pre-Vedic period and of **Rudra** of early Vedic period, is integrated in the worship of lord **Shiva**. As per scholars, the legend of the one of the chief Dravidian warrior-philosopher god, **Murugan** or Subramanya gets integrated with the Kartikeya or Kumar in Puranic culture and his legends find expression in the Skanda-purana. While monism and convergence with the Vedantic philosophy remains the corner stone of Puranas, yet their all-embracing outward manifestation offered sufficient space for numerous faiths and belief systems to flourish and even integrate.

The fountainhead of the culture of Bhakti: While earlier Vedic traditions were centred on the ritualistic culture (karma-kanda) or the profound knowledge (*jnana*) based *Advaitic* spiritualism, the conception of a Supreme manifest with attributes, enabled the evolution of a tradition centred around a personal godhead. Thus **Bhagvata-Purana** (*Srimada Bhagavata* or *Bhagavatam*), amongst the most important and well-known Puranas, is dedicated to the Bhakti (devotion) of Lord Krishna. Many other Puranas are dedicated to Lord Vishnu. **Shiva-Purana, Skanda-Purana, Markandeya-Purana, Linga-Purana** and other Puranas which capture the legends of the Lord Shiva, have formed the central tenets of Shaivism. The **Markandeya-Purana** which incorporates ***Devi Mahatamya*** has been the sacred scripture of Shaktism (worship of Goddess Durga and the numerous forms of female divinities). The conception of the ten incarnations of Lord Vishnu also came in vogue. Of these, the incarnations of Sri Ram and Sri Krishna were the most popular.

The age of Smritis: The Puranic culture also paved the way for the popularity of Smriti texts such as Ramayana, Mahabharata and other traditions which were centred around the **reincarnation of the Godheads**. These Smritis by some accounts are said to have been compiled in this age while some scholars believe them to be of much greater antiquity. However, there is a general acceptance that it was in the Puranic age that the Smritis of Ramayana and Mahabharata became popular. Along with these Smritis emerged a culture inspired by their values and ethics. These manifested in the canonical literature and other tangible elements of this age.

An encyclopedic account of a civilisation: The Puranas were not just a literature reflecting the theological belief of the age. They were indeed more than a treatise on the practice of devotion. Their extensiveness and the bewildering diversity of topics covered by them are truly encyclopaedic. Five key subjects referred to as the *panch-lakshanas* (five signs) are integral to Puranas. These include; the subject of creation of universe ***(Sarga)***; their recreation after dissolution or secondary creation **(*pratisarga*)**; the genealogy of gods and also of sages **(*vansha*)**; the creation of human race and the account of the first human beings (*Manus*) in the numerous secondary creations **(*manvantra*)** and the genealogical and historical account of the solar and lunar dynasties (***vansanucharitam*)**. Thus, they functioned as a repository of cosmological hypothesis as well as a historical account of its age.

The description of the various gods and their incarnations is also an integral element of their composition. The **Bhagavata** comprising of nearly 18000 shlokas (verses) describes the numerous *Avatars* of lord Vishnu (Sri Rama, Sri Krishna, Narsimha etc), besides that of the *bhakta avatars* (incarnation of devotees) such as Prahalad, Narada, Kapila etc. The **Skanda Purana**, the longest of Puranas comprising a mammoth 81,100 verses, recounts the birth of Skanda (also known as Kartikeya and Murugan,) the son of Shiva and Parvati. It describes the narratives of him as the leader of the army of *devas*. The **Garuda Purana,** which centres around lord Vishnu is arranged as a dialogue between the deity (lord Vishnu) and his *vahana* (celestial vehicle) *Garuda*. This Purana covers an astounding range of topics including cosmology, numerous gods and their relationship, philosophies of *Yoga* and *Samkhya*, *moksha*, karmic-cycles, rebirth and even the Upanishadic philosophy. The geography of *Bharatavarsha* (India), sites of pilgrimage, account of the salient rivers, diseases and medicines, astronomy, astrology and Hindu calendar system, architecture of homes and temples, rites of passage, different virtues to be emulated, duties of king and statecraft and even rules of grammar and genre of literature are some of the topics described in its wide array. Thus, the Puranic culture also engendered a tradition of repositing of the diverse social knowledge for posterity.

The Golden Age: This was also the golden age of Hinduism. The Brahmanical religion staged a resurgence. Support of royalty from some of the Kushana rulers and later from the Gupta dynasty fuelled the growth of Hinduism for next half a millennium and more. Although Buddhism and Jainism too remained in reckoning, the Brahmanical religion had again become the mainstream theology. The religious philosophy now incorporated not only the Vedantic thought and the Varnashrama dharma but also the tradition of personal god and devotion to the deity.

Another defining feature of the Puranic age was the conception of the **Dharmasutras** and the **Dharmashastras,** a genre of theological texts which prescribed the codes of righteous conduct, ethics and moral principles (*dharma*). These governed the discharge of individual and social duties for different classes (*varna*) in different stations (*ashramas*) of life, be it for *Brahmancharya* (student-hood), *Grihastha* (house-holdership), *Vanaprastha* (retirement from social affairs) and *Sanyasa* (renunciation). The codes of ethics and duties of different sections, be it the kings or the brahmins etc. were all governed by these treatises. They also contained the rules of inheritance and the laws of civil and criminal justice for the society.

The Dharmashastras are said to be many in number (between18 and100). They themselves emanate from the Dharmasutras, which in term are a part of the Kalpa *Vedanga*. While the Dharmasutras of Apastambha, Gautama, Baudhyayana and Vashistha have survived to this day, the Manu-smriti, Yajnavalkya-smriti, Narada-smriti and Vishnu-smriti are the extant Dharmashastras. Thus, through these treatises, the codes of conduct and specific personal and social laws were codified thus integrating and providing a force of sustenance for the Aryan society. Since their conception in the Puranic age, the **Dharmasutras and Dharmashastras** have shaped the discourse of the Hindu society for the next two millennium.

The Puranic age also encompassed the **Golden period of Indian history** besides that of Hinduism, particularly in the reign of the Guptas (320 CE to 550CE). This was also **the classical age**, the period in which culture, art, sciences, philosophy, economy, literature, mathematics, astronomy, architecture, sculpture, agriculture, trade commerce and administration and other pursuits of human life reached unsurpassed heights. The political stability and sovereignty over a large part of India coupled with an efficient and people-oriented administration heralded an age of prosperity and progress.

This was the age when the **Nalanda Mahavihara** was founded and flourished. Along with the other Mahavihara-universities of this age including the **Vallabhi** (Valabhi) in Gujarat and **Pushpagiri** in Orissa, the dawn of an age of learning took place. The world-famous murals of **Ajanta**, the rock cut caves and sculptures of **Ellora, Elephanata, Udaygiri** and **Khandgiri** were the contributions of this age. The field of sculpture saw the emergence of the indigenous **Mathur**a and **Sarnath** schools of art which were worthy successors of the **Gandhara** and **Amaravati** schools which too flourished in the Puranic age. The beginning of **free-standing temples** as seen in the Dashavatara temple at Deogarh and Chaturmukhlinga temple at Nachna, marked the beginning of a new age of temple construction and architecture.

The Puranic age also witnessed emergence of a range of canonical literature of Hinduism like Puranas, Smritis and Dharmashastras which were either composed or compiled. Buddhist Pitakas and Jain Agams and sutras (like Tattvarthasutra) were the other canonical texts which were compiled in written form and widely propagated.

This was also the age of **classical Sanskrit literature**. Notable literary figures like **Bhasha, Sudraka, Ashvaghosha, Kalidasa, Bharvi, Bhatti, Magha, Vishakadatta, Dandin**, amidst others contributed richly to the Indian literature. *Swapavasvadatta* of Bhasha, *Mrichhaktika* of Sudraka, *Abhijana Shakuntalam* (and other texts) of Kalidasa, *Mudraraksha* of Vishakadatta and many other literary creations of this age are considered all-time great classics.

This was also an era of unprecedented growth of arts, science mathematics, astronomy, medicine and other disciplines. **Natyashashtra** of Bharata a treatise on different art forms, Panini's **Ashtadhyayi** a treatise on Sanskrit grammar, **Kamasutra** of Vatsayayana, **Yogasutra** of Patanjali, **Panchatantra** of Vishnu

Sharma, **Aryabhatiya** of Aryabhatta, **Brihat-Samhita** of Varahmihira and many other singular treatises were composed in this period.

Approximation of the **value of (Pi),** the concept of **earth rotating** on its own axis, explanation of **solar and lunar eclipses** (by Aryabhata), concept of **planetary motion** (by Varahmihira), formal rules for **computing with zero** (by Brahmagupta), writing of numbers in the **decimal system** form and use a circle for zero (by Bhaskara-1)were some such ground breaking concepts which the European nations had to wait for another millennium to understand and discover.

It was an age of great prosperity for the **Dravida region** too, which saw similar progress in all realms of society under the Vakataks in the central India and the Pallavas further south. The region also flourished in the reign of the Chalukyas and the other dynasties. The Puranic age also overlaps with the third of the Sangams which saw unprecedented progress and laid the cultural foundations of the society for the coming centuries. Treatises of the Sangam period extant today including the **Tolkappiam**, the **Pathupattu** and the **Ettutokai** reveal the growth of language and literature. Trade and commerce with kingdoms in Srilanka, Burma (Myanmar) and Mainland Southeast Asia was established eventually leading to the emergence of maritime power of the Cholas in the ensuing centuries.

The Brahmanical traditions also saw an upsurge in the region and by the end of the Puranic age culminated in the **Nayanar** and the **Alvar** movements of Shaivism and Vaishnavism, which heralded the next epoch of the cultural evolution.

The Enduring Legacy: The Puranic aged shaped the coming centuries like no other. It left an enduring legacy in all walks of life, be it, the emergence of the personal god, the cult of devotion, the popularity of the Smritis, the concept of incarnations, the codification of laws in the Dharmasutras, the emergence of grand universities, the free-standing temples, the literary classics, the scientific theories and mathematical concepts or the flourishing trade and commerce. But the most significant legacy of this culture was the **syncretic tradition** of devotion which encompassed even the seemingly divergent beliefs and which proved to be a **singular factor of integration** of the society for the coming millennium and more.

SOLVED QUESTIONS OF PAST YEARS' MAINS (2020 & 2021)

Main Examination 2020

Q.1 *The rock-cut architecture represents one of the most important sources of our knowledge of early Indian art and history. Discuss. (Answer in 150 words)* **(10 marks)**

Ans: Rock cut architecture refers to the creation of structures and objects of art by cutting and removal of stone from solid natural rock. Over 1500 rock cut architectures/structures survive today. The oldest amongst them is the Barabar caves (3rd century BCE) and the grandest is the Kailasa temple at Ellora. Other important structures were the caves at Ajanta, Elephanta, Kanaheri, Guantapalle, Nasik, and Bhaja, besides Mahabalipuram rock cut rathas.

These architectures incorporated Buddhist chaityas, viharas sculpture of Buddha, Boddhisativas, Hindu deities and Jain Tirthankaras and are reflective of the religion philosophy art, architecture and society. The Ajanta caves with Buddhist motifs contains the world-famous mural paintings. The Ellora caves represented a confluence of Buddhist, Brahmanical and Jain subjects. The Kailashnatha temple cut out of a single piece of rock is the largest monolithic temple representing confluence of engineering, art architecture and philosophy.

The Elephanta caves contains the famous sculpture of Trimurti or Maheshmurti image. The Kanaheri caves contained 108 rock cut Buddhist structures mostly viharas, while the Pancha-rathas at Mahabalipuram exhibits the grandeur of Chola art. Thus, these architectures represented different religious thoughts, schools of art and contain a treasure of information about the ancient history and art.

Q.2 *Pala period is the most significant phase in the history of Buddhism in India. Enumerate. (Answer in 150 words)* **(10 marks)**

Ans: Although Buddhism flourished from the 6th century BCE under the patronage of great rulers like Ashoka, Kanishka and Harsha and different dynasties, during the Pala rule (8th to 12th century CE) , it reached great heights with Palas being prominent supporters of Mahayana Buddhism. Under their rule, the Tantric influence also led to flourishing of Vajrayana form of Buddhism, which became a prominent school in North India and even outside India in Tibet, Nepal and adjoining regions.

The great Buddhist Mahaviharas including those of Vikramshila, Odantpuri, Sompura were founded by and flourished under the Pala Patronage, while the Nalanda Mahavihara reached its peak in this period. These Mahaviharas were the epicentres of Buddhist thought philosophy, art and learning. Many noted Buddhist scholars like Atisha, Santaraksita, Saraha, Tilopa and others lived in this period.

Pala bronzes, literature and many Pala period paintings, all of these with largely Mahayana Buddhist subjects and influence, reflect the position of preeminence which Buddhism reached in this period.

Q.3 *Indian Philosophy and tradition played a significant role in conceiving and shaping the monuments and their art in India. Discuss. (Answer in 250 words)* **(15 marks)**

Ans: Indian philosophy and tradition, an integral part of the different religious theologies, have been pluralistic and syncretic. Over the centuries it has influenced and inspired diverse monuments be it the Mauryan architecture which bore the Buddhist influence to Gupta architecture which brought out the Vedic and Puranic traditions and the Jain temples which exuded artistry and simplicity alike. The medieval Islamic architecture was also influenced by the earlier tradition particularly during the reign of Akbar, who syncretized the Indian and Islamic schools. Even in the modern architecture, colonial and the traditional architecture have found a confluence.

The grand stupas of Sanchi and Amravati are a witness to the Buddhist philosophy and tradition and imbued with the Mahayana thought. The life and philosophy of Buddha the events like his birth, renunciation, *Dharmachakra pravartana* and *Nirvana* are all integral to the numerous Buddhist monuments including the Mahaviharas. The dexterous Jain temples depict a rather spartan image of Mahavira or other Tirthankaras, bringing out the emphasis on simplicity and renunciation. The grand temples of the Cholas, Chandelas, Rashtrakutas and other dynasties were imbued with the spirit of Bhakti which swept the medieval period. The large temples with *shikhara* were the abode of gods, a representation of the mythological mount Meru and an integration of the philosophy of *artha, kama, dharma* and *moksha*.

The regional schools of medieval architecture including Malwa, Bengal, Kashmir, Jaunpur, schools, the other schools like Rajput, Sikh, Maratha, Dzong and the hill architecture, all drew inspiration from their regional tradition and philosophies. Coming to the modern age, even the colonial monuments integrated the Gothic and Victorian elements with the centuries old Islamic tradition, the features of Rajput school (like chatris) and the local sensibilities. Monuments of modern India are reflective of its modern yet secular and inclusive philospthy.

Main Examination 2021

Q.1 Evaluate the nature of the Bhakti Literature and its contribution to Indian culture. (Answer in 150 words) **(10 marks)**

Ans. The Bhakti movement was an inclusive, egalitarian, reformative and devotional movement which engendered a wide range of literary works encompassing the teachings and philosophy of the saints from different regions of the country over the centuries.

It propelled the growth of Apbhramsa and the regional languages from which the current day Indian languages evolved. As opposed to Sanskrit, many landmark works like *Yogachintamani* (Ramananda), *Kabir-Bijak* (Kabirdas), *Sur-sagar* (Surdas), *Ramcharitmanas* (Tulsidas) were in Braj and Avadhi. The works of Vidyapati (Maithali) Meera (Braj), Basavanna (Vachnas in Kannada) Jnaneshwar (Jnaneshwai in Marathi) Guru Nanak, Narsimh Mehta, Rahim, Chaitanya were reflective of this trend.

The literature often characterised as *sagun* or *nirgun*, was largely in verse and lead to the growth of poetry. It emphasized on the very essence of Indian philosophy and spiritualism. Through songs, kirtans and other oral means, this literature was propagated among the masses and also lead to the growth of music and other arts. It spread the message of love for God and fellow beings, equality and inclusiveness, eschewing Puranic ritualism and dogmas, while emphasising on simplicity and devotion.